Outpost of Empire

C&C

CAMPAIGNS & COMMANDERS

GREGORY J. W. URWIN, SERIES EDITOR

Campaigns & Commanders

Outpost of Empire

The Napoleonic Occupation of Andalucía, 1810–1812

Charles J. Esdaile

University of Oklahoma Press : Norman

Publication of this book is made possible through the generosity of Edith Kinney Gaylord.

Library of Congress Cataloging-in-Publication Data

Esdaile, Charles J.
Outpost of empire : the Napoleonic occupation of Andalucía, 1810–1812 / Charles J. Esdaile.
p. cm. — (Campaigns & commanders ; v. 33)
Includes bibliographical references and index.
ISBN 978-0-8061-4278-4 (hardcover : alk. paper) 1. Andalusia (Spain)—History—19th century. 2. Spain—History—Napoleonic Conquest, 1808–1813. 3. Joseph Bonaparte, King of Spain, 1768–1844—Travel—Spain—Andalusia. I. Title.
DP302.A52E83 2012
940.2'740946—dc23

2012011094

Outpost of Empire: The Napoleonic Occupation of Andalucía, 1810–1812, is Volume 33 in the Campaigns & Commanders series.

The paper in this book meets the guidelines for permanence and durability of the Committee on Production Guidelines for Book Longevity of the Council on Library Resources, Inc. ∞

1 2 3 4 5 6 7 8 9 10

In memory of my friend,
Richard Hocquellet,
whom I knew for too short a time

Contents

Maps

Preface

Like many others, this book owes its origins to a number of different factors. At the most personal level, there was my desire to revisit previous work and revise it in light of further reading and, indeed, criticism, but beyond that, there was also, first, a recognition that there were certain gaps in the anglophone historiography of the Peninsular War of 1808–14, and, second, the desire both to contribute to and to explore a number of developments in the wider field of Napoleonic history. Finally, underlying all that was a fourth factor in the form of a curious anomaly that would certainly seem to bear further examination: in brief, why was popular resistance in Andalucía seemingly so markedly different in character from that seen in the rest of Spain?

Before discussing the subject of Andalucía, however, we must first consider the general historiography of Napoleonic Europe and, more especially, the construction of the Napoleonic empire. For many years the impression given by most authors writing on the subject was that the whole process of annexation and state building was essentially one that was military and diplomatic. To go this far is perhaps unfair, but such was the emphasis historians placed on campaign and battle narrative that it is difficult not to feel that it was enough for the emperor to triumph at, say, Jena or Friedland for new realms to spring fully fledged from the ashes of his operations. There were always exceptions to this rule—a notable example is H. A. L. Fisher's *Napoleonic Statesmanship: Germany* (1903)—but it was not until the publication of Stuart Woolf's *Napoleon's Integration of Europe* (1991) that the social and political process by which the Napoleonic empire was constructed was made the subject of a scholarly monograph. Woolf's argument is essentially that the expansion of French influence was guided by a common set of ideals imposed with the aid of a common set of tools and accompanied by a common set of practices, including on the one hand administrative integration and on the other economic exploitation. To all this, military victory was certainly an essential precondition, but it did not in itself equate to the massive process of change that followed the proclamation of French control, whether direct or indirect. What mattered was rather the fact that the French knew what to do with their conquests and, all things being equal—which in Spain, of course, they were not—had both the policies and the personnel to take matters in hand. And if they knew what they wanted to do with their conquests, it was because, even before the Revolution, a belief had been growing in France that that nation had become the latest heir to a long tradition of civilizing mission stretching back as far as Ancient Greece, Woolf at times coming very close to suggesting that it was above all this that impelled the wars of the French Revolution and Napoleon alike. This is clearly to go too far—the idea, for example, that the emperor intervened in Spain to save the Spaniards from the clutches of the Inquisition is a fabrication of the Napoleonic legend—but the basic outlines of a reformist agenda, which was a part of the baggage train of all French armies, is nonetheless clear enough. As for the goals of that agenda, these are equally clear: first, to regulate the workings of the state through the introduction of constitutional rule; second, to integrate the people with the institutions of the state; third, to abolish the privileges of the traditional states and corporations; and fourth, to harmonize the workings of the state with the ideas of the Enlightenment.[1]

Nor is Woolf alone in his determination to associate the empire with reform. Another scholar to do this is Michael Broers. In a work that is, perhaps, better known for its argument that, setting aside a few intermediate regions that were an amalgam of the two, the French imperium should be divided into two zones—an "inner empire" (most of present-day France, Holland, Belgium, the Rhineland, most of the former West Germany, Switzerland, and the Kingdom of Italy), where the French were able to impose their control without recourse to military force and, by extension, could push reform to its full extent, and an "outer empire" (Spain; very briefly, Portugal; the Illyrian provinces; Rome; and Naples) that was dogged by serious elite and/or popular resistance that prevented French rule from taking root—he too is insistent that the pressure from Paris and its acolytes was incessant and even inclined to increase as the years wore on: "The final years of Napoleon's rule have often been portrayed as a period of stagnation and increasing conservatism, as a time when the empire began to slip back into the patterns of the *ancien* régime, but nothing could be further from the truth. . . . To the very end, the hereditary empire was fighting the battles of the revolution."[2]

Yet dogmatism has its limits. Having advanced the idea of an all-conquering reformist ideal, Woolf somewhat spoils the effect by immediately saying that, while anything but hostile to the concept of bringing Europe into the light in accordance with the precepts of the philosophes, Napoleon was a pragmatist who refused to allow his hands to be tied by idées fixes: "Unequivocally influenced by the reforming ideals of the Enlightenment, he remained hostile to the dogmatic systems of its more theoretical exponents, whose abstract coherence he regarded as inapplicable to the practical demands of government."[3] Such a qualification is very wise, however. Writing at about the same time, Geoffrey Ellis not only pointed out that the effectiveness of this civilizing mission was very uneven—something with which Woolf does not disagree—but goes on to put the idea very firmly in its place: "We may well ask . . . how far [Napoleon] was inhibited by his financial and military needs from carrying such policies through to their logical conclusion . . . and how far in the event he made a pragmatic compromise with the old feudal structures and privileged élites to extract his imperial spoils."[4] Similarly, even Alexander Grab, an author who is very much inclined to take a positive view of the contribution of the Napoleonic experiment to the history of Europe, is forced to concede that in a number of instances, such as Wespthalia, Switzerland, and the Grand Duchy of Warsaw, the emperor "compromised with conservative élites, allowing them to preserve their privileges as long as they recognised his supreme postion."[5] Such remarks, of course, are not incompatible with the idea of the French having a blueprint for occupation that they applied more or less consistently throughout their domains: we could here cite the creation of new structures of central and local government; the dispatch from Paris of loyal agents of French power as ministers, governor-generals, and chiefs of police; the imposition of conscription on the French model; the co-option of local elites; the socialization of *pays réunies, pays conquis,* and *pays alliés* by means of a sustained campaign of centrally directed propaganda; the ruthless suppression of popular resistance; and where necessary, the substitution of military tribunals and other extraordinary judicial bodies for the civil courts. However consonant with a program of enlightened reform though some of this was, in the aggregate it is difficult not to see it as little more than a scheme to ensure that the empire was milked of the men and money that Napoleon wanted. All the more is this the case if we take into account another of the points that Ellis makes in relation to the empire. As he says, "Two themes are constant: the continuity within the evolving social and political élites of the annexed and subject territories . . . and the often conservative social effects of French policy there."[6]

To put this another way, far from bringing the sort of social and political revolution that is implicit in Woolf's thesis, the French imperium was characterized by a tendency to ally itself with the existing elite and uphold that group's interests. Such a claim, however, chimes in with a major debate in the historiography. A traditional model of the Napoleonic empire, and one congenial to the purveyors of national histories, is that collaboration with French occupation was minimal, and this has tended to be perpetuated by the arguments put forward by Donald Sutherland and others in relation to France to the effect that the notables of France were a powerless force, that what mattered was above all the power of the centralized state. Only ever set out in respect of metropolitan France, this image, however, has been challenged with respect to the wider empire by a variety of scholars, including Michael Rowe, whose work has centered on the Rhineland; Michael Broers, whose work has centered on Piedmont; and John Davis, whose work has centered on Naples. Davis is particularly vigorous in this respect: "At every level the generation that had reached political maturity in the decade of Bourbon absolutism and the republic rallied strongly to the promise of modernity offered by the *grande nation*. . . . To a much greater degree than has been acknowledged, . . . the institutional changes that took place after 1806 came from within the kingdom [of Naples] and were not imposed from above."[7] In all this, then, there lies an obvious opening for the current project, in which respect two questions present themselves, namely the extent to which, first, the local elites formed the bedrock of French rule in Andalucía and, second, the reformist agenda outlined by Woolf remained a live issue with the occupation forces. On top of this, the whole question of occupation policy is worth discussing: in brief, was French practice in Spain, and more particularly Andalucía, sui generis or did it conform to a more general pattern?

So much for the general historiography of Napoleonic Europe, but what of the current author's own work? Over the years I have published a long series of books and articles on the Peninsular War. Broadly speaking, these works have had a strongly revisionist bent, and in 2004 this process came to a head with the publication of *Fighting Napoleon: Guerrillas, Bandits, and Adventurers in Spain, 1808–1814*. In that volume I essentially suggest that the whole issue of the guerrilla resistance during the Peninsular War has been much mythologized, misrepresented, and misunderstood. While the contribution of guerrilla warfare to the overthrow of Joseph Bonaparte and the ejection of the French from Spain is not denied as such, the book raises many questions as to the nature of the "little war" that caused so many problems to the invaders. In brief, I argue that this struggle was in large part the work of the regular Spanish army, or at least local militias, supported on occasion by detachments of the Anglo-Portuguese army of the Duke of Wellington or by landing parties of sailors and marines disembarked from British ships and that the direct involvement of the populace was, by extension, very limited. Of course I admitted that bands of armed civilians also took part in the fighting, but the book raises many doubts as to the value of their contribution, the picture that emerges suggesting, first, that exactly as the French always claimed, many of the more irregular combatants were little more than brigands and, second, that the only cases in which they achieved a measure of success were those in which a steady process of militarization had turned the original guerrilla bands essentially into flying columns of regular troops; indeed, more than that, the book points out that many of the men who have gone down in the older historiography as guerrillas were nothing of the sort, but rather officers of the Spanish army who for one reason or another found themselves conducting irregular operations. Added to all this, meanwhile, are claims that many of the bands that were genuinely raised with a view to fighting the French were formed and sometimes captained by members of the pre-1808 elites and, further, that the war against Napoleon awoke few echoes among the populace, large parts of which remained indifferent or even hostile. To quote from my peroration: "We have here a new analysis of the Spanish guerrillas. Rather than the freedom fighters of legend, they appear rather as a highly complex phenomenon whose military impact has been greatly exaggerated by a combination of muddled thinking, political bias and failure to make use of the full range of primary sources available to the historian."[8]

Yet the Peninsular War was not just a military struggle. In Spain especially, the French armies were fighting not just to beat the last Patriot army, capture the last Patriot fortress, and drive the "hideous leopard" into the sea, but also to establish a new political regime in the form of the Bonaparte Kingdom of Spain. This being the case, it is arguable that the guerrilla war, or, more particularly, its popular aspects, should be looked at in a rather different guise. Let us here reconsider the arguments put forward in *Fighting Napoleon.* Insofar as this work is concerned, there is a clear tendency, first, to reduce the popular element in the guerrilla struggle to a minimum and, second, to argue that, insofar as such an element existed at all, it was essentially devoted to brigandage and consequently had little more than nuisance value. Viewed in terms of the military struggle, these conclusions remain valid, but if the focus is shifted to the construction of the new state, then they should probably be set aside. Thus, mere gangs of bandits, or in the rare instances when they can be so dignified, freedom fighters, could do little to affect the course of the war, but on the local level their actions could be devastating. Much less vulnerable to detection than the more organized forces of such figures as Juan Díaz Porlier, Francisco Espoz y Mina, or Juan Martín Díez, they were a particular threat to the security of the *afrancesados* and other collaborators on whom *josefino* rule depended. If such men were then subjected to intimidation, robbed, or even killed, it was not so much, it may be surmised, because they were seen as traitors, but rather because, as members of the propertied classes, and in many instances keepers of the public purse, they were simply targets that it would have been foolish to ignore. Yet this caveat matters not a whit. What matters is simply that they were attacked, and, further, that the inability of the French forces to halt such attacks could not but discredit them in the eyes of their collaborators and give the latter cause to rethink their conduct. More widely, meanwhile, the anarchy that gripped large parts of the countryside undermined French rule in another sense, for it gave the lie to the social peace for which King Joseph and his ministers claimed to stand and thereby undermined what was in the end their greatest appeal.

If this constant low-level violence shook the structures of collaboration in Spain, it also undermined the morale of the French forces that so evidently failed to protect them. It has often been noted that service in the Iberian Peninsula (or just the Peninsula) was something that was much dreaded on account of, among other factors, the terrible fate that was held to be certain for any man who fell into the hands of the guerrillas. This fear was real enough—there are documented instances of French soldiers shooting themselves rather than allowing themselves to be captured—and to the extent that it had any foundation (something that is certainly open to doubt: most prisoners captured by such men as Espoz y Mina seem rather to have been drafted into their forces),[9] other than in a series of massacres of French invalids and other stragglers that occurred in a number of towns and villages in La Mancha in the panic-stricken days of June 1808, this too was to be found above all in the ways of the low-level brigand-cum-insurgent. For such men it was impossible to assimilate any more foreign recruits than the occasional deserter, while, little better than bandits as they were, they were familiar enough with the torture that was a common feature of attacks by *malhechores:* a frequent experience of the inhabitants of isolated farmhouses visited by such men was to have their feet burned in fires in an attempt to make them reveal their valuables. Such techniques were doubtless also used on Frenchmen who fell into the hands of bandits, and thus it was that, despite the fact that it was a long way from this to torturing men to death by such means as crucifixion, the tale grew in the telling until every last French soldier was convinced that to fall into the hands of the insurgents was tantamount to a death sentence and, with it, a most dreadful fate. We may here cite, perhaps, a story retailed by the cavalry officer Marcellin de Marbot concerning the forced march made by Napoleon's forces in their attempt to catch the army of Sir John Moore during the campaign of La Coruña in 1809: "It is painful to relate that I saw three veteran grenadiers of the guard, unable to march any further and unwilling to fall to the rear at the risk of being tortured and massacred by the peasants, blow out their brains by their own muskets."[10]

Once again, then, one is led back to the activities of men acting without any semblance of military discipline in formations that had no other basis than the gang. All the more is this the case if the matter is considered in political terms. Unlike the larger, more longer-lived, and more militarized bands, whose commanders strove to give them at least a semblance of a uniform as well as to keep them under arms at all times, these genuine irregulars were indistinguishable from the civilian population and might very well live among them, the result being that they very much constituted a hidden enemy and one that was therefore all the more feared. As modern-day conflicts—Vietnam, Lebanon, and Iraq to name but three—testify, it is precisely this situation that is most likely to lead to atrocities. Yet the wholesale massacre of civilians was again something that French and *josefino* authorities could well do without, for this was likely to alienate the inhabitants and, by extension, swell the ranks of the very insurgency it was designed to suppress.

In short, while bands of irregulars probably constituted a minority among the guerrilla movement, at least in Spain as a whole, and at the same time made only a marginal difference to the struggle in military terms, they exercised an influence that was disproportionate to the numbers that they represented, and from this it follows that to revisit some of the conclusions of *Fighting Napoleon* is no means inappropriate. In saying this, moreover, we come to the first reason why Andalucía has been chosen as the subject for this struggle. Whereas in Navarre, the Basque provinces, and Aragón—the only areas whose struggle against Napoleon has been analyzed in any detail in the English-language historiography[11]—the guerrilla war, or at least its popular aspects, increasingly became a matter for large units of an ever more military character, south of the Sierra Morena the struggle was rather, in stereotypical fashion, dominated throughout by small bands of armed civilians. This is most clearly shown by a database I compiled with funding from the Arts and Humanities Research Council and the British Academy. In the first place, Andalucía did not figure especially prominently in the results of the survey, for although the kingdoms of Seville, Córdoba, Jaén, and Granada together had a population of approximately 1,900,000 people (some 18 percent of the population of Spain as a whole), only 290 of the 3,024 combatants listed in the database—9.6 percent—came from those areas. Of course, this may well be a comment on the true extent of popular involvement in armed resistance to the French south of the Sierra Morena, and in the past I have been inclined to view it in this light, but it can also simply suggest that most Andalusians who took up arms did so under the auspices of forms of military organization that were unlikely to leave much of a footprint in the archives. What is certainly the case, however, is that Andalucía accounted for a disproportionate share in the number of guerrilla bands that were traced by the project: of 656 men who were identified as having headed *partidas* of their own, 129 of them—19.7 percent—were associated with that region. In short, guerrilla bands were very numerous in Andalucía, but they were also very small and decidedly irregular in character.[12]

The peculiar nature of the "little war" in Andalucía is not the only issue that makes the region particularly worthy of discussion. On the contrary, added piquancy is lent to the subject by the fact that it offers a very different view of the construction of the Bonaparte Kingdom of Spain (an aspect of the Peninsular War that I had never considered in any detail and therefore welcomed the chance to address). In the existing literature, or at least the

English-language literature, there is a tendency to assume that "Pepe Botellas" never had any chance of establishing his regime on the basis of anything other than French military power. "As long as the basic hostility of the Spanish to the French regime, and hence to Joseph's rule, remained strong," argued Gabriel Lovett, "the King could not possibly establish anything approaching a stable administration."[13] Equally, to quote Michael Ross: "Even Joseph realised he would never be King of Spain until every province was held down by French bayonets. Not only must each corner of the land be conquered, but after conquest it must be garrisoned. Then, perhaps, and then only, would he be able to introduce the enlightened constitution he so desired for the country; only then could his fiscal system be successfully implemented to bring him in sufficient revenue to carry out the reforms he so earnestly desired."[14] Yet was this really true of Andalucía? On the surface there, as much as anywhere else, to maintain order Joseph and his supporters were indeed left with no option but to gird themselves about with the men of the Armée d'Espagne. However, perhaps the line that the invaders could only prevail by means of conquest is too negative. The very heartland of the Patriot war effort between 1808 and 1810, the Kingdoms of Seville, Córdoba, Jaén, and Granada, were also the seat of, in modern parlance, a "failed state" that proved incapable of inspiring the loyalty of elites and populace alike. Invaded by the French in January of the latter year, Andalucía was overrun in no more time than it took for Joseph Bonaparte to march across it from one side to the other. Resistance was nonexistent while the propertied classes hastened to proclaim their loyalty to the new regime. As we shall see, this situation was the result of a killing combination of military exhaustion, governmental incapacity, sectional egotism, social unrest, and political intrigue that reduced the will to resist to a very low ebb. In the words of the Conde de Toreno, "In [Andalucía] . . . the number of the indifferent and those who only wished for peace and quiet was greater than elsewhere."[15]

Without parallel in the annals of the Peninsular War as they are, the extraordinary scenes that greeted the French when they broke through the Sierra Morena in January 1810 are, of course, one more reason to look at Andalucía in some detail. All the more is this the case since there is general agreement that the region was hardly a hotbed of resistance thereafter either. Thus, hardly had the war ended than its chroniclers were noting that responses to the arrival of the French had been decidedly mixed. Here, for example, is Robert Southey: "Fewer guerrilla parties appeared in any other province, although more had been expected there, from the fierier character of the people, and the local circumstances: the land being divided among the cathedrals, a few convents and a few great proprietors, and the greater part of the inhabitants day labourers who were likely to be tempted by the prospect of a predatory life, but Andalucía seemed as if its generous blood had been exhausted in the first years of the war."[16] And here too is Andreas von Schepeler, a Prussian officer who had fled to Spain in 1809 and acquired the rank of colonel in the Spanish army before going on to take up the post of Prussian consul in 1813:

> The reception that the French . . . received in [Seville], and, indeed, in all the other large cities of Andalucía, whisked them from Spain to some enchanted country of repose and friendship. Fanaticism and ignorance both coexisted well enough with the wealth of Andalucía, but a strong preference for a life that was lazy and carefree overcame such feeble impulse as they could impart. The Andalusian believed that, if his province had been conquered, then the same must apply to the whole of Spain, and in consequence he became so devoted to the French that the latter proclaimed Andalucía to be the area of the country that was theirs par excellence. It was there that Joseph received the most sincere homages that were ever paid him, there that he got the bulk of the men who joined his army.[17]

And where the chroniclers led, there followed the historians. In the words of Sir Charles Oman: "The plain-land of Andalucía was undoubtedly the part of the French holding in Spain where the [*josefino*] administration was most successful, and the occupation most thorough. Soult not only built up, but kept together, an *afrancesado* party among the local population which was stronger and more compact than in any other part of the Peninsula. He even succeeded in raising a small permanent force of Spanish auxiliaries, which was decidedly more trustworthy and less given to desertion than the regiments of the same class which King Joseph was perpetually creating in Madrid. . . . On several occasions they fought well against the *guerrilleros* when the latter attempted raids dangerously close to the big cities."[18]

In short, in Andalucía more than anywhere else in Spain, Joseph and his fellow commanders had scope to engage in what today would be termed "peace-support operations" while, as we shall soon discover, they brought to the reconstruction of civil society, which was the key to the restoration of peace, an agenda that was far more sophisticated than they have generally been given credit for (the idea that Soult, Victor, Sébastiani, and the rest were nothing more than rapacious plunderers is one that has been particularly overdrawn). Yet although many of the French generals were soon engaged in a variety of projects designed to give employment to the populace and restore the economy, their efforts never had a chance. Within days of the invaders' arrival at Seville, the incidence of armed resistance was on the increase again: here and there French stragglers began to be picked off, while in such areas as the Serranía de Ronda and the Alpujarras, bands of armed civilians took to the field in considerable numbers. Yet in itself this phenomenon should not have been a problem: at the very time that the French were invading Andalucía, they were just finishing off an entirely similar insurrection in Calabria, and there seems little doubt that the same result could not have been achieved in even such supposed bastions of popular resistance as the Alpujarras or the Serranía de Ronda.[19] As we shall see, however, in Andalucía the problem was much more complex. Economic conditions—the single most important factor in the decision of many peasants, artisans, and day laborers to "take to the hills" were probably no worse in Andalucía than they were anywhere else in occupied Spain, but unfortunately for the French, the region's long coastline and exposed frontiers made it especially vulnerable to penetration on the part of substantial forces of Allied regulars. What might have been a containable problem—even a resolvable problem—therefore spiraled out of control, with the result that peace-support operations became inextricably entangled with counterinsurgency operations. Yet the repression that these entailed rendered the normalization of daily life a near impossibility. In cities such as Seville and Cordoba, something was achieved, but the countryside remained a zone of contention. In conditions such as these, pacification was bound to fail, and yet it is important to remember that popular resistance, such as it was, could not win either, Andalucía only finally being liberated when events in the north of Spain—above all Wellington's victory at Salamanca—forced a most reluctant Marshal Soult to evacuate his dominions or risk being cut off from France. Indeed, the very fact that the commander of what had now become the Army of the South could, at this moment of crisis, advocate digging in in Andalucía and holding it as a bastion of French rule is highly suggestive: Soult may well have been deluding himself as to the extent to which control of his de facto viceroyalty had been established, and yet he clearly did not feel that the region was utterly compromised as a political and military base.

Once again, then, the image emerges of an Andalucía that was strongly *afrancesada*. Yet as with the claims retailed above, this is an image that has never really been subjected to detailed scrutiny. Indeed, the present study fills an obvious gap in the English-language historiography of the Peninsular War. Setting aside the remarks in such general works as Lovett's *Napoleon and the Birth of Modern Spain,* Connelly's *Napoleon's Satellite Kingdoms,* Grab's *Napoleon's Transformation of Europe,* and my own *The Peninsular War: A New History,* sources on *josefino* Spain are few and far between. There is one work that on the surface might seem to offer a potential starting point, Michael Glover's *The Bonaparte Kingdom of Spain* (London, 1971), yet on examination this proves to be little more than a history of the Peninsular War written from the French point of view and has hardly anything to say about the formation or governance of the new state. Beyond that there are two biographies of Joseph Bonaparte—Michael Ross's *The Reluctant King: Joseph Bonaparte: King of the Two Sicilies and Spain* (London, 1976) and Owen Connelly, *The Gentle Bonaparte: A Biography of Joseph, Napoleon's Elder Brother* (New York, 1968)—but while these are interesting enough on *el tío pepe* himself, beyond that they tend to confine themselves to superficialities. Add to this a few specifically military studies, such as Hayman's biography of Marshal Soult and

Alexander's study of French counterinsurgency policy in Aragón, and that is about it. Yet in Spanish the study of Joseph Bonaparte's Spain has taken off apace. Now over fifty years old, Miguel Artola Gallego's pioneering *Los afrancesados* was for a long time the only academic study of any aspect of the latter's rule, but now there are few areas of French-occupied Spain that have not been made the subject of at least one scholarly monograph. That said, the works in question are somewhat variable in quality, but at their best they are the equal of anything available elsewhere, while taken in the round they are a valuable addition to the historiography and certainly deserve to be brought to the attention of an anglophone audience.

As Andalucía is particularly well covered in this new historiography of the war, there is all the more reason for this region to be adopted as our focus.[20] Yet the fact that the field of "occupation studies" has become more prominent is not the only reason why France's attempt to implant a new Bonaparte regime in Spain seems increasingly worthy of attention. Thus, the Peninsular War has become a matter for topical debate. Over the years that have passed since the invasion of Iraq in March 2003, more and more commentators have spotted what they see as parallels between the actions of Napoleon and those of George W. Bush and, more particularly, between the popular resistance faced by the French in Spain and the popular resistance faced by the United States and its allies in Iraq. As I have observed elsewhere, there is much bad history here: in particular, too many of those who have made the comparison have fallen hook, line, and sinker for several much-pushed lines in the emperor's propaganda (specifically, first, that the empire stood for freedom and social reform and, second, that popular resistance to Napoleonic rule was above all the work of the Roman Catholic Church).[21] Yet that said, in the case of Andalucía at least, there are also strange parallels. Like Iraq, Andalucía was overrun by the application of "shock and awe." And as in Iraq, in Andalucía the cause of peace was heavily entwined with that of the restoration of normal civic life: as the American army struggled to restore electric power to Baghdad and the British army to get clean water to Basra, the ghost of Marshal Soult must doubtless have been remarking to its fellows how history has a habit of repeating itself.

As ever, my debts are many and my gratitude heartfelt. First of all, this book could not have happened without the generous financial support of the British Academy, from which I obtained a £7,500 research grant in 2007, and the University of Liverpool. Their faith in me is much appreciated, and I very much hope that the current work will live up to their expectations. Also worthy of mention here are the staffs of the various archives and research libraries in which I have worked, especially the British Library, the Service Historique de la Défence, the Biblióteca Nacional, the Instituto de Historia y Cultura Militar, and the Archivo Histórico Nacional (in this last context particularly Pilar Bravo Lledo, without whose efforts at the head of the Sección de Diversos this book would probably never have been written), as well as my agent at A. M. Heath and Company, Bill Hamilton, and my editor at the University of Oklahoma Press, Chuck Rankin. Beyond such institutional and professional support, there is the institution of friendship. In this respect I am rich indeed. In the academic world many historians looked at drafts of this manuscript, shared their work with me, or gave me copies of their books and articles, this roll of honor including Mark Lawrence, Allan Forrest, Michael Hughes, Jean-Marc Lafon, Antonio Moliner Prada, Nuria Alonso Garcés, Francisco Luis Díaz Torrejón, Manuel Moreno Alonso, José Manuel Cuenca Toribio, Luis Alfonso Limpo Píriz, and Jaime Aragón Gómez (included in this list are only those whose writings are directly relevant to this work—the many other people who have also been so very kind to me are not forgotten). Meanwhile, outside academia, of the many people who gave me companionship and hospitality, special mention is due to Azucena Pedraz Marcos, Jo Klepka, Enrique Mardones, Emilio de Castro, Dolores Schilling, Robin and Joelle Le Mallier, Marie Salgués, and Jesus Maroto, while Leonor Hernández Enviz resumed a past role as a loyal and devoted research assistant. In no case, however, do any of them have any share in any of the faults that may be found in these pages: these are very much "all my own work." And as ever, there is my family, who continue to endure my many failings as a husband and father and are as much owed my apologies as they are my thanks. With Andalucía finally restored to the Patriot cause, perhaps I shall be restored to them.

In ordinary circumstances, it is here that I would end these preliminary remarks, but in the current instance I must add a word of further tribute. This book is dedicated to Richard Hocquellet. A young scholar of great promise and enthusiasm, Richard was the author of the first academic study of the Spanish War of Independence ever to appear in French and latterly was also responsible for a fine modern edition of Toreno's *Historia del levantamiento, guerra y revolución de España;* just as importantly perhaps, he was also a warm and friendly individual who inspired much love among his friends and was a byword for convivial company. To learn, then, that he had perished in a tragic accident came as a great shock, and one that to me was all the sadder as I had but recently got to know him personally. We would probably have disagreed about this book, but for all that, let it serve to perpetuate his memory.

Andalucía during the Campaign of 1810. Map by B. V. Darbishire, 1907.

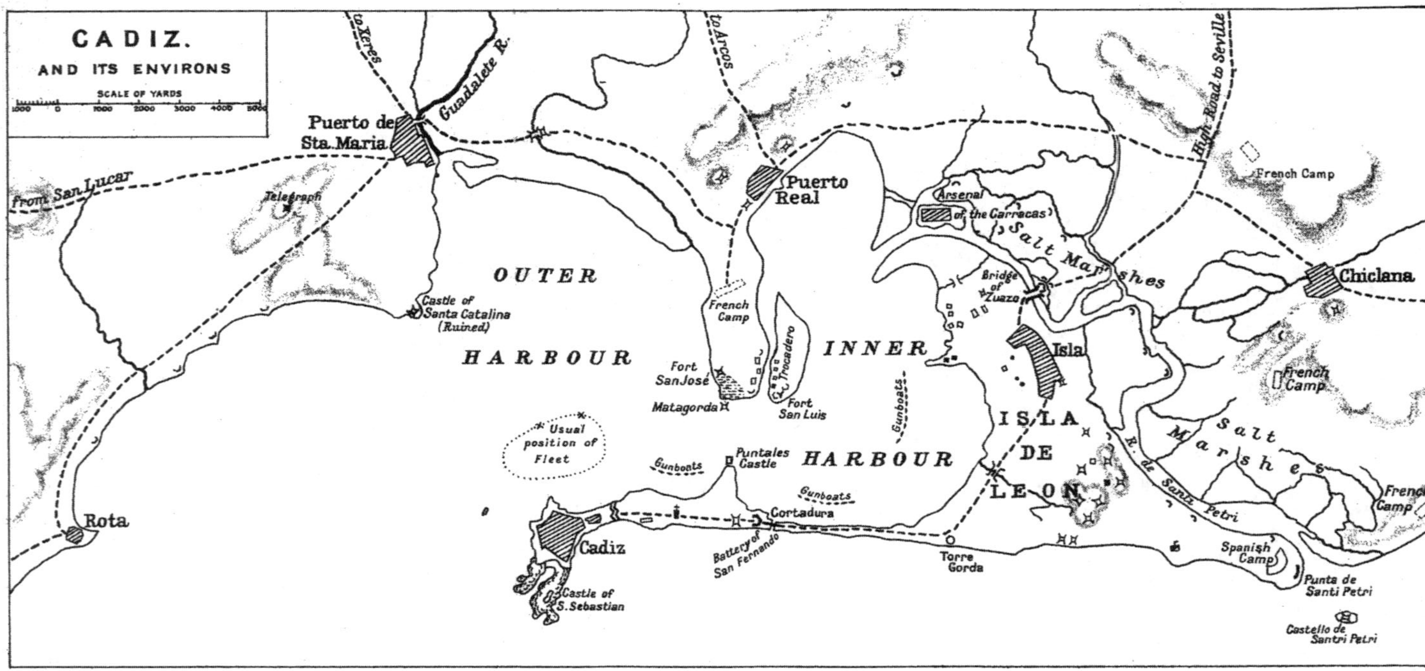

Cádiz and its environs. Map by B. V. Darbishire, 1907.

Outpost of Empire

1

Conquest

By January 1810 the Peninsular War had been raging for almost two years. Following Napoleon's overthrow of the Spanish Bourbons in May 1808, those parts of Spain that were not physically occupied by the French armies had risen in revolt, and this had produced a confused series of military operations in which the fortunes of war had for some weeks swayed to and fro before coming down hard in favor of the Spaniards. Thus, within days of the new king of Spain, Joseph Bonaparte, arriving in Madrid, an entire French army had been forced to surrender at the Battle of Bailén, and the invaders had thereafter been forced on to the defensive and, in particular, to abandon all of Spain south of the River Ebro, including the capital. All this, meanwhile, was coupled with further embarrassments in Portugal, where the army of occupation that had been sent there in 1807 under General Jean Andoche Junot was forced to capitulate, albeit on terms that were extraordinarily generous. Furious at these blows to his prestige, Napoleon responded by pouring fresh troops into Spain, and in November 1808 he personally led his armies in a campaign that in barely one month had shattered the chief Spanish armies and recaptured Madrid. At this point the French might conceivably have overrun the whole of Spain and Portugal as well, but at the last moment, they were distracted by a sudden British offensive that threatened their communications with France in northern Spain. Urged on by an emperor eager to strike a blow at his chief opponent, the invaders turned north and pursued the British into the wilds of Galicia, only for their prey to escape by sea after a sharp rearguard action in which their commander, Sir John Moore, was killed. With the evacuation of Moore's surviving men, the Peninsular War moved into a second period. In essence, in addition to parts of Catalonia, the French now occupied most of the northern and central parts of the Iberian Peninsula, and from these bastions they were constantly trying to expand their area of control westward into Portugal and southward into Extremadura, Andalucía, and the Levante, all of which remained in the hands of the Patriot forces. In this, however, the French were completely unsuccessful for a full year. Having massed a new army at Lisbon under Sir Arthur Wellesley—the real hero of the campaign against Junot—the British were able to repel a fresh invasion of Portugal and start retraining the Portuguese forces so that they too could play their part in the fighting, while in the south and west of Spain, fresh Spanish armies emerged to challenge the invaders. Once again the fighting swayed first one way and then another—if the French captured the isolated fortress of Zaragoza, they were also forced to evacuate Galicia—and it was not until late in the year that Napoleon's forces managed to establish a real measure of predominance and gain the initiative.

It is at this point that our study of the French occupation of Andalucía begins. Stretching for some 250 miles from the frontier of Portugal in the west to those of the Levante in the east, and from 150 to 200 miles from the Sierra Morena to the shores of the Atlantic and the Mediterranean, the four kingdoms of Andalucía—Seville, Granada, Córdoba, and Jaén—had for the past two years been the very heartland of Patriot Spain. In December 1808 the provisional government that had been formed in the wake of the national uprising against the French known as the Junta Suprema Central had taken up residence in the *alcázar* of Seville in the wake of the French capture of Madrid, while Seville also housed Spain's chief artillery foundry and the Patriot zone's only tobacco factory (an important source of revenue given, first, that Spaniards—both men and women—were inveterate smokers and, second, that tobacco was a state monopoly). In Cádiz, meanwhile, the Junta Central had access to Spain's most important port and naval arsenal and thus, through its ships and merchant oligarchies, access to the wealth of Spain's overseas empire. In the fertile basins of the Guadalquivir valley, where wheat, olives, and grapes all grew in abundance, the Patriots possessed one of Spain's few real "bread baskets": while there were, as we shall see, many problems with Andalusian agriculture, in normal times the region accounted for more than a quarter of Spain's agricultural production.[1] Industry, admittedly, had been declining in the course of the eighteenth century, and yet most of the main cities housed a variety of workshops that produced large quantities of weapons and uniforms for the Spanish cause: in Granada, for example, a major armament workshop was established in the summer of 1809 that by the end of the year had constructed 448 complete muskets, 611 musket ramrods, 538 musket locks, 508 musket barrels, and 492 bayonets, while Seville possessed Spain's chief cannon foundry.[2] And finally, in the Sierra Morena there were abundant mineral resources—lead, copper, silver, sulfur, and saltpeter—that could also be turned to good account. On top of all this, meanwhile, there were Andalucía's human resources: Seville and Cádiz were Spain's third- and fourth–largest cities, with populations in 1797—the date of the last census conducted in Spain prior to the Peninsular War—of 96,000 and 75,000 inhabitants respectively, while the region as a whole could claim 1,897,980 inhabitants (for the purposes of comparison, the figures for Galicia and Catalonia, the next most populous regions, were 1,142,630 and 858,818 respectively). Given that the total population of the country was assessed at 10,541,221, something under one in every five Spaniards was an Andaluz.[3] Finally, there was the question of Andalucía's symbolic importance: although Seville was not the headquarters of Spanish Catholicism—that honor rather belonged to Toledo—it was a religious center of major significance and therefore a prize whose capture would signify a major blow in the struggle with "superstition" that French propaganda placed at the heart of the war in the peninsula; by the same token, a successful campaign south of the Sierra Morena would finally exorcise the ghost of Bailén.

From the very beginning, then, it was predictable that the French would sooner or later seek to subdue Andalucía: indeed, the scheme of operations that Napoleon had bequeathed to his generals in the wake of his departure from Spain in January 1809 had specifically laid down the need for just such an advance. Initially, this had had to be postponed in response to difficulties elsewhere, but in the autumn of 1809, it had become clear that the moment was finally at hand. In the first place, the British army of Wellesley—since August Lord Wellington—was no longer a factor of concern. Having expelled the French from Portugal in May 1809, Wellington had gone on to invade Spain and march on Madrid in company with a Spanish army under General Gregorio García de la Cuesta via the valley of the River Tagus. In consequence of this offensive, a considerable victory had been obtained at Talavera de la Reina at the end of July, but then a variety of problems, including most notably the arrival of large numbers of fresh French troops in a position in which they could threaten Wellington's communications, prompted a headlong retreat that ended only when the British reached the River Guadiana at Mérida. Although relations with the Spanish authorities were now under serious pressure, for the time being Wellington was prepared to hold the line of the river between Mérida and the more westerly city of Badajoz; but more than that he would not do. Already, then, the British army was out of the fight, but in November there came news that was even worse, for Wellington announced that he was going to pull his entire army back across the Portuguese frontier and concentrate on protecting Lisbon. That this was the British intention the French could not know, of course, but the complete absence of Wellington's forces from the campaigns of the autumn of 1809 was at the very least highly suggestive.[4]

It is to precisely these campaigns that we must now turn, for it was they that opened the gates to an invasion of Andalucía. To understand the significance of the operations that they encompassed, we must first consider the general military context in which they took place. From January 1809—the moment when the Patriot cause revived in southern and western Spain following the loss of Madrid in December 1808—the defense of Andalucía had essentially been in the hands of two armies. Directly charged with blocking the main high road from Madrid to Seville was the Army of La Mancha, while stationed in and around the fortress city of Badajoz, and thereby blocking the other main route to Seville from northern Spain, was the Army of Extremadura. The two largest armies in Patriot Spain—in July 1809 the former had numbered 27,000 men and the latter 42,000—these forces may be regarded as further evidence of the importance of Andalucía to the Patriot cause, for it was in large part from that region that they were recruited and supplied. Yet substantial though they were, the armies also suffered from serious defects. In both of them the largest single component was the infantry, and yet, in general, Spain's infantry was of very poor quality. Even supposing that the soldiers were willing enough—something that, as we shall see, is open to serious question—their training was by all accounts rudimentary: many men were barely able to load and fire their muskets, while their ability to maneuver on the battlefield was at best limited, all this in part being the product of an officer corps that was all too often made up of clients of the provincial juntas who were as inexperienced as they were unsuitable. Added to this problem was the fact that neither army was constituted in a balanced fashion. First of all, there was the artillery: In the French army, even if this was rarely achieved in Spain, the ideal was five pieces of artillery to every thousand men. Yet in July 1809 the Army of La Mancha could only manage forty guns and the Army of Extremadura thirty, an average of just over one per thousand men. And then there was the cavalry: a force that might number anything up to one-quarter of the strength of a typical French army, in these two Spanish armies combined there were but 10,000 mounted troops (approximately one-seventh of the total), while even these men were poorly equipped and, still worse, poorly mounted.[5]

Except when directly supported by large numbers of British troops (as had been the case at Talavera), to take the field in the open plains of central Spain would have been foolhardy at the best of times, while under the generals inherited from the *antiguo régimen*—for the most part, it has to be said, a collection of nonentities—the chances of success were reduced still further. Yet for political reasons, it was impossible to adopt the defensive strategy that was the only logical course for the Spanish armies covering Andalucía to adopt in the early months of 1809. Under pressure from the very moment of its formation, the Junta Central could only face down its numerous political enemies by obtaining military victory, and thus Spain's forces on the whole maintained an aggressive posture and engaged in a series of offensives against the French. The result, however, was disaster. Whether it was in

Aragón, La Mancha, Extremadura, or Old Castile, Spanish armies were forced to forsake the shelter of the mountain chains that offered their best hope of survival while, spread out around the periphery of the country, they were also operating on external lines and therefore highly vulnerable to sudden French counterstrikes. With the Junta Central's forces also poorly commanded and hopelessly outclassed on the battlefield, to have expected victory would have been optimistic indeed, and in the event what followed was a veritable litany of defeat. In January 1809 the Army of La Mancha was worsted at the Battle of Uclés; in March it was routed at Ciudad Real and the Army of Extremadura all but destroyed at edellín; and in July the Army of La Mancha was trounced at Almonacid de Toledo. Yet even the withdrawal of British support in the autumn of 1809 could not persuade the Junta Central of the necessity for a defensive policy, and on 19 November came a catastrophe that outstripped anything that had gone before. Having advanced yet again from its strongholds in the Sierra Morena, the Army of La Mancha bore down on Madrid, only for its commander—now General Carlos Areizaga—to lose his nerve and dally for some days around the isolated *pueblo* of Ocaña, thereby enabling the French to gather their forces under King Joseph and his newly appointed chief of staff, Marshal Soult, and hurl themselves upon him. Deployed in a an open plain with their right flank completely "in the air," the Spaniards were shattered: while their infantry were pinned down by a frontal attack mounted by their French counterparts, the vastly superior enemy cavalry drove off Areizaga's mounted troops and then wheeled inward to deal with the embattled Spanish foot. Caught in flank and rear, the latter then collapsed amid scenes of the utmost slaughter and panic: by the end of the day, indeed, out of some 51,000 Spaniards who had taken the field, 4,000 had been killed or wounded and another 14,000 taken prisoner. Also gone, meanwhile, were all of Areizaga's baggage and forty of his fifty guns, while many soldiers took the opportunity to desert and simply scattered into the countryside: when the army regrouped in the Sierra Morena, it was found to have lost no fewer than 27,000 men.[6]

The Battle of Ocaña sealed the fate of Andalucía. The series of defeats detailed above had produced terrible losses for the Patriot cause. Fighting in the open and denied an adequate force of cavalry, every time they had been defeated—something that had occurred almost every time they had taken the field—the Spanish armies had necessarily suffered disproportionate losses in terms of both men and guns, a major problem in this latter instance being that the artillery was pulled from place to place not by a militarized corps of drivers, as was the case in the British and French service, but rather by civilian teamsters, who were all too prone to fleeing with their mules and oxen at the first sight of trouble. Uclés had cost 7,000 men and four guns (the only ones the Spaniards had on the field); Ciudad Real, 3,000 men and five guns; Medellín, 10,000 men and thirty guns; and Almonacid, 5,000 men and thirty guns. To all this, moreover, could be added the thousands of men who deserted or fell sick and died (food was always short, and the men had faced the bitter winter of 1808–1809 without adequate supplies of winter clothing, tents, or blankets). Given the problems that the Patriot cause faced in recruiting its armies—something to which we shall return in the next chapter—the resultant gaps in the ranks could not be filled up without the greatest difficulty, while the constant loss of men ensured that the Spaniards were never able to build up a cadre of veteran soldiers, thereby ensuring that their forces never progressed very far in terms of quality.

In the wake of Ocaña, then, Patriot Andalucía was all but defenseless. Its western frontier was still guarded by the Duque de Alburquerque's Army of Extremadura—the one Spanish army that had built up a small record of success by dint of its participation in the Battle of Talavera in July—but that force had been stripped to a mere 12,000 infantry and 1,500 cavalry in order to reinforce the Army of La Mancha, while its effective strength was reduced still further by the need to leave a substantial garrison in Badajoz. Wellington's army, however, was on the brink of leaving Spain—its commander's decision to pull his men out was formally communicated to the Junta Central the day after Ocaña—and the line of the Sierra Morena was protected by nothing more than the remnants of Areizaga's forces, which in January 1810 consisted of no more than 30,000 men. Still worse, these battered and demoralized troops were scattered over a front of some 150 miles in an attempt to block the three main crossing points that led across the mountains to Andalucía. Thus, at Almadén and Pozoblanco the divisions of Francisco Copóns y Navía and Tomás de Zeraín were watching the two minor roads that led from there to Córdoba via the desolate district known as Los Pedroches; at La Carolina the 13,000 men of the divisions of José de Zayas y Chacón, Francisco González de Castejón, Pedro Agustín Girón, and Luis Lacy were blocking the main road from Madrid to Seville at the Puerto del Despenãperros; and finally at Montizón 6,000 more men—the divisions of Gaspar de Vigodet and Adrián Jacomet—had been ordered to check any French advance via Villamanrique over the pass that led down to the upper reaches of the River Guadalquivir around Ubeda and Baeza (none of these passes were especially formidable: all of them, indeed, could easily be bypassed by sending infantry to scale the heights that encompassed them on either side). Behind these men, who were protected by no more than a few half-built redoubts, was almost nothing in the way of reserves other than a few town guards and drafts of conscripts, while they were not backed by a single fortress other than distant Cádiz. In short, the French had only to make the slightest push to the front for the whole of Andalucía to be in danger.[7]

Unfortunately for the Junta Central, far to the north the French high command was casting ambitious eyes on Andalucía. Perhaps surprisingly, the aftermath of Ocaña had not been followed by an immediate invasion. Certainly, an offensive could have been embarked on easily enough—some 60,000 men had been concentrated to defeat Areizaga—while just before the battle the king's chief of staff, Marshal Jean-Baptiste Jourdan, a somewhat lackluster figure who had repeatedly shown a predilection for caution in the campaigns of the summer of 1809, had been replaced by the much more dynamic and aggressive Marshal Soult. Yet a number of issues gave the French pause. Not only were communications between Madrid and the French frontier under constant threat from the growing number of guerrilla bands in Old Castile and the Basque provinces, but it was not clear what Wellington was doing: had he maintained his position at Badajoz and Mérida, he would, after all, have been well placed to strike at the right flank and rear of any French columns operating in the western part of La Mancha. At the same time too, another major Spanish force—the Duque del Parque's Army of the Left—was still in the field in the area of Salamanca, where it had won a minor victory at Alba de Tormes. Initially, then, the French rather resumed a defensive posture, dispersing the troops who had fought at Ocaña over a wide area and sending some of them to chase the guerrillas away from the main road to France. Yet very soon it became clear that there was little need for caution. On 28 November the Army of the Left was soundly defeated at Tamames; at about the same time, it became clear that Wellington was withdrawing his forces into Portugal; the guerrillas were dealt a series of heavy blows by the flying columns that were everywhere dispatched against them; and finally, news arrived that, long promised by Napoleon, large numbers of fresh troops who had been freed up by the defeat of Austria at Wagram were starting to pour across the frontier.[8] In short, nothing now stood between Andalucía and Armageddon. All the more was this the case as the French were receiving reports from south of the Sierra Morena that were encouraging in the extreme: "I have the honor to enclose a translation of a report made by a man who has recently come from Andalucía. Other details that have come in since his arrival suggest that there are great controversies in the home of the insurrection. This quarrel is founded on the rivalry that exists between the Junta Central and its provincial counterparts, particularly those of Valencia and Seville. . . . It appears that there is also no agreement in respect of the manner in which the new government that has been proposed should be formed, and that the defeat of the Spanish armies has thrown these plans into confusion and filled one and all with consternation."[9]

That the French would advance on southern Spain was now highly likely. In the first place, such a plan certainly seemed to chime with what was known of Napoleon's views on how the Peninsular War should be conducted. Admittedly, no orders had been forthcoming from Paris to this effect—Oman suggests the emperor had been deliberately eliding the issue in an attempt to evade the responsibility for failure should the campaign go wrong—but there was plenty of evidence that occupying southern Spain was considered a matter of considerable importance. Prior to leaving Spain in January 1809 after his brief spell of campaigning there,

Napoleon had drawn up a plan that, naturally enough, laid great stress on the need to conquer Andalucía, this indeed having seemingly been envisaged as the very touchstone of victory as well as something that should be achieved, for political reasons, by Joseph himself. As the latter was told: "Since you have expressed the wish to participate in a campaign, the one that you should take part in is the expedition to Andalucía. . . . With two good army corps . . . marching by an unexpected route, you will surprise the enemy and force him to submit. This is an operation which will make an end of the war: I leave the glory of it to you."[10] Equally, in 1808 General Pierre Antoine Dupont's army had crossed the Sierra Morena with the clear intention of occupying Seville and Cádiz, while there seems little doubt that, but for the attempt on the part of Sir John Moore to menace the French forces in Old Castile, which led to the famous "retreat to Corunna," the fall of Madrid would have been followed with another attempt to reach those objectives: at the moment that news arrived of Moore's counteroffensive, Marshal Claude Victor Perrin (always referred to simply as Victor) and his I Corps were poised to plunge southward into La Mancha.[11]

To assume, then, that Napoleon would approve of a march on Seville was not unreasonable. Armed with the benefit of hindsight, a number of British commentators have claimed that the whole campaign was a serious error in strategic terms, that the French should rather have left a small force to watch the Sierra Morena and marched with every man at their disposition on Lisbon in an effort to drive Wellington's army—the chief sustenance, it was supposed, of Spanish and Portuguese resistance—into the sea. On one level this is logical enough, but King Joseph and Marshal Soult were scarcely being derelict in their duty in not marching on Lisbon: behind them, they knew, Napoleon was sending masses of reinforcements whose express task was to invade Portugal, while the emperor had explicitly told Soult that he was coming to Spain to head just such a campaign. On top of this, meanwhile, there was good military reason for a move south, for it was not unreasonable to hope that yet another hammer blow to the Patriot cause might well finish it off altogether and thereby render the British position in Portugal all but untenable. In the circumstances of

1812, certainly, Andalucía would very much prove "a province too far," but at the end of 1809 it was completely impossible to envisage the war on Russia that would make that notion reality. In his memoirs, as British historians regularly point out, Marshal Jourdan was sharply critical of the move, but Jourdan had been the very officer displaced by Soult when he became Joseph's chief of staff: his opinion, then, is scarcely to be relied upon as an objective assessment.[12]

That said, the invasion of Andalucía was not just driven by political imperatives. Let us begin here with King Joseph, who in fact had been talking of such a campaign since at least the previous spring: as he wrote to Napoleon on 2 April 1809, for example, "It is necessary to seize control of Cádiz and the naval squadrons stationed there before despair alone throws the latter into the hands of the English."[13] Nicknamed by historians "the gentle Bonaparte," Joseph had come to come to Spain in 1808 with sincere intentions of doing good. Though in reality no more than the cat's-paw of his brother's imperial designs, *el tío pepe,* as he was known in Spain, wished to improve the lot of his new subjects, wanted to be seen as a genuinely Spanish monarch, and had even originally let himself be convinced that the populace wanted him to ascend the throne. That the reality of his situation was very different was soon made all too clear, but that did not dissuade Joseph from his course. On the one hand, he had worked assiduously to persuade the population of Madrid and such neighboring towns as he could safely reach—Aranjuez, Toledo, and Segovia—to accept him as their ruler, while on the other, the *afrancesado* press had sought to burnish his image in the eyes of a much wider range of Spaniards. As we shall discuss all this at a later moment, for the time being all that needs to be said is that, nearly a year on from the effective start of his reign in January 1809—the moment when he was able to take up permanent residence in Madrid—Joseph remained convinced that, given time, he could still win over the country to his side. Yet with Andalucía still in Patriot hands, large parts of the country remained beyond his reach, and this alone was enough to ensure that Joseph would be keen on a crossing of the Sierra Morena, especially as victory would be accompanied by the opportunity to engage in a display of magnanimity on a grand scale:

there would, after all, be thousands of prisoners of war to pardon and hundreds of repentant officials to confirm in their posts.

At the same time, however, it was not just a matter of winning over the Spaniards or, failing that, overawing them with a smashing victory. On the contrary, *el rey intruso* was anxious to address a number of other issues. Preeminent here was the need to secure control of the reins of government. Situated as he was, Joseph was in a very difficult position. Given the fact that the war continued to rage unabated and that he was entirely dependent on the support of the Armée d'Espagne, he inevitably found himself sharing his kingdom with a veritable kaleidoscope of French commanders, most of them larger-than-life characters who were as greedy for wealth and power as they were jealous of their own authority. Had these men been prepared to cooperate with the king and seen matters in the same fashion as he did, this would not have mattered so very much, but the reality was very different: whereas Joseph wished to pursue a policy of conciliation, their watchword was terror. Still worse, meanwhile, with the connivance of Napoleon and his other representatives in Spain, these officers were able to erect a rival structure of authority. Let us here quote Joseph's close friend and confidante, André Miot de Melito, a French diplomat of great experience who had served as ambassador to Sardinia and Tuscany, governor-general of Corsica, and minister of the interior in Naples, from where he had traveled with Joseph to Spain as his majordomo: "Although the king was [theoretically] in command of the army, the generals . . . nevertheless corresponded directly with the minister of war and often received orders from him that contradicted the ones they got from Madrid. The French ambassador and the official in charge of administering the property that the emperor had ordered to be confiscated, together with the numerous agents that they employed, all of whom were entirely independent of the authority of the royal government, brought to their tasks a rigor that they themselves perhaps lamented, but which they were not allowed to relax, and that rigor completely alienated the minds that the king was so eager to conciliate."[14] Needless to say, Joseph was bitterly resentful of this situation, but with Napoleon himself a partisan of winning Spain over by force rather than persuasion—"I think it necessary that your government, especially at the beginning, must show a bit of vigor toward the mob. The mob only likes and respects those it fears, while the fact that the mob fears you will be the only thing that will make you liked and respected among the rest of the nation"[15]—his protests fell on deaf ears. From all this it followed, then, that if Joseph was ever to get the chance to administer Spain as he wished, he would first have to persuade Napoleon both to trust and to back him, and that in turn meant that he would have to establish himself as a credible leader of the French cause in Spain.

Closely linked to this issue was the constant criticism of which Joseph knew he was the subject, and which for some time had been putting his relationship with Napoleon under strain: surely a victorious campaign in the south could not but persuade the emperor that he was worthy of his trust after all. That Joseph was worried is all too clear from his correspondence. Napoleon, it was learned, was talking of returning to Spain, and rumors began to spread that the emperor intended to transfer his brother to some other post and place the crown on his own head. To quote Miot de Melito again: "The events of the Spanish war had not corresponded to the heights of the ambition of an emperor who had just beaten Austria and signed a peace treaty that marriage with a granddaughter of Maria Teresa would soon cement. He was far, indeed, from sharing in the general satisfaction that reigned in Madrid. . . . The silence that he continued to maintain in respect of the conduct of the king and the last successes that had been obtained announced a discontent that, whether real or simulated, he was keeping in reserve as a pretext for taking whatever measures best suited his interests."[16]

El rey intruso, then, was keen to state his case:

> It is a long time, Sire, since I have had news of Your Majesty. Even the peace [with Austria] I only heard about via the newspapers. The moment that your habitual affection is withdrawn all the glory that it has brought me becomes a heavy burden. If I have lost your friendship, do me the favor of letting me withdraw to the most obscure of retreats, but, if this is denied me, I will find a glorious death amid the dangers in respect of which

> the name that I bear and the troops that I command have never let me experience anything other than victory. Whatever the situation may be, remember that you will never have a friend who could be more worthy of you, nor, indeed, a more tender brother: beware that you do not remember this too late![17]

This letter was penned on the very evening of the Battle of Ocaña. When the news of that great victory produced no other response from Paris than a sharp reproof to the effect that the many captured Spanish colors should have immediately been sent back to France, Joseph wrote to his brother a second time: "All the rumors that are going the rounds here in respect of my fate and that of Spain are holding back the reconciliation of every spirit and obstructing the pacification of the interior. . . . However things work out, may Your Majesty never doubt my tender friendship!"[18]

Further confirmation of Joseph's uncertain state of mind at this point comes in respect of the large number of Patriot prisoners of war taken at Ocaña. In the past, eager both to build a new Spanish army of his own and to give proofs of his clemency and benevolence, *el tío pepe* had advocated a policy of leniency when it came to the treatment of Spanish prisoners of war. Thus after the Battle of Uclés, the many men who were captured by the French were given the choice of either serving in the ranks of Joseph's *juramentados* ("oath-takers") or returning to their own homes (with the proviso, of course, that they swore an oath of loyalty to Joseph). In neither case, however, had the policy been entirely effective. Though it would be wrong to think that there had necessarily been much enthusiasm among the captives to a return to their original colors, desertion among Joseph's turncoats had been enormous, while sufficient men had eventually rejoined the Patriot army or such guerrilla bands as those of El Empecinado and El Médico for the monarch to acquire yet another nickname—*el rey vestuario* (roughly, "the outfitter king"). This being a subject that had led to much criticism of his actions, it is notable that Joseph now adopted a much tougher line. On 27 November he wrote to Soult ordering that a special military tribunal should be formed to deal with the many instances of *juramentados* who had deserted to the Patriots or men who had returned to their homes on parole and then subsequently taken up arms against the government. No punishment was overtly specified for these offences, but as the king stressed the need for "firmness," the implication is clear enough.[19]

By capturing Seville and Cádiz, then, Joseph could well be saving his throne, but even this was not the end of his hopes. By late 1809 the financial situation of the new regime had become distinctly perilous: "Being entirely empty, the public treasury could not meet even the most indispensable expenses. No official could be paid, and thus it was that nobody who had rallied to the new king's party or had been obliged by their position to serve him, was receiving anything. Far from proving a support to him, then, they rather swelled the number of his enemies. At the same time, despite some signs of an amelioration in the state of affairs, all in all there was no guarantee whatsoever of a better future."[20] With much of Spain in the grip of French armies whose commanders held but little respect for the authority of Napoleon's brother, only the relatively small area of territory around Madrid could be relied upon to pay regular sums of money into his treasury. Beyond that there was only such funds as could be raised from the lands and other properties expropriated from the religious orders—now dissolved—and those individuals who had turned their back on Joseph and elected to take up residence in the Patriot zone. All this represented a considerable asset certainly, but even with the French armies in Spain seemingly riding a wave of victory, it was proving impossible to sell them at anything like their full value. To quote Pierre de Lagarde, a senior functionary in the Ministry of General Police who had been sent to the Peninsula to take charge of surveillance operations in Portugal in the wake of its impending conquest: "The walls of Madrid are covered with notices respecting the sale of properties confiscated from the rebels. Not a single person has come forward to purchase anything, in part because nobody has sufficient courage and in part because their value has been estimated as a figure equal to twenty-two times the income that they bring in. It is true that it is possible to pay with *vales* that have now lost around 66 percent of their value, but hardly any of these properties will be sold unless foreign speculators are called in."[21]

On top of the issue of finding buyers, the whole process of disamortization was also extremely difficult to administer. Let us here quote Miot de Melito: "This policy was the only one by which Spain could restore her credit. . . . Yet, being wholly Spanish, the administration was not used to the violent changes with which the Revolution had made us familiar in France, and in consequence only embarked on these ways that were so unknown to it with much delay and reluctance, and much precious time was lost in discussions."[22] This is more than a little unfair—one-sixth of the Spanish Church's property having been disamortized by the regime of Charles IV in the period 1800–1808, the procedure was well-enough understood by Joseph's functionaries—yet taking over the properties concerned was still hardly straightforward, and the king may well have hoped that increasing the amount of property available for expropriation would prove the quickest way of maximizing revenue. In short, could Joseph but capture Seville, he could hope to resolve all his financial problems at a stroke.

For a whole variety of reasons, then, the king was eager to march on Seville, but what of his new chief of staff, Marshal Soult? One of the best commanders that the French Revolution had produced other than Napoleon himself, Jean de Dieu Soult in theory might have been expected to be swayed by thinking that was primarily military; indeed, until the early autumn he had been urging the invasion of Portugal that British observers are so convinced ought to have been France's next move.[23] Yet setting aside the fact that the Duke of Dalmatia—to Wellington's troops he inevitably became the "the Duke of Damnation"—sincerely believed that Portugal was on the brink of being dealt with by the emperor, he too was motivated by other considerations. One such was almost certainly greed, pure and simple. While the marshal was probably by no means the worst plunderer among his fellows, he had certainly not avoided the temptation altogether and beyond doubt regarded Andalucía as a glittering prize. Still more alluring, meanwhile, were the other benefits that might accrue from victory in Andalucía. Thanks to rumors that he had got up an intrigue to have himself crowned king of Portugal (see below), Soult was currently the butt of much humor in the French army—he had become known as "King Nicholas"—while he was also in bad odor with Napoleon: furious not just at the stories that had reached him of his political ambitions but also at his ejection from Portugal at the hands of the British army, the emperor had first sent Soult a stinging rebuke that left him in no doubt that his career was in the balance, then stripped him of his position as chief of staff of the Armée d'Espagne, the latter being given to Napoleon's own chief of staff, Marshal Louis Alexandre Berthier.[24] Capture Seville and Cádiz, however, and it did not seem impossible that past disgrace would be wiped away—indeed, that a grateful emperor might finally lose patience with Joseph and place Soult on the throne of Spain or, at the very least, appoint him as viceroy of Andalucía. Finally, with Napoleon seemingly coming to Spain in a matter of months, the chance of engineering a great victory on his own account, even if only as nothing more than Joseph's chief military adviser, was not to be passed by, for in the presence of their master, the marshals were all little more than underlings. Much here, alas, is pure surmise, but, as Michael Glover writes, judging from the marshal's later conduct: "One thing is beyond all reasonable doubt: Soult did not undertake the expedition under protest as a result of Joseph's written orders. It is certain that he would have had no hesitation about appealing to the emperor over the King's head if he had disapproved of the order."[25] And according to the French general Maximilien Foy, at a great reception that was held in Madrid to mark the New Year, Soult was vigorous in his support for the coming campaign:

> It has now been decided to invade Andalucía; the troops are already moving into position. Many weighty objections have been raised to this expedition: it is said to be unwise since the English, who are still on the borders of Portugal, can, by making a few safe marches, force the army back from Seville and Córdoba to the north bank of the Tagus; it is said that to march the army into Andalucía might prejudice the emperor's plans if he should come to Spain. . . . To this Marshal Soult replies that the invasion of Andalucía is the natural sequel to the victory at Ocaña; that the English will not move on Madrid and that, even if they did, he would not be greatly alarmed; that . . . the emperor . . . was too great a man to find fault with success.[26]

In the French camp, then, all roads led to Seville. In Seville, by contrast, all roads led to perdition. Officially at least, all was still defiance. The Junta Central responded to the crisis with a fine show of activity. While a series of proclamations called for all dissension to be set aside and Spain to gird her loins for a war to the death, frantic efforts were made to energize the war effort. One eyewitness was Andreas von Schepeler, a German officer who had fought in both the Austrian and Prussian armies, fled to England, and finally got himself sent to Spain with the brief of stirring up revolt among the many German troops who had been sent to the Peninsula:

> At the beginning of December, there began to appear a string of orders that may be described as the creature of necessity. The bishops and chapter houses were instructed to comply with the decree of 4 April ordering them to give up all the plate that was not strictly necessary for their services. . . . A 100,000-strong levy of recruits was ordered in which was included widowers without children, novices, ecclesiastics in minor orders, seminarians, . . . even the nobility being accorded no more than the privilege of being allowed to serve as distinguished volunteers. In order to gain fresh horses for the cavalry—which it was hoped to make up to some 30,000 men—and the artillery, the use of private carriages and buggies without prior permission was prohibited. . . . In a proclamation of 20 December, . . . it was further announced that all vacant government offices were to be suppressed, that a loan of 24,000,000 reales was to be raised in Spain and another of 160,000,000 in London; that 100,000 sets of pikes and daggers were to be produced; that the passes of the Sierra Morena were to be inspected by engineers; that the officer corps of each battalion were to be brought up to strength; that all arms in the hands of civilians were to be surrendered to the authorities; and finally, that four of its members were to be sent out to prevent any further misfortunes such as that of Ocaña.[27]

Meanwhile, Patriot Spain's many pamphleteers continued to pour scorn on French efforts to overcome her defenders. One such was Manuel de Zequsina y Arango:

> Despite the heroic character of the Spaniards, and the glorious triumphs that they have obtained over the universal enemy of all nations, at the current moment there is no lack of cynics ready to call the happy success of our endeavors into question. . . . I do not absolutely deny that things will turn out as they predict—thanks to the vicissitudes of fortune Spain might yet succumb and become one of the tyrant's vassal states—but I cannot think of a single reason strong enough to make me think that this will be the case. If we were just to wage war on Bonaparte by raising armies on the same style as his and fighting field battles, I would not give us the least chance, for the enemy has both much more knowledge of the theory of war and a much greater degree of military experience. But this is not the way things are. At the heart of the matter is the fact that Spain wishes to be free, and free she will be because she has thrown the whole of her resources into the struggle. Napoleon's only hope is to make the struggle one of nation against nation, but this prodigy is something that he will never be able to achieve. Whereas he will sacrifice a portion of his treasure, Spain, whose resources are the greatest in the world on account of the wealth of the Americas and the maritime strength of Great Britain, will give up everything she has. Napoleon, then, can attack us with one army after another, but his onrushes will in the end be so many wavelets lapping against a great pinnacle of rock. . . . Indeed, I will go so far as to predict that Napoleon will sooner or later have to abandon his efforts or face revolt in his own dominions, for the latter must inevitably tire of being subjected to so many sacrifices for no other goal than the fortune of him and his family.[28]

In brief, then, all was well. To quote Lord Burghersh, an aide-de-camp of Wellington who had been sent to monitor opinion in Patriot Spain:

> All true Spaniards were yet bound to believe that the battle of Ocaña had been lost from some unforeseen accident, that such was never likely to happen again, and that all the forces that were collected at La Carolina would form an impenetrable barrier to the advance of the French armies and protect the

> Andalucías [*sic*] till the necessary forces were collected to fall with certain destruction on the forces of the invader. If a doubt was stated upon any part of this position, one general answer was given—that a cat could not pass through the defile of Despeñaperros, much less a French army, so that you were now desired to remain convinced that no force the enemy could bring could ever succeed in penetrating to the southward of the Sierra Morena.[29]

Yet such bombast was but a mask. Setting aside the fact that many of the provisions of the Junta Central were patently absurd—the idea, for example, that the unfortunate Spanish levies should be given pikes and daggers in the hope that they would then emulate the prowess of the victorious *tercios* of the sixteenth century would beggar belief were it not for the fact that a similar fascination for cold steel had surfaced in the course of the French Revolution—there was simply no time to put them into effect. Moreover, even if this had not been the case, it is hard to see how much could have been achieved, the new decrees being impeded by "the weakness of the government; the ineptitude, negligence or even treachery of the officials; the laziness or inexperience of the generals; and the anarchy into which much of the government had fallen."[30] The passes of the Sierra Morena, then, remained all but unfortified, and the army not just a skeleton but a skeleton in the wrong place: to his credit the much maligned Areizaga proposed the only sensible course that remained open to him—in brief, the concentration of his scattered forces at Jaén in the hope that he might then be able to defeat the French in detail as they emerged from the defiles of the Sierra Morena—but for political reasons he was overruled, the Junta being far too vulnerable to sanction even the most strategic of retreats.[31] Small wonder, then, that the authorities should have felt constrained to resort to claims of divine protection: "The Junta Suprema . . . could only prove its patriotism by echoing the national warwhoop that they were invincible. Several nuns who believed themselves inspired priestesses were produced to the loyal inhabitants of Seville to assure them that, if ever the French should see the walls of that town, the fire of heaven would fall upon them and destroy them before they should reach its gates. In many other towns the same prophetic inspiration descended upon the nuns. They foretold in every instance the destination that awaited the invaders, but the misfortunes they were themselves to suffer seem not to have been correctly placed before them."[32]

The growing popular unrest, meanwhile, was a particularly serious problem. Beneath the surface, the defeat of Areizaga had produced much turmoil. William Jacob, a British beer magnate and Tory member of Parliament who had chosen the autumn of 1809 to visit Patriot Spain, first heard the news in Cádiz: "Since my last letter we have received intelligence of the defeat of the Army of La Mancha under Areizaga. . . . When the news first arrived, those who were acquainted with it were very anxious to conceal their knowledge, or whispered it as a profound secret to their nearest connections. When it became so generally known that the people could no longer be deceived, it produced gloomy countenances and indignant expressions against the Junta."[33] Also worth citing here is Burghersh, who was in Granada: "So decisive a defeat produced considerable consternation throughout the country: the only considerable army that remained to fight the cause of Spain had been totally destroyed, and to enlightened and unprejudiced minds it was no longer doubtful that the French might at any time march unresisted by any military force to the gates of Cádiz."[34] Finally, in the capital too all was despondency: "I have again had occasion to visit Seville, which I found extremely altered in appearance for the short time I had been absent. During this interval, all the horses and mules had been taken for the use of the troops, so that there were no carriages at the evening promenades and the gatherings of the ladies had few or no visitors, the gentlemen being mostly with the army. The gloomy presages and execrations against the Junta were more openly expressed than at Cádiz: the sensible part of the inhabitants appeared to anticipate a visit from the French."[35] As for popular enthusiasm for the struggle, it was clearly under strain at the very least: "Between Lebrija and Jérez I met some parties of recruits going to the army. They were tied together and guarded by lancemen [*sic*], and at Jérez I found the volunteers on guard at the prison over others who were to be marched forward the next day. I do not, however, mean to infer from this that the young men are generally disinclined to the service; on the contrary, they have usually enlisted very readily, but the late reverses, and the reports of the inattention of the Junta to the comforts of the soldiers circulated among the peasantry have somewhat damped their zeal and rendered force necessary to carry forward the requisition."[36] And everywhere there was much froth but little substance: in Granada, for example, a group of monks proposed the formation of a *freikorps* composed entirely of ecclesiastics, for which they were voted money and arms by the provincial junta, but in the event no such force ever saw the light of day.[37]

While the Junta Central struggled to prepare Andalucía for the coming onslaught, far to the north large French forces were getting into position. In all some 62,000 men were available for the operation: I Corps of Marshal Victor, with three infantry divisions, a light-cavalry brigade, and a dragoon division; IV Corps of General Horace Sébastiani, with one infantry division, one infantry brigade, a light-cavalry brigade, and a dragoon division; V Corps of Marshal Edouard Mortier, with two infantry divisions and a mixed division of hussars, chasseurs, and dragoons; and finally, the independent infantry division of General Jean Dessolles, King Joseph's royal guard, and a brigade of *juramentados*.[38] Various schemes for the invasion of Andalucía had been examined by Marshal Soult, and it was eventually resolved that the thrust should come via two main axes. While Victor's corps concentrated at Ciudad Real and then pushed south for Córdoba via the barren and difficult terrain currently being watched by Copóns and Zeraín, Joseph and Soult would advance on the various passes that led to the upper Guadalquivir.[39] On 7 January 1810, still without word from Napoleon, king and marshal left Madrid for the front, but already thousands of men were moving south. It was an impressive moment, but the police official, Lagarde, was full of foreboding:

> After having for a long time been balanced between the desire personally to subject the south and the fear of angering Your Majesty by acting without orders, the king left for La Mancha yesterday morning. . . . What is remarkable . . . is the unprecedented suite that is accompanying him. Apart from

the personal household of the king, there are four ministers—O'Farrill, Azanza, Urquijo, and Hervas—and twelve councilors of state, all of whom require their own households, their own clerks, their own advisers, their own writing desks, their own printing presses, [and] their own fleet of carriages and wagons. . . . The soldiers look with unfriendly eyes on this swarm of attendants on the grounds that they put everything in doubt, undermine their operations and consume large quantities of such food as is available. . . . As for the spirit of the expedition, it appears less military than conciliatory. Despite all the errors that have been made in this respect, . . . the king's entourage has persuaded him that he has only to show himself for everyone to fall at his feet, and that the people, despite the fury of their leaders, are ready to repent. . . . The result will be, on a multitude of points, continual friction between the civil and military authorities. . . . Yet it is this very mania for implanting the constitution before time, for making the lieutenant general of Your Majesty at every instant take second place to the king, that has ever since your departure . . . inflamed the revolt that has continued to rumble on in the shadow of your outstretched arm. . . . And it is this insistence on believing for a whole year that Spain has been on the point of submission that has led to every efficacious measure being discarded and made it so hard to suppress the ferocious habits of disobedience, brigandage, and murder favored by . . . her mountains and poor communications. . . . It seems to me that, instead of continuing with concessions and sweet words that only serve to embolden the rebels, it would be better to accompany our resumption of offensive operations with the sort of code of conquest that would show every town and village what they had to expect, . . . that would specify the punishment that would be inflicted on any place that defended itself, and on any place where our soldiers were murdered, and . . . terrify the southern imagination. . . . I dare to affirm, even . . . that any other system than that of military government and just severity will perpetuate Spain's troubles instead of curing them. . . . Around the king there is no one, Frenchman or Spaniard, who will give him energetic counsel.[40]

How far Lagarde was to be proved right we shall see in another chapter. For the time being, however, we must consider the march of military operations, which was certainly dramatic. First contact with the defenders came on 19 January, and very soon the French forces—all of them veteran troops with a considerable record of success—were driving in their outposts. On the first day, pressure was heaviest at the easternmost sector of the front in the vicinity of Villamanrique and Montizón, which led Areizaga to send his single reserve division to shore up Vigodet, but this was to no avail: the next day the French—Sébastiani's column—kept coming, and by the afternoon the defense had been broken beyond repair. The Spaniards had made a good fight of it—with 6,000 men, Vigodet had sufficient force at least to delay Sébastiani's 10,000 troops, especially since the pass of Villamanrique was one of the most difficult in the Sierra Morena—and most were able to get away to the southeast. Behind them, however, the defenders left a scene of complete disaster: the 4,000-strong division sent to relieve them marched straight into Sébastiani's arms and was forced to surrender at Arquillos. At the main group of passes centered on that of Despeñaperros, meanwhile, the situation was even worse: on 19 January 15,000 men drawn from the troops of Mortier and Dessolles slammed into just 3,200 Spaniards headed by General Girón and cleared the passes with admirable dispatch, capturing twenty-five cannon in the process.[41] Among those present was Miot de Melito: "The attack began about eleven o'clock. The Spaniards had established two batteries on the further slopes of the mountain that formed the right-hand side of the defile and raised a number of entrenchments blocking the main road in front of the bridge that is encountered just before one reaches the Venta de Cardenas. In less than two hours all these positions were taken and the two batteries overrun by cavalry."[42] Another eyewitness was Antoine Fée, a native of Issoudun and a keen amateur botanist, who had joined the army as a pharmacist in late 1809 and immediately been sent to Spain:

> Before dawn we were on the road. Although a thin covering of snow lay on the ground, we tramped along cheerfully, eager to see the region that we had come to conquer, and picked up the

> main highway a little way north of Santa Cruz [de Mudela]. . . . Smoke from the Spanish campfires was still rising from the summit of the . . . mountains. Dismounted cannon barrels, muskets, sabers, clothing, and munitions of all sorts lay scattered on the ground, while a number of corpses lay scattered among the debris. Everything suggested more that the enemy had taken flight than that he was putting up a real fight. . . . At length La Carolina came into sight with its white houses surrounded by pretty gardens. . . . The inhabitants had fled. The army had fallen on its opponents like a swarm of locusts and devastated everything in sight."[43]

Confirmation of the Spanish rout comes from Alfred de Saint Chamans, the twenty-nine-year-old son of a French viscount who had originally enlisted as a private soldier in the Ninth Dragoons and since risen through the ranks to become a major on the staff of Marshal Soult: "We thought that the remains of the Spanish army that had been beaten at Ocaña would put up some resistance in the defiles of the Sierra Morena. This proved a mistake, however: the only defense they made was to station a few battalions behind some poor-quality breastworks that had been erected so as to block the high road. Beaten before they even fired a shot, the troops concerned took to their heels as soon as they were attacked, and so the passage of the Sierra Morena proved no more than [an] ordinary day's march for the French army."[44]

For the loss of less than 500 men, then, the French had got across the Sierra Morena in just two days of fighting (Spanish casualties in dead, wounded, and prisoners, meanwhile, came to perhaps 6,000). Areizaga and Vigodet managed to get away to the south and on 21 January rallied perhaps 8,000 men at Jaén, where they enjoyed the benefit of a number of fortifications that had been constructed around the city. Here they offered battle to Sébastiani, who had now been ordered to march southward on Jaén, Granada, and Málaga, but when the French arrived on 23 January, the result was an even greater humiliation. Though Sébastiani still had less than 10,000 troops, the defenders broke and fled without firing a shot and dispersed throughout the countryside, leaving behind large quantities of supplies and munitions and no fewer than forty-six guns, a convoy of a further thirty-two guns being overrun on the road to Granada.[45] Meanwhile, Joseph and Soult were heading down the high road that led to Córdoba and Seville, and on 22 January they encountered Victor's corps in the vicinity of Andújar, the latter having brushed aside the divisions of Copóns and Zeraín and come down into the Guadalquivir valley after a wearisome march through some of the loneliest lands in the whole of Spain. In short, 50,000 men were now concentrated less than 100 miles from Seville, and there seemed nothing that could stand in their way. Joseph, meanwhile, was in ecstasy. As he wrote to Napoleon on 25 January: "Tomorrow I will be in Córdoba and a few days after that in Seville. . . . The general pacification of Andalucía is at hand. . . . Sébastiani, Victor, Mortier, Dessolles, these are the honest men who will make the Spaniards friends of France. . . . Soult, too, is rendering us the greatest services."[46]

What made the king particularly happy was the fact that his troops had only to appear before a town for the local authorities to bow the knee to his coming. As for popular resistance, it was notable by its absence. "Córdoba and Jaén have opened their gates to me and sent me embassies," he exulted. "It is inconceivable how advantageous the gross calumnies of the enemy have been to us: the troops are behaving well, and so the populace are in a state of great joy."[47] That things were ostensibly going very well in this respect, there is no doubt. At Bailén, where Joseph spent the night of 21 January, the king was presented with two eagles that had been taken by General Francisco Javier de Castaños's army in 1808; at Montoro a last-minute attempt to revivify its Milicia Honrada—the propertied local guard set up by the Junta Central to combat disorder in the autumn of 1808—did not prevent the town surrendering without a shot being fired; and at Córdoba *el rey intruso* was greeted with a show of popular rejoicing.[48] Despite the fact that the latter city had been sacked in 1808 (see below), the atmosphere there was genuinely positive. "However much the inhabitants may have had good reason to complain of the behavior of the soldiers of General Dupont," wrote Fée, "they had trusted us and remained in their homes. This confidence was not misplaced, and good order reigned on all sides. . . . Asking for ordinary clothes, the monks secularized themselves in an instant. . . .

Once a measure of confidence had arisen between us, something that in most cases took no time at all, they laughed with us at their metamorphosis while yet . . . resuming such part of the life of the cloister as they could."[49]

Nor was the Spanish performance any more impressive in Sébastiani's front. At Jaén not a single man had come forward in response to an attempt to call up the various companies of part-time irregulars that had been set up to combat banditry for service in the Sierra Morena, and the city offered no resistance when the French arrived on 23 January.[50] And at Granada, as the French advanced on the city, the existing administration collapsed, the Junta of Granada dissolving itself and surrendering power to the city's pre-1808 authorities. These immediately issued a declaration proclaiming Granada to be an open city and dispatched two members of the town council to greet the oncoming invaders and beg for mercy. Back in the city, meanwhile, every effort was made to avoid the possibility of armed resistance, the magistrates being given strict orders not to allow any public gatherings, and the few troops remaining there confined to barracks and placed under the command of Colonel Francisco Antonio Cañaveral, the officer who had hitherto headed the urban militia formed in 1808.[51] Thus reassured, on 28 January the French marched in. There was no resistance, and accompanied by the *comisario regio* (royal commissioner) appointed by King Joseph, Miguel José de Azanza, Sébastiani proceeded directly to the palace of the Duques de Gor, which he proceeded to make his headquarters, an integral part of this process being a triumphal procession through the main streets of the city.[52]

At this moment, however, the chief focus of attention was naturally Seville. Once Córdoba had fallen, Joseph and Soult had pushed westward, and on approaching the town of Carmona, they had been confronted by a decision that was to weigh heavily on the history of the rest of the war. In brief, just west of this town the high road along which the French were travelling split in two, with one branch leading westward to Seville and the other heading south toward Utrera and Cádiz. What might have happened had matters fallen out differently cannot be established with any certainty, of course, but it is at least possible to argue that a sudden thrust on the latter by even so much as a division of French troops might have had dramatic results: at this time Cádiz was only defended by a civic militia of extremely dubious combat value (see below), while it is doubtful whether its authorities were any more willing to fight to the death than those of any other Andalusian city. Yet apparently convinced, first, that the fall of Seville would be enough to persuade Cádiz to surrender as well and, second, that Alburquerque's army, which, as we shall see, had hastily been transferred from the Guadiana to the Guadalquivir, was preparing to defend the capital and therefore open to destruction—elements of its cavalry had just been encountered at Ecija—Joseph insisted that the entire army should head straight for Seville.[53]

Though taken on grounds that in the circumstances were logical enough—the destruction of the last Spanish army in the field was beyond question the greatest goal open at this point to *el rey intruso*—this decision was to prove disastrous for the French. To explain this, we must turn to the doings of Alburquerque's Army of Extremadura. This, as we have seen, was scarcely an impressive force, but as soon as its commander had realized that the French were on the move in La Mancha, he had set his men in motion for Andalucía. Initially, his plan had been to join Zeraín and Copóns in the vicinity of Almadén, but very soon news arrived that they were in headlong retreat for Seville, so he too headed for the capital, in the process ignoring orders that arrived from the Junta Central to the effect that he should march on Victor's flank and rear, a demonstration that could have had no effect on the campaign and would have risked the destruction of Alburquerque's army. By dint of forced marches as tough as anything ever seen in the annals of the Peninsular War, by 23 January, now joined by Copóns (the division of Zeraín, by contrast, was held back in the capital as a reserve), his men had reached Carmona and thereby managed to block the high road to Seville. According to the Junta Central, Alburquerque's task was now to recapture Córdoba, but this fresh order was no better than the one that would have taken the duke into Victor's rear in La Mancha: even with the reinforcements it had now picked up, the Army of Extremadura still had no more than 12,000 men, whereas Joseph and Soult had at least 50,000.

Beyond doubt, this was one of the key moments of the Peninsular War, indeed, conceivably of the entire French Wars. Had Alburquerque advanced as he had been directed, he would undoubtedly have led his army to destruction: outnumbered four to one and caught in the open plains of the Guadalquivir valley, it would have been swept away in an instant; equally, had he stood firm at Carmona or fallen back on Seville, the result would again have been a disastrous rout. As all that would have stood between Spain and the complete loss of Andalucía would have been the Cádiz militia, it is therefore just as well that on 27 January news arrived at Alburquerque's headquarters that the Junta Central had fled Seville for Cádiz. Fortunately for the cause of Spain, however, in the duke the Junta Central had something of a "thinking general." Over the course of the past two years, a succession of Spanish commanders, fearful of death at the hands of the crowd or disgrace at the hands of their political superiors, had accepted battle over and over again in the most unfavorable of circumstances and in consequence gone down to inglorious defeat. Alburquerque, though, was different. Considering that his orders had been rendered null and void, the duke immediately put his men on the road again, and, saved from any pursuit by the French insistence on marching on Seville with every man at their disposal—extraordinarily, news of Alburquerque's departure from the area was not picked up until 31 January[54]—by 3 February the Army of Extremadura, further reinforced by a number of battalions of recruits picked up in various towns along the way, was filing across the causeway that carried the high road from Seville to Cádiz across the marshes separating the Isla de León—the island on whose outermost promontory Cádiz stands—from the mainland. Alburquerque, then, had not saved Seville, but it is arguable that he had saved Spain, and with her, in the end, the whole cause of resistance to Napoleon in the Iberian peninsula.[55]

With Alburquerque on the road for Cádiz, it is now time to look at events in the capital. This is not the moment to discuss the politics of Patriot Spain in any depth, but, in brief, the Junta Central had throughout its life been menaced by a powerful coalition of enemies who were determined to bring about its downfall. As to who these forces were, they had three principal foci. Thus, in the first instance we find the leading representatives of the so-called *fernandino* party—that is to say the anti-reformist *fronde* that had been at the center of the *motín de Aranjuez* in 1808 (the palace revolt that had brought down Charles IV and his favorite, Manuel de Godoy, and catapulted Ferdinand VII onto the throne)—in the persons of Francisco Palafox (the younger brother of the famous defender of Zaragoza) and the Conde de Montijo, both of whom were currently in prison on charges of conspiracy and sedition as a result of their earlier coup attempts (discussed in chapter 2). In the second, there was the Marqués de la Romana, the general who had commanded the Spanish division that had been sent to join the *grande armée* in Germany in 1807, and whose return to Spain courtesy of a spectacular maritime rescue by the Royal Navy in the summer of 1808 had been followed by both growing horror at what La Romana saw as the Jacobin tendencies of the Patriot zone and a determination to replace the Junta Central by a council of regency headed by himself. And in the third there was the Junta of Seville—that is to say the revolutionary committee that had emerged as the head of affairs in the city in May 1808—this body having never forgiven the Junta Central for the manner in which the latter had blocked its own plans to assume the government of the whole of Spain. With the Junta Central completely discredited by the advance of the French, the agents of one or other of these hostile tendencies (or perhaps all of them operating in union) mobilized the crowd to take advantage of the situation. Whipped up to a frenzy by paid agitators who accused the Junta Central of treason and called loudly for its replacement by a new regime made up only of true patriots, the populace massed in the streets and demanded both that they be given arms and that Palafox and Montijo should be released. Seeing that their own situation and that of Seville alike were hopeless, on 23 January the Junta Central fled the city. The result was complete chaos. A new government—the so-called Junta Nacional Suprema—was established on the basis of Palafox, Montijo, La Romana, a notoriously reactionary general named Eguía, and the erstwhile minister of the antiguo régimen and luminary of the Junta of Seville, Francisco de Saavedra, but it had no authority whatsoever. An eyewitness to the situation was the famous dissident José Blanco-White:

"When the members of the Junta Suprema [that is, the Junta Central] found themselves obliged to seek safety in flight and could no longer hide the news that the French troops were approaching Seville without encountering the slightest difficulty, the people were seized by a general state of consternation, and turmoil took hold of the city to such an extent that nobody was capable of implementing any of the measures that ought to have been adopted in respect of the defense of the city."[56]

The streets, then, were filled with agitated crowds demanding arms, hunting down spies and traitors, and urging a policy of resistance to the last cartridge upon the authorities, but they were empty of order and direction. Nor, indeed, was there any real chance of doing anything even if it had been possible to get the city under control. There were plenty of arms and munitions certainly, but there were no more than 4,000 troops in Seville—the division of Zeraín plus various battalions that had acted as the personal guards of the Junta Central—and fewer than 200 of them were the trained artillerymen who would play the most crucial part in any siege. Assuming that the apparent zeal of the crowd could be taken at face value, perhaps 20,000 armed civilians might be added to the ranks of the defenders, yet even with this assistance, there would be no chance of holding the city: at great expense Seville had been surrounded by a ring of impressive earthen ramparts, but these were so extensive that they would have required a minimum of 50,000 men to hold with any chance of success. In short, Seville was doomed, and recognizing this, on the night of 28 January, the Junta Nacional fled the city in its turn and dispersed to the four winds (for example, having previously delayed obeying orders he had received to this effect for many weeks, La Romana headed for Extremadura on the pretext that he was needed to take command of the Spanish forces defending Badajoz, while Montijo headed for his estates in Granada on the pretext of raising an army of peasants to march to the relief of Seville).[57]

With Zeraín in the meantime having led the remaining troops out of the city to the west in the hope of reaching safety in the region of Huelva, Seville was quite literally in the hands of the crowd when the first enemy troops appeared before the walls in the late afternoon of 29 January, the only recognized civil authorities of any kind being a few friars who had set themselves up as popular demagogues. Under the latter's leadership, a few hundred of the rioters were prevailed upon to man the ramparts and open an ineffective fire upon the scattered French pickets who constituted the only targets within range, but within a few hours all heart had gone from these last defenders, and they dispersed to their homes. With the French now before the walls in force, Seville's regular authorities—that is to say the city council, the military governor, and the cathedral chapter—were free to seek the best terms of surrender that they could, these being negotiated by an embassy sent to Joseph's headquarters on 31 January.

There followed the same sort of scenes that had already been witnessed elsewhere. At dawn on 1 February some 1,500 French troops—possibly the three battalions of the Eighth Line—entered the city and secured such key points as the arsenal and the *alcázar*—the palace-cum-castle that had been the seat of the Junta Central. This vanguard of occupation was then followed by a group of key staff officers with responsibility for such tasks as securing lodgings for the king and his personal suite, allocating billets, and initiating the inevitable requisitions. Joseph, meanwhile, had spent the night at the nearby *pueblo* of Alcalá de Guadaira and, having already been waited upon by representatives of the civil and military authorities, was by now riding toward the city in his carriage along roads lined by the corps of Marshal Victor. Arriving at the Puerta Nueva de San Fernando, he was met by a delegation of the cathedral chapter, whereupon he mounted a horse and proceeded to ride through the streets to the *alcázar* at the head of his royal guard and, more importantly perhaps, a number of troops drawn from the brown-uniformed Spanish army he had spent the past year endeavoring to form.[58] For a good description of the scene, we may turn to the pharmacist Fée: "Seville surrendered, and the place of the battle that everyone expected was taken by a grand parade. The town . . . opened its gates to King Joseph, who made his entry to the sound of the church bells and found plenty of voices that were happy to welcome him. . . . As for the rest of us, we too got an agreeable reception."[59] Also present was Joseph's friend and councilor, André Miot de Melito:

> The sun was shining with all its force: it lit up the whole of the immense plain in which Seville is situated, and its rays caught the Giralda and the various other church towers that marked the city's skyline. . . . Three quarters of a league from the town, we came up with the corps of Marshal Victor drawn up in battle order on either side of the high road. Dressed as they were in their parade uniforms, the troops were a magnificent sight, while satisfaction at their victory was reflected in every one of their faces. As [Joseph] passed their beautiful lines, he was greeted by the warmest cheers. Preceded by his guard, the King then immediately made his way into the city. He was received . . . by an immense mass of people who filled the streets and squares all the way to the palace. . . . Cries of "Long live the King!" resounded on all sides. Curiosity and fear undoubtedly played a much large role in this spectacle than any other sentiment, but, whatever the true causes may have been, the idea of making for Seville first of all appeared to have been justified: once again the end of the war appeared to be at hand.[60]

Needless to say, this last opinion was shared by Joseph himself. As he wrote to his imperial brother: "Sire: I entered this city yesterday to the acclamations of the whole people. . . . Andalucía is pacified, order is restored; the Junta [Central] is dissolved."[61] In the army too morale was very high:

> We had entered Seville in the most peaceable fashion imaginable: the entire population had stayed in place, and now the city was affording us all the resources of a rich and civiliszed province. In no country have I ever seen anything as beautiful as the countryside of Andalucía. Offered, as we were, the fruits of Europe and Africa alike, we were astonished at its richness. Groves of oranges, aloes, and olives were interspersed with vines and other crops that were native to our own country. As for the immense population, it seemed to have none of the savage air of the other Spanish provinces through which we had passed, and this added to the happy prospect that lay before us. Indeed, in those first days I believe that we had all forgotten . . . the horrors of the Spanish war to such an extent that, offered

> the chance of being magicked away to France, few of us would have taken it.[62]

With Seville in French hands, there is but little left to recount of the sorry tale that was the campaign of January 1810. The day after the triumphal entry into the Andalusian capital, Victor's I Corps marched for Cádiz, only to find that, stiffened by the arrival of Alburquerque, the new Council of Regency that had been formed to rule Spain in place of the Junta Central rejected his summons to surrender. And, while other French units marched on Ayamonte, from whence the last troops who had fled Seville were evacuated to Cádiz by sea, Sébastiani had been moving on Málaga. The last major city to be occupied by the French, this was also the one place that offered serious resistance in the face of the onrushing enemy. Thanks to the detailed account of events there that was kept by a local doctor named José Mendoza y Rico, who already had made a name for himself thanks to the detailed history he had written of the great yellow-fever epidemic of 1803–1804, however, we know that what occurred in Málaga was no last-minute surge of heroism. For reasons that we shall discuss at a later point, the local authorities, and, above all, the provincial junta that ruled the region, were no more popular in Málaga than they were anywhere else in Patriot Spain. In consequence, no sooner had rumors begun to spread that the French had forced the Sierra Morena and taken Córdoba than the populace began "to gather together in the streets, to complain about their rulers and to allege that the Junta Central and General Areizaga had sold out to the enemy."[63] Very soon, meanwhile, matters made still worse by the arrival of large numbers of stragglers from Areizaga's army, not to mention civilian refugees desperate to take ship for Cádiz, Alicante, or Valencia. Fearing that the people were likely to get out of hand—their propensity for violence had already been demonstrated all too clearly in the course of the national uprising of May 1808—on 24 January the junta asked Vicente Abello, a retired infantry officer of Cuban origin who had played an active part in organizing Málaga's volunteers in 1808 and was therefore presumed to have some influence over the crowd, to attempt to calm down the populace. This, however, was a bad move: far from being a loyal servant of the junta, Abello was a deeply embittered man who fancied himself a military genius and believed that he had been repeatedly passed over since 1808. Still worse, he was a close friend of the four San Millán brothers—José, Rafael, Bernardo, and Antonio—all of whom were public notaries with a terrible reputation for fraud, dishonesty, and intrigue. Given that this faction had been scheming for the past year to overthrow the junta, the result was disaster. Quickly gaining the support of a number of clerics, such as a Capuchin friar named Francisco Berrocal, Abello and the San Millán brothers ostensibly set about the task of rallying the crowd behind the junta but so engineered things that very soon demands were being voiced that Abello be appointed captain general. Amid scenes of great disorder—in large part the work of peasants and landless laborers who had been brought in from the surrounding mountains—Abello promptly took control. The junta having been imprisoned, the new ruler made all four of the San Millán brothers generals and appointed the eldest of them military governor, all this being accompanied by a veritable blizzard of patronage, much of it directed at such figures as taverners and smugglers.[64] An eyewitness was the rector of the San Felipe Neri oratory: "The least of it was the plunder and robbery of, as I have heard, men of the greatest wisdom and respect: the ranks of lieutenant and sub-lieutenant were on sale for a couple of gold *onzas*, while one saw effeminate young men, some of them barely past the age of puberty, swaggering around the streets, bedecked with cocked hats, aiguillettes, and pom-poms, carrying sabers under their arms in the French fashion."[65]

Had the new government's conduct of affairs been more efficient than that of its predecessor—the Junta of Málaga, as we shall see, had been a body noted neither for its talents nor its probity—then the coup of 24 January 1810 might be forgiven, but in fact things were if anything even worse than before. With the French bearing down on the city, the only plan that made any sense was to organize a delaying action that would have bought time for the evacuation of the city's treasury, not to mention the contents of its many magazines and warehouses. Yet Abello and his fellows devoted themselves to concentrating inside the city every man, every cannonball, every *real*, and every ounce of supplies that they could lay their hands on, thereby ensuring that when Málaga fell, as it most assuredly would, the French triumph would be even greater. Meanwhile, although the city was wide open to attack, Abello neglected the obvious task of strengthening its defenses in the hope of emulating, say, the defense of Zaragoza in July 1808 and instead concentrated on, first, transforming the *levée en masse* that he had immediately ordered into a field army and, second, placating the inhabitants by spreading rumors of imaginary Spanish victories (though just in case this failed to work, he was also careful to set up a gallows outside his headquarters, which for good measure was ringed by artillery pieces and armed guards).[66]

All this time the French had been coming steadily onward, and at two o'clock in the morning on 2 February, the bubble finally burst with the news that the enemy were through the Boca del Asno pass. The result was complete panic: "The church bells rang the alarm, all the troops were formed up; all the nuns fled their convents, along with those few monks and friars who were still at their posts; infinite numbers of families took ship without the least heed for where they might end up; every vessel in the port put out to sea far enough to ensure that it was out of range of the shore; and finally the common people rushed aimlessly from place to place in a state of absolute panic. In short, the whole place became a veritable Tower of Babel."[67]

As the French did not appear straightaway, the situation soon calmed down a little, and Abello set about trying to get his motley army into a position in which it could defend the city. This, however, was a hopeless task. Almost entirely untrained and in some cases even lacking proper arms, the defenders were in complete confusion, while the Spaniards were also encumbered by large crowds of civilians who had come out to watch the triumph that Abello had continued to promise to the very last. When the French attacked, then, they broke through almost immediately, whereupon Abello and the San Millán brothers promptly turned and fled.[68] The battle, such as it was, having been fought only just outside the city walls, attackers and defenders, soldiers and civilians alike, all now poured through the gates in a single confused mass, with the result that, unlike almost every other city that the French had captured in this lightning campaign, Málaga was thoroughly sacked. As Mendoza complained: "The barbarity of the French reached the extremes of . . . killing the wounded soldiers they found hiding in the houses that they entered and raping every woman whom they caught on their own or had nothing to buy them off with."[69] Such was the fury of the attackers, indeed, that they even looted the houses of prominent members of the French community. Though Sebastiani tried to get his men under control from midnight onward, the violence lasted all night, order only being restored once the victors had drunk themselves into a stupor or collapsed from exhaustion. By that time, Málaga was a shocking sight: "The city evoked horror among all who saw it. It was almost entirely deserted; every door was hanging off its hinges; the streets were stained with blood and strewn with broken weapons, cartridge boxes, and corpses, many of these last our own, and, still worse, beggars and other unfortunates who had had nowhere to hide. The few people one encountered in the streets looked pale and shaken, while their faces were engraved with the horror and misery they had witnessed."[70]

Thus fell Patriot Andalucía. In the space of less than three weeks, the French armies had broken through a major mountain range, advanced hundreds of miles, and captured no fewer than five important cities for the loss of no more than a handful of men. Also lost to the Spaniards were hundreds of guns and immense stores of arms, food, and munitions as well as equally enormous sums of money. Meanwhile, town after town had opened their gates to the invaders without firing a shot, just as the leaders of the Patriot cause had either fled their posts in the hope of reaching safety in Cádiz or elsewhere, or still worse, taken the lead in delivering up the cities and provinces for which they were responsible. In a development of great significance for the future, Cádiz, it was true, had been denied to the invaders while most of the Spanish forces had escaped to fight another day, but in the whole of the Napoleonic Wars, there was little to rival these events other than the equally humiliating political and military collapse that had been played out in Prussia following the twin disasters of Jena and Auerstädt in October 1806. There too resistance had been minimal, and as historian after historian has pointed out, this can be attributed to the complete failure of the Prussian state to engage the loyalty of its population, most of whom had little reason to care whether they were ruled by a Bonaparte or a Hohenzollern. Yet this comparison does not appear to have struck the chord among historians of the Spanish War of Independence that might have been expected. Despite the fact that, in Patriot Spain as much as in Prussia, the sequel to military defeat was a far-reaching reform movement explicitly directed at energizing the population and persuading it to become more closely involved in the fortunes of the state and, still more explicitly, its military endeavors, no one seems to have drawn the obvious conclusion, which is that, at every level, the inhabitants of Andalucía were as lukewarm in their sympathies for their rulers as those of Brandenburg. On the contrary, indeed, over and over again one reads that military defeat was irrelevant—that in effect it said nothing about popular devotion to the war effort and certainly had no influence upon it. With even skeptical contemporary observers who might have been expected to see through this pretense inclined to repeat the same mantra, it is time to pay closer attention to the regime that was so comprehensively savaged in January 1810.

2

The Context of Conquest

Let us begin with the obvious. Not one thing in the previous chapter corresponds with the picture of Spanish resistance presented by the traditional historiography of the Peninsular War. In so far as this last is concerned, the response of the Spanish people to Napoleonic aggression was as sharp as it was unanimous. To the accompaniment of devotion to the exiled *rey deseado* on the one hand and hatred of the invaders on the other, the "intrusive" regime of Joseph Bonaparte was everywhere supposedly resisted, if not to the last bullet, then at least with the utmost ferocity. Earlier in the war and in other parts of Spain, this was in some instances the case, but in Andalucía in 1810, it most assuredly was not. Faced with this difficulty, some historians have attempted to gloss it over or even ignore it altogether, but others have sought refuge in a dictum that, while affording little comfort, at least offers a logical explanation for the collapse of Spanish resistance in the face of King Joseph's crossing of the Sierra Morena. In brief, the idea that Andalucía was inhabited by more *afrancesados* than anywhere else in Spain was coined comparatively early on in the historiography of the war; it is, for example, found in the work of the Conde de Toreno. But whether such words are satisfactory is another matter. While there were certainly cities in Andalucía—Seville for one, Cádiz for another—that were home to pockets of advanced political thought that at least had the potential to line up behind Joseph, the idea that the whole of the south of Spain was sufficiently infected by political *afrancesamiento* to explain the abject scenes of January 1810 is inherently unlikely. Clearly, then, what is needed is an alternative explanation.

Before going any further, however, we need to underline just how marked the contrast was between the behavior of Andalucía in 1810 and that of the rest of Spain. To do this, one can do no better than consider some of the events that marked the year 1808. In a variety of places, of course—Valencia, Zaragoza, Gerona—French attempts to occupy rebellious Spanish cities were met with desperate popular resistance that saw crowds of armed civilians man the walls with whatever arms available and on occasion engage in acts of the most extraordinary heroism: one thinks here particularly of "Agustina of Aragón" taking over her dying husband's cannon at the siege of Zaragoza. Elsewhere, meanwhile, angry villagers tried to protect their homes from French foraging parties or joined hastily raised militias or irregular bands that sought to check or at least harass the march of enemy columns: good examples here are provided by the ferocious fight put up by the *pueblo* of Valdepeñas when it was approached by a regiment of French dragoons or the humiliation inflicted on the column of General François de Schwartz when it was ambushed by Catalan *somatenes* in the pass of El Bruch. Be it noted too, meanwhile, that in 1808 Andalucía had shared in this behavior, one of the reasons why General Dupont adopted the defensive posture that eventually produced the catastrophe at Bailén being his dismay at the extent to which his communication with Madrid had been disrupted by irregular resistance in the Sierra Morena and the valley of the River Guadalquivir. In this last respect perhaps, it is worth quoting the memoirs of Captain Charles François, a company commander in one of the second-line formations that formed the bulk of the first Armée d'Espagne who was sent to the town of Linares to requisition the contents of the local powder mill:

> I arrived . . . at the town, presented myself . . . before the mayor and showed my order. He gave us every assistance . . . and we took half a ton of powder and 1500 pounds of balls, which we put in the carts. My mission being accomplished, I caused bread, meat, rice and a bottle of wine apiece to be given to the soldiers, and they prepared their meal on a plateau overlooking the town. . . . I left at nine p.m., and had hardly

> started . . . when I was attacked on all sides. I formed square with the wagons inside and continued my march, blazing away in all directions . . . until five o'clock in the morning, when I entered a wood where, very fortunately, I found a company of sharpshooters which the general had sent to meet me.[1]

Overt popular resistance of this sort was probably the exception rather than the rule, but even where the French met with no opposition as such, it is clear that their coming was not regarded with any favor. Let us here consider the extraordinary difference in the manner in which the cities of Madrid and Seville first received the figure of Joseph Bonaparte. As we have seen, in Seville *el rey intruso* was greeted by cheering crowds, but in Madrid, 20 July 1808—the day that Joseph first appeared in his capital—was rather an occasion of shame and sorrow. In this respect we can do no better than to begin with the words of José Clemente Carnicero, a priest who kept a journal of daily life in the capital throughout the war:

> On 19 July King Joseph arrived at Chamartín with all the company that had waited on him at Bayonne. Very quickly news spread that he intended to make his public entrance on the following day. Though a few of the more credulous attributed the situation to a stratagem on the part of our generals that was designed to take him prisoner and, with him, his entire army, it is not necessary to ask whether this threw good *madrileños* into confusion. No sooner had the news spread, meanwhile, than an order of the day was circulated to the effect that all the houses along the way should be adorned with decorations and that the people should not be alarmed by the continuous salvos of artillery and peals of church bells that would greet his entrance. This, it was announced, would take place from six o'clock in the evening onward along a route stretching from the Puerta de Recoletos along the Calle de Alcalá and the Calle Mayor to the royal palace, but such [a] difference between his reception and that which greeted our own Don Fernando can hardly be imagined. No citizen hung his balcony with drapes except for two French couturiers. In every other instance the only adornment

> the balconies received was that of the thick linen blinds that . . . kept out . . . the worst of the sunshine. . . . The artillery kept up a constant racket, true enough, but the church bells were rung in so sporadic and mournful a fashion that it sounded as if they were tolling for a funeral. . . . The suite of M. Joseph was reduced to a large escort of infantry and cavalry, a number of his generals and a few Spanish traitors. But what summed up this entry into the city most of all was a gaggle of French agitators who . . . ran along beside the king's carriage, shouting at intervals, "Long live the King! Long live the King!" By contrast all the Spaniards maintained the most profound silence.[2]

It could here be objected that this is the account of someone bitterly opposed to the French occupation—in the years after 1814, Carnicero went on to become a fierce champion of the inquisition—and that it should therefore be treated with some caution. But the truth is that the version that French observers recorded is very similar. Here, for example, is the corresponding extract from a prominent member of Joseph's court named Louis de Girardin:

> At six o'clock in the evening several discharges of artillery announced the departure of the king from Chamartín. His suite was preceded by a strong body of cavalry, and the pavements were lined by French troops. . . . Not a single person could be observed watching the procession from the windows, and the few civilians on the streets were mostly Frenchmen. Not a single "Viva!" was held, while such a ceremony had never been held in such silence. The procession having first processed along the Calle de Alcalá, at eight o'clock in the evening we arrived at the palace once occupied by Charles IV and Ferdinand VII, and alighted from the carriages. No sooner had we done so than the Duke of Rovigo [that is, General Savary] came up to me and said how pleased he was that the entry of the King had gone so well. At this I professed my surprise, but he replied, "You can be as astonished as you like, but I was sure that the King would at the very least have been insulted; indeed, given the distance we had to cover, I expected that at least thirty bullets would be fired at him."[3]

For Joseph Bonaparte this was a moment of tremendous sadness. In the course of his journey from Bayonne to the capital, he had experienced a whole series of snubs and disappointments, but on 14 July the Spanish armies of Galicia and Castile had suffered a serious defeat at Medina de Río Seco, and it appears that he had become convinced that the news of this catastrophe would convince the population of Madrid of the need to acquiesce. Now, however, all hope was gone, and he felt totally defrauded:

> Very soon we will not have a sou: all the provinces are in the hands of the enemy and the latter are to be found on every hand. Henry IV had a party in his favor, and Phillip V only had to contest the throne with a rival, but I have a nation of 12,000,000 inhabitants opposed to me. My assassination is publically spoken of, but it is not this that I fear. . . . If France could put an army of 1,000,000 under arms in the first years of the Revolution, why should not Spain, which is much more united in her anger and hatred, get together 500,000 men and turn them into warriors—indeed, the most splendid warriors—in three months? They could easily have 50,000 men . . . well before that. Meanwhile, neither honest men nor rogues will take my side. No, Sire. You have made a mistake: your glory will be overthrown in Spain. . . . Given that nobody can doubt your love for me, my tomb will form a monument to your impotence.[4]

How can the great difference in the reactions of the two cities be explained? Let us first deal with the question of political *afrancesamiento*. It is the truth that Seville had been a center of liberal thought prior to 1808: thanks to the influence of progressive teaching in the city's university, an entire generation of its intellectual elite had become increasingly critical of the antiguo régimen, and its chief literary and scientific forum, the Sociedad Sevillana de Amigos del País, was therefore dominated by figures noted for their advanced thinking, such as the poets Felix José Reinoso and Alberto Lista. Other products of Seville's proto-liberal circles, meanwhile, were the archetypal dissidents José Marchena and José María Blanco White (the former in 1792 had fled into exile in France, where he went on to become one of the Revolution's chief foreign propagandists; as for the latter, in 1808 a professor at an advanced institute of education founded in Madrid by Manuel de Godoy and despairing of the prospects for reform in Spain, he was ultimately to take up residence in England and turn Utilitarian).[5] However, the same thing could just as well be said of Oviedo, the hometown of such radicals as Agustín Arguelles, José Canga Arguelles, Alvaro Flórez Estrada, and the Conde de Toreno, and yet in all the numerous occasions on which it was entered by the French, the latter city never gave the slightest signs of welcoming their arrival. One may, then, rule out the idea that Andalucía was somehow predisposed to accept French rule, and all the more so as the same turmoil and effervescence was on display south of the Sierra Morena in the wake of the outbreak of the national uprising in May 1808 as was the case in the rest of the country. For a good example, let us here cite the case of Ayamonte. Shortly after the uprising, that town enjoyed a brief visit from a convoy of British troops en route from Gibraltar to Lisbon, among whom was a young ensign named Charles Leslie:

> Being the first English who had landed in Spain since the breaking out of the Patriot cause, we were received with the most enthusiastic demonstrations of joy by the inhabitants. The governor invited all the officers to an entertainment in the evening, and had provided for us billets in all the best houses. The Spanish officers, both of the army and navy, almost crushed us in their fraternal embraces and insisted on carrying us from house to house, and introducing us to all the pretty ladies in the place. These dark beauties gave us the most cordial reception, and sang patriotic songs and warlike hymns, accompanied on the guitar or piano. Some of the naval officers who had been in England repeatedly sang "Rule Britannia" and "God save the King!" Their admiration of England's prowess seemed unaffected. In many houses we observed busts of Mr Pitt. . . . The governor's supper went off with great harmony. Mutual toasts were given, and bumpers drunk to the perpetual harmony of the two nations. . . . The town was crowded with armed peasantry of all ages from seventeen to sixty, eager to enroll themselves under the patriotic banner. . . . They were armed with . . .

> a few muskets, more fowling pieces, some pikes or poles with long bayonets stuck at the end and many pitchforks. There was as little uniformity in dress as in arms. . . . The Patriots having assumed a red cockade, with the cypher FVII worked upon [it], woe to any man who ventured to appear without one. The ladies took a pride in presenting us with this national emblem, embroidered with their own fair hands, as we had been ordered to put them above our black ones.[6]

The scenes witnessed in Ayamonte, however, were as nothing compared to those seen in Málaga. Here events were dramatic indeed. On 4 June a courier arrived from Antequera claiming that there were French soldiers in the nearby town of Benamejí, whereupon 4,000 or more of the inhabitants seized whatever arms they could and marched out to do battle. In the event, of course, this rumor proved false—no troops from Dupont's army ever came closer to Málaga than Jaén—but the crowd refused to disperse and demanded the detention of the city's substantial French community, some members of which they in fact seized of their own accord; the release of the prisoners in the city's jails; and the right to read all incoming mails. To all this the junta gave way, and on 5 June the city's prisons were duly emptied, the prisoners being treated as heroes and in some instances parading through the streets, boasting that they were going to throw the French not just out of Spain but also out of France itself.[7]

Andalucía, then, was not *afrancesada.* Assuming, then, that the welcome accorded Joseph in Seville was neither an invention of French chroniclers nor something that was simply got up in advance of the king's arrival, we need an alternative explanation for what occurred, and for this we might well turn to Marshal Soult. "The cities," the French chief of staff wrote, "received [Joseph] with curiosity, and he allowed himself to be easily deceived by the receptions that were organized to greet him. The propertied classes preferred, it is true, an organized government that would protect their interests to the rule of the mob and the anarchy that must go with it. But . . . the King was above all surrounded with the sort of courtier who in every country throws himself at the feet of whoever is in power in the hope of obtaining favor without any thought of venturing their loyalty beyond mere words."[8] There are, of course, some obvious caveats here, and the historian who does not take them into account would be a fool indeed. Yet at the same time we have a suggestion that the enthusiasm that was on display was based on something more than the desire to curry favor, or to put it another way, place the interests of self and family above those of Spain. Thus we also hear a faint echo of a political choice—in effect, indeed, of a massive vote of no confidence in the Patriot cause, at least insofar as it was identified with the leadership of the Junta Central, and what is more, a vote against the Patriot cause that, given the almost complete absence of popular resistance, must be considered as extending to the common people as well as the elites.

What makes this the more surprising is that the inhabitants of Seville had no more reason than the inhabitants of Madrid to look upon the arrival of the enemy with any equanimity. In July 1808 the latter, of course, were still much moved by memories of the tragic events of 2 May, events that were generally explained in terms of a cold-blooded attempt to massacre them to the last man, woman, and child. The former, however, could rest no easier in their beds, for hanging over them was the specter of what had happened when Dupont's army sacked Córdoba after the action at Alcolea on 7 June. Among those present on that day was an officer of the Regiment of Sailors of the Guard named Pierre Baste:

> It was close to 2.30 pm when the bulk of the division came close to Córdoba. At our approach, the Spanish abandoned their position . . . and our troops launched themselves into the town at the charge. We found it deserted by the Spanish troops, who were fleeing in the greatest disorder. . . . But it became impossible to restrain the greed of the soldiers who, running through the streets with bayonets fixed, forced passage for themselves everywhere and spread throughout the houses in order to pillage. An early column, still marching in closed ranks, arrived in one part of town to be met by musketry from the windows of several houses; this fact led us inevitably to the persuasion that the inhabitants had taken up arms and were defending

> themselves. So a form of street-to-street combat broke out and served as a pretext for our soldiers to sack Córdoba and deliver it up to all the horrors of a town taken by assault. The soldiers scattered by platoons or singly, fully armed and unmoved by any representation made to them. Murder and pillage were soon joined by the rape of women, virgins and nuns, the theft of sacred vessels from the churches—sacrilege accompanied by the most atrocious circumstances. Some officers—even some generals—demeaned themselves by indulging in such dishonour, even when grief-stricken parents sought to solicit the protection of the first officers they encountered. Happily for the name of French honour there were some sensible and generous souls who, in saving more than one family, protected them from the outrageous behaviour of a soldiery even more difficult to rein in once they had broken all the leashes of discipline. I had the good fortune to be able to save several women and some Spanish men who would otherwise have become victim of the soldiers' blind fury. Called to the aid of a woman in the greatest distress, I was almost forced to kill three frenzied members of a light battalion who, despite my efforts and the entreaties of the unfortunate woman, persisted in forcing their brutal attentions on her daughter, a charming young woman. . . . All kinds of disorder characterised this awful day.[9]

Nor was the sack of Córdoba (an experience that was shared in lesser degree by Jaén) an isolated instance of French brutality. On the contrary, as the war continued, the conduct of the invaders continued to be marked by pillage and atrocity: given the conditions in which the war was waged and the immense cultural differences between the combatants, no matter what draconian threats they issued, few French commanders could keep their men in hand. Thus the sack of Córdoba was repeated at Oporto on 29 March 1809, while the passage of Napoleon's forces was everywhere marked by a trail of destruction. Once again the most eloquent accounts come from French observers. Girardin, for example, has left this picture of the retreat of King Joseph and the troops that accompanied him from Madrid to the River Ebro in the wake of the news of Bailén:

> On the first of August the army continued its retreat . . . with the intention of reaching a settlement called San Agustín that lay at a distance of about six leagues from Chamartín. . . . The greatest disorder reigned in the ranks: there did not exist the least spirit of subordination while the voices of the generals inspired neither fear nor respect. In fact, our departure from Madrid resembled more a flight than a retreat: all the inhabitants of San Agustín were pillaged; many of the houses were burned down; more than 2,000 sheep were slaughtered, and the soldiers spent the night indulging in every form of excess. . . . At Lerma . . . the park in which the palace of the Duke of Medinaceli was situated was set alight by our vanguard. Arson is a pleasure our soldiers cannot deny themselves: they set fire to fields of barley that are on the point of being harvested, and the crops have invariably been so baked by the sun that no sooner has the torch been applied than all one sees is a vast crescent of fire. This love of burning was so great that we were hardly out of the hovels in which we spent our nights before they had gone up in flames as well.[10]

These scenes could possibly be put down to the anger and fear felt by a demoralized army on the retreat, but a tendency toward pillage and rapine was also much in evidence when the French swept back across northern Spain in a ferocious counterattack in November. Among those who witnessed the devastation was Joseph's close friend Miot de Melito:

> As we approached Burgos, we crossed the site of the affair of 10 November. It was still strewn with corpses, although the sad spectacle that it presented did not make as painful an impression on me as the state of that great city at the moment of our entrance. Absolutely deserted, almost all the houses had been pillaged and their furniture smashed to pieces and thrown in the mud; part of the city was . . . on fire; a frenzied soldiery was forcing every door and window, breaking down everything that stood in the way, and destroying more than they consumed; all the churches had been stripped; and the streets were encumbered with the dead and dying. In short, although it had not been defended, the city exhibited all the horrors of an assault.[11]

Nor was this conduct moderated as the fighting raged to and fro across La Mancha in the following year. Joseph Naylies, for example, was a lieutenant in the Nineteenth Regiment of Dragoons:

> It was already quite late when we got to Coria. We bivouacked in an olive grove outside the town, but we had no other food than some biscuit we had been given at Galisteo. As soon as sentries had been posted and the horses tethered to trees, the soldiers went into the town, which was deserted. Equipped with great candles that they had stolen from the churches, they battered down the doors with axes and ransacked every chest and cupboard on the pretext of searching for food. . . . The unfortunate place was pillaged all night. Greed knew no limits among our soldiers: inflamed by the tales spread by men whose searches had already proved successful, they did not even respect the sanctity of the grave.[12]

All this, meanwhile, was faithfully reported in Patriot Spain. For a good example of the horror stories that circulated, one might very well turn to the supposed experiences of Toledo following its occupation by the French on 13 December 1808. According to the account received by the Junta Central, the invaders seized large quantities of food, cloth, and footwear; ransacked every house in the city under the pretext of searching for arms; set fire to the main hospital and various other buildings; confiscated the cathedral's plate; and stripped the churches of all their valuables while at the same time wrecking their interiors and mutilating many statues and crucifixes.[13] Such tales were widespread. "Whenever the French come to this village, or, indeed, any other, they commit the greatest atrocities that Your Excellency can imagine," wrote one Martín de la Cerda to the minister of grace and justice, Pedro Rivera. "Three days ago they carried off eight or nine thousand head of livestock of all types belonging to residents of this village, and on the 23rd they took away 714 *fanegas* of barley. While some of them were loading up on this last occasion, meanwhile, others pillaged fifty houses. . . . If I was to list all the crimes they have committed in this district, Your Excellency would be astonished. There is not a chapel that they do not burn, nor a woman that they do not rape. Indeed, sometimes they go so far as to murder the latter, as they also do with those men who do not give them what they want."[14]

Written up in suitably lurid terms, such stories provided the blizzard of anti-French pamphlets and newspaper articles that characterized Patriot Spain with plentiful material. These, of course, were supplemented by the accounts of fugitives from the French zone of occupation. Let us here quote William Jacob: "All who have recently left [Madrid] give shocking accounts of the conduct of the French and the severe sufferings of the *madrileños*. The public places are deserted, and the theatre and the *paseos* left to the French officers. No lady ventures out of her house, and few men who walk in the streets are bold enough to recognise or speak to any of their acquaintance whom they may chance to meet. The houses of the nobility are stripped of their plate, and the furniture, from the want of purchasers, is consumed for firing or is wantonly destroyed. The tradesmen are starving, and the clergy turned out to beg where no-one has anything to bestow."[15] If all this is a little exaggerated, the realities of daily life under enemy occupation were certainly grim enough. Here we might first cite a letter written by one of the many anonymous correspondents who kept the Junta Central supplied with news from the French zone: "The French have adopted the fine art of robbing without scruple, let alone attempting to exasperate the population as little as possible. On the pretext of collecting fines, they now go from shop to shop demanding 500 or more ducados on pain of the owners being sent to prison. . . . The fact is that they think of nothing but terror and robbery. . . . Yesterday there was an execution, while another one is scheduled for today and still others are said to be pending. Indeed, the scaffold is kept permanently in position in the hope of cowing this honorable and generous populace."[16]

One should not imagine, meanwhile, that the invasion of Andalucía was devoid of such unpleasantness. On the contrary, as the French surged across the border, many *pueblos* suffered very badly at the hands of the soldiery: as we have already seen, La Carolina—a colony established in the Sierra Morena by German emigrants under the influence of the reformist Bourbon minister Pablo de Olavide—was thoroughly sacked by the invaders, Miot de Melito admitting that it presented "a picture of devastation."[17] Various veterans of the campaign suggest that these excesses were at their worst in the barren mountains of the Sierra Morena, where the French could not but go short of food, and that the situation was further exacerbated when the populace fled their homes at the approach of the invaders (as was the case at a number of towns, including Bailén), this being something that annoyed the troops and inclined them to show even less restraint in taking what they wanted than would otherwise have been the case. Situated west of Córdoba, for example, the colony of La Carlota was reported by Miot to have suffered no damage, and in his eyes this was due to the fact that the populace had stayed put.[18] However, while the French may have entered most of the larger cities without committing much in the way of disorder, away from the immediate gaze of their commanders, things seem to have gone on pretty much as before. Thus, during the tour of Andalucía that he made following the fall of Seville, when King Joseph stopped for the night at the village of El Bosque, he found that it had been pillaged and partly burned down on the pretext that some of its inhabitants had fired on a party of French dragoons.[19] Finally, in nearby Rota the American consul in Cádiz, José Iznar, complained that his home had been seized as headquarters for the colonel of the French Forty-Fifth Line only minutes after Iznar had entertained King Joseph himself in it in the course of the latter's visit to the town on 22 February 1810.[20]

When the people were not being bullied and robbed, meanwhile, they were being subjected to a regime of tight police control, this being symbolized above all else by the *Reglamento de policia para la entrada, salida y circulación de las personas por Madrid,* which was promulgated on 17 February 1809. Reproduced in full in a pamphlet published in Seville that year, this document consisted of a list of minute rules that regulated every detail of the movements of the people of Madrid and, in particular, communication between the city and the outside world. Thus, assuming that they managed to get to the city at all—Spaniards were not allowed to travel there without a permit from the local commandant—all outsiders were expected to register on arrival with the police in exchange for a pass that allowed them to remain within the city walls for a set time. Equally, no one could leave Madrid without a passport—something that, like the passes issued to outsiders, had to be obtained by payment of a fee—while freedom of movement within the city was only permitted during daylight hours: at night all pedestrians had to carry lamps or torches while they were also enjoined to keep moving and, in particular, not to congregate at such places as street corners.[21] Nor were the French lax in implementing these orders: in a letter dated 28 February 1809, an agent of the junta named Salustiano Andrés de Embite described to its general secretary, Martín de Garay, how the invaders had sentries posted at every corner and were constantly checking everybody's papers.[22]

Underpinning all this was a fear that was in some ways still darker. Thus one of the most potent weapons in the armory of the propagandists of Patriot Spain was the claim that Napoleon's real aim in Spain was to lay hold of all the country's manpower and pack it off to fight in the campaigns of the *grande armée*: in Málaga, for example, a pamphlet appeared that not only insisted that the emperor had intervened in Spain to conscript the population but even included a picture of an "infernal machine"—basically a multiple coffle that could yoke half a dozen recruits together while they were marched off to France—designed to ensure that he got his will.[23] And that this was indeed his will seemed obvious enough. Spain thus far had been spared the rigors of conscription, but how long this grace would survive was a moot point. After all, in 1807 had not an entire division of the regular army been sent to Germany? And by the same token, did not the French troops that had marched across the Pyrenees since the Treaty of Fontainebleau contain a large number of foreign units that were, Patriot pamphleteers supposed, made up of unhappy "slaves" who presumably had been plucked from their homes in other parts of Europe in a manner that was just as brusque?[24]

The fears outlined above were not entirely absent from Andalucía in January 1810. Indeed, it was in large part because of their existence that conspirators such as Abello were able to manipulate the crowd with so much ease. Yet what we see in Seville and Málaga are anything but spontaneous cries of terror and outrage provoked by the advance of a devastating host. In each case the lead was taken rather by elements of the elites engaged in a search for revenge and personal advancement in a manner that was to be absolutely typical of an epoch in which a poor and unsophisticated populace was repeatedly manipulated by powerful interest groups that were firmly entrenched within the structures of political and social power. Indeed, in Seville in particular it appears that conspirators had access to a readymade strike force: "Seville was formerly celebrated for its manufactures of silk, and a considerable quantity of the raw materials was produced in this neighbourhood," wrote William Jacob. "The city was surrounded with mulberry trees, and the worms which fed on them are said to have employed 10,000 looms. At present there are not 500 at work, and those are principally supplied with silk from Granada and Murcia."[25] Just as bad, meanwhile, was the situation that pertained in the tobacco factory, Jacob estimating that by the time that he visited Seville in the autumn of 1809, "either from the reduced consumption or the contraband trade, there is not one eighth of . . . the manufactory employed," a further problem here being the increasingly ruthless discipline to which the remaining workers were subjected: "I was greatly struck with the rigorous examination the workers underwent on their leaving the *fabrica;* they were stripped almost naked and examined almost as closely as if they had been working in a diamond mine."[26] But playing at revolution had had its cost. The violent irruption of the crowd into the political process having been a frightening experience for the propertied classes, there thus emerged the first reason why Joseph Bonaparte received a welcome that was something other than lukewarm. In the words of Charles Oman, "The impression made on the citizens [of Seville] by the conduct of the two juntas, and the turbulence of the mob which had ruled during the last eight days, had been so deplorable that a considerable number of the Sevillians despaired of the national cause and rushed to acknowledge the usurper."[27]

The last days of the Junta Central was not the only occasion in the history of Patriot Andalucía when the crowd had suddenly taken central stage. On the contrary, the period from 1808 to 1810 had been marked by a seemingly endless series of riots and other disturbances. To understand why this was so, it is necessary to return to a discussion of the politics of the Spanish revolution.

As is now generally accepted, the events of 1808 had not been in any sense a spontaneous phenomenon. Throughout Spain the risings had been carefully organized by small groups of conspirators drawn in part from various elements of the traditional elites, in part—albeit here and there only—from men of letters eager to drive forward the cause of political and social reform, and in part from adventurers and malcontents who could either find no place for themselves in the *antiguo régimen* or had fallen out with the authorities (a prime example here is the leader of the revolt in Seville, Nicolás Tap y Núñez), the method that was adopted being in every case to reach out to the crowd through intermediaries who could address the people in their own idiom and spearhead their actions when the moment came to take to the streets.[28] To do this, these agents of revolution were quite prepared to exploit the seething resentment that the veritable calvary represented by the reign of Charles IV—a period marked by epidemic, natural disaster, economic collapse, cultural harassment, ever more lurid stories of corruption at the heart of public life, and almost continuous warfare[29]—had induced among the urban and rural populace alike, and the result was frequently acts of the most savage violence. In Seville itself actual murder should not have been necessary, for any inclination the legitimate authorities may have had to resist the insurrection quickly collapsed in the face of the surging crowds of soldiers and civilians. Yet death was still the result. In what appears to have been an attempt to impress the new authorities with the status that he enjoyed among the crowd, and in particular his ability to use it as a weapon, the day after the uprising the Conde de Tilly, an especially unscrupulous member of the conspiracy, first succeeded in having the city's procurator fiscal, the Conde del Aguila, accused of treason on the flimsiest of pretexts and then instigated his murder: placed in custody in a cell in one of the city's gate towers by the newly formed provincial junta for his own security, Aguila was immediately dragged out and killed by a gang of hired assassins.[30]

Nor was Aguila the only representative of the Andalusian elite to fall at the hands of crowds whipped up by the conspirators. We come here to the case of Francisco Solano, Marqués del Socorro. Captain General of Seville in 1808, Socorro had taken refuge in

Cádiz at the first sign of trouble: like many other generals, he honestly believed that resistance was futile. As Jacob notes, however, Cádiz offered him no greater safety than did Seville:

> As soon as it was known at Seville that Solano had fled to Cádiz, the revolution immediately broke forth. . . . The feelings of Seville were communicated to Jérez, to Santa María, and even to Cádiz, though in the latter their effects were stifled by the efforts of [Solano]. Numbers of people, however, arrived from Seville inspired with feelings of patriotism and vengeance; many entered the city disguised like peasants, and a sufficient number soon arrived to kindle the suppressed patriotism of the *gaditanos.* [Solano] received intimation . . . that the plan of an insurrection was formed, and that he was to be its first victim; he was apprised of the intention to assassinate him on his return from the theatre, and was entreated by his friends not to attend, but he had too much courage to be awed by the intimation, and either the firmness of his disposition or some alteration in the plans of his enemies preserved him . . . from the threatened attack. A party of his friends who [had] adjourned from the theatre to his house, aware of the danger that impended, urged him to seek safety by flight; he rejected their counsel, affected to treat their fears with contempt, and avowed his resolution not to part with his authority but in obedience to the commands of the power from which he had received it. . . . Early on the ensuing morning . . . the populace, irritated by the patriots from Seville, indignant at the treachery of France, and clamorous for the death of the governor, surrounded his habitation. Some parties attacked it with musketry, while others dragged cannon from the ramparts. . . . In the midst of the firing he escaped by the roof of his house and took refuge in an adjoining one, the lady of which, an intimate friend of the family, hid him in a small closet which had been secretly built some years before. When the insurgents . . . discovered his flight, they pursued him to the house where he was concealed, which was searched with diligence but without success. After committing some atrocities and even wounding the lady of the house with a musket ball, they were departing discontented with having

> missed the object of their vengeance, when the party was joined by an artificer who had constructed the secret closet, and who conducted them to the hiding place, where [Solano] was discovered and delivered to the fury of the mob. The general cry of the populace was ""To the gallows! To the gallows!" . . . but such was the indignation of the people that, before he had quitted the house where he was discovered, he was lacerated with knives and his clothes literally torn from his body. Naked and streaming with blood from numberless wounds, he preserved the firm step and manly dignity of an officer . . . till a soldier who had been long under his command, dreading the impending degradation of his old officer, plunged his sword in his heart and terminated his sufferings.[31]

Whipping up the crowd, however, was an extremely dangerous game. Having thus acquired a sense of their own power, the populace were not disposed to allow themselves simply to be dismissed at will. On the contrary, on all sides they were rather chafing at the bit and, in the mass at least, determined to impose their will. To return to the example of Seville, the instigators of the revolution found that they had to spend much time reining in their followers. An immense crowd having assembled in the Plaza de San Francisco in the immediate aftermath of the conspiracy, for example, it began to call for the heads of a number of leading functionaries, the crisis only being resolved when Tap y Núñez rushed to the scene and succeeded in persuading his followers that wholesale massacre would reduce Spain to the same level as France by replicating the scenes witnessed in the latter country during the Revolution.[32] In Jérez de la Frontera, meanwhile, mass killings were only averted by the hasty organization of a Pamplona-style "running of the bulls," which seems to have allowed the crowd to work off its surplus energy.[33] Elsewhere, however, the situation spiraled out of control. Deposed by the people on 4 June, the mayor of Vélez Málaga was imprisoned in a convent in Granada and later dragged out and murdered in the city's main square, along with a prosperous landowner named Bernabé Portillo, who was noted for his attempts to improve his estates through the introduction of the cultivation of cotton (something that may well have earned him the hostility of the lower classes).[34] And finally also in Granada, there perished Pedro Trujillo, a retired general who had served as governor of Málaga and was the brother-in-law of the mistress of the erstwhile royal favorite Manuel de Godoy.[35] In the words of Manuel Moreno Alonso, then: "The masses acted with extreme violence and would be content with nothing less than blood. Yet not the blood of foreigners, but rather that of their own compatriots, and in particular that of the authorities and the wealthy. The fact is that in respect of its demands the uprising was marked by a brutality that was truly exultant."[36]

In general, if the death of French civilians is excluded, the number of killings in the course of the uprising was not great, while Andalucía was not that much affected by the phenomenon: according to Fraser, only about fifty such incidents are known, of which more than half occurred in either Catalonia or Old Castile.[37] Yet for all that, for the propertied classes of the south, and indeed everywhere else, the "revolutionary fiesta" that marked the uprising's first week had still been a frightening experience. Impelled by fears of "treason" that centered as much on a determination to defend the "brave new world" that was felt to have been ushered in by the coming of Ferdinand VII as to root out those who favored Joseph Bonaparte, excited crowds roamed the streets for days on end, carrying arms of every sort, stopping passersby, and sacking such houses as took their fancy (in Ronda the pretext adopted in the case of one prominent army officer was that he supposedly had a guillotine hidden on his property, while in Málaga that of another suffered because he was deemed ipso facto to be a traitor).[38] To compound the problem, meanwhile, within a matter of days, large numbers of men had started to hemorrhage from the many new regiments organized by the provincial juntas: in Seville denunciations of desertion date from as early as 31 May.[39]

What made all this worse, of course, was that throughout Spain the crowd was feared and hated. Thus *populacho*—the very term that was generally used to describe the common people—was symptomatic of the contempt in which they were everywhere held, meaning, as it did, "rabble." And as "rabble," of course, the crowd was ignorant, brutal, irresponsible, and incapable of rational thought and therefore prone to falling under the sway of agitators of the worst sort. To make matters worse, meanwhile, as Adrian Shubert has shown, it was precisely at this time that cultural attitudes to the poor were changing from those of a medieval world, where such problems as poverty were regarded as an immutable part of God's creation, to those of a modern one, in which they were rather subject to rational explanation. In arriving at a rational explanation, however, the elites were incapable of rising above their prejudices: if the poor were poor, it was because they were lazy. Until comparatively recently, then, the correct response to the beggars who filled the streets had been charity—indeed, one could go so far as to say that the poor existed to serve as a pretext for the good works necessary to achieve salvation—but now, in brief, it was correction, the effect of such ideas being to render still more shocking the menacing attitude now affected by the crowd in respect of their "betters."[40] However, if social tensions were strong everywhere, the propertied classes of Andalucía were particularly sensitized in respect of the lower classes by the agricultural system, the result of which was to keep thousands of day laborers and their families vegetating in a permanent state of penury. This system will be looked at in more detail in chapter 3, so it is here sufficient to say no more than that the conditions associated with it were some of the worst in Europe. For a case study in the manner in which the sort of social tensions it engendered were bound up in the rising of 1808, meanwhile, we can do no better than to look at Jaén. In 1808 as much as in 1936, Jaén was a province dominated by great estates. As yet, of course, there was no labor organization of any sort among the *jornaleros* (the day laborers who actually worked the estates), but one may still see the first signs of labor unrest, as in an instance where a group of such men downed tools on the grounds that they were only getting six *reales* per day when other estates nearby were paying six and one-half, this protest being quelled by the promulgation of an order in which it was declared that any further strikes would be punished by four days in prison. Like almost everywhere else in Spain, meanwhile, Jaén was in the grip of serious economic problems in 1808. In part this was the result of serious structural problems centered on the many deficiencies of great-estate farming techniques and the absence of any industrial base, but in addition there had also been disasters of a more immediate variety: having suffered very severely on account of the crop failures of 1803–1804, the region had been hit by a plague of locusts in 1805. In consequence of these latter problems, the harvest of 1808 was a subject of great concern, as witness, for example, an order that was issued by the mayor, Antonio María de Lomas, on 26 January obliging every householder to present the authorities with the bodies of six sparrows within the space of two weeks on pain of a fine of two *reales* for every bird that they failed to deliver. Meanwhile, with bread prices rising rapidly, in the hope that this would tide the populace over and stave off the danger of riots, the town council of Jaén city applied to the cathedral chapter for a loan of 150,000 *reales* that could be used to buy food for the poor.[41]

Despite these efforts on the part of the authorities, difficulties continued, March and April being marked by a prolonged period of heavy rain that delayed the spring sowing and deprived many *jornaleros* of employment: for example, large numbers of such men abandoned their home villages and poured into the capital looking for work. Among the propertied classes, however, such vagrants—the archetypal "sturdy beggars"—were deeply feared, while they were not much better liked by the resident poor with whom they inevitably came into competition. In short, the tension became ever greater—hence, perhaps, the great lengths to which the civil and religious authorities went to celebrate Ferdinand's accession to the throne: in addition to a series of religious processions and high masses, the people were treated with illuminations and six bullfights. Meanwhile, of course, everything possible was done to persuade the populace that all was well—a blind street musician who was heard to sing couplets attacking the French was even arrested—and more practically, to help the hungry, the mayor and various members of the city council appeared in person before the cathedral chapter to beg for money with which to help the unemployed.[42]

With matters in this state, the news of the Dos de Mayo obviously came as a disaster, for it seemed all too clear to the crowd that the populace of Madrid had somehow been betrayed by their betters. To make matters worse, meanwhile, the price of bread was continuing to rise, and this in turn produced a serious riot. In Córdoba, the city council discovered, the response of its counterpart to this situation had been to establish an emergency *junta de tranquilidad* whose object was, in effect, to persuade the populace that something was being done about the crisis while yet straining every muscle to ensure that disorder was averted, but it was resolved that even this move was too dangerous, and to the end the councilors held stubbornly to the path of proclaiming the need to trust Napoleon (prudentially, however, they did attempt to cut the price of bread). Indeed, when orders arrived to send deputies to Bayonne, the council agreed to do so without a murmur, the only difficulty that was raised being the question of how the journey was to be financed.[43]

This position, however, could not be held for very long. On 28 May news arrived of the abdications of Bayonne, while on the twenty-ninth it was heard that Córdoba had risen in revolt. However, the final straw came in the early morning of 30 May. Possibly at the instigation of Fernando María del Prado, the president of the Real Sociedad de los Amigos del País de Jaén and practically the only member of the city council who had argued that Jaén should proclaim its support for Ferdinand VII, a large crowd had gathered in front of Lomas's house to wait for news, and when a messenger duly arrived, it demanded to be allowed to read the letter he carried. As it happened, this was the newly formed Junta of Seville's appeal for the whole of Spain to join it in rising in revolt, and so Lomas sent messengers to all council members ordering them to go to the town hall immediately for an emergency meeting. Seeing this activity, the crowd became still more excited, and when Lomas himself emerged, it followed him to the council chamber, alternatively shouting threats and cheering Ferdinand VII to the echo. Meanwhile, other groups had invaded the cathedral and begun to ring the bells, at which the chapter sent a delegation to meet with the council, which in fact had suspended its sessions in expectation of just such a meeting. The consequent delay, however, proved the last straw: a large crowd was by now filling the Plaza de Santa María and, incensed at the delay, it first invaded the house of the Duque de Montemar and dragged him out by force to act as its spokesman and then assaulted the council chamber itself. Absolutely terrified, Lomas and his fellows were left with no choice and hastily declared the formation of a junta of "public security" composed of Montemar, the intendant, the governor, two representatives of the town council, and an assortment of other officers, clerics, and functionaries, the populace, as everywhere else, being completely excluded (not so, however, the deputies who had been selected to travel to Bayonne, both of whom ended up as members of the new junta).[44]

Whether or not it was against its better judgment, on the surface at least, the new junta proceeded to throw itself into the task of organizing resistance, issuing appropriate proclamations, setting up a patriotic subscription to fund the war effort, ordering the surrender of all weapons held by members of the public, forming a number of irregular bands that proceeded to do all they could to harass the French, and gathering recruits for the regular army. In all this it was strongly backed up by the church: the bishop had fled the city to take refuge in his country residence, but the chapter provided the insurrection with large amounts of financial support, organized a variety of special days of prayer and penitence, and also gave permission for any priests and religious who wanted to do so to take up arms. Yet underlying all this was a strongly conservative theme: the populace were to be mobilized certainly, but they were not to be allowed to take the law into their own hands, the point being driven home still further by the fact that much of the church's propaganda effort was directed at securing an end to what was termed the corruption of the populace's morals, this being a theme that may, of course, be understood to mean that the people were to be weaned away from their growing unruliness and brought back to an acceptance of their station in life. Also important here, of course, was the appearance of a new Milicia Urbana, recruited entirely from the propertied classes, which served both to keep the populace under control and to provide the privileged orders with a way of avoiding service in the field.[45]

In brief then, although there was on the surface a willingness to fight the French, the Junta of Jaén was also driven by other goals, namely the twin determination to protect the privileges of the old elites and to keep the crowd in its place. Indeed, some elements of the original municipal leadership may have gone still further. Lomas had remained in the city after the insurrection and was certainly still there on 14 June, but at some point after this, he slipped away and made contact with the forces of Dupont. No details of what was arranged are available, and all that is known is that on 20 June—the same day that the French attacked Jaén—Lomas was set upon and put to death by an angry mob when he appeared in the village of Valdepeñas de Jaén at the head of a small party of French troops, all of whom were killed as well. Given that the city council later put about a completely false story that Lomas had been killed on 21 June while trying to save the lives of a group of prisoners, it is at least possible that his mission was undertaken with the connivance of powerful elements of the propertied classes—that, in effect, the city authorities had simply been playing for time in the hope that the French would rescue them. Be this as it may, the elites certainly had no real stomach for a fight: no sooner did news arrive that the French were on their way to attack the city than almost all of the town council fled into the countryside (the one exception appears to have been Prado, who had now temporarily assumed the role of mayor).[46]

The case of Jaén, meanwhile, may usefully be compared with that of Granada. Interestingly, in the latter city there was no trouble until the arrival of news of the rising in Seville. At that point, however, the populace took to the streets and, headed by a Jeronimite monk named Padre Puebla, forced Captain General Ventura Escalante to form a junta. As usual, however, this was utterly dominated by the existing elites. Thus, Escalante was president while all but three of the forty ordinary members belonged to either the church, the propertied classes, or the officer corps. Moreover, once again, the emphasis was very much on keeping order: although the junta immediately set about forming an army, terrified by the murder of Trujillo (for which crime three blacks from Santo Domingo were executed as the supposed ringleaders), it also formed a two-battalion-strong Milicia Urbana, recruited from tax-paying residents who were, for whatever reason, exempt from conscription (in respect of which it should be noted that the regulations that were adopted spared anyone deemed to be essential for the smooth running of the city, a clause that in effect allowed the junta to exempt almost anyone it chose). Uniforms of rank and file were to be provided by the junta, but officers were to provide their own, while the junta also formed a Guard of Honor under one Juan José Méndez. Added to this mobilization of the interests of property, meanwhile, were a variety of police measures, such as the imposition of tight controls on the forthcoming Corpus Christi celebrations and the closure of the city's chief theater, not to mention an editorial policy in the new *Diario de Ganada* overtly directed at the suppression of dangerous ideas that might "pervert the opinion of the citizenry and even prove a threat to public order." Yet unlike in Jaén, the authorities did not just go down the road of repression, also trying to win over the crowd through gesture politics—for example, on 11 June the town council voted to forego its salaries for the duration of the war—and trying to control the price of bread, threatening any attempt at speculation with severe punishment and selling off the extensive stocks in the municipal granary at prices that undercut those being obtained by private dealers.[47]

To return to the general picture, had the situation quickly returned to a semblance of normality, the events of the uprising and its aftermath would have been shocking enough, but throughout Spain those areas that remained in the hands of the Patriot cause were plunged into a prolonged period of disorder. In part this was because the populace remained out of control. Though much trouble was also caused by attempts to impose military discipline on the volunteers who had enlisted in the cause of the uprising, at the heart of this situation was the issue of resistance to conscription. The wider reasons for this are examined below, but for the moment let us just note that within a very few weeks of the uprising, many villagers had even less desire to leave their homes than would otherwise have been the case. To quote Ronald Fraser: "There was . . . one very good material reason why the rural populace remained silent and not easily distracted from their daily concerns: in the fields stood the best wheat crop of the first eight years of the new century. This bounty had to be harvested and the grain brought safely in."[48] More prosaically, perhaps, one can argue that the day laborers saw themselves assured of reasonable wages over the summer months and therefore saw no need to enlist. (For the same reason, as Fraser points out, such lists of volunteers as he has been able to track down suggest that day laborers were badly underrepresented in the first men to come forward in Andalucía: instead, recruitment was concentrated among the artisans.) But the problem was not just related to conscription. At issue too was the balance of forces in the countryside. Wildly excited by the millennial hopes aroused by the brief reign of Ferdinand VII, the populace here and there attempted to take the law into their own hands. To quote Fraser again, "The still widely-held Spanish idealization that all social classes were united as one in the struggle was rapidly shown to be no more than a myth."[49]

It would here be possible to spend several pages going through the many instances of agrarian disorder that erupted at one place or another in the Patriot zone in the period 1808–10. Thus, among the examples that we could cite are incidents that occurred at Ribadeo, Oviedo, Don Bénito, Herrera del Duque, Castellón de la Plana, and Calatayud. For the sake of brevity, however, we will simply confine ourselves to events in Andalucía. That said, these were dramatic enough. Let us begin with the case of Carmona. A classic Andalusian agro-town surrounded by immense landed estates, Carmona was dominated by large numbers of day laborers, and with a sharp eye to their best interest, these elements proceeded to take advantage of the fact that many men were leaving the district to join the army, refusing en masse to work in the fields in the hope that they might thereby secure a pay rise from the landowners and then engaging in a furious outbreak of rioting when their employers clubbed together to resist their demands.[50] Threatened with draconian protests by the municipal council, the laborers gradually drifted back to work, but there were plenty of other instances where the authorities did not have matters their own way. In Puerto Real, for example, one of the most prominent men in the district was a substantial landowner of French origins named Estebán Meinadier. Eager to improve his estates, he had immediately before the war brought in a small group of French farmworkers with knowledge of a variety of techniques that he wished to introduce. Whether it was because, as they claimed, they did not want French civilians in their midst or because they rather saw the new arrivals as a threat to their livelihoods, presumably by adopting an attitude of physical menace, the populace first succeeded in having the imported workers confined to the hulks in Cádiz harbor and then subjected Meinadier to a prolonged campaign of extortion, probably with the connivance of the local authorities, who seem to have regarded him as a sacrificial lamb.[51] Meinadier, of course, was identifiably French and therefore a target who was both obvious and vulnerable, and it could certainly be argued that the day laborers of the district were targeting him out of simple patriotism. Yet elsewhere the victims of such tactics were Spaniards who did not have the slightest connection with the invaders: denounced to the authorities as a traitor and subsequently subjected to vigorous investigation, the chief magistrate of Mengíbar was eventually deemed to have been singled out for no better reason than the fact that he had been relatively wealthy and extremely arrogant about it.[52] Finally, there were the series of problems that were experienced at the very similar town of Jérez de la Frontera. Here the problem was once again foreign workers, in this case men who had been taken on the estate belonging to a sherry magnate, James Gordon. The story is retailed by William Jacob:

> Mr Gordon, besides being a wine merchant and a distiller, is a very large farmer: he has purchased 2,400 acres of good land, which is mostly in tillage, and is principally cultivated by the German soldiers who were captured at the surrender of Dupont's army at Bailén: he has also some young men from the Lothians in Scotland, and with these labourers conducts his farms to advantage, and has introduced all the improvements which have recently been practised by the best agriculturalists in Great Britain. . . . At present the demand for men for the army has increased the price of labour excessively and compelled the farmers to give employment to the prisoners, and the Germans, who are laborious and docile, are now preferred to the natives, who are too much attached to their old habits to acquiesce in the improvements which Mr Gordon has introduced. . . . The inhabitants boast of their patriotism and zeal in the cause of their country and express their detestation of the French on all occasions. This detestation has been evinced in the most inhuman manner by the murders committed upon

> several of the prisoners, nor would even those who are on their parole and occupied in the labour of the fields be exempt from apprehension if they ventured to mix with the inhabitants or neglected the precaution of working in parties separate from the Spaniards.[53]

What Jacob here fails to mention is that early in 1809 the presence of the French prisoners of war triggered off a major riot. In brief, on 26 February a large crowd had gathered on the main square and demanded that the prisoners be expelled from the city on pain of death. Yet it was not just the unfortunate enemy soldiers who were the issue: the crowds also waxed furious against the many wealthy inhabitants who had by one means or another succeeded in escaping from conscription and presented the mayor, Joaquín Mergelina, with a long list of grievances.[54]

Much work remains to be done on these issues, but sufficient material is available for the observer to be confident that at least some elements of the agricultural populace seized the opportunity provided by the war to settle old scores, improve their living conditions, or harass the propertied classes. But this was not the only reason why Patriot Spain was gripped by disorder. Also important were the maneuvers that were engaged in by elements of the propertied classes to further their own interests. Pride of place here should probably be given to the *fernandinos*. Thwarted from gaining control of the throne by Napoleon's sequestration of the Spanish royal family, they had then responded to the new situation by throwing themselves into the cause of a national uprising in the hope that this would allow one of their number to establish a regency as an interim solution. However, in the event the plan went wrong. Though representatives of the *fernandino* cause secured control of Zaragoza in the person of Francisco Palafox's elder brother, José, who assumed the role of Captain General of Aragón in a carefully orchestrated insurrection whose success was secured in exactly the same fashion as in Seville and Cádiz, in the rest of Spain its agents were completely swamped. For all the capital that José Palafox made of his successful defense of Zaragoza in July and August 1808, then, no moves were made toward a regency, while the idea was eventually set aside in favor of the committee government represented by the Junta Central. Yet the *fernandinos* were not beaten. It was largely through their doing that the victor of Bailén, Francisco Javier de Castaños—one of the few representatives of the régime of Godoy to have succeeded not only in surviving in a position of power but also in augmenting his reputation—was discredited and removed from the command of the Army of the Center following the Battle of Tudela of 25 November 1808 (a move that was, again in part, achieved through appealing to the power of the street), and by April 1809 they appear to have become convinced that the time was ripe for a coup de main.[55] Insofar as this was concerned, opportunity was soon offered by events in Granada. In brief, like many of its fellows, the Junta of Granada had quickly established a reputation for corruption: a badly written and misspelled denunciation of its activities that was sent to the Junta Central accused it of having stolen at least 5,000,000 *reales,* tolerated a variety of frauds in respect of conscription, and accepted large numbers of bribes from those wishing to escape the army's clutches (significantly, a report later suggested that the events that were to follow were at least in part an anti-conscription riot sparked off by rumors that a large contingent of conscripts were about to be sent off to the Army of Extremadura).[56] Seemingly blind to the risks it was running, however, the junta ignored the growing unrest and, in March 1809, fanned the flames considerably by arresting the city's *síndico del pueblo* (a species of "tribune of the people" who had represented the interests of the populace in the town council). Getting wind of this situation, the Conde de Montijo, who happened to be a prominent local magnate, secured a commission as the commander of an army of reserve that was notionally being established in Granada and traveled to the city. The result was not long in coming: on 16 April a large crowd flooded into the Plaza Nueva and demanded that he be appointed captain general of the province. Possessed of a number of troops loyal to itself in the form of a newly formed battalion of Swiss (more likely, foreign deserters of all sorts), the provincial junta, however, refused to be cowed: cavalry and infantry were sent to clear the streets, and Montijo was arrested and his house searched. Presumably by prior arrangement, just at this point Francisco Palafox also arrived in the city, but he of course had come too late and, rather than taking charge of a full-scale revolt against the Junta Central, was left with no option but to confine himself to a somewhat lame attack on the Junta of Granada.[57]

Defeated in Granada, the *fernandinos* still did not give up, instead hatching a new plot in Seville in the wake of the failure of the Allied armies in the campaign of Talavera in July 1809. Once again, however, the plot was unsuccessful: betrayed to the authorities, Montijo and Francisco Palafox were hastily arrested and flung into the confinement in which they both still languished in January 1810. Yet political dissent was not the only factor making for outbreaks of popular unrest in Patriot Spain. Also significant were the actions of individual adventurers who looked to the crowd as a means of propelling them to high office, splits in the local elites, and local crises rooted in factors that were particular to individual cities. In each case, however, the pattern was the same in that the crowd—and with it street violence—was mobilized in order to secure changes in the political or military situation.

Beginning with the first category, no obvious instances have yet been identified in Andalucía, but in Patriot Spain as a whole there were several episodes in which personal ambition played a major role in stirring up outbreaks of rioting, these then being brought to the attention of at least some members of the elite by means of personal correspondence or coverage in the burgeoning Patriot press. Of these, the most famous is undoubtedly the savage massacre of French civilians that marred the uprising in Valencia: On 5 June 1808, having seen his every attempt to insinuate himself into the provincial junta thwarted by various individuals who had his measure, a Valencian canon of the *madrileño* basilica of San Isdro named Baltasar Calvo, who fancied that he should be a leader of the insurrection and had traveled back to his home city to assume such a role, responded by whipping up an angry crowd by persuading it that the junta was full of traitors and that, if the city's considerable French community had been interned in the citadel, it was only so they could take it over and turn its guns on the inhabitants. Eager to save the city or simply just to run amok, large numbers of men and women promptly burst into the citadel and put most of those inside to death, the whole aim being, of course, to show the junta that Calvo was untouchable and, indeed, that they would suffer the same fate if they did not accede to his every whim. Fortunately for Valencia, however, a number of figures in the regular Patriot leadership had sufficient sangfroid to keep their heads even if, with few troops in the city, they had little option but to call upon the power of the streets themselves. Calvo's followers, having been exhausted by the night of slaughter that had just passed, returned to their homes, leaving the canon temporarily vulnerable to a counterattack on the part of a gang of hired toughs with which the original Valencian conspirators—among them the immensely wealthy Bertrán de Lys merchant dynasty—had made their rising and still maintained at their disposition as the "Company of Public Security." To cut a long story short, then, within a matter of hours Calvo found himself being bundled off to imprisonment and eventual execution in Mallorca.[58]

For a further incident in which an importunate intriguer sought to make his way through the use of violence, we can turn to the Catalan city of Lérida. Here a small group of suspected *afrancesados* had been imprisoned in the citadel following the uprising. There they had been kept safe, but at the end of December, the city was thrown into something of a panic by the arrival of a number of French prisoners of war. Seizing the moment, one Ramón Gómez, an erstwhile farrier who had secured a commission as an artillery officer in the wake of the uprising, provoked a riot. As the hapless governor wrote: "Reinforced by many *migueletes,* the mob seized control of all the defenses in an instant. Laying hold of all the arms they could find, they then forced the cells of the prisoners to the accompaniment of ferocious cries of 'Death to the traitors!'"[59] Cowering behind the locked doors were a judge of the Audiencia of Barcelona named Manuel Fortuny, his wife, Melchora, and their young son; three landowners named José Rubias, José Casals, and José Ignacio Bayona; and the adjutant of the Second Tercio de Migueletes de Lérida, Agustín Sangenis, and within moments all of them had been hacked to pieces. Like Calvo, Gómez had apparently hoped to set himself up as some "tribune of the people," but like him, instead he only met death, along with many of his followers.[60] In all, indeed, at least seven of the rioters were executed in Lérida and sixty-eight in Valencia, the sheer violence of these responses acting as a graphic testimony to the fear that the mob inspired among the upper classes.[61]

Let us now turn to splits in the local elites. Of these the best example, and one rather closer to Patriot Andalucía than Valencia or Lérida, is the insurrection that took place in Murcia in December 1808. In brief, there had been no popular insurrection in Murcia in May 1808: seeing the way in which the wind was blowing, the town council had hastily convened a meeting of all the city's authorities and other leading figures, proclaimed Ferdinand VII king of Spain, and appointed a provincial junta consisting of the bishop; two priors; the leading Bourbon minister, the Conde de Floridablanca; six members of the town council; two officials of the city's law courts; five prominent aristocrats; and five serving or retired army officers, including the military governor. Here as everywhere else, then, the old elites were firmly in control, and for some time Murcia remained reasonably quiet, though under the surface popular grievances were bubbling away as much as anywhere else in Patriot Spain. On the one hand, the junta adopted a particularly draconian attitude toward the populace—just insulting a representative of authority was made punishable by death—while on the other, it governed in a fashion that clearly tended to the benefit of the elites, as witness, for example, its establishment of a regiment of "honorable volunteers" that was protected from service in the field and, as in other such cases, served no other purpose than to allow the propertied classes to play at soldiers. With the lower classes also hit by a new household tax, the streets were understandably less than impressed, but within the junta trouble was also brewing in that, having achieved a measure of predominance, the faction represented by the Conde de Campo Hermoso and his nephew, the Marqués de Vilar, had incurred the jealousy of many other members.

The story of what happened next is extremely confused and sometimes downright contradictory, but in sum, the terrible defeats of November–December 1808 spread panic across southern Spain, and, in Murcia as much as anywhere else, rumors spread that the French were at the gates and that the authorities were traitors. Meanwhile, having originally been dispatched to the Junta

Central as one of Murcia's two representatives, Vilar had been sent back to the city as, in effect, a *répésentent en mission* in the style of those sent out in France in 1793. Though they were certainly in a strong position, Campo Hermoso and his supporters were by no means fully in control—the presidency, for example, was in the hands of the bishop—and they appear to have decided to make use of the growing turmoil to get rid of their opponents. In a carefully staged series of street disturbances—one of their victims later claimed that they were the work of "a small number of malevolent intriguers who to hide their work attributed it to the people," and gave the known ringleaders as an apothecary, two carpenters, a weaver, a notary, a doctor, a surgeon, and a master woodcarver[62]—the intendant and the military governor were forced to resign from their posts altogether (to the accompaniment, be it said, of considerable violence) while an attempt was made to confine the bishop to a friary. Yet the opponents of Campo Hermoso and Vilar were not beaten, and they in turn staged a counterdemonstration in which a crowd was rallied to the equally popular cause of securing the dissolution of the hated "honorable volunteers" (of which the colonel was none other than Campo Hermoso). In the end, then, the result was stalemate: after mediation on the part of the Junta Central, a new junta was established based on much the same personnel as before, though both Campo Hermoso and the old military governor, Retamosa, were excluded. The more things had changed, then, the more they had stayed the same, and the populace, who were not just so many puppets but rather had views and interests of their own, were left seething with anger, as witness the violent anti-conscription riot that took place in the city on 13 March 1809. As one householder complained, indeed, from the moment of Vilar's return to the city onward, Murcia "has not enjoyed a moment's peace; on the contrary, the whole place has been one continuous revolution and hotbed of rumors."[63]

Finally, we have the group of riots that may be regarded as sui generis. Of these the best example is the massive disturbance that gripped Cádiz in February 1809. First discussed by the current author more than twenty years ago in his book on the Spanish army in the Peninsular War, this affair was ascribed by him to Machiavellian maneuvers on the part of the Voluntarios Distinguidos de

Cádiz, the property-owning self-defense force that had been created in the city in similar style to the Voluntarios Honrados de Murcia: "The Volunteers [took] advantage of the riots of 1809 to secure a guarantee that they would never have to serve outside the walls of the city; indeed, there is a strong possibility that its members had fomented the disorder with precisely this end in mind."[64] Quite so, but the author has never told the full story in sufficient detail, and it is to this that we must now turn our attention. Safe on its island in the far southwest of Spain, Cádiz was far removed from the horrors of war and had witnessed neither disorder nor fighting since the uprising of May 1808. As in other cities, however, the rising had been followed by the formation of a junta composed of a variety of local notables, which in turn had gone on to form both a police commission—the Junta de Vigilancia—and the home guard mentioned above. From the start this last affected a particularly swaggering and ostentatious disposition. Composed of five battalions of line infantry, two battalions of light infantry, and a regiment of artillery, or in all some 7,000 men, and were arrayed in some of the gaudiest uniforms in Patriot Spain—a factor that reinforced their social exclusivity given the fact that recruits were only admitted if they could meet the cost of their clothing and equipment—this considerable force was recruited entirely from the wealthier burghers of the city and their clients and dependents.[65] Beyond this force (which incidentally came into being despite the fact that twenty companies of urban militia had existed in the city ever since 1762), recruits were also called for to serve in the regular army, but Cádiz appears to have formed no more than a single battalion of such troops—the Tiradores de Cádiz—although the unit did take part in the campaign of Bailén.[66]

With so disproportionate a force at the service of the city authorities—in November 1808, indeed, it was swelled still further by the formation of various companies of the Milicias Honradas, the security force established in that month by decree of the Junta Central—it might have been thought that Cádiz would have remained quiet, and all the more so as there appears to have been no attempt to impose conscription. Under the surface, however, trouble was brewing. Setting aside general factors common to the whole of Patriot Spain—there was, for example, considerable muttering about the need to punish the "traitors" who were deemed responsible for the disasters of November–December 1808[67]—in the first place, it soon became obvious that, having neatly evaded any need to serve in the field by appropriating the task of defending the city from a French army whose nearest outposts lay many hundreds of miles away, the propertied classes were not carrying out even the minimal duties they had taken on: in January 1809 the commander of the Voluntarios Distinguidos, Pedro de Cardenas, had to issue an edict urging his men to turn out to perform their duties.[68] Far from earning a reputation as heroic defenders of the fatherland, indeed, the Voluntarios were increasingly being viewed as mere parasites: according to one petitioner, the militia was composed of "an indisciplined multitude of men of little worth and bad habits with no interest in the true purposes for which the profession of arms was created who have escaped service in the army by donning the uniform of these battalions of cupids," from whose lips one heard nothing but boasts that "they would not go to the army even though they should be torn to pieces," not to mention claims that "as they had paid for their own uniforms, it was those who could not do so who should go off and fight the French."[69] In the second place, it seems that there was much resentment of the city's customs-house staff, this being regarded as little other than a den of thieves: "These functionaries have no other income but their salary, and yet they get rich and have balconies at the theater. . . . Is it not obvious that there is corruption here?"[70] And in the third place, there was the fact that, while Cádiz was not yet nearly as overcrowded as it was to become during the siege of 1810–12, the population of the city had still risen, this having given rise to fears of substantial increases in the price of food.[71]

In the first weeks of 1809, the growing anger in the streets was inflamed still further by the arrival in the city of the Marqués de Villel. In September 1808 one of Catalonia's two representatives on the Junta Central, Villel has been caricatured in the British historiography as "a very strange character, a sort of nineteenth-century Spanish Puritan, with a taste for playing the benevolent despot." As the same author continues: "He attributed the misfortunes of his country . . . to her moral decadence. . . . He issued an edict commanding all married pairs living apart to re-unite, issued laws repressing theatre-going, late hours, and gambling, legislated concerning the length of ladies' skirts, and organised a grand *battue* against women of light reputation."[72] To ridicule Villel in this fashion is grossly unfair, however. One of the *réprésentents en mission,* like Vilar, sent out by the Junta Suprema Central to take control of affairs on the ground in the dark days of December 1808–January 1809, Villel was no eccentric, but rather an experienced regular soldier who in 1808 had been colonel of the Voluntarios de Barcelona light-infantry regiment. What seems to be a reasonable assessment of his character was provided by Jean-Baptiste de Crossard, a French émigré who had just been sent to Spain as an unofficial envoy by Francis I and happened to arrive in the immediate aftermath of the events described below: "The Marqués de Villel had the reputation of being someone who united a bold spirit with a great deal of ability and skill in the management of affairs; it was said of him, however, that he was something of a busy-body."[73] What was needed, in Villel's eyes, was the vigorous persecution of deserters and draft evaders and, more generally, the imposition of strict controls on the crowd, and to this end he threw himself into the task of imposing strict police regulations upon the city, which included, as implied above, draconian curfews, a variety of restrictions on leisure activities, and an attempt to restore social mores that had been undermined by years of war and economic dislocation. Thus, in a proclamation dated 16 January 1809, while enjoining the populace to be assiduous in the practice of its religion and the education of its children and to be moral in its lifestyle, the junta—acting in this instance as the mouthpiece of Villel, announced that "*habitués* of prohibited games, . . . layabouts, . . . women of no pride, . . . blasphemers, drunks, and those who constantly engage in indecent talk" would be fined, imprisoned, or sent to penal colonies.[74] Underlying all this, of course, was a growing fear of the masses: according to one observer, the "lower class of the people" were "layabouts who are lacking in industry . . . and much inclined to disturb the peace."[75]

These fears soon proved all too apposite. Thus, by the middle of February, tension had reached fresh heights with the arrival in the bay of a convoy of British ships that had suddenly appeared from Lisbon with a brigade of redcoats commanded by John MacKenzie. The presence of this force was entirely fortuitous—in brief, persuaded that the French might invade Andalucía at any time, the current British commander in Portugal, Sir John Cradock, had panicked and taken it into his head to send troops to Cádiz posthaste. Extraordinarily, however, no notice had been given of this move either to the Junta Central or to the local authorities, and the fact that the British government had spent the past month trying without success to persuade Seville to let it garrison the city sparked off fears that MacKenzie's arrival presaged a coup de main designed to secure the port by force or even to turn it into a second Gibraltar (given Napoleon's treachery in 1808, there were many high-ranking Spaniards who could not shake off the idea that Britain too might play Spain false).[76]

Inside the city, the results of this unfortunate affair were dramatic in the extreme. On the one hand, Villel jumped to the conclusion that he was about to be attacked and sent for aid to the nearest regular troops, which happened to be a battalion of Swiss and German veterans of Bailén who had volunteered for service in the Spanish army as a means of escaping a confinement that was at best uncomfortable and at worst downright atrocious. In the city, meanwhile, the Voluntarios Distinguidos viewed the situation with rather different eyes. Knowing that they had been the subject of bitter complaint on the part of Villel, at least some of their number seem to have become convinced that the arrival of the British brigade presaged their immediate dispatch to the front, and the result was yet another complex maneuver in which the crowd was drawn into the politics of the moment. In brief, agitators under the control of the Voluntarios now set out to raise Cádiz in revolt. Reports began to circulate that Villel had swapped the powder in the city's forts and batteries for sand, that the foreign volunteers were in reality a "Trojan horse" designed to secure the city for the French, and that the Voluntarios were all to be disarmed. As the Swiss and Germans marched across the Isla de León toward the city on 22 February, then, the streets were occupied by the populace, Villel's residence surrounded by a menacing crowd, and the gates slammed shut against the oncoming turncoats.[77]

At this point, however, the plot went wrong. In the first place, instead of being murdered like Socorro, Villel was saved by the intervention of a Capuchin friar, the instigators of the revolt therefore having to settle on the marquis being taken into custody while his papers were subjected to a rigorous examination—one that the conspirators knew all too well would turn up absolutely nothing. Still worse, matters now got completely out of hand. The men behind the revolt had wanted only to ensure that the Voluntarios Distinguidos were allowed to continue playing soldiers in the security of their impregnable home, but the populace had an agenda of their own and proceeded to seize the chance to settle a variety of scores both old and new; according to one British eyewitness, indeed, the insurgents "were to the last degree ferocious and bent upon blood."[78] The matter, then, was not allowed to end nearly so tamely as elsewhere. Turning on the hated customs administration, the crowd proceeded to murder its head, José Heredia, on the pretext that he was a nominee of the erstwhile royal favorite Manuel de Godoy and ipso facto a traitor, while moves were also soon afoot to kill the governor, Felix Jones, free all the prisoners in the city, and sack the houses of the propertied classes.[79]

Needless to say, none of this was to the taste of the Voluntarios Distinguidos de Cádiz: the militia was, after all, very much a tool of the merchant oligarchy that dominated the city. Yet in some respects it suited their interests very well, for the growing disorder greatly increased their bargaining power. If logic dictated that they should now turn against the crowd, they could therefore do so on very favorable terms, Jones having to guarantee that the Voluntarios would never have to serve beyond the walls of the city and be given a monopoly of its defense. This done, order was restored soon enough, while the city was once again blanketed with draconian police regulations and threats of reprisal. Yet the rioters had only finally dispersed at the expense of major concessions—most notably, the dissolution of the police commission that Villel had established to watch over law and order and a promise to have the marquis fully investigated by the authorities—the episode therefore beyond doubt adding to the concern that elites felt across Andalucía. According to Crossard, indeed, he found his hosts "plunged into the sort of stupor that comes from having been afflicted by one of those terrifying scenes to which the spirit of revolution is so wont to give birth."[80]

For the propertied classes, then, the disorderly scenes that marked the fall of the Junta Central were the last straw in a chain of events that was pushing them willy-nilly in the direction of collaboration. And with Joseph Bonaparte seemingly a Spanish monarch—we here see the significance of choosing as his escort not French troops but readily identifiable *juramentados*—and very far from being the drunken one-eyed pygmy of Patriot propaganda, it was all the more easy to adopt this course of action. At the gates of Seville, as we have seen, the king disembarked from his carriage and instead mounted a horse so that all might see him. And what they saw was certainly encouraging: recently turned forty-three, Joseph was a smiling and slightly cherubic figure who had none of the brooding intensity that so characterized Napoleon. To quote Fée once more, "For a prince, he certainly had charming manners: although he resembled his brother, his gaze was softer, while he knew how to speak in a gentle fashion, this being something he used to advantage."[81] Although the story comes from Ronda instead of Seville, it is also worth recounting the words of an aide-de-camp of Marshal Soult named Auguste Petiet:

> The King was received with acclamation, and the nobility asked him to restore certain privileges which they had enjoyed heretofore. He then attended Mass in the cathedral. Never have I seen so large a quantity of pretty women concentrated in so small a space: though very devout, they nevertheless pushed and shoved one another to get a view of Joseph, and delivered their opinion of him in loud voices without paying the slightest attention to the divine service. I found myself close to a young woman of great beauty who said to her companion, "They said that he was one-armed and a drunk, and yet he has the prettiest hands in the world while . . . his every aspect denotes a man who is above such gross habits."[82]

Apart from the obvious commentary in respect of Joseph's encouraging physical appearance, in this quotation's reference to the nobility we have another possible reason for the generally favorable reaction to the arrival of the French in that it is possible that some sectors of the privileged classes felt threatened not just by social unrest but also political revolution. However, in reality the period from 1808 onward had seen few radical changes, while the welcome that the French received in Seville was so overwhelming that it is difficult to attribute it only to the reduced group constituted by the beneficiaries of the Old Order. Much more important was the general loathing that was felt in respect of the Junta Central. This body had many enemies, but we will make no reference here to the political jealousies that had precipitated the revolt of 24 January 1810. Even if the ideas on which this latter had been based had been promoted by enemies of the junta, the truth is that by the first months of 1810, there was virtually no element of the educated classes that was not thoroughly disillusioned with the government that had controlled Spain's destinies since September 1808. As William Jacob noted:

> The complaints of the inactivity, selfishness, inability, and intriguing spirit of the members of the Junta are universal. . . . It is . . . commonly asserted that no appointment, either in the army or the state, is given from the merit of the persons appointed, but merely from influence and intrigue. . . . Without dwelling on the fault in the original constitution of the body, a number too great for an executive and too small for a legislature, it is natural to suppose that the Junta would participate in those habits which the state of society to which they were accustomed unavoidably engendered, and were consequently ill-qualified to advance the mighty undertaking which they chose to accomplish; their popularity is now totally lost, and it is the universal wish they may be removed. . . . Many accuse, and perhaps with justice, the most opulent and elevated members of the Junta of disaffection to the cause of their country, and a disposition to aid the views of Bonaparte. Men in their situation, with large estates in that part of Spain occupied by the French, may very naturally wish to return to their homes and their ease even though submission to the enemy should be the necessary consequence. . . . The best informed people here think that a revolution in the government is absolutely necessary to save the country.[83]

The fundamental cause of this disaffection was only in part due to the suspicions of corruption to which Jacob refers. A further problem was the junta's conduct of the war. In the words of a pamphlet published in Cádiz in 1810: "For two years we have been at war, and yet, despite battles, combats, and a thousand minor actions, our soldiers still run in all directions after putting up the briefest of resistance as if it was the very first day they had taken arms."[84] Since the famous battle at Bailén in 1808, the Spanish army had hardly gained a single success, while on more than one occasion—a good example was the campaigns of Talavera de la Reina and Almonacid de Toledo in July–August 1809—it was at least plausible that failure had been due to unwise intervention by the Junta Central in the conduct of operations. That said, however, Spain's generals were more than capable of snatching defeat from the jaws of victory. While it is true that in 1808 the senior ranks had contained little in the way of talent, generals such as Blake, La Peña, Infantado, Venegas, and Areizaga really were some of the very worst that the Napoleonic Wars had to offer. As for Castaños—the one commander of high rank who had obtained success—authorities had for many months kept him shut up in the great monastery of La Cartuja as a scapegoat for the catastrophic defeats of November–December 1808. As an example of the commentaries that were circulating in respect of this point, one can do no better than to cite the newspaper *El Patríota:* "At the sight, for example, of the repeated . . . failures of the Army of the Center—a force that has good troops and excellent officers and yet that gets called the Centrifugal Army even by our very enemies, not to mention the fact that not a single one of its many generals, each of whom has been even more stupid and negligent than his predecessor, has received the slightest punishment—how can the people believe that everything that has happened has happened in good faith rather than as the result of malice or treachery?"[85]

Nor was it just a matter of the generals. If the Spanish army had not been able to face up to the French in battles such as Medellín or Ocaña, then on whom fell the responsibility for introducing the reforms that were so obviously needed? This was a question that could be extended to other subjects as well. From the beginning of the war onward, the Patriot forces had experienced a constant shortage of food, arms, and uniforms, and this was something that, by its very nature, could not be glossed over. As the author of the *gaditano* pamphlet previously quoted remarked: "The unkempt condition of our soldiers has arrived at an extreme that it is impossible to imagine. After so much money . . . has been spent on uniforming and arming them, it breaks one's heart to see them wandering round the streets looking so dreadful, dirty, and repulsive that they appear more like beggars than soldiers."[86] When the British soldiers engaged in the Talavera campaign complained of the appearance of their Spanish allies, then, it seems that they were far from exaggerating: "Falstaff's ragged regiment would have done honour to any force compared with the men before us. They were undisciplined, badly armed, and . . . almost naked. I can assure the reader that it was with the greatest difficulty we could avoid laughing right out of our faces, when officers out at elbows and knees stalked past carrying rusty old swords not worth lifting off the road. Hundreds of men with the most haughty countenances sported coats of many colours, while their inexpressibles bore unmistakable testimony to the difficulty experienced by the wearers in keeping the rags pinned about their legs."[87] Once again the explanation appeared to be government mismanagement. Although he was referring to the slightly different problem of providing the troops with adequate food—something of which they were as deficient as adequate uniforms—the words of the British ambassador, Lord Wellesley, are here as appropriate as anything:

> No magazines or regular depots of provisions have been established, under persons properly qualified to superintend the collection and distribution of provisions. . . . No regular . . . means of transport and movement have been attached to the army or magazines for the purpose of moving supplies from place to place, nor have any persons been regularly appointed to conduct and superintend convoys under the direction of the general commanding the army. No system of sufficient efficiency has been adopted for drawing forth from the rich and abundant provinces the resources which might have been applied, by a connected chain of magazines under due regulation, to relieve the local deficiency of those countries in which

> the army might be compelled to act. Accordingly, the result of the well-intentioned but inefficient zeal of the officers of the government has been totally inadequate to the exigencies of the occasion.[88]

As a result of all these factors, by the beginning of 1809, throughout Andalucía there was great disillusionment regarding the ability of the Junta Central to manage the Spanish war effort, and this could only be reinforced by the apparent attempts of its members to hang on to power and, in particular, to delay the convocation of the new national assembly that most observers saw as the key to reviving the struggle. As a British liaison officer attached to the Army of La Mancha named Phillip Roche wrote to Wellington:

> Nothing can exceed the general discontent, dissatisfaction, and demoralization of the mass of the people and the army. It is a fact, my Lord, beyond contradiction that the eyes and hopes of every good Spaniard are turned towards Lord Wellesley, towards you, and [towards] England, as the only means of salvation from the French, and from the stupid folly and corruption of their government. With this last I do not pretend to have anything to do, but I cannot shut my ears to what I hear repeated a thousand times a day. . . . Besides, how is it possible that anyone who has the faculty of reason can separate the inefficiency, bad organization, and consequent disasters of the army from the source of all these evils in the Junta?[89]

And then on top of all this, there came the disaster of January 1810, the response of the Junta Central, as the much vaunted defenses of the Sierra Morena fell into the hands of the French almost without resistance, being to engage in open falsehoods. The enemy, it admitted, had occupied the strategic point of Almadén, but beyond that the authorities maintained that the Army of La Mancha was resisting the French with great courage and that the Army of Extremadura was marching to its assistance as fast as it could manage in very superior numbers.[90] "We shall work with valor, with order, and with resolution," declared the junta, but in the event its members did not show a single one of these qualities and fled for their lives, leaving in the junta's place the power vacuum that effectively opened the gates to Joseph Bonaparte. As a young functionary of the British embassy who bravely rode out to discover the situation farther up the Guadalquivir valley in an attempt to clarify the situation for the British ambassador—no longer Lord Wellesley but now Bartholomew Frere—wrote: "It will be impossible for those who did not visit the towns and villages between La Carolina and Seville to imagine the hatred of all ranks towards their rulers [or] the language with which they were described."[91]

Returning to the sentiments expressed by Phillip Roche, it is important to underline the fact that they suggest that the feeling of fraud and disillusion that they reveal extended much further than a reduced circle of men of letters, proprietors, functionaries, and caciques. On the contrary, there is a great deal of evidence that among the populace as a whole there was also great disaffection. The first thing to say here, of course, is that the long and cruel struggle into which Spain had been plunged bore no relation to the glib promises of Patriot propaganda, the result being that confidence in the civil authorities was severely undermined. As was logical too, there was great anger at the inability of Spain's generals to defend civil society from the incursions of the French. Yet at the same time the unrest was inflamed by a series of factors that had nothing to do with some supposed determination to resist the French and, more especially, rescue Ferdinand VII. We come here to a War of Independence that is very different from the one that is generally put forward. Thus there is a great deal of evidence that the idea of a spontaneous crusade in favor of "Diós, Rey, y Patria" is little more than an invention, and further, that the disturbances that convulsed Spain in May and June 1808 constituted more a species of *jacquerie* than a military revolt. Within a very few days, the established elites had been able, as in Jaén, to reimpose their authority by means of the creation of the provincial juntas, and one of the first actions of these bodies had been to emasculate the crowd through the introduction of universal military service.[92]

For all that this last measure was accompanied by a tremendous propaganda effort that was designed to persuade the populace of the necessity of marching off to war in some distant province (at this stage most of Spain was still hundreds of miles from the nearest enemy), the reaction of the masses was one of unfeigned hostility. Conscription had never been popular even in the days of the limited call ups of the Bourbons, but the new levies were of a quite unprecedented size, while their administration was marked by great scandal and want of justice. To make matters worse, meanwhile, all too often the members of the juntas inspired little confidence. According to Mendoza, for example, the Junta of Málaga was composed of "the most inept, proud, and ignorant figures imaginable who only thought, not of the good of the fatherland, but of cutting a dash and wielding power."[93] Indeed, Mendoza has left us an acid portrait of many of its members. Thus, the de facto president, Rafael Trujillo, though *teniente del rey* (in effect, military governor), was "an old man with neither resolution nor knowledge, who, though good-hearted enough, was useless at everything"; the Conde de Guadiana "vulgar by upbringing and ill-intentioned by nature"; the Conde de Molina "ignorant, crude, and immoral," not to mention being "a puffed-up, haughty, and ostentatious intriguer and toady, who wished to have his way on everything, . . . obstructed the Junta's every action, and won the votes of many gluttons by virtue of his excellent table"; the cathedral canon, Antonio Corrales, "pleasure-loving, lazy, and completely unsuited to anything that required valor or constancy of spirit"; and the member of the city council, Fernando Ordóñez, "a crude and ignorant man of little talent who was unequalled in his capacity for talking big . . . and stirring up trouble."[94]

At a lower level, matters may have been still worse, if only because the elite of cities such as Málaga possessed at least a veneer of culture and education. In the *pueblos* of Andalucía, however, power was abused in a manner that was utterly naked. For a good case study, we need only look at the instance of Carmona. Here there had been absolutely no popular disturbances of any sort in 1808, and the result was that the local elite, which incidentally did not make a move of any sort until the arrival of orders from the Junta of Seville on 27 May, remained in control of the process throughout. Thus, the new junta that it was required to form was appointed by a meeting of the entire town council, the heads of the town's male religious houses, the town's parish priests, and various other prominent figures and, logically enough, eventually consisted of the mayor, five representatives of the town council, two wealthy landowners, and the head of the local tax office, José de la Concha. Needless to say, the first issue facing the new body was recruitment, and it was not long before it had become quite clear how the landowners who dominated its membership intended to fulfill their mandate. Thus, on 28 May the junta decreed the formation of a battalion of light infantry and a squadron of light cavalry, and within two days 184 men had been assembled for the infantry alone (of patriotic enthusiasm there was still no sign, such genuine volunteers as there were being either local day laborers or Galician migrants attracted by the promise of four *reales* a day, while some of the men were the product of a round-up of migrant workers and unemployed day laborers decreed by the junta). So far, so good, but almost immediately a deep rift opened between the civil and military authorities. A retired officer, Concha had been appointed as the town's commandant, and backed by the fellow ex-officer who had been chosen to lead the light infantry, he tried to insist that only men with previous military service should be given posts as company commanders. However, this was unacceptable to the leading landowners, who, having already secured privileged conditions of service for the propertied classes by decreeing that the cavalry should only accept recruits who could provide their own horses and equipment, had intended that the battalion's officers corps should be monopolized by their various clients. Headed by the wealthy landowner and town councellor Lorenzo Domínguez, the chief citizens therefore employed a variety of methods to intimidate Concha, and eventually succeeded in forcing him to flee to Seville. Victory in this struggle, however, was only the beginning of the story. Thus, the supply of volunteers and levies having very quickly been exhausted, the authorities found themselves being forced to implement the orders issued by, first, the Junta of Seville and, later, the Junta Central to impose conscription. Needless to say, this process was characterized by massive irregularities of all sorts: among other things, families were allowed to buy their sons out of service for sums of 1,000–2,000 *reales*, while the elites protected themselves still further by monopolizing the Milicia Honrada (not that this ever amounted to more than a paper force—entirely officered by representatives of prominent local families and officially composed of 285 men, in reality it never mustered even a tenth of that number).[95]

The result of behavior of this sort was yet more disorder. In Almería, for example, 12 February 1809 saw an angry crowd arm itself with three 3-pounder cannon and besiege the town hall after news spread that a contingent of conscripts from the district, who had been gathered in the city, were to be sent to Catalonia.[96] With the populace—one, it should be remembered, that was marked by very low levels of political consciousness—also hit by high taxes, police regulations that interfered in daily life in the most heavy handed of fashions, the sale of considerable parts of the common lands, and widespread economic disruption, the result was that many of the lower classes were so desperate for peace that they were prepared to turn their back on the struggle and, Joseph Bonaparte or no Joseph Bonaparte, acclaim any solution that might rescue them from the misery that had become the norm.[97]

This desire for peace was all the greater given living conditions in the Patriot zone. In particular, one of least deniable social effects of the War of Independence was the tremendous increase in the number of bandits. Banditry had, of course, been a major problem in many parts of Spain prior to 1808, but thanks to the increased poverty of much of the population, the flight of large numbers of young men from their homes in the face of conscription, and the massive desertion that affected the army, the number of wrongdoers spiraled in the most dramatic fashion.[98] The result—augmented as it was by the pillage engaged in by many starving Spanish soldiers—was impossible to escape. In many parts of Andalucía, travel and commerce became an impossibility, while the victims included not just the propertied but also the poor (among groups who were particularly vulnerable were shepherds, muleteers, and day laborers quartered at the isolated farmsteads known as *cortijos*). For some understanding of the terror that this criminal activity inspired, we can do no better than return to the memoirs of some of the visitors to Patriot Spain. First of all, we have the account of Robert Semple, an American adventurer who traveled from Lisbon to Gibraltar in 1809 and in the course of the journey, had an encounter with a gang of bandits near Córdoba:

At three leagues from Posadas we made a short halt at the Cortijo de los Frailes, a solitary house and almost the only one in all the distance between Almodovar and Córdoba. It was now eight o'clock and the moon, though on the wane, shone with considerable brightness. After a halt of nearly an hour, we pursued our journey over the plain. The . . . silence of the night, the evenness of the ground, and the uniform pace of our mules all tended to lull my companions nearly to sleep. They nodded on their mules, while the ass on which I rode had by degrees advanced to the front, and I found myself the leader of the entire processions. . . . Even by the pale light of the stars the towers of Córdoba were visible at no great distance when two men suddenly rode up to me and pointing their muskets close to my head, called out to me in Spanish to stop. In the first emotions of my surprise I exclaimed I was an Englishman, endeavouring at the same time to get my pistols, which were encumbered by my cloak. "If you touch your arms, you are dead," cried the robber. "Alight instantly or we fire!" In this situation, and unsupported by my companions, I had no alternative but to yield. While this was going on, another robber, wrapped up in a large black cloak, and who appeared to be the captain of the gang, kept riding round the party and driving them nearer and nearer together. The muleteers cried out for mercy, while the woman by turns, sobbed aloud, screamed through terror, or invoked with tears the protection of María Santísima. Meantime, having first taken away my pistols, the robbers ordered me to give up my watch and my money, having done which, they asked me if I had nothing more. I replied that I had only some copper coins of little value . . . which trusted they would leave with me. "Is it only copper? Never mind: give it to me," said the pious robber, "It will do for *las animas* [the souls]."[99] They then went round the whole party, and examined the burdens of the mules. After some time, although I could not see what was going on, I heard the ripping of cords and never doubted it was my unfortunate portmanteau they were cutting open. "Behold me," then said I to myself, "in a strange land without a dollar, change of clothes, or a friend." It was past midnight before we were released. The robbers disappeared with their booty . . . and we proceeded in a kind of mournful silence, the muleteers seeming afraid to open their lips and the woman being still in tears.[100]

A second witness to the level of banditry that characterized the Spanish countryside was the great English political hostess and lady of letters Elizabeth Vassall, who had traveled to Spain with her husband, the erstwhile British Foreign Secretary Lord Holland, to revel in what they had assumed would be the spectacle of a people united in the fight against tyranny. On 11 May 1809 she and her party set out from Seville to travel to Cádiz:

> Set off at four. Reached the Venta de San Antonio . . . near eight. The people of the *venta* [inn] were under some alarm in consequence of a troop of horsemen who had been committing great depredations on the high road in the morning; the robbers were supposed to be lurking in a house . . . about half a league off. As the banditti in Andalusia often force the solitary *ventas* to admit them our soldiers immediately secured the only two gates of entrance and it was determined that we should remain the whole night in order not to encounter any danger of being attacked. . . . At about ten o'clock, just as summer was coming in, I heard the sound of a horse, followed immediately by another. Jokingly, I said to Charles, "Hullo! Here are the robbers!" Lord Holland jumped up immediately and ran to the window, asking, "Who goes there?" The answer was not calculated to set us at rest: "Caballeros! No tengan cuidado, Señor [Gentlemen! Have no fear, sir!]." In an instant the soldiers and servants and muleteers put themselves into a posture of defence, for six or seven horsemen had arrived at the front gate and were clamorous for admittance. Fortunately, no shots were fired, and, when a parley was obtained, it seemed that this was a party of thirteen from Espera [Estepa?] in search of the robbers, who had plundered a house there and committed various excesses. We were not without apprehension, even after they were admitted, that we had let in the rogues. The alarm was very great and justifiable: every face was blanched with fear. The reason for their surrounding the *venta* and posting themselves at the gates was from a supposition that the robbers might have

> quartered themselves there for the night, and unless so circumvented might make their escape.[101]

In neither of these cases are the bandits specifically identified as deserters, but the links are clear enough. For a good example, let us take this report from the Junta de Ecija:

> A considerable number of young men who are perfectly fit for service have spread out across the countryside, taking over the lands and ranches of their owners without anyone being able to make the slightest move to stop them. Many of them have set up camp in the islands that dot the river [Guadalquivir] and are now disturbing this district with the excesses consequent upon hunger, want, and the need to avoid entering any settlement. Only an armed force, and even then one respectable enough to take on gangs of armed men, can put an end to these evils. . . . Proclamations, edicts, communications to the families of the men concerned, everything has been tried, and everything has been in vain.[102]

For another account of the situation, meanwhile, we can turn to the district of Benamargosa near Málaga, the extract that follows being all the more significant as it comes from an area that was later, according to myth at least, to be associated with significant popular resistance to French rule:

> The insubordination and impudence of these *pueblos* has driven me mad to such an extent that I have no option but to trouble Your Excellency in order to ascertain whether by your intervention it might be possible to secure their submission and acquiescence in respect of containing the problem of desertion. . . . Every *pueblo* of this province is full of deserters, of whom some are refugees from the field armies and others men who deserted no sooner than they had reported for duty in Málaga. Added to these there are many men who have evaded the draft altogether, and still others who, although totally fit for service, owe their liberty to their having paid bribes to doctors, surgeons, or go-betweens. . . . Sheltered by their families, such men as these

hang about these *pueblos* in large numbers without there being a single person who can keep them in order.[103]

Full as they are with a sense of tension and unease, these extracts contain the key to the situation. Thus, Patriot Spain was not only a badly governed state caught up in a war that offered few possibilities of victory but also a state in which banditry had reached such a level that, in wide areas of the country, normal life had become an impossibility; indeed, desperate to support their families and in some instances composed of hired thugs with criminal records, even forces that were supposed to keep the peace, such as the Milicias Honradas, were living by brigandage.[104] In this situation the only thing that could be done was to adopt a pragmatic attitude and attempt to find a solution beneath the cape of French occupation, such a way out being all the more attractive in view of the fact that the means the French could call upon to achieve normality and social peace were much more impressive than those that had been available to the Junta Central. There were, of course, other motives for accepting the foreign yoke—defeatism, ideological sympathy, fear of social revolution, and the desire to protect family and status by siding with the new masters—and at least some of these undoubtedly played a part in explaining the presence of the crowds that filled the streets of Seville and cheered Joseph Bonaparte with such enthusiasm. But beyond doubt, what bound rich and poor together was the hope that order and, if not prosperity, then at least the possibility of prosperity might be restored, or to put it still more simply, that daily life would resume its accustomed round. In the very special conditions that reigned in Andalucía in 1810, then, King Joseph and his sponsors had the chance of constructing a new state, even an *afrancesado* state. Yet everything would depend on the ability of the invaders to satisfy the agenda of the inhabitants and give them the security, whether economic or physical, that they so desperately needed. In short, the French had won the campaign, but could they now win the peace?

3

The Conquered Land

For whatever reason, then, by the end of January 1810, most of Andalucía was in the hands of the French. Before embarking on a discussion of the efforts of the invaders to "win the peace," we need first to mount a detailed examination of the lands that Joseph Bonaparte had now entered for the first time, for as has already been intimated, geography was to play a crucial role in the events that followed. On one level, the issue was purely physical: for example, Andalucía's lengthy coastline made it particularly vulnerable to attack from the sea, while the ranges of mountains that ringed it provided a secure refuge for bandits, partisans, and columns of regular troops alike. Yet we cannot just apply ourselves to the nature of the terrain. On the contrary, both resistance and collaboration were conditioned by the shape that had been given to society, and thus it is also necessary to look at such issues as landholding and the pressures generated by the feudal system. When the French crossed the Sierra Morena and left behind winter in La Mancha, they were delighted with their first impressions of their fresh conquest. Kajetan Wojciechowski, for example, was a lieutenant in the lancer regiment belonging to the Legion of the Vistula and participated in the offensive of January 1810 as part of the IV Corps of General Sébastiani.[1] As he wrote: "Although it was the beginning of January [*sic*], we found the trees in flower and the fields green with grass. In the vast plains were to be descried cities, large towns, farms, fields of wheat, and extensive pastures full of livestock."[2] Théophilé Brémond d'Ars, an aristocratic twenty-three-year-old officer of the Twenty-First Chasseurs à Cheval, was even more explicit. As he wrote to his father immediately after crossing the Sierra Morena, "We have been compensated for our fatigues by the pleasure of finding ourselves in a very pretty country under a very different sky: the countryside is charming and completely different from La Mancha; we look upon it, indeed, as the promised land."[3] However, this vision of prosperity was at best partial: in reality, most inhabitants of Andalucía lived in abject poverty, while the relatively developed picture that Wojciechowski and his fellows encountered in the valley of the Guadalquivir could be contrasted with many areas where agriculture functioned at little more than subsistence level. Such a situation was not without its advantages as far as the invaders were concerned, but even so, it was to prove very hard to reconcile the reality with their expectations.

Let us begin, however, with the basic geography of Andalucía. Strictly speaking, in 1808 there was no part of Spain that was officially accorded that title, the region today called Andalucía rather being divided into the four separate kingdoms of Seville, Córdoba, Jaén, and Granada. As we have seen, meanwhile, with almost one-fifth of the total number of Spaniards, the population was considerable. According to the admittedly not very reliable census of 1797—taken as it was in time of war, there seems to have been a general effort on the part of the local authorities to minimize the size of the male population in case conscription should subsequently be imposed—Andalucía had a total of 1,909,422 inhabitants, of whom 749,223 lived in Seville, 252,028 in Córdoba, 213,003 in Jaén, and 695,168 in Granada, the figure for Spain as a whole being 11,595,343.[4] The population, meanwhile, had been increasing steadily during the course of the eighteenth century, although thanks in part to serious subsistence crises in 1762–65, 1780–82, and 1786–87, the rate of increase seemingly had declined significantly during its latter years: according to John Lynch, "[The population of] Andalucía grew by twenty-five per cent in 1717–52, sixteen per cent in 1752–97."[5] With the coastal provinces very badly hit by the terrible yellow-fever epidemic that assailed Spain in 1804—travelers estimated that coastal towns such as Málaga lost between one-third and one-quarter of their inhabitants[6]—the rise may even have been in danger of going into reverse. As in the rest of Spain, meanwhile, the most important occupation was agriculture, but that said, rates of urbanization were significantly higher than elsewhere. Large cities, of course, were few—with 95,000, 70,000, and 55,000 inhabitants respectively, only Seville, Cádiz, and Granada numbered more than 50,000 people—but for reasons that we shall examine later, much of the rural population lived in substantial "agro-towns," such as Utrera, Osuna, and Castro del Río, the result being that of the forty towns and cities in Spain with more than 40,000 people, no fewer than seventeen lay south of the Sierra Morena.[7] Finally, as the above figures show, the population density was distinctively uneven, with more than two-thirds of the inhabitants concentrated, for reasons that will become clear below, in Seville and Granada: Seville, indeed, was one of only six territorial units in the whole Spanish monarchy that is estimated to have had more than forty inhabitants per square kilometer.[8]

As much as 300 miles across and 150 miles deep, Andalucía may be divided into four basic regions, all of which are orientated from east to west.[9] Proceeding from north to south, the first of these consisted of the mountain ranges that separate Andalucía from the rest of Spain. Known generically as the Sierra Morena and buttressed by a number of subranges—the Sierra de Aracena, the Sierra de los Santos, and the Sierra Chimorra—that project to north and south, this stretches all the way from the Portuguese frontier to the very northeastern extremity of the region, where it merges with the Sistema Subbético, the mountain massif that dominates the region of Murcia. In consequence, it is therefore some 250 miles long as well as anything from 20 to 40 miles in breadth. It is neither particularly high—its highest point rises no more than 5,900 feet—nor especially imposing, rather having the aspect of a chain of tangled uplands covered in pine, ilex, and general scrub, but, for all that, it remains a considerable barrier. Communications were poor—in 1810 there were no east–west routes at all and only seven places where an army could pass from north to south, the most famous and dramatic of these being the defile of Despeñaperros, a spot that had already become all too familiar to French troops as the place where the high road from Madrid to Seville crossed the mountains and entered Andalucía. Also the whole area was very thinly populated and therefore incapable of sustaining large forces of troops for any length of time: for example, it has been calculated that in the middle of the nineteenth century—a period little different in demographic terms from that of the Peninsular War—the forty municipalities that embraced the Sierra de Aracena could only boast a population density of fourteen people per square kilometer, while only thirteen of the district capitals had more than 1,000 inhabitants and none of them more than 4,500.[10]

As for economic activity, this centered on pastoral farming—sheep, goats, and fighting bulls—and the harvesting of cork bark, with some scattered pockets of mining—lead was extracted at Linares and copper at Río Tinto—the poverty of the region being such that there was a high incidence of both banditry and smuggling. Deeply aware of this problem, the regime of Charles III had attempted to address the issue by encouraging the establishment of a number of model agricultural colonies, of which the most famous was the one founded on the Madrid–Seville high road near the pass of Despeñaperros by the intendant of Seville, Pablo de Olavide, in 1767 (others included Santa Elena, Guarromán, and Carboneros). Known as La Carolina, this had originally been peopled by Roman Catholic settlers recruited from southern Germany, Alsace, and Savoy. Laid out as a planned settlement, it was an attractive-enough place, with long, straight streets lined with houses of a uniform design crisscrossing one another at right angles, but as early as the 1770s, it was beset with numerous problems. Many of the original settlers had quickly died of disease and, or so it was said, drink—far from being the responsible and experienced tenant farmers envisaged in the original plan, it appears that many of them were in reality destitute vagrants—while those who survived had often had to wait years before getting a plot of land. Forced to work during this time as de facto indentured laborers on the lands of other settlers and initially housed, like everyone else, in squalid camps—it took some years to build the town—they had then frequently seen their plots confiscated after a year or two and given to a Spanish family, the immigrants then being shifted to new allotments on the fringes of the colony. All this, of course, had occasioned much unrest, but any attempts at resistance, or even simply to move elsewhere, had met with severe punishment. As for the attempts that were made to encourage industry—for example, by persuading twenty Catalan cotton manufacturers to move to La Carolina—these had soon run into the problem that the town was far removed from the sea and therefore dogged by production costs that were much higher than those elsewhere. All in all, then, the experiment had hardly been a happy one.[11]

Once the traveler coming from the north had got through the Sierra Morena, however, he came to a very different region in the form of the valley of the Guadalquivir, or to give it its Arabic name, "the great river" (a waterway that is also Andalucía's only navigable river, though ships can only sail up it as far as Seville). Shaped, roughly speaking, like an isosceles triangle, this stretches northeastward from the Atlantic coast between Huelva and Cádiz to the vicinity of Bailén, and, with the exception of the extensive wetlands that fringe the river between Seville and the sea, consists of a more-or-less undulating plain that is for the most part made up of fertile land given over to the cultivation of wheat, grapes, and olives. Such was the terrain spied by Wojciechowski as he rode into Andalucía in 1810, and there can be no doubt that, superficially at least, the countryside offered the appearance of relative prosperity. Here, for example, are the English traveler Henry Swinburne's comments on the area around Córdoba: "The country as you approach Córdoba is all bare, hilly, and arable. The view of the river, city, and woods on the opposite hills is extremely agreeable and picturesque. . . . The environs are delightful and enjoy a rich variety of woods, hillocks, and culture vivified by an abundance of limpid water. The flat land produces olives and corn, and much of it is laid out in gardens where the fruit trees grow to a remarkable size and seem perfectly clean and healthy."[12] It was, moreover, a countryside that was frequently seen by visitors as it was traversed by the single-most important axis of communication in the whole of Andalucía, the high road from Madrid to Cádiz: closely following the river, after leaving the defile of Despeñaperros behind it, this ran westward via Bailén, Andújar, Córdoba, and Ecija and then turned south toward the sea, which it finally reached near the sherry capital of Jérez de la Frontera. Yet appearances were deceptive. On the fringes of the region, for example, there were areas that were as desolate as anywhere in Spain (hence the foundation by Olavide from 1768 onward of fresh colonies, namely the towns of La Carlota and La Luisiana, in the provinces of Córdoba and Seville, though these appear to have been even less successful than the ones in the Sierra Morena: in 1791, for example, La Carlota had a mere sixty inhabitants, while La Luisana was in a state of ruin).[13] "From Osuna to Puebla de Cazalla," complained one traveler, "nothing is to be seen but marshy and uncultivated plains . . . in which there is not so much as a cottage, and the eye meets with nothing to repose on except dirt and thistles."[14] Just as empty, meanwhile, was the countryside that stretched northward from Lebrija toward Seville:

> The country in the immediate vicinity of Lebrija is very rich, abounding in olives, vines, and corn, and for several miles we experienced a pleasant variety of gently swelling hills till we entered on the extensive marshes called the Maresma which are only passable in dry weather. . . . The Maresma is the most extensive tract of . . . pasture I ever beheld: it extends, in the direction we crossed it, almost to Seville, a distance of eight computed Spanish leagues, each of which amounts at least to four English miles. The continuance of dry weather has parched the earth and left but little appearance of vegetation, but, from the deep cracks occasioned by the heat, it is evidently a rich alluvial soil of very considerable depth. The eye is tired by the extent of the horizon, and no object interposes to diversify the scene except the herds of cattle and troops of horses which feed, or rather starve, at this season on a soil which at other times is the most luxuriant known in Spain. . . . On this plain, we found a wretched *venta* [inn], a single house without a neighbour within ten miles, . . . from which no species of refreshment could be procured except bad water for ourselves and barley with chopped straw for the mules.[15]

Similar scenes, meanwhile, were to be witnessed on the road from Jérez to Arcos de la Frontera. Captured en route for the American War of Independence when the convoy he was traveling with was attacked by a French squadron in 1780, a captain of the

Ninety-Ninth Foot named Richard Croker recalled the countryside he passed through as a deserted, sunbaked waste: "Having left the gardens and vineyards in the neighbourhood of Jérez behind us, we journeyed through a country that had the appearance of an arid desert. Nothing green could be seen except here and there some olive groves, and these at a distance from the road. Neither flocks nor herds were there, nor was pasture sufficient for an ass to be found for many miles. . . . In this part of . . . Andalucía it seldom or never rains between February and November; during that space of time, the horizon is clear, and the sun burning; this will sufficiently account for the present face of the country. I do not recollect to have experienced more inconvenience from the heat in any climate than I did this day."[16]

Even in the areas that were more settled, all was not well. In reality, while the valley of the Guadalquivir was certainly one of the most heavily farmed regions in the whole of Spain, productivity was comparatively low and the whole region desperately vulnerable to crop failures and drought. Something of the precarious character of life in the region may be gleaned from a précis of a manifesto penned in January 1837 by the town council of Baeza in protest at the manner in which its town was being consistently forced to pay higher taxes than nearby Jaén:

> The councilors do not understand why less taxation has been imposed on Jaén than on Baeza when the only source of wealth that the latter has is an agriculture that has almost been destroyed by the bad harvests of previous years and can neither be rendered more extensive nor more productive by the agents employed in its respect; when the labor force is employed on land that is wholly lacking in irrigation and is of very poor quality; when its vines are low in yield and productive of a wine of almost no merit; when its olive groves have been reduced to a state of total ruin by the lack of rain; when there are no draught animals of any sort that are capable of helping in the work of tilling the soil for want of both buildings to keep them in and grazing lands to pasture them upon. There is no industry in Baeza that is in any way worthy of note, while such few shopkeepers that it possesses are in extremes for want of goods that

> they can sell. In consequence, the number of inhabitants is rapidly diminishing, while there is a great deal of emigration in the direction of Jaén city.[17]

Even the best that the countryside of Andalucía had to offer, then, was shot through with problems. To these we shall return in due course, but for the time being, let us continue with our tour of the region. Moving on to the third zone into which Andalucía can be divided, we come to the second and more impressive of its upland massifs. Known collectively as the Sistema Penibético, this thrusts southwestward from the Sistema Subbético in a great wedge that separates the Guadalquivir valley from the Mediterranean coast and ends in a sharp point near Ronda. Much more rugged than the Sierra Morena, it includes the highest mountain in mainland Spain—Mulhacén (11,413 feet)—and is made up of a number of separate mountain ranges, including the Sierra de los Filabres, the Sierra Nevada, the Sierra de Baza, the Sierra de Gador, the Sierra de Almijarra, the Sierra Hárama, the Sierra Mágina, the Sierra de Antequera, the Sierra de Bermeja, and the Serranía de Ronda. All of these ranges, which are much lower in the west than they are in the east, thrust upward from an extensive plateau that is on average 1,000 feet above sea level, while they occupy a much wider area than does the Sierra Morena; it is, for example, about 100 miles from Jaén to Almería. On the whole, however, communications were easier: the various ranges are separated from one another by broad upland valleys, such as the *hoya de Guadix* and the *vega de Granada*, and these provided access for a number of major highways, of which the most important was the one that branched off the main road from Madrid to Seville at Andújar and ran from there to Málaga via Jaén and Granada; others included those from Málaga to Ecija via Antequera and from Granada to Murcia via Guadix and Baza. With better roads came more extensive agriculture and a greater density of population (see above), but even so it was a region that was renowned for its wild character. As an example, let us quote the account of a journey made by the French diplomat Jean-François de Bourgoing from Cartagena to Cádiz via Guadix, Granada, Antequera, and Málaga a few years before the outbreak of the Peninsular War.

Here and there were isolated patches where the countryside offered an aspect that was relatively rosy—Bourgoing could not deny the fertility of the *vega de Granada* (the irrigated plain that surrounds the city of that name) and also found Loja to be surrounded by groves of fruit trees of every sort—but on the whole the picture that he paints is one that is dismal in the extreme: "The roads from Lumbreras to Vélez el Rubio are frightful. You travel for five leagues in a *rambla,* or channel of a torrent, seeing nothing but deserts and naked rocks, and surrounded by high mountains, which early in the winter are covered with snow. . . . Depopulation is a terrible scourge to every country. In many parts of Granada the lands have no other ornament than the plants with which nature has governed them. . . . The road from Antequera to Málaga lies principally over high mountains, which present nothing agreeable to the eye."[18]

Typical enough of the towns and villages that dotted the mountains, and one that was to be the scene of sharp fighting in the campaign of Andalucía, was Yunquera. Perched on a rocky spur about twenty miles west of Málaga on the winding mountain track that led from there to Ronda and dominated by the Sierra de las Nieves, in 1810 it was a community of about 1,700 people, all of whom lived in the close-packed streets and alleys that surrounded the parish church. There was a little cottage industry—the nationwide census that had been carried out by the Marqués de Ensenada in 1754 had revealed the presence of several weavers—while there were also a handful of artisans such as shoemakers, but otherwise the population were wholly dependent on the land. As many as half the adult male population were day laborers living on the brink of the utmost poverty, but even the tenant farmers and peasant proprietors were little better off: there was little arable land, and the bulk of the district's produce therefore consisted of such commodities as olives, mulberries, oranges, and chestnuts; indeed, its most valuable export was not agricultural at all, but rather snow gathered from the summits of the mountains and then sent down to Málaga to cool the palates of the wealthy.[19]

So much, then, for the Sistema Penibético. Beyond them and, indeed, running in a great crescent from the frontiers of Murcia to those of Portugal, was the coastal plain that formed the fourth of the geographical areas into which Andalucía could be divided. Some five hundred miles long, this varied in breadth from as much as fifty miles in the present-day province of Huelva to only a mile or two in parts of those of Málaga and Almería. Conditions, meanwhile, differed enormously, from the semi-deserts found in parts of the eastern littoral through the salt flats of Cádiz to the broad wheatlands of the west, while there was also much variation in the density of the population. Between the mouth of the Guadalquivir and the border town of Ayamonte, for example, other than the town of Huelva, the beaches of today's Costa de la Luz were broken by barely half a dozen *pueblos,* whereas around Málaga there were pockets of territory that were dotted with a profusion of small settlements, this being particularly true of the district centered on Vélez Málaga known as La Axarquía. Thanks to the many streams that ran down from the mountains, such areas were frequently heavily cultivated, there being extensive plantations of sugarcane, cotton, and even rice.[20] Most important from the point of view of the years of occupation that were to follow the French invasion, however, were the various ports sprinkled along the coast. Of these the most important were Cádiz, Gibraltar, Algeciras, Málaga, and Almería, but there were many other settlements where troops could be landed in safety, including Ayamonte, Huelva, Puerto de Santa María, and Tarifa, while along the more sheltered coast of the Mediterranean, there were plenty of places, such as Fuengirola and Estepona, where men could even be put ashore on the beach.

As we shall see, this long coastline was to prove the Achilles' heel of French occupation, but to return to the geography, it can be seen that, in general, Andalucía was no wilderness. Yet at the same time, amenities were few and far between. Spanish inns were notorious for their dirt and discomfort, and those south of the Sierra Morena were, it seems, no better:

> The road from Lorca to Lumbreras is tolerably good. It was here I saw the inns of Spain in all their nakedness and poverty. A *posada,* or Spanish inn, merits a particular description. The first room of the house is often a great stable full of asses and mules, through which you must make your way if you wish to

> ask and obtain a lodging. It is with considerable difficulty you get to the kitchen, which is a round or square room, the ceiling of which terminates at a point and is open at the top to leave free passage for the smoke. Round this great chimney is a broad stone bench, which at night serves the family for a bed, but which in the daytime offers a commodious seat to travellers, coachmen, and muleteers, who, seated without distinction with the host and hostess, deprive the air of a part of the smoke by swallowing it. . . . The whole inventory of the kitchen utensils consists in several great frying pans, and everything you eat is fried in bad oil. It is true this is not spared, and abundance is joined to badness of quality to take away the appetite. . . . When you have refreshed and warmed yourself and wish to retire, you are conducted to a damp corner called a chamber. . . . A mattress a foot shorter than it ought to be is thrown upon the ground; the sheets are not much bigger than large napkins, and the counterpane, if by chance you find one, scarcely covers the sides of the wretched pallet.[21]

If the inns were bad, the roads were little better. Some routes, such as that from Seville to Madrid, were well engineered and maintained, but as the eighteenth-century English traveler Henry Swinburne found in the course of a journey from Cádiz to Seville in April 1776, even major highways were unpredictable: "Upon leaving Jérez, we found the roads much the worse for heavy rains, and two days were spent in travelling a few miles through stiff thick clays, where we expected to stick fast every instant as the wheels were clogged to a great height."[22] One route that was particularly bad in this respect was the coastal road that led from Gibraltar to Málaga: little more than a rough track and frequently intersected by ravines running down from the mountains that overlooked it, this was constantly liable to being cut by flash floods that might suspend all movements for days on end (some accounts, indeed, describe it as being completely impassable to wheeled transport).[23] Another notoriously difficult route, meanwhile, was the one that connected Cartagena with Granada via Baza and Guadix. Here, for example, are the memories of the wealthy English traveler Richard Twiss:

> We arrived this morning at the village of Purulena; its inhabitants have dug caves in the soft rock which serve them for dwelling places. We here hired an ass to carry one of the trunks up a mountain we were to pass over as the chaise was too much loaded to be dragged up over such a long ascent . . . and proceeded to Iznalloz where we arrived after having travelled eight leagues through a wild mountainous desert, melancholy, barren, and totally uninhabited. The roads were bad and at times dangerous, being along the edge of precipices. On one side the mountains rose almost perpendicularly, and on the other the fall was equally steep, and the road barely broad enough for the chaise to pass. In these places I always chose to walk. . . . Large stones which had fallen from the rocks frequently blocked up the passage; these stones we were obliged to remove and tumble over the brink which occasioned much delay, so it was quite dark when we got to our night's lodging. . . . The chaise had been once overturned, and much time and trouble was occasioned in setting it up again as we had all the baggage to unload and reload. I was in it when it was overset, but received no hurt.[24]

Nor was it just a matter of bad inns and stony roads. Also to be endured was much personal discomfort. Held prisoner for a while at Arcos de la Frontera, Richard Croker was wry in his account of what he had to suffer. As he wrote in a letter home dated 23 September 1780: "To [the] extreme heat may be added the plague of insects and reptiles always to be found in southern countries. The bug, the mosquito, the lizard, the ant, unite their efforts to make your life miserable. . . . Some of our women have been dangerously ill caused by the venomous bites and stings of these creatures. . . . We have also been most of us disordered in a greater or lesser degree, possibly by the water or, perhaps, too liberal use of the grapes or other fruit. Such are the pleasant effects of the boasted climate of Andalucía."[25]

On the whole, little relief from all this was to be found in the cities of the region. Indeed, these offered a sorry picture. In the High Middle Ages, Andalucía had had an urban life that was highly developed. Industry had flourished in the form of leatherwork, glass, wool, and silk, and the population had been substantial: in the eleventh century—for example, Córdoba may have had a population of 90,000, while that of Andalucía as a whole probably reached 5,000,000. In the wake of the Reconquista, however, the region was struck by economic disaster. The extent of this has been contested, and it is probable that earlier ideas of complete de-urbanization and deindustrialization have been exaggerated. But even so the consequence was serious enough. Cut off from the Muslim world, the industries of Córdoba and its fellows were thrown back on the domestic market, which was not enough to sustain them: on the one hand, the Christian north could not absorb their products, while on the other, the hitherto prosperous countryside of Andalucía experienced an ever greater degree of impoverishment. On top of this, meanwhile, came much heavier taxation that both further squeezed local markets and made investment in industry ever less attractive, while a variety of issues, including not least the influence of the guilds, made it difficult to safeguard profits by cutting labor costs. Meanwhile, in Seville in particular there was a further source of trouble. In the sixteenth century the city had had a de facto monopoly of the colonial trade, and this had brought a degree of revival that had persisted for more than a century: in 1611, for example, it had acquired the cannon foundry mentioned earlier. Yet despite the best efforts of the merchant oligarchs who benefited from it, Seville could not maintain its preeminence, not least because as ships grew larger, so they could not navigate the Guadalquivir so easily. Deprived of employment and hit very heavily by plague and famine, the population fell away, and by 1700 the city was in no better case than most of its fellows, further pain being inflicted with the transfer of its monopoly of the America trade to Cádiz in 1720. As the eighteenth century progressed, some relief was afforded by, first, the establishment in 1757 of the Royal Tobacco Factory, which in the early 1770s was giving employment to some 1,500 men, and, then, a major leatherworks owned by an English entrepreneur named Weatherall, while both soap and silk remained important local products (in 1799 the city had no fewer than 2,318 silk looms), but at best all that could be done was to hold stagnation at bay.[26]

In the wake of the economic turmoil of the sixteenth and seventeenth centuries, what was left was a mere husk. Other than Cádiz and, to a lesser extent, Málaga, which had emerged as Spain's third port in the course of the eighteenth century and since 1808 had been enjoying something of a boom thanks to the greater ease with which it could export the assorted cash crops grown in its vicinity, the one place in Andalucía that may truly be said to have been flourishing was Jérez de la Frontera, where the sherry industry sustained both a population of perhaps 35,000 people and an infrastructure that impressed foreign travelers. "The streets of this city are wider than those of Cádiz," wrote Jacob. "There is a good paved footpath, and it is well lighted; some of the houses are splendid."[27] Elsewhere, however, there was less to admire. Having got to Seville, for example, Swinburne was distinctly unimpressed. The Giralda, he allowed, was fine enough—"extremely noble" even—while he was struck with the square known as the Alameda de Hercules, the Roman aqueduct that supplied the city with water, and the gardens of the alcázar, where he and his party "sauntered near two hours in the groves till we were quite in ecstasy with sweets."[28] But for the rest, Seville was a disappointment:

> The streets . . . are crooked, dirty, and so narrow that in most of them two coaches find it difficult to pass abreast. . . . Most of the churches are built and ornamented in so barbarous a style that I had not the patience to examine them; the cathedral, the capuchins, and the *caridad* are the only sacred edifices really interesting, the first by its antiquity, size, and reputation; the two latter by two *chef d'oeuvres* of Murillo. The cathedral is more cried up than I think it deserves; it is by no means equal to York Minster for lightness, elegance, and gothic delicacy. The . . . pillars are too thick [and] the aisles too narrow, and the choir, by being placed in the centre, spoils the whole *coup d'oeil* and renders the rest of the church little better than a heap of long passages. . . . Not one of the great entrances . . . is finished, and, to disfigure the whole pile, a long range of buildings, in the modern style, has been added to the old part.[29]

Someone else who was less than taken with Seville was William Jacob, who reported himself "not a little disgusted with the filthy appearance of the town" and remarked that in many of the streets, "there is not sufficient room to admit even a single carriage."[30]

Granada and Córdoba, it turns out, were no better. Of the former, Swinburne commented: "The glories of Granada are passed away with its old inhabitants: its streets are choked with filth; its aquaducts crumbled to dust; . . . its trade lost; in a word, everything except the Church and the law is in a most deplorable condition. . . . Most of the streets are narrow and dirty. To the lanes and alleys the common people retire to perform the most filthy of nature's functions. . . . The market place is spacious, but its buildings are horribly ugly."[31] As for Córdoba, viewed from afar the city looked well enough, but like Seville and Granada, its streets were winding and fetid, while Bourgoing remarked that it had "preserved nothing of its ancient grandeur except a vast enclosure full of ruins, and the famous mosque."[32] As for the population, its poverty was all too evident, as witness, for example, Swinburne's claim that "not less than 500" foundling children died each year of starvation and neglect.[33]

Poverty, however, was everywhere, and many remarked upon it. Here, for example, is Richard Twiss: "The beggars who swarm in every part of these kingdoms are as insufferably troublesome as they are in Italy: I have frequently been interrupted while conversing with acquaintances in the streets by the vile paw of a disgusting old woman familiarly placed on my arm, and, on turning to look at the object, have started with horror at the shocking spectacle; these wretches even insolently intrude themselves into churches and coffee houses, and expose their cadaverous and rotten limbs under the nose of the affrighted spectator."[34] Rather less unpleasant in his description of the poor was Richard Croker:

> Although the climate in some degree renders abstinence necessary, the people have a more imperious tyrant, necessity, to compel the observance of it. Wonderful it is to me how they procure the requisites of life, reduced by custom as they are. Trade or manufactures they have none. The only influence that I have seen of anything like industry is in a young shoemaker in my neighbourhood; he is generally at work, and is married to the prettiest woman I have seen at Arcos. . . . Colonel Espinosa, and another gentleman of fortune, distribute their alms to a very considerable number of the poor weekly. I accidentally passed

> through the street today where these people were assembled; they were, many of them, apparently very old, and generally afflicted with leprosy, scrofula, and other cutaneous disorders of the most inveterate kind. . . . Never surely were the severest ills to which human nature is subject more horribly portrayed than in this collection of miserable beings: loathsome and incurable disease, helpless and unregarded old age, and hopeless poverty were here seen in their most abject and extreme state of wretchedness. No ideas equal to this reality ever reached my imagination, and it will not be easy to shake off the impression that the appearance of this group has made. In the street did these poor people wait for several hours, exposed to the burning sun, for sake of receiving a *cuarto* or an *octavo,* the first about the value of a halfpenny, the last a farthing.[35]

Needless to say, though poverty was on occasion confused with virtue—the "frugality" of the populace was much praised—such sights occasioned much sententious comment on the part of foreign visitors. Typical enough was Joseph Townsend. The rector of the Wiltshire town of Pewsey and a renowned polymath with interests ranging from medicine to geology, Townsend visited Spain in 1786–87, and in March of the latter year, he arrived at Málaga, having traveled by sea from Cádiz. What he saw, however, dismayed him in the extreme. "In the city few traces of industry are seen, whilst filth and nastiness, immorality and vice, wretchedness and poverty . . . prevail."[36] More particularly, meanwhile, before the door of each potential benefactor—religious houses, parish churches, or rich merchants—there were to be seen swarms of beggars. "Young and old, the feeble and the robust, men, women, and children, clothed in rags and half-devoured with vermin, . . . they employ themselves in the most disgusting occupation till the hour for distributing the meat and broth arrives, after which they either lie down to sleep or disperse themselves among the streets to beg."[37] Amid such conditions, meanwhile, another problem that could not be avoided was disease. In Málaga, Townsend noted, "diseases of a relaxed fibre . . . debility, tertians, and putrid fevers rage with such violence that more than 3,000 died last year [1786] in the hospital of San Juan de Díos beside multitudes in the city and its environs."[38] As for the cause of all this, Townsend was in no doubt. Witnessing firsthand the distribution of immense amounts of charity to the poor, he drew from this what he deemed to be an obvious conclusion: "With such encouragement for beggars, no wonder that they should abound in Málaga, where the lazy can have no inducement to employ themselves in labour and the profligate, once they have wasted their inheritance, may know for a certainty that they shall never be in want of bread."[39]

Travelers' tales of the poverty to be found in Andalucía form a natural link with the discussion of the region's social structure, to which we must now turn. Insofar as this was concerned, the salient picture was one of the most extreme inequality of wealth and, more especially, landed property. Here the basic picture was affected, first of all, by climate and, secondly, by history. Let us begin with the question of rainfall. Across much of the south of Spain, rainfall is very limited, and there are areas, particularly around Almería, where it is all but nonexistent. During the period of Moorish domination, and before that, in the time of the Romans, this problem had been addressed by widespread schemes of irrigation, but for a variety of reasons these had, except in a very few places such as the *vega de Granada*, been lost almost without trace over the course of the centuries. The consequences, however, were severe, for increasingly the only type of farming that could be practiced with any hope of success was large-scale monoculture, which in Andalucía meant wheat, grapes, or olives. Inherent in the meteorological conditions of southern Spain, then, was a tendency toward the formation of great estates, or *latifundios,* and this was given a further push by the fact that, as the frontiers of Christian dominion expanded in the course of the Reconquista, so successive monarchs handed large quantities of land over to the feudal nobility and the church, and especially the religious orders. Along with this control of the land, meanwhile, went seigneurial rights of various sorts, of which the most important were those of dispensing justice via manorial courts, appointing a wide range of local magistrates and other officials, and exercising a monopoly over such facilities as windmills and olive presses. Not all those involved were titled aristocrats, but even so it was symbolic that some of the most powerful grandees in Spain—men such as the Duques de Medina Sidonia, Arcos, and Osuna—took their titles from towns in Andalucía.

The chief characteristics of rural Andalucía were, then, on the one hand, the concentration of property in a very few hands and, on the other, the absolute dependence of the vast majority of the population on a tiny elite. Taking the region as a whole, 13.5 percent of the land was in the hands of a mere 563 proprietors, while there were many grandees who owned thousands of acres. For a good example of the sort of extremes that might be attained, we might cite the example of the eastern Andalucían municipality of Baeza. Though this town was by no means in the most strongly *latifundista* area of the region, in 1818 there were 156 proprietors owning 42,193 *cuerdas* of land, but of these just six owned 36.4 percent of the total, while various religious houses and charitable institutions possessed another 16 percent.[40] Particularly in the eastern and southeastern parts of Andalucía (as in Baeza), there remained numbers of small and medium proprietors, while in upland regions in particular there was a tendency for large estates to be sublet to more-or-less humble tenant farmers known as *pelentrines,* but the small proprietors had been under serious pressure throughout the eighteenth century and had often been forced by drought to sell their lands, while the latter lived a precarious existence dogged by rack renting and a lack of cheap credit, not to mention the fact that the land set aside from them was invariably the worst and least productive. Another issue, meanwhile, was taxation. In this respect the smallholder was particularly burdened, the worst offender in this respect being the so-called *alcabala,* a tax that was levied at a rate of 6 percent on all items that were brought into market towns for sale and on all items that were purchased there for consumption back in the countryside; the customs officers who enforced this being notorious for their venality, the brunt of the burden inevitably fell most heavily on the poorer classes.[41] For an eyewitness account of the travails of peasant farmers in just one area—that of Jérez de la Frontera—we might cite William Jacob: "The [vine] growers are generally poor and indebted to the merchants of this city, who, by advancing them money before the vintage, are enabled to take advantage of their embarrassed circumstances to purchase at rates which keep those growers in a perpetual state of dependence. This want of capital is felt in still greater degree by the owners of the olive trees, the variable produce of which frequently leaves them too deeply in debt in unfruitful years to enable them to clear themselves in those which are more productive."[42]

As a result of all these pressures, large numbers of peasants were driven from their lands. In 1621, for example, a member of the *cortes* for Granada recorded a dismal picture of the situation in his homeland: "Numerous places have become depopulated and disappeared from the map, . . . their churches decayed, houses in ruins, property wasted, and fields uncultivated. The vassals who formerly cultivated them now wander the roads with their wives and children, searching from district to district for a living and eating herbs and roots to keep alive."[43] This, of course, had considerable implications for the distribution of the population in that the erstwhile smallholders had no option but to congregate in the main towns of each district in search of work, leaving a countryside that was in many areas all but stripped of human habitation; hence the enormous distances that were often to be found between one *pueblo* and the next. As we shall see, this was to present the French with great problems in a military sense, but just as much to the point was the effect that it had upon the nature of the population. Thus, it could not but follow that the dominant social group in most of Andalucía were the *jornaleros* or *braceros*—men who were paid by the day and earned their living working on the great estates—the proportion of the population represented by such figures rising to as much as 75 percent in the valley of the Guadalquivir. In general, this group was viewed with the utmost scorn, and it was perhaps they more than anyone else who gained the Spaniards their reputation for laziness. Writing of Lebrija, for example, Jacob described them as "indolent wretches whom I see . . . loitering in the market place in a state of the most despicable apathy, a set of beings too idle to labour, but who, when their vengeful passions are aroused, are capable of the most horrible deeds of cruelty."[44] That the populace was capable of acts of mob violence is unfortunately true enough—in Lebrija, in particular, on 7 December 1808, eighty prisoners from Dupont's army had been slaughtered in a series of clashes that originated in rumors that the many French soldiers who had been quartered in the town to await the repatriation promised them in the capitulation of Bailén had managed to arm themselves and were planning a massacre of the population[45]—but as the eighteenth-century reformers who had from the 1760s onward began to turn their minds to the problems of Spanish agriculture recognized, accusations that it was naturally idle are unfair. To quote the Conde de Campomanes: "In Andalucía the inhabitants are nearly all simple labourers who have only temporary and precarious occupation and live the rest of the year in poverty, . . . in a wretched starvation which does not correspond to the fertility of the soil and certainly is not caused by their idleness."[46]

What, then, was the cause of the misery that so assailed Andalucía? For a more reasoned explanation than the ones put forward by scornful foreigners, one may here begin with the fact that, given the prevailing weather conditions, huge stretches of even the limited land that was worth cultivating had, over the centuries, been turned over to pastoral farming. So low was the yield of much of the soil that using it to support sheep (especially), goats, horses, and fighting bulls was simply more profitable than it was to use it for raising crops, and all the more so as this both cut down on labor costs—estates used in this fashion obviously supported only a handful of shepherds and stockmen, especially the famous cowherds known as *garrochistas*—and exploited the numerous privileges that were extended by the Spanish monarchy to the powerful interest group represented by pastoral farmers. Only a relatively small amount of land required cultivation, then, and in cereal areas—olive groves and vineyards were a different matter—a good part even of this was not being worked at any given time. We come here to the demands of soil and climate. In brief, with rainfall low and sources of manure minimal, no land could be kept continuously under the plough, and so each estate was divided up into three lots, which were farmed in rotation, with one being used to grow crops, one being left as stubble, and one being left to lie fallow. In this respect olives and grapes offered better chances for laborers, but unfortunately these crops replicated the other great defect of wheat as far as the workforce was concerned in that they only afforded an appreciable amount of employment at certain times of the year. Thus, all three required large numbers of hands at harvest time, while estates given over to wheat also required extra labor at the period of the spring sowing, but for the rest of the time there was almost no work other than a little weeding and hoeing. Almost entirely illiterate, possessed of a life expectancy of no more than thirty years, and crammed together in their miserable *pueblos*—a good example is the riverine settlement of Villa del Río, whose 2,500 inhabitants occupied just 400 houses, one of which appears to have been home to no fewer than twenty-two persons[47]—then, for perhaps two-thirds of each year, the *braceros* were left with no work whatsoever. Indeed, they did not always get even what they could normally regard as their due: heavy rain might cause the spring sowing to be suspended or drought leave estates with nothing to harvest, while a further problem was constituted by the troops of migrant laborers who each year descended on Andalucía from still-more-desperate regions, such as Galicia or the Alemtejo, in search of work. At the same time too, the cultivation of grapes—of the three crops mentioned, the one that required the most labor on account of the need to prune vines twice a year, pile up the soil around the stems during the winter, and excavate a depression around each plant to maximize the water reaching it during the summer—had, or so it was suggested, been generally reduced in favor of wheat because of the minimal profit margin that wine offered.[48] As Pablo de Olavide recognized, the situation of the agricultural laborers was therefore grim indeed:

> The majority of the populace—the group that may be regarded as the crowd—are day laborers, men, indeed, who are the most unfortunate that I know of in the whole of Europe. They are employed on the great estates, . . . but only at such times as their labor is needed and they are summoned by the administrators of each property. In these periods of employment, although they remain all but naked and are given no place to sleep but the floor, they do at least get enough to eat on account of the bread and *gazpacho* that they are given, but, as soon as the slack periods arrive, . . . they are reduced to starvation and have no other option but to turn to charity. In the Andalucían winter,

> then, it is entirely routine for large and small towns alike to be inundated with swarms of laborers . . . begging for money in the streets. . . . In Seville in particular one sees many thousands of such people every year.[49]

For the hundreds of thousands of Andalucíans caught up in this system, life was at best extremely stark. In the first place, living conditions in the agro-towns in which they clustered were near unbearable: few families could boast of more than a one-room cabin, and these were often clustered together in alley-style developments in which ten or more such dwellings would have to share a single communal cooking area. In the second, given the immense distance that separated many of the estates from the *pueblos* that serviced them, it was not practicable for the men concerned to travel to and from their labors every day, the result being that large numbers of them had no option but to live apart from their families. Hired at the start of the harvest or the spring sowing, they would be marched to isolated farm complexes known as *cortijos*. Each one the central nucleus of a *latifundio,* these typically consisted of the house of the estate's administrator; a cluster of cabins for the handful of permanent employees needed to carry out such tasks as looking after the oxen used to pull carts to market or plough the fields; a variety of barns, stables, and storehouses; and finally a barrack block, where the *braceros* were expected to live and sleep. In such places conditions were just as dire as they were back home. As the later English commentator Gerald Brenan wrote, "They slept sometimes a hundred at a time, on the floor of a long room called the *gañanía,* which had a fireplace at one end. The landowner fed them: except at harvest time, when they were given beans, the only dish was *gazpacho,* a soup of oil, vinegar, and water with bread floating on the top. They took it hot for breakfast, cold for lunch, hot again at night."[50]

If the situation in the *cortijos* was particularly grim, no day laborer had an easy life. With the working day customarily sunrise to sunset, in the summer they might have to put in days of sixteen hours, on top of which, in the morning and in the evening alike, there would invariably be a march that might be anything up to several miles long. Temperatures, meanwhile, could easily rise to forty degrees centigrade: "After sunrise," wrote one English traveler, "the weather was so hot that it was with the utmost difficulty I could keep myself awake on my horse. I rode with an umbrella and placed a sheet of white paper between my hat and my head."[51] The labor itself was extremely hard in nature and carried out under the direction of foremen who were not inclined to be anything other than hard taskmasters. And finally, pay was minimal. In Jaén, for example, a *jornalero* earned between four and six *reales* a day, whereas a skilled textile worker got eight and an artisan from seven to eleven (women, of course, got much less: those employed in embroidery and lacemaking, for example, could expect no more than two *reales* and frequently not even that).[52]

As might be expected, such wages were insufficient to support a family of any size, but in most towns of Andalucía, there were few ways in which they could be supplemented. Providing that it was kept within bounds, gleaning was permitted on the great estates: it was customary, for example, to allow the *braceros* to gather fallen olives for their own consumption, while wild garlic and artichokes were also favored items. Equally, a little money might be made by gathering the esparto grass in which southern Spain abounds and plaiting it into baskets and other objects. However, although there were exceptions, such as the embroidery and lacemaking mentioned above, and some pockets of silk and wool production, such as those that survived in Granada, the sort of cottage industry that employed so many women and children in other parts of Europe was for the most part lacking. Nor, meanwhile, did the close-packed *pueblos* of Andalucía have any space for the sort of cottage gardens that were found in English and French villages. Needless to say, the implications of all this were very grim. Let us here once again quote Pablo de Olavide:

> It is very sad to observe how out of a whole family it is only the father who works. Thus, he goes to the fields to earn his pay on every day that he can, and with this he has to maintain his wife and children. As is well known, this cannot be done. There are no factories in which the other members of the family can earn their daily bread, nor any other occupations in which they can engage. The women do not even spin while it is unheard of for

> them to go and work in the fields: it has been many centuries since women and, for that matter, children, labored in the tasks of the countryside, and, in truth, in the current state of things they cannot do so. Being of little strength as she is, how can a woman accompany her husband on a daily journey of two leagues to her place of work, and all the more so when she is carrying a small child? This is one more defect that results from the unfortunate distribution of the population, . . . while the result is that the women and children who make up more than half the population feed on the fruits of others' labor without contributing anything themselves.[53]

If poverty was endemic, escaping from the bondage represented by life as a day laborer was extremely difficult. As we have seen, migration even to major cities such as Seville offered little prospect of improvement as openings were limited and competition from other groups of migrants quite considerable (in most cities of the south of Spain, for example, the Galician porter or water seller had, by the end of the eighteenth century, become a species of stock figure). A better bet, perhaps, was becoming an artisan, but even had the existence of the guild system not posed all sorts of problems in this respect, the average *bracero* had neither the skills, the tools, nor the capital to set himself up in business, while in any case depressed and poverty-stricken Andalucía could support very few such entrepreneurs: according to statistics quoted by John Lynch, in 1787 just 12.7 percent of the populace were employed in handicrafts of any sort.[54] Finally, of course, there was always the hope of somehow being able to rent a plot of land. In theory, this should not have been impossible. Every municipality possessed considerable amounts of common land that could be rented out to individuals, while the owners of the great estates were not averse to renting out a portion of their properties as well. In reality, however, there were serious problems in this respect. In the first place, the common lands were a shrinking resource: over the course of the past 300 or more years, the local notables, who through the system of hereditary seats exercised the same control of the town councils as they did of the land, had absorbed considerable portions of the commons into their own estates. And, in the second, much of the land closest to the towns and villages—the only areas that were really practicable for smallholders to cultivate unless the landowners were prepared to build farmhouses for them to live in—was in the hands of the great estates, the result being that would-be tenants found themselves faced with very high rents (which were usually payable in advance) and very unfavorable leasing arrangements. Once a plot of land had been secured, moreover, there was still the fact that geographical conditions were heavily weighted against the smallholder, the result of all of this being that renting land was really not very much of an option. In practice, indeed, genuine *braceros* could not consider it at all, the only men who could hope to embark upon it being the relatively small subgroup known as the *yunteros*—men who owned no land but possessed some basic agricultural implements and a few oxen and made their living by renting plots on the commons and great estates.[55]

What all this meant for Andalusian society we shall discuss shortly, but before doing so, let us first conclude our discussion of agriculture with some remarks about its productivity. In brief, this was extremely low. Without capital for investment, farming methods remained primitive, while even if more money had been available, the fact that leases were rarely issued for more than three years meant that, whether large or small, tenant farmers had no incentive to improve their holdings. Unprotected by walls or fences thanks to the many privileges that had over many years been extended to pastoral interests, vineyards, olive groves, and wheat fields alike were all vulnerable to damage by herds of sheep or goats. And, finally, given the complete want of prospects for the *braceros,* it was difficult to expect much from them in the way of effort or enthusiasm. To quote Pablo de Olavide: "Everything is left to the care of foremen, mere mercenaries lacking the stimulus of their own interest, who turn up for work with no other motive than that of drawing their pay, and casual laborers who only appear on the scene on those days when they are summoned and again work only for money. In short, then, the fields are cultivated by hands who take no interest in what they do and in general exert themselves no more than they have to."[56]

Given everything that has been said, the conclusion is obvious: however rich Andalucía might appear to the French, there was little chance that it would be able to meet the needs of a large enemy army. Indeed, far from producing the surplus that might have been expected, it was rather a net importer of grain: "The province of Andalucía . . . if properly cultivated, should produce corn sufficient, not only for its own consumption, but for exportation. Yet the wheat annually imported is little less than one million and one half of *fanegas*. . . . Nearly one half this quantity in the year 1787 came from Africa, 85,000 *fanegas* were imported from America, and the remainder was furnished by Naples, Sicily, and Sardinia."[57] For the time being, however, let us confine our discussion to the travails of the indigenous population. As should by now be abundantly clear, in practical terms there was no escape for the *braceros* other than either joining the ranks of the clergy, becoming a bullfighter—something that was, in effect, reserved to men who had grown up on the estates of great stockbreeders—or turning to crime. Of this last option there is evidence aplenty. Let us here begin with the prosaic. In the towns and cities, there was considerable danger from footpads. Here, for example, is another quote from Townsend on Málaga: "For some time I could not conceive the reason why, wherever I had supped, I was constantly attended to my lodging by a servant with a light, but, observing on some occasion, that such attendance would be needless because the stars shone bright . . . I was informed that the servant and the light were not merely for comfort but for safety, for robberies and murders were common in the night. Indeed, when I was there, an officer returning unattended to his lodging was assaulted in the street by thieves and . . . stabbed in the back. . . . In the last sixteen months they reckoned seventy murders for which not one criminal had been brought to justice."[58] Such words are redolent, of course, of social and moral panic, and there is little doubt that the figures Townsend quotes are inflated.[59] Yet the link between poverty and crime is well-enough established for there to be no reason to doubt the basic point, while in the countryside the issue was even more pressing. Banditry, indeed, was a particular threat. Traveling between Málaga and Granada, for example, Townsend found the roads lined with crosses erected in memory of travelers who had been murdered in one attack or another and even came across the body of someone who had been killed the previous night; meanwhile, it was a relief to find himself travelling in a de facto caravan of some fifty people, including no fewer than twenty men carrying arms of some sort or another.[60] For an interesting account of the sort of journey faced by many travelers, meanwhile, we can turn to the writings of Richard Twiss:

> Proceeding four leagues, we arrived at Lorca, which is a pretty large town, containing seven or eight churches. I waited on a colonel to whom I had a letter: he . . . ordered one of his soldiers, equipped with a long gun and a sabre, to accompany us to Granada (which he did on foot, being near 230 miles in five days), because this road is over mountains which are scarcely inhabited and where we frequently travelled without seeing a human being or a house, and sometimes troops of banditti, from twelve to thirty in a company, attack travellers, whom they first murder and then rob, leaving the dead bodies with the carriages on the road, and carrying off the plunder upon the mules. These banditti inhabit caverns among the mountains, and are each armed with a short blunderbuss and half a dozen pistols stuck round their girdle, but, as the whole province is alarmed when they make their incursions, we did not apprehend much danger as we should, of course, be forewarned should they be in the neighbourhood: on those occasions travellers sometimes remain for a week or more in a town waiting for . . . other carriages and guards going the same way, so that there often appears in Granada fourteen or fifteen chaises, forming a kind of caravan. With these precautions, and that of never being on the road before sunrise nor after sunset, we arrived afterwards safe in Granada, having preferred suffering the trifling inconvenience of the heat to the danger of losing our lives. We several times saw two or three men armed with guns lurking [among] the mountains, then join us, walk a league or two, and afterwards, having reconnoitred us, lag behind. . . . At such times I rode before on horseback, the servants walking on each side of the empty chaise . . . and the soldier followed behind.[61]

The reality of Andalusian banditry is open to much discussion. In this respect, the best place to start is with Marxist historian Eric Hobsbawm, who famously argued that bandits were "primitive rebels," men who were hitting back at a system that condemned them and their families to a lifetime of alternating drudgery and starvation.[62] As it happens, Hobsbawm did not discuss Spain in his work, but to a certain extent the same idea is reflected in the Spanish historiography. According to Santos Torres, for example, "If there is one thing that can be said for certain, it is that in Andalucía banditry was in large part a social struggle between the powerful and the oppressed."[63] According to this view, the bandit was not properly speaking a criminal at all, but rather someone who had for some reason or other attracted the wrath of the local elites, or at worst, turned to crime for no other reason than to feed his family. Nor, meanwhile, did he behave as a criminal: the bandit only stole what he needed in order to survive, refrained from acts of gratuitous violence, treated the weak and the innocent with the utmost chivalry, left the poor in peace, shared his gain with those in need, and in general did everything that he could to harass the local elites, even if it was only by cocking a snook at authority (there are many stories, for example, of wanted men engaging in acts of great daring, such as riding into town to have a drink at their favorite tavern, visit their sweethearts, or attend a bullfight). Even if the net result in practice amounted to very little, the simple idea that someone was fighting back could not but be heartening to the desperate peasants and landless laborers, and in this fashion the bandit, or so it was said, became the idol of rural communities, not to mention a symbol of their aspirations and center of their cultural traditions. For many bandits, of course, the end came soon enough in the form of death at the end of a rope, but in paying the ultimate penalty—one to which insult was added to injury by the habit of quartering the victims' bodies and exhibiting them by the roadside—they were transformed into martyrs whose deaths were one more crime to be charged to the score of the hated "big wigs": not for nothing did the government in 1767 decide to ban the ballads based on the supposed last words of the criminals concerned, hawked around the streets by blind beggars after every execution.[64]

With all this, there is but one problem. Thus, in reality, there is little evidence of the relationship between bandits and populace being anything like as rosy as is here painted. Let us take, for example, the case of Diego Corrientes. Born in 1757 to a family of day laborers in Utrera and executed in Seville some twenty-nine years later, Corrientes was beyond doubt the most famous bandit to have been produced by eighteenth-century Andalucía, while his hold on the imagination of the populace is testified to by the fact that, 200 years on, couplets survived that remembered him as a hero who robbed the rich to feed the poor. In fairness to Corrientes, it must be said here that his specialism was such as not to bring him into conflict with the mass of the populace. Thus, to the extent that he engaged in highway robbery at all, he confined himself to holding up carriages—a target naturally associated with the propertied classes—on the high road from Seville to Cádiz, while for the most part rather concentrating on rustling horses from the great estates of present-day Huelva and driving them across the Portuguese frontier for sale in such places as Mértola. Moreover, it is perfectly possible that he always sought to pay his way and even that he might have scattered a handful of coins here and there: such was only good business sense. In typical "good bandit" fashion, meanwhile, he was supposed to have killed no one, while after his death many stories were told of his daring, perhaps the most famous being the tale that related how, discovering that a large reward had been offered to anyone who would turn the person of Diego Corrientes over to the authorities, he tricked his way into the presence of the special emissary of the Spanish state who had been appointed to hunt him down and demanded the money at the point of a blunderbuss on the grounds that he had presented the official concerned with the living person of Diego Corrientes.[65]

The mere existence of these stories proves nothing, however. Like it or not, the fact is that there is no contemporary evidence of Corrientes's popularity with the crowd and that the prominence that he enjoys in bandit hagiography dates from a much later period in which the newly established Gaurdía Civil and the spread of modern communications were gradually reducing brigandage to the status of folk memory. Often referred to though he is as *el bandido generoso,* this nickname in fact only dates from a play that was written about him by José María Gutiérrez de Alba in 1848.[66] What, then, do we really know about banditry in Andalucía at the end of the eighteenth century? Here, of course, the dominant issue is the fact that south of the Sierra Morena, conditions were perfect for the spread of banditry: not only did the *braceros,* who formed the bulk of the populace and provided the cuadrillas with the vast majority of their recruits, exist in a state of the utmost poverty but also the empty nature of much of the countryside, not to mention the presence of two chains of rugged mountains, ensured that men on the run could easily find a hiding place and base from which to operate. From this it follows that, exactly as Townsend says, large parts of the countryside were in the grip of what amounted to a reign of terror: hence Olavide's attempts to colonize the Sierra Morena and the formation by King Charles III of a new security force called the Companías de Escopeteros Voluntarios de Andalucía. So great was the problem, however, that the elimination of even the greatest individual chieftains made little difference. Thus, even though Corrientes perished on the scaffold, other prominent leaders of the day included Francisco Mateos, Pablo Reina, and Bartolomé Gutiérrez, while in 1794 alone the Escopeteros Reales captured no fewer than 364 *malhechores.* Faced by such figures, the regime of Charles IV responded by ordering the deployment of troops, but the fact was that, however many bandits were hunted down, fresh bands sprung to life on every side, the problem in the end proving quite insoluble.[67]

What, then, was the real relationship between the bandits and the populace? Among those who lived out their lives in the larger cities, such as Seville and Granada, and never had much cause to move beyond their walls—people like porters, building laborers, and artisans—it is entirely possible that men such as Corrientes may have enjoyed a certain renown: hence the market for the funerary ballads banned in 1767. It was, however, easy to admire the bandits from a distance: up close was another matter entirely. Let us here begin by quoting Pastor Petit: "The bandit is a highwayman . . . without any other object than filling his pockets. He is neither an idealist, nor a reformer, . . . nor a dreamer, nor an adventurer. . . . The bandit is purely and simply a thief. And, what is more, he has never been a romantic: the image of the bandit who robs from the rich and later divides up his loot among the populace . . . is the invention of poets."[68] Quite so, but from this there follow some very disagreeable conclusions. Unfortunately, we do not have any study of banditry in Andalucía based on the records of the courts, but detailed work that has been done on Galicia shows very conclusively that the idea of the bandit as "primitive rebel" has no basis in reality. Thus, such men might have been the product of an unjust society, but they neither stood up for the people nor were admired by the people. The majority of their victims, certainly, were members of the clergy and the propertied classes, but this was not surprising given the fact that they presented the most promising targets, while humbler folk went anything but unscathed. A favorite tactic of the *cuadrillas,* or bandit gangs, indeed, was to surround isolated farmsteads at night and ransack them for anything worth carrying away—in practice, anything from clothes to cooking pots—while holding the residents at gunpoint, and it was common practice for such incidents to be accompanied by torture, the unfortunate victims being roasted in fires, strung up by their testicles, or burned by hot utensils.[69]

In practice, then, bandits were not shy of attacking the least fortunate members of society, even if all they had was a little food or the clothes that they stood up in, and for this reason in Galicia at least, they were widely hated, in many instances being rounded upon by angry villagers, often with considerable success.[70] Yet, not while the *cuadrillas* were not popular in a general sense, we should move too far in this direction. In order to operate successfully, chieftains had much need of reliable intelligence while they also needed a means of disposing of their spoil. At all times too they were vulnerable to the danger that their hideouts would be betrayed to the local authorities. Much more research is needed on this subject, but, given that terror alone could not have been enough to keep the populace in line, it is difficult not to suspect that bands were in general careful not to prey on settlements in the immediate vicinity of their lairs. A bad hat in one *pueblo* might therefore be a saint in another, and thus it was that, in however far removed a fashion from that envisaged by Hobsbawm, the *cuadrillas* did indeed come to represent, if not a popular response to oppression, then at the very least a means of palliating the misery of daily life.

Though still involved in crime, rather different from bandits were the many gangs of smugglers that operated in most parts of Andalucía. Once again it is Townsend to whom we may turn for a reference: "On these *sierras* the smugglers traverse the country, travelling well-armed and in companies of two or three hundred men with a little field piece loaded with slugs . . . fixed on the saddle of the leading horse. Thus prepared, they have been known to pass unmolested in the presence of the military when in point of numbers they were by no means equal to a contest."[71] The extent of the problem cannot be doubted and was, indeed, remarked upon by Marshal Soult. As the latter wrote in his memoirs: "In some places the population of entire villages had become smugglers. Such men are habituated to a life of constant warfare, while they enjoy a certain respect and are encouraged in what they do by popular prejudices."[72] The origin of this phenomenon was not so much poverty, but rather the fact that throughout Spain, commerce was impeded by an endless series of internal-customs barriers that could not but have the effect of forcing up the price of goods such as tobacco, this being all the more irritating given the fact that in a number of instances, these items were already the subject of state monopolies. In consequence, the smuggler was a much less ambiguous figure than the bandit in that, while he could be mythologized in exactly the same manner as someone who lived outside the law and in general defied and humiliated the authorities, he was not usually guilty of crimes of violence and kept the local inhabitants supplied with goods that were in high demand and would otherwise have been much more expensive.[73]

If bandits and smugglers there were aplenty, in the end, life outside the law was never going to attract more than a fraction of the populace of Andalucía: aside from anything else, it required a degree of energy and initiative that was probably beyond the imagination of most of the depressed and demoralized agricultural proletariat. Nor, of course, could more than a tiny handful of men find a way out through the bullring. For most of the *braceros,* then, life was a matter of little more than day-to-day survival, and this in turn ensured that they could not but remain firmly under the thumb of the propertied classes. In practice, the only way to find work was to adopt an attitude of complete submission, for men who were known as troublemakers would never be taken on, just as men who made any sort of protest in respect of their pay or conditions would find themselves out of a job. Nor was it just a matter of employment, for the wretched cabins that they lived in were also the property of the same elites who owned the land. Everything depended, then, on obtaining the patronage of the owners and thereafter staying in their favor, the only hope being that one day good behavior would be rewarded with the greater security offered by a position on the permanent staff of some *cortijo* or, for that matter, town council. In the meantime, however, humiliation was all but ritual: at the beginning of each hiring season, for example, every *bracero* in town would have to attend a hiring fair in some convenient square—usually the *plaza mayor* (main square)—which was conducted on lines little better than a slave market, after which those men who were not taken on directly would be left with no option but to turn up at the plaza each dawn and stand there for hour after hour in the hope that some foreman would appear and offer them a job. Indeed, even family life was not immune from such pressures, for it was not uncommon to appease the master by inviting him to become the godfather of a laborer's children, while charity too had to be earned by the adoption of a suitably humble demeanor.

Mention of charity cannot but introduce the institution of the church, for it was the church that was the chief support of the destitute, episcopal palaces, religious houses, and parish churches all dispensing limitless quantities of alms, and church-run hospitals taking in the aged, the sick, and the dying by the thousand. If there was one aspect of Andalucía that invariably struck foreign visitors, it was its Roman Catholicism. The church was certainly a force that was always present, though probably no more so than in other parts of Spain. Seville, for example, had a cathedral; a collegiate church; twenty-six parish churches; four auxiliary churches; sixty-eight monasteries, friaries, or convents; and forty-three other religious foundations, while the cathedral chapter alone consisted of eighty-one clergy of various ranks.[74] In addition, one should also mention the *hermandades,* these being lay brotherhoods that performed some of the functions of friendly societies: in 1770 there were no fewer than 1,120 of these bodies.[75] Meanwhile, visitors to Andalucía were invariably struck by the splendor of the masses celebrated in church and cathedral, the pomp and ceremony of the Holy Week processions, the constant intrusion of religion into daily life, and the devotion displayed by the populace when it came to observing the outward signs of religion. Thus, whenever the Blessed Sacrament was carried through the streets to the house of someone who was ill, anyone who was in the vicinity would fall on their knees (and in the case of men, bare their heads) until the procession had passed by; equally, at noon and at five o'clock in the evening, the streets would come to a halt for the recitation of the Angelus and the evening prayer. Meanwhile, even the simplest actions were habitually accompanied by a religious subtext: the worker would cross himself before picking up his tools, the family say grace before every meal, and the caller announce himself with the words "Hail Mary" (to which the response was "Conceived without sin").[76] And finally, faced by natural disaster, the populace had only one recourse—religion: the great earthquake that destroyed Lisbon in 1755 was sufficiently felt in Seville as to induce panic-stricken crowds to besiege parish churches in a desperate bid to secure the sacrament of confession, while in 1758, when Andalucía's crops were threatened by swarms of termites, the dispatch from Pamplona to Seville of the head of San Gregorio Ostiense—a saint whose intercession was much valued as a protection against incidents of this sort—was followed by further outbreaks of mass devotion.[77]

Among the depressed mass of the population, the reach of the Church was not quite as extensive as might have been thought, however. Popular devotion, contemporaries noted, was increasingly a matter of routine, so that the prayers that were supposedly said in every home each night were, according to anecdotal evidence at least, frequently gabbled at high speed in an attempt to get through them as quickly as possible. At the same time, meanwhile, the first stirrings were visible of the anti-clericalism that over the course of the nineteenth century was to become such a feature of radical politics in Spain. If it was, perhaps, but a straw in the wind, in 1802 the parish priest of Jabugo, an isolated *pueblo* in the Sierra de Aracena, petitioned the town council regarding the lack of respect that the populace had been showing the clergy, while English travelers, albeit hardly the most objective source, were quick to note that attitudes toward the Church were at the very least distinctly ambivalent. Here, for example, is William Jacob:

> With all this attachment to forms and ceremonies it might naturally be expected that the clergy would be looked upon as objects of veneration, but, so far as I can judge, this is by no means the case. The language held towards the ministers of religion is not always respectful and is sometimes scurrilous. A few days ago the auxiliary bishop of this city made a tour round his diocese for the purpose of confirmation; from every person confirmed, a small sum of money was required which was either an increase in the customary fee or a novel demand. On his return to the city with the money he had thus collected, he was attacked by a banditti, who robbed him, not only of his extorted wealth, but also of all the clothes and vestments which he carried in his coach. The knowledge of the story excited the jokes and the merriment of the people, mixed with wishes that the clergy were the only victims of robbers. The character and conduct of the friars is generally the object either of virulent reprobation or of ludicrous jocularity. They have lost the esteem of everyone, and, instead of being respected for their seclusion from the world, they are reproached by all classes for their indolence, their voluptuousness and their profligacy; their dispersion is generally looked forward to with pleasing anticipation as an event that must take place if ever the people of Spain are assembled by their representatives, the *cortes*.[78]

If the Church was unpopular, this was hardly surprising. On the one hand, large tracts of land were owned by the religious orders, while on the other, immense sums of money were extracted from the populace by means of the tithes. These were severe enough to merit particular attention: "The tithes collected in Andalucía extend to every agricultural production, and are rigidly exacted, not, as with us, on the ground, but after all the necessary processes to fit it for the use of man. Thus wheat and barley must be not only cut, but threshed and winnowed, before the tithes are taken. . . . The right to tithes has lately been extended to such wild fruits as can be sold even for the smallest sums. Thus, the . . . prickly pears, . . . a wild fruit with which the hedges abound and consequently of little value, have lately been subjected to the tithing system. One tenth also of all the domestic animals is delivered to the tithe collector as well as the wool annually shorn from the sheep."[79] To make matters worse, there was little evidence that much of the Church's income was directed toward the welfare of its parishioners. Large quantities of money was spent on charitable assistance, true, but it was very rare that the clergy took a direct part in such work: rather than involving themselves in teaching and the care of the sick, for example, Spain's thousands of nuns had chosen to confine themselves to their convents and give themselves over to lives of prayer and contemplation. Still worse, Spain's parish priests and curates were easily the section of the ecclesiastical population that was worst provided for in financial terms, where, that is, they were in evidence at all: all over Spain, there was a strong tendency for churchmen to congregate in the larger towns and cities, with the result that many poorer and more remote parishes were left without any spiritual care whatsoever; in 1797, indeed, some 3,000 parishes out of a national total of 19,000 lacked incumbents. In Andalucía this problem was no better than it was anywhere else, but here it was accentuated by a further difficulty in that, for historical reasons, parish sizes were much bigger than they were in the north: in Alava, for example, each priest had the cure of 153 souls, but in Córdoba the figure was 1,115 and in Seville 1,332.[80] If the clergy was often a distant force, then, it was often perceived as a parasitic one. Of some 60,000 ordained priests, almost two-thirds were engaged in administrative work or the education of the clergy, while the monasteries in particular had an evil reputation for laxity, indiscipline, and sexual incontinence. Meanwhile, although the reality was that the vast majority of Spain's clergy survived on very little, an extremely prominent minority, represented by such groups as the canons who staffed the cathedral chapters, enjoyed substantial salaries and were not shy of living lives of considerable self-indulgence. And finally, while it was certainly not true that all bishops, say, were aristocrats, it was all too evident that only the well-educated—and by extension the wealthy—could hope to rise very far in the service of the Church.[81]

How far all this had produced a genuine streak of popular anti-clericalism in Spain in general, or Andalucía in particular, it is difficult to say. What is clear, however, is that, particularly in areas marked by large parishes, the church had great difficulty in reaching out to the mass of the population. Despite intense efforts to improve clerical education in the course of the eighteenth century, most parish priests were men of humble origin who at best could do little more than recite the Mass in mangled Latin. Moreover, with communications as difficult as they were, the supervisory hand of the bishop was very often necessarily forced to exercise a light touch. While some of the men concerned did their best for their flocks, then, many neglected their duties in favor of a life of ease or at the very least failed to achieve the standards expected of them: the number of parish priests who took mistresses is unknown, for example, but it was a common-enough problem for it to occasion considerable complaint among the ecclesiastical hierarchy. To some extent this want of care and, more particularly, catechesis was made up for by the religious orders. In many places more numerous than the secular clergy—in Seville, for example, approximately three-fifths of the city's ecclesiastics were members of religious orders in 1797—orders such as the Franciscans, the Dominicans, and the Capuchins had been founded with a view to taking the faith to the streets and to a certain extent maintained this tradition: in the course of the eighteenth century, the Capuchins in particular were renowned for the great missions that they conducted throughout the country. Yet even here all was not well: too many friars now lived full time in their religious houses and were entirely taken up either with administration or the day-to-day round of communal worship, while in general the religious reformers who had surrounded King Charles III were inclined to be dismissive of the regular clergy as a force that peddled superstition rather than spreading the teachings of true religion.[82]

What, then, can we say of the nature of popular religiosity in Andalucía? That the majority of the population had at least a basic knowledge of the Roman Catholic faith is probable if by that is meant the ability to recite a number of common prayers and retail at least a simple version of the life of Jesus. At the same time too, baptism was near universal and, to go with it, burial in accordance with the rites of the Church, while attendance at Mass and confession both remained high. And finally, preachers such as the renowned Capuchin Fray Diego de Cádiz were capable of both attracting large crowds and whipping them into a state of fervor: in Antequera, indeed, so great was the hysteria that Cádiz provoked on one occasion that, terrified at the thought of the divine vengeance that their town's backsliding might call down upon their heads, the inhabitants threw themselves on its single theater and sacked it out of hand.[83] To imagine, however, either that the Church was in a position of supreme power or that the populace was devoted to it ipso facto is to go too far. It is, of course, dangerous to generalize, but the lower classes regarded the Church with great ambivalence. If its holidays were the only breaks in their routine, its processions an exciting spectacle, its charity an ally in times of need, and its prayers a talisman against the thunderbolts of Heaven, its rents, fees, and tithes were a costly burden and a source of great irritation. In consequence, what it was not was something to die for or even take very much notice of on a day to day basis: implicit in the constant hellfire and damnation preached by Cádiz and his colleagues was a recognition that the Church's influence among large parts of the masses was at best tenuous.

To return to the clergy, this was, of course, only the first and most prominent of Andalucía's elites. Next to them there came the propertied classes, the majority of whom were of noble stock. As we have seen, among these men were numbered a number of titled grandees, but in practice such figures only made infrequent appearances in the region, many of them rather spending their time at court. Much more important, then, were a second rank of figures, including middle-ranking noblemen, who could not afford to reside in the capital but enjoyed sufficient income from their estates to occupy a prominent position in one or other of the region's cities; wealthy notables who, having made a fortune in government service or trade with the Americas, rented land from the Church or the grandees and then either farmed it themselves or sublet it to a variety of tenants; and finally, the swarms of officials, the majority of them landowners in their own right, who acted as bailiffs for the great landowners or staffed the work of local government and the judiciary. To cite just one example, in Granada the law courts gave employment to no fewer than twenty-four judges; 148 prosecutors, defense counsels, and solicitors; forty-seven clerks and notaries; and nine other officers of various sorts, while to these men could be added another sixty functionaries who were in the employ of the town council.[84] As a whole, while there were many who at the very least patronized the arts and affected an interest in the ideas of the Enlightenment, it was not a group with a good reputation: if there was a norm, indeed, it was one of peculation, ignorance, and vulgar ostentation. When Pablo de Olavide took over the reins of government in Seville in 1767, for example, the minister of finance was forthright in his estimation of the task facing him: "Corruption rules everywhere, but in your region it is . . . incomparably worse than it is anywhere else."[85] Meanwhile, amid the general poverty, the elites enjoyed a life of plenty. Here, for example, are Richard Twiss's recollections of a short visit to Córdoba:

> The night after my arrival I was at the Conde de Gabía's *tertulia,* where I had the pleasure of becoming acquainted at once with all these families. They live with great splendour: I never saw such magnificent equipages in any other part of Spain: here are fourteen or fifteen carriages, chariots or phaetons which were lately made in London, and as many more which were procured from Paris. I had an opportunity of seeing all these drawn by four or six beautiful long-tailed prancing . . . horses, as it was at that time the Whitsun fair; the footmen were all in gold and silver-laced liveries. One of the four evenings I remained in Córdoba was spent at the house of the Marchioness of Villaseca: we were first entertained with a concert and afterwards with a ball. . . . The refreshment were first chocolate and afterwards lemonade, ice-creams, cakes and various sorts of wines and liqueurs. The saloon we danced in is very large, hung with crimson damasque and enriched with several of the San

> Ildefonso looking glasses; the ceiling is of white stucco with gilt foliages; the whole of these elegant decorations are executed in the French taste. . . . I observed that a great part of the furniture of these houses was English, such as mahogany chairs and tables, Wilton carpets, etc.[86]

At this time, of course, the landed classes did not have the support of the Guardia Civil, the rural gendarmerie formed to suppress banditry in 1844. That said, however, they were not without their allies. According to Laborde at least, landholders could generally call on the services of the gypsies, "that dangerous and perfidious race, irreligious and dishonest vagabonds without either faith or law who were the curse of Spain, the disgrace of the country which suffered them, [and] the terror of the roads and of the country."[87] Whether this unfortunate group, which was particularly associated with Andalucía, merited such a description is a moot point—they were not, in fact, generally associated with banditry[88]—but according to the same observer, the elites tolerated them, in return for which they "spared . . . their estates, property, persons, servants, and farmers, . . . were the agents of their vengeance, and afforded them as many satellites as there were *gitanos*."[89] At immediate command of the elites too were the large number of servants that they employed in their households. "The houses of gentlemen, and especially of the grandees, swarm with them," complained Laborde. "Often all the servants, or at least all the principal ones, will have their wives and children lodged with them, and fed by their master."[90]

To conclude, then, the wealth of a tiny elite aside, Andalucía was anything but the paradise that the French believed that they saw before them when they emerged from the Sierra Morena. In reality, much of it was desperately poor, with large areas given over to nothing more than rough pasture and most of those tracts that were cultivated distinctly unimpressive in their yield. If the invaders expected that they would be able to live comfortably off the country, then they were much mistaken, while the poor communications, the rugged mountains that occupied roughly half the region's surface area, and the long distances that tended to separate many *pueblos* from their nearest neighbors suggested that maintaining law and order could not but present numerous problems. Also challenging, meanwhile, was the immense length of the Andalucían coast and the many opportunities it offered to an opponent who ruled the waves. Yet the prospect for King Joseph and Marshal Soult was by no means completely bleak. Thus, few parts of Spain were marked by such extreme social tension. On the one hand, even without the traumatic experience of the period 1808–10, the elites lived in fear of the populace, while on the other, even without the equally traumatic experience of being mobilized for a war effort that was universally hated, the populace lived in hatred of the elites. From neither group, meanwhile, was it possible to look for much in the way of ideological commitment: for the bulk of the propertied classes, what mattered more than anything else was all too clearly the maintenance of their privileged positions, while insofar as the peasants and *braceros* were concerned, there is some evidence that even traditional Roman Catholicism was losing its hold among them. The French, perhaps, would not be popular with anybody, but they would also by no means necessarily be rejected out of hand. On the contrary, by the very nature of their situation, the notables were in many instances likely to collaborate with the invaders, while such was the state of dependence in which the *braceros* lived that it was likely that, however sullenly, they might well have no option but to tender at last a degree of submission. Andalucía, in short, was not, say, Navarre, and there was therefore every reason to expect that the history of French occupation in the south of Spain might well be very different.

4

Selling Joseph Bonaparte

In a most literal sense, the invasion of Andalucía in January 1810 was a propaganda offensive. On one level, the idea was purely military: in brief, the Spaniards were to be treated to a display of armed might so terrible that they would finally be convinced that resistance was futile and that in consequence they should lay down their arms. But on another level, it was also political. Spaniards had only to see Joseph Bonaparte in the flesh, or so the argument ran, and they would immediately realize that the hunchbacked drunkard of Patriot propaganda was a pure fiction and that, by extension, they had been lied to and manipulated. No sooner had Joseph entered Andalucía, then, than he had embarked on what was in effect a triumphal progress in which he made every effort to project himself as a benevolent father figure who sought only the well-being and happiness of his subjects. However, appealing though this program was to the ever vain and complacent Joseph—more so than any of the other Bonapartes, Joseph came genuinely to believe in the image that had been crafted of him in Paris—the propaganda of *josefino* Spain was not limited to the mere projection of the figure of the king himself; indeed, given the sheer size of the country and the fact that much of it lay beyond the control of French arms, this would have been a nonsense. On the contrary, *el rey intruso* was backed by a sophisticated propaganda machine that made use of a wide range of techniques and opportunities to push home its message. If the affable and smiling Joseph Bonaparte always remained the most important weapon in the French armory, the brunt of the battle was always waged by newspapers, orders of the day, and proclamations. As to the message that was put forward, this was at base exactly the same as the one being peddled everywhere else in the empire, but happen though this did, at no point was the campaign merely a matter of reprinting articles from *Le Moniteur* or *Le Journal de l'Empire.* On the contrary, Joseph's propagandists, many of them Spaniards themselves, made skillful use of the situation in Spain to give collaboration a rationale that, superficially at least, was quite compelling. If the pen did not prove mightier than the sword in Andalucía, then, it was not for want of imagination on the part of those who wielded it.

Viewed from the French perspective, the idea that presenting the "real" Joseph Bonaparte to the Spanish nation might prove the key to putting an end to its resistance was not so farfetched as it first appears. If there was one area in the whole of Spain where the imposition of French rule had ostensibly been making a little headway prior to 1810, it was that of the capital itself, and it was, of course, precisely there that King Joseph had been most visible. At first things had been grim enough. Joseph's grand equerry, Girardin, for example, had graphic memories of the atmosphere that gripped Madrid in the moment of apparent crisis that beset *el rey intruso* in the first days of January 1809:

> During the first moments of our stay in Madrid, we had many worries in respect of our position. As soon as the emperor marched in pursuit of the English, the capital . . . was menaced by a powerful army commanded by the Duque de Infantado. On 1 January this force crossed the Tagus and advanced to within four leagues of Madrid. Such troops as there were in Madrid made ready to retreat at any moment, while all the employees of the royal household followed their example. Meanwhile, one saw the same agitation that had been on display at the time of our retreat on 29 July 1808. In similar circumstances, all men of discretion will naturally keep silence, but the looks that they threw us . . . betrayed their thoughts, while each fresh piece of news, without being repeated by anyone, was nonetheless known by everyone. Meanwhile, the inhabitants of the capital neglected nothing that might increase our alarm. When a few days went by without any news having been received from

> Napoleon's headquarters, it was immediately put about that the emperor had been defeated by the English. . . . The minister of police, Arribas, who was devoted to King Joseph, assured the king . . . that the disposition of the people was very unfavorable . . . and that a general insurrection could break out at any moment.[1]

Similar scenes were much in evidence when the combined armies of the then Sir Arthur Wellesley and Gregorio García de la Cuesta advanced on Madrid in July 1809—Carnicero speaks of excited groups of men, women, and children actually sallying out of the city to greet the expected liberators[2]—but as one disappointment succeeded another, gradually the capital's inhabitants seemed to accept their lot. Such at least was the opinion of Joseph's principal aide-de-camp, Auguste J. Bigarré:

> After the battles of Talavera de la Reina, Arzobispo, and Almonacid, . . . the British having withdrawn their forces to Portugal, Joseph was left to get on with the legislative and administrative affairs of his kingdom. The ministers of the interior, justice, finance, war, and the marine all submitted various draft decrees to him which he took up as his own. The reorganization of the army was the matter that was of the greatest priority to him, but he also sought to give the ecclesiastical estate all the dignity which it deserved, while yet . . . suppressing an infinity of useless convents and in this fashion giving the body responsible for the sale of the *biens nationaux* the impulse from which so much fruit might be expected later on. Meanwhile, for his part, the secretary of state, Urquijo, worked alongside the counselor of state, Ferri-Pisani, to elaborate a civil code on the base of that of France. At the same time the minister of police suppressed a great many abuses of the most vexatious sort. . . . Eventually the government of King Joseph began to take a good hold of Madrid and the surrounding provinces. The sort of men who in every country of the world enjoy a certain weight among the population on account of their birth, their talents, and their wealth recognized the superiority that Joseph Bonaparte enjoyed over . . . his predecessor, and began

> freely to attach themselves to the new king, and to make many efforts to encourage the still reluctant masses to submit to his authority. . . . Uncertain of their fate and unwilling to compromise their future, the population of Madrid decided at least formally to coexist with the French forces until such time as Spain's destiny had been decided by the march of events.[3]

To some extent, this may have been wishful thinking—indeed, it is specifically denied by other observers, Fée, for example, remembering how the palace in the Plaza de la Villa, where Francis I was housed following his capture at the Battle of Pavía, was throughout the French occupation an object of great pride and consolation to the inhabitants[4]—but it could not be denied that Joseph had worked extremely hard to market himself as the acceptable face of French imperialism since his return to Madrid in January 1809. Whereas Charles IV had spent long hours hunting every day, Joseph was a monarch who took care to be seen to be immersing himself in affairs of state and, even in his leisure moments, sought not seclusion, but visibility:

> When King Joseph was not absent with the army, he ordinarily got up at six or seven o'clock. At nine o'clock he was waited on by the chief members of his household; at half past nine he breakfasted on a couple of eggs or a small piece of fish; at ten o'clock he held audiences with his ministers, with Marshal Jourdan, or any other French or Spanish general who wished to see him; at one o'clock he attended the daily meeting of the Council of State; and at four o'clock he went over to the Casa de Campo, where he dined with Marshal Jourdan, the Comte de Melito, General Belliard, and sometimes various officers of his household or ladies of the court. After the meal there would be a drive in his carriage or a ride on horseback and then a hand of twenty-one, after which he would send off the daily dispatch to Paris and retire to bed.[5]

The king, then, despite a string of mistresses—his favorite was the Marquesa de Montehermoso—was no playboy like his younger brother, Jerome, whose palaces in Westphalia were renowned for their extravagant settings and entertainments (therefore, by extension, he was also no Godoy). Nor was he a coward: indeed, within days of entering his capital for the second time on 21 January 1809, he was riding in his carriage through the streets and visiting its various hospitals and charitable institutions and making frequent appearances at the theater. "The king is employing all the means of popularity with great success," wrote the French ambassador, the Comte de La Forest. "He has been restored in circumstances that are infinitely more favorable than those of his first entry into his capital . . . and, if he demonstrated at that time that he is capable of winning over public opinion, he can today flatter himself that he ought now to be able to do so more effectively. . . . His Majesty is certainly making the attempt. Yesterday he visited the general hospital. There were numerous cries of 'Long live the king!,' and a touching scene took place in the chamber reserved for the Spanish officers who were wounded at Uclés."[6]

Meanwhile, as well as improving the image of the Spanish monarchy and simply making it more visible—as La Forest pointed out, neither Charles III nor Charles IV had ever patronized the theater[7]—Joseph also devoted himself to dispelling the much-vaunted idea that the French were the enemies of Roman Catholicism:

> The king believed that to make himself agreeable to the Spaniards, he had to make a show of being very religious. In consequence, he heard Mass at six o'clock each morning, and obliged me to join him in doing so. In his audiences, meanwhile, he always treated the clergy with marked benevolence. I recall that the day when the heads of the chief monastic orders were accorded the honor of waiting upon him, he detained them for two hours, and made a speech in which the first line was in Spanish and all the rest in Italian (a language that hardly anyone in his audience understood). Adopting a serious manner, the king said, "God is omnipotent: His will alone reigns. That truth being something which it is not permitted to doubt, there is no option but to recognize it and submit to it. That is the duty of a good Catholic. It follows that . . . everything here below bears the imprint of the finger of God. If the Bourbons have been removed from their throne, it is because God has

> marked them with the sign of his reprobation. If my dynasty has replaced theirs, it is because God has permitted it to happen. In consequence, to disobey me is to disobey God, just as to show oneself to be anything other than devoted to me is to show oneself to be a bad Christian."[8]

However, it was with the coming of Holy Week that the king was able to make the greatest play of his Catholicism. Every year Madrid, like every other Spanish city, was the scene of immense processions commemorating the passion of Christ, but from these, again, the royal family had been absent, its members habitually spending the Easter season at Aranjuez. Under Joseph, however, things were different (it is, though, worth noting that the Bourbons' various country residences were not abandoned: on the contrary, the king made a point of making short visits to Aranjuez, El Escorial, and La Granja alike in the hope of maintaining at least a degree of continuity with the traditional movements of the Bourbon royal family). A plan to visit all the major churches of the capital on the Wednesday had to be abandoned due to heavy rain, but on the Friday the king stood for hours on his balcony while confraternity after confraternity—the religious associations responsible for the various floats and tableaux that formed the heart of the processions—passed through the street below in review, Joseph acknowledging each one by going down on his knees and, at least ostensibly, saying a prayer (like Napoleon, he was at best a skeptic).[9]

Finally, if Joseph was Catholic, he was also Spanish, or at least not French. From the beginning, he attempted to avoid speaking French, while he habitually dressed in the uniform of a colonel in his own royal guard, affected the traditional red cockade of Spain, set up a new order of nobility—the Orden Real de España, or Spanish Royal Order—with which to reward members of the elite who would side with his cause, and, insofar as he could attract their services, surrounded himself with Spaniards. As he told General Sébastiani following a heated argument over Girardin's post as grand equerry, for example, "I should not have anyone other than Spaniards around me: things have got to be like that because I am Spanish."[10] In this, moreover, he was to a certain extent successful: there were always many Frenchmen in his entourage, but unusually for the Napoleonic satellite monarchies, of the fifteen men who him served as ministers, not a single one was French, while at a much lowlier level, of his forty pages, no fewer than thirty-nine were Spaniards.[11] Also to be found at the court, meanwhile, were a number of leading grandees and, King Joseph being a genuinely cultured man with a sincere regard for the arts, many of the most prominent writers and artists of the day: among the former were to be found the Conde de Orgaz, the Marqués de Almenara, and the Duque de Osuna, and among the latter Juan Antonio Llorente, Leandro Fernández de Moratín, and even, if only on the periphery, Francisco de Goya.[12]

Joining the men of letters that filled the court were others of a very different stamp. For example, if Joseph patronized the arts, he also patronized bullfighting. Prohibited under Godoy as a pastime that was uncivilized, economically wasteful, and a threat to public order, the bullfight had lost none of its popularity, and no sooner had he arrived in Madrid in July 1808 than Joseph had ordered its rehabilitation. On 27 July, then, the capital was able to patronize the bulls for the first time since 1805, and the populace this time showed none of its previous reserve but instead turned out in its thousands. Further bullfights followed in the course of the autumn under the aegis of the Junta Central, and it might therefore have been thought that Joseph might have rushed to organize a fresh season in 1809. Yet being situated near the Puerta de Alcalá, the bullring had been heavily damaged during the battle of 2 December, while it had also since been pressed into service as a magazine and prisoner-of-war camp. For the time being, then, bullfights were out of the question, but eager to help the king burnish his Hispanic credentials, his Spanish advisers managed to persuade a number of bullfighters and other members of the bullfighting world to become frequent visitors to the court, also organizing an expedition to a ranch near Colmenar Viejo to view the fighting bulls that were being raised there and watch a display of technique.[13]

When he was not patronizing bullfighting, Joseph always had another field in which he could pose as a Spanish monarch. We come here, of course, to the war. On the one hand, this—or to be more precise, the success of French arms—was naturally exploited for all it was worth. Following the victory of Almonacid, for example, Joseph deliberately ensured that his return to Madrid coincided with the feast day of Saint Napoleon on 15 August, and in this manner he made certain that what he regarded as his triumphs in the field could be celebrated in the style he wished without at the same time offending the sensibilities of the emperor (there was a Te Deum, fireworks, and a banquet for 200 guests).[14] Still more pointedly, meanwhile, the thousands of prisoners taken at Ocaña were paraded through the streets of Madrid in a blatant attempt to persuade the inhabitants of the futility of further resistance.[15] Yet the war was not just exploited as a means of emphasizing French military power. Always a kindly and soft-hearted figure, Joseph genuinely hated bloodshed, yet at the same time he also realized that a policy of fire and sword could not win him his kingdom. Angered by the trail of destruction that he had encountered as he rode south toward Madrid in November 1808, he therefore penned what was to be the first in a long series of protests:

> I have arrived in this town [Burgos] to find neither a military commandant nor a chief commissary. . . . The shops have all been pillaged, while at the moment of my arrival the cathedral was just about to suffer the same fate; I sent a few soldiers that I managed to get together to protect it. The clergy and the inhabitants in general have asked me to protect them, but, in truth, I do not have the power to dispose of a single soldier. . . . I see all these disorders, but I can do nothing. Yesterday, as I have been for the past four years, I was at the head of an army, but today I have but the authority of a sub-lieutenant. Given my character, do I deserve to be the laughing stock of the army in the country of which I am supposed to be king?[16]

This letter, of course, was by no means solely the fruit of compassion: Joseph was also moved by hurt pride. But the king had a point, and instructed by Napoleon to begin anew the task of forming a Spanish army, he was glad to have a chance of displaying his generosity toward his defeated enemies by recruiting as many men as he could from the 6,000 Spanish soldiers captured when part of the much-battered Army of the Center was overwhelmed at the town of Uclés on 13 January 1809.[17] Emphasis was given to his enthusiasm, meanwhile, by the fact that the commander of the French forces at Uclés, Marshal Victor, had not only permitted his troops to sack the town unmercifully but also ordered the summary execution of any prisoners who fell behind the column as it hurried the fifty miles that separated the battlefield from Madrid. "On the morning of the fifteenth [of January] we met the Spanish prisoners coming from Uclés on their way to Madrid," wrote one French soldier. "Many of these wretches [were] sunk under their fatigue [while] others died of inanition; when they could march no more, they were shot without mercy."[18] The policy of recruiting Spanish auxiliaries remained a controversial one, for, much to the fury of La Forest and others, many of the recruits simply deserted at the first opportunity—according to Gaspard de Clermont Tonnerre, the royal aide-de-camp placed in charge of its organization, in the first three weeks of its existence, the Regimiento de Irlanda lost 51 of the 411 men it had got together[19]—but by February 1809 Joseph's army, which was deliberately dressed predominantly in brown rather than the blue and green favored by the French, consisted of a regiment of guard infantry, a regiment of guard cavalry, a battery of guard artillery, two regiments of foreign line infantry, two regiments of Spanish line infantry, one regiment of Spanish light infantry, and a squadron of gendarmes.[20]

To all this there was attached a considerable cost in that Joseph's policy of hispanization was inclined to alienate both the French ambassador and the leading French commanders in Spain (interestingly, the only one of them to remain close to Joseph, Marshal Jourdan, who served as his chief of staff in 1808–1809 and 1812–13, was something of an "out" in the French military who had opposed the coup of 18 Brumaire and in consequence since then been out of favor).[21] Nor was Napoleon happy. As he told Pierre-Louis Roederer in February 1809: "The King must be French. Spain must be French. It is for France that I conquered Spain."[22] Yet to the end Joseph retained the courage of his convictions. Ready to alienate the support of the forces that had put him on the throne, he also did not spare himself in other respects. With Spain at war, the king obviously enjoyed only limited freedom of movement, but he nevertheless did what he could to project a favorable image of the new dynasty beyond the gates of Madrid, paying visits to both Segovia and Toledo.[23] And finally, conscious that adopting a purely passive role would win him the respect of neither French nor Spaniard, in the campaigns of the summer and autumn of 1809, he took an extremely active role in the direction of operations, and even if he was never able fully to control the actions of his generals (at the Battle of Talavera, for example, Marshal Victor behaved throughout as if he was the commander in chief rather than the king), Joseph genuinely seems to have come to regard himself as an all-conquering hero: "Sire, at every point the enemy is in full retreat, while we are in pursuit. He is abandoning his wounded: we have already collected more than 4,000 English. I go on horseback and tonight will be in Toledo: the army of Venegas . . . will not be in La Mancha for very much longer."[24]

Just as Napoleon personified the French empire and was the chief agent of its propaganda, then, so Joseph personified the Bonaparte kingdom of Spain. At all events this was the image that the king carried with him when he crossed the Sierra Morena. Indeed, if anything, this aspect of his activity was redoubled: protected by thousands of troops and with the enemy in complete disarray, Joseph was able to engage in precisely the sort of royal progress that he clearly saw as the most important means at his disposal for converting Spain to the new dynasty. From the beginning, then, the campaign in Andalucía was characterized by a marked attempt to win over hearts and minds. Thus, at least according to the official record, at each of the towns he passed through en route for Seville, Joseph was the very model of magnanimity: coming across a hospital at Andújar full of abandoned Spanish sick and wounded, for example, he immediately gave orders for them to be provided with the very best care and attention.[25] At the same time, he was most active in the cause of peace: hearing that the cities of Córdoba and Jaén were considering surrender, he immediately sent two of his chief advisers to reassure them as to his intentions.[26] And if actions speak louder than words, the latter were certainly not neglected: barely a week had passed since his passage through the Sierra Morena before Joseph had issued a manifesto that laid out the legitimacy of the French cause in considerable detail, and in the process made the most unfavorable comparisons between the manliness of *el rey intruso* and the pusillanimity of his predecessors:

> Spaniards! The moment has come when you must hear the truth. This I owe you, while I flatter myself that you will not do so in vain. All men of any sense know that, more than a century ago, the imperious law of circumstance decreed that Spain would be the friend and ally of France. An extraordinary revolution toppled the dynasty that reigned in the latter kingdom from the throne. Unless it wished to suffer the same fate itself one day, the branch of it that reigned in Spain then had but one course of action open to it: either support it by every means or not lay down its arms until it was restored to its original position. Such a course would have been heroic indeed, but instead the Spanish royal house preferred to wait for time to effect what it did not dare to try achieve sword in hand. At length, however, seeing France embroiled in a war in a far country, the palace clique believed that the time had come to throw off the veil and take arms against her, only for its projects to be overthrown by the victory of Jena. In vain did it try to return to the spirit of artifice and act in the same fashion as the men who had negotiated the Treaty of Basel: the conqueror of Europe was not fooled. Not daring to fight, the princes of the royal house of Spain then renounced their rights to the throne, while contenting themselves with securing their own private interests. The grandees of Spain, the generals, the most principal persons of the nation, all recognized these truths, and I myself received the oaths of loyalty that they swore to me in Madrid. The event that took place at Bailén disconcerted everyone, and the weakest fell victim to fear. Only the most enlightened and those fortified by conscience remained loyal. A new continental war and English subsidies have prolonged a futile struggle whose horrors have been experienced by the entire nation. My victory has never been in doubt, but force of arms has now decided the struggle. Who can say what will happen unless peace is restored in Spain in short order? Who can predict the consequences of such

> blind obstinacy? France has every reason to preserve the integrity and independence of Spain if she resumes her character of friend and ally, but, if she instead chooses the path of enmity, she must necessarily seek to weaken her, to dismember her or even to destroy her. Knowing as He does the hearts of all men, God recognizes the sincerity that has animated me in choosing to speak to you in this fashion. Spaniards! The immutable voice of destiny has not yet spoken. Do not allow passions excited by the common enemy to seduce you any longer. Make use of your reason, and this will soon make you see in my soldiers friends who long only to defend you. There is still time: join with me and let this day mark the beginning of a new era of joy and glory for Spain![27]

It was, however, at Córdoba that Joseph was given his first real chance to stamp his mark on Andalucía. No sooner had they entered the city than the French had seized control of the official gazette that had hitherto been published by the local provincial junta, and this was soon publishing a view of the king's stay that may or may not have reflected the true atmosphere of the moment but certainly bears witness to the manner in which he wished to be perceived. Having entered Córdoba amid the same scenes of rejoicing that are so much a feature of French accounts of the invasion of Andalucía, and been immediately waited upon by delegations from the town council, the parish clergy, and the chapters of the cathedral and the collegiate church of San Hipólito, Joseph responded by announcing the award of his Orden Real de España to several ecclesiastics, representatives of the town council, and retired army officers and attending High Mass at the cathedral with his personal suite. Greeted at the main door by the entire chapter, the king processed with them into the church, which is described as being magnificently adorned and packed with people. Having followed Mass with greatest devotion, he then withdrew to the strains of a Te Deum, only to be confronted at the door of the cathedral by a man who burst out of the crowd and flung himself down at his feet, crying out, "Sire, give us work: for a long time we have had neither king nor government." Joseph's response to this appeal, stage managed or otherwise, is not recorded, but with the populace seemingly much taken by him, he did at least promise that only a minimal garrison would be left in Córdoba and that even this would be withdrawn once the city had formed a civic guard. To summarize, then, as king, Joseph would be both a Roman Catholic monarch and a generous one as well as no threat whatsoever to the established order.[28]

Having reached Seville, *el rey intruso* continued to press home the same themes. Hardly had he arrived in the city than he proclaimed his triumph to be the work of divine providence, ordered a Te Deum to be sung in every parish of the archdiocese in recognition of this fact, and decreed an amnesty for all those who had fought against him.[29] From the beginning the proceedings were overlaid by a strongly religious flavor: on 4 February—a Sunday—Joseph again attended a cathedral to hear High Mass. It being the first time that he had appeared in public since his arrival in the city, the king was clearly saying that, next to the affairs of state that had kept him shut up in the royal palace known as the *alcázar* for the last three days, religion was his top priority, while the impression of humility was strengthened by the fact that, despite the pouring rain, he walked the few yards to the cathedral. Meanwhile, the Church had also played its part: the cathedral was draped with its richest hangings, and the king was greeted at the main door by the cathedral chapter and entered the building to the sound of a Te Deum. Inside, meanwhile, there waited a large congregation that had already been primed by a sermon penned by the newly appointed royal commissioner, the Conde de Montarco: in brief, as well as being informed of the free pardon that the new regime was offering to all those who had fought against it, Seville was instructed to give thanks for the manner in which Divine Providence had spared it the horrors of war and at the same time given it a wise, generous, and noble king who wanted only the happiness of his people.[30] Orders having been given for Te Deums to be sung in thanksgiving in all the other churches of Andalucía, it appeared, then, that there was no threat to religion—it helped too that, notwithstanding some initial disorder, the French had, on the whole, behaved with comparative restraint in Seville and placed guards on most the city's major churches[31]—but this was only the beginning of the king's efforts at conciliation. As implied above, some of the first measures to come from Joseph's new headquarters in the *alcázar* were a series of decrees that offered a free pardon to all those who had fought against the French while, having restated the decree of 7 June 1809 that had formally laid down the requirement for all officials, army officers, and members of the clergy to swear an oath of allegiance to King Joseph and given the form in which it should be taken—"I swear obedience to the King, the constitution, and the laws"—on 11 February Joseph confirmed all civil officials who had already sworn such an oath in their jobs, together with any others who conformed to this requirement within three days of the new decree being published.[32] In short, if there was no threat to religion, there was no threat to the established elites either, the latter being given further proof, as in Córdoba, that they could expect to find a niche for themselves in the new order by the issue of the Orden Real de España to some forty-eight prominent officers, officials, churchmen, and local notables, including the city's erstwhile intendant and military governor. Meanwhile, the intendant (or to use the title by which he was known in Seville, *asistente*), Joaquín Leandro de Solis, was appointed *corregidor*—in effect, civil governor—of the city, and numerous nobles given places in a new Guardia de Honor de Sevilla, a species of mounted bodyguard modeled on the old Bourbon Guardia de Corps.[33]

With only ninety-eight men at full strength, the Guardia de Honor was hardly an impressive military force. Far more important in this context was the Guardia Cívica (Civic Guard). Formed by decree on 6 February (this will be looked at more fully at a later moment) but suffice to say that the four battalions of which it should have been composed in Seville offered plentiful opportunities for patronage that again assured many men of more-or-less substance of a place in the new order while at the same time offering a visible guarantee that the interests of property would be defended. However, establishing the Guardia Cívica was not just intended as a means of attracting the support of landed property, for could the French and their supporters but make it a reality, they would be able to offer proof positive that Andalucía was *afrancesada*. Mixed in with all this, meanwhile, was both flattery and an appeal to self-interest, all these themes being summed up by a long speech that Joseph supposedly made at a grand review of the Guardia Cívica on 12 February:

> The speed with which you have answered my call has pleased me greatly, and my confidence in you will be as absolute as the good will that you have shown. You are not only fulfilling your duty as inhabitants of your city, but also giving an example of what every citizen of Spain must do to rescue the nation from the great crisis that it is experiencing. In circumstances such as those of the present, the greater and more determined the service that is offered me, the shorter and less painful will be the sacrifice involved. Until the necessary troops of the line can be organized, it is essential that national [*sic*] guards such as yourselves not only watch over the maintenance of order in the interior, but also make up for the want of regular soldiers. . . . Once order has been restored, the reconstruction of the army will follow, and you will then be asked to do no more than mount guard upon your own cities. From the first moment of my arrival I have visited the many districts of this city almost alone, and shall with the same confidence visit all those places whose inhabitants are devoted to the common interest. This confidence stems from my conscience: in truth, in the least circumstances of my life I am incapable of being guided by anything else. . . . As King of Spain I want more than anyone else among you your independence and prosperity: my happiness and glory are inseparable from them. From this day forward I want the security of this city to be under the safeguard of its own inhabitants, and that, wherever I go, the Guardias de Honor and the *nacionales* [Guardia Cívica] will attend upon my person in the same capacity and with the same status as the royal guard.[34]

The appeal to the propertied classes was completed by a number of other measures. Vague hints, for example, were thrown out that Joseph might spend part of each year in Seville—something that in normal times could certainly be expected to boost the city's prosperity—while a series of royal decrees announced the establishment of a primary school, a girl's secondary school, and an art museum, Seville's chief fora for cultural activities—the

Academía de Bellas Artes and the Real Sociedad de Ciencias—at the same time being favored by generous annual grants.[35] Also favored were the city's antiquarians: deeply impressed by a visit that he made on 8 February to the Roman ruins at Santiponce a few miles north of the city, Joseph ordered that the village should henceforth be referred to by its Roman name of Italica and authorized a grant of 50,000 *reales* toward the excavations that had been underway there since 1785.[36] Shut by the Junta Central as part of its campaign to improve public morals and propitiate the Almighty, meanwhile, on 9 February the city's only theater—the Teatro Principal—was reopened in the presence of the king himself, there following three nights of free performances paid for from municipal funds.[37] And last but not least, good use was made both of Joseph's considerable personal charm and the beautiful setting provided by the *alcázar*. In the words of General Bigarré: "During Joseph's stay in the *alcázar*, . . . he gave various dinners in the gardens under the magnificent orange trees. . . . Every ounce of French art and gallantry went into these meals, while the ladies of Seville who were invited to them found the King of Spain to be as kind as he was attractive. It is undeniable that that prince possessed the gift of pleasing women. I do not know whether it formed a part of his strategy for winning partisans, but, in every town he visited, he made a number of conquests, not just as a king, but as a man."[38]

Joseph, however, was anxious to reach out beyond Seville's elites, for he realized perfectly well that the maintenance of law and order depended to a very large extent on satisfying the needs of the populace. Here the first necessity was work and bread, and it is no coincidence to find that one of Joseph's first measures was to order various repairs to be carried out to the *alcázar*, the cathedral chapter in the meantime being directed to hand over as much money as it could to assist the many artisans who were suffering for want of employment.[39] Reassured by the promise that anything they chose to give would be made up from the proceeds of the state tobacco monopoly, the chapter agreed to hand over 600,000 of the 800,000 *reales* it had in its coffers, but the king did not content himself with mere displays of largesse. To maintain the image of public rejoicing, the principal buildings of the city were illuminated for three nights, while on the morning of 5 February, he embarked on a horseback tour of the city that took in not just the main sights, but also such humble residential districts as Triana. Once again he was accorded a warm welcome: so great was the press, indeed, that it supposedly took the royal party more than six hours to make its circuit of the city.[40] Meanwhile, a delighted Joseph took every opportunity to play to the gallery: "The king stopped on numerous occasions, listened with great kindness to the requests that were made of him, and took care to ask all those who spoke to him what they did, while at the same time telling them that they should return to their accustomed occupations safe in the knowledge that they could do so unmolested. As for those who were without work, he told them that he had given orders for them to be given employment. As His Majesty said, 'I can never forget that I am king not just of the rich and powerful, but also of the artisans and day laborers.'"[41]

What time was left to Joseph in Seville was spent in affecting the appearance of a "king in functions," or in other words, a real king whose time was not just taken up by affairs of state but who also had affairs of state to take it up. Thus, the first three days of his stay in the city were marked by the promulgation of no fewer than twenty royal decrees, and if most of these in fact dealt with matters of first necessity relating specifically to the occupation of Andalucía, it was at the very least no disadvantage for the king to appear to be so assiduous in the performance of his duties. "Legislating was an attribute that was inherent to the dignity of a monarch," writes Díaz Torrejón, "and, given the circumstances, Joseph was doing no more than acting in consonance with his status."[42] Meanwhile, *el rey intruso* was delighted to have the opportunity to hold court and, in particular, to receive the many deputations that now waited on him in his temporary capital. Let us here quote Bigarré once again:

> In the course of Joseph's sojourn in Seville, all the towns of Andalucía hastened to send delegations to congratulate him composed of the most distinguished inhabitants of each place. The priests and monks came to kiss his hand from morning till night, and he told them that he had been sent by God to deliver

> Spain from the ills which she had suffered at the hands of the Bourbon dynasty, and that, under the reign of a prince such as himself, the Spanish monarchy could not fail to become great and majestic once more. For their part the nobles of Andalucía resorted to all sorts of inventions to show the new king . . . their love and devotion. One of them sent him a dozen magnificent fighting bulls as a present and another a beautifully harnessed team of Andalusian horses, while still others put their wives, their daughters, and their very homes at the disposition of His Majesty.[43]

Whether this last remark can be taken at face value in full is a moot point. Be that as it may, the time that Joseph spent in Seville was certainly one of the happiest moments in his entire reign. To have stayed in the Andalusian capital for any length of time, however, would have risked losing momentum, and therefore on 12 February, accompanied by Marshal Soult and a large entourage, he set out on a journey intended as a grand tour of his new domains. As the initial destination was (or so it was hoped) Cádiz, first stop was the town of Utrera, where, according to the *Gazeta de Sevilla* at least, he was accorded a welcome that was superficially just as warm as he had received in Seville:

> The King, our lord, Don José I, entered this town this afternoon accompanied by his royal guard together with the Guardia de Honor de Sevilla. A deputation of the town council had previously met him on the road to offer him its first respects. Every balcony had been decorated with hangings and garlands and the immense crowd that lined the streets showed its joy with repeated cheers and acclamations. The full town council, the *corregidor,* the clergy, the officials of the municipality, the commandant appointed by His Majesty, and various other persons of distinction then had the honor of waiting on His Majesty to pay him their compliments. All the officials begged the King to confirm them in their employment, and His Majesty acceded to this request. At the same time, together with the town council and the clergy, these same individuals swore . . . obedience to His Majesty, the constitution, and the law. Being desirous of

> the establishment of a civic guard, the town council and a number of leading residents then proposed the formation of such a force. . . . Finally, the clergy presented two petitions for the return of various images and other ornaments that had been confiscated from a number of convents that had been suppressed by the previous regime and were needed by the town's parishes.[44]

Having spent the night at Utrera on 13 February and issued a decree (to which we shall return) ordering that all the olive groves belonging to the convents that had been suppressed in Andalucía were to be distributed among the inhabitants of the *pueblos* in which they were situated—another example, this, of the understanding of *el rey intruso* that the occupying forces had a strong interest in addressing social issues—the king and his suite headed south for Jérez de la Frontera. It was a long and wearisome journey—even today the countryside south of Utrera has a particularly bleak and monotonous stamp—but at the end of the day, Joseph was rewarded by much the same scenes as had been witnessed at Utrera in the form of cheering crowds, decorated streets, and obsequious authorities, the governor, an admiral named Salamanca, even going so far as surrendering his cross of the Order of Charles III into Joseph's hands and begging him to exchange it for the new Orden Real de España (to this Joseph responded by not only giving him the insignia that he wore on his own breast but also pinning it on personally). It already being fairly late when the king arrived, the formal business of the visit was postponed until the next day, but all of 15 February was spent in conducting the business of government. Thus, a meeting of the Council of Ministers initiated an attempt to undermine resistance in Cádiz by promulgating a circular enjoining the city's clergy to bring the population to its senses, the town council proceeding to second this by requesting permission to send a delegation to the new Patriot capital to proclaim that anyone who persisted in the cause of resistance was a stranger to true patriotism: not only would such a course achieve nothing, but it would not even be just the inhabitants of Cádiz who would pay the price, for stripped of all its draught animals and beasts of burden and forced to bear the full cost of maintaining Victor's army, the entire region would be ruined. Other than this peace offensive—one that was doomed to failure from the start, given that the authorities in Cádiz had already refused point blank to entertain the forlorn attempts of Marshal Victor to persuade them to lay down their arms—the day was given over to receiving delegations from neighboring *pueblos*, such as Puerto de Santa María, Medina Sidonia, and Sanlúcar de Barrameda, the king rounding off the proceedings by "a long and eloquent discourse" in which he "unburdened himself of his sublime and beneficent ideas with all the frankness of a father speaking to his children," encouraged the inhabitants to form a civic guard, and demonstrated "the want of substance in the terrors spread by enemies of the fatherland . . . that have been the cause of the hostile attitude that is on display in Cádiz."[45]

On 16 February the royal cavalcade moved on again, this time to Puerto de Santa María, the little port that stands across the water from Cádiz. In a passage that was fast becoming repetitive, the *Gazeta de Sevilla* reported the scenes that followed in lyrical terms. Thus, Joseph had entered the town amid scenes of wild excitement: "These having previously been decorated in a manner fit for so auspicious an occasion, the populace lined the streets through which His Majesty had to pass and greeted him with the greatest demonstrations of joy and enthusiasm."[46] The Guardia Cívica having been presented to the king, the latter had then held an audience with all the town's authorities, which had, of course, proved most reassuring to all who attended: "Thanks to the words of peace, clemency, and conciliation addressed to them by the king, all those who attended this audience came away from it filled with a most agreeable impression, His Majesty also stressing how sad it was to him to see the prolongation of a war that was preventing him from devoting himself exclusively to the happiness and prosperity of Spain."[47] The business of the day having thus concluded, the king attended a performance in the town's theater in the presence of "an audience as numerous as it was distinguished."[48] With Joseph now literally in sound and sight of his defiant enemies, 17 February was taken up by a visit to Victor's headquarters and other military affairs, including not least an ostentations review of several thousand troops, but on 18 February the king was once more able to turn to the task of winning over the crowd by attending a bullfight that was "very well attended, set up in an appropriate fashion, and executed with all due ceremony."[49]

The bullfight over, the grand tour rolled on, though so repetitive was its pattern that it is sufficient to simply give an account of the king's progress and to record the impressions of those who took part in it. The former, at least, is easily dealt with: after spending a few days inspecting the siege works before Cádiz and visiting the towns of Sanlúcar de Barrameda, Puerto Real, and Chiclana, on 25 February Joseph returned to Jérez de la Frontera and from there, now protected by 2,000 men of the royal guard, traveled on to Arcos de la Frontera (26 February), El Bosque (27 February), Ronda (28 February–2 March), Casarabonela (3 March), Málaga (4-12 March), Antequera (13-14 March), Loja (15 March), Granada (16–29 March), Alcalá la Real (30 March), Jaén (31 March–2 April), Andújar (3–5 April), Córdoba (6–10 April), and finally Ecija (11 April), from where he returned to Seville the next day.[50] As for eyewitnesses to the journey, one such was the king's aide-de-camp, Bigarré, the picture that he presents being even more inclined to stress popular enthusiasm than the reports we have been following in the *afrancesado* press. Thus:

> Posterity will undoubtedly refuse to believe that the brother of Napoleon was the idol of the peoples of Andalucía in 1810, and yet this is the exact truth. In all the towns and villages through which Joseph traveled on his way from one city to the next, the priests and mayors flocked to him at the head of the whole community to offer him their praise and respect: indeed, many went down on their knees to him, though His Majesty always hastened to have them stand up. Mayors who were known to be good magistrates received particular marks of his esteem, just as priests who had the reputation for being well meaning and devout were given the means of caring for the poor. . . . And how many times did I see this generous philosopher prince strip himself of all the money he had about his person to aid some unfortunate old man or some impoverished mother?[51]

At Málaga, then, "the entire population rushed to show him its good will, its respect, and its devotion," while at Granada, "one of the prettiest women of the town—a member of one of the best families in the province—was so delirious with enthusiasm that she even wrote to him to request the favor of being allowed to visit him in bed" (one may smile at such stories, which may well merely be the product of the common French belief that, bored, repressed, and at the same time excited by the heat of the southern sun, the women of Andalucía were particularly avid for the pleasures of the flesh, but if accounts of the court of Charles IV are to believed, it was by no means uncommon for those seeking favor to plead their case through pretty wives and daughters).[52]

Another participant in the royal progress was Miot de Melito. Herewith his account of Joseph's arrival at Málaga:

> The king made his entrance into that great city on 4 March, and the welcome that he received surpassed anything that could be expected from the devotion of a people of the utmost submission and devotion alike. The streets were strewn with flowers and hung with tapestries; the windows were adorned with beautifully turned-out women waving handkerchiefs in the air; cries of "Long live the King!" resounded on all sides. . . . If Joseph . . . ever really believed himself to be king of Spain, it must have been at this moment. Both a ball and a bullfight were arranged in his honor; in short, nothing that affection, or, in its absence, adulation, could invent to please him was neglected.[53]

For a final word, meanwhile, we can turn to the aide-de-camp, Clermont-Tonnerre. Once again, we find Joseph manipulating the crowd with considerable dexterity: "The morning of his arrival at Ronda, the king pardoned a monk who had been taken prisoner with arms in his possession. The same day he took a walk through the streets accompanied by only three or four other people. Put together, these two actions so excited the inhabitants . . . that they flocked around him, kissing his hands, his feet, his clothes. The women cried for joy and tenderness, while the men cheered without cease."[54] And yet again, there is a strong impression that Málaga extended a welcome that was especially warm:

"The king was received at Málaga by every class of the population with demonstrations of joy that were particularly remarkable. Whether this was because the populace's natural frivolity had made it forget the ills it had suffered when the French had first entered the city, or because the treatment that it had received at the hands of General Sébastiani had genuinely won it over to the side of the king, or, finally, because it hoped that the monarch would make good some of their losses, it is hard to say. One thing that is certainly true, however, is that the senseless resistance that the town had attempted to make was condemned by every inhabitant with anything to lose."[55] As for signs of resistance, they were almost nonexistent, the king generally turning such awkwardness as did occur to good account: at the village of Jamilén, for example, when a small boy darted out of the crowd and shouted "Viva Fernando VII!" he told his guards not to hurt him and threw him a coin, while at Ronda some smugglers apprehended by Joseph's escort were pardoned and given safe conduct to return to their homes, with the admonition that they should henceforth live as good citizens.[56]

Needless to say, Joseph was not just content with smiling and throwing coins. On the contrary, delegation after delegation was treated to detailed exposés of his view of the war. Typical, perhaps, was the speech he delivered to the authorities of Granada on the occasion of his saint's day (19 March):

> The king did not just listen to all the speeches . . . but responded to them . . . with a series of arguments that could not but persuade the least well intentioned among his listeners to adopt his point of view. He detailed the advantages of the constitution that he had brought to Spain and showed them how much it was in their interests and that of the fatherland to join him in good faith and work for the regeneration of Spain. He urged them . . . to organize militia regiments that could answer for the tranquility and obedience of the people and in this fashion spare them the presence of French troops, while at the same time reminding them that, forgetting his responsibility as a French general and thinking only of his sentiments as king of Spain and the father of his people, he had left the greater part

> of his forces on the other side of the mountains [that is, the Serranía de Ronda], this being something that he would have to go back on if he did not receive the help that he was expecting. . . . Meanwhile, if things were bad enough as they were, they could easily get still worse. As the king pointed out, as the emperor had 800,000 men and was at peace with the whole world [*sic*], Spain could find herself literally inundated with French troops unless she rallied to him in a frank and honest manner. Insofar as he himself was concerned, Joseph continued, he had never wanted to be a king and had always much preferred the pleasures of civilian life, while at the same time finding it impossible to envisage happiness other than in the bosom of his family. If he had become king, then, it had been out of an overwhelming sense of honor and the desire to take on the noble task of regenerating Spain: after all, had he not given up a people among whom he was beloved on account of the benefits he had brought them at the very moment when he might have begun to enjoy the fruits of his labors? The people of Spain, he went on, might yet bring down the wrath of the emperor upon their heads by maintaining an insensate resistance and in that case he might in the end be forced to step down. . . . It being all too easy to predict their fate in such a case, he therefore begged them, not as a French general, but as a king who was to all intents and purposes a Spaniard, to join with him, and in this fashion ensure that Spain would merit the preservation of her territorial integrity, and at the same time only have Spaniards as her ministers, generals, intendants, army officers, and other officials.[57]

With Joseph back in Seville, where he was received on 12 April amid a fresh round of ostentatious celebrations, his tour of Andalucía was at an end.[58] How far this was successful as a means of reassuring public opinion and winning support for the French cause is a moot point. For the moment, however, we should note that, pleasant and gracious as the king was, he was not the only weapon that the invaders possessed in the propaganda war. We here come first of all to the issue of the press. Let us here begin with a discussion of the situation in the empire as a whole. With some ten years of the experience of Napoleonic rule behind them, the newspaper editors and journalists of France and the satellite states had long since become a reliable part of the machinery of government. As for the message that they pushed, it was simple and straightforward. At the heart of it, of course, lay the favorable portrayal of Napoleon and the project over which he presided. Thus, the emperor (and at a lower level, satellite monarchs such as Joseph) was wise, benevolent, and utterly devoted to the well-being of his subjects, just as his regime—an entity that was portrayed as being one of great power and majesty—stood for nothing but peace, justice, and prosperity and was in all places striving to bring real improvements in the quality of the life of its citizens. These last in turn responded in kind: while the leading figures in society were everywhere rallying to the empire, the population as a whole was characterized by its submission and contentment. From one end of the empire to the other, then, there reigned nothing but "good order," such problems as banditry being mentioned only to the extent that doing so served to highlight the activity and efficacy of the forces of the state (the counterpoint to this, of course, was the insistence that beyond the frontiers of the empire, the populace was in a constant state of unrest). And needless to say, all this was happening against a backdrop that was highly positive: once again as a result of state intervention—one thinks here, in particular, of the extensive programs of public works that were so much a feature of the regime—trade and industry were invariably portrayed as thriving and the necessities of life as being available in abundance, while the French political system was lauded to the skies as one that had put an end to the turmoil of the Revolution while yet retaining such benefits as equality before the law and representative government (here too there was an obvious contrast with the rest of Europe, the latter invariably being portrayed as being in a state of abject misery). With the empire almost perpetually at war, it was impossible to claim that life was entirely smooth for all of its subjects, but on those occasions that hardship and misfortune were recognized, this was turned into a positive by excoriating Napoleon's enemies and, especially the British, who were invariably portrayed as being the prime movers in all opposition to the empire and, still worse, an evil, hypocritical, and unscrupulous enemy who would stop at nothing, cared only about their own selfish aims, and were bent on eliminating economic competition wherever it raised its head and establishing a world empire. Yet if the British were malevolent, they were also maladroit: time after time their schemes were seen to fail and the empire to emerge triumphant. As for the war, meanwhile, it was nothing but a procession of French victories—victories, of course, whose reportage invariably kept French losses to a minimum and exaggerated those of the enemy while laying immense stress on both the power and the strength of the French army and the personal genius of the emperor, who throughout, it was further claimed, wanted nothing more than peace and stability. To summarize, then, life in the empire was good, life outside it bad, and resistance at any level utterly futile; equally, while the French were fighting a war that was as just as it was successful, their opponents were perpetually mired by injustice and incompetence.[59]

In view of the situation that was to arise in Spain and Portugal in the course of the Peninsular War, it is appropriate to pause for a moment here and pay particular attention to the way the French handled the problem of brigandage. This was too widespread and, indeed, too serious an issue for it to be ignored altogether, and to do it justice, the propaganda of the regime made no attempt to do so. For this there was good reason: whatever the sordid realities of banditry—a phenomenon that in practice made little attempt to differentiate between rich and poor and probably weighed most heavily upon the latter—in legend at least, there were always figures who lived as latter-day "Robin Hoods," robbing the rich to help the poor and constantly defying the authorities with a variety of cheerful daredevilry. In reality, primitive rebels of the sort famously delineated by Eric Hobsbawm did not exist, but that did not stop them from being imagined and in turn becoming a stimulus to desperate young men who might otherwise have endured a life of desperate poverty rather than turning highwayman. Even when matters did not arrive at such extremes, however, the existence of such a counterculture was distinctly disturbing, for in general it could be held to encourage, if not overt defiance, then at least the belief that it was possible to live beyond the reach of the state. Yet in tackling the problem, the Napoleonic authorities had to proceed with some care for fear of disturbing the fiction of the modernizing and prosperous utopia over which they presided, the consequence being that the whole phenomenon was deliberately given an ideological cast. Brigands were certainly the lowest of low—crude, ignorant, and uncivilized outcasts drawn from the poorest and most marginal elements of society and habituated to the most bestial violence. "Bestial," indeed, is a word that is particularly apposite in this context: having placed themselves beyond the pale of civilized society, it followed that bandits were little more than wild animals or even vermin, the language of the texts in which they were discussed invariably reflecting this perception. Yet socially convenient though it was to condemn the poor, it was not just poverty and ignorance that made them brigands but also ideological factors. Behind the phenomenon of brigandage, then, were deemed to lurk the forces of counterrevolution—the Roman Catholic Church, say, or unreconstructed elements of the nobility—this being a theme that was repeated time and again in the course of the Revolutionary and Napoleonic eras, whether it was in the war in the Vendée, the *chouannerie* of Brittainy, the brigandage of the *massif central,* or the risings in southern Belgium in 1798 or Calabria in 1806.[60]

In Spain—a part of the empire in which, for obvious reasons, propaganda assumed even greater importance than it did elsewhere—the chief organ of this propaganda was, from the beginning of 1809 onward, the official bulletin inherited from the Bourbons known as the *Gazeta de Madrid.* As French control spread, however, so other newspapers appeared in those provinces that they occupied, a good example here being the *Gazeta Nacional de Zaragoza.* On a regional level, these were undoubtedly significant, if only because they were more easily accessible than the *Gazeta de Madrid,* but it was always this last that set the general tone (and in fact supplied the regional press with much of its copy). In brief, the format was simple: in any given issue one might find a miscellany of news items from Spain and around the empire (the latter often lifted directly from such French publications as *Le Moniteur*); one or more letters of more-or-less dubious provenance—some were beyond doubt the work of either King Joseph or one of his ministers—that invariably gave accounts of events or situations that were wholly favorable to the French worldview; and a variety of orders of the day, official proclamations, and royal decrees. Typical enough of the contents are a few items that appeared in the spring of 1809. For example, the main news item from Spain in the issue of 18 April is a long account of a typical piece of *josefino* oratory occasioned by the attendance at court of deputations from no fewer than seventeen towns and cities to pledge their allegiance to the new monarch. Thus, Joseph thanked the delegations for their best wishes and urged them all, first, to persuade the inhabitants whom they represented to do all they could to rid the roads of the swarms of bandits that plagued them as the quickest means of getting rid of the burden represented by the French armies and, second, to convince any ecclesiastics who might be stirring up hatred of the French that their behavior not only contradicted the precepts of religion but also was unjust to the king himself. He admitted that all was not as it should be at the current moment, but with the coming of peace, priests would be better supported than had ever been the case before, the ability of the monarch to exercise arbitrary power would be restricted by a modern constitution, all Spaniards would be equal before the law, and, finally, Joseph himself would remain committed to doing all in his power to improve the well-being of every single one of his subjects.[61] Rather similar, meanwhile, was the response to another set of delegations reported in the issue of 1 May. In this the king

> first underlined how great were the means that the same Providence who had set him on the throne of Spain had put in his hands to conserve him upon it, how certain was the triumph of his arms, and how useless were the efforts of those who insisted in continuing to sustain so ruinous a war; then made clear the personal interest that motivated the leaders of the insurrection, reminding his listeners that the same grandees who were . . . shedding so much of the people's blood to keep them under the oppressive yoke of feudalism had been the first to applaud the scandalous abuse that had been made of the sovereign's good faith in the course of the preceding reign; and, finally, urged them with great energy to remember that the war that

> the enemies of Europe [that is, the British] . . . had stirred up in Spain was in reality damaging to no one more than the nation itself given that . . . it was its fields, its towns, and its cities that had to suffer its effects; its treasure that had to nourish it; and its sons who had to lose their lives by the thousand on the field of battle.[62]

In these passages the emphasis was very much on King Joseph. Elsewhere, however, the focus was rather on his subjects. Thus, pride of place in the issue of 2 May was given to a cheerful account of the entry of one of the first regiments of Joseph's Spanish army into Madrid:

> Hitherto in training at Alcalá, the First Infantry yesterday marched into the city to join the garrison. A great crowd assembled to meet it, and the regiment marched through the patio of the royal palace beneath the eyes of the King himself. . . .The excitement of the people who accompanied the regiment on its way and the joy of the soldiers themselves are impossible to express: the King was cheered to the echo, and acknowledged the acclamations of soldiers and civilians alike in the friendliest of fashions. . . . If only all Spaniards shared the sentiments that so imbue the officers and men of this regiment: having witnessed at first hand the abyss into which the fatherland was plunging, they now never cease to give thanks that they have escaped it and are now dedicating themselves to the service of both the nation . . . and the monarch whom Providence has deemed should provide for its felicity.[63]

Even more positive in many respects, meanwhile, was a declaration of support that was reported in the issue of 18 April. Thus, alleging that it did not have the funds to allow it to send a delegation to attend upon Joseph in person, the chapter of a collegiate church at Alcañiz had instead sent an address in which it pledged its loyalty to the new regime on the grounds not just that *el rey intruso* was Spain's legitimate monarch but also that Napoleon had restored the Roman Catholic Church in France and, further, that

Joseph's rule in Naples showed that the king was convinced "that irreligious ideas are impolitic ideas, that every attack on religion is an attack on society as a whole, and that, wherever governments have constantly to fight perverse customs and antisocial habits, law has no effect, authority works in vain, and the bonds that hold society together are dissolved."[64] On 5 May, in an issue dominated by news from abroad, there was only one item relevant to the situation in Spain, but this was significant in that four householders from the Basque *pueblo* of Azcoítia were reported to have seized a young man from Segura who, despite being the son of the local constable, had set himself up as the head of a gang of "bandits and murderers" and attacked a series of isolated French soldiers, the prisoner having been immediately court-martialed and executed.[65] Still more dramatic, meanwhile, were the events that took place in the Castilian *pueblo* of Fuentecén, where, "weary of suffering the vexations caused them by . . . bandits who, on the false pretext of serving the fatherland and molesting the French, have abandoned themselves to every kind of excess and infamy," the inhabitants had set upon one Francisco Pecheromán, the head of "a band of murdering bandits that went under the name of scouts," and tried to take him prisoner, Pecheromán being stabbed to death when he refused to surrender.[66] And finally, on 12 May there was further news from the Basque provinces in that it was reported that, having decided to form a local militia to guard the coast of the province for which he was responsible, the royal commissioner of Guipúzcoa, Francisco Amoros, had been swamped with volunteers and had eventually registered no fewer than 730 men for service in the ranks of the resultant "national coast guards."[67]

So far we have only looked at news from Spain, but the *Gazeta de Madrid* was also keen to keep its readers up to date with news from the rest of Europe. At this point the main issue on the horizon was the new war that had broken out between France and Austria on 8 April 1809, but this was not, it was clear, something that should trouble spirits in Madrid. Thus, on 6 May it was reported, first, that antiwar sentiment was running so high in Vienna that a reign of terror had been imposed to quell it and, second, that an Austrian attempt to build an alliance with Russia and Turkey against France had broken down; for good measure, meanwhile, the Austrians were denounced for making war with illicit means—specifically, attempting to raise the standard of revolt within the frontiers of Bavaria—and acting with a complete want of good faith.[68] As for the war itself, this was portrayed as being in no way the fault of Napoleon: on 8 May the *Gazeta* published a lengthy memorandum penned by the French minister of foreign affairs that argued that, rather than responding with gratitude to the forbearance shown by Napoleon after the Battle of Austerlitz in 1805, Austria had instead from the very beginning armed itself for a fresh conflict, worked against French interests in Italy and the Balkans, and whipped up fear and hatred of France among its own populace.[69] It was, then, the Austrians who had chosen to fight, but in doing so they had made a serious error: on 26 April, indeed, the *Gazeta* had printed a long article pouring scorn on the Austrians' chances of success:

> What can Austria . . . oppose to the 300,000 Frenchmen, Germans, and Italians that Bonaparte will send against her? An army less than half the size of this number; a militia without discipline that has no experience of military life; and a few recruits who at the least reverse will disperse and return to their homes. A treasury that is so entirely exhausted that it does not have the resources to buy the contents of a single London jeweler's. . . . A government composed of courtiers and intriguers, men who are without the slightest talent or morality, and who by their stupidity or ill will have already brought the state very close to the point of ruin, and who by a new excess of temerity, which they call courage, are now going to throw her over the very same precipice.[70]

Immoral and weak, then, the Austrians were heading for disaster. In doing so, however, they were only following the example of Great Britain, whose decision to seize the Danish navy by force the previous year was argued to have shattered the credit of the British state. Here the *Gazeta* gleefully followed arguments that had been voiced in Britain by critics of the Portland administration. Among them was a young William Roscoe: "As well as being iniquitous, the expedition against Copenhagen was essentially anti-political. The object of the constant efforts of Great Britain has always been to maintain a close friendship with the continental powers. . . . The attack on Copenhagen has changed everything. . . .No sooner had Austria received the news . . . than she expelled our ambassador from Vienna. . . . Considering our actions an abdication of all honor and good faith, . . . the emperor of Russia issued a proclamation that amounted to a formal declaration of war."[71] To political disaster there had then been added military defeat. Thus, in the same issue there appeared the last part of a long account of the campaign of La Coruña that had originally been published by the *Journal de l'Empire* in Paris:

> The British retreat to Lisbon being cut off, they had no other way open to them than the road to La Coruña. The shameful circumstances—the haste, the disorder—amid which they arrived at that port are already well known. Pursued incessantly by our troops, they were obliged to abandon 1,500 carts full of munitions and other baggage, 150,000 pounds of powder, sixty pieces of artillery, . . . and 5,000 horses. . . . As for their losses, 6,000 prisoners, . . . 1,500 stragglers lost in the mountains of Galicia (not counting many others murdered by the Spanish peasants), and 2,500 men abandoned in various hospitals . . . prove that they cannot be less than 11,000 men, or one-third of their whole army.[72]

Mention of the campaign of La Coruña, of course, brings us back to events in Spain and, in particular, the war. Here of course the French were making satisfactory progress. In the first place, many successes were being scored against the Spanish regular armies: the *Gazeta* issue of 28 May, for example, has details of both the Battle of Valls—an action in which the Spaniards were claimed to have lost "a large number of pieces of artillery, between 3,000 and 4,000 prisoners, many hundreds of dead, and the important town of Reus and with it considerable magazines of munitions and foodstuffs"—and the occupation of Oviedo by Marshal Ney and General Kellermann, in which respect much was made of the Asturian forces' utter failure to make any resistance and the precipitate flight of the commander of all the Spanish forces in northwest Spain, the Marqués de la Romana.[73] And in the second, the guerrillas were also under much pressure: in the same issue, for example, we read how a Jeronimite friar who had become a prominent guerrilla leader had been arrested and put to death at Barco de Avila (for good measure, it was also reported that the man concerned was suspected to have raped and murdered a young girl who had disappeared at the monastery of Mejorada).[74] More dramatically still, some days later there appeared a report from Bilbao of the capture and execution of "the famous bandit chieftain" Juan Fernando de Echavarría along with two of his followers named José Martín Cabello and Joaquín Zafra:

> An inhabitant of Edillo, . . . Echevarría left his home at the end of last year and descended to the plains of Castile, where he got together a band of criminals and made himself their chieftain, adorning himself on his own authority with the insignia of a lieutenant-captain [*sic*] of the regular army and threatening the local justices with reprisals unless they cooperated with him. Seizing the monies belonging to the public by armed force, he intercepted couriers, arrested and punished those honorable citizens who attempted to oppose his excesses, and caused general horror, as well as dishonoring his own humanity, by executing twenty-four unfortunate soldiers whom he had taken prisoners. . . . Having filled the *pueblos* of Castile with fear and consternation, this criminal then transferred the theater of his operations to the mountains of Santander, where he attempted to spread sedition and disturbed the public peace, occasioning all kinds of vexations among the populace. . . . Eventually cornered by the armed force that was pursuing him, . . . either out of fear or stupidity, he was tolerated by the local justices, and it was only because Divine Providence became weary of having to tolerate such a monster that he was eventually captured. . . . Finding himself behind bars, . . . Echevarría tried to excuse himself by claiming that his operations had throughout had the authorization of the Marqués de la Romana. . . . Yet even supposing that he did in fact possess such authorization, this does not mean that he was any less a criminal, for no general . . .

> would ever sanction the sort of excesses and atrocities that he committed.[75]

Finally, to news items that told their own story, there were added comment, reason, and exhortation. On 23 May, for example, there appeared what may be described as a classic *josefino* harangue:

> If the enemies of our country had not made use of all the means imaginable to keep the peoples of Spain in a state of error and false hope, there is no doubt that the calamities that currently afflict some of her provinces would have been completely over long since. They have not only constantly spread . . . the most absurd and insulting reports in which they entirely falsely make out that the French armies have been suffering continual defeats . . . but they have also taken every possible step to prevent the voice of their legitimate sovereign from being heard by the inhabitants, and this despite the fact that [His Majesty] has constantly called for peace and made it clear that he is always prepared to forget the excesses and mistakes of the past. . . . As they well know, as soon as the populace recognizes the reality of the situation and learns of the many beneficent measures that our monarch has taken, . . . they will be filled with hatred for the authors of their ills and rush to place themselves under the protection of the king. . . . Our beloved sovereign has no other object than to find a prompt and effective remedy for our deep-seated ills, alleviate the evils brought by the war, and cement the happiness of the nation, . . . and His Majesty's every thought has been directed to this end: hence the continuous labor in which he has been engaged with respect to the reorganization of government and other affairs of state ever since his happy return to his capital. . . . But happiness will never be reborn among us unless the peoples of the monarchy quell the voice of passion and, uniting around the throne, ensure that peace and tranquility are restored. Until this happens our provinces, which have unfortunately already suffered grievously enough, will never be free of the burden represented by a numerous foreign army that, however well disciplined, cannot but be very expensive to maintain.[76]

In addition to singing the praises of *el rey intruso,* the *Gazeta* was also eager to paint the darkest possible picture of life in the Patriot zone and, of course, to contrast this with the very different situation that it claimed to characterize the areas governed by King Joseph. Let us here cite the issue of 26 May:

> One of the first effects of the popular revolution in Spain . . . has been to deprive the law of its force. With their authority despised and ignored, magistrates have everywhere been the victim of the . . . hatred and spite of those whose crimes have left them prey to the rigor of the law. . . . This state of social dissolution, which still reigns unchecked in many provinces . . . including, most notably, Andalucía and Valencia, where every moment witnesses scenes of blood and horror sufficient to shock even the most indifferent observer, should make us kiss the beneficent hand of the hero who has saved us from these same dangers. . . . Madrid and many other cities and provinces . . . now enjoy the utmost peace and tranquility. The magistrates can raise their voice in admonition, speak to the people whom they govern in liberty, and ensure that their authority, and indeed, that of the law itself, is respected.[77]

To illustrate the disorder that reigned in Patriot Spain, there were, of course, examples aplenty, but the Cádiz riots of February 1809 made for a particularly dramatic story, and 2 May, therefore, saw the publication of what purported to be an eyewitness account that mixed bitter denunciations of the supposed perfidy of the British with lurid accounts of the savagery of the populace.[78] Also interesting in this respect is a report that was published regarding Valencia: "The oppression and continual harassment that . . . Valencia's propertied classes are suffering at the hands of a ferocious, ignorant, and wild populace that the magistrates and the law alike can barely contain in spite of the exemplary punishments that have been handed down to many of the worst offenders is impossible to express. Suffice to say that in the space of the last ten months, the number of those tried as thieves and murderers has been more than 900. Yet despite this, such crimes remain frequent and all too often gone unpunished. All men of judgment being convinced that these crimes will not cease without the presence of a respectable French army, the appearance of such a force is eagerly awaited."[79]

Such, then, was the picture of Spain, the Peninsular War, and the general situation of the Napoleonic empire that had been put forward up until 1810 by the *josefino* propaganda machine. With Seville and the other major cities of Andalucía all in the hands of the French forces, the torch was now taken up by fresh emissaries. First in the field, as we have seen, were the *Correo Político y Militar de la Ciudad de Córdoba* and the *Gazeta de Gobierno de Sevilla* (almost immediately renamed simply the *Gazeta de Sevilla*), but similar publications soon appeared in Granada, Málaga, and Jérez de la Frontera. Unlike the *Gazeta de Madrid,* however, the focus of those responsible for these publications was always local rather than national or international. Thus, for most of February and March, four topics may be said to have been dominant. In the first place, the military situation was reported in terms that left no doubt as to the futility of resistance; in the second, the royal progress was recounted, as we have seen, in the most loving and obsequious detail; in the third, there was much emphasis on the manner in which life was returning to normal and the social, religious, and political elite submitting to the new regime; and, in the fourth, there was much reportage of the chaos that was supposed to be reigning in Cádiz and the fatal consequences of further resistance. Given that enough has been said to give a fairly clear treatment of the presentation of Joseph's tour of Andalucía, we may here concentrate on the other three.

First of all, let us look at such remarks as were made respecting the advance of the French armies. Given that the first chapter looked at the fall of Málaga in some detail, it is worthwhile to reproduce the account given by the *Gazeta de Gobierno de Sevilla:*

> On the sixth day of this month, the . . . IV Corps entered Málaga. Following the occupation of Granada, a number of . . . British agents attempted to rally resistance, . . . but General Sebastiani did not give them any time to get ready: seizing the . . . pass known as the Boca del Asno, he immediately marched on Málaga. A small group of friars and lawyers had

> the night before arrested . . . the old junta and seized control of the government. Giving themselves ranks and titles of all sorts, . . . they persuaded several thousand of the inhabitants to take up arms. This mob was supported by many cannon, but all that was required to disperse it was a single cavalry charge. . . . Thereupon Málaga was taken by assault . . . and many French prisoners set free. Although it was they who had fanned the flames of sedition, the British had prudently chosen to absent themselves. . . . As for the leaders of the insurrection, they were arrested by the inhabitants of Vélez Málaga and handed over to the authorities, with the request that they be brought to trial.[80]

This passage is worthy of considerable analysis. First of all, it is suggested that Málaga would have submitted to the French without trouble had it not been for British intrigue. Second, in contrast to the vigorous professional soldiers who commanded the French, we learn that the leadership of the insurrection were self-seeking egotists without any military knowledge who, despite plentiful resources, could fashion only the flimsiest of military machines to protect the city. Third, we find that the instigators—British and Spanish alike—made no bones about fleeing the scene as soon as their plans came to grief. And fourth, we see a much misled and repentant populace realizing the error of its ways and turning sharply on those who had so abused its confidence. Not all of this is true, of course—the British had nothing to do with Abello's coup, for example—but there is just sufficient accuracy to give the account the ring of plausibility. Also noteworthy, meanwhile, is what it omits to mention: hardly surprisingly, there is nothing here about the sack of the city by the victorious French troops. If anyone had been guilty of such actions, indeed, it was rather the British, who (wholly without foundation: at this point there was not a single British soldier in Andalucía) were in at least one other article accused of having sacked both Tarifa and Algeciras prior to the arrival of the French army.[81]

Turning now to the restoration of order and the spread of collaboration, on 10 February, for example, the same publication reported, first, the reopening of Seville's theater and, second, King Joseph's interest in the city's few industrial plants:

> The magnificent cannon foundry, the immense tobacco factory, the saltpeter works, . . . and the various concerns owned by private individuals have all been forced to suspend production, throwing thousands of some of the most useful members of society into idleness and misery. Hardly had His Majesty entered Seville than he ordered the Ministry of the Interior to inquire into the state of these establishments in person and to draw up a list of means by which they might be got going again. No delay can be tolerated in the undertaking of this commission, and it has therefore been placed in the hands of a group of intelligent citizens who are interested in the welfare of their country. . . . Meanwhile, in the course of his visit to the cannon foundry and the tobacco factory, His Majesty . . . also ordered that, having not been raised for fifty years, the wages that they pay should be brought into line with the cost of living.[82]

Such measures, it was claimed, brought an instant reward, with so many men supposedly coming forward to join the Guardia Cívica that its full complement had been raised in a matter of days.[83] Nor was it just in Seville that the restoration of order produced an ever greater willingness to cooperate with the French. From Granada too it was reported that large numbers of men had flocked to join its Guardia Cívica and, further, that this force was proving more than willing to undertake such tasks as escorting prisoners, while a letter that appeared in the *Gazeta de Sevilla* on the situation in Puerto de Santa María claimed that, convinced that the French troops were "loyal friends who are ever ready to defend them," the inhabitants were "enjoying the benefits that result from tranquility and good order . . . and going about their business as normal."[84]

One theme that was particularly stressed, of course, was the new regime's determination to root out brigandage. Let us here cite an article that appeared in the *Gazeta de Gobierno de Sevilla* respecting a decree that threatened any *pueblo* that failed either to report the presence of bands of *malhechores* to the military authorities or to do all in their power to resist their demands with severe punishment:

> The penalties that this decree threatens could not be more just. By its provisions, towns and villages are to be held responsible

> for any banditry that is committed within the bounds of their jurisdiction. With this there can be no quarrel. If they . . . give any assistance to those concerned, it follows that they are culpable in respect of any attack that might then follow. Meanwhile, even if they do no more than connive at whatever might go on or take no action to prevent it, given the great importance of this matter, such selfishness or indifference cannot be allowed to go unpunished. If, by contrast, the inhabitants associate themselves with the aims of His Majesty and display the patriotic zeal that can be expected of them, our provinces will soon be free of the plague of outlaws that infests the roads, terrorizes every town and village, and dishonors the Spanish nation. What would the other nations of Europe think of us if we allowed bandits to go on holding pacific inhabitants to ransom and committing more atrocities than Arabs of the desert, and all the more so when the key to the situation les in the hands of the populace itself? We all share an interest in curbing these evildoers and at present have no other enemies to fight: let us, then, make use of all our valor and energy against them.[85]

In this last sentence we come to a further theme that must be highlighted at this point. Thus, the *josefino* project was presented throughout as something that was nonpartisan and even non-ideological with which even such supposedly hidebound groups as the clergy could associate themselves. Indeed, instances of ecclesiastical collaboration were particularly emphasized. Pro-Bonapartist sermons—a prime example is the one delivered in Seville on 4 February by Nicolás Maestre[86]—were therefore featured very prominently along with other demonstrations of clerical support, such as the ode to King Joseph written by a Córdoban cleric that appeared in the very last issue of the *Gazeta de Gobierno de Sevilla:*

> Icy terror has passed away,
> And the happy Spaniard generously offers you eternal loyalty.
> More than the thunderous cannon,
> More than the shining sword,
> More than the armed might of France,
> What swept all before it was your goodness.

> So it is that, rather than lying prostrate with tears bathing her beautiful face,
> Spain is now rejoicing and coming to life again
> Thanks to your presence and the influence of your soul, oh pious king,
> She will live in peace and enjoy its benefits.[87]

Of course, far more important than such sonorous doggerel—the piece reads no better in Spanish—were the pronouncements of the ecclesiastical hierarchy. Hence the importance accorded a pastoral letter written by Miguel Cayetano, bishop of Licopolis (auxiliary bishop of Seville), to the clergy of the diocese of which he was now acting head dated 15 February, the basis of his argument being that the war had been sent to punish Spain for her many sins and that Joseph (who had given him, or so Cayetano claimed, every assurance of his desire to respect the church) had been sent as the answer to the nation's prayers for forgiveness. In short, the coming of King Joseph was the work of Providence: "Know, then, that all this is the work of the secret hand of the Most High, of that God Almighty who we worship and whose people we are."[88]

To return to the four themes that one can identify in the early days of the *josefino* propaganda campaign in Andalucía, the last one that needs to be considered is the state of affairs in Patriot Spain. Let us begin here with the situation of Cádiz itself. As far as this last city was concerned, the picture that was drawn of its situation was, predictably enough, extremely dark. Herewith a report that appeared in the *Gazeta de Sevilla* on 20 February:

> From the accounts of many people who have arrived . . . from the Isla de León and Cádiz, we know that the greater part of their inhabitants disapprove of the attempt that is being made to defend them, this view being shared by all the more substantial elements of the population. The excessive number of people who have congregated in Cádiz . . . has made subsistence impossible for any length of time. . . . The prices of goods of first necessity are rising daily, and they will soon reach such a level that only the rich will be able to buy such products. . . .

> The party of common sense and true patriotism is very great, but terrorized by a mob in the pay of the British, they are waiting on a more favorable opportunity to propagate the ideal of peace and good order.[89]

What made such a move even more desirable, of course, was the fact that, according to the *josefino* press, Cádiz's position was hopeless: Spain was swamped by massive numbers of French troops, and the spirit of resistance crumbling in such few bastions of resistance as remained to the Patriot cause elsewhere. Let us here cite yet another article from the *Gazeta de Sevilla:*

> An army of 60,000 men is in occupation of the four kingdoms of Andalucía. Meanwhile, their capitals are all in a state of perfect tranquility, and their inhabitants hastening to give the kings proofs of their loyalty and adhesion. From Málaga to the Sancti Petri [that is, the creek that separates the Isla de León from the mainland], every port has been occupied: no enemy vessel will be able to enter them, still less pick up supplies for Cádiz. Two army corps have taken possession of the whole of Extremadura, while the forces in Old Castile are pressing in on Ciudad Rodrigo; meanwhile, Oviedo and the rest of Asturias will also soon be occupied by another corps under the command of General Bonet. More than 40,000 men have already replaced those who were sent forward from the Basque provinces and are now on the road for Galicia and Portugal. It is known, too, that still more men could be sent from France if a rapid end to the war does not give the king the satisfaction of being able to keep them beyond the Pyrenees. In Catalonia no Spanish troops remain in the field. . . . Valencia cannot resist and its inhabitants are making prudent efforts to avert the tempest. . . . Cartagena is in no state to resist an attack by land and is thinking of ways of saving itself.[90]

The object of this initial wave of propaganda was, of course, first, either to persuade Cádiz to surrender or to instigate a revolution in the city and, second, to discourage the emergence of resistance in the interior of Andalucía. In neither case was this goal achieved, however: the emissaries sent by Joseph to contact the Patriot authorities were turned back unheard, the war remained unchallenged in Cádiz, and the Serranía de Ronda and the Alpujarras both began to witness serious popular resistance. In consequence, the *Gazeta de Sevilla* and their fellows now shifted their ground. In effect, instead of being minimized or at best treated as something that would fade away in a matter of days, resistance was recognized as a major problem that was likely to be present for the foreseeable future but could achieve nothing and was certain to bring disaster on all concerned, the first hint of this more realistic approach coming in a series of articles that outlined the likely effects of a prolonged defense of Cádiz. One of the first of these appeared in *El Correo Político de Jérez* on 19 February. Thus:

> To be regarded as honorable, the defense of a city has to enjoy at least the possibility of success. What can our unhappy brethren promise themselves, however? Is it really possible that there are none among them who do not see that all this is going to lead to is the horrors of a protracted siege that will end in the extermination of their beautiful city and the death of all its inhabitants? They cannot even console themselves with ideas of eternal glory: the current generation will cover them with opprobrium on account of the ills they will inflict on all their fellow Spaniards and, more particularly, the inhabitants of Andalucía, while its successors will regard them as rebels and enemies of the fatherland. Do they not see that this has been the treatment accorded to the frenetic efforts that were made at Barcelona and Játiva in the War of Succession, and this despite the fact the cause for which the latter were fighting had far more claim to be regarded as being just and reasonable? Posterity judges actions by the utility or otherwise of their results. And what will be the result of this insensate defense? There is nobody who can deny it: the ruin of Cádiz. And who will benefit from it? The British. Is there anyone who can deny this fact? It is for this that the British have struggled with such ardor, have poured out so much money, have employed such iniquitous means of seduction. Fomented and sparked off by these monopolists, the War of Succession gave them possession of Gibraltar and Mahón

> and the great commercial advantages they obtained from the Treaty of Utrecht. The Spaniards who helped them achieve these goals have ever since been the object of execration in the eyes of all good patriots: what will those of the present epoch and those to come say of those who sold Ceuta, that other key to the Straits of Gibraltar, to the natural enemies of Spain, cooperated in the complete ruin of our navy and commercial shipping, and are even now conspiring to make the ruins of Cádiz both a monument to the consummation of Britain's triumph and an eternal record of . . . the most infamous act of treason . . . ever carried out by men calling themselves Spaniards? Those who have directly contributed to putting Cádiz . . . at the mercy of our irreconcilable enemies are guilty of high treason, and this applies just as much to those whose ignominious cowardice has allowed them to be led to the brink of the precipice like some herd of stupid beasts. If they are really set on dying, would it not be more satisfying and more glorious to die in the cause of preserving for the fatherland this glittering emporium than to fall amid its ruins in that of going down in history as venal slaves of Great Britain?[91]

The theme of the disastrous consequences of the continued resistance of Cádiz was thereafter one that was heavily plugged. The city, it was argued, would either first be reduced to ruins by bombardment and then taken by assault and subjected to all the horrors of a sack or be reduced to a British colony—indeed, in one article it was even alleged that it would be annexed to Britain altogether. As such a dependency, however, its future was bleak, for the British were only interested in its ruin as a competitor and would therefore strive might and main to cut it off from the American colonies and strip it of its shipping. As if this were not enough, meanwhile, the inhabitants—a group whose numbers, it was rightly pointed out, had been greatly swelled by the arrival of numerous refugees from the rest of Spain—would be faced not just by bankruptcy and unemployment but also by starvation, it being maintained that there was no way that the British could keep so large a city supplied with adequate food even if they had any interest in doing so. All that resistance would achieve, then, would be to devastate the coastal belt while at the same time providing short-lived aid and succor to the guerrillas, the latter of course being a phenomenon that was excoriated in the extreme.[92]

Insofar as these last were concerned, we have already seen the manner in which irregular combatants were treated in the general propaganda of the empire. This was now repeated still more strongly. On 6 April 1810, for example, a proclamation issued by Blas de Aranza, the royal commissioner appointed by King Joseph to preside over the governance of Seville, described them as "gangs of robbers, . . . thieves, and murderers recruited from the jails . . . and paid by the British."[93] Just as much to the point was the fact that their activities were utterly futile. Let us here first consider a commentary on a skirmish that took place at Torreperogil near Ubeda:

> Of the 300 men who perished in the combat of Torreperogil, more than 200 were poverty-stricken laborers from the *pueblos* roundabout, who had been seduced by a handful of wretches and taken arms without giving a thought to their chances of offering resistance. Many of them were family men with children, this being something that has filled us with the utmost sadness. Let us hope that the incident will open the eyes of many unfortunates who might otherwise fall victim to . . . those who would lead the people to their deaths without giving them the means of putting up a fight worthy of the name. However posterity may choose to judge the cause of the two camps into which Spain has become divided, it will never do other than execrate those who . . . have attempted to force the fatherland to continue a bloody struggle alone notwithstanding the defeat of the party that they have chosen. Conscience . . . might be something that is all very well in an individual who gives up his life for things that, with or without foundation, he believes to be dearer to him than his own existence, but he who sacrifices the lives of others to his beliefs is a murderer, no matter what those beliefs might be. Indeed, if he exposes the fatherland to danger, he becomes a public enemy. Given that these principles of social morality do not admit of any contradiction,

> how should we judge men who command nothing but bandits and defenseless peasants . . . and yet persist in wandering about from place to place, stirring up trouble and impeding the restoration of order?[94]

Setting aside the equally important implication that the rank and file of the *partidas* had been deluded or misled into fighting the French by unscrupulous men who were either agents of the British or mere bandits and adventurers out for plunder and personal gain—a point that is important because it speaks to the notion that a veil would be drawn over the actions of men who laid down their arms and returned to their homes—the lesson was clear enough: only death awaited those who sought to take on the invaders, this point being reinforced by account after account of French punitive columns striking out in all directions and wreaking havoc upon the foe. On 5 April a column that had set out from Ronda under a Colonel Beaussain had stormed Olmeda and put the defenders—"200 *dispersos* and almost the entire population"—to flight for the loss of only two horses; attacking the walled town of Grazalema the next day in the face of determined resistance, the same force had again penetrated the defenses and killed many people: in some houses, it was gleefully noted, there were as many as ten bodies.[95] Meanwhile, as this was happening in the Serranía de Ronda, another column had fallen upon a band of hundreds of insurgents who had taken shelter in the riverside town of Tocina in the Guadalquivir valley: "In less than half an hour, no less cowardly than they were foolish, this rabble had been overthrown. The majority of them were able to escape due to the difficulties we had in getting across the river, but more than 100 of the bandits had been killed without [the loss of] a single one of our own men."[96] As for attacking the French, the result was likely to be just as futile. At El Visillo a detachment of a mere eight soldiers under the command of a corporal had, by dint of retiring to a handy roadside inn, succeeded in fighting off a band of some sixty insurgents, killing four of them and wounding two others, while at Paradas fifty men of the Guardia Cívica of Marchena and a detachment of the Forty-Third Regiment of infantry of the line had attacked a band of rebels who had taken over the town and put them to flight, it being specifically noted that the guardsmen had fought with great courage.[97]

What is striking about many of these accounts is the way that they come close, as in the case of Grazalema, to speaking overtly of outright massacre. Sometimes, indeed, the point was made still more apparent. A good example here is a proclamation issued on 8 May 1810 by Blas de Aranza, who under the terms of the decree of 17 April 1810 (see below) was now prefect of Seville. "Where once there stood Algodonales," he intoned dramatically, "one can now see nothing but ruins." In brief, the story was as follows. According to Aranza, an inhabitant of Algodonales named Romero had set himself up at the head of a large gang of insurgents and, with the support of the local population, made the *pueblo* itself his base.[98] Following an ill-judged attack on a column of French troops, on 2 May 1810 Algodonales had been surrounded and stormed. What followed was clearly grim in the extreme: "The ferocious Romero, who had resolved not to give himself up until the last one of those credulous inhabitants had been put to the sword in payment for letting themselves be seduced by his perfidious counsels, was the last to die."[99] Even such prisoners as were taken in the course of this fighting could expect little mercy, however: all eight of the insurgents captured at Torreperogil were immediately court-martialed and shot, four of them at Ubeda and the other four at Baeza.[100] Equally, from Alcalá de Guadaira it was reported that a court-martial had sentenced two men named Antonio Rodríguez and Bartolomé de los Santos to death by firing squad for the murder of two French soldiers (interestingly, the owner of the house where the killings had taken place, one María Senepe Apri, was accused of complicity and sentenced to a year in prison).[101] Indeed, the *afrancesado* press reads as a veritable litany of death:

> Headed by the mayor, the Guardia Cívica of Fuente Salmera has . . . captured Salvador de Sierra, a bandit chieftain who has been the terror of the countryside; this wretch has been taken to Ecija, where he was immediately condemned to death by a court-martial made up of the officers of the Guardia Cívica. . . . On the 17th of this month the military commission that has its

> seat at Ronda . . . condemned to death Juan de la Cruz Gordillos, an inhabitant of Arriate, and Francisco de Yeguas, an inhabitant of Puebla de Sierra de Yeguas, after finding them guilty of having fought with the bandits that range the countryside at random, robbing, murdering, and making war on the French troops. . . . In accordance with a sentence given on 22 December by a court-martial that had been convened in Córdoba, Antonio Martínez, the commander of a party of insurgents that was taken by surprise at Campanario, . . . has been executed in Córdoba in the presence of the garrison.[102]

In brief, then, both the practice and the propaganda of the regime ensured that insurgents knew full well the price of resistance and, in particular, that armed insurrection would be treated as banditry (by extension, of course, the propertied classes were equally aware that, unlike in Patriot Spain, they could count on the authorities to adopt a tough line in defense of their interests: not for nothing did the invaders do all that they could to conflate armed resistance with mere brigandage). To avoid French retribution, of course, there was one easy answer: in brief, providing the invaders with information, barring the gates against the insurgents, and enlisting in the Guardia Cívica. As we have seen, the growing incidence of collaboration had been a constant theme of *josefino* propaganda from the earliest days of the occupation of Andalucía, but the struggle against the *partidas* served to provide the invaders and their allies with plentiful opportunities to list instances in which townsfolk and villagers had rallied to their cause. From Baeza, then, it was reported that a party of insurgents that had appeared in the town had been set upon by the inhabitants and chased out; from Monturque that a posse of civic guards had been sent out to hunt down a group of Spanish deserters that had been reported as being in the vicinity; and from Belméz that the inhabitants had proved obstructive and defiant in the face of a visitation by the *partidas* of Clemente Arribas and Antonio Bueno.[103] Whether or not any of these stories is true is a moot point, but this is of no account, what matters being that a picture was being painted of an Andalucía in which the space for insurgency was becoming ever more restricted. To quote an article that appeared in the *Gazeta de Sevilla* on 17 August 1810: "Every day the results obtained against the marauders who are scattered across the face of the country are more satisfactory. In every part of Andalucía good order is being established, and public spiritedness making great progress."[104]

If the French were having matters all their own way in the hinterland of Andalucía, the Patriot cause, it was stressed, was doing no better elsewhere. As the need to report the details of Joseph's triumphal progress around Andalucía faded away, so the editors of the occupation press began to fill their pages with stories of French victories in other parts of Spain. One such success story came from Asturias, where it was reported that Bonet had inflicted a heavy defeat on the insurgents at Oviedo on 14 March in which the Spaniards had lost more than 1,000 casualties, while somewhat later the attempt that had been made to capture Badajoz following the fall of Andalucía was reported in considerable detail, the unfortunate fact that the French had never been able to take the city being obscured by lengthy accounts of the demoralization and want of discipline that prevailed amid the defenders.[105] As the spring and summer wore on, however, other fortresses did fall—most notably Astorga and Ciudad Rodrigo—while in August and September, two successive attempts to advance on Seville from Extremadura were thrown back with heavy losses at Villagarcía and Fuente Cantos. On each occasion, of course, the *josefino* press and its controllers were not slow to report what had happened, and once again the emphasis was on the utter inadequacy of the Patriot armies and, more particularly, their leadership. Herewith, for example, the report published by the *Gazeta de Sevilla* in the wake of Villagarcía on 16 August 1810:

> The commander in chief has hastened to announce to the army that on the eleventh day of this month, General Girard's division of the V Corps . . . achieved a brilliant victory over the enemy at Villagarcía. . . . Having got together all the troops in Extremadura, La Romana was foolish enough to take the field. For the next few days he wandered about the province in a fashion that suggested that he had no idea what he was doing, that he had, indeed, no plan whatsoever. He had . . . 12,000

> infantry, 900 cavalry, and a small amount of artillery. General Girard followed his movements and through his skillful dispositions succeeded in bringing them to battle. . . . La Romana took to his heels in the most cowardly fashion at the first volley, while his men only stood long enough to experience complete defeat: 2,000 Spaniards were left lying dead on the battlefield, while another 400 were captured, along with 200 horses and ten guns.[106]

No help, then, was to be expected from the rest of Spain, but what of the outside world, and in particular, what of Great Britain? Here too, it was maintained, there was little hope. Much weight was given, for example, to the bitter parliamentary debates provoked by the disappointments and failures of the summer of 1809—specifically, the abortive advance on Madrid that had culminated in the Battle of Talavera and the disastrous expedition to Walcheren. In reality, these were mere attempts to secure party political advantage that carried little conviction, but the impression given of them in the *josefino* press was inevitably very different. Every attempt was made to stress the considerable criticism that had been voiced of the Spanish armies, while it was even argued that the cause of Spain and Portugal had been given up altogether: according to a letter published by the *Gazeta de Sevilla* on 3 May 1810 that had supposedly been received from a French sympathizer in London, for example, the Perceval administration was only waiting for the French to launch a new invasion of Portugal to pull Wellington's army out of the Peninsula altogether.[107] Even if Wellington stayed put, though, he would be unlikely to stem the onrush, another such letter claiming, first, that the Irish soldiers in his army were deserting in large numbers and, second, that the new Portuguese levies that he had called up to reinforce the redcoats were as yet in no state to take the field.[108] As for active British operations against the French and their allies, these were as immoral as they were futile, being restricted to the capture of a few neutral merchant vessels here and the bombardment of the odd coastal town there, operations, meanwhile, that were often fiercely resisted: according to reports from Copenhagen, for instance, there had been a variety of minor combats off the coast of

Jutland between British and Danish ships, in the course of which several British sloops were taken and two ships of the line that came close inshore in an attempt to seize two Danish merchantmen driven off by the volleys of a company of Danish infantry.[109]

Small wonder, then, that in British-held Sicily, or so it was claimed, the population was becoming increasingly restive at the presence of a foreign garrison that did little other than drink itself to death and think more and more in terms of a revolution, the only indigenous troops that the British had been able to get together consisting of a rabble of erstwhile bandits and smugglers of such low enthusiasm and poor discipline that there was no option but to keep them under lock and key until such time as the forces of Joseph's successor as king of Naples, Joachim Murat, should descend on the island.[110] What else, however, was to be expected of a country that was at one and the same time so inept in its diplomacy and perfidious in its actions, a country, moreover, that at every stage had been the chief culprit in Europe's travails? And that this was the case, there was of course no doubt, as witness, for example, a long article that appeared over several issues of the *Gazeta de Sevilla* entitled "La Inglaterra considerada como causa de las conquistas de Napoleón en el continente" ("Great Britain Considered as the Cause of the Conquests of Napoleon on the Continent"). According to the editor, the literal translation of a pamphlet that had recently been published in England and sold in enormous quantities, this claimed that the British establishment had been carried away by its blind prejudice in respect of the French Revolution and that it had swept the mob along with it by skillful use of propaganda, the popular hatred that it had thereby engendered making it very difficult to arrive at a peace settlement. Combined with all this, meanwhile, had been a determination to maintain control of the seas and destroy all obstacles to Britain's commerce. Thus, it had been Britain that had rejected Napoleon's peace overtures in 1800, Britain that had wrecked the Peace of Amiens, Britain that had stirred up the Third Coalition against Napoleon, Britain that had rejected the chance of peace that she had been offered in 1806, and Britain that had blocked the idea of a general peace conference in 1807. Had all this led to victory, the author continued, then it might have been forgiven, but the war against France had been marked throughout by the gravest misjudgment, of which the most obvious example was the persistent belief of Pitt and his successors that Austrian and Russian armies could beat the French when it was in fact self-evident that the French were infinitely stronger, more effective, and better motivated, while it was also self-evident that Britain had repeatedly failed to give her allies the support that they needed.[111]

Against feeble Britain, meanwhile, there stood the might of the French empire. Insofar as this was concerned, no opportunity was missed of stressing the odds that the Allies faced. On 20 February, for example, the *Gazeta de Sevilla* published a summary of a report that had recently been presented to Napoleon in which it was stated that in 1809 France had been maintaining an army of 900,000 infantry, 100,000 cavalry, and 50,000 gunners and train troops, and, further, that the empire's population amounted to a total of some 38,262,000 people.[112] Thereafter there were frequent references to French troops heading for the Spanish frontier, massing at Bayonne, and arriving at such towns as Valladolid, while, if there were no French victories to report in other parts of Europe, great care was taken to keep Spaniards up to date with the progress made by the Russian army fighting the Turks in the Balkans: in 1810, after all, Russia was still France's chief partner in Europe, and it was therefore grist to the mill to claim that her forces were sweeping all before them and eradicating British influence from the Balkans as surely as France was eradicating it in Spain.[113] Finally, if the French army was at present only active in Spain, the French navy was also taking the war to the enemy: according to a report that appeared in August, two frigates had disembarked a landing party to attack a British trading post on the coast of Sumatra, a battle fleet was threatening to put to sea from Vlissingen, and a squadron of seven ships of the line had appeared off Jamaica.[114]

In the summer of 1810, however, the news story that was most evocative of the power of the French empire concerned the doings of neither Russian armies in the Balkans nor French squadrons off Jamaica. On the contrary, what mattered was above all Napoleon's marriage to the Archduchess Marie-Louise of Austria in a two-day ceremony held at Saint Cloud and the Tuileries on 1–2 April 1810.

As only a year before Austria had been fighting France—had, indeed, been France's most consistent opponent among the continental powers—news of the new alliance could not but come as a bitter blow to the Patriot cause, and the propagandists of Andalucía therefore made much of it, describing the archduchess's journey to Paris and the celebrations that followed in lavish detail, which conjured up fresh visions of power and grandeur, and at the same time stressing the joy of the populace.[115] In France, then, people and throne were united, while the establishment of a Paris-Vienna axis—a development at which Francis I was professed to be delighted[116]—seemed at a stroke to put an end to all hopes of a fresh coalition. As the *Gazeta de Sevilla* put it, "Millions of people will bless this union, for it promises them a happier future."[117] It did not, of course, but that was by the by, and so it was that in Seville, Marshal Soult—now, as we shall see, de facto viceroy of Andalucía—marked the occasion with a Te Deum, three nights of illuminations, the distribution of alms to the poor, and a great banquet that was attended by all the civil and military authorities, not to mention "150 ladies chosen from the best society of the city."[118]

Throughout the French occupation, the public celebration of such events was to remain an important strand in the invaders' attempts to project a positive image of the empire. Typical enough of the sort of thing that went on was the celebration of Napoleon's saint's day in Seville in 1810. At dusk on the evening of 14 August, peals of bells rang out from every church in the city, then at four o'clock the next morning, the city was awoken by a massive salvo of artillery. At ten o'clock High Mass was celebrated in the cathedral to the accompaniment of a Te Deum, and after this alms were distributed to the poor, the cathedral also witnessing the marriage of a number of orphan couples and the presentation of scholarships to a number of children who had been selected as the recipients of municipal apprenticeships. All this was followed by a sumptuous reception in the royal palace at which the guests were presented with special commemorative medals (the garrison, meanwhile, received a double issue of wine). In the afternoon came bullfights, and these in turn were followed by open-air dances, illuminations, and a massive firework display, of which the high point was the release of 2,000 rockets from the Giralda, the elites in the meantime being free to enjoy the banquet and ball laid on in Soult's headquarters. Hardly had the last of the revelers gone to bed than the next round of the festivities began: from eight o'clock in the morning onward, groups of musicians processed around the streets in an attempt to keep up the general mood of excitement, while the afternoon was marked by a horse race and the evening by another reception in Soult's headquarters and a second round of illuminations.[119]

With fireworks exploding in the skies above Seville, we may here conclude this lengthy chapter. In Spain Napoleon's propaganda can be seen to have followed much the same course as it did in the rest of the empire while clearly being cleverly adapted to fit local conditions and to trade on popular concerns and misconceptions. At the center of everything was, of course, the figure of Joseph Bonaparte, whose earnest efforts to play the part of a Spanish monarch and show concern for the welfare of his subjects are almost pathetic in their optimism and sincerity. Yet it cannot be stressed enough that Joseph was in no way isolated in his efforts to win favor with the Spaniards. On the contrary, such behavior was very much in tune with the general style affected by imperial rule, and it therefore seems unfair to pour scorn upon his efforts in the style of self-interested critics such as Marshal Soult. What is true, however, is that even backed up by an extensive propaganda campaign, the exercise of the king's considerable personal charm was not enough to breach the walls of Cádiz. As we shall see, much of Andalucía was brought to accept *josefino* rule, but so long as Cádiz held out, and so long too as much of the population was unable to subsist itself by normal means, there could be no peace.

5

Balls, Banquets, and Bayonets

In the previous chapter it has been shown how the new masters of Andalucía attempted to use propaganda techniques that had already been honed in the rest of occupied Spain, and indeed the grand empire as a whole, to undermine resistance to the rule of Joseph Bonaparte. This task did not just depend on propaganda, however, at least if that is defined only in terms of words and images. Such methods might secure the surrender of some garrison here or turn the coat of some administrator there, but mere words could never be enough to turn Andalucía into a stable bulwark of the Napoleonic Empire. On the contrary, with the countryside overrun with gangs of brigands, be they bandits, deserters, or stragglers from the Spanish armies, what was needed was rather its active pacification, and this in turn meant, first, that law and order had to be restored to the countryside and, second, that structures had to be put in place that would provide the local elites with a means of rallying to the empire as well as a concrete reason for doing so. Andalucía, then, was to be made anew, but however much a part of the aim here was to encourage collaboration, the overall objective was scarcely benevolent. Like any fresh conquest, Joseph's new dominions would have to play their part in supporting the Napoleonic Empire, while *el rey intruso* also coveted their resources for his own benefit, the new structures therefore also being needed to ensure that Andalucía would deliver up what was required of it. With such exploitation, however, would come the risk that pacification would be endangered, and the result, of course, was that the French faced a complex problem whose favorable resolution would require both great good fortune—abundant harvests, for example—and great subtlety. The first, of course, was not within the command of the invaders, but the application of occupation policy was, and in this respect it has to be said that they were not well served. As the French imperium had expanded, so a standard program had developed for the assimilation of each new territory, but in the end no policy is any better than its executors. In short, much would depend on the conduct of the forces charged with bringing Andalucía to heel, and yet, as we shall now see, from top to toe these were imbued with attitudes that were scarcely conducive to success.

At the head of the French chain of command in Andalucía was Jean de Dieu Soult. Born at the village of Saint Amans la Bastide on 29 March 1769, Soult was the son of a notary, but his father died when he was ten, and the family thereafter fell upon hard times, the young man eventually enlisting in the regular army as a private soldier. Quickly promoted on account of his obvious intelligence, by 1791 he was a sergeant and was therefore well placed to take advantage of the expansion of the armed forces brought about by the growing tension with Austria that ultimately led to the outbreak of the French Revolutionary Wars. Thus, awarded a commission in the National Guard, by 1794 Soult had risen to the rank of brigadier. Soon advanced to the role of divisional commander, he distinguished himself in both the Swiss campaign of 1789 and the defense of Genoa in 1800 but played no part in the rise to power of Napoleon Bonaparte: like several other officers associated with the campaign in Andalucía, indeed, he was rather an adherent of Napoleon's archrival, General Jean Moreau. Wilier perhaps than some of his fellows, however, he made no attempt to air any doubts that he may have had, and true to his policy of offering a role to anyone who would accept the new political dispensation no matter what their background, the First Consul responded in 1802 by offering him, first, a senior post in the Consular Guard, then the rank of marshal of the empire, and finally command of a corps in the Grande Armée. There followed two years of distinguished service: at Austerlitz it was Soult's corps that headed the decisive attack on the heights of Prace, while at Jena his troops were again in the thick of the action, this time delivering the massive blow that broke the Prussian left.[1]

Cantoned as he was with his corps in Prussia, Soult played no part in the campaigns of the summer of 1808 and therefore first came to the Peninsula with the reinforcements that Napoleon dispatched to avenge the defeat of Bailén in the course of the autumn. In the campaign that followed, the marshal first looked set to play a minor role in that, rather than spearheading Napoleon's triumphant march on Madrid, his troops were deployed in the central part of Old Castile to protect the emperor's communications with the French frontier. However, very soon circumstances propelled him to the forefront of the action. Thus, unbeknown to the emperor, a substantial British army had been assembling in the vicinity of Salamanca under Sir John Moore, and this suddenly made a stab at Soult's corps in an attempt to distract the attention of the victorious French and prevent them from overrunning the whole of Spain. As Moore had foreseen, this move provoked a massive response on the part of Napoleon, and it was therefore not long before the British were in full retreat for the port of La Coruña. Positioned as he was, Soult could not but be in the forefront of the pursuit, and by the middle of January 1809, he therefore found himself in occupation of the distant province of Galicia.

By now convinced that all that was required was a series of mopping-up operations, Napoleon was on his way back to France. Behind him, however, he had left a plan of campaign that was unrealistic in the extreme. Thus, at the head of no more troops than his own corps and some supporting cavalry, Soult was expected to invade Portugal from the north and occupy first Oporto and then Lisbon; still worse, meanwhile, he was supposed to achieve all this in a mere six weeks. Given that it was the depths of winter, that the roads involved were extremely poor, that the way was studded with fortresses, that a serious revolt had broken out in Galicia, and that a large Portuguese army was blocking the road to Lisbon, Soult therefore did very well to find himself storming Oporto on his fortieth birthday. Beyond that, however, he could not go: the irregular Portuguese militia known as the *ordenança* were harassing his communications, while his men were utterly exhausted. Rather than marching on the capital, the marshal therefore sat down to await developments, in the meantime becoming enmeshed in the complexities of occupation policy.

Insofar as this was concerned, Soult was not without experience. In the Revolutionary Wars, the period 1799–1802 had seen him help put down peasant risings in Switzerland and Piedmont and command an occupying force that was sent to the Neapolitan port of Taranto, while the campaigns of 1805–1807 had ended with him serving in the role of governor of East Prussia. According to his apologists, moreover, in all these activities he had been highly successful in winning the support and respect of the local elites. At all events, for all that the coming of the French had been marked by considerable brutality—Oporto had been thoroughly sacked and some hundreds of the inhabitants killed[2]—in Portugal his policy was essentially one of conciliation. Not least was this visible in his attitude toward the church. For example, the Sunday following his occupation of Braga, Soult attended High Mass in the cathedral, while in the wake of his capture of Oporto, he presented a particularly venerated local shrine with a beautifully wrought lamp and candelabra.[3] At the same time, to the fury of his men, in the aftermath of the sack of Oporto, the troops were made to open their knapsacks and disgorge all the plunder they had taken from the city (though whether any of the money and other valuables concerned was ever restored to the inhabitants is unclear).[4] This stance was not just dictated by the demands of Soult's rather isolated situation, however. A deeply ambitious man, Soult had arrived in Spain with a grievance against Napoleon in that he felt that "Duke of Dalmatia"—the title he had been awarded in 1807—was not sufficiently redolent with the glory he felt himself to deserve (he would have preferred "Duke of Austerlitz"), while he was also deeply aware that his hated rival, Joachim Murat, had in the summer of 1808 been appointed king of Naples. Exactly what happened next remains shrouded in mystery, but it at the very least seems possible that Soult saw himself as a candidate for the throne of Portugal and in consequence made a determined effort to build up a strong local power base to advance this idea. In fairness the marshal's most recent French biographer, Nicole Gotteri, insists that Soult never intended anything of the sort, her view being that, at most, Portuguese place seekers eager to ingratiate themselves with him got up petitions to this effect and paid agitators to shout "Long live King Nicholas!" under the marshal's windows. If Soult was ever afterward known as "King Nicholas" in the French army, it was therefore for no other reason than the fact that the story was taken up by disgruntled elements of his command and, via their evil offices, communicated to ever wider circles of the military.[5]

Well perhaps, though Napoleon, as we have seen, certainly thought otherwise.[6] What does seem to be the case, however, is the fact that Soult was by all accounts a deeply unpleasant individual: the very acme of greed, vanity, and opportunism, it was once said of him that he had no character except on the battlefield. After 1814, for example, he proved a political weathervane who switched his politics with each and every change of regime in France, while in the Peninsular War his lust for plundered works of art was notorious.[7] For a particularly mordant summation of his personality, we might turn to his chief aide-de-camp, Saint Chamans:

> I do not believe that it would be possible to meet a man who knew how to hide so much ability, perspicacity, and finesse in the management of affairs beneath so gross an exterior. . . . In war he loved bold enterprises, and expressed himself with great force once he had settled on a course of action. . . . That said, it was well known that he did not risk his own person too much in that respect. . . . On the contrary, one could accuse him of . . . being too careful in respect of keeping out of danger, this deficiency having grown in proportion with the great fortune that he had amassed (it is not, after all, uncommon to meet officers who do not worry about getting themselves killed when they are mere colonels . . . but later hide behind a marshal's baton).[8]

Still worse from the point of view of the unfortunate King Joseph was Soult's attitude to his Andalusian viceroyalty, the retention of which in the latter's eyes should have become the be-all and end-all of French strategy: following the fall of Badajoz in April 1812, the logical course of action would have been for Soult to evacuate the south of Spain and retire on Madrid, but he not only refused pointblank to consider such a decision but even tried to insist that the king should join him in Seville. As for the style that he affected, it was scarcely calculated to smooth the path of occupation or win over hearts and minds (it should be noted in this respect that the favorable assessment made of him as an occupation commander by such writers as Hayman and Gotteri rests entirely on the account given in Soult's own memoirs). On the contrary, the picture that emerges is one of a haughty and imperious satrap. Even in Oporto the situation had been bad enough, but in Seville it reached new heights. As Fée complained:

> As commander of the Army of the South, the marshal appeared more as the king of Andalucía than as a simple lieutenant of the emperor. No monarch ever surrounded himself with as much majesty, nor was any court ever more servile than his. As Homer said of Jupiter, he could make Olympus tremble with a movement of his head. . . . The marshal was always accompanied by an imposing guard. On Sundays these elite troops formed a corridor leading to the door of the cathedral and presented arms at his passage, while he was followed by the civil authorities and a glittering general staff. . . . Formed in the school of the emperor, meanwhile, he echoed both his gestures and his style of address.[9]

Installed in the splendor of the episcopal palace, then, Soult ran up living costs that threatened to bankrupt his Spanish subjects, while even his own subordinates were the subject of much bullying. Of this, perhaps the worst example came in October 1811, when the unfortunate General Nicolas Godinot received so brutal a dressing down at the hands of the marshal on his return to Seville following the failure of the first French attempt to take Tarifa that, as he left the building, he asked to inspect the musket of one of the sentries posted at the door and, having first calmly asked him if it was loaded, to the poor man's consternation promptly shot himself.[10]

Soult, then, was scarcely a paragon of virtue, but of his talents as an administrator there is no doubt. Thus, as even Saint

Chamans was forced to admit, "He forgot nothing, and was as much abreast of the smallest details as he was of the greatest military operations."[11] Even this could not be said about most of his subordinates, however. Setting Soult aside, the French forces in Andalucía were scarcely well commanded. Let us begin with the three corps commanders.[12] At the head of V Corps, Edouard Mortier, who began his military career as a volunteer in the National Guard in 1789, though well liked and honest, was not known for his intelligence—Napoleon, indeed, called him the least able of his marshals—while his successor, Jean-Baptiste Drouet, was universally regarded as a military nonentity who was much given to attempting to pass the responsibility for major decisions to his unfortunate subordinates. Nor, meanwhile, was I Corps's Claude Victor much better. Famously once upon a time a drummer boy in the Bourbon army, he brought little more to the command of his corps than great physical courage, even his admirers being forced to admit that he was no genius. As for Horace Sébastiani, few of the French army's senior commanders could have been a worse choice for the task that was now in hand. Born in Corsica in November 1772, he had been commissioned as an infantry officer in the army of the ancien régime in 1789, come to the attention of Napoleon during the Italian campaign, and thereafter risen rapidly. Wounded at Austerlitz, by 1806 he was a divisional commander, and already something of an expert on the Middle East—in 1802 he had headed the reconnaissance mission to Egyptian waters that had played a large part in persuading Britain to end the Peace of Amiens—in 1807 he was appointed ambassador to Turkey. Appointed to command a division in the IV Corps of Marshal François Lefebvre in 1808, he took over the corps in February 1809 following its commander's disgrace and thereafter proved competent enough as a general, as witness his defeat of Francisco Javier Venegas at Almonacid (there are, however, suggestions that he was very careless: Auguste de Marmont, for example, paints a picture of a somewhat lackadaisical figure who spent his time reading poetry rather than attending to the details of his command). If his qualities as a commander are disputed, however, his personal qualities are another story. An extremely small man, Sébastiani appears to have been extremely conscious of this fact—Talleyrand claims that he was forever walking on tiptoe in an attempt to make up for his want of stature—and was, in general, noted for his vanity, pride, and ambition. Thus, on the one hand, Sebastiani was inclined to adopt a somewhat Bohemian style, wearing his black hair in flowing curls and habitually affecting an old brown overcoat, and fancy himself as an intellectual, being wont to hold forth in a somewhat ponderous style and dominate the conversation (the ever-catty Talleyrand later remarked that nothing could be more pleasant than to pass time with someone who was happy to talk nonstop and let everybody else catch up on a little rest). On the other, meanwhile, he was bitterly jealous of his fellow officers and extremely greedy. Never had anyone, so one observer said, so justified what had always been said of the arrogance of *parvenus,* while even Napoleon complained of the general's venality. Needless to say, then, as witness the description given by Mendoza, his new subjects were decidedly unimpressed:

> Sébastiani was a small man of no very fine aspect, among other reasons because the natural liveliness that marked . . . his face was contradicted by the air of sternness and gravity that he affected in order to intimidate those around him, the general effect being quite ridiculous. His habits and language were extremely gross, while it made no difference who he was talking to: fine lady or gentleman of rank, his conversation was laced with indecent remarks and obscene words of all sorts, and none of them to the point, at that. His thinking was theatrical, quixotic even, and everything that he set his hand to was done with a certain swagger. As for what he valued, the things he set most store on were really and truly despicable: it was almost as if he were some despot in Asia or Africa. . . . He was generally held to be an intellectual, but if the things he wrote are anything to go by, his talents and knowledge alike were pretty limited. On top of all this, Sébastiani was greedy and covetous—an out-and-out thief indeed—while he possessed the vices of womanizing and gambling to a truly heroic degree.[13]

Unfortunately, such a man was likely to attract the services of officers who were men of the same stamp: his chief of staff, the

Comte de Bouillé, openly boasted that his only goal as a soldier was to build up as large a personal fortune as possible, while his aides-de-camp included the notoriously brutal Jean-Baptiste Berton, a sometime pupil of the military school of Brienne and fanatical supporter of Napoleon who had entered the army as a sublieutenant in 1792 and was to die on the scaffold in 1822 for his part in an abortive rebellion against Louis XVIII, and an officer of an extremely cruel disposition named Bellangé who, while plausible enough, was by all accounts an errant coward (to make matters worse, he had been born and raised in Marbella and was therefore full of resentment at the manner in which the French community in Málaga had been treated in 1808).[14]

Of the various subordinate generals who fought in Andalucía, relatively little is recorded, but few of them stand out as figures of much political sophistication or finesse. In I Corps, for example, a "volunteer of 1792," François Ruffin, was renowned as both a *bon viveur* and the most handsome man in the French army, and Jean Leval, an ex-ranker who had enlisted in the Bourbon army in 1779, as a rough, crude fighting soldier possessed of few social graces and less intellect. Equally, in V Corps François Werlé, Honoré Gazan, and Jean-Baptiste Girard—the first two sometime privates in the Bourbon army and the last a man conscripted in 1793 who was not even commissioned until 1796—all had the reputation of being gallant officers (Girard, indeed, was to be hit three times at Lützen and fall mortally wounded at Leipzig), but little more. The chief of the artillery, Alexandre Sénarmont, was a highly skilled gunner and an efficient staff officer but had never served in a political capacity, while also a cut above the rest was the head of King Joseph's reserve, Jean Dessolles, an officer of some intellectual pretension who had enlisted as a volunteer in 1791 but had fallen out of favor with Napoleon as an associate of Moreau and, in consequence, been left without employment for most of the period leading up to the Peninsular War (hence too the fact that he was even then only given command of a division in the relatively small force assigned to the direct command of King Joseph). As for the commanders of the two cavalry divisions, they too did not inspire much confidence. Edouard Milhaud, the one senior commander who had some experiences in the politics of occupation—he had served as governor of Liguria in 1803—was a sometime *montagnard* who had begun his military career as a private in the marines and then gained a commission in the National Guard before serving as a deputy in the Convention and being promoted to the rank of general for his services in the coup of 18 Brumaire; though brave enough as a soldier—he had fought well at both Austerlitz and Eylau—his chief fame was as a womanizer. As for Marie-Victor Latour Maubourg, while he was a somewhat more attractive figure than many of his colleagues—a titled aristocrat and erstwhile émigré, he was famed for his courage and personal integrity—he had no more political experience than they did and had only risen to the rank of divisional commander in 1808. With other figures who rose to prominence in the course of the occupation, such as Briche, Barrois, Conroux, Maransin, Godinot (yet another general who had begun his career as a private in the Bourbon army, though also one of the few who had served as a military governor in Spain), Soult (the brother of the marshal), and Claparède, men of even less seniority and experience and in one or two instances positively noxious—Claparède, for example, had the reputation of being a vain and avaricious bully—Soult could scarcely be said to have been supported by a staff of skilled technicians.[15]

If the generals who fought in Andalucía were not the best that Napoleonic France had to offer, they were also less than happy in their destiny. Whether it was on account of his near total lack of serious military experience or of his attempts to win over the Spaniards by kindness, King Joseph was universally despised, while matters were not helped by the sense that the Peninsula very much represented a "hardship posting." Far from the emperor's eye and embroiled in a contest that offered few chances for glory and had, in any case, by 1810 receded into the corners of the imperial consciousness, the Peninsular commanders knew that they could not look to their service against the Spaniards and Portuguese as a source of advancement (in this they were quite right: all the Armée d'Espagne's smashing victories produced just one marshal's baton, namely that of Louis Gabriel Suchet). Still worse, the presence in Spain of partisans of Moreau such as Jourdan and Dessolles could not but suggest that service beyond the Pyrenees carried with it the taint of disgrace. Small wonder, then, that it was rumored in the army that many generals were constantly seeking to anger King Joseph in the hope of being relieved of their command, and small wonder too that a lust for plunder should have come to occupy an even greater place in their thinking than might otherwise have been the case. As Albert de Rocca, a Swiss serving as a captain in the Second Hussars wrote, "This Spanish war was ruining France without even interesting the military honor of the nation."[16]

In charge of the campaign in Andalucía, then, was a team that was scarcely the most apposite for the task at hand. In the first place, so led, an army could not but suffer in terms of its discipline and motivation. To quote Fée once more:

> The fertility . . . of Andalucía is a real marvel. Its harvests are abundant and more than surpass the needs of the population. . . . How is it possible, then, that famine could have broken out in a country typified rather by abundance? Why did Andalucía, a region that ordinarily exports so much grain, find it impossible to nourish an increase in population that amounted to a mere 60,000 men . . . spread out over an area of some 2,000 square leagues? Let us have the courage to say that these 60,000 men were great gourmands and that the amount of food they wasted was without equal. Of all the accusations that can be made against Marshal Soult, the least answerable are those that concern his administration: if he had kept a closer eye on the management and consumption of our stocks of grain, we would have enjoyed a state of abundance, while people and army alike would have been spared much trouble. As it was, discipline was not maintained properly: the soldiers wanted only comfort and the officers only riches. As everyone wanted indulgence on their own account, they naturally had to show it to everyone else, and this same indulgence was prejudicial to the true interests of the army.[17]

Even in terms of military talent, the French command was distinctly wanting, while there were also problems on the political front: of the twenty-one senior officers mentioned in the above paragraphs, at least sixteen had either enlisted in the Bourbon army as privates prior to 1789 or entered the military via the National Guard, the volunteers of 1791 or 1792 or the conscripts of 1793.[18] As such, they were truly soldiers of the Revolution and carried with them the violent anti-clericalism that was always the political touchstone of such men in the army of the Grand Empire as the only way open to them of keeping in touch with the ideals of their youth. To innate political prejudice, meanwhile, was added the experience of up to two years' fighting in Spain and Portugal in a war that the French army was convinced was being whipped up by a Roman Catholic Church that was determined to maintain its power and privileges in the face of French-inspired reform and was in large part responsible for the poverty and backwardness in whose midst they found themselves. To quote Bigarré: "The priests . . . knew that with a Bourbon it would always be easy to govern the kingdom to their advantage, whereas with a Bonaparte on the throne they would not be able to be anything other than simple ministers of the gospel. They therefore did everything possible to prevent the people from becoming attached to the new king. In the pulpit and the confessional alike, they denounced him as an atheist and an emissary of Satan."[19]

The army's contempt was not just restricted to the church, however. If the people of Spain, poor and oppressed as they were, were so susceptible to the manipulation of the very church that kept them in subjugation that they were ready to risk annihilation in a suicidal war in its defense, then it must inevitably follow that they were debased beyond hope of redemption. The result, needless to say, was that cultural prejudices from the period prior to 1808 were both confirmed and reinforced. As to what these earlier prejudices were, we have only once more to repair to the work of some of the observers who we have already cited. Perhaps the best example here is the diplomat Bourgoing. In his work, indeed, the accusations come thick and fast, the Spaniard being portrayed as a figure worthy of nothing but contempt. If Bourgoing acquitted him (as we have seen) of the charge of idleness, a characteristic that he pointed out was completely absent in those areas of the country marked by reasonable levels of economic development, in other respects he was less forgiving. Thus: "The

Spanish nation, with some almost modern exceptions, is addicted to religious mummery and is justly accused of superstition. It may even be pronounced . . . that this illegitimate sister of religion has been to the present day either on the throne or very near it. . . . There are . . . several [persons] who have derived from education, their own reflections and travel, very sound ideas of religion, . . . but in the classes where education is neglected (and these are very numerous), where little communication with their betters and few means of enlightening themselves are to be had, superstition and fanaticism are still carried to a degree seldom found in Flanders and Bavaria."[20] To support these views, Bourgoing cited a long list of local traditions—for example, feeding animals with corn blessed by the priest on the feast of St Anthony as a protection against sickness or burying the dead in monastic habits—not to mention the manner in which each and every representative of the church was treated with the most exaggerated veneration and respect, as witness the practice of gentlemen offering a place in their coaches to any priest they encountered carrying the Blessed Sacrament.[21]

Hatred of Roman Catholicism, meanwhile, was further intensified by utterly erroneous ideas of the Inquisition. Centuries before, this had indeed been a force to be reckoned with, but by the early nineteenth century, it was little more than a bureau of censorship whose victims—and none of them mortal—could be numbered on the fingers of one hand. As they advanced across Spain, the French were surprised to find jails encumbered with large numbers of prisoners, and rather than seeing in the latter the natural products of a judicial system that was notoriously protracted in its deliberations, they convinced themselves that the unfortunate inmates were not common criminals but rather victims of clerical tyranny. Such, at least, is the impression conveyed in many memoirs. Here, for example, are the words of a gunner serving in I Corps named Manière: "We opened the prisons of the Inquisition at Burgos, Valladolid, . . . Madrid, Toledo, . . . and many other places. Always it was the same thing: underground cells with poor unfortunates chained up round the middle . . . with no other bed than a stone bench covered with damp straw. Moreover, many of these cells had no light at all, while those that did got the little they enjoyed from a narrow slit that was cut down on a slant from ground level and no more a few inches wide. . . . Almost all the prisoners that we freed had manacles on their feet."[22]

Spain, then, was "the birthplace of mummery and the land of fanaticism and superstition," and if any further proof was needed in this respect it was that, while happy enough to conform with its outward manifestations, Spaniards did not show the slightest sign of living according to the precepts of religious faith.[23] From this idea there flowed yet more invective. Spaniards were, it seems, habitually extremely proud and therefore much given to violence: murders, and especially stabbings, were common, this being something that was much facilitated by the practice of wearing long brown cloaks (see below), while feuds were sometimes resolved by means of ritualized gang battles called *rondallas* or *pedradas.* Yet in none of this was there any honor. As Bourgoing lamented, "The Spaniard of the sixteenth century has disappeared, but his mask remains."[24] Thus, the same long brown cloaks not only physically covered up Spanish daggers but also allowed their owners to approach their victims without the latter knowing that they were in any danger, while the honest and manly duel was by contrast all but unknown, Spanish men being so deaf to the demands of honor that they were quite content to let themselves be cuckolded by all and sundry: "There is no country in Europe that can boast of so few jealous husbands. The women, who were formerly deprived of all intercourse, who could hardly be seen through the grates of their windows, . . . now enjoy perfect liberty. Their veils, the only remains of their ancient slavery, . . . now serve no other purpose than . . . to render them more attractive. . . . Coquetry has made [of them] one of its most seductive items of dress, and, in favoring half-concealment, has indirectly encouraged . . . stolen glances of love. . . . Conquests are become less cruel and dilatory; the husbands are become more tractable, the women more accessible."[25]

That much of this was utter rubbish is beside the point. What matters is that Spaniards were perceived as being cowardly, this point naturally being reemphasized in the French mind, firstly, by the manner in which almost every Spanish army that they had met in fair fight had ended up by fleeing in disorder, and secondly, by *la guerrilla.* This last phenomenon caused particular outrage.

To fight in such a fashion was by very definition to refuse to fight by the rules, indeed, to refuse to fight at all except in circumstances when victory was guaranteed by superiority of numbers, and the fact that the *partidas* invariably decamped in much haste whenever such factors did not pertain bred frustration and with it contempt. Such contempt, meanwhile, could not but be swelled by the fact that many of the victims of the irregulars were comparatively helpless—couriers traveling alone, isolated sentries, or small guard posts. Killing such men was perceived not as waging war, but rather murder—a word that is frequently used is "assassination"—while the perception that the issue was one of crime was strengthened by the belief (not entirely unmerited) that the insurgents were motivated by nothing other than a desire for booty. For soldiers formed in the aggressively masculine culture of Napoleonic France, with its stress on courage, glory, and manliness, such behavior was offensive in the extreme, and it is scarcely surprising that the response should have been one of disgust.[26]

Inextricably linked with the guerrilla war was the issue of cruelty. Long regarded as central to the Spanish character (a tendency in which images of the Inquisition mingled inextricably with those of the bullfight), this characteristic now appeared to have been called to life in its starkest form. Thus, the French army was rife with tales of the horrible fate likely to befall any man who fell into the hands of the Spaniards in general, and the irregular bands in particular, Fée, for example, describing how he was cast down in the course of his journey to Madrid as a new recruit to the forces of occupation by the horror stories with which he was regaled by a number of his fellow travelers who had already served a term in Spain.[27] As we have already seen, how far these stories were true is a moot point. Most of the French soldiers who fell prisoner to Spanish regular troops could rest assured that their lives would be respected, while even the more irregular combatants did not kill all the men they took alive (from the very beginning of the war bounties were paid for every enemy soldier who was handed over to the authorities). Even when prisoners were murdered, moreover, it is unlikely that any of them ever suffered the most extreme tortures that were staples of army rumor: in the famine-ravaged Spain of the Peninsular War, for example, what band of peasants would have had sufficient oil to boil prisoners alive? Yet many atrocities had certainly taken place, and some of the very worst along the very high road along which the French army tramped as it headed for Andalucía in January 1810. Thus, as the army of General Dupont had marched on Córdoba in 1808, it had established field hospitals and supply depots in such towns as Manzanares, Santa Cruz de Mudela, and *Alcázar* de San Juan. Left unprotected by French troops, these had then been fallen upon by bands of insurgents in the wake of the Spanish uprising, and there seems little doubt that the men caught in them had been hacked to pieces without mercy in circumstances that may well have amounted to a veritable frenzy of violence, while some may conceivably have been tortured.[28] Such scenes were never repeated with quite the same intensity, but there is no doubt that, given that torture was an integral part of Spanish banditry, isolated French soldiers who were taken captive by bands of brigands on occasion suffered fates that were quite appalling.[29] And that this was so, many of the troops who marched into Andalucía had witnessed with their own eyes. A sergeant in the 103rd Line, François Lavaux had been in Spain since November 1808 and fought in Aragón and Old Castile: "The brigands attacked us on a number of occasions, but they could never achieve anything. However, whenever they caught one of our men, they made a martyr of him, cutting out his tongue and his eyes, and . . . thrusting his legs into a fire right up to his very midriff."[30]

If Spain, in general, was not a place where the traveler could be expected to be edified by the populace, this was even more true of Andalucía, a region viewed as one in which everything combined to emphasize national characteristics that were on view everywhere. In this respect, we can turn from the views of Bourgoing to those of the equally scathing Alexandre de Laborde. Thus:

> The Andalusians are the Gascons of Spain. . . . They speak a great deal, and particularly of themselves, of their merit, their wealth, or of the valuable or pleasing things which they possess. They have a natural propensity to boasting: their conversation is full of it; the turn of their phrases, their air, their manners, their gestures, their customs carry the stamp of it. . . . Their

> country is a country of boasters, who distinguish themselves from others by their dress; who speak in a high and menacing tone, who bully when they are feared, who fawn when they fail to inspire terror, who are always dangerous when they can strike without risk; in a word of that kind of coxcombs known by the appellation of *majos*.[31]

If Spanish pride, arrogance, and cowardice were more marked among the men of Andalucía, meanwhile, among the women of that region what was to be looked for was heightened sexuality: "A free air, an easy turn, a noble mien, a lively, attracting, animated eye, an arch and pleasing smile, a slender shape, neatness about the feet, a light and elegant dress, various graces, an harmonious voice, a natural softness, and expressive gestures are the attributes of [the women of Andalucía], as dangerous as they are lovely. Skilled in the art of seducing, they are acquainted with all the means of gaining their aim; they use it with address and generally successfully; free in their expressions, and freer still in their behaviour, they allure, they attack, they invite, and it is very difficult to resist them."[32]

Such, then, were the prejudices with which the French entered Andalucía, and once across the Sierra Morena, these were reinforced still further. In this bastion of Spanish Catholicism, for example, it somehow seemed appropriate that the conditions found in the supposed prisons of the Inquisition were even worse than they were elsewhere. At Puerto de Santa María, Manière remembered, the vents that were their dungeons' only source of light "opened onto a muddy courtyard where the jailer was keeping three fat black pigs," the result being that the prisoners were "forced to breathe the most filthy air day and night"; still worse, "in one cell there was a dead body."[33] Something else that struck many observers was the sheer number of ecclesiastics in the streets, and there were those who were not slow to link this with the sexual misconduct associated with Andalucía's women: "The clergy have the people under their thumb. They lay down laws as they please, and, for good or ill, their dictates have to be obeyed. Yet nothing is more odious than the rules that they impose, and dare to claim have come directly from God, who, one is assured, wants things thus. Every priest has a retinue of three or four women who administer to his pleasure without their husbands being able to say a word in protest. If a priest chances to visit one of his concubines, he leaves his shoes or sandals at the door as a warning for the husband; should he come back . . . he is forbidden to enter the house on pain of being brought before the Inquisition."[34]

Here, of course, memory is mingled with imagination, but there is little doubt that the presence of so many clergy struck a jarring note. Nor, on close inspection, were the newcomers particularly impressed with their physical surroundings. A member of Dupont's headquarters staff, Just Roy was one of the many officers captured after Bailén who managed to escape from the Spaniards in a famous episode that we shall detail shortly: "There is a Spanish proverb that says, 'He who has not seen Seville has never seen a marvel.' If Seville is a marvel, then there cannot be many about. The town is large but badly built, while its streets are uneven, twisting, and very narrow. . . . As for the houses, only half are inhabited, the rest having been abandoned."[35] Among Roy's companions, meanwhile, was a pharmacist from Avignon named Sébastien Blaze: "Between the ramparts and the town itself, one treads on a thick carpet of human waste . . . while the banks of the river are covered with manure that has been dumped there to allow the waters to carry it away: apparently, the peasant believes the land to be so fertile . . . that he disdains to make use of this precious resource."[36] Finally, still another disappointed visitor was Hippolyte d'Espinchal, a captain in the Second Regiment of Hussars who arrived with a convoy that was dispatched from Madrid in the spring of 1812: "As gracious as it is famous, [Córdoba] was beloved of the Moors and at each step one comes across the memory of their past glories. Once upon a time some 300,000 strong, the population is now reduced to a mere 15,000, and, where the arts and sciences once flourished, there are now no more than a few skeletal schools that are barely frequented by the ignorant and lazy populace, a populace, what is more, that has no idea that within its walls were born the two Senecas, Lucan, and various other geniuses of this order."[37] With Seville, meanwhile, D'Espinchal was scarcely better pleased. To quote a letter that he wrote to his father on 24 April 1812:

> I cannot yet give you many details of this great city. . . . However, in the three days I have been here, I have not lost time in exploring it, and shall prove it to you by imparting my first impressions. An old Moorish settlement that Spanish pride would have as being without equal, Seville is certainly beautiful enough, but, far from meriting such excessive claims, the only things that really mark it out are its sometime status as a seat of learning, the survival of a few impressive buildings and monuments, its fortunate situation on the left bank of the River Guadalquivir, and its relative proximity to the sea. . . . On wandering around this great city, one is saddened to see nothing but streets that are very narrow, tortuous, and badly paved; meanwhile, the upper stories of the houses lean toward one another so much that at the top a plank of a mere six or seven feet in length could easily make a bridge between them. The result is that both cleanliness and the fresh air that is one of the first needs of the inhabitants is lacking, although the French have made a start on remedying the grave threat to public health that this presents by tearing down various vast convents and turning them into squares.[38]

We here touch upon yet another issue that quickly soured the French in respect of Andalucía. Thus, under the Moors it was common knowledge that Andalucía had been a hub of agriculture and industry, but all that was on view was decay. If this was so of the once-great city of Córdoba, it was also true of the countryside. Thus, save for the two or three areas that had been colonized by Olavide's settlers—"The countryside through which one passes on leaving . . . the beautiful village of La Carlota . . . is, thanks to the activity of the colonists who settled there, one of a sumptuous richness. . . . One travels through immense fields of corn; vineyards bordered with immense aloe hedges; verdant orchards planted with fruit trees of every sort stretching away into the distance"[39]—it seemed that all one saw was waste: "Carmona . . . is placed in the most fortunate of positions in the midst of a great plain that could be the granary of Andalucía if the inhabitants would reform their lazy ways and follow the example of the German colonists. As it is, one sees only a quarter of these fertile lands under cultivation, all the rest serving as nothing more than a pasture for numerous flocks of sheep and goats that feed here and there on patches of weed."[40]

If the civilization of the Moors had been squandered by Spanish sloth and incompetence, two themes survived intact. First of all, there was the near universal belief that Andalucía was a Hispanic Garden of Eden possessed of ground that was so rich and fertile that crops sprung all but unbidden from the ground. "Next to Italy," wrote Joseph's aide-de-camp, Clermont-Tonnerre, "Andalucía is the country most favored by nature. Its sky is as clear as that of Naples, while its fields enjoy a fertility that is surpassed by those of anywhere else in the world. Tropical plants of all sorts flourish there . . . while such crops as tobacco, coffee, and sugar . . . can be introduced with every species of advantage."[41] So ingrained were these ideas, meanwhile, that they were even to be found among the soldiery. Here, for example, is François Lavaux: "To put it in a single line, Andalucía is the wine cellar and granary of Spain. . . . The inhabitants hardly work at all. If they but put in two days a week, they have quite enough to live on. Indeed, the land produces four times more than they could ever need to eat."[42] From such ideas—ideas that, as we have seen, were quite erroneous—there followed consequences that were unfortunate to say the least: in brief, as Andalucía's resources in terms of food production were considered near boundless, pleas for mercy in the face of French requisitioning were unlikely to be entertained even by commanders possessing real humanity.

Andalucía, then, was fecund, but at the same time it was African. Even north of the Sierra Morena, various Frenchmen affected to see African traits in the populace. Here, for example, is Auguste Thirion, a volunteer in the Twenty-Second Dragoons who had served under Soult in the campaigns of La Coruña and Oporto:

> Spain's inclusion in Europe is an error of geography. In her blood, in her customs, in her language, in her lifestyle, and in her manner of fighting, she is African. Her history has been involved with that of Africa for far too long for the constant transfusions of people and habits that were the consequence

> not to have produced such a result: the Carthaginians came to Spain from Africa; the Vandals went to Africa and then returned to Spain; the Moors settled down there for 700 years. . . . If the Spaniard was but to worship Mahommed, indeed, he would be the perfect African; it is therefore only religion that has kept him a European. Consumed by the same fires, given over to the same reserve, the same sobriety, the same silence; as ferocious as he is generous; hospitable and yet implacable in his enmity; naturally lazy and yet indefatigable, no sooner he has been aroused, the Spaniard recalls the Arab devoured by the sun who on the one hand engages in the most bloody banditry and on the other exercises the most generous hospitality, and in this fashion unites in his person the extremes of both barbarity and humanity. What completes the picture, meanwhile, is the similarities in the way they fight. The West associates military honor with precise maneuvers, with impregnable lines, with maintaining an imperturbable front in the presence of the enemy. Indeed, the soldier of the West knows no other direction to march in but forward, and, having reached his assigned position, is forbidden to retire. The soldier of the East, of Africa, of Spain, has long since freed himself from such formalism: for him, there are no such things as lines. Instead, fighting consists in movement, while winning consists of destroying the enemy by any means available. As for flight, this is but a means of self-preservation or a way of leading the enemy into an ambush. At all events, victory is not, as in the West, associated with a given day or a given battlefield. . . . The ideas of glory and honor that are the very soul of the warriors of the West are in the East and South replaced by one concern and one concern only: the destruction of the enemy as the sole object of war.[43]

If comparisons with Africa sprang to the minds of French soldiers who only fought in the north of Spain, how much more likely with those whose campaigns were fought out in the shadow of the Giralda? Over and over again, then, one comes across references to the idea of being on a different continent. Here, for example, is Miot de Melito: "Our journey from Córdoba to Ecija and Carmona . . . was extremely agreeable. New types of vegetation met our gaze, . . . the roads were lined with hedges of prickly-pear and aloes, and from time to time date-palms rose up into the sky. . . . Everything suggested, in fact, that we had reached the extremities of Europe and were approaching Africa."[44] Here D'Espinchal: "Carmona still offers the aspect of a Moorish town, whether it is in the construction of its houses or the bizarre mixture that characterizes the customs and dress of its inhabitants. For example, the women sit on cushions of plaited rushes and swathe their figures in long lengths of cloth that cover everything except their eyes. . . . The houses of Seville are almost all Moorish in construction: they are centered round a small courtyard paved with large slabs of flat stone in the middle of which stands a small tank of water garlanded with plants and shaded by orange trees or cypresses; this refreshes the air, while the walls are also hidden with trellises laden with grapes or citrus fruits."[45] And, finally, here Rocca: "In Andalucía, still more than in any other province in the Peninsula, one meets with traces and monuments of the Arabs at every step. . . . In some convents . . . where the ancient manners are transmitted without alteration, the nuns sit still like the Turks without knowing that they derive the custom from the enemies of the Christian faith. The *mantilla,* a sort of large woolen veil commonly worn by the lower class of women in Andalucía, and which sometimes covers their entire face except their eyes, seems to have originated in the large scarf in which the eastern women wrap themselves when they go out."[46]

Most dramatic of all the influences that began to operate on the French forces after their passage of the Sierra Morena, however, was the confirmation that was received of Spanish cruelty. In the wake of the Battle of Bailén, nearly 20,000 French troops had gone into captivity. Already the repatriation of a few senior officers had ensured that stories were circulating of atrocities and ill treatment, but now the truth of the situation was made all too clear. With Andalucía threatened by invasion, the Spaniards had transferred the prisoners to a series of hulks in the bay of Cádiz, the result being a dramatic decline in their situation: food was limited and of poor quality, while overcrowding was extreme. That said, the prisoners were at least afforded a grandstand view of the corps of Marshal Victor when it arrived on the opposite shore, while they also suddenly found themselves in a situation in which escape was at least a serious possibility. And escape some did, and in dramatic fashion at that. While a few strong swimmers simply dived overboard and struck out for the shore, an officer of the Sailors of the Guard named Grivel and a group of equally intrepid compatriots managed to seize one of the launches that delivered the prisoners' rations and pilot it to safety. Nor was this an end to it. On 6 March a great hurricane struck the bay of Cádiz, and it was noted among the prisoners that the many vessels that were torn from their moorings ended up beached at various points on the coast of the mainland. On at least two ships, then—the *Castilla la Vieja* (a hulk that had entirely been given over to officers) and the *Argonaute*—plots were hatched to put this circumstance to good use. On both the *Castilla la Vieja* and the *Argonaute* these came to fruition. When a storm blew up on the night of 15 May, the inmates of the former turned on their guard and then let slip the ship's moorings. Eventually working out what was afoot, a number of Spanish gunboats gave chase, but the prisoners fought off the various attempts that were made to board their vessel with the aid of such few muskets as they had seized from their guards, not to mention the large number of cannonballs that had been employed as ballast, and the ship at length ran aground close enough to the shore for some 600 men to scramble to safety. On 25 May, meanwhile, the prisoners on board the *Argonaute* tried the same trick, but this time things went badly wrong: the ship ran aground some way out in the bay and was then pounded to pieces by a storm of fire that left few survivors, the only men who got away having been picked up by launches sent out from the shore. In itself, of course, all this was grist to the mill: the image of helpless prisoners being cut down by Allied cannon as they struggled in the water or burning to death in the blazing remains of their prisons was but one more proof of Spanish cruelty, while the stories—not just of life on the hulks but also of a consistent pattern of mistreatment stretching back to Bailén—that such men as Blaze, Roy, and Grivel spread among their compatriots caused universal horror and revulsion.[47]

It was not, of course, just general images of Spain or revulsion at particular instances of that nation's supposed character that contributed to the mentality of the men who marched into Andalucía. On the contrary, the vast majority of them being veteran soldiers who had served in the army for at least two years, if not many more, the French were also products of a long process of indoctrination and acculturalization that was designed to produce a particular type of army.[48] This was, of course, as old as France's military—exactly the same sort of phenomenon had been visible under the Bourbons—but with the coming of the Revolution, there had been a significant change in its direction. No longer, then, were soldiers conditioned to be the loyal servants of an absolute monarch. Fearful of the very idea of a regular army, the leaders of the Revolution had sought to subordinate it to new political norms. In brief, the military were no longer to be a separate corporation inspired above all by the hope of reward in the form of promotion and decorations, but rather an extension of the nation that was motivated to fight by a desire to uphold the common good. Whether this ideal was ever achieved is highly debatable, but exist it certainly did. This, however, was the case only for a relatively short time. With the fall of Robespierre and the coming of the Thermidorian reaction, the conscription introduced to meet the crisis of 1793 was abandoned, and the army increasingly once again became a professional force that was more and more distant—in many cases quite literally—from its parent society. Thanks to the Loi Jourdan, the ballot was reintroduced on an annual basis in 1799, but up till at least 1808 and possibly as late as 1812, neither the flow of conscripts nor the losses suffered by the army were great enough to swamp the cadre of veterans, whose continued presence constituted perhaps the greatest factor in Napoleon's victories. To put it another way, indeed, rather than the army being civilianized by conscription, as Robespierre and his fellows had hoped, the boot was rather on the other foot in that the conscripts were militarized by the army.[49]

But it is not really the soldiery that matters here. The tone of the army—its collective attitudes and habits—was set not by the conscripts, but rather by the officers, and insofar as these last were concerned, one can safely say that by 1810, the ideas of 1793–94 were long since dead. Among at least some of the men who wore the epaulette, as army slang put it, there can sometimes be observed a more-or-less sincere attempt to persuade themselves that they were still fighting for the ideals of the Revolution—that Napoleon indeed was but the Revolution personified. As it happened, such neo-Jacobinism was hardly helpful in terms of the war in Spain, but in reality it was little more than an irrelevance. As the American historian John Lynn put it in a seminal conference paper, the "army of virtue" of 1792 became an "army of honour."[50] In brief, encouraged to think in this matter by an entirely new set of cultural norms, soldiers were no longer fighting for their parent society, but rather for themselves, what governed them being concern not for the good of the nation, but rather for their own standing and personal fortune. At the heart of this issue was the question of glory. Associated with the pomp and grandeur of the army, whether this came in the form of some of gaudiest uniforms in military history, the constant reviews and parades that were so much a hallmark of the regime, or the award of the coveted Legion of Honor, officers were enabled to stand tall in the eyes of their fellow citizens, while by pursuing glory on the battlefield, officers knew that they could advance in the imperial service and secure the patronage of the emperor. It was not, however, just a case of working their way up the ranks. Thus, even the Legion of Honor brought with it a generous pension, while also on offer were substantial landed estates—the so-called *donations*—and numerous titles of nobility. Given that landed estates and titles alike were likely to pertain not to metropolitan France, but to more-or-less far-flung corners of the empire—Soult, after all, was Duke of Dalmatia—the implication was abundantly clear: the grand empire was nothing but a gigantic spoils system that was to be plundered for all it was worth. Concern for military efficiency—the need to ensure that units remained under arms and in good order—ensured that the idea was never rendered wholly explicit, but exist it did and that a fortiori. Nowhere is this clearer than in the many songs that were written by adherents of the regime and that made use of an integral part of the campaign of militarization referred to above. One still hears echoes of 1793–94, to be sure—indeed, many of the songs sung by Napoleon's soldiers were the same as the ones sung by those of the Committee of Public Safety—but there were many newer offerings that stressed the primacy of glory and, with it, all the personal advantages that this would bring, including, not least, the physical conquest, or so it was suggested, of unlimited numbers of beautiful women.[51]

One last factor to consider in this discussion is the past experience of the French army in respect of counterinsurgency operations and, alongside this, the general attitude that prevailed in its ranks with respect to the participation of the populace in military operations. Insofar as this last was concerned, the basic intellectual framework had been laid down under the ancien régime. Thus, logistical concerns, fear of social unrest, and perhaps a realization that small professional armies were simply not strong enough to overawe countries whose populations were up in arms had produced a set of principles that laid great stress on the need for the people to take no part in warfare.[52] So long as the latter confined itself to the pursuit of agriculture and industry and obeyed the dictates of whichever army happened to be in occupation of its homes, the theory was that it had nothing to fear, indeed, that its lives and property would be respected. However, should the populace take up arms, then matters would be very different: entire towns and villages might be burned and their inhabitants put to the sword while, even when matters were not pursued to such extremes, such rebels who were captured alive could expect nothing better than the noose or the firing squad.[53]

French Revolution or no French Revolution, these principles survived after 1789. The people might have invaded politics, but they could not be allowed to invade warfare. If the revolt in the Vendée was put down with exceptional brutality, then, it was not just because the rebels threatened the rule of the Committee of Public Safety but also because they represented a specter that was far more terrifying than mere counterrevolution.[54] For just the same reason, albeit on a much smaller scale, Napoleon responded with exactly the same ferocity when he was confronted by popular insurrection in the Italian city of Pavia in May 1796: "The French troops were given license to sack the town, . . . courts-martial were set up, various ringleaders were shot, and hostages were taken."[55] The story of what happened in Pavia itself has often been exaggerated, but possibly because as peasants, their inhabitants occupied a lower rung in terms of French estimation than town dwellers, a number of villages in the surrounding region suffered much more seriously. At the same time, far worse was to come. Three months after his occupation of Cairo in July 1798, Napoleon was faced by a major popular insurrection in the city. From the very beginning he had made clear to his subordinates that the populace were to be kept down by means of terror, and several villages whose inhabitants were suspected of killing French soldiers had already been razed to the ground. Confronted by rebels who were not just civilians but also Muslims and non-Europeans, the occupying forces responded in a fashion that was all too predictable: having first been bombarded by artillery, the city was taken by assault and subjected to what was probably the worst single atrocity ever committed by a French army in the entire Revolutionary and Napoleonic epoch: as many as 3,000 people were killed on the spot and perhaps another 300 others executed afterward.[56]

The coming of the empire did nothing to quench the capacity of the regime to wreak violence on restive populations. When Calabria rose in revolt following French occupation in January 1806, for example, a pattern of counterinsurgency operations was established that was to form a model for those employed in southern Spain (where the pattern of resistance was in fact very similar). Operating from a network of fortified outposts, French columns scoured the countryside, sacking and burning any villages suspected of harboring insurgents, while prisoners were regularly hanged or shot and the populace coerced into organizing Spanish-style civic guards. Backing up this policy, meanwhile, was an attitude of iron resolution: what finally killed the insurrection—almost literally—was the decision of the then French commander, General Charles Manhes, to order the execution of anyone caught carrying food or wine beyond the confines of their hometowns or villages. Nor, moreover, did it seem that such methods were that counterproductive: by 1810 the insurrection was on its knees, and it is probable that it would have collapsed far earlier had it not been given an untimely boost by the decision of Joachim Murat as king of Naples to introduce conscription in the spring of 1809.[57]

One way or another, then, the forces of occupation were led into a policy that was characterized almost entirely by violence and repression. Yet this, of course, was counterproductive in the extreme. In 1811 a French staff officer named Raymond de Fézensac was sent to Catalonia to write a report on the situation there. His comments, however, are just as applicable—indeed, still more applicable[58]—to Andalucía as they are to that province:

> One can say that Catalonia is in a state of permanent insurrection. We are only masters of the places that we occupy, and can go nowhere except with escorts that often have to be very numerous. . . . The English appear without cease on the coast in order to protect the insurgents. . . . Communications within the province are interrupted. . . . Such a state of affairs leaves . . . little hope of restoring order. To overcome so many obstacles it would be necessary to employ a numerous army that is perfectly disciplined and commanded by experienced generals who are dedicated to the public good Above all, the commander in chief of the army would have to be someone of irreproachable probity who could show the Spaniards indulgence without at the same time being feeble, who could show the Spaniards firmness without at the same time being harsh. The army would also have to be paid in full with money sent from France . . . and the Spaniards shown that we consider them, that they are esteemed and honored, [and] that we are interested in their well-being. In this fashion, decency might obtain what rigor has only served greatly to postpone, and time cure wounds that could not be deeper or more gangrenous.[59]

Fézensac of course was quite right, but unfortunately for the cause of Napoleon, the army that garrisoned Andalucía was very far from being the army that he described. Not only that but it was a force that was almost completely out of control in political terms. Within the French camp, the one highly placed figure who saw matters in different terms was Joseph Bonaparte, but such was the scorn that his imperial brother displayed in his respect that there was little he could do to reign in his military commanders or even some members of the civil administration. As the king's friend Miot had complained (see above), things had been bad even before the French had marched on Andalucía, but now they grew still worse. In January 1810, shaky though his authority was, Joseph had at least been the nominal commander of all the French forces in Spain, but even this was soon to change. Thus, in a series of decrees emitted in the period April–June 1810, a Napoleon impatient with the lack of progress his forces were making in the south of Spain struck one last blow against *el rey intruso.* In brief, the French corps and divisions scattered round Iberia were now formed into a number of regional armies. Thus, the forces that had invaded Andalucía became the Army of the South under Marshal Soult; II, VI, and VIII Corps and the cavalry division of General Louis Montbrun, the Army of Portugal under Marshal André Masséna; VII Corps, the Army of Catalonia under Marshal Charles Augereau; III Corps, the Army of Aragón under Marshal Suchet; a variety of troops that had been in garrison in Old Castile, Navarre, and the Basque provinces or sent as reinforcements from France, the Army of the North under General Jean-Marie Dorsenne; and finally, the royal guard, some stray units that had been left behind by the formations that had invaded Andalucía, and such *juramentados* that the royal administration had managed to keep in being in and around Madrid, the Army of the Center under King Joseph. By now back in Madrid as he was, *el rey intruso* was, in consequence, stripped of all chance of exercising any authority. Setting aside the fact that he had been left with nothing more than a small rump force composed mostly of *juramentados* and foreign auxiliaries (by sheer happenstance one of the chief formations left behind in Madrid in January 1810 had been a division of troops drawn from Holland, Baden, Nassau, and Frankfurt), Joseph was now just one army commander among five others, while Soult, Masséna, and the rest now officially communicated not with him, but with Napoleon's headquarters. In the decree appointing him commander of the Army of the South, Soult, it is true, was enjoined to pay all due respect to Joseph: "I need not remind you of the regard which you must have for the king. Even though you are in reality the general in chief, you must operate in agreement with his representatives." Yet at the same time it was made clear to him that political niceties came second to the needs of the army: "It is the intention of His Majesty [that is, Napoleon] that you should take the most effective measures for attending to the pay and supply of your army. Let your watchword, then, be the principle that war should support war."[60]

Unlike many parts of northern Spain (see below), Andalucía was never made into a "military government" and thereby wholly removed from Joseph's authority. However, by the terms of his appointment—an appointment, be it noted, that in effect both rehabilitated Soult and finally gave official sanction to the campaign of January 1810—the marshal was given more than enough leeway to defy Joseph in the only area in which the king had some chance of exerting his influence. Meanwhile, Soult was only too happy to exploit the opportunities he had been given. Thus, relations between Soult and Joseph had initially been good, but they were rapidly undermined by the French failure to take Cádiz, the king's triumphal tour of Andalucía, and the increasingly decorative nature of the marshal's appointment. Soult also having fallen out with the war minister, Gonzalo O'Farrill, whom he accused of being both incompetent and anti-French, by March 1810 the marshal was chafing at the bit.[61]

King Joseph might have had more of a chance of reining in Soult, Sébastiani, and the rest if he had enjoyed stronger support from the Spanish officials who made up his civil administration, but this was not the case. Rather than adopting a radically different line from the generals, they seem to have viewed the pacification of Spain from a very similar perspective. Missing, of course, was the neo-Jacobinism, the exaggerated militarism, and the contempt for all things Spanish, while there was clearly much jealousy of the manner in which the military dominated events in the *josefino* camp. In other respects, though, there was much common ground, including, not least, fear of the common people and dislike of the Church. Thus, many of the men who formed the bedrock of the royal administration in Andalucía—men such as the Conde de Montarco, who had served as a member of Carlos IV's Consejo de Estado; Miguel José de Azanza, a senior army officer who had served both as minister of war and viceroy of Mexico; and the erstwhile intendants, José Cervera, Fernando de Osorno, Domingo Badía y Leblich, and Joaquín de Solis—had been closely associated with the reformist policies pursued by the Bourbon monarchy prior to 1808. Immediately appointed royal commissioners—in effect civil governors—of one city or another (Azanza, for example, was given Granada), these men on occasion did what they could to ameliorate the consequences of French occupation, but the general picture is one of great congruence with the military. Specifically sent to Andalucía as a species of viceroy in December 1810 with a view to bringing Soult under the control of the throne and ensuring that Andalucía's resources reached Madrid, Montarco in particular soon fell under the marshal's spell. As the French ambassador, La Forest, noted: "The ascendancy that the Duke of Dalmatia has acquired over the Conde de Montarco . . . is such that it has at length become clear that Andalucía will not furnish the king with a single penny. . . . Everything possible to strip an exhausted country . . . of its resources is being rigorously carried out, but the many arrears that have to be paid out, the needs of the moment, and—habitual pretext!—the supposed requirements of the many projects that are still pending together ensure that the marshal keeps everything, . . . while the Conde de Montarco is subjugated to such a degree that he has become his advocate."[62]

From the very beginning, then, French policy in Andalucía was to have the very sharpest of edges. This does not mean, however, that the forces of occupation did nothing but rape, burn, and pillage. Thus, Soult and his fellow commanders were content enough to collaborate with the campaign of propaganda we have examined in the previous chapter and in general were happy with the principle of securing Spain's subjugation by submission rather than outright conquest. Indeed, in the first months of occupation, we often see them corresponding directly with their Spanish counterparts in the hope of getting them to change sides: for example, in the Condado de Niebla, the local French commander, the Duke of Aremberg, in effect tricked the Spanish commander at Ayamonte, Francisco Copóns y Navía, into sending an emissary to his headquarters and, having done this, treated the officer concerned to a long harangue in which he stressed the futility of resistance and promised Copóns the post of governor of Andalucía.[63]

A good example of how French occupation policy worked in practice is constituted by the city of Granada. No sooner had the city fallen without resistance on 28 January 1810, then, than it was subjected to what might be regarded as the basic process of submission and integration. Thus, having declared that it was no longer in a state of rebellion, the city now, in effect, sought to assimilate itself with the rest of *josefino* Spain, the most important step being to organize an oath of obedience to the new regime. The setting for this was a High Mass in the cathedral that was celebrated in the presence of Sébastiani and the royal commissioner, Azanza, on 31 January by the dean, Miguel Clavigne, while the oath itself was sworn not by individuals, but rather by representatives of all the city's institutions and corporations, including the provincial court of justice, the town council, the cathedral chapter, the parish clergy, the nobility, the university, the college of lawyers, the chamber of commerce, and the various guilds.[64] At the same time, a delegation was dispatched to pay homage to King Joseph in the name of the whole city, the men chosen for this purpose including not just representatives of the elite but also of the Third Estate.[65]

With the city almost literally on its knees before them, its new masters guaranteed that all those who had sworn loyalty to King Joseph would be allowed to remain in their existing posts and that all those who laid down their arms would be allowed to return to their homes.[66] At the same time, a grand ball hosted by Sébastiani for the city's leading dignitaries on 12 February confirmed the invaders' respect for the existing social order.[67] Concessions, however, extended no further. Thus, while Azanza immediately declared all measures of the previous administration were null and void and, in line with various decrees that had already been promulgated by the government of King Joseph, ordered the creation of a new town council, the immediate secularization of the religious orders (to which end a committee of sequestration was formed under the city's Bourbon intendant, Fernando Osorno, the latter also being appointed mayor), and the expropriation and sale of all property belonging to those who had gone into exile in Cádiz or elsewhere, Sébastiani imposed the death penalty for all acts of insurgency, directed the populace to surrender any arms that were in its possession, and barred the local authorities and the populace alike from giving food or shelter to brigands, insurgents, or troops loyal to the Patriot regime. Finally, to support his forces and to meet the costs of occupation, in exchange for bonds that were redeemable in terms of confiscated "national properties," Sebastiani also imposed a forced loan of 5,000,000 *reales,* which in theory had to be paid within four days.[68]

To back up these measures, keep the authorities informed of the state of public opinion, and generally maintain order, a new police system was established by a decree promulgated on 6 February. At the head of this organization was a general commissary of police—one Antonio Falcés—who was based in the convent of San Felipe and directly supported by a small number of administrative personnel, thirty-four agents, and a small squad of hired toughs, the city in the meantime being divided into four districts, each of which possessed a police post manned by three more agents of different ranks.[69] To assist in the task of surveillance, meanwhile, in accordance with orders that reached it from Madrid, the town council instigated a census of the population, the justices being instructed to compile two lists, namely, one naming those inhabitants known to be present in the city and another naming those known to be absent; the list of inhabitants having been compiled in this fashion, no one was henceforth to leave the city without a passport from the authorities on pain of paying a heavy fine, it also being laid down that all those who operated inns and lodging houses were to keep the authorities informed at all times of the identity and business of their guests.[70]

Also important to the French was propaganda and the dissemination of information. In order to keep the populace informed of the new regime's measures, on 6 February an official newspaper was established in the form of the *Gazeta del Gobierno de Granada,* and this was soon full of a variety of edicts of which two notable examples are the Bando de Policia (Police Order) of 19 February 1810 and the Reglamento de Teatros (Theater Regulation), which followed it the next day. In brief, in addition to a variety of measures of purely day-to-day import—there were, for example, rules about hanging baskets, the management of bakeries, and the proper care of the city's fountains—the former imposed a strict 11 P.M. curfew on the city (taverns, indeed, had to close even earlier); laid strict controls on the possession, sale, and repair of arms; decreed a weekly levy for the employment of pavement sweepers;

banned the setting up of stalls or the pursuit of trades in the streets; and prohibited gatherings of any sort in cafés and taverns. As for the latter, this was on the surface concerned with matters pertaining purely to the smooth running of the city's theaters—actors were, for example, forbidden to refuse to play the parts assigned to them by directors—but concealed within it there was the same determination to maintain public order, it being laid down that proper decorum was to be maintained at all times and that the general commissary of police should be told in advance of the shows that were to be put on "so that he can make enquiries about them and lay down what is most conducive to the public service and the honest enjoyment of the citizenry."[71] Finally, yet another edict reorganized the city's markets—henceforth, vegetables were to be sold only in the Plaza de Bibarrambla and firewood only in the Plaza de los Lobos—laid down the use of standard-sized tables, and imposed a levy of 100 *reales* a year on all stallholders.[72]

Thus far, we have only spoken of the civil authorities, but this was not an end to it, the activities of the French military governor, General Jean-Pierre Doguereau, also having to be taken into account, and all the more so as his line was even more severe. Thus, among the series of edicts issued by his office, we find orders prohibiting all public gatherings greater than six people, the wearing of capes, and the possession of seditious material of any sort and directing day laborers who needed to find work in the fields around the city to apply for special passes.[73]

The new administration, then, was determined to interfere in respect of the most minute details of daily life: Granada was to be clean, well ordered, free of crime, and perhaps above all, civilized, while residents were also left in no doubt that they had to conform with developments in the rest of *josefino* Spain: hence the series of orders that were published giving details of a variety of royal decrees that had been promulgated in the course of 1809 (to make doubly certain that these were seen by the widest possible audience, many were produced in poster form and pasted up in the streets).[74] In the meantime, of course, anyone who threatened public order was to be dealt with without mercy: on 16 February there came the first of many public executions when three men, including a Capuchin priest, were put to death in front of the cathedral. At first the method used was shooting, but from June 1810 onward, the garrote was employed instead. An eyewitness was the British prisoner Lord Blayney: "In the centre of the square [that is, the Plaza del Triunfo] is . . . a garrote, the mode of execution of which deserves notice. On a platform are placed a number of stools with a perpendicular post behind each: the criminal being seated on the stool, an iron collar is placed round his neck, and the executioner by the turn of a screw puts an end to his existence in a moment. . . . Scarce a day passes without several similar executions."[75] Of course, the mere fact that executions took place in public rendered justice exemplary, but to drive home the cost of brigandage still further, the city was regularly placarded with the sentences handed down in the courts, and the victims having notices labeled "thief," "bandit," or "highwayman" hung round their necks, together very often with the weapons that they had been carrying when they were captured.[76]

If the common people of Granada were to be well policed, the city's elites were to be assimilated with the "masses of granite"—the propertied classes that throughout the empire formed the bedrock of local government. At the heart of this process was an aggressive process of socialization that sought to draw the propertied classes into the orbit of the new regime. At the center of this process, of course, were the quarters allotted to Sébastiani and the French governor in that these became the scene of large numbers of receptions and more informal gatherings, which on the one hand, physically associated the guests with the invaders and, on the other, became yet one more means of singing the glories of the empire. As an officer who had given his parole to his captors, Blayney was treated with all due courtesy and in consequence attended several social events of this sort (not that he seems particularly to have appreciated his inclusion):

> Nothing could be more tiresome than the eternal praises of the emperor which formed the chief topic of conversation at Sebastiani's parties. With a solemnity of countenance and a measured tone, . . . the general would every day at table treat us with a panegyric on the virtues and exploits of his master, of which was the following was naturally the burden. "Gentlemen, the emperor

is a man without fault, and the only person in the world who has so much power against whom nobody can make the slightest reproach." Or, "Gentlemen, the emperor is the greatest of men and the greatest hero the world has ever known." And then he would draw a comparison with Caesar or Alexander, both of whom, of course, were *imbéciles* to Napoleon.[77]

The backdrop to these receptions, luncheons, and banquets was very often one or other of the various *fêtes napoléoniques.* Events such as the saint's days of Napoleon and in Spain King Joseph; the anniversary of Napoleon's coronation; or special occasions such the wedding of Napoleon and Marie-Louise or the birth of the king of Rome, these were celebrated with great pomp and ceremony throughout the Grand Empire, the aim being, of course, on the one hand, to stress the overwhelming might that lay behind French domination, and on the other, to associate the latter with the good things in life, whether they were feasting or social and material advancement. Falling as it does on 19 March, the first of these occasions to affect Granada was the feast day of Saint Joseph, and this was celebrated with all the more enthusiasm on account of the fact that the king himself had arrived in the city in the course of his tour of Andalucía just three days before. Thus, as soon as it was learned that the king would be paying the city a state visit; the town council rushed to prepare no fewer than three different palaces for his use; organized a brilliantly uniformed guard of honor; commissioned a variety of street decorations, including, most notably, a gigantic triumphal arch painted with the legend "To Joseph Bonaparte, the city of Granada—love and loyalty"; ordered the preparation of a number of receptions, banquets, balls, bullfights, and firework displays; and set aside the sum of 4,500 *reales* so that, as was traditional on such occasions, money could be thrown among the crowd.[78] As for the celebrations themselves, these followed a pattern that was absolutely typical. At sunset on 18 March, a twenty-one-gun salute marked the beginning of the celebrations, while the hours of darkness that followed were brightened by the illumination of such prominent buildings as the town hall and the cathedral. The city having been woken at dawn the next morning by a second twenty-one-gun salute, a series of deputations—of the guilds, the town council, the university, the parish and cathedral clergy, and a number of the surrounding *pueblos*—proceeded to wait upon the king in his lodgings in the Chancillería Real, the latter responding with a typical speech in praise of the new Spain. To the sound of church bells and fresh salvos of artillery, Joseph and his suite then made their way along streets lined with troops to the cathedral, where they attended High Mass (complete, of course, with the requisite adulatory sermon and Te Deum) and visited the tombs of Ferdinand and Isabella. There followed a formal luncheon and, in the evening, a banquet and ball in the erstwhile convent of Santo Domingo, together with further illuminations, the only sour note in the proceedings being struck by the fact that, due to pouring rain, a bullfight that had been organized for the afternoon had had to be canceled.[79]

Finally, in recognition, however subconsciously, that poverty and brigandage went hand in hand, some attempt was made to look to the welfare of the increasingly hard-pressed inhabitants (that the arrival of the French had hit the populace very hard there can be no doubt: to meet the forced loan of 5,000,000 *reales*, the town council had had no option but to increase local taxation—the sales tax on meat was doubled, for example—as well as to make use of the fund known as the Pósito Pío, which was traditionally kept as a reserve for use in hard times; in all sorts of ways, meanwhile, the new French police regulations either cost the populace still more money or made it much harder for them to supplement their income by such means as taking lodgers or setting up as peddlers).[80] Thus, if Luis Marcelino Peyreyra (one of Azanza's many successors as Granada's royal commissioner) issued stentorian exhortations for the people to carry on paying the tithes as before (since October 1809 these had been assigned to the needs of the occupying forces), he also ordered those responsible for administering the funds that supported the many hospitals and other charitable foundations that had collapsed on account of the war to render up a strict account of their stewardship and hand over whatever they had in their coffers on the understanding that the money would be disbursed in line with the donors' original intentions.[81] Meanwhile, both as an act of policy and in an attempt to create employment (and in line with developments in Madrid and elsewhere), a number of churches and convents were pulled down to make way for new open spaces, examples of those affected being the convents of the Angel Custodiador, and San Francisco del Alhambra, the churches of San Agustín el Alto, and the hermitages of San Miguel and El Cristo de la Yedra.[82] An interested observer was once again Lord Blayney:

> However the present contest may terminate, it must be admitted that the Spaniards will be indebted to the French for many works both of utility and ornament, which under their old lethargic government would probably never have been thought of. Among other public works commenced by the French at Granada are a bridge of a single arch over the Genil and a theatre, on which a vast number of workmen were now employed in order to finish it before the general's birthday, on which . . . it is to be opened. The contrast between this edifice and the old theatre is striking, the latter being a gloomy and heavy building without ornaments either external or internal, while the former is light and airy with decorations approaching to the tawdry; one reminds of the sober seriousness of the Spaniard, the other of the gay flippancy of the Frenchman. The orchestra in the French theatre is constructed on a new principle, apparently well calculated for the diffusion of sound. The boxes are gaudily painted, and on the fronts alternately are a gilt eagle and an "N."[83]

Also important as a way of providing work for the unemployed was the program of fortification that was begun in and around the Alhambra, which the French made use of as a citadel, the city as a whole being far too large for them to defend properly.[84] Such was the amount of work involved that hundreds of laborers were kept employed for months, but in this instance their endeavors served a double purpose. Looming over the city as they did, the new ramparts were in themselves, of course, an imposing statement of intent—French rule had come to stay—while the guns that protruded from the embrasures were a constant reminder that trouble would be met by the proverbial "whiff of grapeshot."[85]

As in Granada, so in the rest of occupied Spain, the fact being that its experiences were mirrored in all the cities of Andalucía that fell under French occupation.[86] Little by little, meanwhile, the piecemeal process that we have looked at hitherto was incorporated into a common program governed not by local initiative, but by the dictates of King Joseph, Marshal Soult, and from December 1810, the Conde de Montarco. Indeed, hardly had the French set foot in Seville than the first of a veritable stream of directives and proclamations began to emerge from the king's headquarters in the *alcázar*. Initially, these were primarily directed toward the security situation (though there were exceptions, as for example, with the decree that confirmed that all officials who swore an oath of allegiance to Napoleon would be allowed to keep their positions).[87] In brief, while they were assured that intendants and military commanders had the duty to assist them with the task of keeping order, municipalities were warned that it was their duty to do everything they could to frustrate insurgent activity and brigandage on pain of being held responsible for any French or *afrancesado* deaths that took place within their boundaries.[88] Exactly what this meant, meanwhile, was spelled out in an undated instruction that was issued the next month, it being announced that heavy fines would be imposed on the *pueblos* concerned and four of their leading inhabitants held as hostages until the close of hostilities.[89]

Having in this fashion, or at least so it was hoped, shut the gates of the *pueblos* of Andalucía against the irregular bands, the authorities now turned their attention to the bands themselves. A matter of some priority here being to clear the countryside of all those who might end up in such bands, a royal decree of 18 March duly required all *dispersos* (soldiers who had lost their units) to report to a magistrate within the space of fifteen days on pain of being treated as deserters, having done which they would have the option either of enlisting with Joseph's army (for which a variety of rewards were on offer) or being given a passport to return to their homes; meanwhile, as early as 23 January, the thousands of people who had fled their homes in the face of French invasion were warned that if they did not return within the space of eight days, they would be stripped of any property that they might have.[90] Meanwhile, to reassure those who feared French reprisals, no sooner had Joseph entered Seville than it was announced that all those who swore allegiance to the French would be guaranteed a full amnesty for anything that they might have done in the period 1808–10.[91] Finally, logically enough, the rural populace was to be disarmed: according to a royal decree of 17 March 1810, local justices were, first, empowered to pay forty *reales* for every musket that was handed over to them in good working order and, second, ordered after a month's grace to instigate a search for hidden arms.[92]

In his more optimistic moments, Joseph doubtless hoped that these measures in themselves would have been enough to restore order in Andalucía. Yet the possibility that they would not was not ignored. Thus, outright insurgents were to receive no mercy whatsoever. Courts-martial and military firing squads continued to play an important role here, but at the same time, Andalucía was now harmonized with the rest of Bonaparte Spain. In the course of 1809, special tribunals known as *juntas criminales extraordinarias* had been established in Madrid, Bilbao, Pamplona, San Sebastián, and Valladolid on the basis of *afrancesado* members of the judiciary to try such crimes as armed rebellion, sedition, and highway robbery, and these had waged a vigorous war against brigandage (however qualified). With Andalucía arguably in the grip of even worse disorder than the rest of the country, similar institutions were required south of the Sierra Morena, and a decree of 8 May 1810 duly established such juntas in Seville, Granada, Málaga, Córdoba, and Jaén. Empowered to dispense summary justice and sentence their victims to death without the possibility of appeal, these bodies greatly strengthened the machinery of repression while providing yet another way of binding the elites to the new regime.[93]

In order to back up these provisions, security forces of various sorts were obviously necessary, and so we see, first of all, the creation of the Guardia Cívica. In line with developments in the rest of occupied Spain, where the organization of such a force had been initiated by Napoleon himself in December 1808, on 6 February it was decreed that Andalucía should raise a guard on the basis of a pilot scheme that was to be tried out in the cities of Seville, Jaén, Granada, and Córdoba. As to what this last entailed, each of these cities was ordered immediately to form one or more battalions of such troops, the recruits for which were to come from able-bodied men of good character, aged from sixteen to fifty, and drawn from the ranks of the propertied classes (specifically "property owners and their sons and men visibly exercising a trade or profession"). Interestingly, meanwhile, conditions of service were to be extremely generous: for example, battalions would never have to serve outside their own municipalities and yet still in every way rank as regular soldiers.[94]

With this force in place, a royal decree of 20 March hinted at the reestablishment of the old provincial militia by means of a ballot and ordered the formation of eight new regiments of *juramentado* line infantry, named Sevilla, Granada, Córdoba, Jaén, Infantes, Ciudad Real, Alcázar de San Juan, and Toledo. These were, if possible, to be raised by voluntary enlistment, and in particular from among ex-soldiers (to attract such men, it was promised that they would be credited with the time that they had served in the Patriot army). However, each *pueblo* was assigned a quota that it was expected to fulfill, and if sufficient recruits were not forthcoming within fifteen days, then the intendants were authorized to use compulsion, a further spur to efficiency in this respect being a threat that those towns and villages that still had not complied after thirty days would have to provide twice the number of men that would otherwise have fallen to their share.[95] As if this were not enough, meanwhile, on 31 March yet another decree ordered the formation in each province of a security force to be known as the Cazadores de Montaña, or Mountain Rangers: the actual size of this force was left to the military commanders, but the general idea was that it should form part of the army (the Guardia Cívica, by contrast, owed its allegiance to the town councils), take the form of a number of independent companies, and be entirely recruited from volunteers.[96]

Last but not least, in August 1810, orders from Marshal Soult led to the creation of the so-called *brigadas de escopeteros*, or shotgun patrols. In brief, each of these units was to consist of one noncommissioned officer (NCO) and six men, while there was to be one lieutenant for every six patrols and one captain for every twelve. Spread along all the main roads at a distance of no more than three leagues from one another, their job was to go to the assistance of travelers who had been attacked, hunt down bandits, and gather information in respect of the movement of the various gangs. As for the men who made up this rural constabulary, they were to be chosen by the town councils and "citizens of robust constitution . . . and known morality and good conduct," while they were to receive ten *reales* a day (twelve in the case of NCOs), together with one-third of the value of any goods that they might seize from smugglers, although this largesse was expected to cover the costs of their arms and equipment (something that was likely quite considerable—each man was to have a saber, a carbine, and two pistols).[97]

What, though, of the populace as a whole? As we have already seen, the policing of society was at the heart of the new regime's concerns. In the months that followed the passage of the Sierra Morena, a variety of partial regulations were drawn up in this respect, and in October 1811 these were all brought together in a single code that was promulgated by the Conde de Montarco as royal commissioner for Andalucía. In brief, these, in the first place, set up a common structure for the civil police and, in the second, laid down a series of norms that at all times had to be respected by the populace. Taking the chain of command first of all, there would be a general commissary of police in Seville, a principal commissary of police in the capital of each prefecture (see below), and a commissary of police in every other town with a military garrison. As for structure, every village, town, or city would have one or more police posts manned by an appropriate number of agents. Appointed by Montarco, the men concerned would at each level submit regular reports to their superiors while at the same time behaving in exemplary fashion—taking bribes and bearing false witness carried with them the risk of severe punishment—and taking care "to proceed against wrongdoers, deserters, fugitives, prisoners of war, *dispersos,* . . . insurgents, vagabonds, illicit gaming houses, illicit gatherings, the unauthorized possession of arms, espionage, criminal correspondence with the enemy, and anything else that might threaten the security of the state, the health of the public, and the regulations imposed in the name of policing society; to check up on passports and letters of recommendation; to remain vigilant in respect of libels, caricatures, leaflets, and other material attacking the government; and, last but not least, to guard against fraud, contraband, and anything else that might damage the interests of the royal treasury." So much, then, for the police. As for the people, they were to find themselves subject to stricter control than ever. Thus, no one could leave their hometown or village without first obtaining a passport from the local justices and, in those cases where there was a garrison, getting it validated by the military authorities; nobody could have anyone stay in their house without informing the authorities; nobody could open a tavern or a rooming house without getting a permit from the authorities; and above all, nobody would be idle. Thus, "Any individual who does not have a clear job or occupation, who cannot justify his means of subsistence, who is not spoken for by anybody, or who cannot find anyone to speak for him, will be arrested as an idler and handed over to the police, who will investigate his conduct and have him either committed for trial or put to work for the public good." Setting this aside, any infractions of the code were punishable by heavy fines and, in the highly likely event of the accused being unable to find the money to buy themselves out of trouble, lengthy terms of imprisonment (an additional point worth noting here is that, as the system's personnel were all paid from the proceeds of the fines it raised, they had an added motive to ensure that the regulations were enforced in full). And finally, as if all this was not enough, the taverns that were the masses' only regular places of recreation were absorbed into the system of control: thus the official permits mentioned above had to be earned, or so it was implied, by keeping the authorities supplied with a constant stream of information of all sorts.[98]

If the lives of the humbler elements of society became ever more subject to regulation and control, they were also directly affected by a number of reform measures introduced by the French. Given the huge amounts of charity they had disbursed, in no case is this more true than in that of the *josefino* regime's policy of abolishing the religious orders so as to open up their extensive property to being expropriated and put on sale for the benefit of the state. By the time that Andalucía was occupied, this policy was already in full swing in the rest of occupied Spain in that, on 18 August 1809, a royal decree had dissolved all the male religious orders (by contrast, the much smaller group represented by Spain's nuns was left alone, albeit with the provisos, first, that any nun who wished to do so could apply for secularization and, second, that henceforward no new novices were to be accepted by any community, the hope obviously being that over time the problem would simply resolve itself). No sooner had the French entered Andalucía, then, than monasteries and other religious houses began to be torn down on all sides and their inhabitants turned out on the promise of either a new position as a member of the parish clergy or a pension. On 26 February 1810, the prefect of Seville, Blas de Aranza y Doyle, published the decrees suppressing the religious orders and directed that they be put into effect forthwith, while on 6 March he followed this up with an announcement of the impending sale of all their property.[99]

Exactly what the consequences were of these measures we do not know: indeed, one may say that the issue is one that awaits its historian. Potentially, at least, they were massive: in principle, Spain was to be given a new society. Meanwhile, that society was to operate within a new political framework. Most of the decrees that were issued by Joseph Bonaparte in the course of his stay in Andalucía were concerned either with extending legislation that had already been introduced in the rest of the Bonaparte Kingdom of Spain or addressing the turmoil that gripped his new dominions. In a few instances, however, measures were introduced that were directed at the whole of the country, the most important example of this being the radical overhaul that now took place of the country's territorial organization. Prior to 1808 the country had been divided up into a hodgepodge of kingdoms, principalities, provinces, counties, and fiefdoms that differed wildly in terms of their size and systems of law and government and were the product of little other than historical accident. In this Spain was far removed from the rest of the Napoleonic empire, the latter being divided into prefectures of more-or-less equal size whose frontiers were primarily defined by geography. With the decay of medieval institutions such as the *cortes* of Aragón and the Bourbons' imposition of the French system of intendants, a greater degree of order had been imposed on the situation than a quick glance suggests, but even so there remained many anomalies: Extremadura, for example, was little short of 100 times the size of Guipúzcoa, Toro was divided into two separate pieces, and Burgos and Segovia encompassed territorial enclaves belonging to one or other of their neighbors.

Such a situation was hardly likely to survive the rationalizing drive of the Bonapartes—local government, indeed, had already felt its effects[100]—but its end was hastened by political crisis. Thus, in the very midst of King Joseph's tour of Andalucía, he was suddenly assailed by the news that, irritated by the slow progress of Spain's pacification and determined to secure the communications of the major army he was currently concentrating against Portugal, Napoleon had decided to turn the existing provinces of Aragón, Navarre, and Catalonia, together with a new entity formed from the three Basque *señorios* known as Biscay, into military governments over which the king's officials would have no authority. This was a shattering blow, and Joseph responded with a futile gesture of defiance. Thus, turning to his suite for assistance, he quickly produced a plan for Spain's division into thirty-eight prefectures in the French style, each of the new units being named after its capital, headed by a prefect, and divided into between two and four subprefectures. More radical than anything that was to be seen in subsequent years—unlike its *josefino* predecessors, the system of provinces adopted by Spain in the 1830s respected the frontiers of the country's basic historic units—the resultant decree of 17 April 1810 was a clear challenge to Napoleon, and it is scarcely surprising that the latter responded by creating two further military governments out of Burgos, on the one hand, and Toro, Valladolid, Palencia, and Avila, on the other. In the country as a whole, then, the scheme remained a dead letter, but for all that, it did take hold in Andalucía and some other areas. As for what it meant for Andalucía, the latter now had six provinces rather than four: Córdoba, Granada, Jaén, Jérez, Málaga and Seville.[101] As for the prefects, four came from the royal commissioners currently in residence in Andalucía—Francisco Angulo in Córdoba, Luis Marcelino Peyreyra in Granada, Blas de Aranza y Doyle in Seville, and Joaquín María Sotelo in Jérez—while the remaining two were new men, namely Manuel de Echazarreta in Jaén and José Cervera in Málaga. (A good example of the manner in which Bourbon officialdom in many instances collaborated happily with the French, prior to 1810 Cervera had been serving as Málaga's intendant.) Worn out, disillusioned, and in some cases urgently needed elsewhere, by the end of 1810, most of the original faces had disappeared, and the list of prefects become what it was to remain for most of the French occupation. Thus in Seville the prefect was Joaquín de Solis; in Córdoba, Domingo Badía y Leblich; in Granada, Fernando de Osorno; in Jérez, Joaquín Sotelo; in Jaén, Manuel de Echazarreta; and in Málaga, José Cervera.[102]

All the policies we have discussed or otherwise touched upon—the creation of new patterns of public celebration and social integration, the establishment of new security forces and organs of local government, the expansion of the *josefino* army, the wholesale distribution of the "order of the eggplant" (that is, the Orden Real de España), the release onto the market of huge quantities of ecclesiastical property, the restoration of order—were linked together by one main theme. In brief, in line with one of the main principles of French occupation policy as it developed in the rest of the empire, what we see is an attempt to co-opt the local elites, or at least to compromise them to such an extent that they would be forced to uphold the cause of King Joseph willy-nilly. Yet if only thanks to a widespread realization that the restoration of order could not be achieved by the bayonet alone, embodied in the new order was also a certain paternalism and, in particular, a desire to relieve poverty and ensure that the poor were gainfully employed. How far Joseph's instructions in this respect were ever obeyed is another matter, but a royal decree of 13 February 1810 ordered that all the olive groves belonging to the convents that had been suppressed in Andalucía were to be distributed among the inhabitants of the *pueblos* in which they were situated by a junta composed of the mayor, the local public defender, a representative of the town council, and the parish priest.[103] Meanwhile, other measures taken by *el rey intruso* included the abolition of many monopolies and the establishment of new schools in Seville. And where the king led, so the civil authorities followed, and all the more so as the harsh realities of occupation began to bite. In September

1811, for example, alarmed by the prospect of winter, a season that, he noted, "even forgetting our present misfortunes has always been accompanied by want of bread and many other evils that are just as hard to remedy," Peyreyra's successor as prefect of Granada, Fernando de Osorno, summoned a meeting of all the city's civil authorities with the aim of elaborating a plan of action that would "oppose energetic measures to the dreadful spectacle offered . . . every year by the indigent laborers prevented from working by the annual rains or simply left without anything to do." As a result of this meeting, Osorno ordered that each municipality should organize "jobs of one sort or another from which the needy can derive a degree of assistance, whether it be tidying up the streets, improving the roads, or clearing irrigation ditches."[104] In taking this position, of course, Osorno was careful to avoid admitting that the demands of the invaders had anything to do with the situation—this was rather blamed on a combination of the structural problems that beset Andalusian agriculture and the effects of banditry and/or popular resistance[105]—but there is here at least a recognition that pacification depended not just on the sword but also on active measures of social policy. In the city of Granada, indeed, this recognition was formally codified in the form of a set of instructions that laid down the formation of a charitable association consisting of a board of directors and twelve local committees (that is, one for each of the districts into which the city was divided). Composed of the parish priest, the district magistrate, and two prominent citizens, these committees would have the task of forming a list of all those families without support in their district, organizing a monthly subscription and supervising such work as might be carried out, while the central committee watched over the accounts and decided how the money thus raised should actually be spent.[106] Finally, linked to these measures were others that echoed Joseph's recognition that in such circumstances as those in which Andalucía was placed, the rights of private property had their limits: on 14 October 1811 the then mayor, Luis Dávila, issued a proclamation ordering anyone who had any stocks of grain whatsoever to report their existence to the municipality preparatory to a general levy that would be shared out in proportion to the quantities owned by each person.[107]

As witness the example of Sébastiani in Granada, the military authorities certainly did not oppose the efforts at poor relief and other attempts to conciliate the crowd that we have just discussed and, to a considerable extent, even participated in them: in April 1811, for example, Soult proposed that, in view of the very low wages that they received, the workers employed on the fortifications of La Cartuja should receive an ounce of tobacco for free every week.[108] At about the same time, meanwhile, he also issued strict instructions that, in order to protect the needs of agriculture—something that he stressed at all times should be a matter of first concern to every single one of his military governors and commandants—horses, mules, and oxen should only be requisitioned in cases of absolute necessity, and even then only with proper authorization.[109] Still more extraordinarily, on 30 April he announced that he was renouncing the so-called second tithe, this being a duplication of the standard tithe that had been imposed by the regime of Manuel de Godoy as a means of raising extra money.[110] And finally, in the autumn of 1810, the news that yellow fever was once again afflicting the coastal districts of Andalucía led the marshal to assume the same role that prewar Spanish regimes had played in fighting the disease, a series of instructions issued by his headquarters directing that individuals coming from the affected areas were immediately to be placed in quarantine, that isolation hospitals were to be established for the care of the sick, that the houses of all those affected were to be shut up, that money and letters received from the affected zone were be disinfected with vinegar, that those who died of the disease were to be buried in separate cemeteries, and that local authorities were to keep the strictest watch on all roads leading from the Patriot zone.[111]

Yet neither generals, nor royal commissioners, nor even a would-be benevolent monarch ever lost sight of the fact that the chief object of conquest was exploitation. Let us here first discuss the question of Andalucía's harvests. Essential to the well-being of the forces of Marshal Soult—even had adequate reserves of grain and other commodities existed in central or northern Spain, there was no way that they could have been transported to Andalucía—these were effectively placed at the disposition of the invaders. Requisitioning began on an ad hoc basis as soon as the latter crossed the Sierra Morena, but the system was eventually placed on a formal basis by a series of regulations. On paper these were fair enough, it being laid down that the French could take only, first, the produce of all land that had been declared "national property" and remained in the hands of the state; second, all produce that would ordinarily have been made over to the Church in payment of the tithes and other dues; and third, any produce that was left over after due consideration had been taken of the needs of the inhabitants. In this last point lies the rub, however: no mechanism ever seems to have been established for deciding exactly what the inhabitants could be deemed to need, and the result was that the French were, in practice, able to demand whatever they liked.[112]

Nor was it just a question of foodstuffs: from the beginning, Andalucía was to be made to pay for its own subjugation. A prime target, of course, was the Church—this was not just stripped of much property through the abolition of the religious orders and the Inquisition but also hit, first, by the state's appropriation of tithes and, second, the fact that the dioceses of Andalucía were now charged with their share of the 100,000,000-*real* forced loan that had been imposed on the Spanish Church as a whole by Joseph Bonaparte in October 1808—while another source of ready money was found in the large quantities of British goods that were found in Andalucía, on 7 February 1810 Joseph decreeing that all British goods awaiting sale were immediately to be confiscated for sale by the state and, further, that all goods that had already been bought from British merchants could only be sold on payment of a duty of 50 percent of their value.[113]

Such measures could only produce so much in the way of revenue, however, and the result was that no sooner had the French forces entered any given area than it was subjected to enormous financial levies: for example, 1,000,000 *reales* in Córdoba; 5,000,000 *reales*, as we have seen, in Granada; and 12,000,0000 *reales* in Málaga (this last was treated more harshly than most other places on account of the Abello junta's futile attempt at resistance). These "extraordinary contributions," however, were but the start of it, the situation being regularized and rendered permanent in

September 1810 by the establishment of the "ordinary contribution," a set charge that was levied each month on every province of Andalucía in accordance with its population and wealth. The total sums involved were little short of staggering—in all, they have been calculated at 30,748,461 *reales*—while the amounts rose steadily until, by 1812, prefectures were being asked to raise in a single month almost as much as they had been asked to raise in the whole of 1810.[114] Added to these, meanwhile, were not just the periodic fines imposed on municipalities across Andalucía for the depredations of the insurgents but also further "extraordinary contributions" that continued to be levied on a frequent basis right down to the very last days of occupation: on 12 August 1812, Soult imposed a levy of 1,024,410 *reales* on all commercial activities in Seville, this being apportioned among all the city's guilds and corporations right down to their most humble elements (for example, the sellers of secondhand clothes had to find 700 *reales* and the barbers 1,300).[115]

The task of meeting most of these demands fell on the town councils, but these at the same time found themselves having to bear a whole range of other costs. These were many and varied, but not the least of them was that incurred by the celebration of the various *fêtes napoléoniques*, with their banquets, bullfights, fountains flowing with wine, street decorations, and firework displays. For example, taking alone the celebrations occasioned in Seville in April 1810 by the return of King Joseph from his tour of Andalucía, we find the cost of the banquet, the various concerts, the triumphal arch, and the decorations came to 76,710 *reales*. Equally, in March 1811 a lunch hosted by the town council on the occasion of Joseph's saint's day cost 7,000 *reales*; a reception hosted by the Conde de Montarco, 20,000; and the obligatory bullfight, 35,000. And finally, in August 1811 the cost of celebrating Napoleon's saint's day came to 110,000 *reales*.[116] Fortunately, such extravagance came only two or three times a year, but it was underpinned by demands that were less heavy in themselves but also more constant. Somehow, then, money had to be found for the Guardia Cívica, the police, and the various anti-bandit forces; for the muskets and other weapons handed in by the populace; for the construction of fortifications and the demolition of convents;

for cleaning the streets—a major French concern everywhere was public health and hygiene—and regulating the markets; for feeding French garrisons and housing French commanders (immediately following its occupation by the invaders, the town council of Córdoba spent almost 4,000 *reales* on equipping a house for the governor, Dessolles, while, not counting oil, by the end of July, the value of the food consumed by the garrison amounted to 800,000 *reales*); and for a whole array of other tasks ranging from setting up new schools to equipping military hospitals and clearing the sides of all roads of trees, rocks, and scrub that could be used as cover. To raise the money required, town councils obviously had no option but to raise taxes, and in July 1810 that of Córdoba, in particular, duly imposed levies of three *reales* on every *arroba* of flax that came into the city, two *reales* on every *arroba* of hemp, and one *real* on every *fanega* of wheat.[117]

Such measures, however, were not enough, and many town councils faced ever increasing fiscal pressure. Staying with the example of Córdoba, we find that at the beginning of 1811 its arrears were already in the region of 1,000,000 *reales*, and yet for January 1811 alone the ordinary contribution amounted to 541,164 *reales.* Despite desperate efforts, not to mention ever greater threats on part of the prefect, Badía, the council was quite unable to make such payments, and by 2 August the deficit was almost half as much again. As for mercy, there was none, the only response to a petition for the burden on Córdoba to be lessened being a demand for a payment of 1,000,000 *reales* within twenty-four hours.[118] Such a reply was only to be expected from the French, but Badía and his fellow prefects, and beyond him the Conde de Montarco—from December 1810, it will be remembered, royal commissioner for the whole of Andalucía—were just as committed to the requisitioning of Andalucía's resources. Thus, when Soult wrote to Montarco in January 1811 complaining that he had not received a penny of the money that Seville had been due to pay over to the French army, the count immediately issued instructions that it was to be found without delay.[119]

In fairness to Montarco, he was not a complete brute. On the contrary, indeed, his correspondence reveals that time and again he sought to do what he could to soften the burden of French occupation, on one occasion urging the governor of Seville to make fewer arrests and take fewer hostages on the grounds that such a policy could only drive the families affected into the arms of the insurgents, on another supporting a petition from the town of Utrera to the effect that it be let off a fine that had been imposed upon it as a result of some guerrilla raid, and on still another suggesting to Aranza that a separate file be kept of all the many petitions that had been received from the local authorities expounding the misery to which many *pueblos* had been reduced in the hope that presenting Soult with the evidence en masse would persuade him to reduce his demands.[120] Also notable, meanwhile, was the genuine concern that he evinced for the most helpless members of society. In May 1811, for example, he ordered Joaquín Sotelo to take immediate steps to assist the foundling hospital of Sanlucar de Barrameda as it was in a state of complete collapse, while in January 1812 he directed that aid should also be given to the hospital of San Juan de Díos of Jérez de la Frontera, "on account of its limited income and the large number of invalids which it is constantly looking after."[121] And finally, in order to support the *hospital de desfallecidos* (literally, "hospital for the moribund," but in practice a hospice that took in paupers found dying in the streets of hunger and disease) established in Seville in 1812, Montarco organized a raffle, with tickets at twenty-two *reales* a head and prizes consisting of various properties belonging to the national properties.[122]

All this said, Montarco was committed to a *josefino* victory both personally and politically, the result being that, when pushed to the limit, he had no hesitation in proceeding to extremes. Thus: "All other means having been proved to have no effect, it is indispensable that the deficits in your prefecture's payment of its ordinary and extraordinary contributions alike should be made up by the imposition of armed force; that, if the old ones have proved to be inadequate, the *pueblos* should find new ways of meeting the demands that have been made of them; and, finally, that, taking account of every consideration, Your Excellency should yourself propose such measures as appear to be appropriate, necessary, and practical in their execution."[123]

If this was the line taken by the men who might have acted as intermediaries with the occupying forces, the French could scarcely be expected to adopt a more moderate stance. Their response to efforts at protest, indeed, were severe in the extreme. As a first step there was the taking of hostages. For example: "The . . . governor of the province of Granada has received information to the effect that those responsible have not been paying the contributions which are being imposed on them each month. He therefore warns all those who have fallen behind in their payments . . . that they have from this moment until 1 October to pay what they owe on pain of being arrested, imprisoned in the Alhambra, and from thence conducted to France."[124] An alternative, meanwhile, was to billet troops on recalcitrants with orders to meet all their costs until such time as all their debts had been cleared, such a fate eventually befalling the city of Córdoba in May 1812, when a company of dragoons was sent to occupy the town hall for this purpose.[125] And last but not least, places that were not permanently occupied by the French could always be visited by a punitive column: at about this same time, the justices of Galarosa were brusquely informed that if they did not pay over their share of the latest requisition by 20 July, the latter would be levied "militarily"—in other words, their *pueblo* would be sacked.[126]

Given the fact that much of Andalucía was in a state of turmoil and that the French did not have enough troops to impose their will everywhere, the amount of money raised even by these draconian measures never met the full sums demanded of the region. According to Jean-Marc Lafon, indeed, in 1811 Seville paid over some 27 percent of its ordinary contributions, while the same figures for Granada and Jaén were 58 percent and 35 percent. Yet even so the burden was crippling: in all, the figure raised appears to have been something over 242,500,000 *reales*, this working out at roughly four times as much as would have been raised by the pre-1808 Bourbon administration from Andalucía in the same period of time.[127]

That such a figure could have been raised speaks volumes for the realities of French occupation. Couched though this was in the language of benevolence, progress, and emancipation, in practice the needs of the war effort and, beyond that, the Grand Empire came first. To achieve their objectives, meanwhile, the military commanders who were in de facto control of occupation policy were utterly ruthless in their use of force, a good example here being the large numbers of executions generated by their attempts to put down the insurrection. Thus, in the city of Córdoba alone, seventeen men were put to death in 1810, forty-five in 1811, and thirty-three in 1812.[128] How these men fell into the hands of the French is for the most part unknown, but many were certainly the victims of the mobile columns that ravaged the countryside under the command of such figures as the governor of Estepa, François Louis de Bourbon-Busset.[129] As witness the memoirs of François Lavaux, we come here to counterinsurgency operations at their most savage. Lavaux's regiment, the 103rd Line, was a part of the division of General Gazan in Mortier's V Corps. Following the fall of Seville, he initially found himself marching north in an abortive attempt to seize the fortress of Badajoz, but within a few weeks he was back on the Guadalquivir. The troops were exhausted—by the time they reached Seville, they had been four days without bread—but there was no rest. With the countryside up in arms, on 10 April Lavaux's regiment marched northward, together with a few cavalry, with orders to burn down every village that offered resistance and put the entire population, children and babies included, to the sword. After first sacking the town of Branes on the grounds that a few shots had been fired at them, Lavaux and his comrades headed for Constantina, from whence news had reached the French that the insurgents had established a base in the town. The 103rd having come in sight of the *pueblo*, the defenders were offered fair terms, but the latter answered that they would never surrender to the French. Promised by their commanding officer that they would be allowed to sack the place, Lavaux and his comrades immediately fell on with a will, whereupon the defenders fled in panic, many of them being cut down by the French cavalry as they attempted to reach the hills that surrounded the town. Then followed scenes of absolute horror: "We eventually entered the town, the latter immediately being pillaged and reduced to ashes. A number of soldiers entered a convent, and . . . raped and murdered the nuns they found inside. In the evening, after the brigands had dispersed, we were billeted in the town. Hardly anybody was left in any of the buildings, but the few people we did find were immediately bayonetted."[130]

Following the affair at Constantina, the French column returned to Seville only for Lavaux and his comrades to be sent out again, this time against a nearby village in which a number of insurgents had reportedly taken refuge. Sensing that discretion was the better part of valor, most of the band concerned melted away, but a picket of thirty-two men were taken prisoner and executed there and then without further ado. Having done what was required of them, the French returned to Seville for a third time, only almost immediately to march off to war again. On 2 May the 103rd arrived before the town of Algodonales in the Serranía de Ronda. What followed was, as the *afrancesado* press claimed, a bloody affair. In the first charge Lavaux claims that twenty-four men of his own *voltigeur* company fell, but the fire of the insurgents was not sufficient to deter veteran French soldiers forever, and very soon the attackers were advancing through the streets toward the center of the town. Even now, however, the Spaniards did not give up, and their assailants were further enraged to see women carrying ammunition to their husbands and even taking an active part in the defense. The result, needless to say, was wholesale slaughter:

> While we were waiting in the gardens outside the town, the general had ordered us not to spare anyone: even the women and children were to be killed. The horrible carnage that we therefore engaged in had to be seen to be believed. Most of the inhabitants were hiding, and as I advanced, I came across several women and young girls. Out of pity, I spared their lives, but the *voltigeurs* who were following me ran all of them through with their bayonets. Further on I found a number of others who were trying to hide their husbands by lying on the ground and covering them with their own bodies. . . . I leveled my musket at them, but they begged me for mercy so piteously that I could not refuse them. A number of my comrades then came on the scene. . . . Dragging the women aside, they thus revealed their menfolk, some of whom were found still to have guns in their hands. None of those concerned were long for this life: the whole lot were bayonetted. . . . At last we reached the center of the village. All the houses were being set alight, while the soldiers seized everything that they could lay their hands on. The worst thing I saw was in the courtyard of a windmill. This was strewn with eighteen bodies, and among them I saw a little child of no more than three or four years of age lying cradled in

> the arms of its dead mother, the latter having been bayonetted several times. The child was making no cry, but all the same it would let no one carry it away.[131]

Led, as we have seen, by a local insurgent leader named José Romero Alvarez, the so-called Alcalde de Montellano, the insurgents made their last stand in a large house on the main square. Barricading themselves in, they kept up a heavy fire and for some time managed to keep the French at bay. With casualties mounting, the invaders decided to burn Romero and his men out and had soon managed to stack large quantities of wood and hemp against the walls. Still more inflammable material having been thrown onto the balconies and through the windows, the building was duly fired. Very soon it had become an inferno, the flames having spread to a large quantity of olive oil that had been in storage in an adjacent outhouse. Trapped inside, some of the defenders, including Romero, chose to die in the flames, but others rushed out onto the balcony only to be shot down by the vengeful troops waiting aside. With French tempers inflamed by an incident in which a woman had shot a soldier who thought that she was trying to surrender, hardly anyone was allowed to escape, practically the only survivors being Romero's wife and three young children.[132]

Algodonales having been dealt with, it was now the turn of Grazalema, and here too there followed scenes of terrible bloodshed and violence that were mitigated only by the fact that some of the insurgents were able to barricade themselves in a local convent that was too strong to be taken by assault. Yet in the end nothing was achieved: having burned several other *pueblos*, the French column reached Ronda, only to learn that the number of insurgents in the area had been increasing by the day, this being a realization that seems a fitting end to this chapter. The fact is that in Andalucía, techniques that had served the French well in other parts of the empire proved a complete failure. The fire and the sword seen at Algodonales and the other places sacked by Sergeant Lavaux and his fellows was certainly not the only plank on which occupation policy depended. On the contrary, both the military and the civilian authorities made sustained efforts to win the support of the elites and the commonalty alike. In ordinary circumstances these might have been successful, but the circumstances were anything but ordinary. Having for various reasons been prevented from completely eradicating the Allied military presence from Andalucía, the French were forced to make demands of the region that were far higher than might otherwise have been the case. By driving the population ever deeper into poverty, however, this fanned the flames of brigandage and made it still harder for the French to obtain their political, military, and fiscal objectives. With the invaders already in the grip of a series of influences that were not inclined to favor more subtle approaches, the result was an orgy of violence that could destroy places like Algodonales but never bring victory within the grip of Marshal Soult, or at least not until such time as the last Allied regular army had been beaten and the last Allied fortress forced to surrender.

6

Collaboration and Coexistence

At the heart of any study of a period of military occupation must lie the relationship between occupier and occupied. Insofar as this is concerned, the questions are obvious enough. To what extent is the occupier willing or able to elide the harsher aspects of the presence of his forces and ameliorate the demands that they impose on the local economy; to assimilate the interests of the conquered periphery with those of the conquering center; to ensure the continuation of everyday life; and finally, to offer a place—indeed, even a voice—in its administration to established local elites? Equally, to what extent are the occupied able or willing to cling to old loyalties in the face of greater or lesser levels of official pressure and repression; to risk life, limb, family, and friends in acts of overt resistance; to reject tempting opportunities of employment, patronage, or economic advancement; and to deny the human face of the invader? In all cases the answer to these questions will be influenced by a variety of different factors, including the nature of the occupying regime, the relationship between the occupied territory and its previous master, the homogeneity or otherwise of the indigenous culture, and competing perceptions of the military situation, and here the Peninsular War offers us a picture that is no different than that offered by any other conflict. Where the Peninsular War differs, however, is the fact that the history of occupation has, to a large part, been dominated by a discourse that has coincided in wishing to stress a particularly negative view of the situation. On the one hand, ever ready to legitimize their cause, observers favorable to the forces of occupation, not to mention representatives of those forces themselves, on the whole have been anxious to construct an image of the French forces as standard-bearers of European civilization isolated in a hostile land, and to do this it was convenient to portray the peoples of Portugal and Spain as ignorant savages ruled by a church that feared and hated the reforms of the Napoleonic empire, ignorant savages, moreover, who rejected every attempt to better their condition and waged war on the French with the most unrelenting cruelty. Meanwhile, on the other hand, observers favorable to the Patriot cause in Spain and Portugal alike have been just as eager to emphasize the unanimity and determination of resistance (and especially popular resistance) to the Napoleonic imperium and to denigrate and marginalize those who sought to collaborate with the invaders. This chapter, however, will suggest that the reality was far more complex and that, if enthusiastic collaboration was not widespread, in Andalucía it is possible to see the makings of a modus vivendi that, everything else being equal, in time might have allowed the region to become as much a part of what Michael Broers has defined as "the inner empire" as, say, the Rhineland.

In initiating a discussion of this issue, the obvious place to begin is the cheering crowds that greeted King Joseph on the triumphal progress that he embarked upon in the immediate wake of conquest. Ever eager to denigrate *el rey intruso,* in his memoirs Marshal Soult was scathing as to what these crowds represented:

> The king . . . wanted to mount a personal tour of Andalucía. . . . The towns received him with curiosity, and he let himself be easily seduced by the demonstrations of which he was the object. The leisured classes preferred, it is true, a regular government that avoided anarchy and protected property from the rule of the populace. Yet it was never prepared to compromise itself in favor of such a goal. The king became a magnet for the sort of place-hunters who in every system prostrate themselves at the feet of those in power in order to win favors while yet not allowing their loyalties to go beyond mere words. The king loved to believe their promises even when these were belied at every instant. We could not even get towns that had sent delegations to acclaim the king to close their gates against the bands that

> hastened to enter them whenever their garrisons left them unprotected. Both sizeable and rich, the city of Málaga, which had welcomed the king in all due form, had to be left unprotected for a few days while its garrison engaged in operations against the insurgents of the mountains of Ronda. No sooner had they gone than a number of bands who had been hanging around in the area entered it and engaged in all sorts of excesses without the least hand being raised against them. In response to our complaints, we got excuses of every type and fresh protestations of loyalty, but we could no more believe these last than the ones we had received before. The population of the towns were easy enough to govern, but they scarcely offered us a firm foothold. It was in the countryside that the people were truly Spanish—that is to say brutal, almost savage, inured to privation, fond of a life of adventure, used to bearing arms, exalted by the strongest passions.[1]

We have here, then, two separate issues: first of all, that the favorable reception accorded to the king was a matter of show alone, and second, that even if the reaction of the towns could be taken at face value, urban Andalucía was not representative of the region as a whole. Insofar as the first claim is concerned, there is, of course, plenty of evidence that there was nothing spontaneous about what happened when King Joseph arrived in the towns that he visited, and all the more so once a little time had elapsed since the passage of the Sierra Morena. Consider, for example, the account that José Mendoza y Rico gives of the arrival of the royal cavalcade in Málaga, the story that he retails being more or less as follows. From the middle of February onward, rumors had been circulating that Joseph was coming to visit the city, and at the beginning of March, the story was finally confirmed. Immediately there followed a frantic flurry of activity, the town council preparing a lodging for the king in the house of a prominent merchant of French extraction named José María Maury, who had become the commandant of the Guardia Cívica; ordering the erection of triumphal arches at two of the principal gates; organizing a variety of entertainments and other celebrations; and issuing directions to the inhabitants of the houses lining the principal streets to decorate the facades with the usual hangings. On the day of the king's arrival, meanwhile, the screw was turned still further, an order being issued to the effect that the head of any household whose womenfolk did not turn out on their balconies to cheer and throw flowers would be heavily fined and even sent to prison. On the whole these orders produced the desired result—if only because Málaga happened to be the first town where the authorities had thought of having the crowd strew his way with flowers, Joseph was much impressed—but even so the collaborationist faction in the city were taking no chances. Accompanied by the city's new chief of police, Enrique Disdier, Maury went ahead of the royal procession, telling the people to shout "Long live the king!" and threatening them with dire punishments if they did not cheer loudly enough, while agitators in the pay of the chief collaborators mingled with the people so as to ensure that at least some voices were raised in support of the new regime.[2]

In short, the exultant reception that so impressed the French was in reality nothing but a put-up job, and even then one that was by no means entirely successful, Mendoza noting proudly that, despite everything, "the commonalty refused to cheer the king, and only opened their mouths to criticize and insult him."[3] As for the fact that crowds filled the streets, this in itself means nothing, for it can easily be explained away by reference to simple curiosity, the desire to snatch a few of the coins that were habitually flung among the bystanders, or even just the chance of a break in routine: in the dreariness of life in rural Andalucía, a free show complete with a parade, fireworks, bullfights, and illuminations was always a free show. In the first days of the campaign too, the French were crossing territory that was, if not exactly friendly, at the very least sprinkled with families of German origin, for whom the appearance of the French army did not represent quite the same threat that it did to the rest of the populace: as late as 1812, an officer passing through the area of La Carlota described the populace hastening "to welcome the troops with a sympathy that was all the more natural given that the language of those of my men who were Saxons recalled that of their own motherland, the result being that the soldiers passed the night in the midst of joy, pleasure, and numerous libations."[4]

Yet if all these caveats are true enough, it was not just Joseph who was taken in by the cheering crowds. Thus, if we turn, not to Soult's memoirs, but to the reports that he sent to Napoleon via the latter's chief of staff, Marshal Berthier, we find that these are at least as optimistic as anything that emanated from King Joseph. Here, for example, is Soult's account of the first days of King Joseph's tour of Andalucía:

> Having decided that his presence is not required before Cádiz, His Majesty has set out for Málaga, . . . where he intends to organize the region and take various measures that will have the most positive effect in respect of the submission of the whole of Spain. Already the numerous towns that he has visited since his departure from Jérez have shown themselves to be well disposed toward him, and everything suggests that in five or six days the inhabitants of the mountains through which we are now passing, and particularly those of the area around Ronda, . . . will be given sole charge of their police . . . and that they will muster enough armed men to be able to repulse any incursion on the part of foreign troops that might take place. In this fashion, security will be increased, confidence boosted, and the forces of the empire enabled to concentrate their efforts on those points where the enemy is still holding out. . . . It is to be hoped that, despite the resistance of Cádiz and a few other fortresses, this example will be followed elsewhere. The inhabitants of a number of towns and villages have already exchanged fire with bands of smugglers or insurgents. In all the towns of Andalucía the national guard [*sic*] is taking shape and beginning to do its duty. Meanwhile, mounted *compagnies franches* [free companies] are being formed to serve beyond the bounds of the towns and villages, and there is in general such enthusiasm for the king that opposition to his rule may be really said to be nonexistent.[5]

Nor was the marshal any less gushing in his account of Joseph's reception at Málaga: "His Catholic Majesty arrived in Málaga yesterday evening and was received with enthusiasm by its 60,000 inhabitants. Nothing like it has been experienced by him since his arrival in Spain, and it appears that the same sentiment animates the entire population of the Kingdom of Granada."[6]

That Soult should have taken such a line in his dispatches to Napoleon is not, of course, incompatible with a reality that was much darker: the invasion of Andalucía had not been directly sanctioned by the emperor, and the marshal therefore had good reason to present a favorable view of the situation. Even if we accept that Mendoza was partisan in his presentation of events in Málaga, then (and that Mendoza was partisan there can be no doubt: after 1814 it obviously behooved all Spaniards who wrote about the occupation to emphasize the loyalty of their hometowns to Ferdinand VII), we need not believe the wilder flights of *josefino* fancy. In short, even if the elites were on the whole prepared to go along with the demands of occupation, this does not mean that the populace were anything other than bitterly opposed to the French. That this was so is certainly the view of at least some of the invaders. Thus, the Polish officer Wojciechowski later recalled how, in Málaga, to get anyone to attend the social events they organized, the invaders had no option but to send parties of troops round to the houses of the intended guests so that they could claim that they were only attending under duress.[7] Equally, the naval captain and erstwhile prisoner of war Jean-Baptiste Grivel confessed to being much impressed with the attitude of the populace: "The Spaniards . . . are the people of Europe who made the least concessions to their conquerors in respect of fraternization. They endured what they could not free themselves from, but even in the most difficult moments they never flattered us nor sought to hide their resentment and hopes of liberation."[8] Here too we might cite Grivel's fellow captive, Sébastien Blaze: "The people of Seville accepted all the entertainments that King Joseph offered them, but did not detest him any the less for it."[9] And for still further evidence of the extent of popular hostility to occupation, we have only to advert to the scenes that were witnessed when Seville was finally liberated from the French in August 1812. Thus, while the fighting was still going on, small groups of Spanish civilians supposedly seized planks and ran forward to repair the damage that the French had done to the bridge of boats that linked the main part of the city to the suburb of Triana—the initial point of attack—in an attempt to hold back the Allied advance.[10] Once the British, Spanish, and Portuguese troops involved were across the river, then the excitement knew no bounds: thrilled by their impending liberation, the populace rushed into the streets and thronged them to such an extent that pursuit of the French rear guard, which had held out to the last minute on the riverbank, was found to be out of the question. "To describe the joy of the people of Seville is impossible," wrote the Spanish commander, Juan de la Cruz Murgeon. "Any good Spaniard will understand the reactions impelled in them by their patriotism, and . . . imagine for themselves what took place."[11]

For a further suggestion that even in the cities the situation was anything but stable, we may turn to a long report that was sent to the Patriot government in the early summer of 1810 by a spy resident in Seville. Covering the period from February to May 1810 and extending to a length of no fewer than forty-three pages, this mixes military intelligence with a detailed account of life in the city, and in brief paints a very negative picture of the situation, the root cause of the problem being the behavior of the invaders in respect of the civilian population:

> For the first few days the people remained tranquil amid their sorrow . . . but, the soldiers entered their houses in the most despotic fashion, seizing what took their fancy by force, and smashing up anything they could not carry away with them. Many houses were sacked in this manner, while the soldiers put on sale a multitude of goods of every sort. . . . As all the convents of the religious orders had been occupied, even church vestments and sacred vessels . . . appeared in these markets, the religious themselves having to take refuge with the populace. Unable to bear this treatment any longer, the people have become restive and are beginning secretly to conspire against the invaders.[12]

This resistance, the same observer continued, was taking a number of different forms. Individual French soldiers were beginning to disappear at night; the claims made by the *Gazeta de Sevilla* were daily laughed off; and orders that Joseph's saint's day on 19 March should be celebrated by the illumination of every house in the city had been met by a flat refusal to cooperate, hardly one-tenth of the inhabitants complying with the instructions of the authorities. Still more dramatically, on 25 March an attempt on part of the parish priest of Triana to preach a sermon in favor of King Joseph was howled down by the congregation amid cries of "Away with him! Throw him out! Kill him!" (it is but fair to note, however, that the offending priest afterward alleged that the riot had been got up by a fellow cleric who bore him a grudge and was out to do him down). Needless to say, meanwhile, the growing mood of defiance extended to the formation of the Guardia Cívica and Joseph's attempts to raise an army. With respect to the former, the spy continued, the only men who had joined up were the magistrates, while the *juramentado* regiments were no sooner raised than they melted away again, an example that was cited here being that of the Third Regiment of Infantry: brought up to a strength of 400 men on no fewer than three occasions, in between times it sometimes fell to one of as few as thirty. With even the king's most loyal supporters badly divided on matters of occupation policy—according to the report, the city's newly appointed mayor, Joaquín de Goyeneta, had had a furious argument with Aranza regarding whether or not it was politic to impose a financial levy on the city—Joseph in consequence set out to return to Madrid in a state of some despair. Indeed, far from being the gracious address reported in the press, the speech that he made when he took leave of the authorities was one of bitter recrimination: in his eyes his supporters had neither exerted themselves sufficiently nor taken the right measures.[13]

The mention of the Guardia Cívica in this document is worth taking further as there is considerable evidence from the French camp that all was very far from well in this respect. Notwithstanding claims in the *afrancesado* press that have the guard parading in full strength a week earlier (see above), in Seville the organization of this force was set in motion on 15 February 1810 by a proclamation of Goyeneta and the intendant, Joaquín Leandro de Solis: thus, all householders aged between seventeen and fifty were to register, and if necessary present any cases for exemption that they might wish to make, at the town hall on 16 or 17 February on pain of severe punishment.[14] Needless to say, Solis and Goyeneta expressed the hope that this last would not be necessary—that the value of the project was so obvious that cooperation would be universal—but very soon it became clear that their optimism was misplaced. If the string of orders and proclamations that followed is anything to go by, in fact the exact reverse was the case. Thus, on 18 February the registration period had to be extended by two days on the face-saving pretext that, given the short notice, some of those who were supposed to come forward might not have heard of the order in time.[15] Then on 3 March the French governor of the city, Nicholas Guye, issued a proclamation in which he complained that, in general, the inhabitants were proving reticent in coming forward but said that he was, for the time being, assuming that this was because "seditious and ill-intentioned people" had been putting about false accounts of what service entailed; in reality, he continued, men should only have to serve for one day in every twenty-four, the consequence being, first, that there was really no excuse for failing to enlist and, second, that, unless the populace changed its attitude, he would very soon be forced to adopt a much sterner line.[16] All too clearly, however, the populace did not change its attitude: on 16 March 1810 the town council announced that it had asked all the city's guilds to get their members to enlist and assured artisans and tradesmen in general not only that they would be most welcome in the force but also that they would not be treated any worse than anyone else when it came to such matters as assigning guard duty; should such reassurances not produce the desired effect, however, the populace was warned that the city's district magistrates had been ordered to form lists of all the city's inhabitants and to check who had enlisted in the Guardia Cívica, the clear hint being that anyone who still failed to appear would be severely punished.[17]

Initially, then, it is probably true enough that there was some tension: the edge having yet to be taken off them by prolonged social intercourse with the inhabitants, French bullying and harassment were at their worst and Spanish resentment at its highest; hence, perhaps, the tension that marred Seville's annual Holy Week processions in 1810 (in brief, rumors that a large force of guerrillas was about to enter the town came close to provoking so much excitement that the French and their supporters feared that they were facing an insurrection).[18] Yet matters did not remain at such a pitch for very long. Here, for example, is the pharmacist Antoine Fée: "Throughout the occupation, Seville was as quiet as any French city: she had accepted her new destiny, while Joseph had many adherents there. The inhabitants bore our domination as if they were our compatriots. The resident French population—officers of the general staff and the medical services [and] employees of the civil and military administration—all had friends within the walls. . . . The soirées, balls, and dinners given by Marshal Soult were all very much to the taste of the *sevillanos,* and tickets for them were much in demand."[19] In short, while the populace might have hated the invaders, the elites did not (there were, however, exceptions: billeted on a Spanish family of some note in Seville after his escape from captivity, Sébastien Blaze found that his host, one Bénito de la Madrid, was a surly individual who detested the French and insisted on keeping his daughters locked in an upstairs room whenever Blaze was in the house).[20] This does not mean to say, of course, that life was entirely without upset. On the contrary, even in the cities there was inevitably considerable friction between occupier and occupied. Much of this was fairly low level in character, a good example of the sort of issue that could be involved here being recounted by Blaze:

> One evening I went to the theater, and, as I did not know the town, my compatriot, Pascal Tournel, accompanied me home; when we reached my door, it was eleven o'clock. The entire household of Don Bénito had been sound asleep for some time, but he had waited up for me, and came to open the door himself. No sooner had he done so than this ungracious host set about berating me on the late hour of my return, and told me that he went to bed at half-past nine, and that, if I did not fit in with his habits, I would be forced to spend the night in the street. . . . I had been too cruelly . . . persecuted by the Spaniards during my captivity to accept such language now I was free. I answered Don Bénito in the same tone, then, and told him that I would return at whatever time I wanted; that if I found the door locked, I would break it down; and that, if a

French soldier gave an order, a Spanish civilian had no option but to comply.[21]

Some officers, then, were less than tactful, but there were also more serious problems. Among these there was the effect of French reform, which on occasion reached deep into Spanish cultural life. A good instance of this comes with the 1811 decree in respect of the establishment of cemeteries. This policy had already caused much anguish when it was implemented by the Bourbons prior to 1808, and now this was repeated afresh. "Such is the force of habit and prejudice in superstitious lands," wrote Blaze, "that the beautiful Dolores, the daughter of the owner of the house in which I was then staying, came to my chamber in floods of tears. In all good faith she said to me, 'How happy I could be if I could die now.' 'And why would that be?' I asked. 'Because in the future we will not be allowed to be buried in a church.'"[22] Rather more damaging was the drunkenness that was endemic among the French forces—indeed, it was particularly noted among the Polish troops who came to form much of the garrison of Málaga[23]—and this undoubtedly caused much offence in a society where this particular vice was habitually regarded with contempt (the presence of the Poles, meanwhile, was upsetting in another sense: the Lancers of the Vistula, for example, discovered that everywhere they went, the populace shrank before them even more than they did from the other occupation forces on account of rumors to the effect that, as an "Asiatic" people, Poles ate babies).[24]

Another subject that was likely to cause trouble was women. Among the French troops who came to Andalucía, there was undoubtedly much fantasizing, as we have seen, about Spanish women being habitually wanton (this tendency is found in its most extreme form in the memoirs of Sébastien Blaze, who paints a picture of the women of Seville entertaining lovers on a daily basis and even goes so far as to maintain that the iron grills that covered the windows of every house owed their origins to the fears of jealous husbands!).[25] As witness the recollections of Richard Croker, however, the reality was rather different: "I have read in several books accounts of the vitiated conduct of . . . Spanish women in general, but very different indeed is that of the women of Andalucía. . . . Their customs are so extremely modest that they will not allow you to touch the hand of a female, and, as it has not always been found easy to induce an Englishman to confine himself to these restrictions, we have frequently incurred the mild reproof, 'Speak to me; do not touch me.'"[26] Behavior of the sort witnessed by Andrew Blayney, a British general captured by Polish troops at Fuengirola in the course of an ill-starred descent on the coast in the summer of 1810, was therefore unlikely to be any more welcome than it would have been anywhere else: "At Archidona we halted to breakfast. . . . We were attended by four extremely pretty girls, whom the French officers, to show their gallantry, pinched and pulled about until the poor girls were afraid to approach the table, and, although I did not join in tormenting them, I suffered as if I had, and was obliged to assist myself."[27] Given the cultural norms prevalent in the French army, however, such behavior was endemic: set loose in Seville after nearly two years of confinement at the hands of the Spaniards, for example, Blaze appears to have set out to woo literally every woman that he came across.[28]

If the casual womanizing of the French troops caused much offence—the egregious Blaze on one occasion found himself in full flight from an outraged husband and a supporting band of civic guards after being caught in flagrante delicto with the lady of the house and on another was menaced in the street by a gang of *juramentados* who took offence at his gallantry at an open-air dance[29]—their constant plundering was almost equally troublesome to civil-military relations. Let us here consider a story that was recounted by the gunner Manière:

> At the siege of Cádiz we were on quarter rations: in fact, many soldiers deserted so as to get something to eat. We got a three-pound loaf, half of it nothing more than bran, every four days. Some men got through theirs in two, and, until such time as a fresh distribution was made, they had to look to their own subsistence. One day four of us went into a field to gather onions. We were on our hands and knees grubbing them up when suddenly a hail of stones . . . fell around us. Looking up, we saw a dozen peasants running toward us, and in consequence took to our heels in the direction of [Puerto Real]. One man named

> Picart had got hold of a big pumpkin and this prevented him from running fast enough. Setting upon him, the peasants decided to take him to the commandant. Having got safely back to town, I was watching from a street corner when the party arrived. Picart was still carrying his pumpkin, . . . and I therefore shouted to him to throw it away as it was the only evidence of his guilt. This he proceeded to do, but one of his escort recognized me and tried to seize me as well. But I had nothing on me that proved I had been out marauding, and so I called to a group of infantrymen who happened to be nearby, and together we fell on the Spaniards, Picart, meanwhile, taking advantage of the confusion to get clean away.[30]

Such clashes were doubtless repeated many times over in most of the towns of Andalucía, but they are hardly redolent of a people's war, the fact being that the story could in reality have come from almost any part of Napoleonic Europe. The urban lower classes undoubtedly resented the presence of Soult's forces and on occasion showed their teeth: there was the occasional murder—on 1 June 1810, for example, one Francisco León was sentenced to death in Ronda for killing an aged French resident of the town named Domingue Taillau[31]—while more than one French memoir is spattered with accounts of the populace behaving in a threatening manner toward isolated soldiers or engaging in petty acts of resistance, such as serving up donkey for parties of officers instead of beef.[32] Meanwhile, as we shall see, ever-worsening levels of poverty and desperation, not to mention occasional rumors that the French were set to introduce conscription, were to drive considerable numbers of men to forsake their normal lives and seek survival in precisely the same sort of extralegal activity that had been the populace's chief refuge prior to 1808.[33]

Yet in the end, occasional conspiracies aside, such reactions were individual and sporadic rather than communal and continuous. Such at least is the impression that one obtains from reading the account of Edouard Lapène, a French artillery officer serving under Marshal Mortier and who wrote a detailed history of the campaign. Thus, the Andalusians, Lapène asserts, were too accustomed to a life of idleness and ease to make good soldiers, or indeed to want to take up arms at all, while such was the heat to which they were constantly exposed that they were in any case victims of a constant lassitude that at all times tended to keep them close to hearth and home and to dissuade them from anything that smacked of physical activity.[34] All this, of course, is so much nonsense, but what is hard to avoid is the sense that, particularly once the turmoil that inevitably accompanied the first few days of occupation was a thing of the past, the urban populace on the whole remained extremely passive. Setting aside the rather dubious riot in Triana mentioned above, the only serious act of popular resistance in Seville in the whole period of French occupation came in December 1811, when the Casa de la Moneda—the royal mint—was severely damaged by fire the very night a new superintendent who had been sent from Madrid arrived to take up residence within its walls.[35] Equally, in Granada the nearest that the population came to overt resistance was the insistence of a few young men on parading up and down the banks of the River Darro swathed in the heavy brown cloaks that foreigners had always found so sinister and threatening, the futility of this gesture being commemorated in the name by which the spot concerned is known to this day—the Paseo de los Tristes (Promenade of the Melancholy).[36] And finally, in Córdoba the only hint of resistance—if hint indeed it is—was the manner in which the constant French injunctions that each household should regularly sweep and water the portion of street and sidewalk that corresponded to the frontage of its domain appear, as far as possible, to have been ignored.[37] Nor, indeed, were the commonality averse to engaging in attempts to secure the protection of the invaders that were just as groveling as anything engaged in by their social superiors. Hence the famous incident in the course of King Joseph's visit to Arcos de la Frontera when a young day laborer named Juan Girón and his wife, Antonia López, suddenly burst out of the crowd and threw themselves down at the king's feet as he was leaving the parish church after hearing Mass to beg that he accord them the favor of allowing the couple to name their newly born twins after the king and queen, this gesture netting the parents a gratuity of 500 francs.[38]

In view of the fact that the elites were on the whole quite happy to accept French occupation, nothing else is really to be expected.

One is here led back to the iron hand of the great estates. Given the vulnerability of much of the populace to pressure from above, defiance of any sort was likely to have serious consequences in terms of employment and patronage. In the Andalucía of the Junta Central, the full weight of the prevailing system had not been enough to contain popular unrest, but now the state was backed by armed forces and other means of repression that were far more impressive than before, and the result was that the urban populace for the most part endured the presence of the enemy with little demur. As for the elites, even when they disliked the French, they were not always prepared to completely freeze them out, let alone actively resist them. Indeed, even the most violent partisans of the old order were by no means incapable of arriving at a modus vivendi with the forces of occupation. Here it is definitely worth recurring to the memoirs of Antoine Fée. Stationed at the town of Chiclana during the siege of Cádiz, he was billeted in the home of a prominent citizen named Antonio Múñoz and soon discovered that he was scarcely a welcome guest:

> My host . . . had nothing but hatred in his heart. Whenever he and I discussed one or other of the burning questions relating to the future of Spain, he at first made an effort to temper his words, . . . but, little by little, his face would become flushed and his eyes start to burn with a savage gleam, and, driven by the violence of his character, he would completely lose control of himself. . . . In one of these moments of passion . . . he went so far as to say, "Señor Don Antonio, before the war I loved God . . . and desired for my salvation as a Christian, but now I want to burn in hell . . . in order to have the pleasure of seeing that devil Napoleon roast alongside me." Meanwhile, though, truth to tell, he had lost his son in the war; another Spaniard told me that he longed to see the Straits of Gibraltar filled from coast to coast with French blood, and then drown himself in its waves of scarlet.[39]

Yet as Fée soon found, this hatred was in practice tempered by humanity. Múñoz, it transpired, had three daughters, and of these the oldest had married a French captain by the time he arrived, while the youngest was "a flower [who] . . . had not the least idea how to hate." This left just the middle daughter, and here matters first seemed very different: "Maria, had the character of her father and took hatred of the French to a state of exultation. . . . She could never manage to give the name of 'brother' to her sister's husband, and rather always called him by his rank (her sister, meanwhile, became *la capitana*)." Yet even here Fée's cause was not entirely lost, for, as he said, "I tamed this fierce apparition, and, without surrendering her patriotism, she in the end became affectionate enough toward me."[40] In short, bit by bit, Fée, who was clearly a decent and sensitive individual, succeeded in winning over his hosts, so much so, indeed, that they ended up by throwing him a party: "One night I came in and found everything ready for a little get-together. It was . . . my saint's day, and I was very touched by the signs of affection that were lavished upon me. The patio had been illuminated; an elaborate supper, which only the misery of the times prevented from being called sumptuous, was served; and I was presented with bunches of wild flowers, . . . two Roman medals, . . . [and] a drawing of a view of Chiclana. . . . Every face was smiling, even that of the second sister, who for the time being seemed prepared to forget that I was an enemy. . . . It was a delicious evening."[41]

Also interesting, meanwhile, are the experiences of Albert de Rocca. An officer of the Second Hussars, Rocca entered Andalucía with a draft of reinforcements in the immediate aftermath of the fall of Seville and soon found himself, with the rest of his regiment, at Ronda. On 1 May, however, disaster struck when Rocca was badly wounded in a skirmish near Setenil. Helped back to the town by his men, he was suddenly accosted by the couple in whose house he was lodging. Hitherto they had been cold and distant toward him, but now, having heard that he had been hurt, they insisted on having him carried back to their home rather than to the town's general hospital and went to great lengths to make him comfortable. Three days later, meanwhile, this kindness was taken to still greater lengths in that the family made great efforts to ensure that Rocca survived an insurgent attack on the town that temporarily threatened to overrun the district in which he was lodged:

> Balls passed so near my windows that they were obliged to move my bed into the next room. My host and hostess came to tell me, while they endeavoured to remain calm themselves, that the *serranos* were at the end of our street, that they were gaining ground towards us, and that the old town was on the point of being carried by storm: they added that they were going to take precautions to shelter me from the fury of the *serranos* till the arrival of General Serrano Valdenebro, who was their relation. They carefully hid my arms, my military dress, and whatever else might have attracted the attention of the enemy, and, with the assistance of their servants, they carried me to the top of the house behind a little chapel dedicated to the Virgin Mary, looking on that consecrated place as an inviolable asylum. My hosts then brought two priests, who placed themselves at the street door to defend it, and, in case of need, to protect me by their presence. An old lady, the mother of my hostess, remained alone with me, and began praying: she turned the beads of her rosary faster or slower according to the cries of the combatants or the noise of the firearms [that] announced the increase or diminution of the danger.[42]

Rocca ascribed the great kindness shown him to the natural generosity of the Spanish people, but there was also, of course, a degree of self-interest in such actions, for a grateful French officer—indeed, any officer with whom it had proved possible to strike up some sort of personal rapport—was obviously a potential protector and advocate. We may here return to the account of Edouard Lapène:

> Being easy enough to reassure, the Andalusian is very quick to dispose of a touching confidence in others, and at the same time is wholly possessed of the natural instinct to make a patron out of anyone he perceives to be his master. The payment of a few cheap courtesies, then, was quite sufficient to elicit the most unshakeable attachment, the Spaniard being as extreme in his affections as in his hatreds. . . . Very often, then, the Frenchman received as an enemy was on the day of his departure regretted as a friend. . . . In consequence, the

> periodic return of our troops to the same places could not but give rise to genuine warmth. . . . At the approach of a column, the inhabitants would anxiously enquire . . . if it belonged to this or that regiment, while no sooner than some object of their affections was discovered than they would run to him calling his name from afar and carry him in triumph to his old abode. . . . In short, keeping the troops in garrison in one place for long periods paid great dividends, for . . . it established a connection between the soldier and the Spaniard that was of great utility.[43]

Hatred, then, proved to be an emotion difficult to maintain, and all the more so as Fée was far from being the only French officer who, despite the prevailing ethos of the army that he served, was something other than a swaggering braggart. To judge from the many warm letters that he received from Spanish friends and well-wishers when he was invalided out of Andalucía following a serious fall from his horse in an action at Aracena in the spring of 1812, another young man who was much liked by the Spaniards with whom he came into contact was the cavalry officer Théophilé Brémond.[44] Also worthy of note in this context, perhaps, is Petit-Pierre, who as governor of La Cartuja—the citadel constructed by the French on the outskirts of Seville—turned the gardens of the monastery into a model farm and made a detailed study of the botany of the region.[45] There doubtless were exceptions. "Before we reached Martos," wrote Blayney, "we were met by a Monsieur Saul, a German, who, though but a lieutenant, commanded in the town. He . . . did not leave me long in doubt as to his character being that of a ferocious braggadocchio. . . . As we approached Martos, this ruffian pointed out to me two poor wretches hanging at a tree who had recently been executed by his order, observing with an infernal smile [that] 'that was the way to subdue Spain,' to which I could not help replying that 'it would require a vast deal of rope and a great many hangmen to execute eleven million people, and that, if only one remained, revenge would be his motto.' Clenching his fist, knitting his diabolical brow and curling his bushy moustachios, he swore a terrible oath that, if it depended on him, he would not leave one Spaniard in existence."[46] Yet this is scarcely the impression of the French that one generally obtains from British memoirs. Here, for example, is William Grattan, an officer in the Eighty-Eighth Foot who served in the peninsula in the period 1810–12: "It is a singular fact, and I look upon it as degrading one, that the French officers while at Madrid made in the ration of five to one more conquests than we did! How is this to be accounted for? The British officer has the advantage of appearance: his exterior is far before that of a Frenchman; his fortune, generally speaking, ten times as great, but what of all this if the one accommodates himself to the manners, the whims, of those he is thrown amongst, while the other, disregarding all forms, sticks to his national habits, struts about, and not only despises, but lets it be seen that he despises, all he meets save those of his own nation. What a fatal error!"[47]

The obvious place to go from here is the issue of gender relations, but, before considering these, let us first examine the more general issue of social interaction between invaders and invaded. Insofar as these are concerned, it is interesting that Grivel should have noted that, however much they hated the French in general, most of the families that he encountered in towns such as Jérez and Rota regarded the officers that they were forced to lodge in their homes with very different eyes, and that Sebastien Blaze could later write, "Despite their hatred for our nation, every Spaniard was the private friend of some Frenchman, just as every Frenchman had friends in Spain."[48] Very similar words, meanwhile, appear in the memoirs of the staff officer Just Roy, while such are his views that they are worth giving at rather greater length:

> The inhabitants of Seville are more civilized than are those of the majority of Spain's other provinces. The people of good family are most agreeable company, while the lower orders are much less dangerous than they are in Madrid. . . . During the first six months of my stay, . . . I occupied the same lodgings. My host was a canon of the cathedral. . . . He was an educated man, kind-hearted, frank, upright, someone who always spoke his mind straight out, . . . and very soon we were joined by a close friendship, and all the more so as he saw in me a variety of principles and sentiments that were very close to his own. . . . The people detested us, and, it has to be said, not without reason:

> we had hardly conducted ourselves in their country in a manner that was likely to make us popular with them. However, no matter how strong his hatred for France, every Spaniard made some Frenchman the object of his particular friendship, while every Frenchman had friends in Spain, and very often friends of the most proved devotion. . . . I hardly met a single French officer who spent any time in Spain and did not find himself in one of these relationships founded on mutual esteem that so often stood the test of both time and the vicissitudes of war.[49]

To return to the women of Andalucía, meanwhile, whether Grattan's claims really do constitute a fact, singular or otherwise, of course cannot be proven, but the French army certainly did not want for female company. As Fée remarked, for example, "The women paid no attention to nationality, but rather let themselves go wherever their sympathy took them"; hence the fact that, in Blayney's words, "Most of the French senior officers formed a temporary connection with a Spanish lady."[50] What, however, did this phenomenon represent? Given the economic situation, plenty of women were desperate enough to turn to prostitution, or at least to secure protectors among the occupying forces: at Andújar, for example, Blayney encountered "a beautiful Spanish girl of about eighteen, whose elegant shape, perfect head and bosom, shaded by . . . hair falling in graceful ringlets over her shoulders, might have entitled her to sit for the picture of Venus," who had supposedly thrown herself on the protection of the governor, General Blondeau, "to escape the brutality of the brigands" and was now acting as his "housekeeper."[51] That said, however, there are also many stories of more-or-less permanent unions with French officers. We have already mentioned the case in Chiclana noted by Fée, and the same author also describes an incident in Jérez, where an officer caused a great commotion by falling from a window ledge to which he had hauled himself up to speak to a young woman who had caught his eye; though the incident gave rise to much scandal, the couple were eventually married and at length made it back to France, where, we are told, they lived happily ever after.[52]

One question that is impossible to resolve with any degree of certainty here is the extent to which anything else underpinned these liaisons with the French other than the dictates of survival, on the one hand, and love, on the other. There are some observers, certainly, who have professed to see the arrival of the French as a catalyst that, not just in Andalucía but in Spain as a whole, persuaded women that they could break their bonds or at the very least enjoy a moment of diversion, if not sexual adventure.[53] One example of such a case is, perhaps, the wife of the American consul at Rota, an attractive young woman named Margarita and married to a distant relation who was much older than she was. Part French in origin, she spent the years of occupation surrounded by veritable crowds of admirers, among them Captain Grivel of the Sailors of the Guard. "One of the prettiest women in Andalucía," he writes, "[Margarita] lived in a charming villa at the entrance of the town, and entertained many guests. Officers of the highest rank made it their duty to call upon her and pay her homage."[54] Still more interesting, and all the more so as it comes from a Spanish source, is a story from Córdoba. In brief, in September 1810, hearing wild rumors to the effect that an irregular band led by one Francisco Lozano had forced an entire French column to surrender near Lucena, a priest named Francisco de Sales Ramírez made the mistake of remarking to a secularized nun of his acquaintance, whom he happened to meet in the street, that the guerrillas would be in the city any moment. Unknown to him, however, the nun was relishing her freedom and had therefore become a staunch *afrancesada*. What the priest had done being a breach of the rules laid down in respect of passing on news of the enemy, the woman rushed to report him to the occupying forces, and within twenty-four hours the unfortunate priest had been arrested and executed.[55]

Women who were so self-consciously *afrancesada,* however, were beyond doubt very rare. To the extent that there was any bent toward the French at all among the women of Andalucía, it was probably far more the product of French élan, pure and simple. Thus, Grivel positively gloried in the excitement that the improvised company of Sailors of the Guard, of which he was given command following his escape from captivity, generated among the women of Rota (perhaps worth noting here is that the Sailors of the Guard sported a particularly dashing uniform): "I was lodged in the house of an aged notary, . . . but I hardly saw his face, and in truth preferred the society of his family. I often used to chat with his wife and granddaughter. . . . These ladies paid me many compliments on the beauty of my unit. . . . In this they were but the echo of all the women of Rota, and among the young girls it was very much a feather in their cap to have a beau among my men: dressed in brand-new uniforms and perfectly equipped, the Sailors of the Guard possessed an appearance that was irresistible."[56]

Yet preening such as this should not lead us into the trap of overgeneralization. If some Andalusian women literally flung themselves into the arms of the invaders or acted as the agents of *afrancesado* husbands—Mendoza, for example, notes that in Málaga, "almost all the women of any status declared themselves in favor of the French party, and obliged many of their friends to do the same"[57]—others maintained their distance from them, or combined personal civility or even cordiality with an undisguised loyalty to the Patriot cause: Fée, as we have seen, gives evidence of one such case, while even Grivel has to admit that in the household in which he was billeted in Jérez, one of the daughters of the family was a staunch opponent of the French, albeit one who never showed him anything other but courtesy.[58] In a variety of ways, meanwhile, women were able to combine outward conformity with active involvement in the Allied war effort, and this even when the households to which they belonged were ostensibly *afrancesado*. On occasion, this was of quite a dramatic nature—in Ronda, for example, a housewife named María García took it upon herself to set up as a spy and pass information of all kinds to the local partisans[59]—but more often involvement came at the level of the symbolic, whether it was through showing kindness to prisoners of war, refusing to entertain French visitors, or as Rocca witnessed, wearing "English stuffs on which the pictures of Ferdinand VII and the Spanish generals most distinguished in the war against the French were painted."[60]

Setting aside the somewhat specialized issue of the reaction of the women of Andalucía to military occupation, for a case study in the nature of day-to-day relations between occupied and occupier in the region's smaller towns, we could do worse than examine the experiences of Montoro, a pueblo in the valley of the Guadalquivir that was one of the first places to be occupied by the forces of Joseph Bonaparte once they had broken through the Sierra Morena in January 1810. When the French arrived, there was no resistance of any sort—a last-minute attempt to reactivate the town's Milicia Honrada seems to have been directed more at keeping the populace in check than at fighting the French—but this submissive attitude did not spare the inhabitants from considerable disorder when the invaders actually entered the town. Indeed, perhaps spurred on by the imposition of financial levies that together amounted to more than 1,400,000 *reales*, not to mention demands for 3,000 beds and 2,500 blankets, the town council hastened to obey the French, who had established a garrison in the Carmelite convent, in every particular. On 16 February, then, it swore an oath of allegiance to Joseph Bonaparte in the parish church while, in compliance with directions from the governor, it also issued orders for all arms to be handed in immediately, set a guard on the bridge outside the town, and established a watch of forty men drawn from the Milicias Honrada, headed by one Antonio Bénítez, to keep order in the time itself. When orders came for the Guardia Cívica to be established, this too was done, while attempts at flight among the elite appear to have been minimal (the Conde de Robledo and his nephew did disappear for a while, but news that they were likely to be stripped of their property soon brought them back). Nor, meanwhile, was the town council backward in terms of formal courtesies, agreeing both to celebrate Joseph's saint's day on 19 March and to send a delegation to wait upon him in the course of his tour of Andalucía. In short, then, no sooner had the French arrived than the local elites made every effort to maintain order and deliver all that was required of them.[61]

Yet this compliance availed Montoro very little. When Joseph passed through the town for a second time on 6 May 1810 in the course of his definitive return to Madrid—a visit that, among other things, cost the town illuminations, a firework display, and a special play that was put on in its theater—he did turn over a church and a hermitage that had been seized from one or other of the religious orders to the town for use as chapels of ease in respect of the parish church of San Bartolomeo, but, for the rest, the pressure was unremitting. In September the mayor, José Antonio Bordiu, was dismissed from his post in favor of one Manuel

María Ramos y Dazo, while the French insisted not only that the town should keep up with the various financial contributions that had been demanded of it but also supply the occupying forces with large consignments of wheat and other commodities. Very soon Montoro was hopelessly adrift of its targets—by May 1810 alone it owed the French 150,000 *reales*—but desperate pleas for relief were ignored, while fresh demands were heaped upon it, as when the town council was suddenly ordered to raise a 150-strong antibandit patrol. On top of all this, meanwhile, there was also the need to find the pay and table expenses of the French commandant and the rations of the soldiers under his command (in brief, twenty-four ounces of bread, eight ounces of meat, two ounces of vegetables, and three and one-half pints of wine). Desperate to ameliorate matters, in April 1811 the council dispatched the parish priest, the mayor, and a prominent local landowner to Marshal Soult to argue its case, but the only response was that the three men were seized as hostages until such time as Montoro could clear its debts (at that point some 330,000 *reales*). With great difficulty this was duly achieved, but the result was that the town's financial resources were left so exhausted that by June the sum owed had once again risen to some 246,000 *reales.*[62]

In short, collaboration proved almost completely useless as a means of shielding Montoro from the realities of occupation, while this point was driven home still further by the fact that the occupying forces continually interfered in the day-to-day life of the town. Thus, in November 1810 the commandant—one De Prai—ordered that anyone who had to be out on the streets after curfew should carry a light, while in September 1811 set up a system of internal espionage to keep a check on "individuals who have no work and yet spend money as if they had it." Increasingly, however, no one had any money to spend. Indeed, by the beginning of 1812, the populace was on the brink of starvation. As one report complained, "Things have reached such a state that many people are dying of hunger and many others living in the shadow of death." Faced by this situation, the council was left with no option but to establish a charity committee to care for the poor, and yet to the bitter end, it continued to lavish resources on official celebrations: the last feast of Saint Joseph of the French occupation of Andalucía, for example, was celebrated by a play in the garrison's headquarters and an open-air dance in the main square.[63]

Despite unremitting French pressure, then, the major towns and cities of Andalucía remained firmly under imperial control. Indeed, this is very much the message that comes over from Soult's dispatches. Frank enough in their admission of the difficulties the invaders faced in the countryside, as late as the summer of 1812, these reports continued to paint a positive picture of the situation in what the marshal habitually called "the interior of Andalucía"—essentially the valley of the Guadalquivir. A good example here is the dispatch that he penned to Berthier on 27 June 1812. While the French commander admitted that in some areas there was still a considerable amount of disorder—"In the provinces of Granada and Málaga there is still trouble thanks to the existence of powerful bands that I have great difficulty in destroying even when I send a great many troops against them"—he insisted that elsewhere all was quiet: "The interior of Andalucía is tranquil: the inhabitants are devoting themselves to the task of gathering in the harvest and we are already beginning to profit from this. I hope that it will all be got in without difficulty, and that the enemy will not be able to realize the disgraceful plan of putting it to the torch that they have already embarked upon in Extremadura."[64] That Soult was not just whistling in the dark is suggested by events that took place a couple of months earlier. In brief, assailed by the surprise news that Wellington had marched to attack the crucial fortress of Badajoz, Soult had had no option but to mass all the men that he could spare in a forlorn attempt to stave off disaster, but in doing so he had left the rest of his domains, which were left garrisoned only by the most skeletal of forces, dangerously vulnerable to attack. In response to requests from Wellington for the Spaniards to mount diversionary operations, the forces of Morillo and Penne Villemur had advanced on Seville from the Condado de Niebla while Ballesteros had threatened it from the south. With the only troops left in Seville consisting of a few invalids, a handful of regimental depots, a Swiss battalion in the service of King Joseph, the cadres of a few Spanish units, and the Guardia Cívica, the situation looked bleak, for these forces amounted to 2,000 men these were barely adequate for the defenses of the Cartuja citadel. Yet led by the governor, General Antoine Rignoux, the defenders held their ground long enough for Soult's men to retrace their steps. No sooner had they arrived in the vicinity than Morillo and Penne Villemur retreated (Ballesteros, meanwhile, had not pressed his advance farther than Bornos). Meanwhile, there had been neither disorder in the city nor any desertion, and this prompted Soult to speak of the situation in a tone that was positively optimistic: "I have no doubt that the example will be imitated should an occasion for it present itself for a second time. In a few months I also count on being able to put into line the regiment of Spanish lancers commanded by Major Aguedo, together with the unit of gendarmes that he has also organized: these two units are already most handsome, and do their duty in perfect fashion."[65]

Whether Rignoux's civic guards and *juramentados* would actually have defended the walls of the Cartuja had the Spanish generals been more enterprising is another matter: so doubtful was Kajetan Wojciechowski of the value of such troops, for example, that when he was posted to command the garrison of the little town of Mairena de Alcor in 1812, he disarmed the Guardia Cívica on account of "my conviction that that force . . . was more disposed in favor of the nation than it was in favor of the new government, the fact being that in its ranks there was to be found not aid, but rather spies and hidden enemies."[66] And even in Seville the precipitate retreat of the French and their adherents into the Cartuja produced much jeering among the inhabitants, who for some while afterward took considerable delight in making sarcastic remarks about the occupying forces' courage.[67] As for positive cooperation on the part of the crowd, this was scarcely to be looked for. Faced by Soult's orders to form irregular antibandit patrols, the town council of Córdoba timed the necessary recruitment drive to coincide with a feast day, when large numbers of day laborers were likely to be loafing around the town with nothing to do, while at the same time doing all that it could to take the message to the people, yet all its efforts produced no more than thirty men, of whom about half were suspected of having criminal antecedents. Nor did matters improve with bribery: a relaunch of the campaign a few weeks later, with a promise of a bounty of 100 *reales*, produced so few recruits that the town council had no choice but to ask permission to raise the necessary men by means of a ballot.[68]

True enough though all this may be, the evidence that we have suggests that, insofar as the larger towns and cities were concerned, the French could, on the whole, expect passive obedience on the part of the mass of the population. Insofar as this phenomenon is concerned, by far the best evidence that we have comes from Málaga. At the beginning of the chapter, it will be recalled, we came across Marshal Soult complaining bitterly about the manner in which this city was entered by insurgent forces, when it had to be left without a garrison for a few days shortly after the visit of King Joseph, without a shot being fired to defend it. In this, however, he is more than a little unfair. Given that the Guardia Cívica, let alone the regiment of *juramentados* that was being raised to act as the garrison of the city, was at this point a mere skeleton, there was no chance that Málaga could be defended, and before he left, the French governor, General André Perreimond, gave specific orders that no attempt was to be made to do so. What is still more interesting, however, is that left to themselves, the populace made no attempt to take over the city but waited, albeit with growing excitement, to be freed by what was reported to be a liberating army many thousands strong, This was not long in coming, true, but it was nothing like the force that was expected. In reality, the relief force proved to consist of no more than 500 men, all of them civilians armed with little more than knives and fowling pieces, and the majority *serranos* who had been recruited with promises of pillage (some, indeed, were well-known bandits). Much alarmed by their savage appearance, the crowds that were waiting to greet them melted away, and very soon the streets were entirely deserted. Moreover, when the French returned the next day, the inhabitants did not lift a finger to help the *serranos,* and all the more so as the latter had spent most of the previous night looting whatever took their fancy, the result being that the insurgent forces had no option but to take to their heels.[69] Thereafter, moreover, Málaga continued to remain quiet. The experience of French occupation hardly being a pleasant one, the populace were scarcely contented and were, indeed, much excited by news of French defeats: "The inhabitants cheered up at these losses. . . .

The crowd overflowed with joy. . . . This news . . . made the people very happy. . . . Rumors spread among the people that the French were planning to abandon the *sierra* and this pleased them a great deal."[70] Yet it was one thing to enjoy seeing the French in difficulties and quite another actually to fight them, and on two occasions in in the first months of 1812, when news of Spanish successes in the vicinity led to the garrison and its supporters taking refuge in the Gibralfaro fortress, the population again remained quiet.[71] In neither instance did the Spaniards actually appear, but with barely a month to go before the French evacuated the city for good, it was finally attacked by the forces of Francisco Ballesteros. If there was ever a moment for the populace to have come out onto the streets, this was it—Ballesteros and his men occupied the town, the enemy having once again retired to the Gibralfaro—but a handful of individuals aside, once again nothing of the sort occurred.[72]

So much, then, for the people, but what of the elites? Here too the picture is very much one of passive acquiescence—the attempt that was made by a friar named Pedro Antonio Loarte to raise a popular revolt in Granada in the absence of a large part of the garrison in August 1810 was very much an isolated occurrence, for example.[73] Still worse, passive obedience frequently extended to active collaboration: if Loarte was tried and executed, it was because he was betrayed by "a prudent householder of the city."[74] As for the reasons why this was the case, we have first to look to the circumstances of the fall of Andalucía, this last being so precipitate that, even supposing that a general will to do so had existed, few members of the propertied classes had had much chance to escape the occupying forces by fleeing southward to Cádiz or eastward to Murcia and Alicante.[75] Fixed, as it were, in place, the propertied classes found themselves with little option but at the very least to maintain a dialogue with the new authorities: whoever was in power, there were always sons to find positions for, clients to advance, and old scores to settle. And, of course, there were also estates to enlarge, the advertisements for the sale of national properties—houses, farm buildings, mills, vineyards, olive groves—that from the middle of 1810 onward began to fill the pages of the *Gazeta de Sevilla* and the other newspapers of Andalucía being at the very least hard to ignore. To take just one example, members of the established local elite who took part in the scramble in Osuna included the Marqués de Casa-Tamayo, Juan Bejarano Hidalguía, and Cristóbal Govantes y Valdívia, all of whom had served in the pre-1810 town council.[76]

The extent of the dialogue involved is particularly apparent from the register of the petitions that were presented to the Conde de Montarco during his time as royal commissioner of Andalucía between December 1810 and August 1812. Thus, Montarco was deluged with petitions of all sorts on a daily basis. For example, taking several cases at random, the Condesa del Aguila wanted 18,000 *reales* owed in back pay to her husband as an official of the Tesorería Real de Indias; a merchant named José Carvallo wanted permission to send a consignment of 300 casks of wine to Santander; a resident of Villareal del Ariscal named Simón García wanted the bells from one of the convents that had been suppressed in the town; the Conde de Valdecañas asked for permission to sell some entailed property for the purpose of paying his war contributions; a prominent citizen of Jérez named Juan Baéz wanted a property that he claimed to have bought duly made over to him; a retired functionary named José Escobedo wanted a post in the administration; Francisco Noriega y Bada wanted the post of subprefect of Jaén; a sublieutenant of the Guardia Cívica named Francisco Fernández requested that he be exempted from all contributions for a year and granted permission to clear an area of woodland from his estate so as to free up more land for cultivation; a householder of Ecija named Antonio Agustín Méndez wanted safe conduct for a consignment of 180 *fanegas* of wheat that he wished to send to Seville; Francisco and Ana Vazquéz wanted a ruling on a will; Luisa Caballero y León wanted permission to sell a property by public auction so as "to attend to urgent necessities"; Pedro Marquéz wanted permission to postpone payment of a debt of 6,000 *reales*; the Marquesa de Pasiega claimed exemption from a fine that had been imposed on her following the occupation of various *pueblos* in which she had property by guerrilla bands; Antonio Bejarano asked to be allowed to defer payment on a house that he had bought from the administration of national properties; Juan Bautista Velo wanted employment for himself and his sons; Cristóbal Gordillo de la Puerta wanted a retainer "on account of his present services and those which he might offer in the future"; General José de Moctezuma and the Marqués de Casatavares demanded that the residents of Setenil should be made to pay for damage they had done to a woodland by cutting down trees for firewood without permission—the list is literally endless.[77]

Explicit in at least some of these petitions was the desire for personal advancement that could be said to form one of the chief motives for collaboration with the French, and this can be seen still more clearly in the many cases where King Joseph and his commanders were directly approached by members of the local elites (though even then there were sometimes subtexts that suggested a more complex reality: for example, while Francisco de Vargas petitioned Joseph for some post carrying with it a salary big enough to sustain him and his family, he supported his claim with a story of persecution on the most specious of grounds at the hands of the Junta Central).[78] Particularly striking, perhaps, is the case of Francisco Javier de Burgo. Later a leading figure in the monarchy of Isabel II who occupied a succession of ministerial posts, in 1810 Burgo was a young man of twenty-two who, while comfortably off—the scion of a wealthy family, he already had a permanent place on the town council of Motril—had yet to make his way in the wider world. In essence, this meant securing a post in government employ, but as yet he had been unsuccessful, the fact being that the coming of the French therefore represented a major opportunity. Burgo being anything but slow on the uptake, the result was a string of odes in the *Gazeta de Granada* that heaped praises on the French and denounced the Patriot cause in the most violent terms. Having drawn attention to himself in this fashion, the young man duly received an invitation from the town council of Granada to help it lend tone to King Joseph's reception in that city. When the king arrived in Granada on 16 March, then, Burgo was there to welcome him with a suitably grandiloquent poem, a grateful Joseph rewarding him two months later with the post of subprefect of Almería.[79]

Was *afrancesamiento* based on little more than opportunism, then? After 1814 there were certainly plenty of observers who were all too keen to portray the *afrancesados* as unscrupulous adventurers. As an example, we might here look at what Mendoza has to say on the subject of the leading figures in the new administration that took over the government of Málaga, its three most important members being José María Maury, who was the son of a French merchant; the archdeacon of Antequera, Francisco Javier Asenjo; and a failed businessman named Enrique Disdier. Of these Maury was "stunted in stature and ridiculous in appearance, an eternal conspirator [and] a man addicted to the sound of his own voice"; appointed commander of the Guardia Cívica, meanwhile, he was so puffed up with pride that he could "hardly have been any more so had he been made a marshal of the empire." Next came Asenjo. Appointed by Sebastiani as vicar general, he is described as the eternal timeserver, a man who had heaped praises on Napoleon prior to the uprising of 1808, written odes to the victors of Bailén, secured advancement under Abello, and finally been the first to take service with the French. As for his character, this left much to be desired: "[Asenjo] was a man who passed among the multitude as a great intellect, but in reality had a long way to go in this respect, and was at the same time . . . a troublemaker, an intriguer, and a toady, not to mention an egotist who loved people playing court to him." Finally, Disdier was if anything still worse. Chief of the city's police, he was "an unworthy man of no principles, a rogue in every sense of the word . . . who lacked even the idea of shame."[80]

Mendoza is, perhaps, a tainted witness—who knows what petty jealousies might underpin these words—but it is nonetheless hard to acquit the elites of Andalucía of at least a degree of opportunism. Maury and Disdier are easy enough to forgive—they were, after all, both men of French parentage who may well have been exposed to much danger in the course of the revolution of 1808—but Asenjo's evident determination to curry favor with one regime after another is scarcely attractive. Nor is he the only such example. Captured at the Battle of Bailén in 1808, for example, the erstwhile prisoner of war Jean Grivel was, for a little while, billeted at Rota in the house of a doctor named Gallego, who had been violent in his denunciation of Napoleon and all he stood for.

Having escaped from captivity, Grivel was, as we have seen, sent to Rota with a company of Sailors of the Guard. Everything was now very different, however: "I paid a call on my Doctor Gallego, and found that, now [that] we had been all too clearly shown to be the stronger party, he had become the very acme of an *afrancesado.* A true *andaluz,* he had not before time gone from one extreme to the other and become a partisan of King Joseph!"[81]

In such conversions we do not necessarily just see self-interest, however. Also visible is sheer despair. In the circumstances of 1810, indeed, it is entirely understandable that many people should have come to the conclusion that resistance was no longer a viable proposition—that, in effect, it was necessary to obtain peace at any price. That this was so is certainly visible from letters written by French sympathizers, willing or otherwise, in the weeks and months after the fall of Seville. For a good example, we might cite the words of an inhabitant of Arahal named José Zayas:

> This province has suffered greater calamities than anything that has yet been witnessed in the rest of Spain. Thanks to the impolitic resistance of Cádiz, the coast is occupied by a numerous French army that is gradually eating us up. To this can be added the fact that a number of villages of the Serranía de Ronda have also risen against the irresistible forces of the invaders. The latter have severely punished them on more than one occasion, . . . and the result is that every day we hear no other news than that so many people have been put to the sword in one place, or so many slaughtered in another. All people of any sense are hopeful that these examples will put an end to all this turmoil and persuade the small number of troublemakers involved that it is in their best interests to submit to the government and let us all enjoy the benefits of peace. . . . With things as they are, . . . no one has any faith in anything or anyone.[82]

Coupled with the belief that the war was hopeless was utter disillusionment with the Patriot cause, a good example here being the case of one Juan Gallardo de Mendoza. Born in Almería in 1788, Gallardo de Mendoza had secured a commission in one of the new regiments formed in Andalucía at the start of the war and had been sent to Catalonia along with the rest of the division to which he was attached. Like many other officers, he was shocked by the want of commitment to the struggle in Catalonia, and in 1811 he therefore deserted to the French and enlisted in the Régiment de Joseph Napoléon (a unit of Spanish deserters and prisoners of war recruited from various French prison camps that was intended for service elsewhere in Europe). Underpinning all this, however, was the same sense of futility and hopelessness that we have just seen: "At this point nobody foresaw the disasters that would befall the emperor in 1812 and 1813; indeed, he was still at the height of his glory. Not having seen any British troops in Catalonia, I believed that . . . Spain could not resist a France backed by the whole of Europe . . . and that prolonging the war could only lead to the complete ruin of the country. On top of all that, I could not but feel that we were already fighting for a king of French origins. The latter having behaved badly toward his father and his country alike, and abased himself in the most servile fashion before the emperor, I therefore thought that, if we were to have a Frenchman, it might as well be Pepe."[83]

Far away in Catalonia though he was, Gallardo de Mendoza may be regarded an exemplar of the many Spanish officers who rallied to the French in Andalucía in the wake of the disasters of January 1810. Thus, when an officer named Fernando Espinosa Aguilera got back to his home in Ronda following the collapse of Areizaga's army, he turned down an offer of the command of the town's urban militia on the grounds that further resistance was pointless, and instead offered to help negotiate Ronda's surrender, later on volunteering for service in the army of King Joseph.[84] Meanwhile, other pressures were also in operation. First and foremost of these, of course, was the question of the defense of the social order. With the whole of the Patriot zone south of the Sierra Morena in the grip of severe disorder and the tension heightened still further by the onset of the French armies, the propertied classes in many instances rushed to take advantage of the situation. For example, having put up no resistance to French invasion, the town council of Lopera made every effort to comply with the new administration's edicts except in one small detail. This, however, was significant enough. Thus, with respect to the orders that were issued that all arms should be surrendered, it excepted a list of twenty named individuals "of good conduct" and ordained that they should be allowed to use weapons to maintain order and hunt down criminals. Moreover, the mayor, Francisco de Paula Bueno, was a strong supporter of the idea of the Guardia Cívica and on 5 March established a twenty-five-man-strong detachment on the basis of a landowner, two sons of landowners, a carpenter, three master masons, three cobblers, a blacksmith, a butler, three barbers, two tailors, two clerks, two sacristans, and three priests; five days later, moreover, he attended a meeting with the mayors of Marmolejo and Arjonilla at which it was agreed that the other two towns should form such a force as well, support for such initiatives being stimulated by a growing problem of banditry in the area, as witness, for example, a daring attack that was mounted on a mule train bringing a consignment of cloth from Segovia in the vicinity of Montoro on 9 March.[85]

That the propertied classes had much to fear from popular disorder there is little doubt. In at least some instances, indeed, prominent collaborators can be shown to have had some very frightening experiences. Let us here take the example of the prefect of Jérez de la Frontera, Joaquín Sotelo. In 1808 Sotelo was employed as a prosecutor in the Consejo Suprema de Guerra in Madrid. Originally, however, he was from Seville, where he had for some time served as a judge of the high court, in which capacity he had, in his own words, "cleansed that city of more than 400 layabouts in the round-up of 1803, uncovered and proceeded against a number of instances of improper conduct on the part of various agents of the judicial system, and intervened in several other matters of great gravity and importance." That being the case, it was hardly surprising that when Seville rose in revolt, rumors spread in the city that Sotelo was a traitor: having fled Madrid in June 1808, he was forced to throw himself on the mercy of the Junta of Badajoz, which duly investigated his case and publically pronounced him to be guiltless of any charge of collaboration.[86] In fairness to the propertied classes, however, there were also more-altruistic motives for collaboration, not the least of which was a desire to protect their communities. After 1814 it was not uncommon for *afrancesados* to claim that they had done their best to lessen the burden of French reprisals on Spaniards and plead for communities that would otherwise have been subjected to serious punishment: a good example here is the case of one Joaquín de Uriarte, who maintained that, as subprefect of Ronda, he had saved the lives of a large number of hostages from the *pueblo* of Algodonales when they were threatened with execution.[87] As Dallas wrote: "Among the inhabitants who continued in the different towns inhabited by the French, there were many who not only adhered to the cause of the mock king, but who accepted and performed the functions of civil offices under his government. The excuse of such as these as afterward thought it necessary to excuse their conduct was that, being acquainted with the existing laws and customs of their fellow citizens, and partaking of the evils resulting from the intrusion of new ones, they were more likely to reconcile the old with the new state of things and to render the burden less intolerable than a stranger and a foreigner, not to say a Frenchman."[88]

Such stories clearly cannot be accepted without reservation, but there is nonetheless some evidence that something of the sort did take place. Insofar as this is concerned, we can turn to the memoirs of Hippolyte d'Espinchal, a cavalry officer who arrived in Andalucía with a convoy of clothing in the spring of 1812 and was soon appointed to the post of commandant of Arahal:

> My first care . . . was to repair various palisades and other fortifications so as to remove all chance of a surprise, but something else that worried me was the promptitude with which the alcalde leapt to provide for my soldiers' every need, not to mention the welcome accorded them by the inhabitants, among whom were to be found a number of wealthy landowners. Fearing that all this hid something, I therefore resolved to stay on my guard while professing to accept their friendly gestures in all good faith, but I very soon realized that the town's conduct was utterly genuine, and in the course of a whole month in which my men and I were surrounded by a large population in an area that was both swarming with guerrilla bands and a long way from any help, we could have nothing but praise for the inhabitants, the attitude of the latter being confirmed, first,

> by the good conduct . . . of my own men and, second, the vigor with which I resisted an attempt that was made to despoil them some days after my arrival. On the morning of 12 May, . . . there suddenly appeared a major of the Ninety-Sixth Line at the head of a force of his men. Much surprised to find the place occupied by French troops, he told the mayor that he had been sent by General [Nicholas] Conroux to demand a certain quantity of barley, wheat, and wine, together with a number of sheep and cattle, or, failing that, 2,000 duros as their equivalent in money. Yet this demand not being backed up by any written order, this procedure did not appear to me to be at all legitimate, and I therefore told the major that I would send word of his action to Marshal Soult. At this the major retired, though not without threatening that he would very soon be back not just to carry out his orders but also to have a private meeting with me.[89]

In short, then, we see precisely the sort of behavior remarked on by Lapène, the town council of Arahal having in effect co-opted D'Espinchal in the hope—successful as things turned out—that he would protect them from other French commanders with less reason to respect the interests of the inhabitants. Throughout, indeed, the local authorities, as at Montoro, sought frantically to ameliorate the burden on their communities. Here again we can turn to the records of the Conde de Montarco: "The municipality of Torre Don Jimeno manifests the deplorable situation of the inhabitants on accounts of the taxes and forced levies that have been imposed on them by the government, and begs that the sufferings of the population be lessened through the protection of Your Excellency. . . . The same municipality manifests that the financial burden imposed upon it is more than the town's entire income, and that the inhabitants are surrounded on all sides by hunger and want."[90]

Just as honorable as a motive for collaborating with the French, meanwhile, was honest ideological conviction. To take Asenjo as an example, however unscrupulous his behavior may have been, he had had a distinguished academic career prior to 1808 and given many proofs of his advanced opinions; for Díaz Torrejón, indeed, he was the "prototype of the *afrancesado* intellectual."[91]

Certainly the French received the support of a large part of the educated elite. As the noted poet Felix José Reinoso wrote to his old friend, the writer José María Blanco y Crespo (better known as Blanco White), in relation to the doings of the intellectual *tertulia* of which they had both been a part of in Seville in the years prior to 1808: "Almost all your old friends have gone over to King Joseph. . . . Apart from the few people who have taken refuge in Cádiz, you can be assured that there is hardly anyone of any weight in society who is not now a member of his party."[92] In discussing this phenomenon, most authors have been content to confine themselves to the narrow coterie represented by figures such as Reinoso, the writer Justo Matute y Gaviria, the cathedral canon Manuel María Arjona, and the university professor Alberto Lista, a man who had in 1808 flung himself into support for the Patriot cause—he had helped write many proclamations for the Junta Central and been a regular contributor to such publications as *El Espectador Sevillano*—but had been persuaded by the fall of Seville to "turn his coat" and immediately had taken on the task of acting as the editor of the *Gazeta de Sevilla.*[93] Prior to 1808 these men and others like them had been deeply immersed in the writings of the Enlightenment, and their presence in the ranks of the *afrancesados* is therefore logical enough, though ideological collaboration was not just limited to a few men of letters. If the many officials and magistrates who collaborated with the French wanted to keep their jobs, feared social disorder, and believed further resistance to be hopeless, it should not be forgotten that they sprang from a milieu in which many of the ideas of the invaders were anything but new. As Antonio Calvo Maturana has demonstrated, the reign of Charles IV was marked by considerable discussion of the need to police society, to civilize the plebe, and to control and guide public opinion, the aim of all this being, in the first place, to drag Spain into the modern era and, in the second, to give the state greater access to the sinews of power.[94] To implement this policy, the state had had recourse to precisely the same group of educators—the vast majority of them priests or other religious men—magistrates, and functionaries who now formed the bedrock of *afrancesamiento,* indeed had, in effect, called upon the services of some of the very josefino notables whose names we have just mentioned. When Joseph Bonaparte rode into Madrid in 1808, then, the ideas for which he stood—ideas that were in many respects indistinguishable from the thinking that had governed the Spain of Charles IV—were already common currency among the educated classes, while the similarities were driven home still further by the fact that, if the French embarked on the wholesale suppression of the religious orders through the decrees of Chamartín, the Spanish state had already driven out the Jesuits and expropriated and sold off around one-sixth of the lands of the Church.[95]

Given that the Church was one of the most immediate targets of French reform, it might be thought that it would have remained aloof from ideological collaboration, but this was not the case. As we have seen, French soldiers were frequently able to forge firm friendships with individual members of the clergy, while, taking Andalucía as a whole, there is no evidence whatsoever of the church being united in favor of resistance. In the first place, except among the regular clergy, who were, in effect, turned loose to disperse as they wished, there was little in the way of wholesale emigration. If the archbishop of Seville, Cardinal Borbón, fled to the safety of Cádiz in the face of the advancing French army, along with one of his suffragan bishops, the bishop of Loadicea, his other suffragan, the bishop of Licopolis, stayed at his post, along with almost the entire parish clergy.[96] Equally, if the bishop of Guadix abandoned his see, the curates and parish priests of his diocese also for the most part stayed put.[97] And finally, there are the cases of the archbishop of Granada, Juan Moscoso y Peralta, and the bishop of Córdoba, Pedro Antonio Trevilla. With the French bearing down on the city, Moscoso took refuge in a remote village in the Sierra Nevada. Seeing, however, that the French occupation was relatively orderly, within a few days he returned to the city, and on 24 February he swore allegiance to King Joseph in a solemn ceremony in the palace of the Chancillería.[98] As for Trevilla, meanwhile, he not only stayed put but also sent a lengthy pastoral letter to his communicants in which he urged them to accept the new order without question: "Given that it has fixed the destiny our beloved fatherland, nothing is more important in the present state of public affairs than that we submit to the will of

God . . . and cooperate with one accord . . . in the reestablishment of order and tranquillity."[99]

Of course, merely staying put was not in itself proof of *afrancesamiento*: if the parish clergy, in particular, were tied to their churches by their need to care for their flocks, there was nothing to prevent them from engaging in such actions as hiding church plate from the French, acting as spies, passing on Patriot propaganda, or encouraging young men to join the guerrillas. But thanks in part to the influence of Jansenism—a school of thought that sought to reduce the power of the papacy and enhance the authority of the bishops—and in part to their desperate poverty, much of the secular clergy was as penetrated by reformist thinking as the "official" classes.[100] Already conditioned to acting as a mouthpiece of the authorities, large numbers of churchmen therefore went far beyond merely caring for their congregations and acting as a buffer between them and the invaders.[101] We have already mentioned several cases in which priests and bishops spoke up in praise of the new regime, but it is clear that such behavior was quite routine. Flattered, perhaps, by the extremely courteous treatment he was accorded by Sebastiani on his return to his cathedral, the archbishop of Granada issued a fawning statement of support for King Joseph—"My heart . . . is overwhelmed with the sweetest emotions when I consider the very different spectacle that my beloved Granada offers now that it has been joyfully united with its legitimate sovereign and set on the road of happiness and duty"[102]—while various religious authorities regularly condemned attempts to whip up resistance to the French. Typical enough, perhaps, of their general attitude is a letter that was sent by the chapter of the parish church of Chiclana to the Conde de Montarco on 27 April 1812, in which it denounced an insurrectionary proclamation that had recently been promulgated by the Spanish commander, Ballesteros, as being repugnant to the sentiments of peace and goodwill for which it stood, promised to pray without cease for the cause of Joseph Bonaparte, and undertook to pass on all the edicts relating to the subject that had been issued by *josefinos* to every parish in its jurisdiction.[103]

If there was serious trouble among the representatives of the church, it came above all from the dispossessed mass of the monks and friars. Turned loose by the closure of their religious houses, these men had been promised either employment in the structures of the church or a reasonable pension, but in practice they were never adequately provided for, there being far too many of them to be found places as, for example, curates or sacristan and far too little money to pay them what they were owed. In consequence, the large number who could not be taken in by friends and family were, in many instances, reduced to begging in the streets, the result being that many ended up preaching rebellion and in some instances joining the guerrillas; as we have seen, indeed, one of the first executions carried out in Granada by the occupying forces was that of a Capuchin priest.[104] Yet such evidence as there is suggests that in other circumstances even these apparent recalcitrants might have been won over, the papers of the Conde de Montarco containing many petitions from ex-regulars asking for posts as parish priests or chaplains. To take just a few such examples, in October 1811 we find the erstwhile Carmelites Antonio de Negri, Manuel Cuadrado, Francisco García, and Feliz Manuel Acevedo all petitioning Montarco for ecclesiastical posts of one sort or another, it being impossible not to suspect that success would have seen them merge quietly into the ranks of ecclesiastical acquiescence.[105]

In Andalucía, then, the French found many collaborators. At the same time, meanwhile, they also had an important means of bringing them together. With freemasonry very common among French officers, one result of the coming of the invaders had been the establishment of large numbers of masonic lodges; so frequent was this development, indeed, that it has been suggested that it was the fruit of deliberate policy on the part of the invaders: after all, Joseph Bonaparte had been appointed Grand Master of French masonry in 1804. At first, the lodges concerned were wholly military, but it was not long before others began to appear that were wholly formed of members of the indigenous population. Whether the new Spanish brothers were attracted by ideological reasons, the hope of mutual support, or a desire to secure the patronage of the French is unclear, but according to Blaze at least, there were a great many of them:

> Freemasonry made many converts among the Spaniards: they loved anything metaphysical, and the fact that the teachings of masonry are shrouded in the darkest mystery piqued their curiosity, the result being that an infinity of priests, landowners, and members of the bourgeoisie hastened to have themselves initiated. The presence of so many priests astonished us because in France the clergy had never ceased to declaim against an institution about which in reality they knew nothing. How was it, then, that in Spain, the country of superstition and prejudice par excellence, the priests were the first people to become freemasons? The reason . . . is that in Spain the priests . . . are the only people with any learning, and that it requires as much education to oppose popular prejudices as it does courage. . . . It is but fair to say . . . meanwhile, that the Spanish freemasons were the most upright honest people in the world, and that one met among them many . . . true friends.[106]

Whatever the reasons for collaboration, it is clear that it brought together a cross-section of the indigenous elite. Mendoza, for example, lists twenty-nine leading *malagüeño* collaborators other than Maury, Asenjo, and Disdier. Thus, of the twenty-one of whom we have some details in terms of their backgrounds, there were three members of the old town council, one of them a man who had sat on the previous junta and two of them men who had held commissions in the Patriot forces; two priests; the son of a French merchant; two *escribanos;* two merchants; two judicial officials; a surgeon; a schoolteacher; two retired officers (of whom one had become a functionary in the tax administration); and six officers of the army or navy, including the commandant of the port and the erstwhile captain general of Valencia, the Conde de Conquista. Not counting Conquista, of the seven officers who had fought in the Patriot army, one had been captured by the French at Ocaña and then entered their service as a spy; one had taken part in the defense of Málaga and gone over to the French after the city had fallen; one had been a straggler from Areizaga's army who had fled to Málaga; one had been an officer in the Saboya regiment who had returned to Málaga on parole after having been captured in Galicia and become a *juramentado;* one was a colonel of cavalry who had been disgraced by Cuesta following the Battle of Medellín (of the remaining two, we have no details other than the fact that they came from Málaga and were closely connected to the city's merchant oligarchy). Also interesting is the fact that the entire group was marked by a considerable degree of family relationship: no fewer than eight of its members were either related to other members of the group or known to be closely associated with them previously.[107] For an example of this last phenomenon that is even clearer, meanwhile, it is worth citing the case of the Osorno family, Spanish records showing that at least three of its sons became collaborators in one capacity or another (to be precise, Rafael de Osorno served the old and new orders alike as a commissary, Francisco de Osorno became commanding officer of the First Regiment of Line Infantry, and Fernando de Osorno took on the post of prefect of Granada).[108]

Whatever the reasons for collaboration, from all this it is quite clear that sufficient members of the elite were prepared to enter the service of the new regime to give a degree of substance to the *josefino* administration. What, however, of the armed forces? Here the picture was more equivocal. While King Joseph was able to maintain the cadre of a *juramentado* army, this never amounted to anything like the force of his dreams. That this was the case is suggested by a number of returns of strength housed in the French military archives. In this respect, we have two sets of figures. Of these, the first relates to the number of French and Spanish troops stationed in the Kingdom of Seville at different points in 1810 and 1811. On 1 May 1811 the garrison amounted to 541 officers and 12,700 men, but of these only 87 officers and 997 men were Spaniards. Still worse, these *juramentados* represented no fewer than eight separate units—the Guardia Real, the Seventh Line Infantry, the First Swiss, a company of artillery, the Third Cazadores a Caballo, the Cazadores de Montaña, the Escopeteros a Caballo, and the Cuerpo Franco del Guadalquivir—of which only one, the Seventh Line, mustered more than 250 men. Also noticeable is the fact that regular units were seemingly far less popular with recruits than irregulars, the three units that may be counted in the latter category accounting for no fewer than 377 of the rank and file. Finally, it is also evident that, if the cavalry is anything to go by, the *juramentado* army was hardly a battle-ready asset, the four mounted units concerned having only 212 horses for their 529 officers and men. But after a catastrophic drop in strength over the winter of 1810–11 that had seen the number of *juramentados* fall by more than 50 percent, at least the figures remained relatively stable: on 1 October 1811 the total of rank and file who were still with the colors was 921 (although the officers now numbered only 47).[109]

For a more complete picture, we may turn to a report for the whole of Andalucía dated 1 October 1811. This listed no fewer than forty-one separate units, including four regiments of regular cavalry, four battalions of infantry, two companies of artillery, two battalions of invalids, and no fewer than twenty-nine companies of irregulars of one sort or another. In all, these units amounted to a total of 420 officers and 5,008 rank and file, but these figures do not tell the full story. In the first place, there were far too many units, the average size of each one being a mere 132 officers and men. In the second place, the two units of invalids, which together numbered 69 officers and 899 men, or almost 18 percent of the total, are described in the accompanying notes as being useless for anything other than sentry duty. In the third place, even including the invalids, only 2,601—just under half—could be regarded as regular troops (it is noticeable, indeed, that the four battalions of regular infantry were both particularly understrength and particularly overofficered: the Second Light Infantry had 20 officers and 359 men; the Fourth Swiss, 29 officers and 379 men; the Third Line, 50 officers and 296 men; and the Sixth Line, 29 officers and 203 men). In the fourth place, while arms were plentiful enough—between them the *juramentados* had 3,754 muskets, 1,268 pistols, 1,557 swords, and twenty-seven lances—there were serious shortages in other areas: the 1,806 mounted men had only 1,385 horses, while several of the units are described as being very short of uniforms and equipment. And in the fifth place, later returns of strength suggest that the whole edifice was a wasting asset: by 15 November, not counting the invalids, the number of officers and men present with the colors had fallen from 4,457 to 4,083.[110]

As for the motivation of these men, the officers at least were driven by the same sort of thinking as many of the other *afrancesados,* although their reasons were frequently also connected with a variety of circumstances connected with their current situation. For example, on 23 June 1810 a twenty-year-old sublieutenant in the Dragones de Villaviciosa named José Ocaña enlisted in the Sixth Line Infantry, having deserted from the garrison of Cádiz, the fact that he was from Málaga suggesting that, as well as all the other considerations that might have applied, he was either simply homesick or worried about his family (the Sixth Line bore the sobriquet "Fijo de Málaga" and therefore offered a near-guarantee of service in that city), though as a *hijodalgo,* it is conceivable that he might also have become disillusioned by the increasingly liberal atmosphere of Cádiz.[111] Another officer in the same regiment, meanwhile, was José de Vilar. A native of the penal colony known as Peñón de Alhucemas, he had been born in 1790 and in 1808 was a cadet in the Companía Fija del Peñón (that is, its permanent garrison). No explanation is given for his enlistment, but it appears to have been for family reasons: his father, Juan de Vilar, a captain in the Regimiento de Alcalá, was gravely wounded at Ocaña but succeeded in having himself evacuated to Málaga; José having been sent to assist him, both father and son were caught there by the French offensive of January 1810 and in all probability enlisted for want of any other means of subsistence.[112] As witness the following story, to homesickness and want could be added the misery of life in a French prison depot. A *granadiño* captain in the Voluntarios de España infantry regiment, Manuel Ortiz had been sent to the prison camp at Dijon. Receiving news from his mother to the effect that Joseph Bonaparte had personally assured her that he had only to swear loyalty to the new regime and volunteer for service in its army for him to be released immediately, Ortiz duly took the hint, though at the same time he expressed the hope that he might be allowed to serve in his hometown only.[113]

Whatever general patterns are visible in respect of the motivation for enlistment, thanks to the work of Jean-Marc Lafon, we have a fairly clear idea of the background of these *juramentado* officers, albeit one based solely on the records of the Third Line

Regiment. Here three things stand out very clearly. First, of the seventy-five men concerned, thirty-two, including all fifteen of the rank of captain and above, had been officers under the ancien régime and another thirty-two the recipients of commissions in the period 1808–10, this leaving just eleven who had obtained their ranks directly from King Joseph. Second, over two-thirds were of noble origin. Third, almost half came from Andalucía. Quite clearly, then, serving King Joseph was far more about safeguarding existing status than it was about social advancement, just as the *josefino* administration was far more interested in securing the services of the old elite than it was in promoting new men from a wider social sphere. (It is also tempting to conclude that the same figures suggest that collaboration was a particularly Andalusian phenomenon, but to be sure of this, we would need to know far more about the geographical origins of the officer corps of the old Army of La Mancha; it is, however, interesting to note that only twenty-one of the forty-nine infantry battalions that fought at Ocaña were associated in any way with Andalucía, let alone specifically raised there.)[114]

So much for the officers, but what of the rank and file? In this respect it has, of course, been traditional to argue that most of the common soldiers who joined the forces of King Joseph were prisoners of war who took up arms for no other reason than to get back to the armies from which they originated. That the Patriot army was, indeed, the origin of many of the men concerned was true enough, while it is also the case that large numbers of *juramentados* sooner or later deserted from the regiments to which they were assigned: to take just two examples, on 15 May 1811 alone, sixty-three men from four different units disappeared from the garrison of Seville, while a fifty-strong company that was dispatched to help occupy Marbella in the spring of 1810 lost thirteen men in just three days.[115] But to suppose that enlistment was simply a means of getting back into the war against the French is a risky proposition. While it is inherently unlikely that there was ever any ideological engagement with the cause of King Joseph, there is also no firm evidence of a constant stream of *juramentados* presenting themselves at the outposts of such commanders as Copóns and Ballesteros. If erstwhile Patriot soldiers joined the

French, then, it was as likely as not simply to avoid deportation to France as a prisoner of war or to obtain the subsistence that they could not find in any other way. In brief, they joined the French because doing so represented the proverbial lesser evil, and from this it may be surmised that the reason that so many left their service was because it failed to fulfill its promise. Here, for example, is the commanding officer of the Third Regiment of Cazadores a Caballo: "Neither the officers nor the men of the regiment under my command have received any pay for the last month. As for the current month, unless I am authorized to make use of the reserve that has been set aside in case the regiment should go on campaign, I have no idea what to do. The total salary bill comes to 64,000 *reales*, and yet I have received only 19,500, all of which has already been taken up in paying for such things as the replacement of worn-out equipment."[116]

So much for the *josefino* regulars. Yet entering King Joseph's service did not necessarily mean putting on a uniform and enduring the rigors of life as a regular soldier. As we have seen, a large part of the *juramentado* order of battle was made up of companies of irregulars whose chief role was not to take their place in the line of battle, but rather to maintain order and hunt down bandits. As such, they clearly offered an option that was in many ways more attractive than life in one of the line regiments: not only did the recruit have a near guarantee of always serving in his home district, but the service in which the free companies were engaged offered many opportunities for licensed brigandage. Typical enough, perhaps, were the activities of the so-called Cazadores de Montaña de Berja and its commander, Martín Llanos:

> At dawn on 7 May they entered the town [Alcolea], the inhabitants being taken completely by surprised. They behaved like furies, like demons straight out of hell, killing whoever they came across—men, women, and children alike—sacking and burning all the houses and breaking down the doors of the church, where they destroyed the images of Jesus and Mary and killed two elderly priests who had taken refuge in the sacristy. The *serranos* of Berja were all alike guilty of this terrible atrocity, but afterward one of them boasted of having killed twelve

> people by his own hand, and among them a woman and three little children whom he had found hiding in a bed. In the evening, meanwhile, . . . the raiders set off for home weighed down with a glittering haul of clothing, plate, and other things of value, on their arrival being greeted with applause by the majority of the richer part of the population.[117]

The result of such behavior was all too predictable. For men who simply saw banditry as a survival strategy, and particularly men of an unscrupulous disposition, service with such units was obviously preferable to life as a bandit as such, and they therefore flocked to join such figures as Llanos as, to a certain extent at least, did men who already had penal antecedents. Whether entire gangs of smugglers offered to place themselves at the king's command and were in this fashion incorporated into his service as free companies, as is sometimes claimed, is unclear, but what is certainly the case is that there were serious questions to be asked about the antecedents of at least some of the individual recruits: created in 1811, the Partida de Agentes Montados de Polícia de Córdoba included a number of amnestied bandits, of whom several had to be executed the following year after they deserted and returned to a career of highway robbery.[118] Still worse, perhaps, was the free company that appeared at Torremolinos under one Tómas Villarreal, a smuggler who had been in prison awaiting execution when the War of Independence broke out and had been offered his life in exchange for enlisting in the army. Seemingly unwilling to take this chance of turning over a new leaf, Villareal had soon deserted and thereafter lived the life of a bandit in the Serranía de Ronda until he once again fell into the hands of the authorities. This time death seemed certain, but in the event the French arrived in the nick of time, and seizing his chance, Villareal offered to persuade the *serranos* to change sides. In this, of course, he was unsuccessful in a general sense, but he did succeed in persuading a number of bandits to throw in their lot with him and form a counterguerrilla group. As ever, however, ideology was neither here nor there. In the words of Mendoza, "They went over to the French, got themselves amnestied, and, riding out with Villareal, set about plundering town and countryside alike."[119] Nor, alas, was

Villareal the only such figure to join the French in the Málaga area, among the men who rallied to them also being one Mingana, a well-known bandit who was on the run from the law at the time of the French invasion and in September 1810 went on to form his own irregular bands.[120]

Beyond the regular army and the various antibrigand auxiliaries, there was of course the Guardia Cívica. Particularly in the early days of occupation, this was not a force to be reckoned with. "I cannot dissemble, Sire," wrote Marshal Soult. "In the circumstances in which Your Majesty is placed, if I say that not enough is being done in your service, I do but do my duty. Everyone wants to solicit employment, and yet no one wants to commit themselves. If all the officers and functionaries who have been taken into our service were to be forced but to arm their domestics, . . . the result would very soon be the entire submission of Spain."[121] Yet as already noted, things gradually got better. In this respect such incidents as the short-lived liberation of Málaga in March 1810 were an important factor. As Soult wrote: "The population of Málaga played no part in this affair—on the contrary, it showed how delighted it was to be free of the brigands by the cheers with which it welcomed the return of our troops. . . . The insurgents had already made quite a few arrests by the time we returned, and, had we arrived but a little later, there would have been many executions."[122] The problem was never entirely resolved, but by such measures as making membership of the Guardia Cívica a concomitant of holding public office, punishing men who did not turn out for duty, imposing heavy fines on those communities that made no effort to close their gates against parties of insurgents, and actively involving parties of civic guards in antibandit operations, it was at least brought to a pitch in which it sufficed to deal with mere gangs of brigands (a role, of course, in which the propertied classes who formed its mainstay had every interest in pursuing). To quote a letter written by Soult to Marshal Berthier on 15 May 1810, "The landowners have been showing a little more enthusiasm: it would appear that they have discovered that they have an interest in the repression of brigandage."[123] In Osuna, indeed, so great was this *ralliément* that by the end of 1810, the local guard had grown from an initial strength of less than 250 men to one of at least 600.[124] In interpreting how far this development went, of course, we have a problem in that almost all the sources at our disposal in this respect are, of their very nature, pro-French. Reports of the guard enthusiastically hunting down guerrilla bands or defending their *pueblos* against bandit raids must therefore be taken with a grain of salt, but even so, such was the interest of the propertied classes in defending themselves against brigandage that it may be assumed that skeptics like Wojciechowski went more than a little too far.[125]

That said, it is equally possible to go too far the other way. Andalucía's urban elites may have welcomed French protection against social unrest and even been prepared to exert their considerable influence to ensure that the populace remained quiet, but that does not mean that they were necessarily prepared to go along unquestioningly with every aspect of occupation, and in particular, those that bore most heavily upon their own interests. Three issues that need to be considered here in particular are billeting, the heavy financial levies imposed by the French, and the implications of service as a town councilor or local justice. In each of these instances, resistance was considerable. With respect to billeting, Bénito de la Madrid may have resented Blaze's presence because he feared for his daughters, but there were many other reasons why this practice was much disliked. While officers might sometimes be relatively civilized—charming and courteous even—common soldiers were not noted for their manners even when there were no pretty girls to be chased, while the financial costs that were involved could be considerable. Small wonder, then, that a series of orders of the day that were issued in Córdoba suggest that many inhabitants responded by letting stables and other outhouses fall into ruin so that they could not be used to house troops, or even having them demolished altogether, while at the same time making life so uncomfortable for the officers billeted on them that the latter sought alternative accommodation elsewhere.[126] As for the pockets of the elites, right from the beginning they were hit hard—the cost of demolishing the defenses of Seville, for example, was borne by the owners of the various properties that they traversed[127]—and the result was that increasingly desperate efforts were made to hide the real wealth of *pueblos* and individuals alike. As the prefect of Jérez de la Frontera, Joaquín María Sotelo, complained:

> I have been getting in some of the declarations of agricultural and industrial income that the *pueblos* of the prefecture have had to submit in accordance with the regulation that was issued on 20 July. . . . Many of them have still not submitted their figures on account of such pretexts as the large number of their inhabitants, the great extent of their boundaries, the large number of property owners resident elsewhere, and various other things of the same sort. . . . Meanwhile, I regret to say that I have noted little clarity and exactitude in the ones that I have been receiving, the totals stated in them bearing little relation to many details I possess that allow me to calculate the wealth of each *pueblo.*[128]

Finally, there was the issue of service in the new system of local government. Being both extremely time consuming and replete with consequences that were very dangerous, the positions concerned often proved to be less than popular with the men nominated to them, and they therefore frequently tried to withdraw from such commitments: individual examples of such attempts are numerous—in Málaga one Pedro Ortega Monroy even begged to be excused from service on the grounds that he was deaf and therefore could not understand anything that was being said in the council chamber.[129] In June 1811, indeed, the new three-man town council of Puerto de Santa María refused en masse to accept the role that had been thrust upon them and had to be forced to do so by Sotelo.[130]

Irritating as such behavior was as far as the *josefino* regime was concerned, it cannot necessarily be regarded as political: tax evasion, after all, is rife in many Western countries, but that does not mean that those responsible want, say, to overthrow the capitalist system.[131] At the very end, however, the growing inability of the French to provide the elites with a modicum of security coupled with Allied military successes and soaring financial burdens to produce a mixture of disillusionment and even political protest. For example, in Málaga the spring of 1812 saw Disdier both resign his post as commissary of police and the head of the local tax administration and begin to give such help as he could to refugees and fugitives, while a proposal on the part of Maransin to bombard the city in the wake of its occupation by Ballesteros was blocked by Spanish officers, in the meantime all the talk of the *afrancesado* community being of the need to negotiate an amnesty.[132]

Still more interesting, meanwhile, are developments that were witnessed in the spring of 1812 in Córdoba. As in many other places in Andalucía, the last winter of occupation was particularly hard. In first place, fiscal pressure continued unabated. For example, in January the monthly contribution amounted to 557,566 *reales*; in February to 1,115,132 *reales*; and in April to 1,386,432 *reales*, while the inability of the town council to make the requisite payments resulted in heavy fines (1,000,000 *reales* in January and another 1,000,000 in June) together with the occupation of the town hall by a company of troops, which the council was forced to feed and pay until such time as it had met at least a part of its arrears. Then there were all the usual incidental expenses for everything ranging from the postal service to the candles used to light the governor's headquarters (between January and July the city's antibandit patrol alone cost 394,086 *reales*). On top of this the city also made heavy contributions in kind, between January and March handing over 2,175 *fanegas* of wheat, 1,940 *fanegas* of barley, 25 *arrobas* of oil, 108,000 *arrobas* of straw, 30,000 *arrobas* of firewood, 11,000 *arrobas* of meat, and 25,000 *arrobas* of charcoal. All this put appalling strain on the population: the harvest of 1811 having almost completely failed—1812 was a year of famine throughout Spain—by mid-May the *fanega* of wheat had reached 370 *reales*, while many of the poorer inhabitants only survived thanks to such measures as the soup kitchen organized by the charity committee that had been set up by the town council.[133] Meanwhile, if the number of executions are anything to go by, there was no improvement in the security situation:. throughout the period January 1811–August 1812, the rate held steady at about one every week.[134] In short, matters were going from bad to worse, and the result was a surprising development in that, further impelled by Allied military successes such as the recapture of Badajoz, in June, first the bishop; then the erstwhile editor of the gazette and leading man of letters,

Manuel María Arjona; and finally the town council all called for the convocation of a parliament in the style of that of Cádiz as the only means of remedying the situation.[135] Needless to say, no such body was ever convoked in *josefino* Spain, but for all that, the fact that the idea made an appearance suggests that, even in Andalucía, collaboration had its limits.

To conclude this part of our discussion, then, we have to admit that in the cities and larger towns of Andalucía, the French enjoyed a reasonable degree of comfort and security. Considerable parts of the educated classes were either friendly toward the invaders or prepared to tolerate their presence, while the people were so helpless that they could do little more than scowl from the sidelines and engage in the occasional act of symbolic resistance. For the forces of Marshal Soult, then, places such as Seville were at all times something of a haven—"The two years that I spent in Seville," wrote Just Roy, "were without any doubt the happiest period of my time in Spain"[136]—while, particularly at the beginning, there was much optimism among officers and men alike. To return to the comments of Marshal Soult quoted at the beginning of this chapter, however, the essentially urban scene that we have looked at here hardly constituted the whole of Andalucía. Aided by a host of collaborators, the French could dominate Seville and its fellows easily enough, and in fact their rule was never seriously challenged within their walls. More than that, indeed, the forces of Marshal Soult proved sufficiently adaptable in their attitude to the population to form durable relationships with many members of the elites. As we shall now see, however, in the countryside it was another matter.

7

Resistance

Thus far the Andalucía that we have discussed in these pages has hardly presented a flattering picture from the point of view of those who, 200 years on, remain wedded to the notion that Spain responded to French aggression in a spirit of nationalist unity and defiance, in that the rout of January 1810 was succeeded by wholesale political collapse as the region's elites rushed to do the bidding of the invaders or, at the very least, seek to further their interests in their embrace, and the populace of Seville, Córdoba, and other cities subsided into sullen acquiescence. However, as French observers from Marshal Soult downward admitted, the story of Andalucía under French occupation was not just one of collaboration and submission. On the contrary, if the main cities, the valley of the Guadalquivir, and parts of the coastal literal remained quiet, the Serranía de Ronda, the Alpujarras, and the Sierra Morena became the scene of a bitter guerrilla struggle. It is, of course, this aspect of the French occupation of Andalucía that has tended to be recalled most in Spain, and there are many Spanish authors who insist that guerrilla warfare remained the dominant characteristic of the years of occupation. "With the exception of Cádiz," writes Emilio de Diego, "French control was a fact of life in all the main cities, and in this respect Andalucía now differed but little from most of the rest of the country. . . . In the same way as in the rest of the country, however, the French army . . . was incapable of holding down the ground it had conquered. All the more rugged districts . . . remained at the margin of the reach of the Napoleonic administration, while the activity of the Spanish forces, regulars and irregulars alike, . . . limited the authority of the French army to the ground it actually occupied."[1] Here too is Fernando Martínez Laínez: "During the years of French occupation, Andalucía sustained an intense guerrilla struggle. . . . One must discount the idea of an Andalucía in which the guerrillas played little part in events."[2] In this respect, however, pride of place should probably be given to the work of the *granadino* historian Francisco Díaz Torrejón: "It is difficult to know why certain historians have tried to maintain, whether by categorical insistence or simple omission, that Andalucía was not guerrilla territory. . . . Nothing could be more untrue. . . . Superficial ideas to the contrary, Andalucía bore witness to a most intense guerrilla war during the years of French occupation, a guerrilla war moreover that was most productive in terms of its results."[3]

As is apparent from these last words, however, the issue of the "little war" in Andalucía has been the subject of some debate. The French found themselves the subject of constant attack, certainly, but here one has to operate with a degree of caution. While memoirs of French soldiers might speak of the entire countryside springing to arms, there is a degree of imprecision in such words. The impression that is thus created is one of the invaders being confronted from one end of Andalucía to another by nothing but irregular bands made up of armed civilians eager to free their country from the foreign yoke, but in fact one has to proceed with a certain amount of caution in this respect. While many bands of irregulars certainly made an appearance, they were never alone. Thus, the Spanish regular army also remained in the field throughout. In this respect we can speak of three major foci of resistance. To the east the city of Murcia acted as a base for a force of troops that was originally constituted on the basis of the remnants of the men who had defended the Sierra Morena in January 1810 and, following the general reorganization of the Spanish field armies that took place a few months later, became known as the Third Army. Meanwhile, to the southwest the near impregnable bastion of Cádiz and the Isla de León gave refuge to still more regular troops in the form of Alburquerque's Army of Extremadura, this force being denominated as the Fourth Army. And finally, to the northwest lay the fortress of Badajoz, this last becoming the stronghold of yet another force of troops known as the Fifth Army. From three separate directions, then, the French constantly had to fend off the attentions of columns of regular troops whose activities cannot but be regarded as an integral part of *la guerrilla*—indeed, who were for the most part too weak to engage in anything other than glorified guerrilla operations—and from this it follows that the bitter and incessant struggle described by Marshal Soult and his subordinates cannot just be regarded as the work of armed civilians. That this was the case, indeed, was later clearly recognized. In a study of the policies of the last French governor of Málaga written a century after the Peninsular War, for instance, the French military analyst Alphonse Grasset is quite categorical in making a distinction between the two types of resistance. Thus, if he recognized that in September 1811—the moment that he chose to begin his monograph—the region was "overrun by innumerable bands of irregulars," the forces of Marshal Soult, he noted, were also, in effect, faced by three Spanish field armies in the shape of the Third Army (5,000 men) under Joaquín Blake; the Fifth Army (5,000 men) under the victor of Bailén, Francisco-Javier Castaños; and finally a 6,000-man division of the Fourth Army that had just been landed at Algeciras under Francisco Ballesteros.[4]

From all this it follows that simple assertions that Andalucía fought the French are not enough, and that, further, there are a number of research questions that suggest themselves as subjects for discussion. The first of these is obviously the extent to which popular resistance took hold of the region; the second, the share that popular resistance had in harassing the French; and the third, the factors that motivated the formation of the bands of irregulars spoken of by Grasset. In each case there is a traditional answer—in brief, that popular resistance was general, that popular resistance was highly effective, and that popular resistance sprang from hatred of the French and devotion to the cause of, first, Ferdinand VII and, second, the Roman Catholic Church—but in each case it is also a traditional answer that is at the very least wide open to attack. To write too much here would be to anticipate the argument of this chapter, but, given that the matter has already been touched upon in the introduction, let us say a few words about the extent of popular involvement in the struggle. As we have seen in a survey that eventually amassed details of some 3,024 participants in *la guerrilla,* only 290, or somewhat under 10 percent, could be shown to have originated in Andalucía. Meanwhile, these figures have been echoed elsewhere: in a more limited survey of 741 guerrillas, Ronald Fraser suggests that, while 143 of them—some 19 percent—operated at one time or another in Andalucía, only 45 of the 277 whose place of residence could be traced with any certainty were genuine *andaluces.*[5] Particularly when placed beside statistics for other regions, such as Navarre and the Basque provinces, which quite clearly mobilized far more men than their percentage of the population would appear to warrant, these figures are worthy of note (Andalucía, it should be remembered, accounted for approximately 18 percent of the population of Spain as a whole), while, even at the time, popular resistance was a phenomenon that proved surprisingly difficult to trace: asked in 1815 to elaborate a list of the guerrilla bands that had operated in his zone of command, the then captain general of Andalucía could come up with just five.[6]

If no one would deny the fact that numerous guerrilla bands appeared in Andalucía, it is clear that, except in a few instances where particularly corrupt local juntas (one such is that of Ayamonte) set up "guerrilla bands" as private armies or, alternatively, a means of saving their dependents and placemen from service at the front, in the course of 1809, the formation of such forces was intimately linked with the arrival of the French in the localities of rural Andalucía—there was, in short, no rush to take up arms at the news that King Joseph and Marshal Soult had crossed the Sierra Morena. Nor was armed resistance instantaneous even then. Although a French aide-de-camp carrying dispatches named Antoine Curnillon was killed by "brigands" near Carmona as early as 3 February 1810, all the evidence that we have suggests that guerrilla warfare took some weeks to emerge as a significant factor in the situation.[7] Having entered Andalucía a few days after the passage of the main French forces at the head of a draft of reinforcements, for example, the hussar officer Albert de Rocca was able to make his way from the pass of Despeñaperros to Seville without encountering even a hint of trouble.[8] Equally, given the job of carrying news of the fall of Seville to General Sebastiani, an aide-de-camp, Saint Chamans, was able to make it all the way from Seville to Valenzuela via Bujalance and Cañete de los Toros with no more difficulty than that given him by a somewhat refractory mule, and that without the protection of a single French soldier; at both places, admittedly, many of the villagers gathered to see him, but there was nothing in the way of menace—just curiosity and a desire for the latest news. At Valenzuela, true, he was met by a hostile crowd—the *pueblo* had been pillaged the day before by some of Sébastiani's troops, and by sheer ill luck he arrived amid the funeral of a young girl who had been brutally murdered by the raiders—but a combination of foresight and quick-wittedness saved the day, and he was able to continue on his way. Sébastiani, however, was now marching on Málaga, and Saint Chamans, who still had no escort of any sort, was therefore faced with the task of pressing on through the Alpujarras. Infested with bandits as these hills were, this was not a pleasant prospect, and both singly and in groups, he soon began to encounter stragglers from Areizaga's army. Yet these proved not the least threat—most, indeed, were concerned with no more than getting out of his way as fast as possible—and it was only within a few miles of Málaga that Saint Chamans was finally attacked by a group of men who opened fire on him from a cluster of rocks high above the road.[9]

The salient points to emerge from these accounts are threefold: first, Andalucía did not spring to arms as one at the mere news that the French had crossed the Sierra Morena; second, popular hostility was closely linked to cases of French misbehavior; and third, even in areas that were both favorable to guerrilla warfare and swarming with armed men, attacks on the French were at best sporadic in the early stages of occupation. That said, trouble mounted steadily, the growth of irregular resistance being testified to very clearly by the situation reports tendered every few days by the commanders of each of the major French units. Taking those of the division of General Dessolles, which was accorded the task of garrisoning Córdoba and Jaén and had permanent posts at Córdoba, Jaén, Ecija, Osuna, Andújar, and La Carolina, as an example, the first mention of anything resembling an encounter with guerrillas comes in a report of 28 February, in which it is stated that a dragoon acting as an advanced picket for a French column had been killed by a "brigand" near Hornachuelos and that a band of 150 insurgents had been spotted making for Fuente Ovejuna in the Sierra Morena. Thereafter, however, mention of the irregular bands becomes more and more frequent. Thus, on 5 March it was admitted that parties of brigands had been reported at Anora and Jugosa and that a number of troops had had to be dispatched from Córdoba to chase away a further party that had temporarily occupied Montilla, and on 9 March that a small detachment of troops that had been sent to Villanueva del Arzobispo to collect supplies had been and forced to flee, with the loss of five dead. In the face of all this, Dessolles remained primly upbeat—as he pointed out, an action at Torreperogil in which a force of 700–800 insurgents was scattered by a French column was but one of a whole series of defeats that was inflicted on the Spaniards.

Yet as fast as the French dealt with one threat, others sprang up: on 27 March came tales of a force of eighty French cavalry and Spanish *juramentados* that had had to be rescued after being besieged in a house in Morón as well as a patrol of eight French soldiers that had to fight off another attack at El Visillo, while on 18 April it was reported that troops that had been sent to raid Hinojosa and Belalcázar had been attacked by the bands of Ventura and Caracol. The fact was that, with the French hampered by insufficient resources and poor coordination, no progress was being made whatsoever. Something of the flavor of that constant activity that was going on is suggested by a general report of 20 June:

> A number of parties that had been approaching from the direction of Extremadura having shown some intention of menacing Belalcázar, the column at the orders of *chef du bataillon* Bony quitted Pozoblanco in order to march to meet them, only for the enemy to fall back before them. A band of brigands crossed the River Genil and moved to attack Santa Ella: despite a gallant defense on the part of its Guardia Cívica, which cost it a number of dead, the brigands got into the town. The column of Captain Robin was then sent to occupy Puente Don Gonzalez, a point via which the enemy was hoping to retreat, and the latter were eventually attacked and dispersed by a party of the Twenty-Seventh Chasseurs à Cheval. A number of soldiers of

> the Fifty-Fifth [Line] attacked Cazorla on 4 June. . . . Headed by their colonel himself, they occupied the town easily enough, only to find that this was because the enemy had evacuated the place the night before, leaving behind no more than a few stragglers. . . . In the course of this affair, the strong chance of an attack on Jaén led to a number of troops from the garrison of Andújar having to go to the assistance of the men stationed there. Having been informed that a band of 150 mounted brigands had been spotted at the foot of Mount Pelagares [?], the commandant at Alcaudete, Captain Dalmon of the Fifty-Fifth, immediately made to attack them. In the skirmish that followed he managed to kill around fifteen of the insurgents, . . . in addition to which the enemy had a number of wounded, as well as losing six horses killed and twenty-three captured, together with the greater part of their baggage. . . . Insurgent movements in the direction of Alcalá la Real have forced the column patrolling the *campina* [that is, the district surrounding the city of Córdoba itself] to go to the aid of the town of Priego as there were fears that it was about to be attacked. Several large bands that emerged in the area of Vilches, Arquillos, and Monpasson [?] . . . having been thrown back on Ibroz and Baeza, the troops stationed at Ubeda marched to intercept them as quickly as possible, but the insurgents, who were all mounted, took flight, though not before they had loaded their horses with all the money in the place. . . . Finally, every day the outposts at La Carolina exchange shots with small parties of raiders who suddenly appear on the high road.[10]

For some weeks after the fall of Seville, Soult had remained unremittingly optimistic in his account of events in Andalucía in the regular reports that he wrote for Marshal Berthier as the Armée d'Espagne's nominal chief of staff, but as early as the middle of March, he had evidently decided that matters had reached such a point that they could no longer be covered up. On the seventeenth, then, Soult reported that King Joseph had the day before entered Granada and been welcomed by an ecstatic crowd and that it seemed likely that it would be possible to form an entire division from the large numbers of ex-soldiers living in the area.

At the same time in the province of Málaga also, or so he claimed, everything was going well: the establishment of the Guardia Cívica was proceeding so rapidly, indeed, that it had been deemed possible to leave the city entirely in its hands. However, at same time, although he expressed the hope that the area would soon be pacified, he also had no option but to report that Ronda had had to be evacuated by its garrison and to admit that the threat to public order was becoming increasingly serious:

> In the days to come it will be very difficult to protect ourselves against the intrigues that are being mounted in the mountains by British agents unless we occupy the Campo de San Roque [that is, the area of land encompassing the British enclave of Gibraltar]. . . . His Catholic Majesty would have posted the division of General Dessolles among them had it not been necessary to use it to protect the lines of communication that link Granada and Seville with the Sierra Morena and to sustain the numerous towns of the Kingdoms of Jaén and Córdoba. At present these last are tormented by thousands of smugglers and soldiers who have become separated from their regiments. Unable as we have been to round the latter up, they have turned to brigandage, while, all told, the total number of smugglers and stragglers together has been calculated at more than 30,000 men.

Nor, meanwhile, was the Serranía de Ronda the only area to be affected by the revolt. "Thanks to the use of threats, torture, and the destruction of entire villages, not to mention the dispatch of a column of troops from Almería in the direction of Motril, General Blake, . . . who must himself therefore be regarded as nothing other than a brigand, has managed to incite the inhabitants of the Alpujarras to take up arms."[11]

As is already explicit, this activity was closely linked to the formation of guerrilla bands. This had certainly been an integral part of the strategy of the Junta Central, and the French had no sooner broken through the Sierra Morena than attempts began to be made to put such a scheme into practice, a good example of this being the manner in which the Marqués de Villafranca y los Vélez proclaimed his intention to form a party of sixty mounted priests and religious men at his own expense.[12] Nor were the military authorities remiss in this respect. On 10 February 1810, for example, Joaquín Blake, the general who had replaced Areizaga in command of the wreckage of the Army of La Mancha (now, as we have seen, renamed the Third Army), dispatched a number of officers to stir up popular resistance in the eastern reaches of the province of Jaén, the most important being Brigadier Antonio Osorio Calvache and a captain of the Regimiento de Cazadores de Barbastro named Hermenegildo Bielsa, while Colonel José Valdivia managed to gather a group of fugitives from Areizaga's forces at Marbella.[13] How far these efforts bore direct fruit is a moot point—the crowds of ecclesiastics, stragglers, peasants, and day laborers that such men got together were invariably routed by the French with much slaughter almost as soon as they took the field[14]—but by the summer, guerrilla bands of one sort or another had come into being in abundance, guerrilla bands, meanwhile, that were entirely separate from the Patriot war effort proper. Thus: "Colonel Beaussain reports that none of the parties he has encountered have presented any trace of regular troops, all of them having rather been composed of stragglers and peasants from villages in the mountains."[15] In Jaén, for example, not counting the commanders of bands based in La Mancha who from time to time crossed the Sierra Morena to raid such towns as Bailén—examples include Juan Antonio Orobio, Francisco Abad Moreno ("Chaleco"), Vicente Giraldo, and the priest Francisco Ureña—the best-known leaders were the brothers Juan and Francisco Uribe, the priest Antonio Moya de la Torre, and three otherwise unknown individuals named Lorenzo Terreros, Andrés Diego, and Valeriano Rodríguez.[16]

Elsewhere, meanwhile, we hear of still more leaders. In Córdoba recorded chieftains include the priest Clemente Arribas, the friar Miguel Herrero, the gypsy Francisco Salazar, and a number of figures of whom we know little more than their names, namely Antonio Bueno, Francisco Espín ("Tamborlán"), Francisco Díaz ("el Cojo de Torremilano"), Alonso Gómez ("el Manco"), and Juan Manuel ("Ronquillo").[17] In Granada, if one discounts ad hoc forces of regular troops, such as the roving band of cavalry headed by Lieutenant Colonel José Miguel Villalobos y Cabrera under the denomination of the "Guerrillas del Tercer Ejército," the most noted figures were the mayor of Otivar, Juan Fernández Cañas ("Tío Caridad"); the mayor of Ohanés, Francisco Moreno; and the officer of the customs guard, Francisco García.[18] In Huelva two leaders of whom we know at least a little are one Juan Santana Bolaños and a monk named Antonio Jiménez, while on 17 August 1810, the so-called Compania de Contrabandistas—an irregular formation established by the Junta of Ayamonte prior to the French invasion and headed by one Donaso González Cortes—was reported to have attacked a detachment of enemy cavalry at Almonte.[19] And in Málaga chieftains often mentioned in the literature encompass the priest Antonio Muñoz, the peasant José Segovia, the regular-army officers Vicente Moreno and Antonio de Luque, the notary Francisco de Roa, the senior bureaucrat Manuel Jiménez Guazo, José Ruíz Falcón ("Juan Soldado"), and finally Manuel Santaella.[20]

Popular resistance did not just take the form of the formation of guerrilla bands, however. In the Serranía de Ronda, by contrast, we see a phenomenon that was rather different. Though quickly penetrated by the French—the town of Ronda itself was occupied on 10 February 1810—many of the smaller *pueblos* in the region remained free, and it was not long before a variety of figures in the Allied camp had come to realize that the rugged mountains of the district were an ideal base for guerrilla warfare. As early as 6 February, the commandant general of the Campo del Gibraltar, Adrián Jacomet, commissioned a supernumerary officer named Francisco González Peinado to range the interior of the Serranía with the aim of raising the inhabitants in revolt. Accompanied by a small group of regular-army officers and the parish priest of Algeciras, Peinado duly visited such *pueblos* as Algatocín and Jubrique, while he was very quickly joined by a small British mission that had been dispatched to the area for the very same purpose by the governor of Gibraltar, Colin Campbell.[21] These emissaries found the area in a state of considerable ferment. If things had, on occasion, been difficult in the larger towns and cities, in more remote districts such as the Serranía, the French had been far less inclined to respect the norms of discipline, and the inhabitants in consequence had been subjected to considerable brutality.

To take just one example, in Ronda itself an apothecary named Salvador Aguila, who had just given all the money he had available in his house to another soldier, was murdered by a trumpeter of the Second Hussars who was aggrieved at the fact that there was nothing left for him.[22] With the area swarming with bandits and dispersed soldiers, meanwhile, it was inevitable that here and there French soldiers should have begun to fall victim to knives and bullets, and to this the governor of Ronda, Gilbert Vinot, responded as if he was already faced with a full-scale insurrection. Among the *pueblos* to feel his wrath was Gaucín. As a priest named José Guerrero Palacio noted: "On 28 [*sic,* 22] February 1810 the French army entered the district and waged the most cruel war upon it, killing its inhabitants and pillaging or destroying all that they came across, their fury being such that they did not even spare its holy churches."[23]

Anger at the French, as we shall see, was not the only factor in the events that followed, but González Peinado and his fellow agents were able to secure a ready hearing. At the same time, the insurgents had already secured a leader of their own. Among the inhabitants of Gaucín who had fled their homes at the approach of the French was José Serrano Valdenebro. Born in 1742, Serrano Valdenebro had enlisted in the Guardias Walones in 1767 and then transferred into the marines ten years later. Severely wounded several times, badly disfigured—it appears that he had suffered significant burns at the siege of Gibraltar—and finally deprived of the use of one of his hands by frostbite, he retired from the navy in 1796 and spent the next few years writing commentaries on the art of war. Returning to active service in 1808, at the end of 1809 he was given command of a hastily improvised Legión Real de Marina, only to suffer a serious fall that forced him to take a leave of absence and retire to his home in Gaucín.[24] Hearing of the approach of the enemy, Serrano Valdenebro fled and took shelter in a shepherd's hut some distance away, and there he remained for some days. Around him, however, the insurrection was rapidly gathering strength, and on 28 February a large force of peasants armed with nothing more than pitchforks and fowling pieces fell on the small garrison that had been left in Gaucín and drove it out. Realizing, perhaps, that they were in dire need of assistance, the local elites now turned to Serrano Valdenebro and begged him to take command. To this the latter agreed, and on 1 March he in effect proclaimed himself to be the leader of the revolt.[25]

At the behest of González Peinado and Serrano Valdenebro, the *serranos* were soon massing for an attack on Ronda. This is an affair to which we shall return at a later point, a more important matter at the current moment being the form that the insurrection took. Here and there adventurers of one sort or another attempted to form guerrilla bands—one such was Andrés Ortiz de Zarate, a teacher of mathematics who had taken refuge in Gibraltar and joined the mission sent out to the Serranía de Ronda by General Campbell as an interpreter[26]—but in effect the form of military organization favored by the insurrection was that of a local home guard organized in parish companies that were mobilized for the purpose of specific military operations or the defense of their own *pueblos.* Eventually confirmed by the Regency as the military commander of the district, Serrano Valdenebro immediately divided it up into six zones denominated *cuartones,* each of which grouped together between four and six municipalities. As for the militia companies that were supposed to be fielded by each municipality, these were commanded by assorted local notables. Full details of the men concerned are not available, but the one list that has been compiled gives the names of some fifty-five officers, of whom nine were priests or friars, four sometime officers in the Milicias Honradas, one a regular-army officer, one a judicial official, and one a village doctor.[27]

Whether these arrangements were ever very successful in controlling the insurrection is a moot point, the need to impose a greater degree of control being suggested by an ordinance submitted to the Cádiz government in November 1810 by the mayor of Mojocar, Ramón Somalo, which basically proposed that the de facto home guard that had emerged during the fighting should be levied by conscription at a rate of ten men for every thousand householders from among those groups of the populace—married men, for example—not already liable to conscription, that the families of the men conscripted should be given public assistance, and that recruits should be formed into battalions under the command of respected local notables.[28] Be that as it may, from the beginning the war in the Serranía was rather different from its counterpart in the rest of Andalucía, the manner in which the system functioned being exemplified by two dispatches written by Serrano Valdenebro in the early summer of 1810. The first of these concerns an action that took place on 5 May. In brief, several companies of *serranos,* including those of Cortes de la Frontera, Gaucín, Casares, and Igualeja, had gathered in the vicinity of Arriate to attack a French force that was on its way from Ronda when they became aware of a party of forty dragoons that was bringing in a consignment of hay and other goods requisitioned at the town of Setenil. Making use of a convenient gully, they were able to steal up on the French and open fire at close range, routing them with the loss of eight dead and six prisoners and eventually seizing no fewer than nineteen of their mules.[29] As for the second action, this time the focus was a strong French punitive column that left Ronda in the direction of Marbella on 26 May. In response to this threat, Serrano Valdenebro called to arms the men of Casares, Manilba, Jímena, and Gaucín while a number of patrols did what they could to harass the French column, which, having occupied Manilba, was now marching on Gaucín in a bid to regain Ronda. Seeing that the French were in retreat, and having received eighty reinforcements from Ubrique, the Spanish commander directed his forces to close in on the column. Attacked from all sides, the French pressed on, but their losses were mounting while they were also unable to prevent the Spaniards from repeatedly getting in among the cattle they had collected and driving off a number of beasts. At length, however, they could go no further:

> By the time they reached the spring of La Piedra, they found that they might just as well have been shut up in a sack, for the heights on their left flank had been occupied by the forces pursuing them, while those ahead had been occupied by parties from the villages of Juscar and Cartajima. At this they became greatly alarmed, and it is possible that they might have thrown down their arms had it not been for the implacable hatred clearly visible among the populace. As it was, for about an hour they remained clumped together under fire from all sides, the musketry to which they were subjected being so intense that

> they were scarcely able to fire a shot in return. . . . At length they once more advanced on the pass. Here, however, they were met by the contingents of Tarajàn, Pujerra, and Igualeja. Commanded by Don Juan Becerra, these greeted them with heavy fire, whereupon they lost all formation, some of the men also trying to escape by means of various tracks that crossed the hillside.[30]

For a French view of the fighting, we can do no better than turn to the memoirs of Albert de Rocca, who in early March 1810 found himself under attack from the *serranos* as he sought to reach Ronda with his column of reinforcements:

> The Spaniards kept up a brisk fire of musketry upon the detachment from the rocks and the windows of the houses at that end of the village which we must pass. Having no hope of succour we resolved to cut our way through the enemy. My horse received a ball through the neck and fell. I succeeded in raising him immediately and [rejoined] the detachment. Shortly afterwards, my comrade had his arm broken, [and] we saw almost all the hussars fall successively around us. Women, or rather furies let loose, threw themselves with horrible shrieks upon the wounded, and disputed who should kill them by the most cruel tortures. They stabbed their eyes with knives and scissors and seemed to exult with ferocious joy at the sight of their blood. . . . We pushed on our horses . . . and fortunately passed the defile. We were soon after surrounded by a cloud of peasants detached from the main body. . . . They followed us along the rocks without daring to approach nearer than musket-shot for fear of not being able to regain the mountain if we charged. Priests and alcaldes were riding on horseback along the heights to direct the movements of the crowd. Such of our wounded as had the misfortune to fall off their horses were stabbed behind us without mercy. One alone escaped, for he had the presence of mind to give the bystanders to understand that he wished to confess before he died, and the priest of Setenil saved him from the fury of his enemies.[31]

These scenes of mass mobilization and, indeed, people's war were not repeated elsewhere (though a variant on the theme may have been attempted by both Bielsa and Osorio, the guerrilla bands associated with these commanders seem rather to have been "crowd armies"—assemblies of peasants and day laborers who, instead of engaging in hit-and-run attacks, sought rather to engage the French in open battle). A more classic pattern is that seen in the case of the band headed by Juan Fernández Cañas. As we have seen, Fernández Cañas was alcalde of the village of Otivar at the time of the arrival of the French forces and, according to his own account, took to the hills in June 1810 after getting involved in a fight with some *juramentado* irregulars who sought to take a horse from him. Very soon he had gathered a small group of *dispersos* around him, and having first joined up with another chieftain named Luis Negro, by the middle of July he was in action against the French, ambushing a strong column near Nerja, capturing a supply column at the Venta de Lachar, and capturing the garrison of a small coastal battery at La Herradura. There followed many other attacks, and within a year Fernández Cañas had secured the rank of colonel, though, unlike many similar commanders in La Mancha and the north of Spain, he never seems to have succeeded in militarizing his band by transforming it into a regular unit. Despite this, what emerges is the picture of a permanent force of perhaps 500 men that sustained itself by what it could seize from the French or requisition from the populace, a force, indeed, that lived separately from the populace.[32] Moreover, if Fernández Cañas did not succeed in militarizing his forces, there were evidently other Andalusian chieftains who did. Attacked near Guarromán at the head of a large convoy en route from Madrid to Seville in the spring of 1812, for example, Hippolyte d'Espinchal remembered the enemy as having been dressed in at least an approximation of military uniform:

> According to the information that we received about what had happened, it transpired that we had been attacked by about 3,000 men commanded by the Marquesito. . . . The troops involved had been composed of both infantry and cavalry,

> the latter being mounted on horses of a pretty scrawny build, some of which were equipped with high Spanish saddles and others with the type issued to French dragoons and hussars. The clothing and armament of the cavalrymen corresponded to the bizarre nature of their mounts' harness: one saw French helmets, infantry shakos, busbies, Spanish hats with their brims turned up at one side, and lances, muskets, and sabers of many different kinds. All of this seemed to suggest that they were troops of a very irregular character, and yet their dress had a degree of uniformity: almost all of them were dressed in a brown jacket adorned with red turnbacks and frogging. . . . As for the infantry, they were armed with a mixture of British, Spanish, and French muskets (a considerable number of them without bayonets) and a variety of sabers and hangers. A few of them had cartridge boxes, but the majority favored special belts instead, while their clothing consisted of brown jackets and trousers of every color imaginable; their footwear, meanwhile, was in the worst state imaginable.[33]

Such, then, was the guerrilla movement in Andalucía. What, however, were its effects? A good place to start here might be the casualties that the insurgents inflicted on the French forces. Given the incessant activity that we have recorded, it might be thought that French losses ran into many thousands, while King Joseph's aide-de-camp, Bigarré, who after all experienced the campaign in Andalucía firsthand, actually claims that the bands accounted for as many as 180,000 of the invaders.[34] However, in reality, a study of such records as are available suggests that, if such a hecatomb took place, it did not do so south of the Sierra Morena, a good place to start in reaching this conclusion being the returns of strength submitted by all divisional commanders every month. Let us start with the corps of Marshal Victor. If we take Ruffin's division as an example, on 1 February 1810 it numbered a total of 5,624 officers and men, whereas by 1 December it was down to 4,977; equally, that of General Leval numbered 8,268 men in February 1810 and 7,513 in December.[35] Given that Victor's troops were primarily engaged in the siege of Cádiz and therefore far removed from the worst ravages of the guerrilla war, it may be more useful to examine Sebastiani's corps, which was, as we have seen, rather trying to hold down such districts as the Alpujarras. Here on 31 January the division of General Rey had 11,078 officers and men, whereas by 15 November (the last date for which figures are available) it was down to 9,889; equally, the Polish division commanded by Werlé numbered 6,144 officers and men on 31 January, but 5,892 on 15 December, and 5,459 on 1 June 1811; on 1 September, the last return prior to the changes that resulted from the creation of the new division of reserve established by Marshal Soult, it still had 5,390 men.[36] Finally, there is V Corps of Marshal Mortier. Here we have Girard's and Gazan's divisions. On 1 February 1810 these had 8,805 and 8,164 officers and men respectively, whereas on 16 December their totals had fallen to 7,610 and 7,334. Given that both these divisions were involved in the capture of Badajoz and suffered heavy losses at the Battle of Albuera on 16 May 1811, it is best to avoid the next six months, but for the twelve-month period that followed, the only field action of any significance in which either was engaged was that of Arroyomolinos de Montánchez.[37] Unfortunately, a full run of figures is not available for this period, but on 15 July, having in the meantime received significant reinforcements, Girard's division was back up to 8,800 men and Gazan's (now under Claparède) to 9,164; on 15 January 1812, by contrast, now under Dembowski and Darricau respectively, they were down to 6,724 and 8,252, though the heavy losses suffered by the former were almost entirely the result of Arroyomolinos.[38] If we exclude major battles, then, we may say that the wastage suffered by the French forces in Andalucía averaged something less than 10 percent a year (the actual figures for the period February–December 1810 come out at 9.78 percent). This, however, represents losses due to all causes, the result being that guerrilla warfare can only be credited with a relatively limited number of casualties.[39]

For an alternative view of the same question that accords the guerrillas rather more credit, we may look at the figures that may be derived from the tables compiled by the French military historian Aristide Martinien in his *Tableaux par corps et par batailles des officiers tués et blesses pendant les guerres de l'empire, 1803–1815*. Published in 1899, this extraordinary work of reference suggests that

2,732 French officers were killed or mortally wounded in Spain and Portugal between 1808 and 1814, and by extrapolation, it has been calculated by the Spanish historian Jorge Planas that, assuming that these figures are correct, the total cost of the Peninsular War to Napoleon's forces in terms of combat losses was around 37,000 men (by contrast, in the British army the equivalent figure was 10,500 and in the Portuguese some 8,000).[40] Of the 2,732 French officers who fell, meanwhile, some 492, or 18 percent of the whole, are reckoned by Planas to have fallen victim to irregular opponents of one form or another. Yet a consideration of the results for Andalucía in particular paints a picture that is rather different. Here the number of French officers who were assassinated or fell in combat between February 1810 and August 1812 was 124, but of these 34, or 27 percent, may definitely be said to have been accounted for by irregular resistance, while another 23, or some 18 percent, are "possibles." In short, in proportionate terms more French soldiers fell to irregulars in Andalucía than was the case elsewhere. Yet this is hardly surprising given that the French forces in Andalucía had neither to fight many field actions nor besiege many fortresses: discounting the blockade of Cádiz, the chief exceptions were the Battle of Barrosa (5 March 1811) and the siege of Tarifa (20 December 1811–5 January 1812). Moreover, even taking them to their greatest extreme, they suggest guerrilla warfare only accounted for something over 800 dead. To these, of course, must be added the wounded. Counting officers only, these numbered some 395, of whom a minimum of 87 (22 percent) and a maximum of 183 (46 percent) were hurt in clashes with irregulars, the total number of wounded therefore probably numbering somewhere in the region of 2,000.[41] In short, regrettable though the casualties that they caused were, the guerrillas scarcely caused the losses with which they have been credited, the really significant blows to Soult's manpower rather coming in the Battles of Barrosa and Albuera, of which the former cost the French 2,380 casualties and the latter as many as 7,900.

The effect of the *partidas* should not just be computed in terms of "body count," however. Constantly forced to march hither and yon through some of the wildest terrain in Spain, the troops became ever more prone to exhaustion and demoralization. As cavalry officer Théophilé Brémond wrote to his mother in June 1810, "We are wandering around the Sierra Morena without a moment's rest, waging a guerrilla war that really is most trying, not least because of lack of sleep and the state of alert in which we are constantly kept."[42] Another cavalryman, meanwhile, was the Polish lancer Kajetan Wojciechowski: "Much reduced, our regiment was stationed for more than a year in the town of Baza. Despite this, the incessant expeditions to chase the partisans, gather food, and collect the people's financial contributions did not allow us to rest for an instant. . . . Every day our duties grew more difficult. What with the constant alarms and the need to remain on the alert the whole time, we never got a moment's peace."[43] Also Polish was Andrzej Daleki, a peasant from the district of Krotoszyn who was conscripted into the Polish army then being formed by Napoleon at the end of 1806 and sent to Spain in 1808 and now found himself serving as part of the garrison of Málaga: "For two weeks [after the capture of Málaga] we wandered to and fro in the mountains hunting down the Spaniards who had taken shelter among them. But to the devil with a war in which a regular soldier has to fight against an entire nation! As fast as we chased them out of a place, they simply came back in again. All that we managed to do, in fact, was to use up our own men: insofar as Spain was concerned, the only ground that we occupied was that beneath our feet, and even that was lost as soon as we moved on again."[44] Finally, Just Roy, as we have seen, was serving in Seville on the staff of Marshal Soult: "The guerrillas harassed us without cease and did us terrible harm: every day they carried off some detachment, some petty convoy, some little post, and, put together, these losses amounted to a total that was quite considerable."[45]

That Roy's view was statistically very far from being the truth is neither here nor there, what matters being rather the perceptions of the officers and men of the army of occupation. In reality, the bands were neither ubiquitous nor capable of inflicting that much in the way of damage, but veterans of the campaign remembered the matter very differently, while fuel was added to the flames by the constant stories of torture and murder, the result being that few French soldiers were free from an ever-present fear of sudden death. "At that time," wrote the pharmacist Fée, "one traveled in

Spain in the same fashion as one did in Arabia: woe to him who strayed from the caravan. The inhabitants, who after all still had some drops of African blood flowing through their veins, turned Bedouin, stalked their prey, and, more through love of plunder than patriotic devotion, flung themselves upon it. Having quickly seized whatever came to hand, they then disappeared among the rocks to divide up their booty and torture their prisoners. . . . Ravines, clumps of trees, ruined buildings, rocky outcrops, all these alike could suddenly be swarming with our assailants, and in just ten minutes one could find oneself a prisoner."[46] To quote Fée, indeed, there was no safety even in places in which there were relatively large numbers of French troops, one such being the town of Jérez:

> After the Battle of Chiclana [Barrosa], the hospitals were full of wounded, and I was called to Jérez to help look after them. . . . One could not move beyond the last houses of the town without danger. Beyond the walls the guerrillas prowled around without cease in the manner of hunters stalking their prey. At dusk in particular, well-mounted horsemen would suddenly gallop in close, armed with grappling irons that were attached by long cords to the pommels of their saddles. Choosing some unfortunate sentry, they would ignore the single shot that was all that he would have time to get off and hurl their grappling irons at him, these having only to catch on some part of his clothing or equipment for him to be dragged away and hacked to pieces. Even in the middle of the day one had to be prudent. Whenever I needed to go off and gather herbs, for example, I always kept my horse nearby and ensured that I was accompanied by a servant, whose task it was to keep watch: no sooner had he spotted riders in the distance, or anyone else, than I would be in the saddle.[47]

All this, meanwhile, was experienced amid a country in which campaigning was harsh in the extreme. Among the French troops patrolling the Sierra Morena, for example, was a twenty-two-year-old trooper of the Twentieth Dragoons named Louis Antoine Gougeat:

> We left Córdoba on 12 May [1811] . . . but, instead of continuing to descend the valley of the Guadalquivir, we turned sharply to the right and entered the mountains of Extremadura. We marched for the greater part of the day, more often on foot than on horseback, through a horrible country in which one saw little more than rocks. . . . The heat was overwhelming. At last . . . we arrived at a spring where we made camp. . . . It was high time: we were dying of thirst. The commandant then waited for fresh orders. Had he lost his documents, or was he just trying to confuse the enemy's spies? I have no idea, but what is true is that, when the regiment finally got back on the road again, it seemed to me that we several times retraced our steps along roads that we had already taken. We seemed, indeed, to be marching at random. This went on for three days and nights, but very soon our supplies were exhausted. The men began to complain, and demanded that they either be given bread or given an enemy to fight. . . . Pretty soon vermin of all sorts had added themselves to the ills that afflicted us: we were seriously incommoded, while all our efforts to rid ourselves of the problem proved useless.[48]

Even when the troops were neither in any danger nor being forced endlessly to tramp the sierras in pursuit of an elusive foe, their lot was one of boredom and misery. Food was usually short, while the men faced endless months in lonely garrisons or primitive cantonments. Fée, for example, has left us a graphic picture of life in the French lines in front of Cádiz:

> Our men were picked off by enemy fire, by illness, sometimes even by suicide. Homesickness, that incurable melancholy, . . . carried off a good few more. . . . Nobody had a care for the pleasures of the soldiers. . . . In those times our men did not receive a free ration . . . of tobacco, and yet they also lacked the money to buy it. In consequence, the entire First Corps smoked less in a year than the students of a military academy now do in six months. Food was never abundant, while the strong, thick wine distributed to the troops swelled the head without nourishing the body. The army could beat the Spaniards and fight

> with success against the British, but a still more redoubtable enemy was gradually undermining its strength. Little by little, boredom—something that kills and stupefies just as surely as a narcotic—took control of the best soldiers. . . . Meanwhile, the bitterness of our situation was increased still further by the sad fact that we almost never received any mail from our families. . . . Nor did we know anything that was happening in France or the rest of Europe. Newspapers or fresh copies of periodicals were rarities. . . . Though free on the surface, in reality we were . . . poor exiles in a foreign land.[49]

On top of boredom, there was also heat:

> In the month of May the heat became excessive and the thermometer marked forty degrees centigrade in the shade. . . . If you lie perfectly still in a closed room provided with porous water pots . . . that give off a little humidity, and refresh [yourself] with oranges and cold water, . . . you can just about stand it, but even these measures are not enough when the wind is in the east. This wind—the *solano*—comes from Africa, where it passes across the sands of the great desert. . . . If it blows for several days, the heat becomes stifling, while the nights do nothing to cool things down. At such times streams run dry, plants wither, and animals die of asphyxia. . . . Man too cannot escape its influence. . . . He can hardly breathe and is devoured by an ardent thirst. . . . It is, then, all too easy to imagine the sufferings of our soldiers, living, as they were, in the open air and with no better cover than their rough shelters.[50]

The result of all this, of course, was a growing sense of futility and demoralization among the troops, and with it ever greater indiscipline. Angry and unhappy, the soldiers were brutalized by their experiences and rendered ever more likely to revenge themselves on the hapless populace, thereby driving ever more villagers into the arms of the insurgents. At the village of El Fondón, for example, the execution by firing squad of five men suspected of involvement with the bands was reportedly accompanied by the rape of their wives and daughters in the public washhouse.[51] Indeed, as Lord Blayney discovered when he was captured in the course of an abortive British landing at Fuengirola, even regular soldiers were likely to be given short shrift if they fell into their hands:

> I soon . . . observed a column close in from the left, on whose caps I perceived the number "four" with an eagle, and which proved to be the *quatrième polonais.* The troops with me, after firing a few rounds, charge this column, and a very severe conflict ensued, which unfortunately ended in my being made prisoner, having but nine men remaining of those that advanced with me. Those only who have suffered a similar fate can form any idea of my sensations at being thus obliged to surrender to a ferocious banditti, who loaded me with every vile epithet, but in whose outrageous violence I in great measure found my personal safety, for they crowded so thick on me that they had not room to give force to their blows. They tore my clothes, rifled my pockets, and attempted to pull off my epaulets, and the resistance I made to this last indignity procured me several blows from the butt ends of their muskets that covered me with contusions. . . . The scene that presented itself at this moment can never be effaced from my memory: both officers and soldiers had all the appearance of those desperate banditti; their long moustachios, their faces blackened by smoke and gunpowder, and their bloody and torn clothes giving to their whole appearance a degree of indescribable ferocity.[52]

Fear, meanwhile, also played its part in ensuring that the invaders did not observe many niceties. Taken to Granada by his captors, for example, Blayney on the way observed a group of his guards literally shoot first and ask questions afterward:

> A few horsemen appearing on the summit of a hill, a detachment of lancers . . . was ordered to reconnoitre them, while the convoy halted to take some refreshment at a small house on the road side. The Poles ascended the hill with great rapidity

> and soon returned with five horses, reporting that they had belonged to the brigands, of whom they had killed seven. The general with an air of triumph bade me observe the cattle on which our allies were mounted. . . . These animals were indeed most wretched, and a kind of pad on which the country people convey their things to market served for saddles. I firmly believe that these brigands were in reality nothing more than a party of inoffensive peasants whom the Poles had robbed of their horses in order to corroborate the detail of their prowess. Besides, it was considered as a sufficient proof of brigandage for the peasants to be found in the smallest number at any distance from their villages.[53]

The chief effect of popular resistance in Andalucía was therefore not so much the direct impact it had upon the French armies in military terms but rather the way in which it pushed the invaders into policies that were counterproductive. To quote Blayney again:

> At the commencement the Spaniards were lukewarm in their own cause, and would probably have remained so had not the cruelties and excesses of the French roused them to resistance and revenge, . . . for it is a general order that the inhabitants of a place where . . . a crime is committed are to be put to the sword without exception of age or sex, and their habitations burned to the ground, nor is any enquiry ever made into the provocation that may have committed these excesses. By this system of terror and extermination the French have created the bands which they name brigands, for the inhabitants of a village who are fortunate enough to escape from these military execution, having no place of refuge, join the first armed party they meet, and, urged by revenge and desperation, commit the greatest cruelties on the enemies that fall into their hands. . . . Indeed, it requires little penetration to discover that the exterminating system of warfare adopted by France, although it might succeed in a country where the inhabitants could be hemmed into a little space, must inevitably fail in one so extensive and naturally strong as Spain.[54]

Instability, then, begat instability, and this is further evident in the experiences of those who actively collaborated with the French. Particularly in areas outside the control of the invaders' garrisons, such men, and their families too, were in constant danger of reprisals either against themselves or their property. As an example, we may cite here a telling reference from the casebook of the Conde de Montarco: "Don Salvador Sabina, resident of Olvera and captain of the Guardia Cívica, claims that he has suffered grave injuries in respect of his fortune at the hands of the insurgents on account of his service in this force and requests indemnification in the form of properties expropriated from émigrés."[55] In fact this source is rather more sparse in the light it sheds upon this problem than might be expected—in the period January–May 1811, for example, there are, including possibles, no more than ten mentions of guerrilla warfare—but it might also be relevant that in the same period no fewer than twelve mayors sought to resign their posts.[56] Whether this last was because of fear of reprisals is unclear, but there is much evidence to suggest that the *afrancesados* did indeed come under direct attack. One well-known incident took place on the high road from Antequera to Málaga in May 1810, when that city's entire Extraordinary Criminal Tribunal was captured by the band of José Ruiz Falcón and packed off to General Jacomet in San Roque for trial.[57] Meanwhile, on 14 June the band of Pedro Alcalde descended on the *pueblo* of Alcalá la Real and murdered the mayor, the next day seeing Alcalde in Ybros, where he wounded the town clerk.[58] On 1 June 1811 the chieftain Pedro Saldivar ("Palmetín") rode into San Lucar de Barrameda and killed an inhabitant named Fernández who had presented Joseph Bonaparte with six launches that could be used as gunboats in the bay of Cádiz and in return had received the Orden Real de España.[59] Finally, less grim but no less telling was a story that was doing the rounds in Cádiz in 1812 to the effect that the wife of a leading inhabitant of Jérez was accosted by a band—possibly that of the same Saldivar—while out riding with a group of French officers (who, so it was said, most ungallantly galloped to safety and left her to her fate) and was tied to a tree and soundly birched with a bundle of furze.[60] Of course, such attacks could be just as counterproductive as French repression, for as we shall see, they were by no means necessarily a political act, but the fact remains that beyond the walls of the larger towns and cities, no collaborators could think themselves safe.

None of this was remotely compatible with the successful implantation of French rule in Andalucía, and yet aware though the invaders were of the need to tackle the conditions that gave rise to the constant disorder, be it mere brigandage or otherwise, their hands were tied by two issues whose effects were wholly inescapable. In the first place, right across Andalucía the result of the war was economic disruption of the highest order. To take just one example, Blayney has left us a striking account of the situation in Málaga:

> The population of Málaga is between thirty and forty thousand souls, and though it still retains some external appearance of its former prosperity, it is but the unsubstantial shadow of departed reality. The total cessation of commerce, and the losses consequent on the war, have produced innumerable bankruptcies and universal distress; the port, which is daily growing shallower from the mud carried into it by the Guadalmedina, has lost all appearance of commercial life, some fishing boats alone being seen in movement, while a few . . . feluccas and other smaller craft are laid up rotting. What a contrast with the former flourishing state of this city, whose annual exports were valued at near half a million sterling in wines, brandy, oil, fruits, anchovies, and . . . silks. Such have been the devastating effect of the unprovoked and unjustifiable invasion of the French.[61]

To the effects of war were added those of natural catastrophe. From 1811 onward, large parts of Andalucía were gripped by yet another epidemic of yellow fever, which not only badly hit the work force but also disrupted communications even more than they were already on account of the various quarantine measures that the French were forced to introduce, while that same year saw the onset of a terrible drought. So severe was the situation, indeed, that even Soult was forced to admit that the countryside was in no state to bear the demands of the war: "No one can remember an autumn as baking as the one that we are experiencing. No rain has fallen; the fields are parched; the animals can find no pasture and are dying in scores. Together with the fears inspired among the inhabitants by the contagion that reigns in Murcia and the poor result of the last harvest, this calamity has occasioned a progressive rise in the price of commodities of the first necessity. A great deal of careful management and, above all, help from abroad, will be necessary to preserve . . . the south of Spain from, if not famine, then at least great want."[62] Of careful management there was little, however, and of foreign help even less, the result being a veritable crescendo of misery:

> Our difficulties increased and hunger became as widespread as it was horrific: there were no supplies for the troops and still less for the common people. The town council attempted to force the merchants to fix the price of such food as they obtained, but . . . the latter refused. . . . On the eighth of April [1812], a double contribution was imposed for the current month. This augmented emigration to such an extent among those who could escape that, in addition to the want of food in the markets on account of the stall holders' failure to appear, consternation became general, for the hunger being experienced by the poor was now truly dreadful. Persons of every class and condition fought one another for a stalk of lettuce, a cabbage leaf, or some miserable fragment of food that had been discovered among the rubbish thrown from some house or other; lemons and bitter oranges were bought and sold as the most exquisite delicacies; and the very bones that fell from the tables of the French and their followers were snatched from the mouths of dogs so that humans could continue to chew upon them. On all sides one saw wild-eyed specters . . . pleading either to be given bread or to be allowed to die, and the city appeared more like a cemetery that had come to life than a bustling center of commerce. . . . The populace was gripped by fear and alarm: more than 100 persons were dying of want each day, and the streets were inundated with figures on the point of death. . . . There was not a single person who was not revolted at such sights, and the very French were . . . eaten up by an inner guilt that lent a bitter taste to all their pleasures. As for emigration, it became a

torrent: while good Spaniards fled to the mountains, or when they had them at the very least took shelter in their country houses, the *afrancesados* journeyed to Antequera to seek refuge with the garrison there.[63]

Yet in the face of this situation, the French remained utterly inflexible, and this for one simple reason. In brief, war had to be made to support war. There being no way of dispatching large quantities of food to southern Spain, the occupation forces had perforce to be fed from the resources of Andalucía. Nor was the situation any better when it came to finance. Unlike food, gold and silver presented no difficulties in terms of transport, but here there were political problems. In brief, the imperial regime was utterly averse to meeting the financial costs of occupation, while the little money that did arrive in Spain was filtered through the *josefino* government in Madrid. King Joseph, Marshal Soult complained, received 2,000,000 francs a month from France to cover the pay of the various armies, but of this only 530,000 was allotted to Seville, this being rather less than half of what the Army of the South needed, and even this sum was frequently not dispatched in full.[64] Where he could, Soult fought back—Napoleon having decreed that all goods and other resources confiscated from the enemy should be sold in benefit of the French war effort, the marshal refused pointblank to accede to Joseph's demands that a part of the proceeds of such sales should be remitted to Madrid[65]—but such windfalls were of their very nature distinctly erratic. In terms of food and money alike, then, everything the French needed had to come from Andalucía, and that despite the fact that the populace had been reduced to penury. In respect of this attitude, we can do know better than to cite a letter from General Maransin to his colleague General Leval: "Poor even in ordinary times, . . . the district of Coín today lacks everything. Obliged to receive friends and enemies alternately and to furnish them with their necessities and, in addition, pay the contributions that they exact, each day augments the violence of their situation. . . . Nevertheless, I have ordered a redoubling of vigor and have authorized the use of whatever means are judged to be convenient. Obtaining results being extremely difficult at the current moment, the fact is that all means have become legitimate."[66]

What all this meant was that, even assuming that they had any real desire to do so, the local elites had no hope of protecting the populace, their collaboration therefore serving only to stoke the fuel of social unrest. This is a point to which we shall return, but for the time being, it is sufficient to note that the net result of French occupation was still further to blur the already very indistinct boundary between life within and without the law in the Andalusian countryside. In all the wilder parts of the region—the Sierra Morena, the Serranía de Ronda, the Alpujarras—and even some of the more accessible areas as well, the bandit was already a common figure when the French marched in, while the defeat of Areizaga's army meant that the countryside also became scattered with desperate bands of fugitives, all of whom in effect had little option but to turn, if only temporarily, to brigandage. Prior to January 1810, brigandage had been just that, in that the lives of crime led by those involved had had as their backdrop the existing structure of Spanish state and society, but the arrival of King Joseph and the French armies led to an automatic change in that backdrop. The result of this was to introduce an element of ambiguity into the situation. Despite the fond imaginings of patriotic Spanish writers, bandits did not turn from highway robbery to freedom fighting as soon as the enemy appeared at the gates. As a case in point, we have the story of Juan Masias. A native of Pradolongo in León, Masias had migrated to Andalucía in 1795 and settled in the town of Carmona, where he appears to have eked out a living as a day laborer and herdsman. Yet for reasons that remain unknown, in 1809 he turned to banditry in company with a number of other men from the same district. Increasingly suspected by the Patriot authorities, he was arrested in September of that year, along with two men named Manuel Fernández and Francisco Estebán, and was put on trial, only to be let off with a warning for want of proof. Undaunted by this narrow escape, at the beginning of July 1810, Masias reformed his gang and held up a carriage containing a number of travelers, who were not just robbed but also subjected to considerable violence. But Masias was evidently not much of a chieftain in that, on the night of 21 July, the gang was surprised by a patrol of *josefino* irregulars headed by one Ignacio San Vicente in the act of robbing a number of muleteers. Captured in the ensuing skirmish, Masias, Fernández, Estebán, and a fourth man named Manuel Jiménez were put on trial in Seville, all four of them being executed on 2 October 1810.[67] Clearly, Masias and his band can hardly be classed as freedom fighters. Yet given the identification of so much of the local elite with the cause of collaboration or, at least, acquiescence, any crime directed against a member of the propertied classes automatically assumed a patriotic hue, this being still more the case when, naturally enough given the fact that they had arms and, often enough, horses and money to boot, French soldiers began to fall victim to robbery and the murder that was its usual concomitant. With every robbed magistrate and every dead infantryman or aide-de-camp in objective terms a blow for the Patriot cause, guerrilla warfare in Andalucía can therefore be seen to have had at least a part of its origins in crime. To quote Soult, "Making war was but an excuse for crimes against property."[68]

Of course, as even a rapid glance at its cast of characters suggests, the guerrilla war was not just rooted in banditry. To revert to some of the details given earlier, most of the chieftains of whom we know some personal details were representatives of the antiguo regimen, or at least the ranks of property, status, and education. Thus, Moya de la Torre, Arribas, Herrero, Jiménez, and Muñoz were priests or monks; Fernández Cañas and Francisco Moreno alcaldes; García, Moreno, and Luque army officers or gendarmes; Roa and Jiménez Guazo functionaries; and Ortiz de Zarate a teacher (by contrast, we hear of just two men—the one a peasant and the other a gypsy—who were very clearly representatives of Spain's more marginalized elements). There are obvious distortions at work here—as ever, we are always likely to know more about men of property than men of poverty—and it is not to be thought that the command of the bands was wholly elite based. At least in principle, however, these were men with a stake in society who had something to fight for, or to put it another way, something to fear. While doubts might hang over one or two of them—if Vicente Moreno won fame in the wake of his execution in Granada in August 1810, there is some circumstantial evidence to suggest that he was no patriotic hero but rather an adventurer who took advantage of the chaos that beset Andalucía in the wake of the French invasion to strike out on his own[69]—it therefore has to be conceded that the "little war" was not entirely devoid of political commitment. All the more is this the case if we concede that the rank and file also contained men for whom fighting the French was a genuine impulse, a good example being the five Capuchin friars who killed in action when the band of Manuel Jiménez Guazo—the so-called Cruzada del Obispado de Málaga (see above)—was taken by surprise by enemy troops at the isolated Convento del Santo Desierto de las Nieves.[70]

Setting aside the figure of the warrior-monk, however, enthusiasm for the war among the populace remained as limited as ever, the chief factor needed to galvanize popular resistance being the presence of the French themselves. Nowhere is this clearer than in the Condado de Niebla, an isolated corner of the modern-day province of Huelva. Insofar as this area was concerned, the French did not have sufficient troops to establish much of a base there when they invaded Andalucía in 1810. Setting aside a tour de force that saw a detachment of troops from the corps of Marshal Mortier sack the towns of Cartaya, Villanueva de los Castillejos, and finally Aracena, the enemy presence was therefore confined to a single regiment of chasseurs commanded by the Duke of Aremberg that, having first raided as far as Ayamonte, established garrisons at Moguer and Niebla, this latter post later being taken over by a battalion of Swiss infantry drawn from the *josefino* Régiment Royal-Etranger. In consequence, on 14 April 1810 Francisco Copóns y Navía was able to land a small force of troops at Ayamonte, which had become the headquarters of the fugitive junta of Seville, and restore most the western part of the region to Patriot control behind the protection of a line of outposts stretching from Paymogo to Gibraleón. For the next nine months, Copóns concentrated on gathering in the swarms of *dispersos* who had fled to the area, in which respect he managed to increase his initial 850 men to a total of more than 3,700.[71] To put it mildly, it was an uphill struggle, however. As the chronicler of Copóns's operations wrote:

> All energy and patriotism were gone. The egoism of many landowners, . . . the fear and ignorance of the mass of the people, and the sagacity of the enemy, who had been both buying the hearts of the rich and . . . terrifying the spirits of the poor,

> ensured that many *pueblos* submitted to the yoke of *el rey intruso.* As for those places that remained free, they suffered from the same egotism, their justices acting in an arbitrary manner that recognized . . . no other law than that of their caprice. . . . From this it followed that in every *pueblo,* many stragglers and deserters were hidden without either the justices or, much less, their parents . . . making any attempt to get them to return to their regiments.[72]

As for Copóns himself, he was close to despair. No sooner had he arrived at Ayamonte than he was complaining: "The *pueblos* of the Condado de Niebla lack the patriotic ardor that once moved them. Although they sigh for their liberty and cry out for the enemy to be defeated, nobody is doing anything."[73]

We here return to the basic fact that participation in the Spanish war effort was above all a response to economic pressure. Safe behind Copóns's picket lines, the populace of Ayamonte and its hinterland were happy to sit out the fighting in relative peace, but only a few miles away the situation was very different. The terrain being far more open, there were fewer bands in the Condado de Niebla than elsewhere, but they nonetheless sprang up in considerable numbers, the reason for this being that, in brief, life became quite insupportable. For towns that were more-or-less permanently in the hands of the invaders, the situation was bad enough—on 12 July 1810, for example, the justices of Niebla reported that so heavy was the pressure induced by French requisitioning that the populace had been reduced to begging for alms—but in places that were caught in no-man's-land, the situation was downright catastrophic. For example, in May 1811 Cartaya was faced by a sudden order that it should henceforth every day send 350 rations of bread, 100 pounds of meat, forty *arrobas* of straw, four *fanegas* of barley, and 40 pounds of vegetables to Ayamonte, while in 1810 alone the town of Cañaveral de León supplied Ballesteros with 4,000 rations of bread, 200 rations of chickpeas, forty-three *fanegas* of wheat, fifty-one *fanegas* of barley, sixty-eight *arrobas* of fat, 214 quintals of fodder, nineteen oxen, twenty cows, 353 goats, considerable quantities of wine and brandy, and a cash payment of

6,000 *reales.* Yet the French too were absolutely merciless: to take just one example, by March 1812 Valverde del Camino had paid them 189,367 *reales.* Desperate measures to alleviate the situation notwithstanding—at Almonte the municipality ordered several tracts of common grazing land to be brought under the plough, appropriated a considerable sum of money belonging to one of the town's two religious houses, and offered a Seville merchant named José Bénito de Torres generous terms in exchange for securing a regular supply of foodstuffs from Huelva—such pressures were not be endured, and all the more so given that trade and agriculture were all but paralyzed. Faced by the near certainty of starvation, then, considerable parts of the population sought safety in flight: for example, El Cerro de Andévalo reported the loss of 164 householders to emigration in the course of the war, and Beas, which was burned by the French on three separate occasions, another 50.[74]

From flight, of course, it was but a short leap to participation in *la guerrilla*: how else were the refugees to feed themselves? Yet emigration was not just caused by economic desperation, another factor that played its part being fears of conscription. There was no intention to introduce this in Spain in the first instance, of course, but clumsy attempts to encourage the enlistment of *dispersos,* not to mention standing orders that they should register with the local authorities, spread panic among the populace: "Hearing that Marshal Victor was out to enlist them, the young men of Jérez and the other *pueblos* of the district abandoned their homes . . . and, rounding up as many horses as they could from farm and pasture, joined together and took up arms against their oppressors."[75] Needless to say, such fears were ruthlessly exploited by the Patriots, a good example being events in the Serranía de Ronda, where the rising against the French appears in part to have been the work of agents who spread rumors that occupation would be followed by the conscription of the entire male populace and put it about that the invaders had brought with them whole wagon-loads of manacles for this purpose.[76] Let us not delude ourselves, however: the fact that flight was inextricably linked with French occupation does not mean that it was a political action. Unlike the parish home guards set up by Serrano Valdenebro, more-genuine bands of necessity operated at a distance from their homes and were therefore by definition abandoning them to the fury of the invaders, the fact being that enlisting with some *cabecilla,* or even setting up as one, did not necessarily betoken a conscious decision to fight the French, but rather the adoption of a traditional survival strategy that could as easily be substituted by the idea of taking service with the invaders. Thus, in November 1810 the second in command of the Companía de Controbandistas de Ayamonte deserted to the French after having first helped himself to the entire contents of the unit's pay chest, while in September 1811 a Patriot spy reported that several bands of irregulars had gone over to the French at Córdoba.[77]

The opportunistic nature of popular participation in *la guerrilla* in Andalucía is by no means undermined by the sincerity of some of the latter's leaders. In brief, even if one accepts that men like Clemente Arribas and Juan Fernández Cañas were genuinely heroic in their opposition to the French, it does not necessarily follow that the same applies to their followers. Taking the case of the band of Vicente Moreno as an example, no fewer than thirty of the thirty-three men who were under Moreno's command when he was captured in August 1810 were stragglers from the army, and while it may be that each and every one of them wanted nothing more than to avenge themselves for the defeats they had suffered at Ocaña and in the Sierra Morena, it has to be observed that such a pattern of behavior was hardly the norm among the *dispersos* who they represented. Another member of the band, meanwhile, was Francisco Herrera, a young man from Vélez Málaga who had been in jail awaiting trial for murder when the French arrived in January 1810. Still incarcerated seven months later, on 13 July he was released when Moreno raided the town and, naturally enough, decided to join his liberators.[78] Once again, we cannot quite rule out the possibility that such men found in the war an opportunity to turn over a new leaf, but to imagine that they all did, and still more so that they did not feel themselves free to slip away and set up in the business of banditry on their own account, would be naive in the extreme. After all, was not personal freedom and, with it, the ability to recruit a band of followers of one's own the whole point of being a bandit (the only definition of the path that they had embarked upon that would have meant anything to men such as Herrera)?

Let us be generous, however, and say, first, that the myriad gangs of smugglers and bandits who were already operating in Andalucía at the moment of the French arrival were instantly converted in each and every case into heroic freedom fighters and, second, that the many bands that instantly sprang into being were all of them panting to hurl themselves upon the invaders—that the heroic myth, in other words, holds good. If banditry was not part of the picture at the beginning, it could not but soon become a part of it. To survive, the bands needed food, and in a situation in which a region that was for the most part desperately poor in the first place was being both forced to sustain a rapacious army of occupation and held to account for any assistance that it gave to the insurgency, it could not be long before even the most upright and committed chieftains were being forced to resort to forced requisitioning to keep their followers together. The extent to which this process went varied from band to band, and in general it is probably true to say that those leaders who consistently waged war upon the French were able to take enough food from the enemy to maintain discipline and spare the civilian population the worst effects of living off the country: hence, perhaps, the fact that the guerrilla band headed by Pedro Saldivar was after the war reported to enjoy "a very good reputation."[79] Yet a mere glance at the copious detail provided by Díaz Torrejón is sufficient to suggest that such cases were far from the norm—that French accusations that the bands were mere brigands are uncomfortably close to the truth. For example, though possessed of a reasonably active record, the band of Francisco Lozano ("Bolsero") was by the middle of 1811 sacking *pueblos* such as Iznájar, while a year later we read of the partida of Ramón Torralvo meting out exactly the same treatment to Montalbán.[80] Still worse, meanwhile, were other bands that, while killing the occasional Frenchman, embedded such activities in lives that became ever more sordid in their violence and criminality. For example, originally led by a day laborer from El Rubio named Miguel Hidalgo, the so-called *partida de las Guerras* (so named because of a family named Guerra that came to dominate it) slid into a career of robbery and murder, whose victims included not just several local notables who may or may not have been collaborators but also such figures as a young goatherder named Juan de los Angeles Machuca; not surprisingly, although its members all survived the years of French occupation, they one by one ended their days on the scaffold in the period after 1813.[81]

If this "Guerra gang" is an extreme example, there were many bands that inhabited a no-man's-land of ambiguity, among those so defined by Díaz Torrejón being those of Bartolomé Gómez ("Bartolo"), José Alonso ("Malacara"), Antonio Díaz, José Segovia, Juan Guerra, Juan de Díos Bellido, Antonio de Campos, Manuel Santaella, and Francisco de Roa (a figure who, for all his status as a notary and a mayor, research has shown to have in 1806 been put on trial for murder).[82] Like the Guerras, most of these barely known figures ended up in trouble with the Spanish authorities in the years after the French evacuation of Andalucía, but at least they at some point or other fought the French. That said, the latter cannot but be forgiven for describing all their irregular opponents as "brigands," while it cannot be denied that there were still other bands that literally were never more than bandits.[83] So grave was the problem of criminality, indeed, that at times Andalucía seemed in the grip not of a guerrilla struggle, but a mere orgy of pillage, the result being that on occasion the beleaguered Patriot authorities left with no choice but, in effect, to do the work of the invaders for them. Arriving in Algeciras in 1811, for example, General Ballesteros gave short shrift to the inhabitants of the Serranía de Ronda: "The . . . guerrilla bands that infested the region were one of the objects that called for my consideration. Not only had questions been raised as to the services that they had rendered, but the *pueblos* of the district were loudly complaining of their excesses. . . . I examined the truth of these representations in person. . . . Convinced that the bands existing in the district under my command were both militarily useless and prejudicial to the nation, I immediately ordered their disbandment."[84]

This reaction may have been overly harsh—as we have seen, some of the chieftains were just as much defenders of the fatherland as Ballesteros was—but the fact was that, even had their very existence not encouraged desertion among forces of regular troops such as the one the general commanded, the bands who ranged Andalucía had other things on their minds than simply expelling the French. In some areas, in fact, we can go still further. Nowhere is this more true than the Serranía de Ronda. Here, close examination reveals not a guerrilla insurrection, but a jacquerie. At first the disturbances that broke out in the area after it was occupied in February 1810 aroused much hope among Patriot authorities. "The uprising of the Serranía de Ronda is a glorious affair," wrote General Castaños. "Put on the right footing, it could be of major help to future operations."[85] However, sent to get the *serranos* together in order to use them to assist the operations of a division that was to be disembarked from the sea under Luis Lacy, Ambrosio de la Cuadra found that "the right footing" was not something that was to be attained with any ease. In the first place, an interview with the supposed leader of the rebels proved a depressing experience: "[Serrano] Valdenebro arrived today. He is very gloomy about the state of affairs in the sierra and foresees all sorts of difficulties about assembling the peasants. In a word . . . the *serranos* do not want to leave their villages and are not doing anything of any use."[86] As La Cuadra observed, then: "We cannot count on any aid from the Sierra, whether in terms of men, mules or anything else."[87] The inhabitants would defend their villages from French foraging parties and punitive expeditions and fall upon such targets as couriers and unprotected parties of civilians, but they would not take part in formal military operations. Nor was La Cuadra the only Allied officer to discover this. When Lord Blayney landed at Fuengirola in 1810, for example, hopes that his handful of troops would be supported by the inhabitants of the neighboring Serranía de Ronda proved unfounded, and that despite the fact that the whole area had seemingly taken arms against the French. Thus: "Previous to marching I had some conversation with Captain Miller of the Ninety-Fifth Regiment, who, with several other officers, had been latterly employed in organising the Spanish peasants. He informed me that a considerable quantity of arms and ammunition had been distributed amongst them, and consequently that I might expect a number to join me immediately. In this, however, I was entirely disappointed, not more than ten or twelve making their appearance."[88]

But this was not the end of the problem. To return to La Cuadra, he did not just voice reservations as to the military value of the insurrection but also expressed grave doubts in respect of the direction that it was taking. "The state of anarchy that prevails among the inhabitants ought to alarm us rather than give us hope."[89] As to what he meant, this is best approached through the experiences of Ronda. As we have seen, early in March 1810 Serrano Valdenebro managed to mass a large force of peasants against the garrison. Seeing the latter's campfires dotting the hills overlooking the town, the governor, Colonel Vinot, concluded that he was hopelessly outnumbered and pulled out without a fight. What happened next is recorded by Albert de Rocca: "The very day . . . we left Ronda, the mountaineeers entered it, . . . shouting with joy and discharging their pieces exultingly in the streets. The inhabitants of each village arrived together marching without order, and . . . loaded their asses with whatever they found . . . till the poor beasts were ready to sink under the weight of the booty. . . . The prisons were forced, and the . . . criminals they contained ran instantly to take revenge on their judges and accusers. Debtors obtained receipts from their creditors by forcible means, and all the public papers were burned in order to annul the mortgages that the inhabitants of the town had upon the mountaineers."[90] For a Spanish view, meanwhile, we have the account given by a prominent nineteenth-century antiquarian named Juan José Moreti, who was the son of an Italian printer who had come to Spain to serve the regime of Joseph Bonaparte and stayed behind in Ronda after the retreat of the French forces:

> Predisposed . . . against Ronda for no other reason than that it was the seat of the local law courts, the *serranos* entered the town and, to the astonishment of all, inflicted much damage upon it, thereby sullying the sacred cause that had brought them together. As many of them had legal cases outstanding against them in the city's notorial offices, . . . they broke open their archives and seized all sorts of documents, which they then piled up in a heap and put to the torch. . . . As the town

> hall was located in the same square, and their object to burn everything that was written down on paper that they could lay their hands on, the municipal archive suffered the same fate.[91]

Man of order and authority as he was, Serrano Valdenebro was deeply shocked. As he later wrote: "The atrocious conduct of the peasantry . . . reduced me to tears. Much impressed with the problems of making headway at the head of such unruly followers, I took my leave, and returned to my family to await whatever the future might bring."[92] To make matters worse, meanwhile, the *serranos* could not even hold the town: on 21 March General Perreimond arrived from Málaga at the head of a substantial column of French troops and engaged in ferocious reprisals. This brings us, of course, to a further problem with the insurrection in that, militarily speaking, it could never hope to prevail. A scholarly individual who had written widely on the art of war, Serrano Valdenebro was well aware of this problem. Already deeply perturbed by the wayward nature of his followers, he was not much reassured by their fighting abilities: "Although war is being waged in these mountains in the style of Viriato, flattering results cannot be expected. . . . The peasants are little more than unmanageable. There is little union or regularity . . . in their movements. This is not to be surprised at: among troops who have not been fashioned by the strictest discipline, these qualities cannot be achieved. . . . Valiant in skirmishing, they do not understand that shock action is the chief weapon on the battlefield. . . . So long as troops do not realize that battles are won by the sword and bayonet, all is lost. Fire is only a chimera. . . . Advancing on the enemy with union and bravery . . . is what brings victory."[93] Such combatants, Serrano Valdenebro reasoned, might well be able to cause the French great difficulties: "A band of patriots situated in mountains that are almost inaccessible will hold off the bravest soldiers."[94] Warfare, though, was not just a matter of harassing French columns as they tramped through rugged mountain passes or defending hilltop villages. If victory was ever to be attained, the war would sooner or later have to be carried to the enemy, and this entailed fighting battles that the insurgents could not hope to win: "Should the latter fall back to more accessible terrain, the picture changes. . . .

The peasant wages a petty war. . . . How can this man fight in a terrain where infantry can press upon him or cavalry ride him down?"[95]

It will be argued, of course, that guerilla bands of the sort that fought the French in the south of Spain had no business fighting the invaders in terrain where they could suffer such a fate. Yet this begs a series of questions in respect of what guerrilla warfare as classically imagined could contribute to the Patriot cause. All too clearly, the bands could not drive the French from Andalucía: as the miserable fate of the peasant horde that followed Bielsa to destruction at Torreperogil showed, that was a task that could only be undertaken, if then, by the various forces of regular troops that clung on throughout the years of French occupation around the periphery of the region, including most notably at Cádiz. Given the fact that Spain never had to rely on the bands for its liberation, this qualification, it will be argued, does not signify: stiffened by a degree of Anglo-Portuguese support, the Allied armies always remained capable of taking the field, while even had this not been the case, from the middle of 1811, the forces of the Duke of Wellington were a constant presence on the frontiers of Extremadura and León and, what is more, a constant presence that increasingly had the capacity to wreak havoc on the arrangements of the French in southern Spain from afar. In this context, all that the bands had to do was to avoid destruction and prevent the forces of Marshal Soult from either crushing one or more of their more regular adversaries or sending overwhelming numbers of reinforcements to take part in the distant struggle with Wellington. In this they evidently succeeded brilliantly, and so accept though we might the evidence that many of the guerrillas were little more than bandits—indeed, that in many instances they quite literally were bandits—and further, that they inflicted little damage in terms of actual casualties, it is therefore self-evident that the contribution that they made to the Spanish war effort was wholly positive, and not just that but possibly absolutely vital.

In a military sense, no one can object to this judgment. It is certainly possible to issue caveats with respect, for example, to the manner in which the existence of the bands encouraged desertion, while it would certainly not be going too far to say that the disorder that they engendered in the Andalusian countryside was a major reason for the inability of the Spaniards to mobilize the resources of the region for the campaigns of 1813 (see below). Without the bands, however, the outcome of the war might have been different, while it is clear that such was the level of collaboration among the local elites that the rule of King Joseph would probably have become a reality. That said, however, it is not possible wholly to sustain the conventional view of the Andalusian guerrillas. In the first place, the fact that they were not a patriotic phenomenon is self-evident: insofar as can be judged, the majority of the rank and file were motivated not by love of king and country, or still less, religion, but rather by a desperate search for the wherewithal of survival; indeed, so severe did the situation become by 1812 that it was in some areas quite literally a case of turn bandit or die. As for fighting the French, meanwhile, it was at best a necessary concomitant of this strategy and certainly not the main aim of its adoption: on the contrary, the *dispersos* who were the mainstay of the first bands and remained prominent in the ranks of *la guerrilla* in many instances wanted nothing more than to put soldiering behind them for good. In the second place, while the consequences of French occupation might have been such as to force many men in effect to take up arms, the idea of the formation of guerrilla bands per se was very much an elite affair in terms of both conception and personnel, though even then questions hang over the motivation of some of those involved: was Vicente Moreno, for example, a selfless hero who deserves the unique accolade paid to him by the *cortes* of Cádiz, or was he rather an adventurer who sought to achieve fame and advancement by freeing himself from the bonds of life in the regular army?[96] And in the third place, one cannot but note the fact that the depredations of the bands in some respects actually may have strengthened the cause of collaboration, by on the one hand, reaffirming men of property in their fear of the populace and, on the other, exposing the *pueblos* to constant reprisals against which they could do nothing to protect themselves and in effect drove them to become de facto counterguerrillas: the chieftain Antonio Díaz, we are told, met his end in January 1812, when villagers from a number of the places he had preyed upon joined together to form a posse and launched a surprise attack on his band.[97]

In short, one is left with a decidedly mixed impression. Although the bands certainly played an important role in the war in Andalucía, their effect was by no means wholly positive in that, setting aside a minority of more-or-less honorable exceptions, many of them were essentially bandits rather than freedom fighters and as such essentially only took on the French in the context of an agenda that was very different from that of some supposed crusade for God, king, and fatherland, at the same time actually undermining the Spanish war effort. Thus, how many *dispersos* might not ultimately have rejoined their regiments had it not been for the presence of the irregulars? Equally, how many deserters might have stayed with their units had the bands not given them somewhere to run? Nor, meanwhile, were the partisans the only Spanish forces in the field. On the contrary in fact, throughout the French occupation, Spain's soldiers continued to maintain a presence in the hinterland of Andalucía and thereby to keep the cause of conventional war alive and with it, incidentally, many irregulars who would otherwise almost certainly have ended their lives on the scaffold. That being the case, it is to the largely unknown story of Patriot Spain's forgotten armies that we must now turn.

8

Fights and Forced Marches

If the story of the French occupation of Andalucía is a study in failure, as it is, it is for one reason and one reason alone. Once the *josefino* yoke had started to bite and the fabric of society began to disintegrate in the face of economic collapse, popular resistance quickly became a considerable nuisance, albeit a nuisance that was rooted in long traditions of banditry rather than patriotic outrage at French occupation, let alone the kidnap and overthrow of Ferdinand VII. For the next two years, that same resistance prevented the invaders from realizing their objectives in Andalucía, and whatever the caveats that can be made about it, it would therefore be foolish to deny its historical importance. Yet, whether freedom fighters or brigands, the armed civilians that ranged the countryside in such numbers were never entirely dependent on their own resources. Thus, the French were also faced by large numbers of Spanish regulars. These troops themselves, of course, played a part in the guerrilla war by engaging in daring mobile operations deep in the hinterland of Andalucía, while their forays ensured that at no point could the French concentrate on the counterinsurgent operations on which the consolidation of their rule depended. More than this, indeed, comparing developments in Spain with those that took place elsewhere, including most notably the Tyrol and Calabria, suggests that the Spanish regulars saved the insurrection from destruction: had they been acting in isolation, even the most determined and heroic armed civilians would have been quite incapable of resisting the French war machine on their own for more than a limited period. The story of the unsung heroes of the Spanish army having thus far gone largely untold, it is therefore but justice that, along with some of the other factors that prevented the French from consolidating the successes of January 1810, they should now receive some recognition.[1]

At the forefront of our consideration here must be the Allied retention of the fortress city of Cádiz. As city after city surrendered to the triumphant French armies and the tatterdemalion Spanish Army of La Mancha scattered to the four winds, King Joseph had, as we have seen, simply assumed that its defenders—at this point mainly the same urban militia whose determination to avoid serving in the field had caused the riots of February 1809—would capitulate in their turn. In consequence, rather than having the corps of Marshal Victor head directly for the sea, he had turned aside in favor of a triumphal entry into Seville. This was, perhaps, the greatest single error of the Peninsular War. Entirely unbeknown to the French, the Duque de Alburquerque was at that very moment leading his Army of Extremadura, by now the only Spanish army left in the field in the south of Spain, in an epic march to save the city that, since the fall of Seville, had become the de facto capital of the Patriot cause. On 3 February he and his men reached the coast and filed across the causeway that formed the only landward access to the island on which Cádiz was built, the result being that when the French finally arrived the next day, they found the defenses bristling with troops.

And what defenses: in practice the city was impregnable. Situated at the end of a sand spit nearly five miles long jutting out from a triangular piece of land known as the Isla de León, which is separated from the mainland by a wide strip of creeks and salt marshes—the Río Sancti Petri—and could only be reached in 1810 by means of a narrow causeway-cum-bridge known as the Puente de Suazo, Cádiz was barely in range of the only possible site for a siege battery. Even this last—a peninsula that half closed the mouth of the great harbor protected by the Isla de León—was soon held by troops ensconced at its seaward end in the fort of Matagorda. Batteries and redoubts commanded the entire length of the Sancti Petri, the Puente de Suazo had been blown up after Alburquerque's men had marched across it, the isthmus was studded with defenses, and Cádiz was itself protected by massive eighteenth-century walls. Visiting the city in November 1809, William Jacob was much impressed:

> The fortifications of this city on the land side are well constructed: there is only one entrance and that is very narrow, so that, if the water be smooth, gunboats may flank an approaching army on both sides. The walls near the gate are so constructed that, though, from the extent of the glacis, they do not appear lofty, yet no part of the city is visible from without the land gate. The fortifications are all bomb-proofed and casemated and the glacis is mined throughout, which, added to the narrowness of the front, makes it capable of a very vigorous defence. In order, however, to prevent the possibility of an attack on the city itself, a new battery is constructing across the isthmus, which, when finished, will render the approach extremely difficult. The spot on which it is erecting is at such a distance from the city that, until it be taken, an enemy cannot construct mortar batteries near enough to throw shells into the town. . . . The expense of this battery has been enormous: the soil being sandy, they have been obliged to construct a foundation of solid masonry seventy-five feet under the surface. The part above the ground is formed of sandbags which are walled up to the top of the parapet. A ditch is to be formed in front, and if proper defences be placed to prevent cavalry turning the flanks when the tide is low, this *cortadura,* as it is called, will add considerably to the security of this important place. . . . The end of the Isla de León towards the continent is remarkably strong, both by nature and art, and may be considered as one of the principal defences of Cádiz. The navigable River Sancti Petri intersects the land, and is crossed by a bridge flanked with batteries. . . . The road beyond the bridge is made through marshes, which except by this causeway are impassable, and it is intersected by two deep rivers.[2]

Nor was all this an end to it: with the harbor full of British and Spanish warships, any attempt to push along the isthmus toward the city was liable to be hit from both flanks by deadly broadsides.[3]

Faced by such defenses, even the normally bullheaded Victor realized that a head-on attack was out of the question, but having taken the decision not to attempt a storm, the French were faced by a difficult problem.[4] Thus, had Cádiz been a tiny place manned by a few hundred men only, it might have been possible to screen it with a token force of troops and leave it to its own devices. Yet Cádiz was not such a place. On the contrary, not counting the Voluntarios Distinguidos, who could only be counted on, at best, to man the innermost defenses of the city, it was already held by an army of some 12,000 men, while the broad expanses of the Isla de León and the Allies' control of the sea meant that an almost infinite number of reinforcements could be brought in from elsewhere. Very soon, indeed, while the defenses of the city were strengthened still further by the improvisation of a flotilla of gunboats from the launches of the fleet, men began to pour into Cádiz and its environs. From Ayamonte, for example, came 3,000 soldiers who had fled Seville and been evacuated by sea, while the defenders were further reinforced by a strong Anglo-Portuguese brigade commanded by General William Stewart (shaken by their experiences, the Spaniards had abandoned their earlier scruples in respect of admitting foreign troops to Cádiz, the Anglo-Portuguese contingent eventually being augmented to the size of a full division under the command of General Thomas Graham). Although the local authorities refused pointblank to sanction recruitment to the regular army—all men between the ages of sixteen and fifty-five were mobilized certainly, but depending on their resources, they were rather sent to join either the privileged Voluntarios Distinguidos or the prewar urban militia—men therefore existed in plenty, and Marshal Victor was therefore left facing the very real possibility that, unless a substantial force was stationed to contain Cádiz, the defenders might sally forth and win a major victory that could force the evacuation of the whole of Andalucía.

There followed, then, a curious reversal of the position hitherto. The French certainly did not abandon their plans for an attack on Cádiz: on the contrary, the cannon foundry at Seville was set to constructing a number of specially designed giant mortars that could lob bombs across the bay into the city, large numbers of small boats were collected to form the basis of an amphibious assault, the infantry of Victor's corps was furnished with improvised flotation devices made from envelopes of leather, messages were dispatched to Napoleon begging for the dispatch of a fleet, and active operations were begun against the isolated Allied bridgehead at Matagorda. Yet with the best will in the world, it was quite clear that the French could not hope to launch a major attack on Cádiz for many months: aside from anything else, though the stores captured in Seville provided them with much of the material needed for a siege, there were still shortages of certain key items, of which some could only be made up by the dispatch of special convoys from France. With money short, meanwhile, even readily available local resources proved hard to obtain: if the invaders eventually put together a fleet of 193 pinnaces for the invasion of the Isla de León, for long periods work on the project had to be abandoned for want of money.[5] As Soult himself admitted in the wake of an abortive attempt on his part to open negotiations with Alburquerque: "Everything suggests that this will be a long contest and that the result will be decided by force."[6] If there was to be no quick victory, however, I Corps was going to have to maintain its current position on the shores of the bay of Cádiz ad infinitum, for only thus could the Allied threat be successfully contained. Not only that, meanwhile, but the larger numbers that could potentially be massed by the Allies at any one point along the coastline meant that the French had to start throwing up fortifications themselves. From Rota to Puerto Real, then, lines of entrenchments and batteries crept across the landscape. In theory, of course, these could be described as siege works, while the French also claimed that they were designed to seal off the coast to smuggling, but the truth was plain for all to see: the invaders had at last lost the initiative, while it began to look as if those who were actually under siege were not the defenders of Cádiz, but rather the troops of Marshal Victor.[7]

The forced immobilization of I Corps on the shores of the bay of Cádiz was soon followed by a blow to the cause of the invaders of Andalucía that was almost as serious. To the north of Seville, of course, there stretched the province of Extremadura. Well aware of the potential threat that the area posed to his conquests, immediately after the fall of Seville, Soult had ordered Marshal Mortier to march on Badajoz with part of his corps in the apparent hope that Alburquerque's departure would have left that fortress uncovered and demoralized. In the event, however, the gamble failed, for realizing that it had to be safeguarded at all costs, the new commander of Spanish forces in León, the Marqués de la Romana, led several divisions to save the city, leaving the outnumbered Mortier with no option but to withdraw. For the time being, the situation was not too bad in that La Romana was neutralized by a French force that had appeared from an entirely different direction. Thus, initially stationed in the Tagus valley, the corps temporarily commanded by General Etienne Heudelet de Bierre had been ordered to march to assist Mortier. Finding that the latter had already departed by the time he reached the Guadiana, the general therefore contented himself with merely occupying the area around Mérida. Though Heudelet was scarcely the most aggressive of commanders, his presence alone was sufficient to keep La Romana in check, but in the early summer, there came a sudden hammer blow. Crucial though their presence in Extremadura was, Heudelet's men were marched north to join in the operations that preceded Masséna's invasion of Portugal. Frantic at what he saw as an act of betrayal that threatened disaster, Soult protested bitterly and even tried to persuade Napoleon that Masséna should march not on Lisbon, but rather on Badajoz, but it was to no avail: henceforth Extremadura was to be the concern of Soult and Soult alone.[8]

To understand the significance of this situation, we need to turn to the narrative of the campaigns that took place in the Army of the South's area of operations in the period 1810–12. Essentially these pitted the forces of occupation against a variety of small field armies and independent divisions of Spanish troops that operated against the French from every direction of the compass. First in the field in this respect was General Francisco Ballesteros. In 1808 a thirty-eight-year-old officer of the customs guard in Asturias, Ballesteros had already fought the French in the campaign of 1793–95, and in the aftermath of the Spanish uprising, he was appointed by the provincial junta established in Oviedo to the rank of, first, brigadier and, then, major general, taking command of a division in the Army of Asturias.[9] Assigned to home defense, he and his men saw no action until May 1809, when the French marched on Asturias. Débâcle for the Spaniards though this was, Ballesteros had nonetheless emerged from the affair with some credit. Bypassed by the invaders, he led his

10,000 men in a desperate march to save Oviedo, but seeing that he could not arrive in time, he resolved to launch a surprise attack on Santander, which had been left almost undefended by the French. This duly succeeded, but the invaders almost immediately returned in force, Ballesteros being left with no option but to take to the sea in a small fishing boat while those of his men who managed to get away—some 3,000 were captured—fled into the hills.[10] Unfortunate though this affair had been, Ballesteros nevertheless returned to Oviedo as a hero and was soon again at the head of a division. There followed more adventures: in September 1809 Ballesteros was summoned to join the main Spanish field army in northwestern Spain, a move that involved a 150-mile journey through the wastes of León across territory that was wide open to enemy attack. Moving via Miranda de Duero and Ledesma, the Spanish commander reached his destination safely, only immediately to be plunged into the disastrous campaign of Alba de Tormes. In this he could have, like most of the rest of the forces he had just joined, received a serious mauling, but by sheer good fortune his division escaped the battlefield without suffering serious harm. There followed a miserable winter spent in the desolate Sierra de Gata—of the 26,000 men who had escaped from Alba de Tormes, by January 1810 some 9,000 had died of illness or starvation—but the privations that the soldiers endured were such that at least those who survived were transformed into hardened veterans, and all the more so as, unusually, many of them had been under arms for six months or even a year. In the words of the Conde de Toreno: "The bulk of this division came from the one that its commander had brought down from Asturias in 1809, while it still had all of its original officers apart from those few who had perished or been called away on other duties."[11]

This is, perhaps, the key to what happened next. Ballesteros's men—the Navarra, La Princesa, Oviedo, Covadonga, Villaviciosa, Candas y Luanco, Castropol, Pravía, Cangas de Tineo, Grado, Infiesto, and Lena regiments—were no mere levies but seasoned soldiers (a few of them may even have served in the prewar Spanish army). At the same time, undefeated in battle, they also had a commander who, if ambitious and vainglorious, was also a genuinely inspirational leader who was hungry to make his name. It was a potent combination. Indeed, when La Romana looked for a force with which to harass the French in the wake of Mortier's retreat from Badajoz, he could not have picked a better formation. At all events Ballesteros threw himself into the mission with considerable gusto. Marching by the remote route that led into western Andalucía from Extremadura via Fregenal and Aracena, on the night of 19 March he launched a surprise attack on the cavalry brigade of General Beauregarde at Valverde and put it to flight, with the loss of its commander. Six days later he was at Ronquillo, just twenty miles north of Seville, but much to the delight of the *Gazeta de Sevilla,* here he was less successful in that a French infantry brigade managed to drive him off, this being an event that was exploited for all it was worth:

> The armies that some dreamers believed they could see from the tower of the cathedral, the same armies that certain vile creatures persuaded the gullible to have defeated the French and were on the point of entering Seville, have had the good sense to retire on Badajoz at the double. A division of the valorous troops of the V Corps has pursued them as far as . . . Monasterio, where their commanders have learned from various inhabitants of good sense that Ballesteros, the presumptuous general who led the Spaniards, had promised his men that they could sack Seville. . . . And who has saved you from this treat? Ask yourselves this: has it not been the French? You can be sure that without their help . . . this beautiful capital would have been converted into a chamber of horrors. . . . Open the eyes of understanding and accept that these much vaunted armies are but gangs of wretches who scarcely have any refuge left in the whole of Spain, and whose only means of subsistence are the pillage of her towns and villages and the robbery and murder of the individuals they encounter on her highways.[12]

At this point, perhaps, Ballesteros should have cut his losses and fallen back on Extremadura, but instead he lingered on the River Tinto. This was a rash decision: Marshal Mortier had sallied forth against him at the head of the division of General Girard, and after an initial skirmish at Aracena that cost the French 120 men, on 15

April this force attacked him at Zalamea after a fierce fight that saw the Spaniards attempt to stave off the French from the shelter of a ridge studded with rocky outcrops. Yet defeated though Ballesteros may have been, his division was not destroyed: at most only some 900 Spaniards had fallen. Moreover, instead of pressing on in pursuit, Mortier turned aside to launch a sweep of the plains between Huelva and the sea and was then forced to return to Seville for fear that otherwise the insurgents would get out of hand. In consequence, Ballesteros was left free to rebuild his forces in the shelter of the Sierra de Aracena, and very soon he was ready for further mischief.[13]

His chance came soon enough. Until the month of July, the bulk of La Romana's forces had been pinned down in the vicinity of Badajoz by the continued presence in the area of Mérida of the French II Corps under, first, Heudelet, and then his replacement, Jean Reynier. Indeed, on 6 July the latter commander succeeded in inflicting a considerable reverse on one of La Romana's outlying divisions at Jérez de los Caballeros.[14] Later that same month, however, as we have seen, Reynier marched north to join Masséna's invasion of Portugal. La Romana, then, was once again free to engage in offensive action. Calling in Ballesteros from the Sierra de Aracena, he concentrated 11,000 men and advanced southeastward with evident intention of threatening Seville from the direction of the mountainous district around Guadalcanal. Keeping to the shelter of the mountains as it did, this in itself was by no means a bad move, but La Romana had not counted on the vigor of Marshal Soult. Initially, the way to Seville had been barred by the single division of General Gazan, and that had been much weakened by the fact that a part of its strength had been detached to the Condado de Niebla far to the southwest. However, just at the opportune moment, Gazan was joined by the division of General Girard, which had in April been marched south to help pacify the Sierra de Ronda and had now been hastily recalled. The result was a second reverse for La Romana. Hastening north, Gazan and Girard attacked him at Villagarcía near Llerena, and in a fierce action drove him back with severe casualties, the leading role in the affair being played by Gazan's division: "Throwing itself upon the enemy without hesitation, notwithstanding the latter's resistance, it routed them completely, and killed or took prisoner more than 3,000 men, before pursuing them as far as Zafra, where it captured considerable quantities of supplies."[15]

At this point La Romana might have been in serious trouble, for Marshal Mortier had now come up with orders to pursue the beaten Spaniards with the forces of Gazan and Girard. Yet even at this early stage, the French simply did not have enough men to capitalize on their advantages. To concentrate so many troops against the Spanish forces in Extremadura, Soult had had to make use of virtually all the mobile reserves that he had to hand—in effect, the division of General Girard—and therefore found himself powerless to guard against any other threat (at the same time, of course, transferring Girard from the vicinity of Ronda to the frontiers of Extremadura had taken the pressure off the *serranos,* whose various bands were able to resume their previous activities). Yet the unfortunate marshal soon found himself facing just such a menace. Thus, such was the position of the French in Andalucía that Spanish forces could very easily appear at any moment from virtually any direction. To compound the problem, having recovered from the first shock of defeat, the Regency that had replaced the overthrown Junta Central as the head of the Spanish state had adopted the most aggressive posture that it could. All the forces left in Andalucía and Murcia were placed under the command of Joaquín Blake, a general of Irish ancestry who had played no part in the defeats of January 1810, and designated the Army of the Center, while with Cádiz safe, some of the surplus troops in the city were made use of to launch spoiling attacks along the coast.[16] Badly stretched as they were, the French could hardly keep an effective watch on five hundred miles of beach, while there were a number of coastal towns that had thus far remained outside their control altogether, the two most important being Ayamonte and Tarifa. Possessed of both abundant shipping and total control of the sea, the Regency was therefore quick to make use of its opportunities. As early as 14 April 1810, then, General Copóns landed at Ayamonte at the head of a force of 700 men and quickly reimposed Patriot control in the western half of what is today the province of Huelva, though feeling that he was too weak to challenge even the very limited forces the French possessed in the region—a few hundred men at Niebla and Palos de Moguer—he eschewed military action in favor of gathering in some of the swarms of stragglers who infested the region, in which respect he managed to add some 3,000 men to his forces.[17]

Rather more important were the events that took place on the coast of present-day Málaga. Eager to further the cause of insurrection in the Serranía de Ronda and the Alpujarras, the Regency had, as we have seen, already sent a number of officers to stir up revolt in the area. Now, however, it went still further: on 19 June a division of 3,000 men was disembarked at Algeciras under another general of Irish descent named Luis Lacy. In the event, Lacy did not achieve very much in the Serranía: advancing in the direction of Ronda, he quickly became disgusted with the disorderly behavior of the *serranos* and almost immediately fell back on his port of arrival, though not without having dispatched a garrison to the town of Marbella. From Algeciras, however, he was ferried to Huelva, where he disembarked on 23 August. Given the weakness of the French forces in the area, this was a major threat: indeed, recognizing the inability of his forces to make head against Lacy, the commander of the garrison had promptly pulled out all his men and fallen back in the direction of Seville. Greatly alarmed, Soult knew he had no option but to expel Lacy, but the price of doing so was giving up his operations against La Romana, the only troops that he had to hand to deal with the threat being those of Marshal Mortier. Far from being allowed to pursue the troops defeated at Villagarcía, the latter was therefore ordered to adopt a defensive posture and dispatch the division of General Gazan to search out Lacy and defeat him. All the advantages that had been gained on the frontiers of Extremadura were therefore lost, while Soult in the event did not even secure any compensation in the Condado de Niebla: for reasons that have never been entirely clear, after just six days Lacy had re-embarked his troops and returned to Cádiz, leaving Gazan's men with little to do other than round up a few irregulars.[18]

Just as La Romana had disrupted operations against the *serranos*, then, so Lacy had now disrupted operations against La Romana. Freed from the threat of attack, indeed, the marquis promptly returned to the fray. Retracing his steps, in early September he once again appeared on the northern frontiers of Extremadura, having first secured some reinforcements in the form of a brigade of Portuguese cavalry that had been lent him by Wellington. Fortunately for Soult, Gazan had just arrived back from his fruitless expedition to the Condado de Niebla so that the whole of the corps of Marshal Mortier was available to take the offensive. For a second time in as many months, then, La Romana found himself facing far more troops than he could possibly hope to vanquish, and he therefore fled northward as fast as his men could march, with Mortier in hot pursuit. Indeed, much alarmed by a cavalry action at Fuente Cantos on 15 September that emphasized just how vulnerable his troops were to the French, he did not content himself with retiring on Badajoz but fled still farther northward to Montijo. As Oman observes, the whole of Extremadura was now at Soult's feet, but unlike in 1811 there was no pressing reason to besiege Badajoz, while Mortier in any case was desperately needed back in Andalucía. Very soon, then, the French forces were falling back once more, a whole summer of marching and countermarching having therefore achieved precisely nothing.[19]

The long and complex story of the Spanish army's operations in Andalucía in 1810 does not end with the retreat of La Romana. Far to the east, General Sébastiani had, for the last few months, been fighting his own war on the frontiers of Murcia. As will be recalled, in January 1810 a considerable fragment of Areizaga's army had escaped in this direction. Preoccupied with the *partidas,* however, the French commander had been able to do little about this threat other than launching two brief raids against the city of Murcia, neither of which had produced very much in the way of results. As a result the Spanish forces in the region—by now denominated, as we have seen, as the Third Army—were gradually able to rebuild their strength. In August Blake had traveled to the area from Cádiz to take over command from Manuel Freyre, and having amassed some 10,000 men, at the beginning of November he led his troops forward to challenge Sébastiani. This, however, proved to be a grievous error. In the short term the French could scrape together no more than 1,300 cavalry and 2,000 infantry, but the local commander, General Édouard Milhaud, was an officer of a singularly resolute stamp and therefore decided to risk attacking the Spaniards straightaway rather than waiting for reinforcements. There followed what has gone down in the history of the war as the rout of Baza. On the morning of 4 November, Blake was advancing to occupy that town, with his forces spread out over a considerable length of high road, when Milhaud suddenly burst upon him at the head of his cavalry. Taken completely by surprise, the leading Spaniards turned and ran, and they in turn swept away the men behind them. Realizing that to do so would be to risk disaster, Milhaud did not press the pursuit too far, with the result that, excluding deserters, Blake's casualties in terms of killed, wounded, and missing amounted to no more than 1,500 men. All the same, even ignoring the Spanish commander's carelessness, it had been a depressing affair: in brief, it was all too obvious that at this stage the French could not be challenged in open battle.[20]

In Andalucía and on the frontiers of Extremadura, then, Spain's soldiers continued to lose battle after battle. Yet their campaigns were not without their effect. In the words of the Conde de Toreno: "Amid reverses and *contretemps,* Spanish tenacity and, in particular, the innumerable series of combats that took place on every side exhausted the French. . . . Well-directed battles, it is true, did not make much of a dent in their ranks, but they were still worn down . . . by the constant marches and countermarches."[21] In his headquarters in Seville, meanwhile, Soult was becoming more and more alarmed. As he later admitted:

> The emperor had imposed on my army a task that it could not fulfill. The corps of which it was composed were simply too weak. . . . On 15 September 1810, IV Corps, which was estimated as having a strength of 19,190 men, in reality counted no more than 12,579, while the V Corps had less than 10,000 men in the ranks out of a full strength of about the same number. As for I Corps, its infantry battalions had no more than 360 men under arms. Since their invasion of Andalucía, none of the three had received any of the reinforcements that had been sent across the border from France, the detachments that they were supposed to have got having been detained along the way, whether it was by the king or the generals through whose districts they traveled. The clearest orders—indeed, the liveliest

> supplications, did not succeed in securing their presence, and so, being unable to make good its needs, the Army of the South, enfeebled by illness and constant fighting alike, melted away at a rate that was positively frightening. . . . And yet, although it was smaller in force than [the emperor] believed, it was this same army that was expected to assure the submission of the whole region stretching from the frontier of Portugal to the kingdom of Valencia. As to what this task entailed, it included the following: prosecuting the siege of Cádiz; masking Gibraltar in the center, Badajoz in the west, and Cartagena in the east; . . . keeping watch on the coast from the Algarve to Alicante; and putting down the insurrections that continued to flare up in the mountains.[22]

Justified though Soult was in his complaints about the manner in which drafts intended for his forces were being detained en route in northern and central Spain, it was not just a shortage of men that plagued him, however. Also very difficult were his relationships with his subordinate commanders. In part, as Soult admitted, this was the inescapable result of the situation in which the Army of the South was placed:

> The constant labor, frequent combats, and near-daily forced marches represented a service that was very hard indeed and left our troops very tired. The three army corps were spread out all over the place, and their commanders made the most bitter protests against this state of affairs. Mortier complained that V Corps had been broken up, that its component divisions were spending all their time marching from one end of Andalucía to another, and that he had been left without any command to exercise. Victor reported that I Corps was much weakened due to the constant detachment of troops to the mountains of Ronda or the right bank of the Guadalquivir; that he no longer had sufficient troops to guard the immense extent of the siege lines; and that, once they were aware of his weakness, the enemy would be able to break out whenever they chose. As for General Sébastiani, forced to split his troops between Murcia, where there was a Spanish army, the mountains of Jaén, which

> were infested with brigands, . . . and the coast of Málaga, he could no longer dispose even of the division he had hitherto kept in reserve. Meanwhile, all three of them were reporting their effectives were diminishing very fast and that their daily losses were not being replaced. These complaints were only too well founded, but it was not in my power to satisfy them in any way. There was no dramatic maneuver that could be undertaken anywhere. We were condemned to forever keeping watch on a vast circumference while at the same time on all sides conducting an endless *guerre de détail*. . . . I could only keep my troops going by means of a series of ever-changing expedients, whether military or administrative, that merely damaged everyone's long-term interests.[23]

True though this was, there were other issues too. As haughty and imperious as he was cold and distant, Soult did little to win the trust and confidence of those around him, but it has also to be said that his subordinate commanders were scarcely the most malleable of individuals. Sébastiani, at least, Soult clearly outranked, but both Victor and Mortier were as much marshals of the empire as he was, and indeed, as much dukes as he was too (to be precise, Victor was Duke of Belluno and Mortier Duke of Treviso). Initially, of course, Soult could count on his position as Joseph's chief of staff, but hardly had the campaign of Andalucía begun when news arrived that Napoleon had stripped him of the job and given it to Berthier instead. For some weeks, then, Soult was left in limbo, with no position of authority whatsoever other than his de facto status as King Joseph's chief military adviser.[24] With even that role taken away from him by the departure of *el rey intruso* for Madrid, Soult was saved by the creation of the Army of the South, but there remained the facts, first, that the civil administration was officially subject to his authority only in those matters that directly pertained to the needs of the army (a phrase that was, of course, constantly open to debate) and, second, that Victor and Mortier were bitterly jealous of his appointment. That the situation was an extremely unhappy one was clear enough from the experiences of the aide-de-camp Lejeune. Sent to Spain in February 1811 to report on the situation and chivvy on the French commanders,

Lejeune encountered an atmosphere that was positively poisonous. On the one hand, interviewed in late March following his return from Badajoz (see below), Soult could hardly contain himself:

> Marshal Soult was especially bitter at having to command men of equal rank with himself, and said he was often very much worried by being obliged to show so much consideration for them. "Of course," he said, "I feel greatly flattered at having Marshals de Treviso [Mortier] and de Belluno [Victor] under my orders, but I should much prefer generals on whose passive obedience I could rely." . . . Then, his excitement increasing, Soult added in a voice full of emotion, "Would you believe it? I am surrounded by jealous men, eager for my recall; I am badly seconded by officers of too high rank to obey me without criticism; and I have not a single friend in whom I can confide."[25]

Yet on the other, Victor (Lejeune did not see Mortier or Sébastiani) was no more pleased with Soult than Soult was with him. At Puerto de Santa María, then, the emperor's emissary was given a very hearty welcome and told a tale of great activity and enterprise, the underlying message being very clearly that, if the siege of Cádiz was making no progress, it was because Soult was not giving it sufficient support. Indeed, Victor does not seem to have been shy in making the point quite explicit: "Marshal Victor gave me a long account of the necessities of his army, and told me how important it was that the emperor should come in person to settle the affairs of Spain."[26]

Of course, none of this is to say that things were very much better in the Patriot camp. The establishment of a national assembly in Cádiz had done nothing to invigorate such matters as conscription and taxation. In such towns and cities as remained in Patriot hands, local juntas that were as ambitious as they were self-serving had sought to challenge hard-pressed military commanders and exploit the war effort for their own ends. As the rout of Baza showed, many Patriot troops were barely fit to take the field, while, with the exception of Ballesteros, few of their commanders had shown much in the way of even basic competence.

Meanwhile, it is worth recalling that the constant marches and countermarches that gave Soult so much trouble were just as wearing to his opponents. Estanislao Salvador, for example, was the commander of a battalion of the Princesa infantry regiment: "We have had to put up with seven days of the most horrible heat in the open without once entering a town or village, without anything to eat and without a moment of repose, and the result is that we officers are so shattered that we hardly know ourselves. . . . Nobody can imagine all that we have had to suffer physically."[27] At the same time, leading the invaders a merry dance though their columns did, they were rarely free of danger. As Ballesteros wrote to a trusted correspondent: "We are, my friend, constantly under arms, for the French are in far greater strength than we are."[28] Desertion, then, was a constant problem, but the Patriot armies were still in the war, the fact being that, so long as this remained the case, Soult could not hope to suppress the disorder that gripped the Andalusian countryside.

For neither the French nor the Spaniards did the year 1811 bring any relief. On the contrary, the military campaigning raged unabated. The new year was scarcely a day old, then, when Soult launched a full-scale invasion of Extremadura. The origin of this operation lay in part in the constant skirmishing of 1810: though the French had checked Ballesteros and ultimately worsted La Romana, it was quite plain that, so long as the Spaniards held Badajoz, they could continue to harass Soult ad infinitum. So serious were the implications of an attempt to take that fortress, however, that it seems unlikely that such an operation would have been launched without the influence of events in the rest of Iberia (while Soult may have made a similar attempt a year earlier, he did so in the context of a situation that suggested that Spanish resistance was on the point of complete collapse). In particular, late July had seen the invasion of Portugal by Marshal Masséna. Cut off by the depredations of the Portuguese militia and home guard, that commander had soon been lost to sight in the wilds of Beira, but far away in France, Napoleon was well aware that even Masséna—by reputation the best of his marshals—might have difficulty in taking Lisbon. From late September, then, he began to take an interest in ways in which Soult could assist the Army of

Portugal. Initially, the plan was simply to have him demonstrate against Extremadura so as to tie down La Romana, but before Soult could act on this, the marquis marched to join Wellington at Lisbon with a large part of his troops. Discovering that this was the case, the emperor ordered Soult to have Mortier march on the Portuguese capital so as to threaten it from the south. As the commander of the Army of the South knew well enough, this scheme could not possibly be put into effect: aside from anything else, the road to Lisbon was blocked by the fortresses of Badajoz and Elvas. In consequence, the idea was quickly dropped in favor of the somewhat less visionary plan of an attack on Badajoz: if carried through successfully, this would put an end to the endless game of attack and retreat in the Sierra Morena while giving a major boost to French prestige; at the same time, Soult would be enabled to claim that he had done his best to aid Masséna.[29]

In the first week of January 1811, then, Soult set off from Seville at the head of an army of 20,000 men.[30] To concentrate such a force, however, the French commander had had to make some dangerous decisions. The core of the invasion forces consisted of the corps of Marshal Mortier, but the troops concerned were scarcely free for deployment elsewhere as they had, in effect, been responsible for the security of a great band of territory stretching from Huelva to the easternmost frontiers of Seville. Left behind after their departure were only a few *juramentados* and convalescents, and thus it was that both Victor and the governor of Córdoba, Dessolles, found themselves having to send men to take the place of Mortier's forces. Yet this was not the only call on the troops holding the rest of Andalucía; to bring his strike force up to a reasonable size, Soult had called in four regiments of cavalry and one of infantry from Victor's corps and still another regiment of cavalry from that of Sébastiani. In short, the capacity to take the offensive was achieved only by means of paring the troops left to hold Andalucía to the bone. With the situation before Cádiz particularly difficult—there were just 19,000 men left to keep the 25,000-strong garrison in check—Soult knew that he was taking a great risk. As he later wrote: "Victor had an extremely delicate mission to fulfill. . . . I could only hope that it would be a short campaign and that I would soon be able to return to Andalucía to finish off my projects before Cádiz."[31]

A speedy victory was not to be had, however. In the first place, the advance on Badajoz was conducted in conditions that were as bad as anything the French ever had to face in Spain:

> Although the winter was far advanced, the weather at first seemed favorable, but all at once an enormous storm of the most violent sort blew up and placed great obstacles in the way of the advance. The rain and hail that fell were so heavy that great torrents swept away the roads, and the situation became so terrible that the soldiers became completely demoralized. More than 300 carts loaded with beef were abandoned by their drivers, and a large part of the supplies and munitions were lost. . . . Meanwhile, the countryside that the army was traversing was a wilderness that offered nothing more than barren heathland devoid of all resources: one scarcely saw a human habitation. Covered in mud and deprived of all shelter, the men could not even light fires to dry their ruined clothes.[32]

Nor was it just the weather that dogged the march on Badajoz. By sheer coincidence, just as Soult set out from Seville, Ballesteros received orders from Cádiz ordering him to transfer his forces to the Sierra de Aracena and place himself under the command of the Fourth Army. Within a few days, then, the Spanish commander found himself a few miles to the west of the enemy columns toiling northward toward Badajoz. In the event, the French seem to have discovered his presence before he did theirs, for a detachment that was hastily dispatched from Mortier's corps to see off the new threat appears to have managed to take him by surprise near Monasterio. However, Ballesteros managed to get away with the bulk of his men, and this in turn left Soult in a difficult situation: either he pressed on regardless and hoped that the troops he had left behind proved sufficient to contain his Spanish opponent, or he detached a substantial force of troops to hunt him down and thereby jeopardized progress in Extremadura. Hoping that the Spaniards would not put up much of a fight, Soult opted for the latter option and ordered the whole of Gazan's infantry to turn aside and deal with Ballesteros. That said, the French commander was less than happy with his situation:

> The emperor has done me the honor of asking whether Cádiz will ever fall. I have replied in the affirmative, but for this to happen I will need more resources. . . . What can I do with the troops I have available? The territories that I am occupying are more than 150 leagues from France, while I cannot reduce their extent without compromising everything. On the left I have to defend myself against the forces that month after month appear in Murcia and threaten an invasion, while in the center I have to contain the British garrison in Gibraltar and push on with operations against Cádiz, held though this is by 20,000 troops. Not only that, but I am maintaining one third of Spain in its duty and have also mounted a considerable diversion of the army that has invaded Portugal, and that at sixty leagues from my own line of operations. Once again, then, I appeal to the emperor to send an agent worthy of his confidence to examine what I have done and even take my place. . . . For my part I cannot see how I can obtain any advantage, the only thing that I aspire to, then, being a glorious death.[33]

Nor did Soult's woes show any signs of diminishing. Aside from anything else, finishing off Ballesteros proved easier said than done. To quote Oman, the decision to pursue the Spanish general led Gazan "into three weeks of desperate mountain-marching and semi-starvation at the worst season of the year, for Ballesteros, who showed considerable skill in drawing his enemy on, moved ever south and westwards towards the lower Guadiana."[34] Both sides having received a few reinforcements—Ballesteros was joined by the troops of General Copóns and Gazan by those available to the French governor of the Condado de Niebla, André Rémond—battle was finally joined at Villanueva de los Castillejos on 24 January 1811. Far from running away, however, the Spaniards put up a good fight: "Ballesteros deployed his men in two lines and, though attacked by both Gazan and Rémond, held his positions until nightfall."[35] Still worse, meanwhile, they also got away: under cover of darkness, the Spanish commander forded the Guadiana and retreated some miles into Portugal. Unwilling to pursue him any farther, Gazan was left with no option but to break off the campaign and hasten to rejoin his parent corps in Extremadura. This he eventually did, but in his absence Soult had been near paralyzed for want of infantry: operations against Badajoz did not even begin until 30 January, and even then the fortress held out until 10 March (indeed, it would probably have held out still longer had not a lucky French shot struck down its vigorous and determined governor, Rafael Menacho, and handed control of the defense to an officer named Imaz, who seems at best to have been utterly incapable of meeting the responsibility that was thereby thrust upon him).[36]

The delay in taking Badajoz was all but fatal, however, and it was only by sheer good fortune that disaster was avoided. Thus far, the Allies had made but little use of either their seapower or their great mass of troops—some 20,000 Spaniards and 5,000 Anglo-Portuguese—that were holding Cádiz and the Isla de León. A number of small expeditions had been organized to the mainland certainly, but none of these had been prosecuted very vigorously, while the latest—a raid on the town of Fuengirola in October 1810 by an ad hoc brigade composed of two British infantry battalions and one Spanish one—had ended in disaster when the troops concerned were taken by surprise and forced to re-embark amid scenes of the utmost confusion, with the loss of their commander, Lord Blayney, who was taken prisoner.[37] With Soult away in Extremadura, however, the Spanish government finally woke up to the possibilities that it had to hand. The result was the campaign of Barrosa. In brief, the Anglo-Portuguese division that had been helping garrison Cádiz under the command of Thomas Graham was embarked with a strong force of Spanish regular troops and sent to Algeciras. United under the command of the Spanish general La Peña, the combined army was soon marching west to do battle with Victor, the plan being that he would be caught between the garrison of Cádiz and the army of La Peña. Fortunately for the French, however, the expedition miscarried. A commander noted for timidity and ineptitude alike, La Peña steered a course that kept him very close to the sea and, in this fashion, contrived to spare Victor the fate that had been planned for him. Thus, rather than taking him in the rear, the Allied expeditionary force rather confined itself to trying to get into touch with the troops left to hold Cádiz. Although this placed the French in a much better position than might otherwise have been the case, even now they might have been dealt a severe blow, for La Peña could have fallen on them from the south with his 15,000 men while the troops in Cádiz launched an amphibious operation against, say, Puerto de Santa María. This, however, would have required more vigor than La Peña was capable of, while his fellows in Cádiz also squandered their opportunities by eschewing a descent on Puerto de Santa María in favor of laying a pontoon bridge across the Sancti Petri at its southern extremity so that they could get in touch with the expeditionary force.[38]

The result of these successive blunders was all too predictable in that the whole Allied army ended up jammed together in a narrow strip of land encompassed by the sea on one side and an arm of the Sancti Petri on the other. Still worse, meanwhile, Victor was handed the initiative. Leaving a skeleton force of gunners, engineers, and marines to man the siege lines, he used one of his three infantry divisions to contain the front of La Peña's column while sending the other two to swing round behind its right flank and come down on its rear. By sheer good fortune it so happened that the troops that it met were not the Spaniards—a force of doubtful quality that might have been routed with incalculable consequences—but rather the division of General Graham. Turning on the enemy masses that suddenly appeared in its rear with great courage, this saved the day and turned what could have been a major disaster into a considerable defensive victory. Thus, while one of its two brigades assaulted a prominent hill crowned by an old Moorish watchtower that had been seized by the division of General Ruffin, the other attacked that of General Leval. Though Graham's forces were outnumbered by six to five, they yet managed to prevail. Within two hours, indeed, the entire French force was in full retreat, having lost around a third of its men, including Ruffin, who was mortally wounded. The British were scarcely in better case—they had, indeed, lost a quarter of their strength—but with the French in disarray, a still greater success might have been obtained had La Peña but marched to the support of Graham with every man he possessed. No such movement was forthcoming, however: in the face of the enemy, the Spanish commander seemed all but paralyzed, and the end result was that the campaign ended on the tamest possible note, with the entire Allied force withdrawing across the Sancti Petri into the Isla de León amid a cacophony of mutual recriminations of such violence that it effectively put an end to any chance of such an operation ever being repeated.[39]

Fought on 5 March 1811, the Battle of Barrosa was therefore something of a strategic triumph for the French, however much this may have been through no merit of their own. In their camps, indeed, it was represented as "a brilliant victory in which . . . they baffled the schemes of their enemies and forced them to retreat."[40] Yet their situation remained as problematic as ever. In particular, Ballesteros had taken the field yet again. After Villanueva de los Castillejos, he had, as we have seen, taken shelter in Portugal, but he now came forward yet again and attacked the outnumbered Rémond at the River Tinto at the point where it is crossed by the road from Valverde del Camino. Forced to flee in disorder, Rémond fell back on Seville and took up a blocking position at La Palma del Condado, where he was joined by the current governor of Seville, General Augustin Darricau, with the 1,600 men that were all that could be spared from the city as a field force. As Ballesteros had some 4,000 troops with him, it is probable that he might still have overcome the French, but just at this point—5 March—the Spanish commander got news that a French force was bearing down on him from the direction of Extremadura. In the event, this news proved false—no French troops departed Badajoz to return to Andalucía prior to 13 March—but Ballesteros was not to know this and therefore retreated in haste so as to take shelter behind the Tinto. Discovering his mistake, the Spanish general immediately retraced his steps, and on 9 March he fell on Rémond at La Palma. No longer supported by Darricau, who had returned in haste to Seville as soon as the threat from Ballesteros appeared to have receded, and according to tradition attacked by the townspeople as well, Rémond was routed and fell back to Seville, with the Spaniards in hot pursuit.[41] What might have happened next is unclear, but Darricau and Rémond were at least potentially open to attack and were probably only saved from serious misfortune by the arrival of rumors from the north—this time all too correct—that Badajoz had fallen and that substantial French forces were marching south to save Seville, the result of this news being to persuade Ballesteros to retrace his steps and make all haste for the safety of Niebla.[42]

With Soult now back in Seville at the head of most of Gazan's division and a brigade of dragoons, the immediate danger was at an end. Yet the French commander realized that Ballesteros remained a threat, and all the more so given the fact that he could easily be reinforced from the sea and might in any case strike again at any moment. Still worse, at the end of March, news arrived that the division of veteran Spanish infantry commanded by General José de Zayas y Chacón had disembarked at Moguer. Correctly seeing this as a major threat, Soult once again acted with great promptitude: within a matter of days, a task force was on the road from Seville with orders to throw Zayas into the sea before he could join up with Ballesteros. In this it was successful: no sooner had the French column appeared than the new arrivals reembarked in haste. This was not an end of the campaign, however. Having initially come down to meet Zayas, Ballesteros was now in full flight for the Sierra Morena. But the commander of the troops who had been sent to vanquish Zayas, the particularly tough and thrusting Jean-Pierre Maransin, decided that the opportunity was too good to miss and, having sent back the few cavalry and artillery pieces that had accompanied his expedition to Seville, gave chase. Pursued ever farther northward, Ballesteros eventually turned at bay at Fregenal, only to be badly defeated. Help, however, was at hand, for in the course of these operations, a large Anglo-Portuguese army commanded by William Beresford had appeared in Extremadura and closed in on Badajoz while sending out a covering force of mounted troops to watch the road to Seville, a somewhat chastened Ballesteros being grateful enough to take shelter in the rear of the cavalry screen while Maransin, who, completely unaware that other Allied troops were in the area, had almost marched headlong into the midst of the new arrivals, fled posthaste for the safety of Andalucía, and eventually succeeded in linking up with the covering force of Latour-Maubourg (see below).

Meanwhile, the appearance of Beresford's forces in Andalucía prompted the Spanish authorities in Cádiz to make an attempt to resume conventional operations. Thus, the two best divisions of the Fourth Army, those of Zayas and General Miguel Lardízabal y Uribe, were embarked on ships and transported to Ayamonte, from where, commanded by General Blake, they marched north into Extremadura and in early May joined up with not only Ballesteros but also what remained of the old Fifth Army (the force that had formed the basis of La Romana's command in 1810—placed under the command of Gabriel de Mendízabal following the sudden death of the marquis from natural causes in January 1811, it had been badly beaten before the walls of Badajoz in the course of the siege and forced to flee into Portugal, where it was taken over by the victor of Bailén, Francisco Javier Castaños). Still worse, having reached Extremadura, they were able to link up with Beresford. To explain the presence of this commander, we need to revert to Soult's attack on Badajoz. Hearing that the Spanish fortress was in danger, Wellington had ordered Beresford to march to its relief at the head of three divisions of British and Portuguese infantry, a brigade of German riflemen, and two brigades of dragoons. In the event, these men had not arrived in time, but they were quickly able to invest Badajoz and thereby threaten everything that Soult had just taken so many risks to gain.[43]

We come here to the real nub of the issue. Despite his protests, Soult had enough troops more or less to dominate Andalucía without help from elsewhere, but holding down Extremadura was another matter. To protect the province, Soult had left behind 11,000 men of V Corps under the temporary command of General Latour-Maubourg (following the conclusion of the siege of Badajoz, Mortier had returned to France), but though a very serious loss in terms of garrisoning Andalucía, this force was scarcely sufficient to hold down a region as large as Extremadura, the garrison of Badajoz alone absorbing some 3,000 troops.[44] Nor, meanwhile, could so small an army hope to hold off a substantial relief force, and certainly not one as big as the one that had just taken the field, Beresford's column consisting of no fewer than 18,000 men. In short, Wellington had only to decide to retake Badajoz for it to be in serious danger, the only way that Soult could forestall this being to bring up so many men from Andalucía that his dominions there would be in almost equal trouble. As at least some of the French commanders in Spain realized, the problem was at root insoluble. Let us here quote the then commander of the Army of the North, Marshal Bessières: "The entire world knows the vicious nature of our operations. . . . We occupy too much ground; we use up our means without profit or need; we cling on to dreams. Cádiz and Badajoz absorb all our resources: Cádiz because it cannot be taken, and Badajoz because it needs an army to support it. The latter should be blown up and the former renounced for the time being."[45] The strategy postulated here is an interesting one. In brief, what Bessières appears to be hinting is that the French should give up most of their conquests; concentrate the bulk of their forces around, say, Madrid; and tempt the Allied forces into attacking them and thereby fighting the war on their terms. Whether such a plan would have worked cannot be known (though in fact it presents many problems: how, for example, would the French have sustained so large a mass of troops?). For Soult, however, it represented such a massive confession of failure that it was unthinkable, while even giving up Badajoz was not something to be entertained with any degree of levity, and all the more so as its conquest had at least ensured that the repeated Spanish incursions of the summer of 1810 were a thing of the past.[46] That said, however, Badajoz was also a constant hostage to fortune, for its loss would constitute a devastating blow to French prestige. If attacked, then, Badajoz had to be relieved at all costs, but this would necessarily mean assembling a large force from the troops available in Andalucía and thereby putting the situation there in jeopardy. That this would be the case, meanwhile, had been rendered all too obvious by events in the heartland of French Andalucía during the Extremadura campaign. With some difficulty, Ballesteros had been fended off, but he had not been the only enemy to have threatened the stability of the valley of the Guadalquivir. Thus, the irregulars of the Serranía de Ronda had also made their mark. As Soult had complained to Berthier on 8 February:

> Driven by misery and the desire to pillage . . . almost all the insurgents and smugglers of the mountains between Ronda and the Campo de San Roque have descended on the plains and committed a number of excesses. Various mobile columns have been dispatched in their pursuit, but they have only been able to drive them away for a brief moment, while few of the insurgents have been caught. It only having been possible to give Utrera a feeble garrison, on 13 January brigands entered the town and committed a number of murders and robberies. On top of this, they have raided Trebujena and other towns in the provinces of Seville and Jérez, while they almost succeeded in seizing the castle of Zahara. . . . The weakness of the garrison of Seville does not permit it to make any detachments, and knowing that I have sent this unit back from Extremadura, General Darricau is awaiting the arrival of the Sixty-Third Line with impatience.[47]

In many ways, then, the capture of Badajoz was a strategic disaster for the French cause, and from the spring of 1811 onward, it was to place the French position in Andalucía under serious strain. This was evident from the moment of Beresford's arrival before Badajoz. There was no immediate danger of the fortress falling: it was well provisioned and garrisoned, while its governor, General Armand Philippon, turned out to be the bravest and most resourceful of leaders; at the same time, though Soult was not to know this, Beresford did not have access to an adequate siege train. Yet for all that, delay was not advisable, and so Soult had scarcely returned to Seville before he was once again casting round for a field army. With some difficulty, seventeen battalions of infantry and seven regiments of cavalry were scraped together from various sources, and on the night of 8 May, this relief force set out from Seville. Picking up Latour-Maubourg, who had managed to escape to the fringes of the Sierra Morena without a fight, Soult marched north for a week and on 15 May ran into the combined forces of Beresford, Blake, and Castaños arrayed across the highroad to Badajoz on a range of low hills centered on the village of La Albuera. The story of the ferocious battle that ensued the next day has been told many times, and there is no need to do so again now. In brief, however, Soult—a master of grand tactics if nothing else—attempted to hook round the unprotected Allied right flank, only to see his troops first checked by a thin line of Spanish infantry and then driven back by the relentless counterattacks directed against them, not so much by Beresford (who appears to have lost all control of the battle), but rather his subordinates. By the end of the day, then, Soult was right back where he started, while his army was in such a state of disorganization that he soon realized he had no option but to fall back on Seville. The cost to the Allied armies had been terrible—British losses were 4,189 killed, wounded, and taken prisoner, while between them, the Spaniards and Portuguese had lost another 1,667 men—but the French army's condition was infinitely worse. A figure often quoted for its losses is 7,900 men, or roughly 10 percent of the entire Army of the South. Return to duty though some of the wounded eventually did, the whole edifice of French control had been badly shaken.[48]

Terribly damaging though it was to the French position in Andalucía, the Battle of Albuera was but the start of the seemingly endless strain that the attempt to hold Badajoz was to pose on Soult's resources. Thus, no sooner had the marshal's battered army fallen back on Seville than the Anglo-Portuguese forces resumed the siege of Badajoz, this time under the command of Wellington in person and with the assistance of far more troops (instead of the three infantry divisions commanded by Beresford, there were now five). For a variety of reasons, the pace of operations was very slow, but it was clear enough to all concerned that sooner or later starvation alone would be enough to bring Philippon to his knees. Fortunately for Soult, who had fallen back with what was left of the army that had fought at Albuera to the area of Llerena, one person who was as aware of the danger as he was Marshal Marmont, the new commander of the Army of Portugal. Just before he had marched on Badajoz, "King Nicholas" had written to Masséna informing him that saving the city might require the assistance of his forces. Had this missive arrived while Masséna was still in command, it might well have been ignored, but Marmont was fresh to the Peninsula and eager to make his mark upon the course of the war and therefore sent a message to

Soult from his headquarters in Salamanca saying that he would, if necessary, come south with his entire army. More than that, hearing the news of Albuera, rather than waiting for further word of Soult, he began to move south of his own volition. Informed of this, the commander of the Army of the South began to move north in his turn. Choosing as he did to take not the road for Badajoz, but rather that for Mérida, the march was not molested in any way, and on 18 June Soult's forces successfully made contact with those of Marmont. The result was an impressive concentration of troops—some 60,000—and this was quite enough to persuade Wellington to abandon his siege and pull his forces back to a strong defensive position on the River Caya, just inside the frontiers of Portugal (even once every possible man had been shifted down from the vicinity of Almeida in response to Marmont's march south, the British commander's strength only came to 54,000 men). However, in the end all this came to nothing: having reconnoitered Wellington's position, Soult and Marmont decided that it could not be forced and simply sat down to contain the Anglo-Portuguese army while the garrison of Badajoz hastily filled in all the trenches left by the besieging forces and did what it could to repair the walls and restock the fortress's magazines. Yet in the barren wastes of Extremadura, masses of troops of the sort that had been got together by Soult and Marmont could not be maintained for very long, while even had there been more food to hand, hardly any time had passed before the former was receiving very bad news from Andalucía. In brief, the insurrection in the Serranía de Ronda had once again flared up; armed bands were menacing Seville, where General Darricau had abandoned the main part of the city and withdrawn the few men he had available into the Cartuja; and the Third Army was again pressing in on the frontiers of Granada, where Sébastiani had been left with no more than 9,000 men. Faced by this challenge, Soult wanted to return to Seville with the whole force he had got together to succor Badajoz, but Marmont responded violently to this suggestion, which he correctly interpreted as an attempt to get him to take charge of Extremadura on a permanent basis, and threatened immediately to return to León with all his men. His bluff called, an angry Soult caved in, and on 28 June he departed for Seville with only those troops that belonged to I and IV Corps, the whole of V Corps being left behind with Marmont and under the command of the newly arrived Jean-Baptiste Drouet.[49]

Mention of this last figure brings us to the one welcome development that had taken place in the whole situation. While engaged in the relief of Badajoz, Soult had received the one substantial reinforcement reached him in the whole period from January 1810 to August 1812. This was not, however, the fruit of any relaxation of the emperor's insistence that the marshal had enough men both to take Cádiz and hold down Andalucía and Extremadura. Rather, the story is as follows. Up until 1809, every French infantry regiment had consisted of three field battalions and one depot battalion, and every cavalry regiment three field squadrons and one depot squadron. However, such were the numbers of conscripts that an ever more aggressive recruitment policy had begun to force into the army that, by the middle of 1809, sufficient recruits were available to increase the number of field battalions and squadrons per regiment from three to four. In all, this change should have brought Soult no fewer than twenty-two battalions of infantry and nineteen squadrons of cavalry, but, while a few of the units concerned were dispatched to Spain, the majority were held back and used to form a new corps.[50] Commanded by Drouet, this force was initially sent to support Masséna's invasion of Portugal, but, with the failure of this operation, there seemed no reason why its component units could not be sent to their parent regiments. In consequence, in May 1811 it was duly split up, and the eighteen battalions of infantry and six squadrons of cavalry that belonged to I, IV, and V Corps packed off to Andalucía in the charge of Drouet. Having got to Córdoba, however, Drouet discovered that Soult was in Extremadura, and so, having already trudged all the way from Salamanca, his unfortunate men were faced with another long march, this time to Badajoz. Here they were split up yet again, the units belonging to V Corps being left in Extremadura and the remainder taken away by Soult when he returned to Seville.[51]

To the travails of V Corps, we shall return soon enough. In the meantime, however, it should be noted that Soult had been away from Seville for the better part of two months with a third of his forces. During this time, the troops left behind had held on easily enough, but they were now once again in great danger. Thus, following Albuera, Wellington had suggested to General Blake that he take his Fourth Army expeditionary force and return to Andalucía. Marching via Portuguese territory, Blake duly moved south again and in late June crossed the frontier into the present-day province of Huelva. With the road to Seville wide open, a more enterprising commander might have made a dash for Soult's capital, but Blake was not the world's greatest strategist and had also suffered such a surfeit of disaster that he had become excessively timid. Rather than heading straight for the Guadalquivir, he rather presented himself before the walls of Niebla, which was garrisoned by a mere 600 men of the *josefino* Régiment Royal-Etranger under a Swiss major named Fritzherz. Though the French had done what they could to reinforce the defenses, these were hopelessly inadequate, consisting of little more than the original medieval *enceinte* and its attendant castle, but Blake had brought no guns of any sort with him, while, though pressed home with some spirit—the Spaniards suffered some 200 casualties—an attempt to storm the town by escalade failed for want of adequate scaling ladders. Left unsuccored, the garrison would sooner or later have succumbed to starvation, but Soult had no intention of letting his opponents secure the propaganda coup that would have been afforded them by even the capture of so insignificant a post as Niebla. Hearing of Blake's offensive while en route to Seville from Badajoz, he therefore sent all the infantry he had with him to attack the besieging forces. The plan adopted was promising enough in theory—while one column marched on Niebla from the north, another circled round to the west in an attempt to take the Spaniards in the rear—but Blake quickly got wind of what was in store for him and hastily retreated to Ayamonte, whence he took ship for Cádiz with the two divisions he had taken with him to Extremadura in the first place, though not without having first ordered Ballesteros to resume his old station in the Sierra de Aracena.[52]

Yet another crisis had been faced down, then, but no sooner had Niebla been saved than trouble erupted elsewhere. Far to the east the Spanish forces holding the Murcia region—the Third Army—had spent the winter of 1810–11 recovering from the rout of Baza and, by the spring of 1811, could count on a field force of some 13,500 men. Commanded once more by Manuel Freyre, these troops had taken advantage of the absence of some of Sébastiani's troops for Extremadura to close in on Granada. Forced in self-defense to concentrate most of the troops that they had in eastern Andalusia around the city, the French had in consequence been forced to give up such outposts as Almería, their general sense of insecurity being increased still further by the fact that Sébastiani, increasingly frustrated by the campaign in Andalusia, had at this very moment secured leave to resign his command and return to France. This was alarming enough—among other things, Sébastiani's replacement, Jean Leval, was little suited to a corps command—but still worse was to follow. Thus, having sailed with his two divisions from Ayamonte to Cádiz, in an excess of confidence that was probably brought on by Albuera (a battle that was being widely represented as a great Spanish victory), Blake suddenly demanded that he be given command not only of the Fourth Army but also of the Second (the garrison of Valencia) and the Third, thereby reviving and even expanding upon the military structures that had come into being in February 1810. This arrangement being sanctioned easily enough, by the last week of July, Blake was sailing with the same two divisions as before to Almería, from whence he marched to join Freyre, the latter's headquarters now being at Baza. Much alarmed at this news, Soult rushed most of the troops he had brought back from Badajoz to Granada and managed to take Freyre and Blake's forces unawares. Beaten in minor actions at the River Guadal and Las Vertientes on 9–10 August, the Spaniards retreated in haste to Murcia, having lost something in the region of 2,000 casualties, though the French made no effort to pursue them, preferring instead to use the troops they had got together to reoccupy Almería and attempt to wreak havoc on the insurgents of such areas as the Alpujarras.[53]

Until the summer of 1811, the Army of the South may be judged roughly to have been holding its own against its many opponents. This had not been achieved without much hard fighting and even more hard marching, while toward the end of the period, disaster had only been avoided thanks to the timely intervention of the

Army of Portugal, but every attempt to challenge Soult's control of the chief bastions of occupation had, in the end, been repulsed. From now on, however, the situation was to change dramatically. To the very end the French would be able to hang on to their main strongholds, but with their troops hopelessly overextended by the capture of Badajoz, their capacity to take offensive action was to be, first, reduced very severely and, second, eradicated altogether. As we shall see, meanwhile, the late summer of 1811 was also a watershed in a number of other respects, being marked by significant changes in both the organization of the occupying forces and the chief focus of military operations. That being the case, it is perhaps a convenient moment to take stock of the situation of the occupying forces and their opponents.

In brief, the situation was more or less as follows. Not counting the irregular bands and the garrison of Cádiz—setting aside the useless Voluntarios Distinguidos, some 20,000 men, of whom 5,000 were British or Portuguese—there were three Allied forces operating against the troops of Marshal Soult: the Fifth Army, the remains of the old Army of the Left, under Castaños (5,000 men); the mixture of troops from the Third and Fourth Armies that had just been defeated on the frontiers of Murcia (15,000 men); and finally the division of Ballesteros (6,000 men). To face these enemies, Soult in theory had some 77,000 men, but of these around 8,500 were sick in hospital and nearly 10,000 more detached, leaving no more than 58,000 men available for service. Moreover, even much of this force was tied down in essential duties of a sort that could not be neglected. Thus, the majority of the infantry of Marshal Victor's I Corps was permanently employed in the siege lines facing Cádiz so that its only contribution to the garrisoning of Andalucía was to keep such towns as Puerto Real, Puerto de Santa María, Jérez de la Frontera, Medina Sidonia, Arcos de la Frontera, and Chiclana out of the hands of the insurgents. Equally, half of V Corps—the infantry division of Eugène Villatte and the light cavalry brigade of André Briche—was absorbed by the occupation of Extremadura and, unlike I Corps, made no contribution to the defense of Andalucía at all. With still other French troops tied to the vicinity of Seville, Córdoba, Granada, Jaén, and Málaga, the largest *masse de manoeuvre* that Soult could count upon numbered a mere 20,000 men, though weary of the difficulties that had sometimes been caused by his subordinate commanders, the marshal had attempted to ensure that he could always count on at least this force by designating certain troops for an army reserve that notionally consisted of two divisions of infantry and one of cavalry.

Let us now examine the position of the French army in more detail. Two of the three infantry divisions—those of Nicolas Conroux and Villatte—of I Corps were, as already implied, deployed in an arc along the coast from Puerto Real to Chiclana, while aside from two battalions that had been left at Puerto Real, the third was split between Ronda, Osuna, and Seville as part of the army reserve (the regiments involved were the Sixteenth Light and the Eighth, Forty-Fifth, and Fifty-Fourth Line). Of IV Corps, its French infantry division was stationed at Granada, Motril, Antequera, Málaga, and Alcalá la Real with the proviso that two of its four regiments—the Twelfth Light and the Fifty-Eighth Line—could be required as part of the Army of the South's reserve at any moment, while its Polish division was split between Jaén, Granada, Córdoba, Antequera, and Ismalles, with the troops at Córdoba—the Grand Duchy of Warsaw's Fourth Regiment of Line Infantry—again being assigned to the reserve. As for its brigade of light cavalry, meanwhile, one regiment was at Lumbreras and the other at Seville, again as part of the army reserve. Of V Corps, setting aside the many troops deployed in Extremadura, there were left but eleven infantry battalions, all of them from the division of General Michel Claparède, including five at Jérez, three at Seville, and three at Constantina. Of the army-level cavalry, Latour-Maubourg's division of dragoons was stationed at Niebla, Ecija, Arcos de la Frontera, Jérez, and Conil and Milhaud's at Lumbreras, Granada, Jaén, Vélez Blanco, Málaga, and Córdoba, but once again a good half of this force was earmarked for service with the reserve, so it could be withdrawn at any moment. Finally, aside from the various troops already mentioned, Córdoba was held by a nine-battalion-strong infantry brigade, while one should also not forget the various Spanish units stationed at Seville and a number of other places. In short, the French were scattered broadcast across hundreds of miles of territory, the only substantial concentrations of troops that were to be found being those holding

Seville, Granada, and the siege lines facing Cádiz. Note too, meanwhile, that even those troops notionally earmarked for the reserve generally had garrison duties as well so that any attempt to draw on their services could not but run the risk of fresh difficulties.[54]

Thus far, energy, good fortune, and hard fighting had together sufficed to paper over the cracks in the edifice of French occupation. As the events of the autumn of 1811 were to show, however, Marshal Soult's luck had at last run out. Trouble began with the disembarkation of the hard-marching and hard-fighting division of General Ballesteros at Algeciras in the first few days of September. As the Spanish commander could very easily march from there to occupy Ronda and the surrounding district, this was obviously a major threat, and one that posed the French many problems: setting aside the fact that the area was all but inaccessible, Ballesteros could count on getting supplies by sea and also being evacuated should he come under too much pressure, while he might even be able to threaten Seville. Moreover, the arrival of the general led to a resurgence of resistance: much encouraged by the appearance of Ballesteros's forces, the insurgents of the Serranía de Ronda congregated in such villages as Benaoján, Torox, and Yunquera in considerable numbers and prepared to sally forth against the French.[55] That this was so was at least in part due the new arrival's grandiloquent rhetoric, the fact being that Ballesteros had long since learned that this was a key weapon in the cause of advancing his interests in Cádiz. Here, for example, is the text of the address that he issued to his troops on landing at Algeciras:

> Soldiers! You are going to march against the enemy, and I am resolved not to halt until I am in a position to force him to do battle. I know your enthusiasm and your desire: like me, you wish to give the fatherland indelible proofs of the warrior spirit that animates the soldiers of the Fourth Army, the same soldiers who have so often shown that they know how to win renown with their deeds of valor. I believe with all my heart that the enemy will soon evacuate Andalucía, and that this land that you have so watered with your blood, this land in which you have displayed a constancy that will be the wonder of future centuries,

> will reward you with the gratitude and recognition that are the mark of a populace that has . . . given me so many testimonies of its loyalty, of its patriotism, and finally, of the love that it bears for you. This beautiful country whose liberty you have been so anxious to restore, is impatiently awaiting the happy day when it will be able to unite its sons to our banners with the same enthusiasm that we saw in the course of our glorious campaign on the Guadalquivir in the month of April. The same people that embraced you amid the bayonets of the enemy now cannot wait to show you its gratitude in complete liberty. As for me, meanwhile, I aspire to nothing more than the common weal, and to having the pleasure of watching the brotherhood that is so proper to the feelings of a nation whose one desire from the beginning of our struggle has been to conquer or die for the salvation of the fatherland.[56]

In another context it would be interesting to deconstruct the coded messages hidden in this document. For the time being, suffice to say that for the next few months, a number of circumstances were to make the Serranía de Ronda and its surroundings the epicenter of the war in Andalucía. In Granada IV Corps received much relief from the fact that the autumn of 1811 saw Marshal Suchet, the commander of the French forces in Aragón and Catalonia, launch a great offensive against Valencia that distracted the attention of Blake and drew away a large part of the Spanish forces in Murcia; in Cádiz the garrison continued to sit quietly behind its defenses; and in Extremadura the bulk of the Anglo-Portuguese army had marched away to set about the capture of distant Ciudad Rodrigo. Meanwhile, not only had the division of Ballesteros—by far the most active component of the Patriot forces—been transferred to Algeciras, but the city of Málaga was also currently looming very large in Soult's preoccupations. It being ever more clear that Andalucía could not even support itself, let alone the French forces of occupation, securing additional supplies of grain were vital, but there was but one means of doing this, which was somehow to open up a line of communications with Morocco, whose merchants had traditionally exported large quantities of grain to Spain and Portugal alike. The only major port in French hands on the coast of Andalucía, Málaga clearly had an important role to play in this respect, and toward the end of August, a new commander had been sent there in the person of Jean-Pierre Maransin, a vigorous officer whom we previously met chasing Ballesteros from Andalucía in the weeks leading up to the Battle of Albuera. Provided with a small task force of troops drawn from Soult's central reserve in the form of two battalions of the Fifty-Eighth Line, a squadron of the Twenty-First Dragoons, and a detachment of artillery, Maransin was ordered do what he could to pacify the area with the aid of Málaga's existing garrison of a regiment of *josefino* infantry and two squadrons of French dragoons. However, much more to the point were the rest of Maransin's orders. In brief, the new commander was instructed to fit out a fleet of twelve "corsairs," fast sailing vessels that could operate from Málaga and both seize Allied shipping and protect friendly vessels from the enemy, the whole squadron being placed under a Spanish naval officer named Babastro. Soult, in short, was henceforth to have not just an army but also a navy.[57]

Given that the appearance of Ballesteros was such a major threat, it might have been thought that Soult would have flung his every available man against him. Yet short of both food and money though he was, Soult appears to have decided that, with the harvest in the fields, he could not afford to let significant stretches of country fall into the hands of the insurgents simply because he happened to be engaged in conventional operations elsewhere (it may be too that he had little respect for Ballesteros, the conduct of the latter having on a number of occasions suggested that his fiery oratory was little matched by his daring).[58] In consequence, Soult chose to make the initial target not Ballesteros, but rather the *serranos*. Thus, forming two columns from his reserve under Generals Louis Cassagne and Antoine Rignoux, he ordered them to march on Yunquera, this last having become the chief center of the insurrection. This, however, was an extremely risky move: Cassagne had no more than 1,600 men and Rignoux only 3,000, and the fact was that Ballesteros could easily have fallen on either of them; indeed, apparently unknown to Soult, the Spanish general was himself marching on Yunquera. In the event, no such disaster occurred—no sooner had he occupied Yunquera than Ballesteros heard of the advance of the French and, apparently convinced that they were present in much larger numbers than was actually the case, fell back on Ubrique. Indeed, it was rather the French who were able to claim a victory. On 14 September Cassagne and Rignoux assaulted Yunquera and wiped out the 600 men who had been left behind as a rear guard, capturing large quantities of arms and supplies in the process. Over the next two or three days, various other towns were stormed or otherwise occupied, and the result was a temporary decline in popular resistance in that many of the insurgents fled into the mountains.

Having carried out their orders, Cassagne and Rignoux now halted their operations and, indeed, pulled back many of their troops, but Ballesteros was still at large, having fallen back from Ubrique to Jimena de la Frontera. Once again the French had been very lucky, for the Spanish general had been toying with the idea of mounting a counterattack on his pursuers, only to hear at the last minute that a large French force was marching on his communications from the west. In brief, however, this was a misapprehension: there were, indeed, French movements afoot to the west, but in reality the situation was far less serious than Ballesteros feared. Thus far, I Corps had taken no part in the campaign, the cause of this being the very poor relations that existed between Victor and Soult: Soult was jealous of Victor and had accordingly drawn particularly heavily on his forces in respect of the formation of the reserve, while Victor resented Soult and was not inclined to exert himself to obey his orders or to assist him. The logical thing to have done, of course, would have been to rush as many troops as possible to Jimena de la Frontera to cut off Ballesteros's retreat while he was still in the mountains, but instead all that Victor did was to send 1,500 men under a Colonel Combelles to expel the 200-man garrison the Spaniards had immediately installed in the castle of Alcalá de los Gazules. Just as with the earlier moves of Cassagne and Rignoux, this was most dangerous as Ballesteros might easily have destroyed Combelles as well, but the Spanish commander missed his chance and instead dispatched a mere reconnaissance that the colonel promptly pounced on and routed before going on to secure the surrender of the castle. At last apprised that the enemy force to the west was only tiny, Ballesteros now marched on Alcalá de los Gazules with all his forces. There followed a sharp fight, but Combelles seems to have been a skillful commander and held out long enough to extract his little command without too many losses.

The castle, meanwhile, was still in French hands, and unwilling to see matters end in a defeat for his corps, Victor therefore resolved on a counterstroke. Thus, having sent Combelles a small force of cavalry, he sent a message to Rignoux, as the nearest French commander, asking him to march on Jimena de la Frontera so as to cut off Ballesteros. Rignoux, it seems, was happy enough to comply, but whereas Victor had imagined that he would be followed by the whole of the division to which belonged, in reality he headed south with no more than his own brigade, while, just to compound matters, Victor also failed to instruct Combelles to press on beyond Alcalá de los Gazules should he find out that Ballesteros had fallen back. This, indeed, he had, at first marching as far east as Casares, only then to double back once more as soon as he heard that he was not being followed. Thus it was that for a third time, an outnumbered French force found itself marching straight into the path of his army. This time, however, there was no escape: a letter that Victor sent countermanding Rignoux's march as soon as he realized that Combelles had not advanced beyond Alcalá never arrived, while a rescue force dispatched by Soult as soon as he realized what was going on only got as far as Alcalá. Reaching Jimena de la Frontera without coming up with Ballesteros, Rignoux was informed that his quarry had disappeared into the mountains in the direction of Ronda. Unwilling to risk destruction in some defile, he therefore resolved to turn west in the hope of linking up with Combelles, only to find the Spanish general lying in wait for him at the point where the Alcalá road crossed the River Guadiaro a few miles to the west of Jimena. By dint of hard fighting, Rignoux managed to cut his way through, with the loss of 150 men, and eventually made it to safety, but the whole campaign had very much been a "near-run thing."[59]

Needless to say, the campaign of September 1811 put the relationship between Soult and Victor under fresh strain: indeed, incensed by the former's attempts to throw all the blame on him, the latter now wrote to Napoleon appealing to be transferred to another command. Meanwhile, it also offers a prime example of the difficulties that the French had to face in Andalucía. The whole campaign had been conducted in baking heat; the French troops had had to march great distances in some of the most mountainous terrain in Spain for no appreciable gain—between 12 and 26 September, Rignoux's brigade marched at least 200 miles (Málaga–Yunquera; Yunquera–Ubrique; Ubrique–Montellano; Montellano–Jimena; Jimena–Bornos)—and all that had been achieved was to inflict a few hundred casualties on the Spaniards, burn a few rebel villages and capture some supplies. Still worse, operating from bases that were a hundred or more miles apart from one another, the French commanders had had great difficulty in coordinating their operations and for much of the time had been completely unaware of Ballesteros's real whereabouts; Soult, indeed, appears at the crucial moment completely to have lost control of the situation. All too apparent was the jealousy that bedeviled relations between the French commanders: having been left by Soult to play a subordinate role in affairs, Victor responded by grabbing the first chance he had of some glory without any thought for the consequences of his actions. And last but not least, all the marching and countermarching of the French columns altered the situation in the *serranía* not a whit, as witness, for example, the stark words of the report directed by Maransin to Soult on 27 September:

> The bands of Luque, the Crusade, Roda, and Bessera are still in occupation of Yunquera. Some small parties appeared before Alhaurín de la Torre but were driven off by the mobile column commanded by Captain Serra with the loss of two men and three horses. On 24 September a party of 300 troops of the line composed of both infantry and cavalry entered Alora and seized some supplies before then moving on in the direction of El Valle. The day before, two columns had set out from Vélez. Of these, the first, which was commanded by Major Bellangé, headed for Benamócarra . . . while the second, which was commanded by Captain Ricart of the Fifty-Eighth Line, marched on Canillas. . . . Having joined with the bands of a number of other commanders, Segovia attacked Ricart's column at the defile of

> Algarrobo, the skirmish that resulted costing the latter twelve dead and four wounded. . . . Meanwhile, whether it is achieved through volunteering or impressment, the incorporation into the bands of deserters, stragglers, and civilians capable of taking up arms is steadily increasing the strength of the brigands.[60]

If anything, the French position had been worsened by the campaign of September 1811. Despite all the efforts of Soult's propagandists, for example, the skirmish at Jimena de la Frontera quickly became a major source of inspiration among the populace. As Maransin complained: "Exaggerated accounts are being published of the successes obtained by Ballesteros. Proof of their veracity having ostensibly been offered by the latter's official report, stories are going round to the effect the brigade of General Rignoux has been entirely destroyed with the loss of 1,000 dead and wounded and many prisoners."[61] Of course, there was not just the issue of prestige but also that of repression. As even the French had to admit, counterinsurgency was not a pleasant business. On 24 September, for example, the village of Algarrobo found itself the subject of punitive action on account of the ambush that had taken place nearby the day before. To quote Maransin again: "On 24 September Bellangé marched on Algarrobo to destroy the bands that had occupied the surrounding heights. His mere appearance being sufficient to disperse the brigands, the troops were able to occupy the village without resistance. Despite the orders of their commander, they then committed a number of excesses, having been incited to commit acts of violence by the French blood that had been shed with so much savagery in the same spot."[62]

Clearly, then, the French were faced by a classic dilemma. Rugged though it was, substantial columns of troops could penetrate the heartland of insurrection with little more difficulty than that offered by the state of the district's roads—the columns of Cassagne and Rignoux had crisscrossed the *serranía* several times without once being attacked by the enemy—but this meant nothing: rather than try conclusions with forces much stronger than themselves, the bands simply melted away into the mountains, leaving the French to vent their fury on such unfortunate *pueblos* as Algarrobo. However, if only because of the simple fact that brigandage in effect became the only means of subsistence left to the population, every village that was sacked and burned merely produced fresh recruits for the insurgents. Still worse, meanwhile, no sooner had the French columns moved on than the partisans simply moved back to their old haunts and continued in the same fashion as before. Faced by what was in effect a classic guerrilla campaign, the invaders could only hope to win by establishing a permanent presence in every mountain village and at the same time so saturating the countryside with punitive columns that the bands were left with nowhere to hide. To do this, however, they had first to defeat the Spanish regular forces, this being something that had over and over again been shown to be beyond their power.

By the autumn of 1811, then, it was becoming clear that the struggle to control Andalucía could produce at best nothing more than stalemate. If the correspondence of Jean-Pierre Maransin is anything to go by, the French were well aware of this. On the one hand, one finds endless lamentations in respect of the inability of the three punitive columns that were endlessly roaming the hinterland of Málaga to put an end to the insurrection, of the manner in which Ballesteros was building up his forces unchecked at Algeciras, and of the damage the endless fighting was having on the countryside's ability to support the costs of French occupation. And on the other, there is what looks like an ever greater tendency to clutch at straws, the submission of a handful of insurgents here or the heroism of a small French post there being given the sort of attention worthy of major news items.[63] Yet the futile marching and countermarching continued without let up. To return to the military situation, Soult had decided that the next object of the campaign ought to be the capture of Tarifa and the defeat of Ballesteros. To this end, 8,000 men were scraped together from various sources, placed under the command of General Godinot, and pushed forward into the territory held by Ballesteros. Yet this operation proved utterly fruitless, for the Spanish commander simply retired beneath the guns of Gibraltar and took up so strong a position that the French did not dare attack him. Desperate to salvage something from the situation, Godinot sent some troops to reconnoiter Tarifa, but this force only reached the vicinity of the town with great difficulty—among other things suffering a guerrilla attack that cost it almost all the 300 head of cattle that it had brought along as food—and then discovered that, while certainly not perfect, the defenses were far too strong for them simply to be rushed. In short, the whole operation had proved utterly pointless, while it had been achieved at the cost of weakening the French elsewhere and thereby exposing them to fresh attacks. In the end, the *quietus* was given to the enterprise by Marshal Soult, who alarmed, among other things, that the British might be planning a fresh attack on Badajoz, sent word that the troops concerned should pull back immediately unless they could definitely obtain hold of Tarifa and Algeciras, though it is probable that shortage of food would very soon have forced them to retreat anyway. Had they been able to hang on a few days more, it is just possible that they might have obtained some result, for Ballesteros was very short of both food and water and might therefore have been forced either to risk a defeat by coming out fighting or to take ship for Cádiz, but as it was, the whole campaign had been a disaster, and all the more so as it had been accompanied by the usual scenes of disorder. Among Godinot's troops was the pharmacist Sébastian Blaze, who had been pressed into service as part of a scratch squadron of cavalry composed entirely of supernumerary officers left over from the great prisoner-of-war escapes of May 1810. It should be noted, however, that his account was marked by a considerable degree of special pleading.

> At midday on 14 October, the division arrived before San Roque. . . . Ballesteros having taken shelter beneath the walls of Gibraltar, the town was only held by a small party of cavalry that had been left behind to protect the retreat of his army. Moreover, these horsemen soon gave way before us: there was, then, no more than a brief skirmish at the gates of the town. . . . A number of women and old people were found to have shut themselves up in the church: they were invited to return to their homes, and the latter were respected. Yet otherwise the town was all but deserted, and General Godinot could not prevent the houses of those inhabitants who had fled from being

> pillaged: the soldiers broke down the doors to look for food and fodder and, while searching for these commodities, seized whatever took their fancy, in which respect be it said that these gentlemen are not fussy. If the inhabitants of San Roque had stayed in their homes, the majority of the houses would not have been sacked, burned down, or knocked to pieces in the manner that actually occurred, but eager to increase the inhabitants' hatred of the French, Ballesteros had forced them to follow him in order to ensure that the town was pillaged.[64]

Returning to Seville, the unfortunate Godinot was subjected to such a tirade of abuse by a frustrated Soult that, as we have seen, he shot himself. The effect of the expedition to Tarifa, meanwhile, was uniformly negative. On the one hand, relations between Soult and Victor became still more strained—in brief, the former felt that the latter had not done enough to support the expedition, while the latter felt that too much of a strain had been placed on his resources—while on the other, the guerrillas had been able to overrun the whole district between Málaga and Yunquera; indeed, the troops who had been pulled out of western Málaga to take part in the expedition literally had to fight their way back to the capital. Once they were back, however, the position soon stabilized itself, Maransin being able drive back the insurgents from the vicinity of the city, while troops sent from the frontier of Murcía by General Leval reduced the pressure in the eastern part of the province. On one level, then, all was much as it had been before, and yet the episode had badly shaken the whole edifice of French occupation: much grumbling and a general lack of enthusiasm notwithstanding, hitherto Málaga had paid its contributions more or less on time, while the authorities had cooperated with the French well enough, but now there was a growing sense that the power of the occupation forces was distinctly limited and that they might therefore be defied, if not with impunity, then with at least some chance of success.[65] Among the French, by contrast, there was a growing sense of despair, and this was now reinforced by the receipt of dire news from Extremadura. In brief, discovering that General Girard had marched on Caceres with the bulk of the troops that had been detached from V Corps to hold Extremadura and was completely out of touch with any other French forces, on 28 October the commander of the Anglo-Portuguese forces that had been left to watch the Portuguese frontier, Sir Rowland Hill, pounced on him at the town of Arroyomolinos de Montánchez, the result being a disaster that cost Girard more than 2,000 casualties.[66]

To say that Soult reacted with shock and anger to the news of Arroyomolinos is an understatement: "The event . . . is so extraordinary and humiliating that I know neither how to explain it nor how to describe it. . . . I am full of shame. . . . I am not very hopeful that General Girard will return to us: it is said that he has been killed or gravely wounded. But if he does get back, I will have him stripped of his command and brought before a court-martial."[67] If this was so, it was entirely understandable, while news of the reverse was soon after followed by another unwelcome development. As if it was not bad enough that the two regiments that had been most badly hit at Arroyomolinos were marched off to be recruited back up to strength in France and Soult instructed to send two fresh regiments up from Andalucía in their place, in January 1812 fresh orders were received from Paris: in brief, with war looming in the east, Napoleon had decided to draw on the considerable reservoir of forces that he possessed in Spain, the Army of the South's share of the cull amounting to the four regiments—three of line infantry and one of lancers—belonging to the Grand Duchy of Warsaw that had come to Andalucía as part of Sébastiani's IV Corps in 1810. The 6,000 troops that these units amounted to did not represent as great a loss as that suffered by some of the other French commanders in Spain—Dorsenne's Army of the North lost as many as 14,000 men—but even so they were all veteran soldiers, and their loss was to be much felt.[68] Far away in France, however, Napoleon simply would not accept the fact that Soult did not have enough men to hold down Andalucía. Typical enough was his reaction to the news of Arroyomolinos:

> You will convey to the Duke of Dalmatia my discontent at the flank march that General Girard embarked upon in the face of the enemy. . . . This should have been protected by a strong detachment. It is unfortunate that, with an army of 80,000 men, dispositions of a sort that might have prevented an affront at

> the hands of a mere 6,000 British troops were not made—dispositions, moreover, that ordinary prudence alone should have been sufficient to dictate. Tell him that I remain very firm in my opinion: whenever battle is given, and all the more so against the British, one should never divide one's forces. That being the case, he should unite his forces and confront the enemy with imposing masses, and all the more so as any troops who are left in their garrisons run the risk of being beaten in detail or forced to abandon their posts.[69]

How Soult felt on receiving these words of wisdom is best left to the imagination, the fact being that they demonstrate an utter want of understanding on the part of the emperor. Meanwhile, matters were further complicated by the fact that the Army of the South had just embarked on fresh offensive operations. In brief, insult having been added to injury by a surprise raid that Ballesteros had launched on the garrison of Bornos, Soult had resolved to attack Tarifa, a target that was particularly attractive on account of the fact, first, that its garrison included a brigade of British troops led by a Colonel Skerret, which had of late shown signs of taking an active part in Ballesteros's operations, and, second, that its capture would open up close links with the Moorish coast and, with them, access to the large stocks of wheat with which that state had traditionally exported to Spain and Portugal.[70] This time, however, it was to be no mere reconnaissance in force. On the contrary, some 8,000 men were got together from various sources in Córdoba and Granada and another 7,000 from the lines in front of Cádiz, the latter also supplying the expeditionary force with a small train of artillery; in command, meanwhile, was Marshal Victor. Recognizing that he could do little to stop such an onslaught, Ballesteros once again retreated under the guns of Gibraltar, and though much delayed by torrential rains that turned the coastal plains into a swamp, by 20 December the French had closed in on the town. What followed, however, was a fiasco. Protected only by weak medieval walls that were wide open to bombardment and provided with relatively few cannon, Tarifa should have fallen with the greatest ease, but heavy rain continued to delay operations. Not until 29 December, then, were the French guns ready to open fire on the town, but when they did, they proved more than sufficient for the task: within a few hours a wide breach had been blown in the northern walls and the defenders' artillery almost entirely silenced. So overawed was Skerret at these events that he proposed evacuating the town and falling back to a small hummock that rose out of the waters of the Mediterranean just off the coast (connected to the mainland by a narrow causeway and ringed by several newly built batteries, this had been converted into a makeshift citadel). Fortunately, however, a council of war attended by all the senior officers of the garrison vetoed this plan, and instead, every effort was made to prepare for an assault. After a night of torrential rain that caused both sides much misery and, crucially, caused the French to postpone any action until full daylight, on the morning of 31 December, this duly came in the form of two columns of grenadiers and *voltigeurs* who hurled themselves at the walls with great courage, only to encounter a hail of musketry that cut down many men before they had advanced more than a few yards. As a result, not a single man penetrated the breach, French losses by the end of the day amounting to at least 400 soldiers. With morale among his troops as low as it could get, Victor tried to continue the siege for a few days more, but his trenches were flooded by continued heavy rain, while food began to run out on account of the fact that all the roads that the French had used in their approach to the town had been blocked by flooding. As dark fell on 4 January 1812, then, the invaders abandoned their lines and fell back northward, having been first forced to abandon almost all their heavy guns, the ground now so waterlogged that it was impossible to move them.[71]

If the campaign of October 1811 had shaken the French grip on Andalucía, the failure before Tarifa was well-nigh catastrophic. As Soult wrote, "I cannot deplore this reverse enough, not just because of the losses that it has occasioned us but also because of the consequences that will stem from it."[72] Though the human cost—no more than 500 dead and an indeterminate number of sick and wounded—had not been very great, the troops who had taken part in the siege were exhausted and demoralized, Oman describing them as being "so tired out and war worn that for several weeks they continued to fill the hospitals . . . with sick, and were incapable of further active service."[73] Needless to say, the blow to French prestige was also enormous. Around Málaga, in particular, such was the upsurge of disorder to which the defeat gave rise that Maransin's flying columns were hard put to maintain any sort of order, while the governor's problems were quickly worsened by the fact that, no sooner had the French retreated from Tarifa, than Ballesteros once more advanced into the interior. Early in February, then, he occupied the town of Coín with some 5,000 men. All that Maransin had to oppose him in the first instance was 1,500 troops, of whom a number were unreliable Spanish *juramentados* and irregulars. Another force was coming up on Ballesteros's left flank commanded by General Rey, and it would clearly have been better to await its arrival. Maransin, however, was nothing if not a fiery figure, and on 16 February he foolishly accepted battle on his own at Cartama. Hardly surprisingly, the result was disaster: furiously assailed by Ballesteros's men, the French initially put up a good fight, but then Maransin was wounded leading a counter-attack, the result being a panic that soon had his entire force fleeing in rout. Discovering Rey's approaching troops in the moment of victory, Ballesteros hastily retreated in his turn, so that in the end little damage was done—as the Spaniards had demonstrably lost more men in the battle as well as a number of prisoners in the subsequent retreat, the French were even able to claim a victory—but it was now clear that even in the field, the invaders could no longer expect to worst the Spaniards on every occasion.[74]

No thanks to Maransin, then, that French had got off lightly at Cartama. That said, coming as it did in the wake of the disquieting news that Wellington's forces had stormed the border fortress of Ciudad Rodrigo, the victory had a powerful moral effect on the cause of collaboration in Málaga. As in every other city in Andalucía, the official press had continued to be relentless in its proclamation of victory, and the sight of panic-stricken fugitives streaming into the city therefore came as a grave shock. To quote the doctor, Mendoza:

> After a little while, large numbers of wounded and stragglers began to arrive. The enemy were seized by blind panic. Utterly bewildered, they did not know what to do. . . . Fearing that the

> Spaniards might appear before the walls, the hundred-odd troops who were in the town took up positions overlooking the banks of the Guadalmedina. . . . Meanwhile, the supporters of the French took refuge in the castle or hid themselves. . . . As for . . . the crews of the corsairs, they embarked on their ships with all their belongings. All this was executed with such haste and confusion that the large crowds that had come out to watch the humiliation of the French fell into a panic and shut the gates, running about the streets to such an extent that the whole town was soon in an uproar.[75]

These events are worthy of further consideration. Once the confusion had subsided, the French tried to punish Málaga for its supposed rebellion, claiming among other things that women had been seen sharpening knives on the sills of their front doors. But the town council succeeded in persuading them that there had been no rebellion and that the crowds had simply been running in panic.[76] What we see, then, is a situation in which it appears that, although the occupying forces were clearly thoroughly disliked, there was also great fear of the likely consequences of liberation: far from flinging open the gates to the *serranos,* the townsfolk rather slammed them in their faces. That said, Cartama clearly came as a moment of truth for many *afrancesados.* Not only was the military threat to their position much greater, but it had also suddenly become much grimmer. While the fate of those who fell into the hands of the bands could sometimes be terrible, the Patriot regulars had until now generally spared their opponents. In the wake of Cartama, however, Ballesteros suddenly changed the rules of the game. In brief, finding that his prisoners included a dozen members of the *josefino* line-infantry regiment stationed in Málaga, the general had them all executed. The French responded in kind—when thirteen of Ballesteros's soldiers were captured in a skirmish at Alozaina a few days later, they were executed in turn—but among the *juramentados* there was general consternation: "The Málaga regiment has been very badly shaken by the news of the treatment that was meted out to the prisoners who had fallen into Ballesteros's power. Ill will has seized upon this episode as a means of perverting the spirit of the soldiers and . . .

inciting them to desert. A glorious death and, after that, paradise: such are the rewards that are held to fall to the soldiers of Ballesteros. For those men who remain loyal to His Catholic Majesty [King Joseph], there will be nothing but ignominy and hellfire."[77]

Needless to say, the response of many *juramentados* to this situation was to try to escape while the going was good, but such was the manpower situation that Maransin could not spare the services even of a few turncoats, the departure of IV Corps's Polish division for Russia having come as a particularly grievous blow. Beyond the walls of Málaga, then, the invaders were only able to maintain permanent posts at Alhaurín and El Burgo. However, as the French presence in the countryside dwindled away, so the starving saw less and less reason not to turn to banditry or flock to the cause of insurrection. Politically, meanwhile, loyalty to Joseph Bonaparte simply ceased to be an option, for the French could no longer protect such groups as members of the Guardia Cívica. The result was inevitable: in brief the disorder snowballed. The three punitive columns operating with Málaga as their base continued to ravage the countryside, even scoring the odd success, but they could not be everywhere at once, while so many of the populace had now taken up arms that, being quite small. For a case in point, we can cite the experiences of the force commanded by Major Chaillot. Composed of 150 infantry, twenty dragoons, and thirty-five Spanish irregulars, on 5 March this was routed with substantial losses at Arenas by a force of 1,000 Spaniards, including 250 regular troops who had been landed by sea with orders to stir up rebellion.[78]

Quite clearly, then, the hinterland of Málaga was slipping ever further from the French grasp. As Maransin admitted: "At two o'clock in the afternoon of 1 March, one of my servants led my two saddle horses out of the city to give them some exercise. Within a quarter of an hour of him passing the Vélez gate, five robbers surrounded him and seized the two horses. Carried away as a prisoner, the man was then murdered in a ravine on the far side of the Gibralfaro fortress. . . . The spirit of insurrection is manifesting itself on all sides, while a number of well-organized conspiracies are only awaiting the arrival of Ballesteros's troops to burst forth. . . . Momentarily extinguished, the fire . . . is on the point of flaring up once more."[79] Losing control of the countryside was not something the French could afford, however. As we have seen, the harvest of 1811 had been very bad, the result being that the situation in Málaga was already extremely difficult. As the French consul in the city reported to Napoleon's minister of marine, Admiral Decrès:

> The bands of brigands who have emerged in the eastern part of the province and are infesting the roads that lead to Granada and [Almería] are multiplying by the day, the few troops that we have being insufficient to pursue them into the mountains, where they have a sure refuge. . . . It is rumored that the garrisons stationed at Motril and Almería are to be withdrawn to Granada, while every day we expect to hear that Almería has also been evacuated. . . . If the eastern coast . . . really is abandoned in this fashion, it will give every facility to smugglers to bring in all sorts of merchandise prohibited by imperial decree and at the same time to export much in the way of both foodstuffs and revenue. Yet things are bad enough as they are. . . . The greater part of the shops are shut for want of custom, while misery is already at the zenith. A considerable number of unfortunates have arrived from villages in the interior, and more than 6,000 strong, they throng the streets and squares, while the deplorable state to which they have been reduced is such as to excite horror and compassion. A *fanega* of wheat now costs anything from 200 to 360 *reales* instead of 90. . . . The terrible situation of the province is in consequence the chief subject of the public's attention at the present time. Over the last few days, indeed, groups of people have frequently been seen discussing the famine, though it has to be said that they have not as yet given rise to any cause for suspicion.[80]

At this precise moment, however, fresh disaster struck the French cause. To return to a point made earlier, one of the briefs that Maransin had brought with him to his new command was to reinforce French naval power in the Strait of Gibraltar. At the time of his arrival in Málaga, this had been absolutely minimal—in a year and a half of occupation, the French had managed to equip no more than a single gunboat, named the *Sébastiani,* together with a small number of privateers that had been commissioned under the aegis of one José, a Genovese who prior to 1810 had been a merchant in Gibraltar but had now come over to the French[81]—and shortage of money had ensured that Maransin had not been able to make much progress. However, men, at least, were not in short supply—on the contrary, Málaga contained considerable numbers of Croat, Italian, Maltese, and Gibraltarian mariners who the collapse in trade since 1810 had consigned to a state of the utmost misery—and Maransin therefore managed to get a further seven vessels ready for sea. Soult's navy, then, was never very great, but it was yet sufficient to ensure that a number of shiploads of Moroccan wheat were brought safely into the harbor, this doing at least a little to take the edge off the subsistence crisis. Also helpful, meanwhile, were various cargos of food that were found on board several British and Moroccan vessels that were captured en route for Sicily and other destinations. On the night of 29 April 1812, however, even this small succor was taken away. Thus, in a daring commando-style operation, a small British squadron consisting of two sloops, a brig, and a gun-brig commanded by Captain Thomas Usher sailed into the port and disembarked a number of landing parties, which proceeded to wreck some of the defenses and cut out several vessels as prizes. Though taken by surprise, the garrison fought back hard—British casualties amounted to fifteen dead and fifty-three wounded—but their best efforts could not disguise the extent of the catastrophe, nor still less, alter the fact that henceforth Málaga was kept under close blockade, the result being that Moroccan wheat came there no more.[82]

With the French hold on Málaga clearly crumbling, a determined effort on the part of Ballesteros might have achieved dramatic results. Fortunately, however, the aftermath of Cartama saw that commander distracted by a series of festivities, and it was not until the end of March that he took the field once more. Even then he did not march on Málaga, choosing instead to threaten Seville, in which respect he was supported by a further force of 4,000 men that had appeared in the Condado de Niebla in the shape of the Fifth Army, this having just been ordered south from Extremadura. The march on Seville was well timed: having heard that Badajoz was in danger from Wellington, Soult had just marched north with his reserve, leaving the city guarded by a mere 800 invalids and civic guards. This being the case, Ballesteros, who by 5 April had got as far as Utrera, might easily have taken the city, and all the more so as the troops that arrived from Extremadura were bearing down upon it from the west, but at the last moment he hesitated, giving Soult just time enough to retrace his steps and bring his men back to protect his capital. By then the commander of the Fourth Army was well away—receiving an entirely false report that the French troops stationed between Seville and Cádiz were about to fall upon him, Ballesteros had immediately set off for safety and within two days had covered some sixty miles, his only aggressive action being to send a detachment of troops to attack the garrison of Osuna.[83] This led to a minor defeat: while some soldiers found refuge in the tower of the cathedral, the bulk of the garrison retreated into the citadel that had been prepared for such eventualities and repelled every attempt to dislodge them, the Spaniards eventually being driven away by the timely arrival of a relief column headed by Marshal Soult himself. However, having regrouped his men at Setenil, the Spaniard then hit back by launching a surprise attack on a small French force that had occupied Alora under General Rey, who first proceeded to retreat posthaste to the outskirts of Málaga and then, without informing Maransin, suddenly made off for Antequera in the dead of night. Much alarmed at this betrayal, Maransin barricaded himself into the castle with such few troops as he had in the city—a mere 300 men—but he need not have worried, for Ballesteros was once more falling back, having heard that Soult was about to fall upon his rear. For a short while it looked as if he might make a stand in the area of Alozaina and Yunquera, but when the French showed signs of closing in on him from several sides at once, he immediately retired on Algeciras.[84]

This mini-campaign is difficult to evaluate insofar as what it says about Ballesteros himself—was he a master of strategy or simply a braggart whose only idea was to avoid defeat?—but insofar as the situation as a whole was concerned, it had served well enough: though short of many stragglers, Ballesteros's army was still intact, while Soult had been called back from marching to relieve Badajoz (not that he could have done very much even had he done so). Mention of Badajoz, meanwhile, compels us to turn aside from Málaga to look at the wider war. As we have seen, in the autumn of 1811, Wellington had transferred his attention from Extremadura to León, and on 19 January 1812, his efforts had been rewarded by the capture of Ciudad Rodrigo. Given his intention of launching a full-scale invasion of Spain, his next target had to be Badajoz, and by mid-March the fortress had been invested by the bulk of his forces. Insofar as meeting this threat was concerned, Soult was in a slightly better position than before in that Victor had been called back to France to take part in the invasion of Russia, this not only removing a serious threat to the marshal's authority but also allowing him to abolish the old corps structure and give the Army of the South a less cumbersome organization (in brief, six infantry divisions and three cavalry divisions, the commanders of which all reported to the marshal himself).[85] However, if Soult could now dispose of his troops pretty much as he wished, nothing could alter the fact that he still did not have enough of them. Hearing that Badajoz was under threat, he had, by the usual process of stripping his garrisons in Andalucía to the bone, been able to put together a field force of 13,000 men. To these could be added the 12,000 men who had hitherto been holding southern Extremadura, but Wellington had massed no fewer than 55,000 men against Badajoz: on his own, then, Soult was helpless. To achieve anything, he would therefore once again require the assistance of the Army of Portugal, and he had, in fact, marched north in the expectation that Marmont would once again come south from León. Unlike in 1811, however, this help did not appear: Napoleon having sent Marmont orders that he should respond to any British move on Badajoz by invading northern Portugal as a diversion, no troops appeared from the direction of the Tagus. Still worse, knowing full well that Marmont had no siege train nor, still less, the wherewithal to maintain himself for long in the empty wastes of Beira, Wellington simply ignored his movements and concentrated on besieging Badajoz, which was finally stormed with great loss of life on 6 April 1812.[86]

The loss of Badajoz was entirely predictable. As Soult had written to Berthier on 15 March: "I cannot preserve both Andalucía and Extremadura by myself. . . . I must have reinforcements. . . . Unless the emperor puts 25,000 fresh troops at my disposal, I foresee nothing but misfortunes of a sort from which it will be very difficult to recover."[87] In the short term, however, it had little effect on his situation. Far from embarking on an invasion of Andalucía that would necessarily have swept all before it, Wellington rather resolved on the alternative course of an advance in León and therefore withdrew the bulk of his forces from Extremadura. Though now almost certainly doomed, French rule therefore lasted for a few months longer. That said, the situation was no quieter than it had ever been. Away from the major cities and the lowlands of the Guadalquivir valley, the irregulars were as a great a problem as ever, while Ballesteros was merely biding his time to make another bid for glory. Having regrouped his forces at Algeciras, in late May he struck again, marching northward to attack the French-held town of Bornos in accordance with orders that he had received to effect a diversion in favor of Wellington's forthcoming offensive in León. The result was the Battle of Bornos. Fought on 1 June 1812, this was the biggest single clash between the French and the Spaniards in the whole of the struggle in Andalucía, pitting as it did 4,500 Frenchmen—the bulk of the division of General Conroux—against perhaps 9,000 Spaniards. Having marched his command no fewer than sixty miles in just two days, he crossed the River Guadalete and, protected by a thick fog, launched a dawn attack on the entrenchments that protected the French camp. Instead of just maintaining a passive defense, Conroux hurled his troops directly at the Spanish center. This maneuver caught Ballesteros completely by surprise—he had spread his men out in a thin cordon in an attempt to envelop the enemy—while his troops were in any case extremely tired, and the result was that the Spaniards broke and ran. An eyewitness was the recently arrived Hippolyte d'Espinchal: "The Ninth Light and the Ninety-Sixth Line sallied out from their positions and fell on the enemy with great courage and resolution. Well aware that they had to win the fight, they swept aside the Spaniards, who until then had been fighting well but could not resist so terrible an onset. Despite their great superiority in numbers, they were therefore . . . pursued from ridge to ridge as far as the river. Not allowed a moment's respite, . . . many drowned in the water, while the rest only got away in the greatest disorder."[88]

Bornos was beyond doubt a serious reverse for Ballesteros. According to Soult, the Spanish commander lost four guns, 1,500 muskets, three standards, 600 prisoners, and 1,100 dead and wounded on the battlefield alone, together with many other men who were drowned trying to escape across the River Guadalete; furthermore, after the battle "deserters came in entire bands."[89] This was possibly something of an exaggeration—the fact that French loss came to at least 400 suggests that the battle was less one sided than Soult's figures suggest—but even so, for a few weeks Ballesteros was out of the fight. Yet this did not mean that the invaders were free to carry on the struggle against the insurgents. Even now there was evidence that this was not a lost cause. Thus, on 31 May Maransin had reported that on 26 May a band headed by one Roda that had appeared at Molina had been put to flight by the inhabitants and, further, that four days later the proprietors of Almogía had banded together to apprehend a small gang of brigands who were operating in the area.[90] Two weeks later there was more good news: not only were the proprietors of the areas organizing private security forces to safeguard their interests, but many muleteers were also asking for arms so that they could defend their cargos as they traveled from one place to another.[91] The trouble was that, as ever, the French were not in a position to exploit such incipient war weariness. At the very moment that Ballesteros was falling back from Bornos, the Extremaduran front flared up once more. In accordance with prearranged plans to prevent the French from concentrating their forces against Wellington's forthcoming offensive in León, the Anglo-Portuguese forces that had been left to watch over Badajoz under Sir Rowland Hill pushed forward southeastward toward the frontiers of Extremadura. Soult being concerned to avoid another Arroyomolinos de Montánchez, the whole of his disposable reserve—the infantry division of Pierre Barrois and the cavalry division headed by the marshal's brother, Pierre—were soon marching north to join the two infantry divisions that had hitherto been observing Hill from the safety of southern Extremadura. Placed under the command of Drouet, for the next few weeks the resultant task force was tied down in a series of complicated operations that saw it first advance as far as Albuera and then retire almost to the Sierra Morena, the result being, of course, that in Andalucía Soult was left without the slightest ability to pursue any advantage that he might have derived from Bornos.

The result of this situation was all too foreseeable. Little more than a month after Bornos, Ballesteros was back in the field once more. Eager to make up for his defeat, the Spaniard now resolved to launch a raid on Málaga. Having received considerable reinforcements from Cádiz, he had some 18,000 men at Algeciras, but such were the supply difficulties posed by operations in the interior that less than half of these could be utilized in field operations. It was, then, only with 9,000 men that on 2 July he marched out of Algeciras and took the road for Málaga. In an attempt to keep his advance hidden from the French, he marched only by night and in this fashion reached Coín on 8 July. The garrison was easily driven out, but the enemy commander responsible for the district, General Leval, had guessed that Ballesteros might try something of the sort and had therefore concentrated as many troops as he could at Málaga, waiting there for him with a force of six and a half battalions of infantry, five squadrons of cavalry, and twelve guns. In fact, this was not such a large force—Leval had only 3,500 men—but Cartama and Bornos suggested that the French had at the very least a fighting chance of victory, and it was therefore just as well for Ballesteros that, with battle imminent, Leval suddenly decamped with all his troops, having received an urgent summons from Soult to join him at Seville, apparently because the marshal had heard rumors that Wellington was about to descend on him with all his troops. In the event, Leval only got as far as Antequera before a fresh dispatch arrived from Soult to the effect that all was well and that his services were not wanted after all, but in the meantime Málaga had been completely uncovered and Maransin left with no option but to retire into the castle with the 400 men left to him. With Leval out of the way, Ballesteros was exaltant. "Frenchmen," he proclaimed, "For five years you have been shedding your blood to secure the crown [of Spain] for the brother of the monster who . . . has dragged you from your homes to die far from everything that you love. . . . Fly, then, . . . to abandon these eagles that . . . have converted you into instruments of tyranny. . . . Your fate is no longer in doubt: either perish loaded down with the execrations of all men of good will, or adopt the sentiments of those who know how to conquer or die for the cause of independence." Having duly softened up the defenders, on 14 July the general entered Málaga with all his men, and immediately set about both imposing a contribution of 400,000 *reales* and stripping the city of all its supplies of food. So far, so good, but in the process Ballesteros's troops got out of hand and began to sack the houses of all the wealthier inhabitants, in which activity they were joined by elements of the lower classes. With the growing chaos fully visible from the castle, Maransin decided on a most daring move. Profiting from the general disorder, the bulk of the castle's defenders suddenly sallied out into the city in two columns and drove all before them. At length the startled Spaniards rallied and forced the French to fall back once more, but Ballesteros had been much shaken, and that same night he retreated to Coín, the only fruit of his venture having been a few wagons of grain. Still worse, meanwhile, while he had been away, Soult, who coincidently had come down to Victor's headquarters at Puerto de Santa María, had dispatched the division of General Villatte to occupy Algeciras, the garrison of which had slipped away without a fight and taken refuge at Gibraltar.[92]

Hearing of this disaster, Ballesteros took refuge at Yunquera. Yet though there were now French forces virtually on all sides—in addition to Villatte's division, Leval was marching on him from Granada at the head of 3,000 men—he realized that his only hope was to keep moving and, further, that it was necessary to boost the morale of his men, who were, it seems, increasingly dissatisfied with his leadership. In consequence, in yet another rapid night march, the general led his troops to Osuna, where having forced the garrison to take refuge in a fort outside the town, he gave his men permission to sack the houses of the French and their supporters, imposed another contribution, and as at Málaga, ordered such foodstuffs as could be found to be removed from the town.

All this having been achieved without hindrance from the French, the next night he marched for Casares, where he received word that a division commanded by Murgeon was about to land at Algeciras. This force duly disembarked near the town on 2 August, whereupon Villatte hastily fell back to the northwest. In the event, Murgeon's men were quickly withdrawn once more, but their intervention nonetheless sufficed to allow Ballesteros to get his troops together again—now some 20,000 all told—and recover control of his old territorial base.[93]

What might have happened next is open to debate. In theory, a field army of 20,000 Spanish regulars of the sort now commanded by Ballesteros ought to have been able to pose serious problems for Soult, for its defeat would have required the services of at least three of the marshal's nine divisions. However, there is some doubt as to whether so large a force could ever have taken the field, while Ballesteros himself was clearly at his happiest playing the role of a mere divisional commander. In the event, however, circumstances outside Andalucía now intervened in such a manner as to ensure that the experiment was never put to the test. In brief, all the campaigning of the period June–July 1812 had taken place against a background of Wellington's invasion of León. Commencing on 13 June, this culminated in a general action at Salamanca on 22 July. Sometimes known as "Wellington's masterpiece," this affair was certainly one of the greatest victories of his career. Fighting without the support of any of the other French armies in Spain, Marmont had initially surpassed himself, outmaneuvering Wellington and forcing him to retire from the Duero to the Tormes. Having reached the latter river, however, the commander of the Army of Portugal overreached himself and opened the way to a massive counterstroke that, by the end of the day, had cost him as many as 14,000 casualties. With the remnants of Marmont's forces fleeing in the direction of Burgos, this was a blow that the French could not recover from with any ease. Thus, King Joseph hung on for a little while in Madrid at the head of the Army of the Center, but the latter was composed of no more than 15,000 men, and, as soon as he heard that Wellington had decided to follow up his victory at Salamanca by marching on Madrid, he ordered the evacuation of the capital and headed eastward for Valencia.

Events of this magnitude, of course, could not pass unnoticed in Andalucía. From as early as late May, Joseph had been bombarding Soult with letters demanding that he send at least a part of his forces to join the Army of the Center, but these orders had been completely ignored on the pretexts, first, that Wellington was in reality marching not on Salamanca but Seville and, second, that the Army of the South was already doing all that it could in containing Hill. As Joseph got more pressing, meanwhile, Soult responded with a completely fresh plan of campaign: in brief, the king should evacuate Madrid and join him in Andalucía, this being the only region, Soult insisted, in which the French could subsist a large army for any length of time.[94] Though much excoriated by observers such as Oman, this was not perhaps quite so visionary a plan as has often been claimed: Wellington would have been forced to march into Andalucía and thereby be distracted from exploiting his success in other directions, while left with little option but to seek a pitched battle with the combined forces of Soult and Joseph, he might even have been vanquished. That said, it was at the very least a very risky scheme—the consequences of a serious defeat could have been scarcely less than a second Bailén—while to have had any hope of success, it would have entailed giving up the whole of Andalucía. To speculate on such matters is useless, however, King Joseph killing the plan stone dead by his decision to retire on Valencia rather than Andalucía.[95]

Hearing of this decision, even Soult had to recognize that the game was finally up: after two and a half years of struggle, Andalucía would finally have to be abandoned. Despite one last protest to Joseph, in which he pointed out that surrendering southern Spain almost certainly meant saying goodbye to it for good, on 12 August—the same day that Wellington finally entered Madrid—Soult ordered the Army of the South to abandon its positions and concentrate on Seville and Granada prior to evacuating the region. To the end, however, Soult remained defiant, as witness, for example, the order of the day in which the news was announced to the army:

> The army must make ready to go on campaign. The commanders of each unit must immediately distribute to the troops such

> clothing and footwear as they may be lacking and assure themselves that they have all that they need. Those regiments that lack sufficient shoes for each man to have a spare pair in his pack or that are in need of any other effects . . . will requisition what they need from the countryside. . . . Each regiment will also conduct a most stringent review to establish the needs of the soldiers and at the same time get rid of any frivolous objects that they might have so as to reduce the amount they have to carry on the march. . . . All drummers, musicians, domestic servants, and camp followers should be issued with as many muskets, carbines, or pistols as the stores of ordnance will permit. . . . All officers and members of the civil administration of whatever rank who have soldier-servants must immediately return them to their units on pain of severe punishment. . . . Each regiment is also to ensure that its baggage is reduced to what is strictly necessary: anything more than this . . . just gets in the way, while it is better to get rid of things before the campaign starts than to be forced to abandon them after first having dragged them along for a while. And in no case is any regiment to have more than three wagons or to fail to attach their wagons to the baggage train.[96]

Meanwhile, 15 August being the saint's day of Napoleon himself, the day was celebrated with as much pomp and splendor as ever. To quote Fée: "The marshal bade farewell to the inhabitants of Seville with a splendid banquet and a magnificent ball. . . . All the powder that was going to have to be abandoned was used up in fireworks and the quantity was prodigious. There was music, dancing, games, illuminations, everything, indeed, that could be wished for."[97]

This last show, however, was very much the swan song of Napoleonic rule in Andalucía. Over the next few days, garrison after garrison said goodbye to many of its Spanish womenfolk, blew up its defenses, and destroyed such stores and guns as it could not carry with it. As can be imagined, the scenes around the bay of Cádiz were particularly dramatic, the miles of hutments making for enormous conflagrations that were observed with awe from the defenses. What, though, had brought down Soult's rule? As this chapter has revealed, the palm here must first go to the Spanish regular army. Despite, first, the appalling defeats of January 1810, second, the qualitative superiority of the occupying forces, third, crippling logistical problems that ensured that many Spanish soldiers continually went both barefoot and hungry, and fourth, leadership that was frequently barely competent, thousands of officers and men not only stuck to their guns but repeatedly carried the war to the enemy, who were in consequence never able to concentrate their full strength against the bands of brigands and insurgents who sprang to such violent life in the shelter of such areas as the Serranía de Ronda. This is not to say that the many bands of armed civilians made no contribution to the French defeat. On the contrary, time and again their depredations forced the French to turn back from the pursuit of La Romana, Blake, or Ballesteros. That said, however, they could not have held out for long on their own, while as we have seen, they inflicted far less damage on the French than did their regular fellows. In the end, then, the much derided regular army was at the heart of the survival of the Patriot cause in Andalucía. Yet dedicated though it was, this force was aided by other factors. In the first place, we have the accidents of geography: Andalucía's long coastline and many mountains, not to mention the near impregnable fastness constituted by the Isla de Leon, all rendered the task of the invaders very difficult. And, in the second, was British aid: it was British control of the sea that allowed Spanish expeditionary forces to land at such scattered points as Ayamonte and Tarifa, kept Cádiz supplied with food, and cut off the French from Moroccan wheat; it was British arms and uniforms that allowed Spanish soldiers to take the field; and it was largely British soldiers who wrought such havoc on the French cause at Barrosa, Albuera, Badajoz, and finally Salamanca. In Andalucía, as everywhere else, then, even the most dedicated patriotism was not enough.

Conclusion

To return to a train of thought that we discussed in the introduction, if there was ever a part of the Napoleonic imperium that deserves to be labeled as part of the "outer empire," it is Andalucía. Situated at the very frontier of Napoleon's domains, it was only under French control for a relatively short period of time—two and one-half years—and was never in a position to experience the normal functioning of French rule. Indeed, with the exception of the main cities (and not even all of them, Cádiz never falling to the invaders at all), much of the region only experienced French soldiers as a more-or-less transitory presence, albeit one that was frequently as destructive as it was traumatic. Indeed, for all its formal assimilation into the structure of the Bonaparte Kingdom of Spain, Andalucía was not so much a province of the empire as a theater of war: sometimes supported by the Anglo-Portuguese forces stationed in Cádiz, Spanish troops repeatedly penetrated the region and occupied various parts of its territory for months at a time: indeed, places such as Ayamonte and Algeciras saw more of the forces of Patriot Spain than they did those of Napoleon Bonaparte. In short, maybe even "outer empire" is too generous a term: perhaps we should rather be thinking of Andalucía as a species of no-man's-land.

In the face of these considerations, the departure of the forces of Marshal Soult from Andalucía in September 1812 might seem to be a foregone conclusion. Meanwhile, if French failure is held to be certain, it is tempting to argue that the whole occupation was the fruit of nothing more than greed, opportunism, and self-aggrandizement—in short, that Andalucía was invaded in 1810 for no other motive than Joseph Bonaparte's determination to refurbish his tattered authority and satisfy a master whose strategy could be argued to consist of little more than a series of démarches that aimed to do little more than augment the glory of their progenitor, a master who conquered for no other reason than that it was necessary that he should do so. To argue thus is very much to do with the benefit of hindsight, however. In the winter of 1809–10, there was good reason to believe that invading the south of Spain made a great deal of sense. With Andalucía very much the most important bastion of Spanish resistance to Napoleon, there was every reason to hope that its conquest would put an end to *la guerre d'Espagne,* and that this in turn would force the British to evacuate Portugal. Indeed, given the perennial weakness of the succession of Tory administrations that had governed Britain since 1807, there was even some hope that so massive a blow to British intervention in the Iberian Peninsula would precipitate a political crisis that might bring in the Whigs and, with them, the possibility of a compromise peace that would, in effect, amount to a British surrender. And, finally, the fact is that for Napoleon, glory mattered: so damaging were his policies to the interests of the eastern powers that the French army had little option but to keep adding to the battle honors that decorated its standards, in which connection it might be noted that invading Andalucía would finally kill off the humiliation of Bailén.

Add to this the facts, first, that substantial French forces ended 1809 in geographical locations that could not have been more suited to a descent on Seville, second, that the chief Spanish army defending Andalucía had just sustained a shattering defeat at the Battle of Ocaña, and third, that there was clear evidence that the Patriot administration was in a state of utter disarray, and it can hardly be considered surprising that on 19 January 1810, two full corps d'armée and part of a third, not to mention various other units, marched across the Sierra Morena. Nor, alas, is there any reason to be surprised at what followed: outnumbered, badly officered, half-starved, and demoralized, the troops in the path of the torrent broke and ran, leaving the victorious French forces free to fan out across Andalucía and capture town after town without resistance. Only at Cádiz were the invaders frustrated, and then only because the Duque de Alburquerque managed just in time to line the defenses with a force of troops that had escaped the initial disaster. Even then, however, military crisis led directly to political crisis in that the provisional government that had been in control of the fortunes of Patriot Spain was brought down by a revolution inspired by its enemies.

Mercifully for the Patriot cause, the overthrow of the Junta Central led only to the formation of a regime that, if not always very effectual, was absolutely single-minded in its determination to resist the French. Every effort to persuade Cádiz to surrender, then, foundered, while within weeks the Patriot forces had started to hit back. This narrative of defiance is very much a cornerstone of the Spanish national myth, but in the interior of Andalucía, it was mirrored but imperfectly. Thus, if a phenomenon took hold that is commonly assumed to have amounted to guerrilla warfare, for large parts of the population—the propertied classes especially, but also many humbler folk—the arrival of the French came as a welcome relief, and there is no reason to doubt that at least some of the excitement that greeted Joseph Bonaparte when he rode into, first, Córdoba, and then Seville was genuine. To explain why this was so, we have to consider the reality of Patriot Andalucía. According to the Spanish national myth, the great revolt that inaugurated the Peninsular War was above all a popular affair, an affair in which a people numerous and armed had risen spontaneously to restore the Bourbon monarchy in the person of Ferdinand VII and, as some at least would argue, to regain the primitive liberty lost in the course of centuries of despotism.

Refurbished by the patriotic rodomontade of the bicentenary of the events of 1808, this view of events still holds sway in much of the Spanish historiography. Yet empirical research has suggested that it is difficult to sustain this view. There was great popular turmoil in 1808 certainly, but it was not in and of itself focused on Napoleon. What was in the air was rather revolution, or to be more precise, an ever-growing feeling of anger and despair at the misery into which Spain had been plunged by fifteen years of war, epidemic, natural disaster, and economic collapse, these problems being blamed in the popular mind on the royal favorite, Manuel de Godoy. Thanks to the byzantine intrigues of the Spanish court, by the beginning of 1808, popular hopes of a better Spain had become focused on the person of the crown prince, Ferdinand. Brought to the throne by a military coup on 19 March in the so-called *motín de Aranjuez*, Ferdinand was greeted by wild rejoicing that frequently slid over the line into sack and pillage (in the little Andalusian town of San Lucar de Barrameda, for example, a botanical garden that had been established by Godoy was wrecked by a mob). By the same token, then, when news spread that Napoleon had deposed Ferdinand—that the much hoped-for "golden age" with which wishful thinking associated the young monarch had, in effect, been stifled at its very birth—the land was gripped by real fury.

In this fury lies the origin of a Spanish crusade against Napoleon. But what role did anti-French feeling actually play in the disturbances? Here and there, isolated French civilians were murdered certainly, while 2 May 1808 witnessed what at first sight looks like a serious insurrection in the Spanish capital, but to the extent that it existed at all, hatred of France was not based on what the emperor had done in respect of the Spanish monarchy. Rather, if the French were hated, it was because they had, in effect, acted as the protectors of Godoy and stood in the way of the torrent of righteous anger that had looked set to sweep away all those the crowd held to be responsible for their many ills, while the feeling in the streets was further whipped up by small groups of conspirators who regarded the crisis provoked by French intervention—and, more particularly, the events of the Dos de Mayo—as a means of forcing their way into the corridors of power or addressing other sectional agendas. Confronted by this wave of unrest, the established elites had few options, for any attempt at temporizing, let alone opposition, was wont to see them confronted by a lynch mob, and with varying degrees of enthusiasm, they therefore placed themselves at the head of the anti-French movement and, insofar as possible, muzzled the demagogues who had temporarily seized control of the streets (in Seville, for example, it was not long before Nicolas Tap y Núñez found himself under arrest). Having thus secured their position, meanwhile—throughout not just Andalucía, but the whole of Spain, the provincial juntas that had been formed to fill the vacuum resulting from the de facto collapse of the Spanish state were dominated by such dignitaries as bishops, abbots, captains general, and military governors—the established authorities and their clients threw themselves into the task of diverting the fury of the crowd into safer channels. This meant, on the one hand, demonizing the French and, on the other, using military discipline to bring the streets under control while flattering the people with glowing references to their courage and generosity.

It might be thought that war with France was an inherent part of all this, and the traditional version of events certainly assumes that this was so. In reality, however, this was very far from being the case. In May 1808 the vast majority of Spain was free of French troops, while excepting the Dos de Mayo—an affair that was in any case more a mass panic than an insurrection—no risings took place in those areas where enemy forces were actually present. In consequence, rising against the French was not linked in the popular mind with going to war, while the leaders of the insurrection reinforced this misconception by claiming that a mere show of force would be quite enough to settle the matter—that confronted by Spanish heroism, Napoleon would back off in alarm. When the first calls went out for volunteers, then, there was some response from the crowd: not only did soldiering seem to consist solely of mounting guard, parading through the streets, and hounding adherents of Godoy, but the pay on offer was very generous, while May was in general a slack period of the agricultural year and therefore one when large numbers of day laborers were unemployed. That said, one should not go too far in this respect: there is plenty of evidence that some men were pressured into serving by social superiors or simply impressed willy-nilly (one group that was particularly vulnerable here were the crowds of migrant laborers who every year set out from impoverished regions such as Galicia in search of work, while in Badajoz a foreign legion—the so-called Legión de Extranjeros—was organized from the many Portuguese who had come across the frontier for the same reason); at the same time, of course, the very fact that junta after junta had very quickly to introduce the principle of universal conscription is hardly lacking in significance.

From the beginning, then, the idea that the populace was solidly behind a war against France was questionable, and no sooner had it become apparent that the uprising had plunged Spain into a major war, and that military service would mean not just real soldiering but real soldiering in foreign parts (that is, other provinces of Spain), than the gulf between myth and reality became all too apparent. Within a matter of days desertion had become a major problem, while the new levies frequently struggled hard to avoid the imposition of military discipline and in at least one instance murdered the unfortunate general who had been appointed to command them. As for the draft, meanwhile, it was bitterly resisted—there were, for example, a number of anticonscription riots as well as widespread evasion—while from all sides the authorities were showered with appeals for exemption and remonstrances against having been selected. To make matters worse, meanwhile, the new authorities in many cases seem to have shown great partiality in the manner in which they called up the soldiers they needed, the net result being that the chief burden of the struggle fell overwhelmingly on the laboring poor: if conscription had, in principle, been declared to be universal, it cannot but be felt that this was only done in order to offer a sop to the crowd, there being no intention whatsoever to making this provision stick.

In short, the outbreak of war everywhere sharpened social tension in Spain, and as Spain's generals started to suffer defeat after defeat, so popular anger grew accordingly. With the people also under great economic pressure thanks to the exigencies of war and the collapse of commerce, the result was numerous outbreaks of riot that sometimes had strong elements of social protest. As if this was not enough, the intrigues that characterized the politics of the elite only added to the general instability: time and again one faction or another attempted to attain its goals through the aid of an alliance with the streets that all too often ended in murder and mayhem. That said, political intrigue and popular discontent were not the only sources of disorder. While these factors were certainly of importance in the larger towns and cities, in rural areas the problem was the very different one of brigandage. As has already been implied, the response of many Spanish soldiers to the danger and hardship of life in the ranks was desertion, while every defeat tended to leave thousands of fugitives and stragglers scattered broadside over the face of the countryside as *dispersos,* the only practical answer that either of these groups had to staying alive in the short term being to turn to brigandage. Meanwhile, as artisans, peasants, and agricultural laborers became ever more desperate in the face of requisitioning, increased taxation, and economic disaster, so they too took to the hills to seek a living from criminal activity, the final ingredient in this devil's brew being the many young men who ran away from their home villages to avoid conscription.

The internal history of the whole of Patriot Spain is therefore one of great turmoil, but Andalucía suffered particularly badly. Cádiz, Granada, Málaga, and Seville had all witnessed serious disturbances in the course of the uprising, while the autumn and winter of 1808 saw agrarian disorder grip towns such as Carmona and Jérez de la Frontera. Then came the great insurrection in Cádiz in February 1809 and, finally, the insurrection in Seville that brought down the Junta Central as the French moved in at the end of January 1810. On top of all this, meanwhile, the countryside was gripped by a banditry that weighed heavily on rich and poor alike, the authorities being quite unable to do anything about it. With the Junta Central deeply discredited by both the propaganda of its political opponents and the evidence of its utter incapacity, the fact is that by the time the French advanced across the Sierra Morena, Patriot Andalucía was to all intents and purposes a failed state. Hence the almost total lack of popular resistance as the invaders fanned out south and west; hence the cheering crowds that filled the streets of Córdoba and Seville; and hence too the eager manner in which large numbers of the elite suddenly discovered *afrancesado* sympathies the moment that French troops appeared on their doorsteps. Or rather, perhaps, they rediscovered them: the political ideas that underpinned the Napoleonic empire were very far from being alien to much of Spanish educated opinion, and there was therefore little difficulty in moving from one camp to the other.

From a failed state, however, we move to a failed occupation. Whether the French could ever have turned Andalucía into a solid bastion of their empire is a moot point. As witness, first, Joseph Bonaparte's decision to follow up military victory with a triumphal progress round his new domains that positively oozed with affability and benevolence, second, the manner in which his propagandists either took over existing local newspapers or established new ones of their own and proceeded to lambast the Patriot cause and at the same time stress the social and political advantages of the new order, and third, the desperate efforts that were made at the Hispanization of the forces of occupation, on the political level there was no want of understanding of the policies that needed to be implemented were success to be achieved. Also worth noting, meanwhile, is the manner in which the social structure of Andalucía tended to favor the French: whether they were day laborers, peasant farmers, artisans, cattle herders, or even bullfighters, the vast majority of andaluces lived in a situation of such dependence on the tiny handful of *señores* who owned so much of the land that in normal circumstances the elites had a very good chance of backing up whatever political choices they made with at the very least the sullen acquiescence of the populace.

Unfortunately for the hapless Joseph, however, a series of factors stood in the way of achieving the peaceful integration of Andalucía into his kingdom that was his aim. In the first place, of course, there was the impoverished nature of his new domains. Contrary to what the French had been led to believe, Andalucía was not some Garden of Eden in which produce literally sprang from the ground. Instead, much of it was uncultivated waste, while even those areas that were farmed for the most part only produced the most limited of yields. In consequence, supplying the French armies was a constant problem, and given that their faulty assumptions about the geography of their new conquests suggested that the only explanation must be either recalcitrance or laziness, the military commanders responded with a policy of the utmost ruthlessness: suffer though Andalucía might, it would meet the costs of French occupation. Nurtured in this attitude by and an emperor who was ever more contemptuous of Joseph and a military culture of a particularly harmful nature, Soult, Sébastiani, Mortier, and the rest therefore came to adopt a policy that was utterly opposed to that of the king, the latter's authority being weakened still further by the fact that in May 1810 he set out for Madrid, never to return. This is not to say that French policy in

Andalucía was utterly devoid of positive aspects as witness the fact that in Granada and a number of other cities, serious attempts were made to provide employment for the population through a policy of public works and poor relief. Yet, as ever, the road to hell is paved with good intentions: as the cost of these projects were largely born by the city councils involved, the only effect was to increase the burden of occupation still further; meanwhile, of course, such was the ever-deepening poverty that they made little difference to the socioeconomic situation.

The net result of French occupation, then, was everywhere a mixture of trauma and deprivation. With the invading forces forced to live off the country from the earliest days of the campaign, while at the same time engaging in the unlimited pillage and rapine characteristic of Napoleon's soldiery, the result was a series of sporadic acts of resistance that attracted violent reprisals of a sort that could not but exacerbate the general disorder: in brief, even where personal vengeance was not an issue, what was left for villagers whose homes had been destroyed but a life of brigandage? In this manner, never wholly unmixed with fear—in the countryside the populace had often abandoned their homes in the face of invasion—the relief and even anticipation with which the French had, on occasion, been greeted in January 1810 was quickly dissipated, while a number of other factors ensured that hostility and disillusion was quickly turned into something rather more serious. Thus, from the safety of Cádiz, the new regime that had been established in the wake of the fall of the Junta Central sent out a number of agents with the task of whipping up popular resistance to the invaders, while here and there place seekers, adventurers, or genuine patriots emerged who attempted to form guerrilla bands dedicated to harassing the French, the best examples, perhaps, being the army officer Moreno and the struggling tutor in mathematics Ortiz de Zarate.

One should not exaggerate the importance of this phenomenon. In the first place, even the most dedicated of the *partidas* were of little more than nuisance value in military terms; in the second, the mobs of stragglers and armed civilians gathered together by the agents of the Spanish government were easy prey for the occupying forces; and in the third, hatred of the French, though present, was not the only emotion that moved the populace. Thus, it cannot but be suspected that many of those who flocked to join the new captains of resistance were interested in little more than pillage, or to put it in less judgmental terms, feeding their families, while in the Serranía de Ronda, in particular, it appears that what has ever since been viewed as wholesale armed resistance was rather an agrarian revolt directed against the local elites. Meanwhile, fighting the French could well be an extension of longstanding patterns of behavior. Most importantly, the coming of the French did not suddenly put an end to banditry. On the contrary, this phenomenon continued unabated. Men who had been bandits prior to January 1810 in many instances simply went on being bandits, while their ranks were swelled by fresh recruits as ever-larger numbers of the inhabitants were forced to try to make ends meet by turning to crime, even if only on an occasional basis. Among this rural underworld, devotion to Ferdinand VII or even the Roman Catholic Church in all probability counted for little, and yet even setting aside the fact that French soldiers were as tempting a target as anyone else, from brigandage it was but a small step to guerrilla warfare. Though many outlaw gangs remained tiny, other groups banded together for self-protection, and in this guise the constant need for food forced them to engage in requisitioning and to adopt a more military style, just as certain chieftains realized that the benefits of banditry could be realized just as easily, and with no greater a degree of risk, by assuming the guise of freedom fighters. The militarization seen in the north of Spain was rarely apparent, but even so, the gangs remained an obvious threat to French authority: only able to take on enemy columns in the most favorable of circumstances, they were yet very difficult to exterminate, while also being a constant threat to the safety of the propertied classes and the credibility of Bonaparte rule alike.

Very soon, then, the countryside of Andalucía was in a state of turmoil that a combination of the near collapse of ordinary economic life and a spiral of reprisal and counterreprisal combined to render ever deeper: if the French were not universally hated by the populace when they entered Andalucía in January 1810, a few months of rapine, repression, and requisitioning at the very least did nothing to improve their image. Yet in itself this did not mean that the war was lost for the invaders. Though scarcely ideologically committed to the Napoleonic empire, the elites on the whole remained quiescent, the chief factors in this situation being ambition, fear of the crowd, and the need to interact with the invaders on a day-to-day basis. Duck and dive for all they were worth in respect of such burdens as taxation and requisitioning though they might, then, they were unwilling to forge the alliance with the streets that was the only way that they could seek to challenge the French. Meanwhile, shaken though the bonds of Andalusian society had been, their economic power remained such as to ensure that, when it suited their interests, they could mobilize a considerable number of clients. Despite the doubts that its reliability raised in the eyes of many French soldiers, then, the Civic Guard proved something other than a complete failure, not only serving as an urban watch but also helping hunt down bandits.

There was always, then, a certain social and political base from which the French could work in Andalucía, while popular resistance was shot through with so many ambiguities that there were plenty of means by which it could be subverted: thus, much of the populace being interested in survival and economic gain far more than they were in ideology, entire gangs of bandits were frequently co-opted as auxiliaries, even though the savagery with which such men were inclined to behave was such that they probably added greater fuel to the insurgency than they ever denied it. At the same time, for all their highly damaging cultural attitudes, the occupying forces also brought with them a wealth of experience in the suppression of banditry: after all, brigandage of precisely the same sort that the French faced in Andalucía had been a constant feature of some eighteen years of campaigning in Italy, while similar problems had been experienced in Brittany and the Vendée. What is more, although restoring order had often taken a fair degree of time, French arms had always proved more than equal to the task: in Calabria, where a particularly ferocious popular revolt had broken out in 1806, rebellion was on its last legs by the time that the French occupied Seville.

In the end, then, the French occupation of Andalucía was not doomed to failure on account of the weight of popular resistance that it faced: left to their own devices, indeed, in the end the invaders might well have triumphed. What wrecked the chances of King Joseph and Marshal Soult, then, were rather other factors. In the first place, there was the geography of Andalucía in that the invaders were, from the very beginning, literally girdled by the threat of enemy operations: Extremadura, the Algarve, Murcia, and Cádiz could all serve as bases for British, Spanish, and Portuguese troops, while British control of the sea combined with the sheer length of the Andalusian coast to ensure that powerful expeditionary forces could appear almost anywhere. To a certain extent, this threat could be reduced by military action—in March 1811, for example, Badajoz was taken by troops dispatched from Seville, while there was no reason in principle why an outpost might not also have been established at Murcia. Yet such operations could only be achieved at the cost of gravely weakening the troops who were endeavoring to hold down Andalucía itself. Thus, the fact was that the troops who shortly after the conquest of Seville became the Army of the South were, from the beginning, burdened by the need to keep a very strong force before the impregnable island fortress of Cádiz, the failure to take this city while the invaders had the chance being a key moment—indeed, *the* key moment—in the history of Napoleonic Andalucía. Meanwhile, substantial numbers of troops upon whom Soult had relied to neutralize the Spanish forces in Extremadura and keep down the guerrillas of La Mancha were pulled away to take part in campaigns in León and, ultimately, northern and central Portugal. With wastage among the troops very high and reinforcements limited, the Army of the South would therefore have had some difficulty keeping order even had it only had to deal with mere brigandage.

The point is, however, that it did not just have to deal with mere brigandage. From the beginning the authorities in Cádiz—from the end of January 1810, the seat of the Patriot government—maintained a most aggressive posture, sending out force after force to land on the Andalusian coast, while the commanders of the Spanish armies based in Extremadura and Murcia mounted repeated offensives that, if always repelled in the end, often caused Soult considerable alarm. Meanwhile, an entire division of troops under Ballesteros was kept stationed more-or-less permanently in districts that the French found hard to dominate, and this acted as a "flying column" whose rapid marches from place to place tied down large numbers of the invaders. Last but not least, on several occasions the mix was added to by powerful forces of Anglo-Portuguese troops that, unlike the tatterdemalion Spanish armies, were capable of inflicting serious damage on the invaders (in two and a half years of fighting in Andalucía and Extremadura, indeed, the only French losses of any consequence came in the Battles of Barrosa, Albuera, and Arroyomolinos de Montánchez, all three of which were in large part the work of British soldiers).

The threats represented by all these regular troops were rarely so serious that they could not be faced down, while even when they were not, the French were saved by extraneous factors, such as divisions in the Allied ranks or the arrival of help from elsewhere. However, this is by the by: what matters is that by their very presence, they prevented the invaders from concentrating on the counterinsurgency operations that could beyond doubt have restored order in Andalucía. To have any hope of even partial success—the best that could be hoped for given the continued resistance of Cádiz—Soult needed more resources, but of this there was little hope. If this last was so, meanwhile, there was but one person to blame. As commander of the Army of the South, Soult has often been faulted for attempting to occupy the whole of Andalucía and, in his earlier incarnation as Joseph Bonaparte's chief of staff, permitting the invasion of the region in the first place. This criticism, however, is to a great extent unfair. Unlike many of his detractors, Soult realized that Napoleon's wars were above all political conflicts in which what mattered almost more than anything else was the prestige of the empire. In 1810, then, logic dictated the invasion of Andalucía, just as in 1811 and 1812 that same logic dictated that it could not be given up. Within these parameters it must be said that Soult performed extremely well: despite his ever-dwindling resources, to the very end the heartland of French-ruled Andalucía remained firmly under his control, while crisis after crisis was met with a mixture of energy, courage, and sheer determination. If the French failed in Andalucía, then, it was scarcely the fault of Marshal Soult. Instead, the finger must point at Napoleon. Thus, it was the emperor who failed to veto the invasion of Andalucía, just as it was the emperor who failed to give Soult the additional resources that were his only hope of victory, pushed him into further advances that were strategically untenable, and, in the end, denied him the support of the Army of Portugal. As Soult observed in his memoirs: "Dominated . . . by the belief that all that was left to do in the south of Spain was to hunt down a few bands of brigands, [the emperor] pooh-poohed the Spaniards and minimized their chances of resistance. But it was not just a question of guerrilla bands."[1]

From a failed state we moved to a failed occupation. From a failed occupation, though, we must now move to a failed liberation. In the autumn of 1812, it seemed that Andalucía was once again set to become the motor of the Spanish war effort, and it was certainly the hope of the Duke of Wellington that Spanish armies based in that province would play a major part in the campaign of 1813. Yet nothing of the sort occurred. No troops from Andalucía reached the theater of war—by then the Pyrenees—until well after the decisive battle of Vitoria. The reasons for this were manifold. First of all, there is the issue of Anglo-Spanish relations. In September 1812 Wellington had been offered the command of the Spanish field armies, but there had always been a degree of resistance to this among the military—on 31 October, indeed, Ballesteros had "pronounced" against the move at Granada—while by the time that the British commander had formally agreed to the new role, the military situation had changed; indeed, Wellington had suffered the embarrassment of having been forced to vacate much of his Spanish conquests and retreat into Portugal. Stimulated by the bitter protests that emanated from Ballesteros, who was now incarcerated in Ceuta, resistance to Wellington's appointment therefore grew, and all the more so as the new commander in chief responded to the chaotic situation that he found he had inherited by demanding administrative powers that appeared to threaten the provisions of the constitution that Spain had acquired in 1812.[2]

Yet the failure of troops from Andalucía to take the field in any number in the first half of 1813 was not just the result of friction between Wellington and Cádiz. Just as important was the impact of war. Thus, after two and one-half years of constant campaigning, Andalucía had been reduced to ruin. Trade and commerce were at a standstill; many towns and villages had been reduced to blackened shells, the countryside had been stripped of its resources, the populace was in a state of semi-starvation, banditry was rife, and yellow fever had wrought dreadful havoc in all the coastal provinces. At the most basic level, then, it was near impossible to mobilize Andalucía for a war beyond its frontiers: as Wellington quickly discovered, for example, the carts, mules, and draught animals that would have been needed to get even such troops as were under arms on the move for northern Spain were simply not to be had. As for conscription, this too was problematic. All across Andalucía the municipal authorities on whom the process depended had been disrupted by, first, the imposition of new models of town council by the Constitution of 1812 and, second, the numerous recriminations that were unleashed among the elites in respect of such matters as collaboration with the invaders. When they were not fighting with each other, meanwhile, the elites were fighting with Cádiz: the imposition of new civil governors—*jefes políticos*—was often deeply resented, while many of the reforms pushed through by the *cortes* in the course of 1813 (an obvious example is the abolition of the Inquisition) were inclined to push potential allies of the government into a position of noncooperation, if not open resistance.[3] And then too there was the matter of the human cost of the war. According to recent estimates, this was not at as high as has sometimes been assumed, and certainly not as great as the ravages of harvest failure and epidemic in the period 1801–1807, but the situation was still bad enough: between 1808 and 1814 lower Andalucía—roughly the area stretching from Córdoba to Huelva and Cádiz—is calculated to have lost over 7 percent of its population, while the population of the city of Granada fell from 55,000 in 1804 to 49,000 in 1817.[4]

To discuss the matter in this fashion, however, is to ignore the role of the people. Yet the latter were anything but passive agents in the situation. On the contrary, it was not long before it showed itself to be as reluctant to participate in the war effort as it had been in 1808. Under the pressure of enemy occupation, true, there had been considerable engagement with the cause of resistance, but this had been greatly eased by the blurred distinctions between banditry, jacquerie, and guerrilla warfare, not to mention the fact that service in, say, the forces of General Ballesteros or participation in *la guerrilla* had represented an important means of survival. Nor, meanwhile, had most combatants ever had to move very far from their homes. Now, however, fighting the French meant serving in the regular army, and serving in the regular army meant fighting beyond the confines of Andalucía, on top of this there being the fact that conscription pressed upon the populace with the same injustice as it had in 1808–1809. To add insult to injury, thanks to the introduction of a new system of taxation by the *cortes* of Cádiz, taxation was often heavier than before, while the people were also confronted by a situation in which many of those who had collaborated with the French were able to slide effortlessly back into positions of power and authority. As Jean-Marc Lafon has written: "Although the subject has not been studied very much, it appears that purges were not very extensive. . . . We have some examples from the rest of Spain . . . and one or two from Andalucía, the most important being those relating to Baena and Jaén. From these it can be deduced that the cleanup was little more than a joke."[5] However, if the *afrancesados* were left alone, the populace were not: in many places stringent police measures were introduced that severely restricted their freedom of movement, their leisure activities, and their ability to make a living from such marginal activities as prostitution and games of chance.[6] And finally, there was the issue of the end of *la guerrilla*: even those who had genuinely fought the French in the irregular bands found that their attempts to gain preferment met with considerable difficulty—one such was the *malagüeño* chieftain Antonio Múñoz[7]—while those who had either never been more than bandits or who now found themselves with no other means of support than banditry discovered that the Patriot authorities were no more sparing in their use of garrote and firing squad than the French had been: on 10 June 1813, for instance, Rafael Pidilla, Antonio Toral, Francisco Martínez, and Francisco del Río were shot by firing squad in Jaén as "thieves, deserters, murderers, and members of the criminal gang that has been infesting the . . .

paths and roads around the *pueblos* of Quesada, Pozo Alcón, Cazorla, Hinojares, and Belerda."[8]

In 1812–13 as much as in 1808–1809, then, the result was bitter resistance: large numbers of *mozos* fled their homes rather than serve in the army, while in March 1813 a battalion of the Savoya infantry regiment that was marching to take ship for America mutinied at Montoro and dispersed in bands of up to sixty strong.[9] All this was mixed up with considerable anger at the limitations of the reforms introduced by the Cortes of Cádiz from 1810 onward: not only had the power of the oligarchy been cemented by the introduction of a system of indirect elections that ensured that only men with substantial local influence or patronage would be elected to parliament, but also feudalism had been abolished in such a way that most of the old feudal dues were simply translated into rents. With land redistribution of any sort nonexistent, the result was a spate of riots and uprisings: at El Coronil, for example, an angry crowd assaulted the manorial court and tore down the arms of their feudal overlord.[10] Meanwhile, it is beyond doubt, at least in part in this same spirit of anger and social unrest, that we should interpret the widespread anti-liberal disturbances that greeted the return of Ferdinand VII in 1814: exactly as in 1808, the crowd interpreted *el rey deseado* as the harbinger of a new era of social justice in which their ills would be attended and their enemies swept away.[11]

From all this it can be seen that the war in Andalucía cannot but be open to reassessment. In the end, if the French faced considerable levels of popular violence in Andalucía, it was because their military culture placed few bounds on the violence and molestation that could be offered to civilians, because both policy and circumstance directed that their armies should attempt to live off a country whose resources were not equal to the task, because the Andalusian economy collapsed under the weight of war and occupation, and finally, because Andalucía united a long tradition of banditry with the physical characteristics necessary for that tradition to flourish. But was popular violence the same as popular resistance? When the French were in occupation of the region, in one sense the answer cannot but be "yes," though everything we know about the periods from 1808 to 1810 and 1812 to 1814 suggests that even the direct experience of enemy occupation and atrocity was not enough to make the French so hated that the populace wished only to fling themselves upon them. Despite the efforts of certain committed individuals, *andaluces* took part in mass rebellions because they associated them with traditional acts of rural protest, just as they saw in the *partidas* not guerrilla bands, but traditional gangs of bandits. This does not mean that popular disorder had no effect, or even that it was not widespread: a Frenchman who fell to a bandit was just as dead as one who fell to a guerrilla, while there is no doubt that the constant irregular warfare was at the very least a serious irritant. However, it does mean that there were always limits on what could be achieved, and in effect, that in Andalucía as much as in the rest of Spain, exaltation of the *partidas* has gone too far.

Notes

Abbreviations

ACA-JSC	Archivo de la Corona de Aragón (Barcelona), Junta Suprema de Cataluña
AGS-GJ	Archivo General de Segovia (Segovia), Sección de Gracia y Justicia
AHN-SC	Archivo Histórico Nacional (Madrid), Sección de Consejos
AHN-SDC	Archivo Histórico Nacional (Madrid), Sección de Diversos (Colecciones)
AHN-SE	Archivo Histórico Nacional (Madrid), Sección de Estado
BN	Biblioteca Nacional (Madrid)
BN-CGI	Biblioteca Nacional (Madrid), Colección Gómez Imaz
HMM	Hemeróteca Municipal de Madrid
IHCM-CDF	Instituto de Historia y Cultura Militar (Madrid), Colección Documental del Fraile
IHCM-CGB	Instituto de Historia y Cultura Militar (Madrid), Colección del General Blake
MCPMRJ	Casse, *Mémoires et correspondance politique et militaire du Roi Joseph*
RAH	Real Academía de Historia (Madrid)
SHD-ST	Service Historique de la Défence (Paris), Section de la Terre

Preface

1. See S. Woolf, *Napoleon's Integration of Europe* (London, 1991), 8–13.
2. M. Broers, *Europe under Napoleon, 1799–1815* (London, 1996), 180.
3. Woolf, *Napoleon's Integration of Europe*, 20–21.
4. G. Ellis, *The Napoleonic Empire*, 2nd ed. (1991; London, 2003), 91.
5. A. Grab, *Napoleon and the Transformation of Europe* (Basingstoke, 2003), 23.
6. Ellis, *Napoleonic Empire*, 94. For a more trenchant statement of Ellis's views, see G. Ellis, "The Nature of Napoleonic Imperialism," in *Napoleon and Europe*, ed. P. Dwyer (London, 2001), 97–117.
7. J. Davis, *Naples and Napoleon: Southern Italy and the European Revolutions, 1780–1860* (Oxford, 2006), 162. For the views of Rowe and Broers, see M. Rowe, "Resistance, Collaboration, or Third Way? Responses to Napoleonic Rule in Germany," in C. J. Esdaile, ed. *Popular Resistance in the French Wars: Patriots, Partisans,*

and Land Pirates (Houndmills, 2005), 67–90; and M. Broers, *Napoleonic Imperialism and the Savoyard Monarchy, 1773–1821: State Building in Piedmont* (Lewiston, N.Y., 1997).

8. C. J. Esdaile, *Fighting Napoleon: Guerrillas, Bandits, and Adventurers in Spain, 1808–1814* (London, 2004), 204. For a recent European-wide study of popular resistance to the French Revolution and Napoleon, see M. Broers, *Napoleon's Other War: Bandits, Rebels, and Their Pusuers in the Age of Revolutions* (Oxford, 2010). Unwilling entirely to shed the notion that rural *résistants* were driven by ideological concerns, Broers nevertheless admits that they were inextricably linked with banditry: "When resistance to the new régime . . . rooted itself in the countryside, . . . peasants fought like the best fighters they knew—men they feared, respected, did business with, fled, drank with, and often were part-time: bandits." Ibid., xiv.

9. Such references are numerous. For example, according to a report received in June 1812 from a French soldier who had been taken prisoner by the guerrillas but had then got away: "Almost all [Espoz y] Mina's cavalry is composed of deserters from the armies of the French and their allies, while there are around 300 other such men in the infantry." Also worth noting is a report of 16 October of the same year that mentions that the band of El Pastor—a force that at this time comprised three infantry battalions organized on the basis of one grenadier, four center, and one light companies—included a grenadier company made up entirely of Frenchmen. See Précis of Reports Received by General Thouvenot, 18 June, 19 Oct. 1812, Instituto de Historia y Cultura Militar, Ejército del Norte, 7343.49/50.

10. M. de Marbot, *The Memoirs of Baron de Marbot, Late Lieutenant General in the French Army*, 2 vols. (London, 1892), 1:354.

11. For example, see J. L. Tone, *The Fatal Knot: The Guerrilla War in Navarre and the Defeat of Napoleon in Spain* (Chapel Hill, N.C., 1994).

12. See C. J. Esdaile and L. Hernández Enviz, "Anatomy of a Research Project: The Sociology of the Guerrilla War in Spain, 1808–1814," in Esdaile, *Popular Resistance in the French Wars*, 123–24.

13. G. Lovett, *Napoleon and the Birth of Modern Spain* (New York, 1965), 509.

14. M. Ross, *The Reluctant King: Joseph Bonaparte, King of the Two Sicilies and Spain* (London, 1976), 184.

15. Conde de Toreno, *Historia de la guerra, levantamiento, y revolución de España*, ed. R. Hocquellet (Pamplona, 2008) 530.

16. R. W. Southey, *History of the Peninsular War*, 6 vols., new ed. (London, 1828–37), 5:48.

17. A. von Schepeler, *Histoire de la guerre d'Espagne et de Portugal ainsi que de la guerre qui en resulta*. 3 vols. (Liège, 1829–32), 2:519.

18. C. Oman, *A History of the Peninsular War*, 7 vols. (Oxford, 1902–1930), 3:317–18.

19. For the Calabrian insurrection of 1806–1810, see M. Finley, *The Most Monstrous of Wars: Napoleonic Guerrilla War in Southern Italy, 1806–1811* (Colombia, S.C., 1994).

20. For an excellent bibliographical essay, see R. Sánchez Mantero, "Los estudios sobre la Guerra de la Independencia en Andalucía," in J. M. Cuenca Toribio, ed., *Andalucía en la Guerra de la Independencia* (Córdoba, 2009), 9–15. Two works that are of particular significance, meanwhile, are F. L. Díaz Torrejón,

Guerrilla, contraguerrilla, y delincuencia en la Andalucía napoleónica, 1810–1812, 3 vols. (Granada, 2004); and J. M. Lafon, *L'Andalousie et Napoléon: Contre-insurrection, collaboration, et resistance dans le midi d'Espagne, 1808–1812* (Paris, 2007).

21. For a discussion of these issues, see C. J. Esdaile, ed., "Spain 1808–Iraq 2003: Some Thoughts on the Use and Abuse of History," *Journal of Military History* 74, no. 1 (Jan. 2010): 173–88.

Chapter 1

1. J. Lynch, *Bourbon Spain, 1700–1808* (Oxford, 1989), 204–205.

2. A. Guillén Gómez, "La Junta de Gobierno de Granada y su contribución al apoyo logístico de los ejércitos nacionales: La fábrica de armas de fuego, junio de 1808–enero 1810," *Cuadernos del bicentenario,* no. 4 (Dec. 2008): 28–29.

3. For these figures, see J. Vicens Vives, *Historia de España y America social y económica,* 2nd ed., 5 vols. (Madrid, 1971), 4:5–7.

4. The aftermath of the Talavera campaign, insofar as the British forces are concerned, is discussed in J. K. Severn, *A Wellesley Affair: Richard Marquess Wellesley and the Conduct of Anglo-Spanish Diplomacy, 1809–1812* (Gainesville, Fla., 1981), 51–70.

5. For a discussion of the Spanish armies mobilized by the Junta Central, see C. J. Esdaile, *The Spanish Army in the Peninsular War* (Manchester, 1988), 118–23.

6. For details of the Battle of Ocaña, see Oman, *Peninsular War,* 3:92–96.

7. Ibid., 3:68–69, 111–13.

8. Ibid., 3:115–19.

9. J. D. Soult to H. Clarke, 8 Dec. 1809, MCPMRJ, 7:109.

10. Napoleon to Joseph Bonaparte, 11 Jan. 1809, ibid., 5:331.

11. Oman, *Peninsular War,* 1:481.

12. For a spirited defence of the decision to invade Andalucía, see P. Hayman, *Soult: Napoleon's Maligned Marshal* (London, 1990), 138–41.

13. Joseph to Napoleon, 2 Apr. 1809, MCPMRJ, 6:147.

14. A. Miot de Melito, *Mémoires du Comte Miot de Melito, ancien ministre, ambassadeur, conseilleur d'*état, *et membre de l'istitut,* 3 vols. (Paris, 1858), 3:48.

15. Napoleon to Joseph Bonaparte, 16 Jan. 1809, MCPMRJ, 5:359.

16. Miot de Melito, *Mémoires,* 3:74–79.

17. Joseph Bonaparte to Napoleon, 19 Nov. 1809, MCPMRJ, 7:88.

18. Joseph Bonaparte to Napoleon, 3 Dec. 1809, ibid., 7:107–108.

19. Joseph Bonaparte to J. D. Soult, 27 Nov. 1808, ibid., 7:105.

20. Miot de Melito, *Mémoires,* 3:49.

21. Lagarde to Napoleon, 8 Sept. 1809, in N. Gotteri, ed., *La mission de Lagarde, policier de l'empereur, pendant la Guwerre d'Espagne, 1809–1811,* (Paris, 1991), 126.

22. Miot de Melito, *Mémoires,* 3:50.

23. Soult's baptismal name is usually given as "Nicolas Jean de Dieu," but the "Nicolas" appears to have been a nickname he acquired while serving in the Rhineland in the mid-1790s. For reasons that are not clear but may well have been rooted in irony, the populace started referring to him as the *wundermann,* or "wonder-worker"; this being a title that was locally accorded to Saint Nicholas, the troops picked up on this, and so the name stuck.

24. Napoleon to J. Soult, 26 Sept. 1809, in H. Plon and J. Dumaine, eds., *Correspondance de Napoléon Ier publiée par ordre de l'Empereur Napoléon III, 32 vols.* (Paris,

1858–69), 18:527–28; Napoleon to A. Berthier, 28 Nov. 1809, in ibid., 19:47–48. Initially the plan was for Berthier to travel to Spain, but for reasons that are not quite clear, he never did so. For full details of events in Oporto, see below.

25. Glover, *Legacy of Glory,* 153.

26. Ibid., 151. According to Miot de Melito, however, for all Soult's confidence, he nonetheless insisted that Joseph should provide him with a written order to the effect that Andalucía should be invaded: in the event of the emperor's displeasure, it would therefore be the king who would be first in line for blame. See *Mémoires,* 3:80.

27. Schepeler, *Histoire de la guerre d'Espagne et de Portugal,* 2:496–97.

28. M. de Zequsina y Arango, *Paralelo militar entre España y Francia con varias reflexiones sobre el éxito feliz de nuestra independencia contra las usurpaciones de Bonaparte* (Cádiz, 1809), BN-CGI, R60781, pp. 5–6.

29. Earl of Westmoreland, "Memoir of the Early Campaigns of the Duke of Wellington," n.d., BN, MSS/23087, f. 182.

30. Schepeler, *Histoire de la guerre d'Espagne et de Portugal,* 2:497.

31. M. López Pérez and I. Lara Martín-Portugués, *Entre la guerra y la paz: Jaén, 1808–1814* (Granada, 1993), 286–87.

32. Westmoreland, "Early Campaigns of the Duke of Wellington," 190.

33. W. Jacob, *Travels in the South of Spain in Letters Written A.D. 1809 and 1810* (London, 1811), 189.

34. Westmoreland, "Early Campaigns of the Duke of Wellington," 180.

35. Jacob, *Travels in the South of Spain,* 190.

36. Ibid., 191.

37. Schepeler, *Histoire de la guerre d'Espagne et de Portugal,* 2:500.

38. For the organization of the French forces that invaded Andalucía, see Oman, *Peninsular War,* 3:532–37. Sébastiani's corps was incomplete, one of its two infantry divisions having been detached to escort the prisoners of Ocaña back to the French frontier and half of another held back to help garrison Madrid.

39. Ibid., 3:123–25.

40. Lagarde to Napoleon, 9 Jan. 1810, in Gotteri, *Mission de Lagarde,* 148–52.

41. Oman, *Peninsular War,* 3:130–32.

42. Miot de Melito, *Mémoires,* 3:85.

43. A. L. A. Fée, *Souvenirs de la Guerre d'Espagne, dite de l'independence, 1809–1813* (Paris, 1856), 49–50.

44. A. de Saint-Chamans, *Mémoires du Général Comte de Saint-Chamans, ancien aide de camp du Maréchal Soult, 1802–1832* (Paris, 1896), 166.

45. J. D. Soult to A. Berthier, 25 Jan. 1810, MCPMRJ, 7:237; Schepeler, *Histoire de la guerre d'Espagne et de Portugal,* 2:507.

46. Joseph Bonaparte to Napoleon, 25 Jan. 1810, MCPMRJ, 7:236.

47. Ibid.

48. Ross, *Reluctant King,* 188–89; A. Delgado García, *Montoro en la Guerra de la Independencia* (Montoro, 2006), 93.

49. Fée, *Souvenirs,* 56–57.

50. López and Lara, *Entre la guerra y la paz,* 272, 293.

51. A, Gallego y Burín, *Granada en la Guerra de la Independencia* (Granada, 1923), 65–66; A. Martínez Ruiz, *El reino de Granada en la Guerra de la Inpendencia* (Granada, 1977), 85–86. Azanza, who appears to have been regarded by Joseph as a species of "hitman," only remained royal commissioner until the middle of

February, at which point he was replaced by one Estanislao de Lugo. For reasons that are not entirely clear, Lugo was replaced almost equally quickly by Andrés Romero Valdés, while on 9 May there was yet another change when the post went to Luis Marcelino Peyreyra.

52. C. Viñes Millet, *Granada ante la invasión francesa* (Granada, 2004), 51–55.

53. That it was Joseph who was responsible for this much-criticised decision is clear from J. D.Soult to A. Berthier, 27 Jan. 1810, SHD-ST, C8–146, ff. 56–58. This letter, of course, is highly convenient to Soult, but the fact that it was written before anyone realized the significance of the mistake that had been made tends greatly to strengthen its veracity. As for claims that the decision was Soult's, the only source that they can cite is Joseph's loyal friend, Miot de Melito (*Mémoires,* 3:99). If anyone really said "Let somebody answer to me for Seville, and I will answer for Cádiz!," it was therefore probably the king. In fairness to Joseph, however, one must point out that, in a letter he wrote to Marshal Ney that same day, Soult shared his assessment of Alburquerque's intentions, so it may well be that he concurred in the decision. See J. D. Soult to M. Ney, 27 Jan. 1810, ibid., ff. 54–56.

54. J. D. Soult to A. Berthier, 31 Jan. 1810, ibid., ff. 59–61.

55. The operations of the Army of Extremadura are discussed in Oman, *Peninsular War,* 3:135–38. For Alburquerque's own account of his arrival in Cádiz, meanwhile, see the manifesto that he penned in the course of the bitter disputes that broke out between him and the local authorities after his arrival in the city: *Manifiesto del Duque de Alburquerque acerca de su conducta con la Junta de Cádiz y arribo del ejército de su cargo a aquella plaza* (London, 1810), BN-CGI, 60013-4.

56. M. Moreno Alonso, *Sevilla napoleónica* (Sevilla, 1995), 15.

57. Oman, *Peninsular War,* 3:141–42.

58. The most detailed account of King Joseph's entry into Seville is that found in F. L. Díaz Torrejón, *José Napoleón I en el sur de España: Un viaje regio por Andalucía, enero–mayo 1810* (Córdoba, 2008), 96–98.

59. Fée, *Souvenirs,* 62.

60. Miot de Melito, *Mémoires,* 3:100–101.

61. Joseph Bonaparte to Napoleon, 2 Feb. 1810, MCPMRJ, 7:249.

62. Saint-Chamans, *Mémoires,* 167–68.

63. J. Mendoza y Rico, *Historia de Málaga durante la revolución santa que agita a España desde marzo de 1808,* ed. M. Olmedo Checa (Málaga, 2003), 93.

64. Ibid., 93–96. See also R. de Mazariego, *Manifiesto que publica el ayuntamiento de la ciudad de Málaga sobre las ocurrencias que precedieron en ella a la entrada de las tropas francesas* (Málaga, n.d.), 5–9. With respect to Abello in particular, see V. Abello, *Manifiesto que hace a su patria Don Vicente Abello, Capitán General aclamado por el lealísimo pueblo de la ciudad de Málaga el día 24 de enero de 1810* (Isla de León, 1811), 10–18.

65. M. S. Santos Arrebola, "Incidencias de la ocupación francesa en la congregación de San Felipe Neri de Málaga," in M. Reder Gadow and E. Mendoza García, eds. *La Guerra de la Independencia en Málaga y su provincia 1808–1814* (Málaga, 2005), 583–90.

66. Mendoza y Rico, *Historia de Málaga,* 96–100.

67. Ibid., 102–103.

68. Ibid., 104–107.

69. Ibid., 107–108.

70. Ibid., 109. Among the dead was Juan José del Castillo, a retired officer who was the grandfather of the later Spanish statesman Antonio Cánovas del Castillo. As witness the version of events contained in E. Alcántara Alcaide's work, a concomitant of the sack of Málaga was the emergence of many stories of desperate popular resistance in the streets. See E. Alcántara Alcalde, *Málaga frente a la Guerra de la Independencia 1808–1812* (Málaga, 1966),72–74. It is difficult, however, to give these much credit even if it is by no means impossible that, to pick up on one feature of the legend, the odd French soldier had a pan of boiling water hurled in his face by some desperate housewife.

Chapter 2

1. R. Douglas, ed., *From Valmy to Waterloo: Extracts from the Diary of Captain Charles François, a Soldier of the Revolution and the Empire* (London, 1906), 185–86.

2. J. C. Carnicero Toribio, *Historia razonada de los principales sucesos de la gloriosa revolución de España,* 4 vols. (Madrid, 1814), 1:152–55.

3. L. S. de Girardin, *Journal et souvenirs, discuors et opinions de S. Girardin,* 4 vols. (Paris, 1828), 4:122–23. For another French account, see G. de Clermont-Tonnerre, *L'expédition d'Espagne, 1808–1810,* ed. C. Desparte (Paris, 1983), 94–95.

4. Joseph Bonaparte to Napoleón, 24 July 1808, MCPMRJ, 5:382–83.

5. For some details, see M. Martínez Quinteiro, *Los grupos liberales antes de la cortes de Cádiz* (Madrid, 1977), 22–23; and Moreno Alonso, *Sevilla napoleónica,* 127–29.

6. C. Leslie, *Military Journal of Colonel Leslie, K.H., of Balquhain, whilst Serving with the Twenty-Ninth Regiment in the Peninsula and the Sixtieth Rifles in Canada, etc., 1807–1832* (Aberdeen, 1887), 25–26, 29–30.

7. Mendoza y Rico, *Historia de Málaga,* 80–83.

8. L. Saint Pierre and A. Saint Pierre, eds., *Mémoires du Maréchal Soult: Espagne et Portugal* (Paris, 1955), 175–76.

9. Baste's memoirs were originally published in A. de Beauchamp, *Collection des mémoires relatifs aux revolutions d'Espagne* (Paris, 1824). This translation, however, is that provided in T. Mahon, "Recollections of Capitaine de Frégate Pierre Baste," Nov. 2006, Napoleon Series, http://napoleon-series.org/military/battles/baste/c_baste1.htm.

10. Girardin, *Journal et souvenirs,* 4:152–53, 161.

11. Miot de Melito, *Mémoires,* 3:22.

12. J. J. de Naylies, *Mémoires sur la guerre d'Espagne pendant les années 1808, 1809, 1810, et 1811* (Paris, 1817), 183–85.

13. Anonymous memorandum, 13 Jan. 1809, AHN-SE, 40-F, no. 258-2.

14. M. de la Cerda to P. Rivero, n.d., ibid., no. 228.

15. Jacob, *Travels in the South of Spain,* 144.

16. Anonymous letter, 24 May 1809, AHN-SE, 40-B, no. 29.

17. Miot de Melito, *Mémoires,* 3:87.

18. Ibid., 3:96.

19. Clermont-Tonnerre, *Expédition d'Espagne,* 338.

20. Memorial of J. Iznar, 22 Feb. 1810, AHN-SE, 2952.

21. For these regulations, see Anonymous, *Gritos de Madrid cautivo a los pueblos de España* (Seville, 1809), BN-CGI, R60124-8.

22. S. A. de Embite to M. de Garay, 28 Feb. 1809, AHN-SE, 16-1, ff. 38–43.

23. See *Invención de la maquina de Napoleón para esclavizar la España* (Málaga, 1808), BN-CGI, R60043-75.

24. As well as the famous Mamelukes, of which there were a mere troop of perhaps thirty men, the forces that occupied Madrid at the start of the war had included six foreign infantry battalions—three Swiss, two German, and one Irish. Of these, the Swiss were volunteers recruited by contract with the cantonal authorities, and the Germans and Irish—the latter in many instances actually Germans too—prisoners of war who had joined the French forces rather than languish in jail. Even here, then, Spanish perceptions were confused.

25. Jacob, *Travels in the South of Spain,* 166.

26. Ibid., 73.

27. Oman, *Peninsular War,* 3:143.

28. For the uprising in Seville, in particular, see M. Moreno Alonso, *La revolución "santa" de Sevilla (la revuelta popular de 1808)* (Seville, 1997). For two contrasting general discussions, cf. Esdaile, *Spanish Army in the Peninsular War,* 75–89; and R. Fraser, *Napoleon's Cursed War: Popular Resistance in the Spanish Peninsular War* (London, 2008), 82–123.

29. For an introduction to the social and economic background, see C. J. Esdaile, *The Peninsular War: A New History* (London, 2002), 9–22; and Lynch, *Bourbon Spain,* 394–418.

30. Toreno, *Guerra, levantamiento, y revolución,* 64; Schepeler, *Histoire de la guerre d'Espagne et de Portugal,* 1:268–69.

31. Jacob, *Travels in the South of Spain,* 28–30. See also Toreno, *Guerra, levantamiento, y revolución,* 66; and Schepeler, *Histoire de la guerre d'Espagne et de Portugal,* 1:273–75. According to another account, the woman who tried to protect Socorro confronted the mob single-handed with a pistol, only to be attacked and badly wounded. Cf. J. B. L. de Crossard, *Mémoires militaires et historiques du Baron de Crossard pour servir a l'histoire de la guerre depuis 1792 jusqu'en 1815 inclusivement,* 6 vols. (Paris, 1829), 3:285.

32. Moreno Alonso, *Revolución "santa" de Sevilla,* 173.

33. Fraser, *Napoleon's Cursed War,* 123.

34. F. Montoro Fernández, "Mayo–junio de 1808 en la Axarquía: Destitución y muerte del corregidor de Vélez Málaga," in Reder Gadow and Mendoza García, *Guerra de la Independencia en Málaga,* 509–18.

35. Toreno, *Guerra, levantamiento, y revolución,* 68.

36. Moreno Alonso, *Revolución "santa" de Sevilla,* 173.

37. Fraser, *Napoleon's Cursed War,* 121–22.

38. P. A. Girón, *Memorias de la vida de Don Pedro Agustín Girón,* ed. A. Berazaluce, 3 vols. (Pamplona, 1978), 1:217; Mendoza y Rico, *Historia de Málaga,* 84.

39. See Proclamation of the Junta of Seville, 31 May 1808, IHCM-CDF, 864.

40. For an introduction to elite attitudes toward poverty, see A. Shubert, *A Social History of Modern Spain* (London, 1990), 52–53. See also R. M. Pérez Estévez, *El problema de los vagos en la España del siglo XVIII* (Madrid, 1976), 55–78.

41. F. Valenzuela Saavedra, *La sociedad de Jaén ante la invasión napoleónica, 1808* (Jaén, 2000), 28–38.

42. Ibid., 40–44.

43. Ibid., 45–48.

44. Ibid., 53–55.

45. Ibid., 58–68.

46. Ibid., 85.

47. Martínez Ruiz, *Granada en la Guerra de la Independenica,* 41–57 passim.

48. Fraser, *Napoleon's Cursed War,* 119.

49. Ibid., 181.

50. Ibid., 182–83; J. M. Navarro Domínguez, "Las juntas de gobierno locales en una comarca rural sevillana: Los Alcores en 1808," in Cuenca Toribio, *Andalucía en la Guerra de la Independencia,* 120–21. Social tension in Carmona appears to have been particularly intense. In brief, prior to 1808 the town council had been engaged in a scheme designed to improve the municipal lands at the expense of the rural poor. Thus, in general, the only lands it rented out were plots of very low quality. Desperate to make a living, the hapless individuals to whom these went would put immense amounts of energy into improving them, only to find that they could not make them pay, the result being that they were evicted and the same lands rented out at a higher price to another bidder. See Bernal, *Lucha por la tierra,* 173.

51. Fraser, *Napoleon's Cursed War,* 187.

52. See Conde del Pinar to M. de Garay, 7 Aug. 1809, AHN-SE, 61-T, no. 420.

53. Jacob, *Travels in the South of Spain,* 39–43.

54. J. Mergelina to Junta Central, 28 Feb. 1809, AHN-SE, 31-E, no. 127. See also Junta of Jérez de la Frontera to Junta Central, 1 Mar. 1809, ibid., no. 129.

55. For the intrigues of the Palafoxist party in the autumn of 1808, see Esdaile, *Spanish Army in the Peninsular War,* 127–32.

56. Anonymous to Junta Suprema Central, n.d., AHN-SE, 52-G, no. 353; Report, Anonymous to Junta de Seguridad Pública, n.d., AHN-SE, 31-D, no. 125.

57. Schepeler, *Histoire de la guerre d'Espagne et de Portugal,* 2:385–86. See F. Palafox to Junta Central, 2 May 1809, AHN-SE, 17/6, ff. 31–32. For a defense of the uprising, see Manifesto of "El pueblo de Granada," 20 June 1809, AHN-SE, 52-E, no. 273.

58. The best modern account of this sanguinary affair is to be found in M. Ardit Lucas, *Revolución liberal y revuelta campesina: Un ensayo sobre la desintegración del régimen feudal en el país valenciano, 1793–1840* (Barcelona, 1977), 127–34. Please note too the pamphlet literature that made this event public property in Patriot Spain: see, for example, Anonymous, *Causa contra el canónigo Calvo* (Valencia, 1808), BN-CGI, R60087-11. Ronald Fraser claims that further riots, some of them equally fatal, that took place at Segorbe, Sagunto, Jérica, Ayora, and Castellón were also instigated by Calvo or, at the very least, his connections, but the fact that at least some of these disturbances took place before the Valencian killings suggests that the canon's role in them was limited—indeed, that he rather made use of a general climate of insecurity and inflamed passion as a basis for his coup. See *Napoleon's Cursed War,* 149.

59. J. Castro de Lavalle to T. Reding, 18 Jan. 1809, ACA-JSC, 4.

60. For a graphic contemporary account of the Lérida affair, see *Noticias de Lérida* (Lérida, 1809), BN-CGI, R60292-7.

61. For these executions, see Fraser, *Napoleon's Cursed War,* 149, 234.

62. C. Campos to Junta Suprema Central, 7 Jan. 1809, AHN-SE, 31-H, no. 173.

63. A. García to Junta Suprema Central, 4 Feb. 1809, ibid., no. 161. The best account in English of the Murcia affair is contained in Fraser, *Napoleon's Cursed War,* 235–39. See also Jiménez de Gregorio, *Murcia en los dos primeros años de la Guerra de la Independencia,* 39–89 passim. For the accounts of Villar and Campo

Hermoso, see Marqués de Villar to Junta Suprema Central, 14 Mar. 1809, AHN-SE, 31-H, no. 164; and Conde de Campo Hermoso to Junta Suprema Central, 3 Jan. 1809, ibid., no. 170-2.

64. Esdaile, *Spanish Army in the Peninsular War,* 175.

65. The imposing physical appearance of the Voluntarios Distinguidos de Cádiz is best observed in J. M.Bueno, *Uniformes militares de la Guerra de la Independencia* (Madrid, 1989), 118–25.

66. For the recruitment of volunteers, see J. Aragón Gómez, *La vida cotidiana durante la Guerra de la Independencia en la provincia de Cádiz* (Cádiz, 2005), 233.

67. Anonymous petition, 13 Jan. 1809, AHN-SE, 30-E, no. 237.

68. Order of Pedro de Cardenas, 18 Jan. 1809, BN-CGI, R60002-5.

69. Anonymous to Junta Suprema Central, n.d. AHN-SE, 52-A, no. 27.

70. Anonymous to Junta Suprema Central, n.d., ibid., 52-G, no. 206. That there was such corruption is confirmed by a number of observers who visited the city prior to 1808. One such was Jean-François Bourgoing, who described the customs officials of Cádiz as "wretched mercenaries, who, for the value of half a crown, would suffer all the smugglers on earth to pass them un-noticed while they are scrupulously careful to empty the pockets of every honest man" and complained that "they have the impudence, if you only pass the gate of the city to get to the pier, to ask you for something to drink in a tone that plainly signifies 'give or we will search you.'" J. F. de Bourgoing, *Modern State of Spain Exhibiting a Complete View of its Topography, Government, Laws, Religion, Finances, Naval and Military Establishments, and of Society, Manners, Arts, Sciences, Agriculture, and Commerce in That Country,* 4 vols. (London, 1808), 4:213–14.

71. Junta de Vigilancia de Cádiz to Marqués de Villel, 1 Feb. 1809, AHN-SE, 14-A, no. 10-1, ff. 55–56.

72. Oman, *Peninsular War,* 2:29–30. In fairness, Oman does but echo the language of contemporary British observers, as witness, for example, Earl of Ilchester, ed., *The Spanish Journal of Elizabeth, Lady Holland* (London, 1910), 289–90.

73. Crossard, *Mémoires,* 3:292.

74. Proclamation of the Junta of Cádiz, 16 Jan. 1809, BN-CGI, R60002-4.

75. J. de Miranda to M. de Garay, 19 Mar. 1809, AHN-SE, 16-3 (2), f. 58.

76. For the background to the crisis of February 1809, see Oman, *Peninsular War,* 2:27–28.

77. It is worth noting here that another theory floated after the riots was that they were instigated not by the Voluntarios Distinguidos, but rather by officials of the customs administration, the theory being that the men concerned feared that Villel's determination to root out corruption was on the point of landing them in serious trouble. If so, however, they were truly hoist with their own petard, for it was on the customs administration that the rioters expended the bulk of their fury. See Anonymous to Junta Central, n.d., AHN-SE, 31-C, no. 38 (2). A particularly notable feature of the revolt, meanwhile, was the part taken in it by women, British eyewitnesses remarking at the presence in the crowd of both large numbers of what may be inferred to have been prostitutes furious at the manner in which Villel had been threatening their livelihood and a smattering of society women who objected to the very idea that a man could tell them what to wear. See Ilchester, *Spanish Journal of Elizabeth, Lady Holland,* 386; and Lady Jackson, ed., *The Diaries and Letters of Sir George Jackson, K. C. H., from the Peace of Amiens to the Battle of Talavera,* 2 vols. (London, 1872), 2:386–87.

78. Ilchester, *Spanish Journal of Elizabeth, Lady Holland,* 386.

79. Despite his name, Jones was wholly Spanish, being a descendent of one of the many Jacobite exiles who had fled to Spain in the 1690s.

80. Crossard, *Mémoires,* 3:284. For the aftermath of the riots, meanwhile, see the extensive documentation in AHN-SE, 31-C, nos. 38–81 passim. See also Marqués de Villel to T. Reding, 28 Feb. 1809, ACA-JSC, 4; proclamation of the Junta Central, 24 Feb. 1809, ibid.; and proclamation of the *alcalde mayor* of Cádiz, 28 Feb. 1809, BN-CGI, R6000-11. As promised, meanwhile, Villel's conduct was duly investigated by a species of public inquiry, but the lengthy report that this produced is not very enlightening: while Villel was completely exhonerated of all wrongdoing, and not just that but also praised for the energy he had shown in such matters as strengthening the city's defenses and establishing a small-arms manufactory, the causes of the revolt are glossed over, the one point that does come through very strongly being the presence in the crowd of numerous members of the Voluntarios Distinguidos de Cádiz dressed in civilian clothes. See S. Sánchez, ed., *Expediente formado en virtud del Real Orden de la Suprema Junta Central y Gubernátiva del Reino, por la que sirvió dar comisión a los Señores D. Miguel Alfonso Villagómez y D. Tomás Moyano del Consejo de S.M. en el Real y Supremo de Castilla para examinar la conducta del Excelentísimo SeñorMarqués de Villel, Conde de Darius, Grande de España de primera clase, gentilhombre de cara de S.M., con ejercicio, vocal de la misma suprema junta y su comisionado en esta plaza* (Cádiz, 1809), BN-CGI, R60013-3.

81. Fée, *Souvenirs,* 63.

82. F. Valdés Fernández, *La Guerra de la Independencia en Badajoz: Fuentes francesas, I—memorias* (Badajoz, 2003), 152.

83. Jacob, *Travels in the South of Spain,* 32–60 passim. For an even more negative description of the atmosphere that reigned in Seville under the Junta Central, see Schepeler, *Histoire de la guerre d'Espagne et de Portugal,* 2:387–89.

84. Anonymous, *El duende de nuestro ejército descubierto por un buen patríota* (Cádiz, 1810), 5, BN-CGI, R60087.

85. *El Patríota,* n.d., no. 1, p. 4, HMM, AH1-5 (no. 158).

86. *El duende de nuestros ejércitos,* 21.

87. A. Haley, ed., *The Soldier Who Walked Away: Autobiography of Andrew Pearson, a Peninsula-War Veteran* (Liverpool, n.d.), 65.

88. Lord Wellesley to M. de Garay, 21 Aug. 1809, in M. Martin, *The Dispatches and Correspondence of Richard Marquess of Wellesley during His Mission to Spain in 1809* (London, 1838), 46–48. For a general denunciation of the actions and efficacy of the junta, see *El Español,* 30 Apr. 1810, 23.

89. Roche to Lord Wellington, 10 Oct. 1809, in Second Duke of Wellington, ed., *Supplementary Despatches, Correspondence, and Memoranda of Field Marshal Arthur Duke of Wellington, K.G.,* 4 vols. (London, 1858–72), 6:394.

90. *El Espectador Sevillano,* 20 Jan. 1810, 439–40.

91. "Notebook in the Hand of Richard Wellesley II of Events in Spain and Portugal, October 1809–January 1810," University of Southampton, Carver MSS, no. 53.

92. For a detailed discussion of conscription in Spain in the period 1808–10, see C. J. Esdaile, "Conscription in Spain in the Napoleonic Era," in D. Stoker, F. C. Schneid, and H. D. Blanton, eds., *Conscription in the Napoleonic Era: A Revolution in Military Affairs?* (Abingdon, 2009), 102–21.

93. Mendoza y Rico, *Historia de Málaga,* 77.

94. Ibid., 77–78.

95. For the troubles of Carmona, see Navarro, "Juntas locales," 109–20. Meanwhile, the disastrous state of the Milicia Honrada, which was mirrored in other towns, such as Palma del Río, is abundantly testfied to by a proclamation that issued was issued by the captain general of Andalucía, Ventura Escalante, in September 1809: "Every day a mass of petitions reaches me . . . asking for exemption from service in the Milicia Honrada. Some of their authors claim, entirely falsely, that they are prevented from serving by age or infirmity; others cite their dedication to their career or to the posts that they occupy; and still others make out that service as a common soldier is incompatible with their rank in society. As if all this was not enough, there are also those, and not just a few of them at that, who compete for decorations or appointments in the militia while at at the same time having not the slightest intention of serving in its ranks. And one and all accompany their applications with pompous references, matters such as their name and family, that do not have the slightest connection with the patriotism and illustration that ought to be the guide of all good Spaniards at the current moment." Order of the day of V.Escalante Rodríguez, 13 Sept. 1809, BN-CGI, R60002-32. For the situation in Palma del Río, see B. Pareja Cano, "El reglamento para la formación de la Milicia Honrada: El caso de la villa de Palma y su partido, 1808–1809," in Cuenca Toribio, *Andalucía en la Guerra de la Independencia,* 123–31.

96. J. de Sandoval to M. de Garay, 13 Jan. 1809, AHN-SE, 31-A, no. 1.

97. For all this, see A. Moliner Prada, "La conflictividad social en la Guerra de la Independencia," *Trienio* 35 (May 2000): 81–115; and Esdaile, *Fighting Napoleon,* 61–89. For a good example of the sort of regulation and control to which the populace were regularly subjected, one has only to turn to various orders of the days that were issued in Seville in April 1809. Having first been subjected to a census that should have provided the authorities with the address of every man, woman, and child in the city, the populace found themselves under the heel of a regime that was at least the equal of anything that the French introduced in, say, Madrid. Thus, no one could leave the city for more than twenty-four hours or move from one house to another without obtaining the permission of the authorities, just as no one could have anyone stay under their roof without informing the authorities of their presence. See proclamation of Eusebio de Herrera, 22 Apr. 1809, BN-CGI, 60002-19. Still worse, meanwhile, was an order that appeared in the town of Isla de León in July of the same year, this imposing a strict curfew, subjecting such groups as beggars and street vendors to the constant threat of arrest, and prohibiting the playing even of such games as were deemed pemissable—chess, draughts, and *alquerque*—in public. See proclamation of Sebastián de Solis, Isla de León, 18 July 1809, BN-CGI, R60002-29.

98. For a general discussion of this phenomenon, see E. Martínez Ruiz, "Desertores y dispersos a comienzos de la Guerra de la Independencia: Su reflejo en Málaga," in Reder Gadow and Mendoza García, *Guerra de la Independencia en Málaga,* 145–63.

99. The reference is to the regular collection taken up in Spanish churches to pay for masses to be said for the souls of the dead.

100. Semple, *Second Journey in Spain,* 108–10.

101. Ilchester, *Spanish Journal of Elizabeth, Lady Holland,* 332–33.

102. Junta of Ecija to Junta Suprema Central, 13 June 1809, AHN-SE, 82-C, no. 335.

103. J. Pinto y Palacios to M. de Garay, 24 July 1809, ibid., 62-F, no. 168.

104. For example, A. Gil de la Parra to M. de Garay, 18 June 1809, ibid., no. 167.

Chapter 3

1. The presence of Polish troops is explained by the fact that considerable numbers of the French troops who served in Spain were in reality not French at all, but rather representatives of one or other of the various satellite states. Most of these forces did not fight in Andalucía, but the Poles were there in substantial numbers: one of Sébastiani's two infantry divisions was made up entirely of six battalions drawn from the army of the Grand Duchy of Warsaw, while, as noted, his light cavalry brigade included the Lancers of the Vistula, this being a unit formed from Poles serving in the Prussian army who had been taken prisoner in 1806 and volunteered to join the French army. See C. González Caizán, "La participación polaca en la ocupación de Andalucía por el ejército imperial: Estado de la investigación," *Cuadernos del bicentenario,* 10 (Dec. 2010): 5–24.

2. K. Wojciechowski, *Mis memorias de España,* ed. J. S. Ciechanowski et al. (Madrid, 2009) 110.

3. A. Brémond d'Ars, ed., *Historique du 21e Régiment de Chasseurs à Cheval 1792–1814: Souvenirs militaires* (Paris, 1903), 203–204.

4. M. Moreno Alonso, *Historia general de Andalucía* (Sevilla, 1981), 390. The real figure has been estimated as something between 2,000,000 and 2,500,000 people.

5. Lynch, *Bourbon Spain,* 196.

6. Jacob, *Travels in the South of Spain,* 236.

7. Vicens Vives, *Historia de España y América social y económica,* 4:7.

8. Ibid., 4:5.

9. The most complete and, indeed, objective contemporary account of the geography of Andalucía is Laborde, *View of Spain,* 2:1–150.

10. M. Moreno Alonso, "La Sierra de Aracena en el siglo XIX: Contribución a la historia real de España," in *Andalucía contemporánea, siglos XIX y XX: Actas del I Congreso de Historia de Andalucía* (Córdoba, 1979), 2:106.

11. The best accounts of the construction of La Carolina may be found in M. Capel, *La Carolina, capital de las nuevas poblaciones: Un ensayo de reforma socio-económica de España en el siglo XVIII* (Jaén, 1970), 97–112; and J. Hauben, "The First Decade of an Agrarian Experiment in Bourbon Spain: The New Towns of the Sierra Morena and Andalucía, 1766–76," *Agricultural History* 39, no. 1 (Jan. 1965): 34–40. See also M. Defourneaux, *Pablo de Olavide ou l'afrancesado, 1725–1803* (Paris, 1959), 175–245. For the views of three foreign visitors, see H. Swinburne, *Travels through Spain in the Years 1775 and 1776* (Dublin, 1779), 327–31; W. Dalrymple, *Travels through Spain and Portugal in 1774 with a Short Account of the Spanish Expedition against Algiers in 1775* (London, 1777), 24–27; and J. Townsend, *A Journey through Spain and Portugal in the Years 1786 and 1787 with Particular Attention to the Agriculture, Manufactures, Commerce, Population, Taxes, and Revenue of the Country and Remarks in Passing through a Part of France,* 2 vols. (London, 1792), 2:289–96. Strictly speaking, although located within the boundaries of Córdoba and Jaén, the *nuevas poblaciones* (new settlements, as they were called) were not part of those provinces but were subject to the Madrid-based Intendencia

General de Nuevas Poblaciones, while their inhabitants also enjoyed a privileged legal status (among other things, they were exempt from military service).

12. Swinburne, *Travels through Spain,* 291–93. See also Townsend, *Journey through Spain,* 2:300.

13. Bourgoing, *Modern State of Spain,* 3:125–27.

14. Ibid., 4:209.

15. Jacob, *Travels in the South of Spain,* 54–55.

16. Croker, *Travels,* 87–89.

17. M. Matthys, "Baeza en el siglo XIX: Un estudio de demografia social," in *Andalucía contemporánea, siglos XIX y XX: Actas del I Congreso de Historia de Andalucía* (Córdoba, 1979), 2:87.

18. Bourgoing, *Modern State of Spain,* 4:128, 134, 206.

19. See F. J. Oliva Flores, "Yunquera en los años previos a la Guerra de la Independencia," in Reder Gadow and Mendoza García, *Guerra de la Independencia en Málaga,* 259–65.

20. According to some observers, the cultivation of sugar cane at such places as Motril was experiencing a sharp decline on account of the heavy duties that were levied upon it. See Swinburne, *Travels through Spain,* 181.

21. Ibid., 126–27. For an equally uncomfortable stopping place at Gaucín, see Dalrymple, *Travels through Spain and Portugal,* 2–3.

22. Swinburne, *Travels through Spain,* 265–66.

23. For a description of this route, see Jacob, *Travels in the South of Spain,* 219–24.

24. R. Twiss, *Travels through Portugal and Spain in 1772 and 1773* (London, 1775), 231–32. Another traveler on this same stretch of road was Henry Swinburne: "Yesterday afternoon we had nothing but rapid ascents and descents, rendered incredibly greasy and fatigueing by the heavy rain of the proceeding night. . . . The Cuesta de Yerma . . . is perhaps not to be matched for badness on any carriage road in the world. All our mules yoked together were scarce able to . . . drag [the carriages] up the almost perpendicular parts of this abominable mountain." *Travels through Spain,* 144–45.

25. Croker, *Travels,* 105–106.

26. Details of the silk industry in Seville may be found in G. Desdevises du Dézert, *La España del antiguo régimen* (Madrid, 1989), 677; and Townsend, *Journey through Spain,* 2:332–34. Weatherall's enterprise is mentioned in Jacob, *Travels in the South of Spain,* 165. For the tobacco factory, meanwhile, see Twiss, *Travels through Portugal and Spain,* 306–307. Finally, Córdoba is discussed in J. Lynch, *Spain, 1516–1598: From Nation State to World Empire* (Oxford, 1991), 167–68.

27. Jacob, *Travels in the South of Spain,* 39. Swinburne is much less appreciative, complaining of "winding streets and horrible kennels of black stagnated water . . . [from which] there arose an almost suffocating stench." *Travels through Spain,* 228. Equally, Bourgoing notes that the rest of its manufactures were minimal, the town only being able to boast of a mere twenty looms that produced "some linen and ribbons." *Modern State of Spain,* 3:141. Meanwhile, as the French never entered Cádiz, no attempt is made to describe it here. However, Bourgoing describes it as an "insufferably stinking" warren of a city much troubled by both petty crime and swarms of rats that ran about the streets each night, being "extremely troublesome to those that walk late." Ibid., 3:231–40 passim.

28. Swinburne, *Travels through Spain,* 268, 281.

29. Ibid., 279–80.

30. Jacob, *Travels in the South of Spain,* 56, 71.

31. Swinburne, *Travels through Spain,* 179–80, 203–204. The extent of Granada's decline may well have been exaggerated by Swinburne and other observers, modern research having suggested that the second half of the eighteenth century actually witnessed a modest economic revival based on the cultivation of such cash crops as hemp and flax (both raw materials that were in much demand for naval construction) and the demands of the colonial trade. Yet the basis of this period of relative prosperity was extremely weak—if the production of both silk and wool were flourishing, for example, they really only did so because of the captive market represented by the Americas. War with Britain from 1796, then, brought economic disaster: between 1797 and 1804 the population of the city of Granada declined from 65,000–70,000 to 55,000 people. See E. Díaz Lobón, *Granada durante la crisis del antiguo régimen* (Granada, 1982), 17–100 passim.

32. Bourgoing, *Modern State of Spain,* 4:223. For a slightly more favourable account, see Dalrymple, *Travels through Spain and Portugal,* 14–15. The mosque Bourgoing refers to is, of course, the cathedral.

33. Swinburne, *Travels through Spain,* 321. See also Townsend, *Journey through Spain,* 2:301.

34. Twiss, *Travels through Portugal and Spain,* 332.

35. Croker, *Travels,* 121–23. The Colonel Espinosa referred to was a retired Spanish officer who had befriended Croker and his fellow prisoners.

36. Townsend, *Journey through Spain,* 3:17.

37. Ibid., 3:16. Swinburne describes the paupers he saw in Granada as "sturdy, able-bodied rascals that live by alms and conventual donations." *Travels through Spain,* 209–10.

38. Townsend, *Journey through Spain,* 3:23. As this suggests, the mortality from sickness was at all times extremely high. What Townsend ignores, however, is the vulnerability of Andalucía to repeated episodes of epidemic disease, the most recent of these being the outbreaks of yellow fever that ravaged the coastal littoral and part of the interior between 1801 and 1804. In 1801 alone, 14,685 people died of this cause in Seville and 7,195 in Cádiz. See Bourgoing, *Modern State of Spain,* 3:131, 185.

39. Townsend, *Journey through Spain,* 3:17. Passing through Cádiz prior to his visit to Málaga, Townsend was much struck by the city's workhouse, the only institution of its kind in the whole of Andalucía, which at the time of his visit housed no fewer than 834 inmates, including ninety-seven who had been forcibly incarcerated there "under correction"; typically enough, however, he lamented its management as being too lenient, and expressed the opinion that, rather than being encouraged to work through the promise of pay, the paupers should be denied food until they had performed a set amount of work. Cf. ibid., 2:377–83.

40. Lynch, *Bourbon Spain,* 204; Matthys, "Baeza en el siglo XIX," 2:89–90.

41. See Jacob, *Travels in the South of Spain,* 169. The *alcabala* did not just hit smallholders but also drove up food prices: "The people [of Córdoba] complain much of the imposts; they say [that] by going two or three leagues out of the town to any of the villages, bread, the chief aliment of the Spaniards, is to be had three or four *cuartos* a pound cheaper." Dalrymple, *Travels through Spain and Portugal,* 20.

42. Dalrymple, *Travels through Spain and Portugal,* 40–41.

43. J. Lynch, *The Hispanic World in Crisis and Change, 1598–1700* (Oxford, 1992), 203.

44. Ibid., 49.

45. For the Lebrija massacre, see J. Cortines, ed., *Felipe Cortines Murube: De la independencia—los franceses en Lebrija y otros escritos* (Lebrija, 2008), 13–28. Interestingly, the incident took place against a backdrop of rising social tension: in the course of the autumn, the prisoners had been used to bring in the olive crop, and this had forced down the wages paid to the local *braceros*.

46. G. Brenan, *The Spanish Labyrinth* (Cambridge, 1943), 122.

47. R. Agüera Espejo-Saavedra, *Villa del Río, 1810–1812: El padrón de los franceses* (Córdoba, 2003), 70–71.

48. Townsend, *Journey through Spain*, 3:27–28.

49. P. de Olavide, "Informe sobre la ley agraria," in E. Núñez, ed., *Pablo de Olavide: Obras selectas* (Lima, 1987), 492.

50. Brenan, *Spanish Labyrinth*, 121.

51. Twiss, *Travels through Portugal and Spain*, 266.

52. Valenzuela Saavedra, *Jaén ante la invasion francesa*, 28.

53. Olavide, "Informe sobre la ley agraria," 493.

54. Lynch, *Bourbon Spain*, 205.

55. See Olavide, "Informe sobre la ley agraria," 491–92.

56. Ibid., 487–88.

57. Townsend, *Journey through Spain*, 2:421. The *fanega* was a measure of grain equivalent to approximately one hundredweight.

58. Ibid., 3:17–18.

59. A further aspect of popular violence that needs to be considered here, however, is that of the common brawl. Spanish society was, as we have seen, generally deemed to be incorrigibly violent, and in Andalucía this problem was held to be particularly acute on account of the hot winds that blew from Africa and supposedly inflamed the natural irascibility of the populace. While this is not to be taken too literally, the miserable conditions endured by the *braceros* probably gave rise to many vicious arguments that ended in stabbings and even blood feuds. See Bourgoing, *Modern State of Spain*, 1:281–82; and Laborde, *View of Spain*, 2:148.

60. Townsend, *Journey through Spain*, 3:47, 51.

61. Twiss, *Travels through Portugal and Spain*, 228–29.

62. See E. Hobsbawm, *Primitive Rebels: Studies in Archaic Social Movements in the Nineteenth and Twentieth Centuries* (Manchester, 1971).

63. J. Santos Torres, *El bandolerismo en España: Una historia fuera del ley* (Madrid, 1995), 57.

64. Ibid., 17–29.

65. See "La leyenda de Diego Corrientes Mateos," accessed 30 Nov. 2009, http://www.juntadeandalucia.es/averroes/ceipcastilblanco/novedad/leyenda3.htm.

66. J. F. Botrel, "'El que a los ricos robaba': Diego Corrientes, el bandido generoso y la opinión pública," Biblióteca Virtual Miguel de Cervantes, accessed 30 Nov. 2009, http://www.cervantesvirtual.com/servlet/SirveObras/12937733117075979643624/p0000001.htm.

67. J. Santos Torres, *El bandolerismo en Andalucía, I: Sevilla y su antiguo reino* (Seville, 1991), 149–97 passim.

68. D. Pastor Petit, *El bandolerismo en España: Cinco siglos de desequilibrio social y de bandolerismo* (Barcelona, 1979), 21.
69. B. López Morán, *El bandolerismo gallego en la primera mitad del siglo XIX* (La Coruña, 1995), 48–54, 173–209.
70. Ibid., 55–57.
71. Townsend, *Travels in Spain,* 3:52.
72. Saint Pierre and Saint Pierre, *Mémoires du Maréchal Soult,* 177.
73. Despite these obvious reservations, there were still links between smuggling and banditry. As Townsend observed, smugglers whose bands had been broken up by the authorities, or who found themselves destitute and deprived of their previous followings as a result of a term of imprisonment, might very well turn to more violent forms of crime as their only means of sustenance. See Townsend, *Journey through Spain,* 3:306–307.
74. Desdevises du Dézert, *España del antiguo regimen,* 44.
75. Defourneaux, *Pablo de Olavide,* 269.
76. For some interesting remarks in this respect, see Jacob, *Travels in the South of Spain,* 90–93; and Croker, *Travels,* 126–33.
77. See W. Callahan, *Church, Politics, and Society in Spain, 1750–1874* (Cambridge, Mass., 1984), 66.
78. Ibid., 93. For events at Jabugo, see Moreno Alonso, "Sierra de Aracena en el siglo XIX," 110.
79. Jacob, *Travels in the South of Spain,* 99–100.
80. Callahan, *Church, Politics, and Society,* 10.
81. Ibid., 6–46 passim.
82. Ibid., 15–16, 23–24, 63–64.
83. Ibid., 64.
84. Townsend, *Journey through Spain,* 3:81–82.
85. Defourneaux, *Pablo de Olavide,* 252.
86. Twiss, *Travels through Portugal and Spain,* 254–55.
87. Laborde, *View of Spain,* 2:149.
88. Swinburne, *Travels through Spain,* 244–46.
89. Laborde, *View of Spain,* 2:149.
90. Ibid., 5:295.

Chapter 4

1. Girardin, *Journal et souvenirs,* 4:287–88.
2. See Carnicero Toribio, *Historia razonada,* 2:80. For a French point of view, see Miot de Melito, *Mémoires,* 3:59–60.
3. A. J. Bigarré, *Mémoires du Général Bigarré, aide-de-camp du Roi Joseph, 1775–1813* (Paris, 1903), 256–62.
4. Fée, *Souvenirs,* 36. See also Miot de Melito, *Mémoires,* 3:74.
5. Bigarré, *Mémoires,* 251.
6. See Comte de La Forest to J. B. de Champagny, 27 Jan. 1809, in G. de Grandmaison, *Correspondance du Comte de la Forest ambassadeur de France en Espagne, 1808–1813,* 7 vols. (Paris, 1905–13) , 2:23.
7. Comte de La Forest to J. B. de Champagny, 1 Feb. 1809, in ibid., 37.
8. Girardin, *Journal et souvenirs,* 4:131–32.
9. Comte de La Forest to J. B. de Champagny, 1 Apr. 1809, in Grandmaison, *Correspondance du Comte de la Forest,* 2:133.

10. Girardin, *Journal et souvenirs,* 4:263.

11. Connelly, *Napoleon's Satellite Kingdoms,* 237–38; Ross, *Reluctant King,* 175.

12. The most recent general discussion of the phenomenon of *afrancesamiento* is constituted by J. López Tabar, *Los famosos traidores: Los afrancesados durante la crisis del antiguo regimen, 1808–1833* (Madrid, 2001). For Goya in particular, see G. Dufour, *Goya durante la Guerra de la Independencia* (Madrid, 2008). The issue of the extent of Goya's *afrancesamiento* has been the subject of much debate; the truth appears to be that, while the Aragonese painter was no enthusiast for French intervention in Spain, he was at the same time far from enamored by the Patriot cause: the famous engravings known as *The Disasters of War,* for example, were originally entitled *The Fatal Consequences of the Bloody War in Spain against Napoleon.*

13. E. Asín Cormán, *Los toros josefinos: Corridas de toros en la Guerra de la Independencia bajo el reinado de José I Bonaparte, 1808–1814* (Zaragoza, 2008), 135–39.

14. Miot de Melito, *Mémoires,* 3:66–67.

15. Ibid., 3:77–78.

16. Joseph Bonaparte to Napoleon, 10 Nov. 1808, MCPMRJ, 5:267.

17. For Napoleon's support for the formation of a Spanish army, see Napoleon to Joseph Bonaparte, 7 Jan. 1809, ibid., 5:317.

18. P. Haythornthwaite, ed., *In the Peninsula with a French Hussar: Memoirs of the War of the French in Spain* (London, 1990), 69.

19. Clermont-Tonnerre, *Expédition d'Espagne,* 251–52.

20. L. Sorando Muzas, "El ejército español del Rey José I: Componentes, efectivos, y uniformidad," in Dirección General de Relaciones Institucionales, ed., *La Guerra de la Independencia, 1808–1814: El pueblo español, su ejército, y sus aliados frente a la ocupación napoleónica* (Madrid, 2008), 367–72. It here deserves to be said that, according to Clermont-Tonnerre, of the 5,600 rank and file who were taken at Uclés, only 3,000 actually enlisted with the French, the remainder either succeeding in making their escape or electing to remain in captivity rather than fight against their former comrades. At least in the regular army, then, it is arguable that popular devotion to the cause of Ferdinand VII was much greater than is sometimes argued. It is therefore probably just as well that initially the number of Spaniards required was not very great: the royal guard was formed on the basis of the escort of Neapolitan troops who had accompanied Joseph to Bayonne; the two foreign infantry regiments in part from remnants of the Swiss, Walloon, and Irish regiments of the armed forces of Charles IV and in part from deserters from the British army; and the gendarmes from men seconded from the Imperial Guard.

21. A hero of the Revolutionary Wars, Jourdan had been given his marshal's baton in 1804 as a sop to Jacobin opinion but had been denied both the dukedom given to most of his fellows and employment in Napoleon's campaigns. For a brief life of Marshal Jourdan, see M. Glover, "'The True Patriot'—Jourdan," in *Napoleon's Marshals,* ed. D. G. Chandler (New York, 1987), 156–75.

22. Lovett, *Napoleon and the Birth of Modern Spain,* 503.

23. For Joseph's visit to Segovia, see Miot de Melito, *Mémoires,* 3:71–72.

24. Joseph Bonaparte to Napoleon, 7 Aug. 1809, MCPMRJ, 6:300.

25. *Correo Polítíco y Militar de la Ciudad de Córdoba,* 27 Jan. 1810, 2.

26. Ibid., 1.

27. Proclamation of Joseph Bonaparte, 27 Jan. 1810.

28. *Correo Político y Militar de la Ciudad de Córdoba,* 28 Jan. 1810, 1–3, ibid.

29. *Circular del Ministro de Negocios Eclesiásticos a todos los obispos, arzobispos, abades, párrocos y demas prelados,* 3 Feb. 1810, BN-CGI, R60014-7.

30. For the religious ceremony of 4 February, see Díaz Torrejón, *José Napoleón I en el sur de España,* 107–109; and Moreno Alonso, *Sevilla napoleónica,* 38–41. Meanwhile, some idea of the planning that was involved in such ceremonies may be obtained by the orders issued the day before by the town council in accordance with the instructions that had been received by Francisco Amoros, the city's newly appointed superintendent of police: in brief, the streets were to be cleaned and cleared of all obstructions, every house decorated in as fine a manner as possible, notices put up to warn the populace what was going on, and lists prepared of members of the"deserving poor" to whom the king could distribute alms. See proclamation of the town council of Seville, 3 Feb. 1810, BN-CGI, R60014-66.

31. How far they were respected is impossible to say, but the advance of the French had been marked by the issue of strict orders against looting. For example, see Order of the day of Marshal Soult, 25 Jan. 1810, *Correo Político y Militar de la Ciudad de Córdoba,* 28 Jan. 1810, 3–4.

32. Royal Decrees, 7 June 1809, 11 Feb. 1811, in *Gazeta de Sevilla,* 13 Feb. 1811, 1, 5.

33. Díaz Torrejón, *José Napoleón I en el sur de España,* 112–13.

34. *Gazeta de Sevilla,* 13 Feb. 1810, 7–8. There being clear evidence that not a single *cívica* had been enlisted at this point, we may conclude that no such grand review took place. That this was so, however, was immaterial, what mattered at this point being to paint a picture of *andaluces* of every class rushing to enlist with the cause of King Joseph.

35. Ibid., 5–6; Díaz Torrejón, *José Napoleón I en el sur de España,* 105.

36. "Real decreto por el que restituye el nombre de Itálica a la ciudad que se nombra así en el tiempo de los romanos y se consignan rentas para las excavaciones," 8 Feb. 1810, in Anonymous, *Prontuario de las leyes y decretos del Rey Nuestro Señor Don José Napoleón I,* 2:27. See also Miot de Melito, *Mémoires,* 3:109.

37. Díaz Torrejón, *José Napoleón I en el sur de España,* 105.

38. Bigarré, *Mémoires,* 269–70.

39. *Gazeta de Sevilla,* 13 Feb. 1811, 8.

40. Díaz Torrejón, *José Napoleón I en el sur de España,* 110–11.

41. *Gazeta del Gobierno de Sevilla,* 6 Feb. 1810, 1–2.

42. Díaz Torrejón, *José Napoleón I en el sur de España,* 106.

43. Bigarré, *Mémoires,* 266.

44. *Gazeta de Sevilla,* 16 Feb. 1810, 14–15.

45. Ibid., 20 Feb. 1810, 20–21; Díaz Torrejón, *José Napoleón I en el sur de España,* 140–44.

46. *Gazeta de Sevilla,* 20 Feb. 1810, 22. What the *Gazeta de Sevilla* did not report was the scornful response returned by the Duque de Alburquerque to the formal invitation to surrender that was extended him in the course of the royal visit to Puerto de Santa María. See *Contestación dada por el Capitán General de los cuatro reinos de Andalucía y jefe del ejército, Duque de Alburquerque, a la carta recibida del general francés Duque de Dalmacía por parlamentario dirijido desde Chiclana en 16 de febrero de 1810* (Seville, 1810), BN-CGI, R60002-54.

47. *Gazeta de Sevilla,* 20 Feb. 1810, 23.

48. Ibid.

49. Ibid., 23 Feb. 1810, 27. Joseph appears to have returned from Andalucía absolutely convinced of the need to make bullfighting a central plank of his public relations. At all events, no sooner had he returned to Madrid than he gave orders for a full season of *corridas* to be organized as soon as was decently possible. This took some time—not only were the necessary horses and bulls lacking but also the war had dispersed the greatest names in bullfighting to the four winds—but by 24 June all was ready: no fewer than 190,000 reales had been invested in repairing the *plaza de toros*, over 100 bulls had been brought into the city from various places in the Tagus valley, and as fine a company of *toreros* and *picadores* had been assembled as had ever taken to an arena—among the names concerned are to be found some of the greatest of the day, including Juan Núñez ("Sentimientos"), Francisco Herrera ("Curro Guillén), Alfonso Alarcón (El Pocho), Jerónimo Cándido, and José Romero. There followed no fewer than twelve bullfights in what remained of 1810, while many others were held in 1811 and 1812, those that coincided with *fêtes napoléoniques* being both particularly lavish and free to the public. What is interesting here, however, is the extent to which the bullfighting world seems to have collaborated quite happily with the *josefino* authorities: the only concerns that were raised by the *toreros* related to the amount they would get paid and, in the case of those who had to come from Andalucía—seemingly the majority—the dangers that they might face on the road (that this was a sensible concern was demonstrated by the fact that a party of twelve *toreros* and *picadores* who had elected to travel to Madrid together were set upon by bandits on the road near Santa Cruz de Mudela and robbed of 15,900 reales). Truly, then, these were swords for hire, though not at the cost of Joseph Bonaparte: as Asín points out, the whole season was paid for by the town council of Madrid. For all this, see Asín Cormán, *Toros josefinos,* 154–99 passim.

50. For all this, see ibid., 151–317 passim. Joseph's return to Seville having coincided with Holy Week, the king immediately flung himself into the traditional round of processions for which Seville is so famous. Miot de Melito, *Mémoires,* 3:141.

51. Bigarré, *Mémoires,* 272–74.

52. Ibid., 272–73.

53. Miot de Melito, *Mémoires,* 3:118–19.

54. Clermont-Tonnerre, *Expédition d'Espagne,* 350–51.

55. Ibid., 352.

56. Ibid., 390. For the incident with the smugglers at Ronda, see *Gazeta de Sevilla,* 9 Mar. 1809, 63.

57. Clermont–Tonnerre, *Expédition d'Espagne,* 370–71.

58. *Gazeta de Sevilla,* 13 Apr. 1810, 143–44.

59. For an excellent discussion of the general outline of the message pushed by Napoleon and his acolytes, see R. Holtman, *Napoleonic Propaganda* (New York, 1950), 1–36.

60. For a detailed discussion of the themes outlined in this paragraph, see A. Forrest, "The Ubiquitous Brigand: The Language and Politics of Repression," in Esdaile, *Popular Resistance in the French Wars,* 25–44.

61. *Gazeta de Madrid,* 17 Apr. 1809, 535.

62. Ibid., 1 May 1809, 580.

63. Ibid., 2 May 1809, 581.

64. Ibid., 18 Apr. 1809, 520.

65. Ibid., 5 May 1809, 597–98.
66. Ibid., 16 May 1809, 647.
67. Ibid., 12 May 1809, 627.
68. Ibid., 6 May 1809, 599–601.
69. Ibid., 8 May 1809, 608–10.
70. Ibid., 26 Apr. 1809, 554–55.
71. Ibid., 22 Apr. 1809, 540.
72. Ibid., 539. In reality, British losses in the course of the campaign were no more than about 6,000 men, while even after the horrors of the retreat—admittedly a grim business—Sir John Moore's army proved capable of more than holding its own when the French finally came up with it at La Coruña. As for material losses, while many horses and wagons and copious stores of food and munitions certainly had to be abandoned, none of the army's guns were lost, the artillery pieces referred to consisting either of the weapons stationed on the walls of La Coruña or others that had been sent from England to equip the Spanish army.
73. Ibid., 28 May 1809, 694–95. The insertion of a news report of a battle that was actually fought on 18 February at this point may seem odd, but it should be remembered that, with Tortosa, Tarragona, Lérida, and Huesca all still in the hands of the Patriot forces at this point, there was no direct communication between the French forces in Catalonia and those in central Spain, the result being that news of the French victory could only have reached King Joseph via Paris. As for the contents of the report, these are clearly exaggerated: though heavily defeated at Valls, the Spaniards lost only 3,000 men at most, while the "large number of artillery pieces" turns out to have been just eight.
74. Ibid., 695.
75. Ibid., 2 June 1809, 718.
76. Ibid., 23 May 1809, 676.
77. Ibid., 26 May 1809, 688.
78. Ibid., 2 May 1809, 581–83.
79. Ibid., 28 May 1809, 695.
80. *Gazeta de Gobierno de Sevilla,* 11 Feb. 1810, 4–5.
81. See *Gazeta de Sevilla,* 23 Feb. 1810, 23, ibid.
82. *Gazeta de Gobierno de Sevilla,* 10 Feb. 1810, 7, ibid. In addition to the more obvious aspects of this passage, we see here a clever attempt to stress a strong measure of continuity with the past. Thus, the individuals who made up the commission established by the minister of the interior are described in the original as *hombres inteligentes y amigos de su país,* this being a clear echo of the network of the numerous *sociedades de amigos de su país* that sprang up as intellectual discussion groups and forcing houses of reform in the late eighteenth century.
83. Ibid., 8 Feb. 1810, 3.
84. *Gazeta de Sevilla,* 23 Feb. 1810, 27, ibid. For the claims in respect of the Guardia Cívica of Granada, see ibid., 28.
85. *Gazeta del Gobierno de Sevilla,* 8 Feb. 1810, 4, ibid.
86. For the text of Maestre's sermon, see ibid., 6 Feb. 1810, 2–4.
87. Ibid., 11 Feb. 1810, 5–6.
88. For the full text of this encyclical, see *Gazeta de Sevilla,* 27 Feb. 1810, 37–40, ibid.
89. Ibid., 20 Feb. 1810, 22.
90. Ibid., 23 Feb. 1810, 30–31.
91. Ibid., 6 Mar. 1810, 51–53.

92. For all this, see, for example, ibid., 13 Mar. 1810, 67–71. Very similar sentiments are expressed by an article entitled “Carta de un granadino” that first appeared in the *Gazeta de Granada* but was later reprinted in a number of other *afrancesado* newspapers. See *Gazeta de Oficio del Gobierno de Vizcaya,* 10 Aug. 1810, 2–4.

93. Proclamation of B. de Aranza, 6 Apr. 1810, in *Gazeta de Sevilla,* 6 Apr. 1810, 127.

94. Ibid., 124–25.

95. Ibid., 22 Apr. 1810, 188–90.

96. Ibid., 10 Apr. 1810, 132.

97. Ibid., 6 Apr. 1810, 124.

98. In fact Romero—his full name was José Romero Alvarez—had been living in the nearby town of Montellano, where despite a ten-year term of imprisonment imposed for the murder of a captain in the regular army in 1797, he had, at the beginning of 1810, occupied the post of mayor. On 22 April, however, the French had burned Montellano, whereupon Romero had fled to Algodonales.

99. Proclamation of B. de Aranza, 8 May 1810, AHN-SE, 2994. For a full account of the Algodonales affair, see below.

100. *Gazeta de Sevilla,* 23 Mar. 1810, 95. For good measure Ubeda was also forced to pay a fine of 300,000 reales.

101. Ibid., 11 May 1810, 328.

102. Proclamation of B. de Aranza, 17 July 1810, in *Gazeta del Oficio del Gobierno de Vizcaya,* 15 Aug. 1810, 4, BN, Z/11558; *Gazeta de Sevilla,* 28 Sept. 1810, 724; ibid., 28 Dec. 1810, 932.

103. *Gazeta Extraordinaria de Sevilla,* 2 May 1810, 282; 16 Apr. 1810, 153; 28 Apr. 1810, 268–69.

104. *Gazeta de Sevilla,* 17 Aug. 1810, 607, ibid.

105. Ibid., 30 Mar. 1810, 108; 29 May 1810, 381–86.

106. Ibid., 17 Aug. 1810, 609. The Spaniards returned their losses as 600 men, while French casualties are estimated at 200. See Oman, *Peninsular War,* 3:331.

107. *Gazeta Extraordinaria de Sevilla,* 3 May 1810, 289.

108. *Gazeta de Sevilla,* 12 June 1810, 424, ibid.

109. *Gazeta Extraordinaria de Sevilla,* 25 June 1810, 453–54, ibid.

110. *Gazeta de Sevilla,* 25 May 1810, 376–77, ibid.

111. Ibid., 30 Apr. 1810, 269–72; 1 May 1810, 277–78; 4 May 1810, 301–304; 11 May 1810, 322–24.

112. Ibid., 20 Feb. 1810, 19–20.

113. Ibid., 18 May 1810, 337–38.

114. Ibid., 2 Aug. 1810, 573–74.

115. See, for example, ibid., 24 Apr. 1810, 217–20.

116. See ibid., 20 Apr. 1810, 173–74.

117. Ibid., 13 Apr. 1810, 138.

118. Ibid., 22 May 1810, 358–60.

119. See *Programa para el aniversario de S.M. el Emperador y Rey Napoleón, y de SM la Emperatriz y Reyna María Luisa, celebrado sobre las orillas del Betis por las tropas imperiales y galo-europeas el 15 y 16 de agosto de 1810* (Seville, 1810), BN-CGI, R60014-8. For a similar bill of fare dating from the celebration of Joseph's saint's day in 1812, see *Programa para la festividad de los días del Rey Nuestro Señor, Don Josef Napoleón I* (Seville, 1812), ibid. Broadly speaking, this was much the same except that in this case there was specific reference to the distribution of bread, meat,

vegetables, and *sopa económica* to lists of "deserving" poor drawn up by the town council, with the assistance of the city's parish priests. The mention of groups of musicians playing popular fandangos and the like is interesting. As María José de la Torre Molina has shown, music was an integral part of public ceremonies in the course of the French occupation. However, whereas the cathedral choirs and military bands that were their most obvious musical backdrop stressed the themes of the divinity of kingship and imperial glory, we here see music chosen not to overawe the populace, but rather to connect with them: indeed, it seems that in Málaga the street was appeased not just with bullfights but also displays of "gypsy dancing" (i.e., flamenco). See M. J. de la Torre Medina, "La música en las ceremonias públicas malaguenãs durante la ocupación napoleónica," in Reder Gadow and Mendoza García, *Guerra de la Independencia en Málaga,* 655–63.

Chapter 5

1. For full details of Soult's life prior to the Peninsular War, see Hayman, *Soult,* 17–83.

2. The sack of Oporto is remembered above all for the misfortunes of several hundred fugitive civilians who were caught on the city's quayside by French cavalry as they tried to flee across the bridge of boats linking the city with the suburb of Vila Nova de Gaia and were swept away by the current when their weight swamped several of the pontoons. It has often been said (not least by the current author) that the casualties of this incident alone ran into several thousands, but in fact the city's archives suggest that the total number of dead for the whole day was no more than 400. That said, the capture of the city was a grim affair that offers a marked contrast to the fall of Seville.

3. For Soult's policies in Oporto, see N. Gotteri, *Le maréchal Soult* (Paris, 2000), 317–18.

4. A. Thirion, *Souvenirs militaires* (Paris, 1892), 80–82.

5. Gotteri, *Maréchal Soult,* 317–28.

6. For a very different version of events, see the admittedly deeply hostile Saint-Chamans: according to him, Soult had hardly occupied Oporto before he was making use of a variety of agents to build up a party in support of his being given the throne. *Mémoires,* 133–34. A compromise position put forward by Hayman is that, in line with instructions from Napoleon that he should do everything in his power to break the hold of the Bragança dynasty, Soult encouraged the local elites to petition the French authorities for the transformation of Portugal into a French satellite, in exchange promising them his protection. See *Soult,* 112–13. In fairness to Soult, meanwhile, it has to be said that the idea that he should be offered the throne was hardly out of line with wider imperial policy at this stage—that he may, in fact, genuinely have believed that he was acting in the best interests of the French empire.

7. Or at least so it is always said. In the course of the Peninsular War and, more specifically, the campaign in Andalucía, Soult certainly amassed a large art collection that brought his descendents a fortune when it was dispersed after his death, but rather than literally being plundered, the paintings involved may rather have been the fruit of the expropriation and sale of the property of the religious orders, many of whose houses were adorned with a variety of masterpieces.

8. Saint-Chamans, *Mémoires,* 34–35. In accusing Soult of cowardice, Saint-Chamans, an embittered individual who seems to have been convinced that the marshal could have done more to further his career, may have gone too far, but it is clear that in battle Soult had a habit of producing ambitious plans and then failing to see that they were executed effectively, while at Albuera in particular his absence from the critical point on the battlefield—an absence, indeed, that may have been crucial in the loss of the battle—was particularly noticeable. For a more balanced assessment, it is worth citing Hippolyte d'Espinchal: "The Duke of Dalmatia could certainly be severe, brusque, and on occasion, greedy, but he had the essential qualities that merited the esteem, the confidence, and the devotion of the troops that fought at his orders. Attentive to the welfare of the soldier, for whom he nourished a genuine affection, as well as being careful to be sparing of his blood, he was just, fair, and contemptuous of all intrigue. At the same time, meanwhile, appreciative of true merit, he never forgot any officer fortunate enough to have attracted his attention." *Souvenirs Militaires,* 2:46–48.

9. Fée, *Souvenirs,* 135–36.

10. L. Lejeune, *Memoirs of Baron Lejeune, Aide-de-Camp to Marshals Berthier, Davout, and Oudinot,* ed. N. Bell, 2 vols.(London, 1897), 2:74; S. Blaze, *Mémoires d'un apothicaire sur le guerre d'Espagne pendant les années 1808 à 1814,* 2 vols. (Paris, 1828), 2:216. Edouard Lapène's version of the story, however, is rather less dramatic: according to him, Godinot rather shot himself in his billet and, at the same time, was motivated not so much by brutality on the part of Soult, but rather depression brought about by prolonged separation from his family. See E. Lapène, *Conquête de l'Andalousie: Campagne de 1810 et 1811 dans le midi d'Espagne* (Paris, 1823), 267–68.

11. Saint-Chamans, *Mémoires,* 34. Soult's administrative ability is best revealed by the events of July 1813. Ordered to take over the army that Wellington had decisively defeated at Vitoria on 21 June with the loss of all its cannon and baggage, within a month the marshal had managed to ready it for a counteroffensive that all but reached the gates of Pamplona before it was turned back at Sorauren.

12. The starting point for all biographical information on matters relating to the personnel of the empire is J. Tulard, *Dictonnaire Napoléon* (Paris, 1989). On the marshals in particular, however, see Chandler, *Napoleon's Marshals.*

13. Mendoza y Rico, *Historia de Málaga,* 118.

14. Ibid., 119, 144–46.

15. For all this, see Tulard, *Dictionnaire Napoléon;* and A. Pigeard, *Les etoiles de Napoléon* (Paris, 1996), 192–692 passim. Both Barrois and Claparède had enlisted as volunteers in 1792.

16. Haythornthwaite, ed., *Memoirs of the War of the French in Spain,* 92–93.

17. Fée, *Souvenirs,* 132. Another French observer who complains bitterly of the corruption that reigned in the military administration is the artilleryman Edouard Lapène: "The corps . . . , indeed, even the divisions, were encumbered with swarms of functionaries of every conceivable rank and employment. It is, perhaps, necessary to look among this swollen bureaucracy . . . for the origins of the many difficulties that hampered the supply of food." *Conquête de l'Andalousie,* 187.

18. In this Soult's forces do not appear to have been unusual. It is interesting in this respect to compare the three corps that invaded Andalucía in January 1810 with the similar force that invaded Portugal some six months later. Like

Soult, the overall commander, André Masséna, and his three corps commanders (Reynier, Ney, Junot) had all started their military careers as privates in either the Bourbon army or the forces of the Revolution, while of the eleven commanders of divisions or independent cavalry brigades (Merle, Heudelet, Marchand, Mermet, Loison, Clausel, Solignac, Montbrun, Soult, Lamotte, and Saint Croix), only one—Montbrun—had definitely held a commission under Louis XVI, though one or two others—Clausel, for example—came from backgrounds that would probably have enabled them to become officers had they been of an age to do so prior to 1789.

19. Bigarré, *Mémoires,* 233–34.

20. Bourgoing, *Modern State of Spain,* 2:260.

21. Ibid., 2:261–74.

22. G. Babst, ed., *Souvenirs d'un canonnier de l'Armée d'Espagne, 1808–1814* (Paris, 1892), 17–18.

23. Bourgoing, *Modern State of Spain,* 2:275–77.

24. Ibid., 2:250.

25. Ibid, 2:288.

26. For a good example, see Bigarré, *Mémoires,* 235–36.

27. Fée, *Souvenirs,* 3.

28. For a discussion of these massacres, see J. de Haro Malpesa, *Guerra de la Independencia: La Mancha, 1808—diarios, memorias, y cartas* (Alcázar de San Juan, 2000), 104–13. Some attempt has latterly been made to downplay their extent, but a private letter published in Andalucía as a pamphlet in the summer of 1808 says clearly that 400 French stragglers had been massacred at Valdepeñas and that a general and six other officers had been killed at the Puerto del Rey near La Carolina. See Anonymous, *Aviso en carta de Andujar de 9 de junio* (n.p., 1808), BN-CGI, R62280.

29. At its most functional, torture was a means of getting victims of banditry to reveal the hiding places of their valuables. However, given that it seems to have been employed even in circumstances where such factors clearly did not apply, it is probable that it was also resorted to as a macabre process of bonding.

30. F. Lavaux, *Mémoires du campagne, 1793–1814,* ed. C. Bourachot (Paris, 2004), 137. Many of the accounts of torture that one finds in French memoirs appear to be based on hearsay, while others were almost certainly invented altogether. Lavaux, however, is a singularly honest observer whose memoirs carry with them a strong ring of truth, while the reference to the victims' legs being thrust into fires—a traditional method of torture among Spanish bandits—suggests that in this particular at least, he can be relied upon. For more typical treatments of the subject, see Blaze, *Mémoires,* 2:90–91; and E. Blaze, *Life in Napoleon's Army: The Memoirs of Captain Elzéar Blaze,* ed. P. Haythornthwaite (London, 1995), 88–89.

31. Laborde, *View of Spain,* 2:148–49.

32. Ibid., 2:149.

33. Babst, *Souvenirs d'un canonnier,* 18.

34. Lavaux, *Mémoires du campagne,* 147–48.

35. J. Roy, *Les français en Espagne: Souvenirs des guerres de la Péninsule* (Tours, 1856), 204–206.

36. Blaze, *Mémoires,* 2:148.

37. D'Espinchal, *Souvenirs militaires,* 1:382.

38. Ibid., 2:2–3. D'Espinchal exaggerates the extent of French urban renewal here: in fact only one *sevillano* convent was torn down to create a new square.

39. Ibid., 1:384.

40. Ibid., 1:385.

41. Clermont-Tonnerre, *Expédition d'Espagne,* 333.

42. Lavaux, *Mémoires du campagne,* 145–46.

43. Thirion, *Souvenirs militaires,* 61–62.

44. Miot de Melito, *Mémoires,* 3:96–97.

45. D'Espinchal, *Souvenirs militaires,* 1:385, 2:2.

46. Haythornthwaite, ed., *Memoirs of the War of the French in Spain,* 117–20. For a general discussion of French views of Andalucía, or at least a part thereof, see J. R. Aymes, "La Andalucía del sur-este en la correspondencia del Mariscal Soult y las memorias de militares napoleónicos," in Reder Gadow and Mendoza García, *Guerra de la Independencia en Málaga,* 15–35.

47. The best account of the affair of the *Castilla la Vieja* and the *Argonaute* may be found in Oman, *Peninsular War,* 3:321–22. For a near contemporary French account, see Anonymous, *Evasion des prisoniers français détenus á bord du ponton* Castille la Vieille (Paris, 1818). It has to be observed that French anger at the bombardment to which the two vessels were subjected is more than a little synthetic, the hurricane of 6–9 March having seen their shore batteries bombard three Spanish ships of the line that were driven ashore with red-hot shot and then use canister to cut down the survivors as they struggled ashore.

48. It is difficult to establish how many of Soult's forces were veterans. But only Victor's corps and part of Sebastiani's had been involved in the Battle of Talavera—the one field action in which the French army had thus far suffered significant casualties—and, notwithstanding the wastage suffered on account of disease and the "little war," it may therefore be presumed that as many as three-quarters of the men concerned had already been serving in the army when I, IV, and V Corps were sent to Spain in the autumn of 1808; at all events, the troops were not the miserable conscripts with only a few months' service who had characterized the forces that had gone down to defeat at Bailén.

49. One may go too far here. As both Michael Hughes and Alan Forrest have convincingly shown, the letters written home by common soldiers are full of suggestions that, for the most part, they were never more than resigned to their fate, while many of them also remained deeply Roman Catholic in both outlook and belief. Yet the fact that desertion rates remained comparatively low (and were inclined to fall the longer one remained in the army), not to mention the heroic behavior of many French soldiers, suggest that the army's capacity for conditioning its recruits was greater than it has been given credit for. As Hughes puts it, indeed, they became "*grognards* in spite of themselves." See M. Hughes, "Vive la République! Vive l'empereur!: Military Culture and Motivation in the Armies of Napoleon, 1803–1808" (Ph.D. diss., University of Illinois Urbana-Champaign, 2005), 375–87.

50. See J. Lynn, "Toward an Army of Honour: The Moral Evolution of the French Army, 1789–1815," *French Historical Studies* 16, no. 1 (Spring 1989): 152–82.

51. M. Hughes, "Images of the *Grognard:* Songs, French Soldiers, and Military Culture in the Armies of Napoleon," presented at the annual Consortium on Revolutionary Europe, 2003 (this paper has yet to be published and is cited here with the kind permission of the author). For a more general discussion of the

ethos of Napoleon's army, see A. Forrest, "The Military Culture of Napoleonic France," in *Napoleon and Europe,* ed. P. Dwyer (London, 2001), 43–59.

52. A further consideration here was the need to forestall domestic rebellion: whether it was in the Highlands of Scotland or the steppes of the Ukraine, the populace knew that the consequences of revolt were likely to be horrific in the extreme.

53. For some interesting discussions of the position of the civilian population in respect to military operations in the eighteenth century, see J. Childs, *Armies and Warfare in Europe, 1648–1789* (Manchester, 1982), 143–73 passim; and C. Duffy, *The Military Experience in the Age of Reason* (New York, 1988), 304–308. Needless to say, the "laws of war" had a habit of being relaxed when it came to the conduct of Europe's armies but enforced with the utmost severity when it came to that of the populace.

54. A recent verdict is that of David Bell: "From a strictly military point of view, Turreau's 'hell columns' had no serious purpose at all. His plan was a witches' brew of hatred, fear, fantasy, and pure folly; its execution an unmitigated horror and counterproductive to the extent it spurred further resistance." See D. A. Bell, *The First Total War: Napoleon's Europe and the Birth of Warfare as We Know It* (New York, 2007), 184.

55. M. Boycott-Brown, "Guerrilla Warfare *Avant la Lettre:* Northern Italy, 1792–97," in Esdaile, *Popular Resistance in the French Wars,* 58–59.

56. See P. Dwyer, *Napoleon: The Path to Power, 1769–1799* (London, 2007), 391–404 passim.

57. For all this, see Finley, *Most Monstrous of Wars.*

58. There is abundant evidence that by 1811, popular resistance in Catalonia was at a very low ebb and, further, that it had never been anything like as enthusiastic as is often claimed.

59. R. de Fézensac, *Souvenirs militaires de 1804 à 1814* (Paris, 1863), 197–200.

60. A. Berthier to J. D. Soult, 14 June 1810, MCMPRJ, 7:293–94.

61. See Gotteri, *Maréchal Soult,* 378–79.

62. La Forest to Napoleon, 11 Apr. 1811, in Grandmaison, *Correspondence du Comte de la Forest,* 5:18–19.

63. F. Copóns y Navía, to E. de Bardaji, 23 June 1810, AHN-SE, 2994, no. 18.

64. Gallego y Burín, *Granada en la Guerra de la Independencia,* 68. For the full text of the *acta de juramento,* see ibid., 154–55.

65. Ibid., 68.

66. For the policy of the authorities in respect of the soldiers of the Patriot armies, see Proclamation of Fernando de Osorno, 9 May 1810, AHN-SE, 2993. In brief, any *dispersos* who chose to return to their homes were welcome to do so provided that they stayed within the law, worked quietly at their accustomed occupations, and submitted to any conscription that might later be ordered for the forces of King Joseph; such men, moreover, would also enjoy the protection of the *josefino* authorities in the face of any attempt to force them back into the service of the Patriots.

67. Gallego y Burín, *Granada en la Guerra de la Independencia,* 74.

68. Ibid., 68–69. For the order to sweep the countryside for abandoned weapons and equipment, see circular of F. de Osorno, 20 Feb. 1810, AHN-SE, 2993.

69. Gallego y Burín, *Granada en la Guerra de la Independencia,* 73.

70. Proclamation of Fernando de Osorno, 26 May 1810, AHN-SE, 2993.

71. For the text of these two decrees, see Gallego y Burín, *Granada en la Guerra de la Independencia,* 155–58.

72. Ibid., 74.

73. Ibid., 82–83.

74. For a good example, see Order of Estanislao de Lugo, 21 Feb. 1810, AHN-SE, 2993. In this document, as current royal commissioner, Lugo published the contents of no fewer than four royal decrees, in which respect it was, perhaps, significant that two of them were concerned with tightening up the treatment of cases of smuggling while a third was the order that replaced hanging with execution by the garrotte. Yet as ever, the stick was balanced by the carrot: in a second order of the same day, Lugo published three decrees that painted a picture of the regime that was rather less bleak: thus, the three measures chosen were those guaranteeing freedom of occupation, suspending the sale of any lands entailed to the support of such charitable institutions as hospitals, and abolishing the punishment of running the gauntlet in the army. Ibid. For an examples of a poster, see the large notice containing brief details of no fewer than seven royal decrees, most of them relating to the establishment of the principle of the freedom of occupation—for example, one was a decree ending all restrictions on the manufacture and sale of playing cards—that appeared in the streets on 7 February. Ibid.

75. A. Blayney, *Narrative of a Forced Journey through Spain and France as a Prisoner of War in the Years 1810 to 1814,* 2 vols. (London, 1814), 1:73–74. It has to be said, however, that *pace* Blayney, the number of deaths was relatively low: in all only some twenty-seven people seem to have been put to death in this fashion by the end of the year, the most famous victim being Vicente Moreno (discussed below). See Gallego y Burín, *Granada en la Guerra de la Independencia,* 84–86.

76. The number of people executed in Granada seems to have been smaller than in some of the other cities in Andalucía. In Málaga, for example, 42 executions took place in 1810 alone, the total for the whole period 1810–12 being 101. Unlike in Granada, however, most executions seem to have taken place inside the city's jail, though the bodies were generally put on display by hanging them from its windows. See M. Reder Gadow, "Violencia y sociedad en la Guerra de la Independencia," in *Guerra, sociedad, y política, 1808–1814,* ed. F. Miranda Rubio, 2 vols. (Pamplona, 2008), 1:573–77.

77. Blayney, *Narrative,* 1:95–96.

78. Gallego y Burín, *Granada en la Guerra de la Independencia,* 75–76.

79. Díaz Torrejón, *José Napoleón I en el sur de España,* 262–77.

80. For the increase in taxation, see ibid., 72.

81. Proclamations of Luis Marcelino Peyreyra, 25, 27 May 1810, AHN-SE, 2993.

82. Gallego y Burín, *Granada en la Guerra de la Independencia,* 70–71.

83. Blayney, *Narrative,* 1:104–105. An *afrancesado* account of the works described by Blayney is found in an anonymously written letter: "In order to feed the people and keep them from turning to crime, the general in chief has embarked upon . . . a variety of public works. These include the construction of the Teatro Napoleón (which is now finished), the laying out of a beautiful promenade, . . . the improvement of the bridge over the River Darro, and the destruction of many old houses so as to create public squares. . . . All this has been funded by the income of various convents and a subscription that has been

supported by a number of officers of the garrison and prominent local citizens." Anonymous letter, n.d., AHN-SDC, legajo 134.

84. The construction of such fortifications was a feature of French policy throughout occupied Spain. Begun at Burgos, where Napoleon noted that the old mediaeval castle overlooking the town would make an ideal nucleus for a powerful citadel that could overawe the city and, in case of need, serve the garrison as a refuge (otherwise the city was only defended by flimsy mediaeval walls susceptible of being breached by even field artillery), by 1810 it had been extended to Madrid, Salamanca, and many other towns under French domination. Setting aside the case of Granada, in Andalucía cases may be found in Seville, Málaga, and Jaén (respectively, the convent of La Cartuja, the Gibralfaro fortress, and the castle of Santa Catalina). For an interesting archaeological survey of one of the sites affected, see J. C. Castillo Armenteros and M. C. Pérez Martínez, "Del castillo medieval a fortificación francesa: El castillo de Santa Catalina (Jaén) durante la Guerra de la Independencia," in *La Guerra de la Independencia (1808–1814)—perspéctivas desde Europe: Actas de las terceras jornadas sobre la batalla de Bailén y la España comtemporánea,* ed. F. Acosta Ramírez (Jaén, 2002), 171–238. For a specific study of the Alhambra, see B. Vincent, "La ocupación de la Alhambra, 1810–1812," in J. M. Delgado Barrado and M. A. Lopéz Arandía, eds., *Andalucía en guerra, 1808–1814* (Jaén, 2012), 163–70.

85. "I had a good view of the field works constructing above the Alhambra; they were . . . palisaded round [and] mounted thirty-six pieces of ordnance." Blayney, *Narrative,* 1:129.

86. For purposes of comparison, see, for example, M. A. Ortí Belmonte, *Córdoba durante la Guerra de la Independencia, 1808–1813* (Córdoba, 1930), 89–109 passim; and the numerous orders pertaining to Seville in BN-CGI, 60014.

87. Royal Decree, 11 Feb. 1810, in *Gazeta de Sevilla,* 13 Feb. 1810, 5, BN-CGI, R60051.

88. Royal Decree, 5 Feb. 1810, in *Gazeta de Gobierno de Sevilla,* 6 Feb. 1810, 4, ibid.

89. See *Gazeta de Sevilla,* 20 Mar. 1810, 87–88, ibid. Prompted by the continued disorder, Soult was eventually led formally to codify these provisions: in brief, any *pueblo* that failed to establish a militia would have to meet the living costs of their garrisons and in addition pay a fine amounting to three times the value of anything seized by the guerrillas within their boundaries; any *pueblo* plundered by guerrillas would have to pay a fine equivalent to three times the value of anything that was taken by them unless it could prove that it had both put up a fight and that its assailants had numbered at least half the number of the inhabitants; and, finally, any *pueblo* that voluntarily supplied food or drink to the *partidas* would again have to pay a fine equivalent to three times the value of anything they handed over. See Proclamation of Marshal Soult, 8 May 1812, AHN-SE, 2994, ff. 317–19.

90. Royal Decree, 18 Mar. 1810, AHN-SE, 2994, ff. 119–20; Royal Decree, 3 Apr. 1810, ibid.; Royal Decree, 23 Jan. 1810, BN-CGI, 62297.

91. Royal Decree, 2 Feb. 1810, BN-CGI, 62297.

92. Royal Decree, 17 Mar. 1810, AHN-SE, 2993. The consequences of the discovery of hidden weapons were grim: anyone found with them in their possession was to be tried by court-martial and the pueblos concerned to pay a fine of 200 reales per weapon.

93. See L. Hernández Enviz, "Medios de control social en la España de la independencia: El Tribunal de Seguridad Pública del régimen patriota y las Juntas criminales bonapartistas," in *Conflicto y sociedad civil en la España napoleónica: Actas de las quintas jornadas sobre la batalla de Bailén y la España contemporánea,* ed. F. Acosta Ramírez (Jaén, 2004), 77–118. In fairness to the *juntas criminales,* it has to be said that they did not behave entirely arbitrarily: 11 percent of the prisoners who appeared before the five tribunals established in Andalucía were acquitted, while the one based in Seville became embroiled in a fierce dispute with Marshal Soult when a man that it had refused to proceed against on the grounds that he was a regular soldier was seized by French troops and shot by firing squad. See T. Escudero to Conde de Montarco, 28 Nov. 1811, AGS-GJ, 1080.

94. Royal Decree, 6 Feb. 1810, AHN-SE, 2993. To complete our picture of events in Granada, this last city raised two battalions of *cívicas* on the basis of the similar Milicia Urbana that it had possessed under the Junta Central: no fewer than fifteen of the Guardia Cívica's officers had served in this force, while its command was given to the same Francisco Cañaveral y Ponce who had commanded the *urbanas.* See Martínez Ruiz, *Granada en la Guerra de la Independencia,* 94–95. For the origins of the Guardia Cívica in occupied Spain as a whole, meanwhile, see Mercader Riba, *José Bonaparte,* 301–302.

95. Royal Decree, 20 Mar. 1810, in *Gazeta de Sevilla,* 10 Apr. 1810, 133–34, BN-CGI, R60051. This decree is of some importance, constituting proof, as it does, that, in contrast to what is often argued by Spanish apologists for Napoleon, *josefino* Spain would not have remained exempt from the conscription that ravaged the rest of the Grand Empire. For reasons that are not quite clear, the regiment that was supposed to be raised in Granada had its base transferred to Málaga and thereafter bore the name of that city.

96. Royal Decree, 31 Mar. 1810, in ibid., 134–36.

97. Proclamation of Marshal Soult, 11 Aug. 1810, AHN-SE, 2993. In reality, Soult's counterinsurgency policies represented little more than an incremental advance on those already introduced by King Joseph. But it is the opinion of two leading experts on the war in Andalucía that, ever more frustrated by his inability to restore order, the marshal greatly intensified the ferocity that the French brought to the task. See F. L. Díaz Torrejón, "La obsesión de Mariscal Soult: Medidas contra-guerrillas en la Andalucía napoleónica," *Cuadernos para el bicentenario* 10 (Dec. 2010): 65–79; and J. M. Lafon, "Contra-insurrección y/o guerra total? Estudio de la política 'pacificadora' desplegada por Soult en Andalucía en el nuevo marco bélico," ibid., 175–90.

98. "Reglamento de Policia," 28 Oct. 1811, AGS-GJ, 1081. For some details on how the police actually functioned, see M. Turrado Vidal, "Información policial y contraguerilla en la Andalucía ocupada, 1810–1812: El caso de Córdoba," *Cuadernos para el bicentenario* 10 (Dec. 2010): 137–74.

99. Proclamation of B. de Aranza, 26 Feb. 1810, BN-CGI, R60014-17; proclamation of B. de Aranza, 6 Mar. 1810, ibid., R60014-20. A particularly radical follower of King Joseph, Aranza was especially enthusiastic in waging war on the religious orders. Thus, in a proclamation of 22 June, he announced that, in conformity with a decree that Joseph had just issued in Madrid on 6 June, ex-regulars could draw the pensions assigned to them from the municipalities in which they had decided to reside (usually either their hometowns or the towns in which their convents had been situated). However, entirely on his own initiative, he

added a number of conditions that went far beyond anything seen in the decree of 6 June in that those concerned would have, in effect, to prove that they had lived quietly in their cloisters throughout the period 1808–10 or, alternatively, that if the fortunes of war had forced them to flee, they at least had settled in some appropriate refuge and taken no part in the fighting, the object of all this being, of course, to ensure that any monk or friar who had enlisted in a *partida* should be excluded from the system of compensation. Proclamation of Blas de Aranza, 22 June 1810, ibid., R60014-23.

100. The policy of the *josefino* regime in respect of local government was defined by royal decrees of 21 August and 4 September 1809. In brief, these dissolved all existing town councils and replaced them with new bodies elected by assemblies of all the taxpayers of each municipality. In municipalities of up to 2,000 inhabitants, the people could select the members as they wished, but in those of more than 2,000 they could only present lists of candidates to the local intendant, who would either determine the composition of the town councils himself or, in the case of settlements with more than 5,000 inhabitants, refer the matter to the king. As for the question of composition, meanwhile, there was to be a *corregidor,* or mayor, and either two, four, or sixteen *regidores,* according to the size of the population. For a discussion of one example of the imposition of the new system in Andalucia, see S. Baena et al., "El ayuntamiento de Córdoba en 1810," in Cuenca Toribio, *Andalucía en la Guerra de la Independencia,* 19–31. See also "Nomina de los individuos que componen la municipalidad de Sevilla desde el dia 11 de junio de 1810 en que fueron nombrados por el Excmo. Sr. Consejero de Estado, D. Blas de Aranza, Comisario Regio Prefecto de esta ciudad, en virtud de las facultades concedidasal efecto por S.M.C. el Sr. D. José Primero en su real decreto de 4 de septiembre de 1809," BN-CGI, R60014-65.

101. Mercader Riba, *José Bonaparte,* 230–34.

102. Ibid., 236–38. Of these figures, Osorno in 1810 had been intendant of Granada; Badía y Leblich, an extraordinary figure who had spent the period 1803–1808 traveling in Morocco, North Africa, and the Middle East under the pseudonym of Ali-Bey, intendant of Segovia; Cervera, as we have just seen, intendant of Málaga; Sotelo an official of the Consejo Suprema de Guerra; and Solis a member of King Joseph's Council of State. (Echezarreta, alas, has defeated all attempts to establish his background.)

103. *Gazeta de Sevilla,* 20 Feb. 1810, 23, BN-CGI, R60051.

104. Circular of Fernando de Osorno, Sept. 1811, AHN-SDC, 134.

105. Proclamation of Fernando de Osorno, 1 Oct. 1811, ibid.

106. "Reglamento para reunir caudales y soccorrer en el próximo invierno las clases desválidos de Granada," 1 Oct. 1811, ibid. In introducing these measures, it should be noted, the authorities were careful to restrict the assistance on offer to a bare minimum. Thus, the pay to be received by each *jornalero* was fixed at 4 *reales* (or 4.5 if the man concerned brought his own tools), this being at best two-thirds of what one might have received in 1808, while the employment of those who had any sort of trade—men, in short, who ought in theory to be able to support themselves without assistance—was specifically prohibited. It will also be noted that the authorities did not themselves assume the responsibility for poor relief; instead, this was to be funded by public subscription.

107. Proclamation of L. Dávila, 14 Oct. 1811, AHN-SDC, 135.

108. See Conde de Montarco to B. de Aranza, 18 Apr. 1811, AHN-SC, *libro* 1742, f. 59.

109. Order of the day of Marshal Soult, 28 Apr. 1811, BN-CGI, R60016-1(10).

110. Proclamation of Marshal Soult, 30 Apr. 1811, AHN-SE, 2993.

111. Orders of the day of Marshal Soult, 24 Sept., 7 Oct. 1810, ibid. Be it noted that there was a certain duality of purpose here: while Soult's rules and regulations were of obvious relevance in respect of the spread of disease, they also served to subject the populace to yet another system of controls.

112. See Order of the day of Marshal Soult, 5 May 1812, BN-CGI, R60016-1(11).

113. Royal Decree, 7 Feb. 1810, ibid., R60014/72.

114. See Lafon, *Andalousie et Napoléon,* 472–73.

115. Order of Junta Municipal de Repartimientos de Sevilla, 12 Aug. 1812, BN-CGI, R60014-80.

116. See various accounts, ibid., R63188.

117. For all this, see Ortí Belmonte, *Córdoba durante la Guerra de la Independencia,* 131–38 passim. It should be remembered here that the demands of the new order did not supplant those of the old one but were rather bolted on to them, the populace being expected to go on paying all the same taxes as before. See proclamation of Blas de Aranza, 14 May 1810, BN-CGI, R60014-22.

118. Ortí Belmonte, *Córdoba durante la Guerra de la Independencia,* 153–60. For a detailed study of another example, see L. Pérez Frias, "La gestión económica en el ambito municipal: Caso del ayuntamiento de Málaga," in F. Miranda Rubio, ed., *Guerra, sociedad, y política, 1808–1814,* 1:507–47. As the author writes, "Eight months after the occupation of Málaga by the Napoleonic army, the economic situation of the municipality was worrying: the city was facing great difficulties with respect to the requirements of the *josefino* authorities." Ibid., 534.

119. For example, see Conde de Montarco to B. de Aranza, 22 Jan. 1811, AHN-SC, *libro* 1742, f. 5.

120. See Conde de Montarco to A. Darricau, 22 Jan. 1811, ibid., ff. 7–8; Conde de Montarco to F.J. Aspiroz, 4 Mar. 1811, ibid., f. 47; Conde de Montarco to B. de Aranza, 2 Apr. 1811, ibid., ff. 53–54.

121. Conde de Montarco to J. M. Sotelo, 21 May 1811, AHN-SC, *libro* 1745, f. 44; Conde de Montarco to J. M. Sotelo, 22 Jan. 1812, ibid., f. 98.

122. Proclamation of Conde de Montarco, 26 May 1812, BN-CGI, R60016-1(14).

123. Conde de Montarco to B. de Aranza, 16 May 1811, AHN-SC, *libro* 1742, ff. 105–106.

124. Proclamation of General Dufour, 25 Sept. 1811, AHN-SDC, 135. Even *afrancesados* did not escape such treatment: for example, in February 1811 the administrador de *bienes nacionales* of Jérez de la Frontera, Bartolomé Angulo, complained to Montarco that the French governor had placed him under house arrest when he fell behind with his contributions, a furious Montarco having to send the provincial prefect orders to have him released immediately. See Conde de Montarco, to J. M. Sotelo, 16 Feb. 1811, AHN-SC, *libro* 1745, ff. 8–9.

125. Ortí Belmonte, *Córdoba durante la Guerra de la Independencia,* 204.

126. See General Barrié to justices of Galarosa, 14 July 1812, AHN-SDC, 135.

127. See Lafon, *Andalousie et Napoléon,* 472–83.

128. Ortí Belmonte, *Córdoba durante la Guerra de la Independencia,* 151, 201–202, 210. It may here be worth offering such limited information as is available as to the identities of the victims. Thus, of the twenty-six men whose occupations are known, five were priests or religious, one a watchman employed on some landed estate, six Spanish deserters or *dispersos,* nine French soldiers who had

presumably deserted to the enemy or turned to banditry themselves, and three members of the local auxiliary unit known as the Francos de Córdoba.

129. For some details on this figure, see F. L. Díaz Torrejón, "Un Borbón en la Estepa napoleónica," *Cuadernos del Bicentenario* 8 (Apr. 2010): 83–122.

130. Lavaux, *Mémoires du campagne,* 152–53.

131. Ibid., 153–55. Lavaux, alas, is not exaggerating here: in 1814 the parish priest compiled a list of no fewer than 239 victims, including a child just three days old. See Díaz Torrejón, *Guerrilla, contraguerrilla, y delincuencia,* 3:163.

132. Lavaux, *Mémoires du campagne,* 155–56.

Chapter 6

1. Saint Pierre and Saint Pierre, *Mémoires du Maréchal Soult,* 175–76.

2. Mendoza y Rico, *Historia de Málaga,* 132.

3. Ibid.

4. D'Espinchal, *Souvenirs militaires,* 1:384. See also Wojciechowski, *Memorias de España,* 110–11.

5. J. D. Soult to A. Berthier, 1 Mar. 1810, SHD-ST, C8-146, ff. 117–25. The term *compagnies franches*—literally "free companies"—requires some explanation. Usually referred to in English by the German term *freikorps,* these were units of irregulars who were traditionally employed as scouts and raiders; in Spain, however, they were above all employed as auxiliary police and antibandit forces.

6. J. D. Soult to A. Berthier, 6 Mar. 1810, ibid., ff. 126–29.

7. Wojciechowski, *Memorias de España,* 106.

8. J. Grivel, *Mémoires du Vice-Admiral Baron Grivel, ed. M. G. Lacour-Gayet (Paris, 1914),* 235.

9. Blaze, *Mémoires,* 2:137.

10. A. Dallas, *Felix Alvarez; or Manners in Spain, Containing Descriptive Accounts of Some of the Prominent Events of the Late Peninsular War; and Authentic Anecdotes Illustrative of the Spanish Character* . . . . 3 vols. (London, 1818), 3:71.

11. J. C. Murgeon to J. Moscoso, 29 Aug. 1812, AHN-SDC, 82, no. 12.

12. Anonymous, "Noticias de Sevilla," n.d., AHN-SE, 2994, no. 4.

13. Ibid.

14. Proclamation of Joaquín Leandro de Solis and Joaquín Goyeneta, 15 Feb. 1810, BN-CGI, R60014-48.

15. Proclamation of the town council of Seville, 18 Feb. 1810, ibid., R60014-49.

16. Proclamation of Nicholas Guye, 3 Mar. 1810, ibid, R60014-50.

17. Proclamation of the town council of Seville, 16 Mar. 1810, ibid, R60014-70.

18. Blaze, *Mémoires,* 1:396. Dramatic testimony of the extent of these fears is afforded by a proclamation of the criminal division of the high court of Seville dated 7 March 1810 (BN-CGI, R60014-63), which denounced the insurgents and warned against their efforts to make use of "impostures as ridiculous as they are malevolent to persuade the incautious . . . to follow in their wake."

19. Fée, *Souvenirs,* 110–11.

20. Blaze, *Mémoires,* 1:325.

21. Ibid., 1:325–26.

22. Ibid., 1:402. The issue here was the ingrained belief that no one could achieve eternal life unless they were buried within the confines of a church. By contrast, according to Sébastien Blaze at least, one French reform that may have secured some approbation among the lower classes was the suppression of the

monasteries. "It they want to eat now," the crowd reportedly remarked of the erstwhile religious, "they will have to flog themselves to death like the rest of us." See ibid., 2:86.

23. At the Battle of La Albuera (16 May 1811), a number of British witnesses contended that the Lancers of the Vistula were drunk when they launched the famous flank attack that destroyed three of Beresford's British infantry battalions. See, for example, C. Oman, ed., "A Prisoner of Albuera: The Journal of Major William Brooke from 16 May to 28 September 1811," in C. Oman, *Studies in the Napoleonic Wars* (Oxford, 1929), 178.

24. For an interesting discussion of Spanish views of drunkenness, see Croker, *Travels,* 117–18. For Spanish view of the Poles, see Wojciechowski, *Memorias de España,* 118.

25. Blaze, *Mémoires,* 2:168–71.

26. Croker, *Travels,* 234.

27. Blayney, *Narrative,* 1:69. See also a story that Alexander Dallas claims to have got from a Belgian officer whom he met in the course of the Waterloo campaign. In brief, stationed in a small village with two other officers, he ordered the local mayor to provide him with three pretty girls, including, not least, his own daughter. The girls being duly delivered, they were then seemingly kept as sex slaves. Two of them apparently became reconciled to their new masters, but the daughter of the mayor proved so irreconcilable that she was released. Shamed by her experiences, however, she never returned home and instead took refuge with five old nuns who were clinging on in a nearby convent. *Felix Alvarez,* 2:114–18, 257–58.

28. For an entertaining, if doubtless semifictionalized, account of his career as a philanderer, see Blaze, *Mémoires,* 2:108–35. Marked as it is by frequent changes of billet—in brief, every time that he got into trouble, Blaze claims that he simply found somewhere else to stay—its plausibility is somewhat undermined by the tight regulations that controlled the system of billeting. See "Ordre pour le logement des militaires chez les habitans," 5 Feb. 1810, BN-CGI, R60002-50.

29. Blaze, *Mémoires,* 2:124–25, 184.

30. Babst, *Souvenirs d'un canonnier,* 29–30.

31. Proclamation of B. de Aranza, 1 June 1810, BN-CGI, R60002-66.

32. For example, see Haythornthwaite, ed., *Memoirs of the War of the French in Spain,* 123–29.

33. For an example, we can here cite a case that was tried by a court-martial in January 1811. In brief, four workers from the cannon factory were accused of having been incited to run away to join the guerrillas by an underground recruitment agency operated by a notary named José González and an embroiderer named Bernardo Palacio. See "Sentencia dada por la comisión militar especial creada en Sevilla en nombre del Emperador y del Rey," 8 Jan. 1811, BN-CGI, R60014-79.

34. Lapène, *Conquête de l'Andalousie,* 22–23.

35. Dallas, *Felix Alvarez,* 2:197–202. It should be noted here that the evidence that the fire was the work of arson is, at best, circumstantial.

36. Martínez Ruiz, *Granada en la Guerra de la Independencia,* 95.

37. Ortí Belmonte, *Córdoba durante la Guerra de la Independencia,* 208.

38. Clermont Tonnerre, *Expédition d'Espagne,* 339. At first sight this story looks more than somewhat doubtful, but Díaz Torrejón has traced the resultant entry in the baptismal register, and it transpires that a couple named Juan Girón and

Antonia López really did have twins on the day that Joseph visited Arcos de la Frontera and, further, that the children were duly christened José Napoleón and Josefa Julia, with King Joseph himself as godfather. See Díaz Torrejón, *José Napoleón I en el sur de España,* 169.

39. Fée, *Souvenirs,* 89.

40. Ibid., 66–69.

41. Ibid., 80.

42. Haythornthwaite, ed., *Memoirs of the War of the French in Spain,* 161–62. Serrano Valdenebro was one of the principal leaders of the insurrection in the district of Ronda (see below).

43. Lapène, *Conquête de l'Andalousie,* 60–61.

44. Brémond d'Ars, *21e Régiment de Chasseurs à Cheval,* 284–90.

45. Blaze, *Mémoires,* 2:145–47.

46. Blayney, *Narrative,* 1:142–43.

47. W. Grattan, *Adventures of the Connaught Rangers from 1808 to 1814,* 2 vols. (London, 1847), 2:95–96.

48. Grivel, *Mémoires,* 233; Blaze, *Mémoires,* 1:411. Blaze himself became close friends with a canon of the cathedral of Seville who, while a functionary of the Inquisition, was yet a bitter critic of its operations and the proud owner of a large library of forbidden books. See ibid., 344–51.

49. Roy, *Français en Espagne,* 204–11.

50. Fée, *Souvenirs,* 111; Blayney, *Narrative,* 1:117.

51. Blayney, *Narrative,* 1:157.

52. Fée, *Souvenirs,* 104–105.

53. See, for example, J. Elting, *Swords around a Throne: Napoleon's Grande Armée* (London, 1988), 611.

54. Grivel, *Mémoires,* 239–40.

55. Ortí Belmonte, *Córdoba durante la Guerra de la Independencia,* 148–49. Such, at least, is the story that was related in the family, Ramírez's nephew being the distinguished Cordoban antiquarian Luís María Ramírez de la Casas Deza.

56. Ibid., 240.

57. Mendoza y Rico, *Historia de Málaga,* 117.

58. Grivel, *Mémoires,* 233.

59. See M. Reder Gadow, "Espionaje y represión en la Serranía de Ronda: María García, 'La Tinajera,' un ejemplo de coraje ante los franceses," in I. Castells et al., eds., *Heroínas y patriotas: mujeres de 1808* (Madrid, 2009), 175–92.

60. Haythornthwaite, ed., *Memoirs of the War of the French in Spain,* 123; Mendoza y Rico, *Historia de Málaga,* 118; Oman, "Prisoner of Albuera," 185–86.

61. A. Delgado García, *Montoro en la Guerra de la Independencia* (Montoro, 2006), 93–100.

62. Ibid., 101–103.

63. Ibid., 103–105.

64. J. D. Soult to A. Berthier, 27 June 1812, SHD-ST, C8-148, ff. 167–71.

65. J. D. Soult to A. Berthier, 14 Apr. 1812, ibid., ff. 97–105. Soult's comments may, of course, be regarded as being dubious in their veracity, but the court was evidently impressed enough by what had occurred to issue a circular letter to the magistrates of the province in which it spoke highly of the attitude of the city: "The court has seen with great satisfaction the manner in which, despite the constant increase of evils of every sort on account of the length of the war, each and every one of the inhabitants . . . has given public . . . proofs of their adhesion to

the ideas of peace, law, and good order." See circular letter of the high court of Seville, 18 Apr. 1812, BN-CGI, R60014-31.

66. Wojciechowki, *Memorias de España,* 107.

67. Blaze, *Mémoires,* 2:231.

68. Ortí Belmonte, *Córdoba durante la Guerra de la Independencia,* 141–42.

69. Mendoza y Rico, *Historia de Málaga,* 137–41.

70. Ibid., 150–59.

71. Ibid., 204–206, 210–11.

72. Ibid., 215–18.

73. Díaz Torrejón, *Guerrilla, contraguerrilla, y delincuencia,* 2:182. After the French had evacuated Andalucía, stories circulated of the existence of a secret resistance organization called the Congreso Secreto Hispalense, but even the deeply patriotic Manuel Moreno Alonso cannot bring himself to claim that this ever amounted to anything, even if it existed at all. See *Sevilla napoleónica,* 293–95. Periodically, however, one does come across cases of espionage: setting aside the case of María García that we have already noted, in April 1811 one Ramón Trullas was executed for this offence in Badajoz. See "Jugement rendu par la commission militaire speciale séante á Badajoz," 11 Apr. 1811, AHN-SE, 2993.

74. Wojciechowski, *Memorias de España,* 112. The term *vecino* is usually translated "resident" or "inhabitant," but at the time of the Peninsular War, it was applied only to householders who paid a certain level of taxation.

75. This case is made very strongly in an anonymous pamphlet published in Seville in the immediate aftermath of the French evacuation of Andalucía. As the author points out, for men with families to support and, especially, those with limited incomes, flight was simply not an option, while even getting by in Cádiz would have been at the very least quite difficult. To argue, however, that those who emigrated were egoists and cowards and that the real heroes of the hour were those who stayed behind was daring to say the least. See Anonymous, *Carta en defensa de los que se quedaron en Sevilla sirviendo sus empleos* (Seville, 1812), BN-CGI, R61212.

76. F. L. Díaz-Torrejón, *Osuna napoleónica 1810–1812* (Seville, 2001), 181–83. That the estates on offer were tempting, there is no doubt. To take just one example, on 26 June 1810 six properties in the province of Seville were put up for sale, the combined income that they offered being computed at 147,217 reales. See *Aviso al público,* 26 June 1810, BN-CGI, R60014-58.

77. For all these examples, see "Libro donde se sientan los decretos expedidos por el Excmo Sr. Conde de Montarco, Comisario Regio General de las Andalucías por SMC, a las instancias dirigidas a SE colectiva e individualmente como así mismo las ordenes generales e instrucciones dictadas por SE," AHN-SC, *libro* 1741, ff. 1–50.

78. See Lovett, *Napoleon and the Birth of Modern Spain,* 580.

79. J. Castillo Cano, *Almería en la crisis del antiguo régimen: La Guerra de la Independencia en la ciudad, 1787–1814* (Almería, 1987), 127–28.

80. Mendoza y Rico, *Historia de Málaga,* 122–24.

81. Grivel, *Mémoires,* 238.

82. J. Zayas to D. García Trevilla, 9 May 1810, AHN-SE, 3119. For some other examples, see Lovett, *Napoleon and the Birth of Modern Spain,* 576–81.

83. R. Peyre, ed., *Mémoires du Major Gallardo de Mendoza,* in *Miscellanea Napoleónica,* ed. A. Lumbroso, ser. 3–4 (Rome, 1898), 382–83. Given the general tendency to sing the praises of Catalan resistance, Gallardo de Mendoza's claims

might be regarded as being open to challenge at the very least, but there is considerable archival evidence to suggest that he is telling the exact truth, including, not least, in letters written by other Andalusian officers who were sent to Catalonia. See Esdaile, *Fighting Napoleon,* 81–83.

84. M. Reder Gadow, "Violencia y sociedad en la Guerra de la Independencia," in Miranda Rubio, ed., *Guerra, sociedad, y política,* 1:566.

85. J. Herrador Haro, "La invasión francesa en el sur-este de la provincia de Jaén: El caso particular de Lopera," in Cuenca Toribio, *Andalucía en la Guerra de la Independencia,* 89–92.

86. For all this, see J. M. Sotelo, *Discursos presentados a la Junta Suprema de Extremadura por Don Joaquín María Sotelo, fiscal del Supremo Consejo de la Guerra* (Badajoz, 1808), BN-CGI, R62274-1.

87. See Lovett, *Napoleon and the Birth of Modern Spain,* 583.

88. Dallas, *Felix Alvarez,* 2:216–17.

89. D'Espinchal, *Souvenirs militaires,* 2:6–7.

90. Petition of town council of Torre Don Jimeno, "Libro donde se sientan los decretos expedidos por el Excmo Sr. Conde de Montarco, Comisario Regio General de las Andalucías por SMC, a las instancias dirigidas a SE colectiva e individualmente como así mismo las ordenes generales e instrucciones dictadas por SE," n.d., AHN-SC, *libro* 1741, f. 36. See also the very similar petitions submitted by the town councils or mayors of Aguadulce, Jimena, Pozo Alcón, Linares, Pruna, Martos, and Fuente del Rey, ibid., ff. 52–54, 59, 60, 62.

91. Díaz Torrejón, *José Bonaparte I en el sur de España,* 216.

92. Moreno Alonso, *Sevilla napoleónica,* 153.

93. For example, see ibid., 145–62.

94. See A. J. Calvo Maturana, *"Aquel que manda las consciencias": Iglesia y adoctrinamiento político en la monarquía hispánica preconstitucional, 1780–1808* (Cádiz, 2011).

95. For a summary of this argument, see A. J. Calvo Maturana, "Propaganda y control de consciencias en el reinado de Carlos IV" (Ph.D. diss., Universidad Complutense de Madrid, 2009), 527–39.

96. Moreno Alonso, *Sevilla napoleónica,* 253–61.

97. S. Pérez López, *Guadix y su obispado en la Guerra de la Independencia: Quebranto económico y ruptura social en un dióceses de la Alta Andalucía, 1801–1814* (Córdoba, 1998), 113–20.

98. Gallego y Burín, *Granada en la Guerra de la Independencia,* 158.

99. Ortí Belmonte, *Córdoba durante la Guerra de la Independencia,* 97–98.

100. For a detailed discussion of the many tensions that beset the Spanish Church during the reign of Charles IV, see Callahan, *Church, Politics, and Society,* 79–85.

101. For a general discussion of *afrancesamiento* among the clergy of Andalucía, see G. Dufour, "Clero afrancesado en Andalucía," in Delgado Barrado and López Arandía, *Andalucía en guerra,* 79–87. See also Reder Gadow, "Ambigüedad de la iglesia malagueña durante la Guerra de la Independencia," 2:677–88.

102. Gallego y Burín, *Granada en la Guerra de Independencia,* 84–86.

103. "Arenga del cuerpo eclesiastico ante una carta amenazadora interceptada a Ballesteros," in J. Aragón Gómez, *Chiclana de la Frontera bajo el gobierno de José Napoleón, 1810–1812* (Chiclana de la Frontera, 2007), 202–203.

104. Pérez López, *Guadix,* 84.

105. See "Libro donde se sientan los decretos expedidos por el Excmo Sr. Conde de Montarco, Comisario Regio General de las Andalucías por SMC, a las instancias dirigidas a SE colectiva e individualmente como así mismo las ordenes generales e instrucciones dictadas por SE," AHN-SC, *libro* 1741, ff. 172, 174, 179.

106. Blaze, *Mémoires,* 1:364–66. For a general discussion of masonry in *josefino* Spain, see J. A. Ferrer Benimeli, *Masonería espanõla contemporánea, I: 1800–1868* (Madrid, 1980), 38–109. It should be noted, however, that Ferrer Benimeli insists that indigenous participation in French lodges was minimal, and that Spaniards rather chose to form their own lodges and insisted that these should be independent of French masonry: whereas the latter was headed by the so-called Grand Orient, Spanish masonry was headed by the Gran Logia Nacional de España (Grand National Lodge of Spain).

107. Mendoza y Rico, *Historia de Málaga,* 124–30. For a more scientific treatment of this subject, one can refer to the work of Jean-Marc Lafon. Based on an analysis of 926 men identified by him as *afrancesados,* this again suggests that collaboration was a common phenomenon among the propertied classes, though with the caveat that active participation in the political, military, and judicial structures of the *josefino* state was confined to a relatively small minority, something that is very suggestive here being the fact that, of the 177 *andaluces* decorated with the Orden Real de España who were still alive in 1812, only ninety-five fled with the French army. See J. M. Lafon, "Sociología y motivaciones del colaboracionismo en la Andalucía napoleónica," in *Bailén a las puertas del bicentenario: Revisión y nuevas aportaciones—actas de las septimas jornadas sobre la batalla de Bailén y la España contemporánea,* ed F. Acosta Ramírez (Jaén, 2008), 25–54.

108. See Petition of R. de Osorno, 3 Aug. 1810, AHN-SE, 3119.

109. "Situation des troupes francaises et espagnoles stationées dans l'étendue de la province de Seville à l'époque du 15e octobre de 1810," SHD-ST, C-8, 399; "Situation des troupes francaises et espagnoles stationées dans l'étendue de la province de Seville à l'époque du 1er mai de 1811," ibid.; "Situation des troupes francaises et espagnoles stationées dans l'étendue de la province de Seville à l'époque du 1er octobre de 1811," ibid.

110. "Situation sommaire en presents sur les armes des troupes espagnoles stationées dans l'arrondissement de l'Armée Imperiale du Midi à l'époque du 1er octobre de 1811," ibid., 356; "Situation sommaire en presents sur les armes des troupes espagnoles stationées dans l'arrondissement de l'Armée Imperiale du Midi à l'époque du 15e novembre de 1811," ibid. Note that three units—the Seventh Line, the Royal Guard, and the Guardias de Honor—that are shown in the returns of strength for Seville are missing from the general return; the latter's figures, then, should be increased by perhaps as many as 500 officers and men. Meanwhile, for the difficulties involved in clothing and equipping the troops, see Conde de Montarco to General Marti, 9 Apr. 1811, AHN-SC, *libro* 1742, ff. 80–81.

111. Service records of D. José de Ocaña, AHN-SE, 3119.

112. Service records of D. José de Villar, ibid; Service records of Juan de Villar, ibid.

113. Petition of M. Ortiz, 3 July 1810, ibid.

114. Lafon, *Andalousie et Napoléon,* 232–35.

115. Moreno Alonso, *Sevilla napoleónica,* 211; Mendoza y Rico, *Historia de Málaga,* 147–48.

116. Report of commanding officer of Tercer Regimineto de Cazadores a Caballo, 4 May 1811, AHN-SC, *libro* 1742, ff. 87–88.

117. V. Sánchez Ramos, ed., *Las memorias de un alpujarreño: Don Juan Gabriel del Moral Villalobos entre Fondón y Berja, 1796–1826* (Mojácar, 1999), 83.

118. See M. Turrado Vidal, *De malhechores a gente de orden: Historia de una partida bonapartista codobesa* (Madrid, 2005), 126–35.

119. Ibid., 150.

120. Ibid., 167.

121. J. D. Soult to Joseph Bonaparte, 18 Mar. 1810, SHD-ST, C-8, 146, ff. 144–45.

122. J. D. Soult to A. Berthier, 23 Mar. 1810, ibid., ff. 157–59.

123. J. D. Soult to A. Berthier, 15 May 1810, ibid., ff. 250–52. For the situation in Seville, see Moreno Alonso, *Sevilla napoleónica,* 202–205.

124. Díaz Torrejón, *Osuna napoleónica,* 137–43. The commander of the Osuna *cívicas,* meanwhile, was one Miguel de Soto, a prominent local resident who had served from 1808 to 1810 as *sargento mayor*—in effect, adjutant—of one of the volunteer battalions raised in Seville at the outbreak of the uprising and returned to his home following the disintegration of his unit in the wake of the passage of the Sierra Morena.

125. One incident that has reached us more or less "in the raw" is a skirmish that took place near the village of Lantejuela on 18 January 1811, in which a mounted patrol of the Guardia Cívica of Fuentes scattered a bandit gang headed by one Bartolo and took five prisoners for the loss of one man killed. Conde de Montarco to Commandant of Guardia Cívica of Marchena, 27 Jan. 1811, AHN-SC, *libro* 1742, ff. 12–13; G. O'Farrill to Conde de Montarco, 13 Feb. 1811, ibid., f. 44.

126. Ortí Belmonte, *Córdoba durante la Guerra de la Independencia,* 180–81.

127. Order of the Governor of Seville, 5 Feb. 1810, BN-CGI, R60014-41.

128. Circular of Joaquín María Sotelo, 20 Sept. 1811, ibid., R60002-98.

129. See Conde de Montarco to Conde de Vistahermoso, 19 Oct. 1811, AHN-SC, *libro* 1744, f. 66.

130. Conde de Montarco to J. M. Sotelo, 2 July 1811, AHN-SC, *libro* 1745, f. 61.

131. Here and there, however, individual town councils did prove capable of being extremely obstreperous. For example, in the early months of 1811, relations between the town council of Jérez de la Frontera and Joaquín Sotelo deteriorated to such an extent that the latter had all its members arrested. See Conde de Montarco to J. M. Sotelo, 12 Apr. 1811, ibid., ff. 27–28.

132. Mendoza y Rico, *Historia de Málaga,* 214–15, 218.

133. Ortí Belmonte, *Córdoba durante la Guerra de la Independencia,* 203–207.

134. Ibid., 201–202, 210.

135. Ibid., 211.

136. Roy, *Français en Espagne,* 224.

Chapter 7

1. E. de Diego, *España, el infierno de Napoleón, 1808–1814: Una historia de la Guerra de la Independencia* (Madrid, 2008), 348–49.

2. F. Martínez Laínez, *Como lobos hambrientos: Los guerrilleros en la Guerra de la Independencia, 1808–1814* (Madrid, 2007), 381.

3. F. L. Díaz Torrejón, "Aproximación al movimiento guerrillero en Andalucía," in Reder Gadow and Mendoza García, *Guerra de la Independencia en Málaga,*

108. For the very acme of Andalusian pride in the guerrilla struggle, however, see Alcántara Alcaide's *Málaga frente a la Guerra de la Independencia.*

4. A. Grasset, *Málaga: Provinvia francesa, 1811–1812,* trans. and ed. M. C. Toledano (Málaga, 1996), 38.

5. Fraser, *Napoleon's Cursed War,* 499.

6. See "Capitanía General de Andalucía: Noticia de las partidas de guerrilla o cuerpos francos que se formaron en los Reinos de Sevilla, Córdoba, y Jaén en los años de 1809, 1810, 1811, 1812, y 1813 en la pasada campaña," 1 Aug. 1817, AHN-SDC, 124, no. 50.

7. The death of Curnillon, who was almost certainly the first victim of the Andalusian guerrilla, is mentioned by Saint-Chamans. See *Mémoires,* 169.

8. Haythornthwaite, ed., Memoirs of the War of the French in Spain, 122.

9. Saint-Chamans, *Mémoires,* 169–75.

10. "Rapport Général du Division Dessolles," 28 June 1810, SHD-ST, C8-356. For the period February–June, see the similar reports that were written on 28 February, 5 March, 9 March, 20 March, 27 March, 14 April, 18 April, 10 May, 14 May, 24 May, and 5 June.

11. J. D. Soult to A. Berthier, 17 Mar. 1810, SHD-ST, C8-146, ff. 136–42.

12. Proclamation of Marqués de Villafranca y Los Vélez, 23 Jan. 1810, IHCM-CGB, 3/28.

13. Díaz Torrejón, *Guerrilla, contraguerrilla, y delincuencia,* 1:202, 3:18–20.

14. Valdivia was defeated and captured at Ojén on 15 July, while it was Bielsa who suffered the disaster at Torreperogil mentioned above. As for Osorio Calvache, after suffering several defeats in the spring and summer of 1810, he was killed in an unsuccessful attack on the French garrison of Villacarrillo in November. *Gazeta de Sevilla,* 6 Apr. 1810, 124–25; 24 July 1810, 550; 13 Nov. 1810, 826–27.

15. Ibid., 11 May 1810, 328.

16. Díaz Torrejón, *Guerrilla, contraguerrilla, y delincuencia,* 2:44–51; López and Lara, *Entre la guerra y la paz,* 395–97.

17. Díaz Torrejón, *Guerilla, contraguerrilla, y delicuencia,* 2:51–65.

18. Ibid., 2:208–31. The title given to Villalobos's force—a hodgepodge of detachments from at least seven different cavalry regiments—highlights a semantic difficulty that has long caused difficulty with respect to the analysis of the "little war." In brief, prior to the Peninsular War, the Spanish word "guerrilla" was employed to describe not irregular bands of armed civilians, but rather regular soldiers deployed as skirmishers, scouts, or advanced guards. An accurate translation of "Guerrillas del Tercer Ejército" might therefore be "Outriders of the Third Army."

19. M. Peña Guerrero, *El tiempo de los franceses: La Guerra de la Independencia en il suroeste español* (Almonte, 2000), 49; A. E. Jiménez, *Queja de un patríota al supremo consejo nacional en que manifiesta la alevosia con que se persigue a las partidas de guerrilla y los defensores mas celosos de la patria* (Cádiz, 1811), BN-CGI, R61148. For the doings of González Cortes and his followers, see Junta of Ayamonte to F. Copóns y Navía, 25 Aug. 1810, RAH, 9-31-6:6968.

20. Díaz Torrejón, *Guerrilla, contraguerrilla, y delincuencia,* 2:59–124 passim. The career of Múñoz in particular may be studied in F. L. Díaz Torrejón, *Antonio Múñoz, el Cura de Riogordo: Un guerrillero malagueño contra Napoleón* (Málaga, 2011). Known as the "Cruzada del Obispado de Málaga" as it was, the band of Manuel Jiménez Guazo is worthy of special mention here as, in conformity with many stereotypes, it was raised at the suggestion of a number of bishops and

other clergy who had found refuge in Cádiz and was originally supposed to be recruited entirely from priests, monks, and friars. Whether this aim was ever achieved is a moot point—though a number of religious certainly served in its ranks, it is clear that it also included many members of the laity—but beyond this it should be pointed out that the band was very much an exception: while several others were headed by priests or monks, the Cruzada was the only such force that was so specifically religious in its conception. In short, claims that the guerrilla war was captained by the Church are greatly exaggerated.

21. Díaz Torrejón, *Guerrilla, contraguerrilla, y delincuencia,* 3:164–68.

22. J. J. Moreti, *Historia de L.M.N.Y.M.L ciudad de Ronda* (Ronda, 1867), 596.

23. J. M. de Molina Bautista, *Historia de Alhaurín de la Torre en la edad moderna, 1489–1812* (Alhaurín de la Torre, 2000), 231.

24. Martín de Molina, *Gaucín,* 60–87.

25. Ibid., 114–21. See also J. Serrano Valdenebro, *Manifiesto de los servicios hechos a la patria por el Jefe de Escuadra, Don Jose Serrano Valdenebro, desde el movimiento de la nación a la justa defensa contra la invasión que nos tiraniza hasta su remoción del mando de la Sierra Meridional en 2 de julio de 1811* (Algeciras, 1811), 12–13, BN-CGI, R61110. Credence is given here to the idea that there was indeed a general revolt in the Serranía de Ronda. That said, the episode was beyond doubt much mythologized. For a critical analysis of one of the many memorials on which the heroic account is based, see J. M. Bernal Gutiérrez, "La defensa de Casares como mito de la Guerra de la Independencia," in *1808–1812: Los emblemas de la libertad,* ed. A. Ramos Santana and A. Romero Ferrer (Cádiz, 2009), 193–201.

26. Díaz Torrejón, *Guerrilla, contraguerrilla, y delincuencia,* 3:225.

27. Gutiérrez Tellez, *D. José Serrano Valdenebro,* 80–81.

28. "Reglamento para la formación de cuerpos patríotas que hagan el servicio de guerrilla en el Reino de Granada interín su ocupación por el enemigo," AHN-SDC, 124, no. 28.

29. J. Serrano Valdenebro to A. Jacomet, 5 May 1810, ibid., 94, no. 1.

30. J. Serrano Valdenebro to A. Jacomet, 2 June 1810, ibid.

31. Haythornthwaite, ed., *Memoirs of the War of the French in Spain,* 134–35.

32. Díaz Torrejón, *Guerrilla, contraguerrilla, y delincuencia,* 2:214–19.

33. Espinchal, *Souvenirs militaires,* 379–80.

34. Bigarré, *Mémoires,* 278.

35. "Situation des troupes composant le 1er Corps de l'Armee d'Espagne à l'époque du 1 février 1810," SHD-ST, C-8, 354; "Situation des troupes composant le 1er Corps de l'Armee d'Espagne à l'époque du 1 décembre 1810," ibid.

36. "Situation des troupes composant le 4e Corps d'Armée à l'époque du 31 janvier 1810," ibid., 359; "Situation des troupes composant le 4e Corps d'Armée à l'époque du 15 décembre 1810," ibid.; "Situation des troupes composant le 4e Corps d'Armée à l'époque du 1 juin 1811," ibid.; "Situation des troupes composant le 4e Corps d'Armée à l'époque du 1 septembre 1811," ibid. None of these figures are distorted by major actions such as Barrosa and Albuera.

37. The details of this action need not concern us here, but in brief, on 28 October 1811 a mixed force of British, Portuguese, and Spanish troops under General Hill pounced on the division of General Girard in an isolated spot in what is today the province of Caceres and inflicted over 2,000 casualties.

38. "Situation des troupes composant le 5e Corps d'Armée à l'époque du 1 février 1810," SHD-ST, C-8, 360; "Situation des troupes composant le 5e Corps d'Armée à l'époque du 16 décembre 1810," ibid.; "Situation des troupes

composant le 5e Corps d'Armée à l'époque du 15 juillet 1811," ibid.; "Situation des troupes composant le 5e Corps d'Armée à l'époque du 15 janvier 1812," ibid.

39. One issue that needs to be taken into account here, but that is in reality almost impossible to quantify, is that of reinforcements and replacements. That Soult received at least some fresh troops cannot be denied, but, as his correspondence is replete with complaints at the manner in which his drafts were constantly being pressed into service by other French commanders in the course of their march across Spain, one may assume that the numbers that reached him were not very great and, by extension, that there is no hidden deficit in the above figures.

40. J. Planas Campos, "La contribución británica en la Guerra de la Independencia: Una aproximación cuantitativa," *Trienio,* 54 (Nov. 2009): 5–21. Please note that these figures exclude the battles that took place during Wellington's invasion of France in 1814; if these are included, the figure for Britain's losses rises to approximately 12,000 men.

41. For all these figures I am deeply indebted to my friend and colleague Jorge Planas Campos, whose work on the statistics of the Peninsular War I look forward to seeing in print at an early date.

42. Brémond d'Ars, *21e Régiment de Chasseurs à Cheval,* 210.

43. Wojciechowski, *Memorias de España,* 112–13.

44. F. G. Bak Presa González, A. Matyjaszczyk Grenda, and R. Monforte Dupret, eds. *Soldados polacos en España durante la Guerra de la Independencia Española, 1808–1814* (Madrid, 2004), 70.

45. Roy, *Français en Espagne,* 226.

46. Fée, *Souvenirs,* 18–19.

47. Ibid., 99.

48. L. A. Gougeat, "Mémoires d'un cavalier d'ordonnance de 20e Dragons, 1810–1814," in Anonymous, *Mémoires sur les campagnes d'Espagne* (Paris, 1997), 97–105 passim.

49. Fée, *Souvenirs,* 71–72.

50. Ibid., 74–75.

51. Sánchez Ramos, *Memorias de un alpujarreño,* 84–85.

52. Blayney, *Narrative,* 1:35–38. For a particularly grim account of counterinsurgency operations from the point of view of a French infantryman, see Lavaux, *Mémoires du campagne,* 150–57.

53. Blayney, *Narrative,* 1:60–62.

54. Ibid., 139.

55. "Libro donde se sientan los decretos expedidos por el Excmo Sr. Conde de Montarco, Comisario Regio General de las Andalucías por SMC, a las instancias dirigidas a SE colectiva e individualmente como así mismo las ordenes generales e instrucciones dictadas por SE," AHN-SC, *libro* 1741-E, f. 2.

56. Ibid., ff. 1–124 passim.

57. R. de Mazariegos to A. Romero Valdés, 19 May 1810, AGS-GJ, 1086; Díaz Torrejón, *Guerrilla, contraguerrilla, y delincuencia,* 3:105–106.

58. Report of G. Valdés, 17 June 1810, AGS-GJ, 1076.

59. Anonymous report, 3 June 1811, AHN-SE, 3146.

60. Dallas, *Felix Alvarez,* 2:217–20, 270.

61. Blayney, *Narrative,* 1:57–58.

62. J. D. Soult to A. Berthier, 15 Oct. 1811, SHD-ST, C8-147, ff. 389–83.

63. Mendoza y Rico, *Historia de Málaga,* 207–208, 214.

64. Saint Pierre and Saint Pierre, *Mémoires du Maréchal Soult,* 181.

65. Ibid., 182.

66. J. Maransin to J. Leval, 25 Jan. 1812, in Grasset, *Málaga,* 343.

67. *Gazeta de Sevilla,* 5 Oct. 1810, 738–39, BN-CGI, R60051.

68. Saint Pierre and Saint Pierre, *Mémoires du Maréchal Soult,* 184. Such a judgment might well be expected of Marshal Soult, but even Spanish observers now admit that many of the guerrilla bands in Andalucía were in reality nothing more than bandits. Let us here quote Marion Reder Gadow: "In Andalucía the list of the victims of bandit attacks that were later confused with, or justified as, guerrilla raids is a very long one. . . . The countryside of Jaén . . . felt the effects of a gang of bandits headed by the brothers Cristóbal Perea (alias "Cara Vaca") and Juan Perea (alias "Navidad"). . . . In this case as in so many others, the war against the French yoke was no more than a pretext to launch attacks on property. . . . Today, there is no one who would doubt the insurgent movement's links with crime." "Violencia y sociedad en la Guerra de la Independencia," in Miranda Rubio, ed., *Guerra, sociedad, y política,* 1:570–71.

69. For a discussion of the complicated case of Vicente Moreno, see Esdaile, *Fighting Napoleon,* 103.

70. See A. de Valencina, *Los capuchinos de Andalucía en la Guerra de la Independencia* (Seville, 1910), 139–46. The monks concerned are recorded as Pablo de Jérez, Diego de Teba, Francisco de Cádiz, Gabriel de Samalo, and Elias de Santander.

71. Peña Guerrero, *Tiempo de los franceses,* 23–28; Díaz Torrejón, *Guerrilla, contraguerrilla, y delincuencia,* 3:246–55.

72. J. Ibánez, *Diario de operaciones de la división del Condado de Niebla que mandó el Mariscal de Campo, Don Francisco de Copóns y Navía, desde el dia 14 de abril de 1810, que tomó el mando, hasta el 24 de enero de 1811, que pasó este general al Quinto Ejército* (Faro, 1811), 3–4, IHCM-CDF, 342.

73. F. Copóns to F. Eguía, 14 Apr. 1810, RAH, 9:6966. In view of the lackluster perfomance of the Condado de Niebla hitherto, the reference to patriotic ardor may seem puzzling, but Copóns was probably referring not to the Napoleonic period, but to that of *los reyes católicos,* many towns in the district having played a leading role in the voyages of Christopher Columbus.

74. Peña Guerrero, *Tiempo de los franceses,* 47–83 passim.

75. Anonymous report, n.d., AHN-SE, 2994. For the caution of the *josefino* administration with regard to any mention of compulsory military service, see circular of G. O'Farrill, 24 Mar. 1810, AGS-GJ, 1163.

76. Report of M. J. Martínez Valcarcel, 4 Aug. 1810, AGS-GJ, 1078; Anonymous report, 29 Aug. 1810, ibid.

77. J. Heredia to F. Copóns, 21 Dec. 1810, RAH, 9:6967; anonymous report, 25 Sept. 1811, AHN-SE, 3146.

78. L. Guerrero to M. Romero, 25 Jan. 1811, AGS-GJ, 1082.

79. "Capitanía General de Andalucía: Noticia de las partidas de guerrilla o cuerpos francos que se formaron en los Reinos de Sevilla, Córdoba y Jaén en los años de 1809, 1810, 1811, 1812, y 1813 en la pasada campaña," 1 Aug. 1817, AHN-SDC, 124, no. 50.

80. Díaz Torrejón, *Guerrilla, contraguerrilla, y delincuencia,* 2:122, 132.

81. Ibid., 2:140–44.

82. For all this, see ibid., 2:146–49, 225–31, 3:59–126 passim.

83. For numerous examples, see ibid., 3:127–37.

84. F. Ballesteros, *Respetuosos descargos que el Teniente General Don Francisco Ballesteros ofrece a la generosa nación española en contestación a los cargos que S.A. la Regencia del Reino se ha servido hacerle en su manifiesto del 12 de diciembre del año pasado de 1812 dirigido a la misma para su inteligencia* (Cádiz, 1813), 21–22, IHCM-CDF, 154.

85. F. J. de Castaños to J. Blake, 28 Mar. 1810, IHCM-CGB, 3/25.

86. A. de la Cuadra to F. Abadia, 13 June 1810, ibid.

87. Ibid.

88. Blayney, *Narrative,* 1:13–14. According to Blayney, the presence of Miller and the other officers, of whom the most prominent appear to have been two lieutenant colonels named Basset and Warrington, was the work of the Duque del Infantado, the latter having prevailed on the British government to send a number of officers to organize the *serranos.* Ibid., 1:26–27.

89. A. de la Cuadra to F. Abadia, 13 June 1810, IHCM-CGB, 3/25.

90. *Haythornthwaite, ed., Memoirs of the War of the French in Spain,* 150–51.

91. Moreti, *L.M.N.Y.M.L ciudad de Ronda,* 598–99. It was not just legal documents that were burned: also consigned to the flames was a large quantity of *bulas de cruzada* (roughly speaking, certificates buying exemption from purgatory sold to raise money for the expences of the church) that were seized in the house of Antonio Gómez Barroso, the latter being the official responsible for their sale. See Conde de Montarco to J. M. Sotelo, 12 Feb. 1812, AHN-SC, *libro* 1745, f. 104.

92. Serrano Valdenebro, *Manifiesto,* 18.

93. J. Serrano Valdenebro to J. M. Carvajal, 4 Apr. 1811, *Diario de Algeciras,* 24 Apr. 1811, 357–61. Viriato—more commonly Viriatus—was a leader of resistance to the Roman Empire among the tribes of modern-day Portugal.

94. Ibid.

95. Ibid.

96. To this day the name of Vicente Moreno is inscribed in letters of gold on the walls of the lower chamber of the Spanish parliament. In brief, the story is as follows. Among the measures decided on by the *cortes* of Cádiz was that the walls of the chamber should be placarded with the names of prominent heroes who had distinguished themselves in the struggle against the French, those chosen initially being the artillery officers Daoiz and Velarde, both of whom had died in the revolt of the Dos de Mayo, and the defender of Zaragoza, Francisco Palafox. Following his execution by the French in August 1810, however, Moreno's wife traveled to Cádiz to secure public assistance for herself and her children. Her case having been taken up by several deputies, in December 1810 the *cortes* resolved not merely to grant her a pension and pay for the education of her son, but also to accord Moreno himself certain honors, not the least of which was the inclusion of his name alongside those of Daoiz, Velarde, and Palafox. For all this, see R. Fernández de Castro, *Apuntes históricos-biográficos del insigne patríota, capitán de infantería, Don Vicente Moreno, héroe de la Guerra de la Independencia* (Melilla, 1908).

97. Díaz Torrejón, *Guerrilla, contraguerrilla, y delincuencia,* 3:228.

Chapter 8

1. To this day there is no narrative study of the campaign in Andalucía, whose events have rather to be reconstructed from the relevant sections of such sources as Oman, Gómez de Arteche, Toreno, and Schepeler. However, there are a

number of local studies, of which the most detailed cover the region of Málaga. For two examples, see J. Bernal Gutiérrez, "La costa occidental de la provincia de Málaga durante la invasion francesa en la Guerra Peninsular: Marbella, Estepona, Casares, y Manilva, 1808–1812," in Reder Gadow and Mendoza García, *Guerra de la Independencia en Málaga,* 539–52; and S. D. Pérez González, "La Guerra de la Independencia en Alhaurín el Grande," in ibid., 553–70.

2. Jacob, *Travels in the South of Spain,* 182–83, 195–96.

3. For the role of the Spanish navy in the defence of Cádiz, see A. Guimera Ravina, "La armada y el sitio de Cádiz," in Delgado Barrado and López Arandía, *Andalucía en guerra,* 153–62. Meanwhile, for naval matters in general, see C. D. Hall, *Wellington's Navy: Seapower and the Peninsular War, 1807–1814* (London, 2004).

4. In fact, particularly in the early days, the situation was not quite as bleak as this suggests. Thus, Alburquerque's army was exhausted and demoralized, the Spanish navy unprepared for action, and many of the lesser defenses unfinished or even barely begun, while the new administration that had seized power in Cádiz in the wake of the collapse of the Junta Central proved less than energetic in its response to the crisis. Symptomatic of the panic in the city is the fact that the crucial fort of Matagorda was blown up and evacuated, true though it is that its ruins were, within a few days, reoccupied and repaired with sandbag barricades. Had the French attacked, it is therefore possible that they might just have broken through. The Spanish commander, indeed, was the first to own this point: "Cádiz's only real outwork though it may have been, when I occupied the Isla de León with my little army, its defenses were so weak that, had the French troops who were following us attempted to launch a determined attack, it would surely have fallen, and with it but a short time afterward Cádiz as well." Alburquerque, *Manifiesto del Duque de Alburquerque,* BN-CGI, 60013-4, ix. See also Schepeler, *Histoire de la guerre d'Espagne et de Portugal,* 2:521. The French émigré J. B. L. de Crossard, however, is more positive: visiting the defenses of the Isla de León immediately prior to his return to Austria in the autumn of 1809, he pronounced them to be in a reasonable state of readiness. See *Mémoires,* 4:195–96.

5. For example, see J. J. Salcedo to Conde de Montarco, 14 May 1811, AHN-SC, *libro* 1745, f. 41.

6. J. D. Soult to A. Berthier, 21 Feb. 1810, SHD-ST, C8-146, ff. 99–102. For Soult's attempt to persuade Alburquerque to surrender, see J. D. Soult to Duque de Alburquerque, 16, 19 Feb. 1810, ibid., ff. 89–90, 97–99.

7. For an excellent French account of the occupation of the coastline and the preparations for a future assault on Cádiz, see Lapène, *Conquête de l'Andalousie,* 28–29.

8. For Soult's views on the departure of Heudelet from Extremadura, see J. D. Soult to A. Berthier, 24 June 1810, SHD-ST, C8-146, ff. 286–88. It has been traditional to attribute the expression of such complaints to selfishness and want of strategic vision, but the strategy that is implied in Soult's correspondence at his point—in essence, containing Wellington's army in Portugal while knocking Spain out of the war—was probably the only one that offered Napoleon the hope of victory in the Peninsular War.

9. For some details of Ballesteros's early career, see Ballesteros, *Respetuosos descargos,* 5–6.

10. For Ballesteros's attack on Santander, see Oman, *Peninsular War,* 2:386–87.

11. Toreno, *Guerra, levantamiento, y revolución,* 689.

12. *Gazeta de Sevilla,* 10 Apr. 1810, 132–33, BN-CGI, R60051.

13. Oman, *Peninsular War,* 3:214–15; Lapène, *Conquête de l'Andalousie,* 40–41. See also J. D. Soult to A. Berthier, 20 Apr. 1810, SHD-ST, C8-146, ff. 212–14. It should be noted that from an early date, Ballesteros proved a controversial figure in that he was adopted by champions of the cause of Spanish liberalism as the very prototype of the new-model generals who they believed were Spain's best hope in the struggle against France, the resultant adulation both flattering his considerable ambitions and upsetting other Spanish commanders, such as the governor of Ayamonte, Francisco de Copóns y Navía. See Díaz Torrejón, *Guerrilla, contraguerrilla, y delincuencia,* 3:256–57.

14. Lapène, *Conquête de l'Andalousie,* 42–43.

15. Saint Pierre and Saint Pierre, *Mémoires du Maréchal Soult,* 196; Lapène, *Conquète d'Andalousie,* 43–44; Oman, *Peninsular War,* 3:331. The number of Spanish losses was in reality probably no more than 600.

16. Implicit in the creation of the Army of the Center was the suppression of the commands of both Areizaga and Albuerquerque, the former being simply dismissed and the latter dispatched as ambassador to London, where he died a few months later from the effects of a brain tumor. However, the new organization did not prove practical: from the very beginning, Blake was forced to delegate command of the forces in Murcia to the erstwhile commander of Areizaga's cavalry, General Manuel Freyre, while, in the summer of 1810, a major reorganization of all the Spanish land forces saw the troops based in Murcia and Cádiz redesignated as the Third and Fourth Armies.

17. Peña Guerrero, *Tiempo de los franceses,* 23–24.

18. For all this, see Oman, *Peninsular War,* 3:328–30; Schepeler, *Histoire de la guerre d'Espagne et de Portugal,* 2:546–47; and Toreno, *Guerra, levantamiento, y revolución,* 586–88.

19. Oman, *Peninsular War,* 3:332–33.

20. Ibid., 3:337–38.

21. Toreno, *Guerra, levantamiento, y revolución,* 593.

22. Saint Pierre and Saint Pierre, *Mémoires du Maréchal Soult,* 187.

23. Ibid., 187–92.

24. For Soult's travails in the initial stages of the occupation, see Gotteri, *Maréchal Soult,* 378–79.

25. Lejeune, *Memoirs,* 2:58, 73.

26. Ibid., 2:70.

27. E. Salvador to J. O'Donnell, 5 July 1810, AHN-SDC, 133. This passage refers to the campaign of La Romana's army in southern Extremadura and, in particular, the action at Jérez de los Caballeros.

28. F. Ballesteros to V. Letona, 12 Dec. 1810, BN-CGI, R62741.

29. For the origins of the invasion of Extremadura, see Oman, *Peninsular War,* 4:23–26.

30. The organization of the expeditionary force is discussed in Lapène, *Conquête de l'Andalousie,* 70–71. Insofar as its direction was concerned, Soult seems to have behaved with his usual lack of generosity: as Lapène points out, while Mortier was given the day-to-day direction of operations (and with it the responsibility for failure), Soult insisted on accompanying the march on Badajoz so as to ensure that it would be him who took the credit for victory.

31. Saint Pierre and Saint Pierre, *Mémoires du Maréchal Soult,* 201.

32. J. Belmas, *Journaux des sièges faits ou soutenus par les français dans la péninsule de 1807 a 1814,* 4 vols. (Paris, 1836), 1:158. For further details of the extreme difficulty that dogged the march on Badajoz, see Lapène, *Conquête de l'Andalousie,* 74–76.

33. J. D. Soult to A. Berthier, 25 Jan. 1811, SHD-ST, C8-347, ff. 17–21.

34. Oman, *Peninsular War,* 4:35.

35. Toreno, *Guerra, levantamiento, y revolución,* 689.

36. For the siege of Badajoz, see Lapène, *Conquête de l'Andalousie,* 80–99.

37. See Blayney, *Narrative,* 1: 35–38. For two modern accounts, see C. Posac Mon, "El castillo de Fuengirola, baluarte imperial en la Guerra de la Independencia," in Reder Gadow and Mendoza García, *Guerra de la Independencia en Málaga,* 93–104; and T. M. Barker, "A Debacle of the Peninsular War: The British-led Amphibious Assault against Fort Fuengirola [*sic*], 14–15 October 1810," *Journal of Military History* 64, no. 1 (Jan. 2000): 9–52.

38. It is a commonplace of the British historiography to abuse La Peña for the catastrophic errors that wrecked the chances of Allied success in this campaign, but even the Spanish sources have few good words to say about him, Toreno, for example, openly describing him as a coward. See *Guerra, levantamiento, y revolución,* 696.

39. For a succinct and largely honest French account of Barrosa, see Lapène, *Conquête de l'Andalousie,* 112–19. What would have happened had La Peña and Graham pressed their advantage is hard to predict. The siege of Cádiz would have had to be abandoned certainly, but Victor would probably have been able to retire on Seville, where he would presumably have been joined by large parts of the forces that had been left behind to hold Granada, Córdoba, and the Condado de Niebla. To have remained in the field in the face of the 30,000 men that might have been involved would have been madness, and so the best bet is that, in the end, the Allies would have fallen back on Cádiz, thereby leaving the French to carry on as before. That said, one can assume that the French siege lines would have been levelled and that the flotilla of boats collected in the mouth of the Guadalquivir for a possible amphibious assault put to the torch, while it is not impossible that Ballesteros might have temporarily seized Seville or Blake Granada. As the effect of such events on the *afrancesado* community would, beyond doubt, have been traumatic in the extreme, the whole basis of French control must necessarily have been gravely undermined. Yet there are alternative scenarios. What would have happened, for example, had faulty intelligence led to La Peña and Graham suffering a heavy defeat at Utrera or Jérez de la Frontera? In short, the end result might just as easily have been disaster for the Allied cause.

40. Lejeune, *Memoirs,* 2: 68. This was undoubtedly the case, but in the wake of the battle itself, the feeling in I Corps was very different. To quote Lapène: "A mournful spirit of consternation reigned . . . throughout the line and the most fearful rumors that the siege works were to be abandoned and destroyed passed from mouth to mouth." *Conquête de l'Andalousie,* 121.

41. According to local tradition, the hero of the popular uprising was a tavern keeper of the Calle de Escalones named María Marcos (or to use her nickname, "Marímarcos"). At some point in the nineteenth century, the street in which she lived was renamed in her honor, but there is no evidence that the story has a basis in anything other than legend. What is true, however, is that Ballesteros could

not have maintained himself in the wilds of the Sierra Morena for as long as he did without at least a modicum of civilian support, a key figure here apparently being Vicente Letona, the chief administrator of the royal copper mines at Río Tinto. See Jepane to La guerra de la independencia en Huelva message board, 2 May 2008, http://riotinto.mforos.com/555733/7523687-la-guerra-de-la-independencia-en-huelva/ (accessed 16 Nov. 2011). According to local tradition, Letona supplied Ballesteros with large quantities of food as well as military intelligence of all sorts while raising a guerrilla band that was paid a bounty for every pair of French ears that its members brought him. Yet Ballesteros also appears to have been utterly ruthless in his treatment of the civilian population. Herewith, for example, the remarks of a British liaison officer who served with his division: "Of all the unworthies produced by Spain during this war (and God knows there were plenty of them), this man was the greatest impostor and charlatan. . . . He certainly kept a body of men together, but they proved only a curse to the inhabitants . . . [and] appeared to be composed of the débris of defeated and dispersed armies, men who would not fight, yet reassembled to obtain food because they were too idle or too dissipated to work. Whenever the French retired, the Spaniards followed, composing and reciting songs of victory, but at too respectable a distance to disquiet the enemy. If the French . . . attempted to pursue them, they soon found how vain was the undertaking." T. Bunbury, *Reminiscences of a Veteran, being Personal and Military Adventures in Portugal, Spain, France, Malta, Norfolk Island, New Zealand, Anderman Islands and India,* 3 vols. (London, 1861), 1:111–12.

42. Oman, *Peninsular War,* 4:128–29. The operations of Ballesteros were the most serious challenge the French faced elsewhere in Andalucía during the course of the Barrosa campaign. However, it should be noted that, far from the coast though they were, Dessolles and Sébastiani were so alarmed at the news that a substantial Allied army had been put ashore that they hastily concentrated as many troops as they could manage, thereby ensuring an immediate upsurge in brigandage. See Lapène, *Conquête de l'Andalousie,* 110–11.

43. From January 1810 until March 1811, Soult had not had to worry about the possibility of direct intervention in Andalucía on the part of Wellington's army, for the latter had been wholly neutralized by the activities of the Army of Portugal and had ultimately retreated inside the impregnable Lines of Torres Vedras. In March 1811, however, Masséna was driven to retreat by starvation, and with the marshal's army in tatters, Wellington was free to think about the possibility of campaigns in Extremadura and even Andalucía.

44. A further issue to be considered here was the effects of being stationed in Extremadura on the morale of the troops concerned. As Lapène points out, it was a desolate and lonely region that was alternately drenched by winter rains and scorched by the summer sun, lacked even Andalucía's few comforts, and possessed almost nothing in the way of resources: on campaign, indeed, the troops often could not even find wood for their campfires. All this the garrison endured with great stoicism, Lapène contends, but it cannot be suspected that the reality was very different. See *Conquête de l'Andalousie,* 101–103.

45. Belmas, *Journaux des sièges,* 1:560–61.

46. If Badajoz presented Soult with a very difficult problem, its capture was far from unimportant. On the contrary, its possession was vital both to the protection of Andalucía and to the pursuit of victory in the Peninsular War.

47. J. D. Soult to A. Berthier, 8 Feb. 1811, SHD-ST, C8-147, ff. 32–35.

48. The most recent work on the much studied Battle of Albuera is G. Dempsey, *Albuera 1811: The Bloodiest Battle of the Peninsular War* (London, 2008).

49. Fortunately for Soult, the detachment of the whole of V Corps to Extremadura proved to be only a temporary necessity in that Marmont eventually agreed to keep a single infantry division stationed in northern Extremadura. As a result, left to hold only the southern part of the region, Drouet was able to send back one of his two infantry divisions to Seville.

50. Whether any of the units sent to Spain actually reached Andalucía is another matter. Rather, it seems likely that, like the "march battalions" (in brief, drafts of conscripts belonging to different regiments that had been put together for the journey to their regiments) destined for his command, the majority were detained in the north of Spain and employed in counterinsurgency operations against commanders such as Mina.

51. Oman, *Peninsular War,* 4:441. By the time that they arrived at their final destination, the men who marched south with Drouet would have covered a distance of 600 miles in a space of less than six weeks.

52. Oman, *Peninsular War,* 4:475–76; Peña Guerrero, *Tiempo de los franceses,* 31–42; Lapène, *Conquête de l'Andalousie,* 238–39.

53. Oman, *Peninsular War,* 4:479–81.

54. For all this, see "Situation et emplacement des corps de l'Armée du Midi, 1er septembre 1811," in Grasset, *Málaga,* 573–77.

55. Ibid., 47–48. It appears that the inhabitants of the area were already in a state of considerable excitement thanks to the efforts of the notorious *frondeur* Montijo, who had been sent out from Cádiz with order to make use of the local connections derived from the considerable estates he owned in the region to revivify the resistance. Possessed of a well-proven ability to whip up the crowd—in March 1808 he had taken a leading part in the revolt that had overthrown the regime of Charles IV and Godoy—he appears to have had some success, on 31 August inflicting an embarrassing reverse on the French by capturing two companies of Polish infantry at Motril. One of the men taken captive was the peasant Andrzej Daleki: "They shut us up in a cemetery and stripped us of everything down to the very clothes we were wearing. . . . The heat was insupportable, and a great crowd of people had gathered as if it were a theater. They had come to laugh at us, . . . and as if that were not enough, we were led through the streets from one side of the town to the other and back again to punish us still further. Only God knows the shame I felt. I cast my eyes on the ground and in a low voice prayed to God to free me from this humiliation . . . and, if that could not be, then to take me out of this world on the spot. If I had had some sort of weapon in my hand, I would have hurled myself on the whole of the inhabitants singlehanded—indeed, on a whole enemy army—so that I could die and in this fashion save myself from my shame. But I had nothing, and so there was nothing I could do." Presa González et al., *Soldados Polacos en España,* 79.

56. Order of the day of Francisco Ballesteros, 24 Aug. 1811, BN-CGI, R60003-20.

57. For all this, see J. D. Soult to J. Maransin, 11 Sept. 1811, in Grasset, *Málaga,* 242–44.

58. According to Lapène, indeed, such was the disruption and depopulation in parts of the countryside that many French troops actually had to be sent out to gather in the harvest. See *Conquête de l'Andalousie,* 186.

59. For all this, see Grasset, *Málaga,* 49–62. See also J. D. Soult to A. Berthier, 24, 25 Sept. 1811, SHD-ST, C8-147, ff. 330–34, 351–53; and A. Rignoult to J. D. Soult, 25 Sept. 1811, ibid., ff. 380–88.

60. J. Maransin to J. D. Soult, 27 Sept. 1811, in Grasset, *Málaga,* 249–51.

61. J. Maransin to J. D. Soult, 5 Oct. 1811, in ibid., 270.

62. J. Maransin to J. D. Soult, 27 Sept. 1811, in ibid., 250.

63. For all this, see especially Maransin's dispatches to Soult for the month of October 1811, these being reproduced in full as an appendix to Grasset's *Málaga.* It should be noted, however, that the picture that emerges of events in the Patriot camp is by no means one that fits comfortably with notions of a great crusade against the French. Thus, if Ballesteros was gathering recruits from the countryside, he is represented as having to use force to do so. As for the *partidas,* meanwhile, they continue to be represented as mere brigands intent on nothing more than terror and extortion.

64. Blaze, *Mémoires,* 2:197–98. For details of the campaign, see Grasset, *Málaga,* 73–84.

65. Grasset, *Málaga,* 84–91.

66. For the action at Arroyomolinos de Montánchez, See Oman, *Peninsular War,* 4:599–605. See also R. Burnham, "The Battle of Arroyos dos Molinos [*sic*], 28 October 1811," The Napoleon Series, http://www.napoleon-series.org/military/virtual/c_molinos.html (accessed 28 Sept. 2010).

67. J. D. Soult to A. Berthier, 1 Nov. 1811, SHD-ST, C8-147, ff. 419–23.

68. Oman, *Peninsular War,* 5:83.

69. Napoleon to A. Berthier, 6 Dec. 1811, in Plon and Dumaine, *Correspondance de Napoléon,* 23:58–59.

70. So confident was Soult that he would be able to take Tarifa that he had, in fact, already had his agents purchase 50,000 quintals of grain at Tangier ready for immediate shipment across the Strait of Gibraltar. See J. D. Soult to A. Berthier, 1 Jan. 1812, SHD-ST, C8-148, ff. 3–6. The strategic significance of taking the town in this respect, meanwhile, is self-evident: Tarifa being the southernmost point of Spain, it is only twelve miles from the Moroccan coast, whereas the voyage from Málaga is almost ten times that distance.

71. For the siege of Tarifa, see Oman, *Peninsular War,* 5:111–29.

72. J. D. Soult to A. Berthier, 11 Jan. 1812, SHD-ST, C8-148, ff. 9–11.

73. Oman, *Peninsular War,* 5:129. Certainly the sufferings of the French at Tarifa were very great. Let us here quote Alexander Dallas: "Since the conclusion of the peace, chance has thrown me into the company of an officer who was present at the siege of Tarifa, and the account that he gives of the miserable situation of the besieging army exceeds even the distress which they were supposed by those within the walls to have suffered. He assured me that for several days the greater part of the army lived entirely upon oranges . . . and that the rinds of the fruit was the only substance given to the horses during the same time." *Felix Alvarez,* 2:273.

74. Grasset, *Málaga,* 130–53. See also J. D. Soult to A. Berthier, 27 Feb. 1812, SHD-ST, C8-148, ff. 72–74.

75. Mendoza y Rico, *Historia de Málaga,* 204–205. The original being neither well written nor well structured, the translation given here is a fairly free rendition. Mendoza's text reads as follows: "Un terror pánico se apoderó de los negros que, atolondrados, no sabían que hacerse; a poco rato principiaron a entrar

heridos y dispersos en gran número . . . y, como venían perseguidos por Ballesteros, se alborotó el pueblo. Unos 100 hombres que habían en ésta se parapetaron en los paredones de Guadalmedina, temiendo llegaran los españoles hasta aquí. Esto fue ejecutado con tanta precipitación y atolondro que las gentes que en gran número salieron ver la vergonzosa entrada de los franceses se amedrentó y corrió en términos que se alborotó toda la población y se cerraron las puertas. Los afrancesados se subieron al castillo . . . [o] se escondieron y mudaron de domicilio. Los genoveses y piratas de los corsarios se embarcaron con todos sus equipajes y se pusieron en franquía."

76. Ibid., 206.

77. J. Maransin to J. D. Soult, 1 Mar. 1812, in Grasset, *Málaga,* 423. Needless to say, the French and their adherents made much use of the executions as a means of blackening Ballesteros. See Proclamation of the Conde del Montarco, 25 Mar. 1812, BN-CGI, R60014-13.

78. Grasset, *Málaga,* 166.

79. J. Maransin to J. D. Soult, 7 Mar. 1812, in ibid., 435.

80. Pruharan to D. Decrès, 4 Apr. 1812, AHN-SDC, 134.

81. Mendoza y Rico, *Historia de Málaga,* 147.

82. For the naval attack on Málaga, see ibid., 212–13; and Grasset, *Málaga,* 184–85. For some interesting remarks on the problems of building a squadron at Málaga, see J. Maransin to J. D. Soult, 21, 27 Sept. 1811, in Grasset, *Málaga,* 247–50.

83. This was the crisis referred to in chapter 6 in respect of the loyalty of the Guardia Cívica. Commanded by Morillo and Penne Villemur, the troops of the Fifth Army showed rather greater courage, demonstrating before the defenses of the Cartuja for several days and only giving way when Soult was within striking distance of the city.

84. Grasset, *Málaga,* 169–81. See also J. D. Soult to A. Berthier, 21 Apr. 1812, SHD-ST, C8-148, ff. 117–21.

85. For Soult's reorganization of the Army of the South, see Oman, *Peninsular War,* 5:108–109. In Extremadura a vestige of the old system was retained in that Drouet, who in theory had been reduced to the status of a mere divisional commander, continued to exercise the command not just of his own troops but also those who were sent from time to time to reinforce him.

86. For the background to the fall of Badajoz, see ibid., 5:264–73.

87. J. D. Soult to A. Berthier, 15 Mar. 1812, SHD-ST, C-148, ff. 84–87.

88. D'Espinchal, *Souvenirs militaires,* 2:11. For details of the battle, see Oman, *Peninsular War,* 5:521–22.

89. J. D. Soult to A. Berthier, 1 June 1812, SHD-ST, C8-148, ff. 149–50.

90. J. Maransin to J. D. Soult, 31 May 1812, in Grasset, *Málaga,* 483.

91. J. Maransin to J. D. Soult, 15 June 1812, in ibid., 489.

92. Ibid., 196–206; Mendoza y Rico, *Historia de Málaga,* 215–18. For the text of Ballesteros' proclamation, see BN-CGI, R60003-19. Malága, meanwhile, paid dearly for the raid: not only was the city forced to pay for everything that was taken but also three men and—exceptionally—three women were executed for their part in the disturbances. See J. Maransin to J. D. Soult, 31 July 1812, in Grasset, *Málaga,* 530; and Reder Gadow, "Violencia y sociedad," 587.

93. Grasset, *Málaga,* 211–20.

94. J. D. Soult to Joseph Bonaparte, 16 July 1812, MCPMRJ, 9:45–47. See also J. D. Soult to A. Berthier, 27 June 1812, SHD-ST, C8-148, ff. 167–71.

95. For all this, see Oman, *Peninsular War,* 5:492–94.
96. General Order of the Army of the South, 15 Aug. 1812, AHN-SDC, 134.
97. Fée, *Souvenirs,* 138.

Conclusion

1. Saint Pierre and Saint Pierre, *Mémoires du Maréchal Soult,* 187.
2. For Wellington's travails with respect to Andalucía, see C. J. Esdaile, *The Duke of Wellington and the Command of the Spanish Army* (Basingstoke, 1990), 59–135 passim.
3. For some general remarks on the political legacy of French occupation, see Esdaile, *Peninsular War,* 472–74. There are few studies of postliberation Andalucía, but one is A. M. Espinar Casajú, *Málaga durante la primera etapa liberal, 1812–1814* (Málaga, 1994).
4. Fraser, *Napoleon's Cursed War,* 513–18; E. Díaz Lobón, *Granada durante la crisis del antiguo régimen* (Granada, 1982), 95.
5. Lafon, "Sociología y motivaciones del colaboracionismo en la Andalucía napoleónica," 53.
6. Espinar Casajú, *Málaga durante la primera etapa liberal,* 90–95.
7. Díaz Torrejón, *Antonio Múñoz,* 294–320.
8. Proclamation of the Commandant General of Jaén, 15 June 1813, BN-CGI, R60016-23.
9. R. Agüera Espejo-Saavedra, "Consecuencias de la Guerra de la Independencia en la comarca del alto Guadalquivir," in Cuenca Toribio, *Andalucía en la Guerra de la Independencia,* 221–22.
10. See Bernal, *Lucha por la tierra,* 74. Other Andalusian towns affected by these disturbances include Vejer, Conil, and San Lucar de Barrameda. See S. de Moxo, *La disolución del regimen señorial en España* (Madrid, 1965), 56–60.
11. For the disturbances of May 1814, of which there were examples in both Granada and Málaga, see Esdaile, *Peninsular War,* 499.

Select Bibliography

Archival Sources

Archivo Histórico Nacional (Madrid). Sección de Consejos, libros 1741, 1742, 1743, 1744, 1745, 1746.

Archivo Histórico Nacional (Madrid). Sección de Diversos (Colecciones), legajos 100, 124, 129, 132, 133, 134, 135.

Archivo Histórico Nacional (Madrid). Sección de Estado, legajos 14, 16, 20, 30, 31, 40, 52, 62, 82, 2952, 2993, 2994, 3003, 3067, 3078, 3079, 3080, 3119.

Biblioteca Nacional (Madrid). Colección Gómez Imaz, carpetas R60002, R60003, R60005, R60013, R60014, R60016, R60036, R60087, R60781, R61212, R61284, R61547, R62297, R62741, R62306, R62314, R62774, R63188, R63192.

Service Historique de la Défence (Paris). Section de la Terre, serie C–8, cartons 146, 147, 148, 354, 356, 359, 360, 399.

Newspapers and Periodicals

Correo de Málaga

Correo Político y Militar de la Ciudad de Córdoba

Gazeta de Madrid

Gazeta de Sevilla

Published Primary Sources

Anonymous. *Prontuario de las leyes y decretos del Rey Nuestro Señor Don José Napoleón I desde el año de 1808.* 3 vols. (Madrid, 1810–12).

Anonymous. *Témoignages sur les campagnes d'Espagne et de Portugal: Extraits du "Carnets de la Sabretache," années 1899, 1902, 1908, 1920* (Paris, 1999).

Anonymous, ed. *Mémoires sur les campagnes d'Espagne* (Paris, 1997).

Babst, G., ed. *Souvenirs d'un canonnier de l'Armée d'Espagne, 1808–1814* (Paris, 1892).

Barrès, M., ed. *Memoirs of a French Napoleonic Officer: Jean-Baptiste Barrès* (London, 1925).

Berazaluce, A., ed. *Recuerdos de la vida de Don Pedro Agustín Girón.* 2 vols. (Pamplona, 1978).

Bigarré, A. J. *Mémoires du Général Bigarré, aide-de-camp du Roi Joseph, 1775–1813* (Paris, 1903).

Blanco White, J. *Letters from Spain* (London, 1828).

Blayney, A. *Narrative of a Forced Journey through Spain and France as a Prisoner of War in the Years 1810 to 1814.* 2 vols. (London, 1814).

Blaze, S. *Mémoires d'un apothicaire sur le guerre d'Espagne pendant les années 1808 à 1814.* 2 vols. (Paris, 1828).

Bourgoing, J. F. de. *Modern State of Spain Exhibiting a Complete View of its Topography, Government, Laws, Religion, Finances, Naval and Military Establishments, and of Society, Manners, Arts, Sciences, Agriculture, and Commerce in That Country.* 4 vols. (London, 1808).

Brémond d'Ars, A., ed. *Historique du 21e Régiment de Chasseurs à Cheval, 1792–1814: Souvenirs militaires* (Paris, 1903).

Casse, A. du, ed. *Mémoires et correspondance politique et militaire du Roi Joseph.* 10 vols. (Paris, 1854).

Clermont-Tonnerre, G. de. *L'expédition d'Espagne, 1808–1810.* Edited by C. Desparte (Paris, 1983).

Croker, R. *Travels through Several Provinces of Spain and Portugal* (London, 1799).

Dallas, A. *Felix Alvarez; or Manners in Spain, Containing Descriptive Accounts of Some of the Prominent Events of the Late Peninsular War; and Authentic Anecdotes Illustrative of the Spanish Character* . . . . 3 vols. (London, 1818).

Dalrymple, W. *Travels through Spain and Portugal in 1774 with a Short Account of the Spanish Expedition against Algiers in 1775* (London, 1777).

D'Espinchal, H. *Souvenirs militaires, 1792–1814.* Edited by F. Masson and E. Boyer. 2 vols. (Paris, 1901).

Fée, A. L. A. *Souvenirs de la Guerre d'Espagne, dite de l'Independance, 1809–1813* (Paris, 1856).

Gille, L. F. *Les prisonniers de Cabrera:* Mémoires d'*un conscript de 1808.* Edited by P. Gille (Paris, 1892).

Girardin, L. S. de. *Journal et souvenirs, discours et opinions de S. Girardin.* 4 vols. (Paris, 1828).

Gotteri, N., ed. *La mission de Lagarde, policier de l'empereur, pendant la Guerre d'Espagne, 1809–1811* (Paris, 1991).

Grandmaison, G. de, ed. *Correspondance du Comte de la Forest, ambassadeur de France en Espagne, 1808–1813.* 7 vols. (Paris, 1905–13).

Grivel, J. *Mémoires du Vice-Amiral Baron Grivel.* Edited by M. G. Lacour-Gayet (Paris, 1914).

Haro Malpensa, J. de, ed. *Guerra de la Independencia: La Mancha, 1808—Diarios, Memorias, y Cartas* (Alcázar de San Juan, 2000).

Haythornthwaite, ed. *In the Peninsula with a French Hussar: Memoirs of the War of the French in Spain.* (London, 1990).

Hulot, J. L. *Souvenirs militaires du Baron Hulot,* général d'*artillerie, 1773–1843* (Paris, 1886).

Ilchester, Earl of, ed. *The Spanish Journal of Elizabeth, Lady Holland* (London, 1910).

Jackson, Lady, ed. *The Diaries and Letters of Sir George Jackson, K.C.H., from the Peace of Amiens to the Battle of Talavera.* 2 vols. (London, 1872).

Jacob, W. *Travels in the South of Spain in Letters Written A.D. 1809 and 1810* (London, 1811).

Laborde, A. de. *A View of Spain Comprising a Descriptive Itinerary of Each Province and a General Statstical Account of the Country Including Its Population, Agriculture, Manufactures, Commerce, and Finances; Its Government, Civil, and Ecclesiastical Establishments; the State of the Arts, Sciences, and Literature; Its Manners, Customs, Natural History, etc.* 5 vols. (London, 1809).

Lagneau, L. *Journal d'un chirugien de la Grande Armée, 1803–1815.* Edited by C. Bourachot (Paris, 2000).

Lapène, E. *Conquête de l'Andalousie: Campagne de 1810 et 1811 dans le midi d'Espagne* (Paris, 1823).

Lavaux, F. *Mémoires du campagne, 1793–1814.* Edited by C. Bourachot (Paris, 2004).

Lejeune, L. *Memoirs of Baron Lejeune, Aide-de-Camp to Marshals Berthier, Davout, and Oudinot.* Edited by N. Bell. 2 vols. (London, 1897).

Martin, M. *The Dispatches and Correspondence of Richard Marquess of Wellesley during His Mission to Spain in 1809* (London, 1838).

Mendoza y Rico, J. *Historia de Málaga durante la revolución santa que agita a España desde marzo de 1808.* Edited by M. Olmedo Checa (Málaga, 2003).

Miot de Melito, A. *Mémoires du Comte Miot de Melito, ancien ministre, ambassadeur, conseilleur d'*état, *et membre de l'institut.* 3 vols. (Paris, 1858).

Núñez, E., ed. *Pablo de Olavide: Obras selectas* (Lima, 1987).

Plon, H., and J. Dumaine, eds. *Correspondance de Napoléon Ier publiée par ordre de l'Empereur Napoléon III.* 32 vols. (Paris, 1858–69).

Presa González, F., G. Bak, A. Matyjaszczyk Grenda, and R. Monforte Dupret, eds. *Soldados Polacos en España durante la Guerra de la Independencia Española, 1808–1814* (Madrid, 2004).

Rouillard, T., ed. *Relations de la campagne d'Andalousie, 1808* (La Vouivre, 1999).

Roy, J. *Les français en Espagne: Souvenirs des guerres de la Péninsule* (Tours, 1856).

Saint-Chamans, A. de. *Mémoires du Général Comte de Saint-Chamans, ancien aide de camp du Maréchal Soult, 1802–1832* (Paris, 1896).

Saint Pierre, L., and A. Saint Pierre, eds. *Mémoires du Maréchal Soult: Espagne et Portugal* (Paris, 1955).

Sánchez Ramos, V., ed. *Las memorias de un alpujarreño: Don Juan Gabriel del Moral Villalobos entre Fondón y Berja, 1796–1826* (Mojácar, 1999).

Sanz Hermida, J., ed. *Monjas en guerra, 1808–1814: Testimonios de mujeres desde el claustro* (Madrid, 2009).

Schepeler, A. von. *Histoire de la révolution d'Espagne et de Portugal ainsi que de la guerre qui en resulta.* 3 vols. (Liège, 1829–32).

Semple, R. *A Second Journey in Spain in the Spring of 1809 from Lisbon through the Western Skirts of the Sierra Morena to Sevilla, Córdoba, Granada, Málaga, and Gibraltar, and Thence to Tetuan and Tangiers* (London, 1809).

Swinburne, H. *Travels through Spain in the Years 1775 and 1776* (Dublin, 1779).

Thirion, A. *Souvenirs militaires* (Paris, 1892).

Toreno, Conde de. *Historia de la guerra, levantamiento, y revolución de España.* Edited by R. Hocquellet (Pamplona, 2008).

Townsend, J. *A Journey through Spain and Portugal in the Years 1786 and 1787 with Particular Attention to the Agriculture, Manufactures, Commerce, Population, Taxes, and Revenue of the Country and Remarks in Passing through a Part of France.* 2 vols. (London, 1792).

Twiss, R. *Travels through Portugal and Spain in 1772 and 1773* (London, 1775).

Weigall, R., ed. *Correspondence of Lord Burghersh, Afterwards Eleventh Earl of Westmorland, 1808–1840* (London, 1912).
Wojciechowski, K. *Mis memorias de España.* Edited by J. S. Ciechanowski et al. (Madrid, 2009).

Secondary Sources

Abella, R. *La vida y epoca de José Bonaparte* (Barcelona, 1997).
Abella, R., and J. Nart. *Guerrilleros: El pueblo español en armas contra Napoleón, 1808–1814* (Madrid, 2007).
Agüera Espejo-Saavedra, R. *Villa del Río, 1810–1812: El padrón de los franceses* (Córdoba, 2003).
Aguilar Gavilán, E. *Andalucía durante la Guerra de la Independencia* (Granada, 2008).
Alcántara Alcalde, E. *Málaga frente a la Guerra de la Independencia, 1808–1812* (Málaga, 1966).
Alexander, D. "The Impact of Guerrilla Warfare in Spain on French Combat Strength." *Consortium on Revolutionary Europe Proceedings* 5 (1975): 91–98.
Aragón Gómez, J. *Chiclana de la Frontera bajo el gobierno de José Napoleón, 1810–1812* (Chiclana de la Frontera, 2007).
Aragón Gómez, J., J. Paz Pasamar, and A. Souto Fernández. *Conil durante la ocupación francesa* (Conil, 2004).
Artola, M. *Los afrancesados* (Madrid, 1976).
Asín Cormán, E. *Los toros josefinos: Corridas de toros en la Guerra de la Independencia bajo el reinado de José I Bonaparte, 1808–1814* (Zaragoza, 2008).
Aymes, J. *La Guerra de la Independencia en España, 1808–1814* (Madrid, 1975).
Bell, D. A. *The First Total War: Napoleon's Europe and the Birth of Warfare as We Know It* (New York, 2007).
Bernal, A. *La lucha por la tierra en la crisis del antiguo régimen* (Madrid, 1979).
———. *La propiedad de la tierra y las luchas agrarias andaluzas* (Barcelona, 1974).
Broers, M. *Europe under Napoleon, 1799–1815* (London, 1996).
———. *Napoleon's Other War: Bandits, Rebels, and Their Pursuers in the Age of Revolutions* (Oxford, 2010).
Callahan, W. *Church, Politics, and Society in Spain, 1750–1874* (Cambridge, Mass., 1984).
———. "The Origins of the Conservative Church in Spain, 1789–1823." *European Studies Review* 10, no. 2 (April 1980): 199–223.
Cambronero, C. *El rey intruso: Apuntes históricos referentes á José Bonaparte y á su gobierno en España* (Madrid, 1909).
Canales Gil, E. "La deserción en España durante la Guerra de la Independencia." In *Bicentenari de la Revolucio Francesa (1789–1989): Le Jacobinisme,* 211–30 (Barcelona, 1990).
———. *Patriotismo y deserción durante la Guerra de la Independencia en Cataluña* (Coimbra, 1988).
Castillo Cano, J. *Almería en la crisis del antiguo regimen: La Guerra de la Indepedencia en la ciudad, 1787–1814* (Almería, 1987).
Connelly, O. *The Gentle Bonaparte: A Biography of Joseph, Napoleon's Elder Brother* (New York, 1968).

———. *Napoleon's Satellite Kingdoms* (New York, 1965).
Cortines, J., ed. *Felipe Cortines Murube: De la independencia—los franceses en Lebrija y otros escritos* (Lebrija, 2008).
Cuenca Toribio, J. M., ed. *Andalucía en la Guerra de la Independencia* (Córdoba, 2009).
Delgado Barrado, J. M., and M. A. Lopéz Arandía, eds. *Andalucía en guerra, 1808–1814* (Jaén, 2010).
Delgado García, A. *Montoro en la Guerra de la Independencia* (Montoro, 2006).
Demerson, J. *José María de Lanz, Prefecto de Córdoba* (Madrid, 1990).
Díaz Torrejón, F. L. *Guerrilla, contraguerrilla, y delincuencia en la Andalucía napoleónica, 1810–1812.* 3 vols. (Granada, 2004).
———. *José Napoleón I en el sur de España: Un viaje regio por Andalucía, enero–mayo 1810* (Córdoba, 2008).
———. *Osuna napoleónica, 1810–1812* (Seville, 2001).
Diego, E. de. *España, el infierno de Napoleón, 1808–1814: Una historia de la Guerra de la Independencia* (Madrid, 2008).
Dufour, G. *La Guerra de la Independencia* (Madrid, 1999).
Ellis, G. *The Napoleonic Empire,* 2nd ed. (1991; London, 2003).
Esdaile, C. J. *Fighting Napoleon: Guerrillas, Bandits, and Adventurers in Spain, 1808–1814* (London, 2004).
———. "Heroes or Villains? The Spanish Guerrillas in the Peninsular War." *History Today* 38, no. 4 (April 1988): 29–35.
———. *The Peninsular War: A New History* (London, 2002).
———, ed. *Popular Resistance in the French Wars: Patriots, Partisans, and Land Pirates* (Houndmills, 2005).
———. *The Spanish Army in the Peninsular War* (Manchester, 1988).
———. "War and Politics in Spain, 1808–1814." *Historical Journal* 31, no. 2 (1988): 295–317.
———. *The Wars of Napoleon* (London, 1995).
Flores Manzano, F. *El bandolerismo en Extremadura* (Badajoz, 1992).
———. *La guerrilla patriótica en Extremadura, 1808–1812* (Mérida, 2009).
Fraser, R. *Napoleon's Cursed War: Popular Resistance in the Spanish Peninsular War* (London, 2008).
Gallego y Burín, A. *Granada en la Guerra de la Independencia* (Granada, 1923).
Girod de l'Ain, G. *Joseph Bonaparte, le roi malgré-lui* (Paris, 1970).
Glover, M. *Legacy of Glory: The Bonaparte Kingdom of Spain* (London, 1971).
González Cruz, D. *De la Revolución Francesa a la Guerra de la Independencia: Huelva a fines de la Edad Moderna* (Huelva, 2002).
Goodman, E. "Spanish Nationalism in the Struggle against Napoleon." *Review of Politics* 20, no. 3 (July 1958): 330–46.
Gotteri, N. *Le maréchal Soult* (Paris, 2000).
Grasset, A. *Málaga: Provincia francesa, 1811–1812.* Translated and edited by M. C. Toledano (Málaga, 1996).
Gutiérrez Tellez, D. *Biografía de D. José Serrano Valdenebro, Jefe de Escuadra de la Real Armada Española, 1743–1814* (Cortes de la Frontera, 2008).
Hayman, P. *Soult: Napoleon's Maligned Marshal* (London, 1990).
Herr, R. "Good, Evil, and Spain's Uprising against Napoleon." In *Ideas in History,* edited by R. Herr and H. Parker, 157–81 (Durham, N.C., 1965).

Holtman, R. *Napoleonic Propaganda* (New York, 1950).

Jiménez de Gregorio, F. *Murcia en los dos primeros años de la Guerra por la Independencia* (Murcia, 1947).

Lafon, J. M. *L'Andalousie et Napoléon: Contre-insurrection, collaboration, et résistance dans le midi d'Espagne, 1808–1812* (Paris, 2007).

López Pérez, M., and I. Lara Martín Portugués. *Entre la guerra y la paz: Jaén, 1808–1814* (Granada, 1993).

López Tabar, J. *Los famosos traidores: Los afrancesados durante la crisis del antiguo régimen, 1808–1833* (Madrid, 2001).

Lorente, L. *Agitación urbana y crisis económica durante la Guerra de la Independencia, 1808–1814* (Cuenca, 1993).

———. *Poder y miseria: Oligarcas y campesinos en la España señorial, 1760–1868* (Madrid, 1994).

Lovett, G. *Napoleon and the Birth of Modern Spain* (New York, 1965).

———. "The Spanish Guerrillas and Napoleon." *Consortium on Revolutionary Europe Proceedings* 5 (1975): 80–90.

Madrid del Camacho, M. *Un barcelonés prefecto de Córdoba con José Bonaparte* (Córdoba, 1972).

Martín de Molina, S. *Gaucín: 1742–1814: Vida, trabajos, avatares, gesta, y vindicación del Brigadier, Jefe de Escuadra de la Real Armada, Comandante Extremadura al mando del Duque de Alburquerque, Mariscal de Campo, diputado en las Cortes Generales y Extraordinarias de Cádiz, Maestrante de la Real Maestranza de Caballería de Ronda, gobernador militar y político de Cartagena, Don Josef Serrano Valdenebro, jefe de la guerrilla de la sierra meridional con cuartel general en la mencionada villa malagueña de Gaucín durante la guerra contra el invasor francés* (Córdoba, 2005).

Martínez Laínez, F, *Como lobos hambrientos: Los guerrilleros en la Guerra de la Independencia, 1808–1814* (Madrid, 2007).

Martínez Ruiz, A. *El reino de Granada en la Guerra de la Independencia* (Granada, 1977).

———, ed. *II Seminario Internacional sobre la Guerra de la Independencia: Madrid, 24–26 de Octubre de 1994* (Madrid, 1995).

Martín Mas, M. *Los guerrilleros, 1808–1814: La pesadilla española de Napoleón* (Madrid, 2005).

Mercader Riba, J. *José Bonaparte, rey de España, 1808–13: Estructura del estado Español bonapartista* (Madrid, 1983).

———. *José Bonaparte, rey de España, 1808–13: Historia externa del reinado* (Madrid, 1971).

Moliner Prada, A. *La guerrilla en la Guerra de la Independencia* (Madrid, 2004).

———. "La peculiaridad de la revolución española de 1808." *Hispania* 166 (May 1987): 632–46.

———. "Las juntas corregimentales de Cataluña en la guerra del francès." *Hispania* 158 (September 1984): 549–82.

———. *Revolución burguesa y movimiento juntero en España* (Lerida, 1997).

Moreno Alonso, M. *La batalla de Bailén: El surgimiento de una nación* (Madrid, 2008).

———. *Los españoles durante la ocupación napoleónica: La vida cotidiana en la vorágine* (Málaga, 1997).

———. *José Bonaparte: Un rey republicano en España* (Madrid, 2008).
———. *La Junta Suprema de Sevilla* (Seville, 2001).
———. *El nacimiento de una nación: Sevilla, 1808–1810—la capital de una nación en guerra* (Madrid, 2010).
———. *La revolución "santa" de Sevilla (la revuelta popular de 1808)* (Seville, 1997).
———. *Sevilla napoleónica* (Sevilla, 1995).
Moreti, J. J. *Historia de L.M.N.Y.M.L Ciudad de Ronda* (Ronda, 1867).
Múñoz del Bustillo, C. "Bayona frente a Cádiz: Gobierno y administración en la prefectura de Jérez." PhD diss., University of Cádiz, 1989.
Nabonne, B. *Joseph Bonaparte: Le roi-philosophe* (Paris, 1949).
Oman, C. *A History of the Peninsular War,* 7 vols. (Oxford, 1902–1930).
Ortí Belmonte, M. A. *Córdoba durante la Guerra de la Independencia, 1808–1813* (Córdoba, 1930).
Pastor Petit, D. *El bandolerismo en España: Cinco siglos de desequilibrio social y de bandolerismo* (Barcelona, 1979).
Peña Guerrero, M. *El tiempo de los franceses: La Guerra de la Independencia en el suroeste español* (Almonte, 2000).
Pérez López, S. *Guadix y su obispado en la Guerra de la Independencia: Quebranto económico y ruptura social en un diócesis de la Alta Andalucía, 1808–1814* (Córdoba, 1998).
Priego López, J. *Guerra de la Independencia, 1808–1814* (Madrid, 1972–2000).
Read, J. *War in the Peninsula* (London, 1977).
Reder Gadow, M. "Ambigüedad de la iglesia malagüeña durante la Guerra de la Independencia." In *La Guerra de la Independencia: Estudios,* edited by J. A. Armillas, 2 vols., 2:677–88. (Zaragoza, 2001).
Reder Gadow, M., and E. Mendoza García, eds. *La Guerra de la Independencia en Málaga y su provincia, 1808–1814* (Málaga, 2005).
Rodríguez Cancho, M. *La Guerra de la Independencia en Badajoz, 1808–1814* (Badajoz, 2008).
Rodríguez Solis, E. *Los guerrilleros de 1808: Historia popular de la Guerra de la Independencia* (Madrid, 1887).
Romero Romero, F. *Guerra de la Independencia en Villamartín* (Córdoba, 2003).
Ross, M. *The Reluctant King: Joseph Bonaparte, King of the Two Sicilies and Spain* (London, 1976).
Ruíz Rodríguez, J. A. *Don Benito durante la Guerra de la Independencia Española, 1808–1814* (Don Benito, 2008).
Sánchez Fernández, J. "El ejército contra las guerrillas: La jefatura militar frente al fenómeno guerrillero durante la Guerra de la Independencia." *Revista de Historia Militar,* no. 87 (July 1999): 149–74.
Santos Torres, J. *El bandolerismo en Andalucía, I: Sevilla y su antiguo reino* (Seville, 1991).
———. *El bandolerismo en España: Una historia fuera del ley* (Madrid, 1995).
Turrado Vidal, M. *De malhechores a gente de orden: Historia de una partida bonapartista cordobesa* (Madrid, 2005).
Valencina, A. de. *Los capuchinos de Andalucía en la Guerra de la Independencia* (Seville, 1910).
Valenzuela Saavedra, F. *La sociedad de Jaén ante la invasión napoleónica, 1808* (Jaén, 2000).

Vidal Delgado, R. *Historia de la Guerra de la Independencia en el Campo de Gibraltar* (Cádiz, 1975).
Vilar, P. *Hidalgos, amotinados, y guerrilleros: Pueblo y poderes en la historia de España* (Barcelona, 1999).
Viñes Millet, C. *Granada ante la invasión francesa* (Granada, 2004).
Woolf, S. *Napoleon's Integration of Europe* (London, 1991).

Index